A New Look at the Ancient Path ... ... UALITY

Most people are vague in appealing for help from the Cosmic Beings, which leads them to contact the wrong energy source—if they are able to make contact at all—and their petitions go unanswered.

To successfully call on the energies of the Ancient Ones, you need a firm basis of knowledge of their powers. By educating yourself about the pantheons of deities and examining the meaning behind ancient spiritual beliefs, you can rediscover some of the deep spiritual truths expressed through the rituals of your ancestors. This book makes it possible for you to correctly define the powers of the Gods or Goddesses upon whom you intend to call, and to develop effective personal rituals to enrich your spiritual life.

Magick of the Gods & Goddesses is a study of the principal ancient pantheons of the world, differing in two major aspects from other studies: this book points out the underlying similarities among the energies symbolized by the Gods and Goddesses—*and* focuses on the practical application of these energies. It is a straightforward reference tool that provides the necessary information for everyone to worship and use the Ultimate Creative Power. A discussion of the importance of ritual and magick is included to deepen your understanding, as well as explanations concerning the ritualistic practices of Witchcraft, Ceremonial Magick, Shamanism, and the Qabala. Each chapter concludes with a bibliography, as a gateway to further study.

We are all on a quest for fulfillment, whatever our cultural or religious backgrounds. What better means of achieving that quest, than to discover and draw upon the same powerful energies that our ancestors knew of? The ancient pools of energy created and fed by centuries of belief and worship of the deities still exist ... and these energies can help us attain not only material, earthly benefits, but spiritual illumination and contentment, as well.

About the Author

D. J. Conway was born in Hood River, Oregon, to a family of Irish-North Germanic-Native North American descent. She began her quest for knowledge of the occult more than 25 years ago, and has been involved in many aspects of New Age religion from the teachings of Yogananda to study of the Qabala, healing, herbs, and Wicca. Although an ordained minister in two New Age churches and holder of a Doctor of Divinity degree, Conway claims that her heart lies within the Pagan cultures. No longer actively lecturing and teaching as she did for years, Conway has centered her energies on writing. Several of her stories have been published in magazines, such as *Encounters*, which pertain to the field of science fantasy.

To Write to the Author

If you wish to contact the author or would like more information about this book, please write to the author in care of Llewellyn Worldwide, and we will forward your request. Both the author and publisher appreciate hearing from you and learning of your enjoyment of this book and how it has helped you. Llewellyn Worldwide cannot guarantee that every letter written to the author can be answered, but all will be forwarded. Please write to:

D. J. Conway
c/o Llewellyn Worldwide
P.O. Box 64383, Dept. L170-9, St. Paul, MN 55164-0383, U.S.A.

Please enclosed a self-addressed, stamped envelope or $1.00 to cover costs.
If outside the U.S.A., enclose international postal reply coupon.

LLEWELLYN'S WORLD MAGIC SERIES

MAGICK OF THE
GODS
&
GODDESSES

(Previously titled: *Ancient & Shining Ones*)

HOW TO INVOKE THEIR POWERS

D. J. CONWAY

1997
Llewellyn Publications
St. Paul, Minnesota 55164-0383, U.S.A.

FIRST EDITION
First Printing, 1997
(Previously titled: *Ancient & Shining Ones*)

Cover Art & Design: Anne Marie Garrison
Maps: Alexandra Lumen
Book Design and Layout: Jessica Thoreson

Illustration credits begin on page 433

Library of Congress Cataloging-in-Publication Data
 Conway, D. J. (Deanna J.)
 [Ancient & shining ones]
  Magick of the gods & goddesses : how to invoke their powers / D. J. Conway
   p. cm. —
 Originally published: The ancient /& shining ones, 1993, in series: Llewellyn's world magic series.
  Includes bibliographical references and index.
  ISBN: 1-56718-179-1
  1. Gods — Miscellanea. 2. Goddesses — Miscellanea — 3 Magic —
 I. Title.
 BF1623.G63C66 1997
 291.2'11 — dc21   97-174388
                      CIP

Llewellyn Publications
A Division of Llewellyn Worldwide, Ltd.
P. O. Box 64383, St. Paul, MN 55164-0383

Printed in the United States of America

Llewellyn's World Magic Series

At the core of every religion, at the foundation of every culture, there is MAGIC.

Magic sees the world as alive, as the home which humanity shares with beings and powers both visible and invisible with whom and which we can interface to either our advantage or disadvantage—depending upon our awareness and intention.

Religious worship and communion is one kind of magic, and just as there are many religions in the world, so are there many magical systems.

Religion, and magic, are ways of seeing and relating to the creative powers, the living energies, the all-pervading spirit, the underlying intelligence that is the universe within which we and all else exist.

Neither religion nor magic conflict with science. All share the same goals and the same limitations: always seeking truth, forever haunted by human limitations in perceiving that truth. Magic is "technology" based upon experience and extrasensory insight, providing its practitioners with methods of greater influence and control over the world of the invisible before it impinges on the world of the visible.

The study of world magic not only enhances your understanding of the world in which you live, and hence your ability to live better, but brings you into touch with the inner essence of your long evolutionary heritage and most particularly—as in the case of the magical system identified most closely with your genetic inheritance—with the archetypal images and forces most alive in your whole consciousness.

ALSO BY D. J. CONWAY
Norse Magic
Celtic Magic
Maid, Mother, Crone
Dancing with Dragons
By Oak, Ash and Thorn
Animal Magick
Flying Without a Broom
Moon Magick
Falcon Feather & Valkyrie Sword
Astral Love
Magickal, Mythical Beasts
Lord of Light & Shadow

FICTION
The Dream Warrior
Soothslayer

FORTHCOMING
Mysterious Magickal Cat
Warrior of Shadows (fiction)

In memory of my grandmother,
Clara Fern Long née Corbin,
who first read me the ancient stories.

CONTENTS

CHAPTER ONE

INTRODUCTION

A scholar at work, Paris, 1820

THE FIRST draft of this book was finished in the late summer of 1979. The manuscript has been a very long time in completion to the satisfaction of everyone concerned. This book has been a labor of love; it is an effort to compile as much as possible of the necessary magickal correspondence information on world deities in one volume. Of course, it is impossible to include every tidbit of information on every ancient deity and ritual system. One is always bound to miss something. The chapters on magickal and belief systems are by no means complete; they are intended only as an introduction and springboard to further study.

Pythagoras, the Greek philosopher, called the Supreme Mind the Power within all things, the Cause of all things. In his writings, he described the body of God as composed of light.[1]

We know what light is and is not, but we do not truly understand the total nature of light. And spiritual Light, as opposed to the physical light, is even more difficult to begin to understand. A clearer knowledge of the Ancient and Shining Ones is the first step on that path.

I have not included the religious ideas of the Christians, Moslems, and Hebrews because I felt that their belief systems and mythologies would be better treated in a separate book. Because of the similarities of these religious beliefs in one

1

god and their common racial history (especially at the beginning of each religion), I felt that these three systems could be more fully explored in-depth in another volume at another time. The same applies to Voodoo, which is a Westernization of African beliefs.[2]

In the mythologies of each ancient religion, I have chosen the myths that best illustrated a particular deity. In no way is it possible to include every myth from around the world. Also, the mythical stories all have more than one level of meaning; each has a spiritual meaning hidden under symbols. The myths chosen are ones I consider interesting and reflective of each culture.

The costume details listed for each culture are included for their interest and their potential use in rituals. By surrounding one's self with symbols of a particular pantheon, whether cultural symbols or magickal symbols, the magician activates areas of the subconscious mind that make magick viable and successful. This is the practical reason behind the wearing of robes and ritual attire. Until the subconscious mind is actively engaged, work done in magickal rituals and spellworking will not be consistent or have a high rate of success.

The reason and drive behind writing this book is simple. For many years there has been a growing interest in, and need for, personal magick and religion. But when the novice begins to look for information, he or she must wade through hundreds of books, many of dubious value, to find the necessary magickal and mythological facts. Although the inner spiritual drive to find that new and unique path is strong, the seeker can become extremely frustrated in the search. This book, with its bibliographies at the end of each chapter, was written to aid in that search, to make things a little easier in a world that is not generally helpful in the search down ancient paths of spirituality.

Thousands of people of this New Age[3] are dissatisfied with what they see and hear in the religions currently accepted by society. There is an emptiness, an inner seeking for a more fulfilling, personal way of worship. More and more people are returning to the Old Religions, not exactly as they were hundreds and thousands of years ago, but brought forward into the needs and understanding of the New Age times. These paths are re-creations and, in some instances, creations; they meet individual spiritual needs better than the staid religions.

No religious philosophy can afford to remain static. If it does not change, progress, evolve, then it begins to solidify and eventually dies. It is the same in Nature. Plants and animals that become overspecialized and cannot adapt to changing conditions become extinct.

There must always be room for self-expression of the individual in religion, room for new interpretations and insights. Without positive evolution, religions tend to become hard and demanding, power hungry and controlling, instead of joyful and enlightening. Followers begin to drop away because their needs are not met. Few new members are added.

Many "no-change" adherents to these philosophies become fanatical, losing sight of the original spiritual intentions. Theirs is declared to be "the only way." So rigid does their thinking become that anyone who believes differently is in danger of being persecuted, with the religious persecutions fully justified and ordained by whatever deity they serve, in the minds of the perpetrators.

The Gateway to Eternal Wisdom, Heinrich Khunrath, Hanau, 1609

Religious worship should never again be totally governed by ecclesiastic organizations with wide-reaching powers. That era should be gone forever. Humankind finally is beginning to realize the greatest of all spiritual mysteries: the search for Goddess/God/the Cosmic Source cannot be "out there" somewhere, but must be an individual search within each person. And each person will find and see Goddess/God/the Cosmic Source in a different way. Therefore, no church government has the right to judge how a person can and should worship. There is a piece of the truth in all beliefs; no one ideology holds all the truth.

There is no one right way to approach and worship the Divine Creator. Written over the entrance of one of the Tibetan lamaseries is the phrase: "A thousand monks, a thousand religions." Each person has unique spiritual needs that can be fulfilled only by religious worship tailored to the individual.

The powers behind the Old Gods and Goddesses are still very much alive, for which we should be thankful. Properly used and adapted to modern living, the ancient legends and ritual methods can greatly enrich our lives.

Civilization is no longer so narrowly area-centered, family or clan-centered, or race-centered, as it was for centuries. We realize we are all part of one family, the

3

family of Earth. We are reaching out to the stars where some day we may find other civilizations and beings who also worship, in many different ways, the Divine Source. If we try to understand the truth behind our own past legends and deities, then we will be better able to see the same truths hidden behind the galactic ways of worship.

Humankind instinctively seeks that which will aid them in their development. A growing interest in rediscovering the Old Gods/Goddesses is the first step in preparing humankind for what is to come. By being open-minded and sensitive to the spiritual ideas of other cultures, other races, other worlds, we will find ourselves on new, exciting spiritual thresholds. We must move closer to that ultimate discovery—finding and recognizing God/Goddess/the Divine Source within ourselves, thus discovering our true identity.

I have chosen to spell magick with a "k" to differentiate it from stage magicians' sleight-of-hand tricks. Magick has absolutely nothing to do with magic. *Magic* is a business of deceiving people. *Magick* is a personal ritual system.

To avoid tedious repetition, I have chosen not to be consistent in using he/she when speaking of a person. This does not mean I am insensitive to the gender issue; it simply means I find it boring and unnecessary to keep repeating such a phrase. In my opinion, it perpetuates rather than solves the centuries-old problem of sexual discrimination by emphasizing the separateness of genders. Unfortunately, the English language does not have a pronoun that describes both sexes in one word. However, I have chosen to use the term "humankind" in place of "mankind," as this seems a reasonable substitution.

The descriptions of costume given in each chapter are just basics. In European countries, for instance, costume should be described as to era and locality; that would be a whole book in itself. Space simply does not allow that luxury here, so I have chosen to give a thumbnail sketch, without regard to time or the many various localities and customs. The descriptions are for the practitioner who might wish to enhance his nationally-flavored rituals by costume.

The ancient Mystery Religions taught that even the Gods[4] could understand only a little of the glorious Light that was their source of being. Therefore, we humans cannot hope completely to understand the Gods. Each seeker must pursue the Light of the deities as far as he is able.

When studying the Old Gods—the Ancient and Shining Ones—remember the Wiccan saying:

All Gods are one God, and all Goddesses are one Goddess, and both are One.

This does not mean that Pagans believe in the one God of the Christians, but that they acknowledge there is one Prime Creative Source of Power that brought everything into being in the beginning of all things. Scientists call this the Big Bang Theory.

As to the many religious/spiritual avenues of pursuit of this knowledge, Rudyard Kipling said it best in his poem "In the Neolitic Age": "There are nine and sixty ways of constructing tribal lays, And every single one of them is right."

ENDNOTES

1. Hall, Manly P. *The Secret Teachings of All Ages.* Los Angeles, CA: Philosophical Research, 1977.
2. Some useful books on this are Bertiauz, Michael, *The Voudoun Gnostic Workbook*, NY: Magickal Childe, Inc., 1988. Denning, Melita, and Phillips, Osborne, *Voudoun Fire*, St. Paul, MN: Llewellyn Publications, 1979. Metraux, Alfred, *Voodoo in Haiti*, NY: Schocken Books, 1972.
3. When the term *New Age* began to be used, it meant the dawning of a new era where people were once again open to the investigation and practice of the psychic sciences and Pagan religions. In my opinion, it has unfortunately degenerated into a term which now primarily is a catch-word for fence-sitters who want to dabble but not make a commitment to the Pagan world. Perhaps it is time for those who are committed to Paganism to come up with a different term to describe themselves and their movement, leaving the words *New Age* to those who frequent psychic fairs and belong to Christian-oriented churches (and no, I am not running down all psychic fairs).
4. Hall, Manly P. *The Secret Teachings of All Ages.*

GENERAL BIBLIOGRAPHY

These books contain material pertinent to all or nearly all of the following chapters.

Arrowsmith, Nancy, and Moorse, George. *A Field Guide to the Little People.* NY: Pocket Books, 1977.

Batterberry, Michael and Ariane. *Fashion: The Mirror of History.* NY: Greenwich House, 1977.

Baumgartner, Anne S. *A Comprehensive Dictionary of the Gods.* NY: University Books, 1984.

Bibby, Geoffrey. *Four Thousand Years Ago.* NY: Alfred Knopf, 1961.

Bibby, Geoffrey. *The Testimony of the Spade.* NY: Alfred A. Knopf, 1956.

Blavatsky, H. P. *Isis Unveiled.* Pasadena, CA: Theosophical University Press, 1976.

Blavatsky, H. P. *The Secret Doctrine.* Wheaton, IL: Theosophical Publishing House, 1978.

Bradshaw, Angela. *World Costume.* NY: Macmillan, 1952.

Braun and Schneider. *Historic Costume in Pictures.* NY: Dover 1975.

Budge, E. A. Wallis. *Amulets and Superstitions.* NY: Dover Publications, 1978.

Bulfinch, Thomas. *Bulfinch's Mythology.* NY: Avenel Books, 1978.

Campbell, Joseph. *The Hero with a Thousand Faces*. Princeton, NJ: Princeton University Press, 1968.

Campbell, Joseph. *The Inner Reaches of Outer Space*. NY: Harper & Row, 1986.

Campbell, Joseph. *The Masks of God: Primitive, Oriental, Occidental and Creative Mythology*. UK: Penguin Books, 1968.

Campbell, Joseph. *The Mythic Image*. NJ: Princeton University Press, 1981.

Campbell, Joseph. *Myths to Live By*. NY: Bantam Books, 1988.

Campbell, Joseph. *The Power of Myth*. NY: Doubleday, 1988.

Campbell, Joseph. *Transformation of Myth Through Time*. NY: Harper & Row, 1990.

Carlyon, Richard. *A Guide to the Gods*. NY: Wm. Morrow & Co., 1982.

Cavendish, Richard, ed. *Mythology: An Illustrated Encyclopedia*. NY: Rizzoli, 1980.

Cirlot, J. E. *A Dictionary of Symbols*. NY: Philosophical Library, 1978.

Cotterell, Arthur. *A Dictionary of World Mythology*. NY: Perigee Books, 1979.

Cotterell, Arthur, ed. *Macmillan Illustrated Encyclopedia of Myths and Legends*. NY: Macmillan, 1989.

D'Alviella, Count Goblet. *Migration of Symbols*. UK: Aquarian Press, 1979.

Eichler, Lillian. *The Customs of Mankind*. NY: Nelson Doubleday, 1924.

Farrar, Janet and Stewart. *The Witches' God*. Custer, WA: Phoenix Publishing, 1989.

Farrar, Janet and Stewart. *The Witches' Goddess*. UK: Robert Hale, 1987.

Frazer, James G. *The Golden Bough*. NY: Macmillan, 1963.

Goodrich, Norma Lorre. *Ancient Myths*. NY: New American Library, 1960.

Goodrich, Norma Lorre. *Myths of the Hero*. NY: Orion Press, 1962.

Gorsline, Douglas. *What People Wore*. NY: Bonanze Books, 1962.

Graves, Robert. *The White Goddess*. NY: Farrar, Straus & Giroux, 1980.

Guirand, Felix, ed. Trans. Richard Aldington and Delano Ames. *New Larousse Encyclopedia of Mythology*. UK: Hamlyn, 1978.

Hall, Manly P. *The Secret Teachings of All Ages*. Los Angeles, CA: Philosophical Research Society, 1977.

Hamilton, Edith. *Mythology*. Boston, MA: Little, Brown & Co., 1942.

Harris, Christie, and Johnston, Moira. *Figleafing Through History*. NY: Atheneum, 1971.

Hawkes, Jacquetta. *Atlas of Early Man*. NY: St. Martins, 1976.

Hawkes, Jacquetta. *The World of the Past*. NY: Alfred Knopf, 1963.

Herrmann, Paul. *Conquest by Man*. NY: Harper & Brothers, 1954.

Keightley, Thomas. *The World Guide to Gnomes, Fairies, Elves and Other Little People.* NY: Avenel Books, 1978. (Originally published 1880.)

Kohler, Carl. *A History of Costume.* NY: Dover, 1963.

Lehr, Ernst. *Symbols, Signs and Signets.* NY: Dover Publications, 1950.

Lippman, Deborah, and Colin, Paul. *How to Make Amulets, Charms and Talismans.* NY: M. Evans & Co., 1974.

Lum, Peter. *Fabulous Beasts.* NY: Pantheon Books, 1951.

Lurker, Manfred. *Dictionary of Gods and Goddesses, Devils and Demons.* NY: Routledge & Kegan Paul, 1987.

Monaghan, Patricia. *The Book of Goddesses and Heroines.* St. Paul, MN: Llewellyn Publications, 1990.

Murray, Alexander S. *Who's Who in Mythology.* NY: Bonanza Books, 1988.

National Geographic. *Everyday Life in Ancient Times.* Washington, D. C., 1955.

Newmann, Erich. *The Great Mother: An Analysis of the Archetype.* Princeton, NJ: Princeton University Press, 1963.

Page, Michael, and Ingpen, Robert. *Encyclopedia of Things That Never Were.* NY: Viking Penguin, 1987.

Parrinder, Geoffrey. *A Dictionary of Non-Christian Religions.* Philadelphia, PA: Westminster Press, 1971.

Purce, Jill. *The Mystic Spiral: Journey of the Soul.* NY: Thames & Hudson, 1974.

Selbie, Robert. *The Anatomy of Costume.* NY: Crescent, 1977.

Sjoo, Monica, and Mor, Barbara. *The Great Cosmic Mother: Rediscovering the Religion of the Earth.* San Francisco, CA: Harper & Row, 1987.

Stone, Merlin. *Ancient Mirrors of Womanhood.* Boston, MA: Beacon, 1984.

Stone, Merlin. *When God Was a Woman.* NY: Harcourt Brace Jovanovich, 1976.

Thomas, William, and Pavitt, Kate. *The Book of Talismans, Amulets and Zodiacal Gems.* North Hollywood, CA: Wilshire Book Co., 1970.

Walker, Barbara. *The Woman's Dictionary of Symbols and Sacred Objects.* San Francisco, CA: Harper & Row, 1988.

Walker, Barbara. *The Woman's Encyclopedia of Myths and Secrets.* NY: Harper & Row, 1983.

Wells, H. G. *The Outline of History.* NY: Garden City Books, 1961.

Yarwood, Doreen. *Encyclopedia of World Costume.* NY: Scribners, 1986.

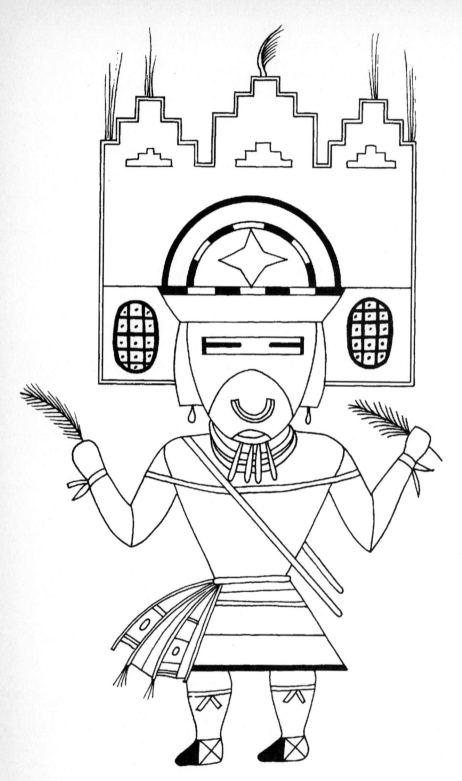

Hopi messenger of the gods

CHAPTER TWO

WHO AND WHAT ARE THE GODS?

*Incarnation of Vishnu
imparting wisdom*

THE GODS are a reality, but not necessarily in the way we think of reality. The Ideals, or Archetypal Images, behind the Gods have been in the minds of humans for thousands of years and will remain for thousands more. They have influenced every aspect of humankind's thinking and progress, actions, and social laws.

The many Gods/Goddesses each represent an aspect of the Ideal of the whole Ultimate Creating Force behind all that exists.[1] By personifying each separate Ideal, humankind is better able to relate to the whole. Contemplation of the Ultimate Creating Force in its entirety is beyond the comprehension of humankind. This Force is so abstract there is nothing to which it can be compared. Although humankind is capable of dealing in abstract thought, there must always be some point of reference for there to be understanding.[2] If a person could expand his mental universe so he could comprehend this Ultimate Force in all its aspects and glory, that individual would cease to exist. He would have become an equal of the Force and therefore no longer in limited physical form.

There are as many ways of defining the Gods as there are people. Some believe that the Gods are actual beings, much more powerful than we are, who came into existence at the creation of the universe and who live on another plane. They believe that these Gods have a lifespan infinitely longer than ours, and that they can influence and manipulate events with vast powers that cross dimension and time.

Others believe that humankind's thought-forms[3] created the Gods, that continual centuries of belief and worship deposited great power in those thought-forms until they became a type of living creature.[4]

It is like the old argument of which came first, the chicken or the egg. It is my personal belief that the answer probably lies somewhere in the middle of these ideas. However, the important thing is not how the Gods came into being, but that they do exist and have great powers. That their existence cannot be proven is unimportant; the universe itself acts as though they do.[5]

Intense, concentrated thoughts over a long period of time are very powerful things, having tremendous energies to create or destroy; this is especially true of ritualistic thought-patterns. The realities behind the Gods and Goddesses are vast pools of energy, fed by intense, emotion-filled worship by humankind. These energy pools still exist and can be used, if correctly called upon. Present day rituals and worship revitalize and replenish these ancient energies, awakening them from their long sleep of disuse.[6]

But, like the Ultimate Source, they are not found by searching "out there." They must be contacted deep within the Self. To do this, you must study the old myths and legends told of these deities so that your subconscious mind will awaken to its potential of contacting these Ideals and using their energies. An alert subconscious will delve into the universal memory pool, or race mind, or the collective unconsciousness hypothesized by Carl Jung,[7] gathering information necessary for your growth.

These archetypes (first forms or patterns) of Ideals can provide clues to dealing with everyday problems and people. If this seems impossible, consider the Hermetic teaching:[8] "As above, so below." Simply put, this means that everything on a spiritual or even a universal level is repeated in humankind and our immediate surroundings in a scaled-down form.

The characteristics symbolized by deities the world over are all to be found in the human personality, some stronger than others.

Humankind has an inborn need for religious or spiritual expression in some form or another. Being uniquely individual, all people have different needs to be satisfied. It is rather like asking ten witnesses to describe a robbery; you will get ten different descriptions of the same event, some of which are vastly different.

Some people still feel a need to be part of a strictly-structured church system; others never set foot inside an orthodox church. Still others, because of deep conditioning, feel compelled to attend a rigid group service, yet always have an empty spot inside them that remains unfulfilled. It is time people realized that to worship in any manner, as long as it harms no creature, is their right. There is no right way or wrong way to approach spiritual enlightenment and development; there is only the individual way. A melody to one person may be out of tune to another.

Greek Pantheon in Psyche Received into Olympus *from the painting by Caravaggio*

In later chapters I will present some of the similarities and differences between the various pantheons. It may surprise you to find interconnecting threads of spiritual thoughts running through them all. This, in itself, is proof that spiritual, religious ideas and Ideals are not unique to any one system, but are part of a universal pool of wisdom that has been, and still can be, drawn upon by humankind. Each pantheon was individually suited in some unique way, beyond the basic truths and Ideals, to the racial, geographic, and cultural aspects of the people who worshipped it.

I also will explain some of the correspondences between the pantheons, such as which Gods/Goddesses represent similar Ideals, yet have degrees of differences that make them unique. All this information has one goal: to provide each person with a variety of doorways to spiritual growth and development.

All ritual, even in the orthodox churches, is a spiritual play in which you are both watcher and participant. Its purpose is to stimulate areas of your mind that you do not use in ordinary activities. It is necessary to activate these areas of the mind so they become connecting links between the Ultimate Source and yourself. I believe we must offer people a theological/spiritual alternative for opening these connections.

Finding a Personal Pantheon

There are a number of ways to decide which pantheon is most suited to you as an individual. You may choose one because of family conditioning and previous religious training; your ancestral heritage;[9] geographic connections, such as the area in which you live or have lived; or your personal interests and goals.

Many people are raised with a religious background that is rich in symbolism and Ideals (Gods and Goddesses). To become aware of all this requires an in-depth look at something you have taken for granted all your life, and probably go through the worship with half your mind somewhere else. Seeing the value of the very familiar is often difficult.

Ancestral heritage is a wide field. Some families take pride in clinging to the old beliefs and practices, while others convert to a new religion and lose the old. Even if you are of mixed racial background, and most people are, it can be worthwhile to trace the religious background of each race. You will find a wealth of information that will aid your spiritual development.

My grandmother read me Scandinavian, Celtic, and Greek/Roman myths when I was quite small. She stirred an interest in me that has lasted for years. The fact that my family is Irish-German-Native North American also prompted me to study the cultures of those races. I firmly believe that everyone should be acquainted with the background of their particular racial heritage. If such study does not spark an interest for you, continue reading the myths and legends of other cultures. Somewhere in the vast pantheons of this world you will discover what speaks to you.

Hopi mother goddess Hahhaiwugti

The history of the area in which you presently live can also be a treasure trove of ancient cultures and beliefs. You can benefit greatly by showing some interest in your immediate environmental past. Any information gained makes you that much stronger.

Perhaps none of the mentioned ways of finding a pantheon have produced any that appeals to you. If this is the case, consider your personal goals, remembering that as your goals change, you may want to change pantheons. If your goals are primarily spiritual, for example, you might consider the deities of Egypt, China, India, or Celtic realms. Mental goals could use the pantheons of Greece, Rome, or North America. Physical gains could call upon the gods of Nordic-Germanic tradition, the Pacific

Ocean, or Japan. Of course, these are just examples as all pantheons serve more than one level of goals. So do the Angels and Archangels, Elementals, and Planetary Forces.

Beginners on the path of spiritual growth will find the information in this book interesting for browsing, a "get acquainted" form of reading. Advanced ritualists can use this for a quick method of review and a ready-reference for determining the Ideals most useful for ceremonies.

One important factor to keep in mind while reading is that Goddess-oriented cultures were the oldest form of religious worship and civilization. The original cultures gave their prime worship to the Great Mother and Her consort. Lineage and inheritance were traced through the females, not the males. When the God-oriented cultures overran them, the Goddesses were made secondary to the Gods, and many of their aspects and functions were changed or taken away from them.

Humankind has come full circle. Most people no longer think that armed might and warfare contribute anything positive to human development or spiritual growth. Now that humankind stands on a great new threshold—the exploration and possible colonization of space—we are once again changing our attitudes toward worship and personal spiritual expression. We had best go into space with an open mind and a willingness to allow others "out there" the freedom of worship that fits their needs, if we wish to keep that freedom for ourselves.

ENDNOTES

1. Joseph Campbell, in *Transformations of Myth Through Time*, says that believing fanatically that "God" is either one or many is misleading; one and many are only concepts or categories of thought. The term "God" is supposed to go beyond a personality to a transcendence of thought. The Pagan/Wiccan view of "God behind the Gods" does not mean acceptance of or belief in the Christian deity. It is an acknowledgement of the unknowable force which created the universe and everything in it.

2. Joseph Cambell, ibid., says that one of the reasons we have run into trouble is that we tend to make the symbols of spiritual thinking concrete. For example, the Moslems believe they have to make a pilgrimage to Mecca, the Christians to Bethlehem. Although we use symbols to understand abstract spiritual ideas, they should be flexible.

3. Margot Adler, in *Drawing Down the Moon*, describes them as thought-forms and Shining Ones. She writes that the universe is such a complex originator of such diverse creations that "gods" are well within the realm of possibility. We call these eternal beings "gods" because that is the only way we can understand them.

4. *Leaves of Yggdrasil*, St. Paul, MN: Llewellyn Publications, 1990, by Freya Aswynn. Aswynn concludes that the gods, nature spirits, and probably other life-forms as yet unknown to us were likely all evolved from the original consciousness that evolved when creation began. She further writes that human

consciousness and the human mind later gave these beings their forms and names. Because the gods must act through the human mind they eventually become "humanized," or seen as having human personalities and failings.

5. King, Frances, and Skinner, Stephen. *Techniques of High Magic.* The same argument can be applied to the existence of evil forces. The aspects symbolized by deities are also aspects of thought and behavior of humans. Therefore "evil," or more precisely, "negative" aspects would exist. Some, such as the Christian Devil, have been fed on a regular basis by belief of worshippers, even if that belief is only fear.

6. The Gods/Goddesses stay the same over the centuries, although they do change slightly as humankind itself changes. Like religion, the deities either change and grow, or die when they become outdated.

7. Jung, C. G. *The Archetypes and the Collective Unconscious.* Jung says that this collective unconscious is not individual but universal in nature.

8. *The Kybalion: Hermetic Philosophy*, by Three Initiates, published by the Yogi Publication Society, Chicago, IL, 1940, is the primary text used in study of the Kybalion (which is not the same as the Qabala). This book gives an in-depth discussion of this phrase, as well as other metaphysical thoughts. This book is also mentioned by Shah, Indris, in *The Sufis*, UK: Octagon Press, 1964, and in Shumaker, Wayne, *The Occult Sciences in the Renaissance*, Berkeley, CA: University of California Press, 1972.

9. Little is known of the DNA structure and what it contains. It is theoretically possible that somewhere in the DNA is the past record of inherited racial beliefs. Scientists know that certain protective behaviors appear to be inherited. An example of this is the instinctive hunkering down or running of young chicks when a hawk flies overhead. The chicks will do this whether or not they have been raised with their mother. Another unknown aspect among humans is the makeup and workings of the mind. The brain is not the mind; the brain is a physical organ that operates rather like a computer or machine that processes data. The mind appears to be able to transcend literal time and space, among other accomplishments. Excellent examples of this difference can be found in the stories of recovering stroke victims. These people all relate similar incidents where their minds are clear and functioning, while their brains are short-circuiting and refusing to work properly. For more on this, see *The Natural History of the Mind* by Gordon Rattray Taylor, NY: E. P. Dutton, 1979.

CHAPTER THREE

THE IMPORTANCE OF WORSHIP TO HUMANKIND

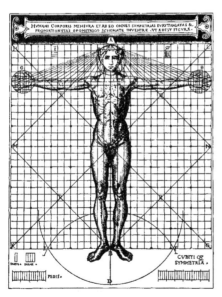

The mystery of the Macrocosm

FROM THE very beginning of humankind's history, worship has been an important part of our species' development and spiritual growth. We have always worshipped and revered tangible objects as symbols of the infinite, unknowable Creator.[1] The Christians, although originally borrowing heavily from the symbols and symbolic rituals of the ancient Pagan Mysteries, have tried to switch from these symbols to totally abstract ideas, without much success, I must say.

Humankind is a species that relies upon its physical senses to survive in this world and as a method of comparison to concepts of an invisible spiritual nature. Even the visions of the highly spiritually evolved human are experienced and described as if perceived by physical senses of sight, sound, smell, touch, and taste. It is the only way in which we can begin to understand and assimilate spiritual experiences, let alone share those experiences

Ancient horned figure

with others. So, to help humans who seldom or never activated their visualization processes, the ancient spiritual leaders (most often the priests and priestesses) devised concrete visual symbols to aid in worship of the Divine. The first symbols were paintings on the walls of sacred caves and little clay and mammoth ivory Paleolithic figures such as the Venus of Lespugue, France, carved about 24,000 BC.

The initiates of ancient beliefs warned their followers that an image was not a reality; they spoke of images as visual symbols of subjective ideas. The images of the gods were not intended to be worshipped; they were to be regarded simply as visual reminders of certain aspects of spiritual, invisible Divine principles. Unfortunately, many people did not, or could not, understand this form of abstract reasoning. Their spiritual growth had not evolved to the point where they could comprehend or differentiate between the idea of a physically formed God and an abstract Archetype.

One thing is apparent throughout all of humankind's history of worship. We do not seem to be able to live in our universe without some belief in a Supreme Being, a Creator of logic and power, however remote. Complete understanding of that Deity is not required, for we see the evidence of creation all about us. As Socrates said, he did not know what God was, but he knew what He was not.

The sad part of humankind's search for God/Goddess/Creator is that so many will fervently worship in their own sanctuaries in their own particular way, but will criticize and try to destroy the way others worship. If these people would only read the mythologies of this world with an open mind, they would find that all of the mythological motifs are revered in one way or another by all peoples of this planet. In the deepest sense, humankind needs to acknowledge that the basis of all spiritual belief comes from the same Source. In fact, the very basis of human development and evolution comes from an acknowledgement in some way of that Source. Any group of humans that has denounced an active belief in the Source has suffered a loss of commitment to and cohesion of their social structure.[2] And when belief becomes religion with a mere priestly function, truth is lost.

Basically there are two major types of "religion." The type that is called Paganism is polytheism, or belief in a plurality of gods. The other type is monotheism, or belief there is only one god. Three major religions have come out of the Middle East; all are monotheistic. Two of these three have a history of aggressive tendencies towards the rest of the world that worships differently, as well as toward each other. Polytheistic religions tend to be more open-minded about spiritual seeking by the individual.

C. G. Jung writes that the human psyche has within itself all the images that are the basis for creating a myth. He states that these images reside within the collective unconscious.[3] Jung goes on to clarify the difference between the collective unconscious and the subconscious. The subconscious, he writes, is the depository of each person's experiences, even if not remembered. The collective unconscious is a collection of archaic or primordial, universal images that have existed since the first humans[4] and are the same within each person regardless of race or religious belief.

The archetype behind any religious idea has a specific energy. It does not lose any of this energy if the human mind ignores it. The power may lie dormant, but certainly does not cease to exist, no more than does a disbelief in the Creator make it become non-existent.

It is also wise to note that all archetypes have positive, favorable aspects and negative, unfavorable aspects. It is up to each individual to choose to follow and emulate the positive aspects of any archetype in whatever form of religion one professes. Unfortunately, especially in the Western world, religion has too often been a means of oppression instead of a guide to better living. Churches gain power and status by supporting the powerful. Examples of this can be seen in the historical support of the churches for cruel monarchies and dictators. If the churches would concentrate on helping people to understand and experience spiritual growth, wars would greatly diminish and the lives of the average people would improve considerably.

Plato in *Phaedrus* wrote that not one person who decided in his youth to hold the opinion that there were no gods ever came to the end of his life with that conviction. Deep down within the soul, humankind "knows" there is a Supreme Creator. It is this

Execution of Witches in England

17

instinct that compels us to acknowledge in a multitude of ways the existence of that Being. It is an instinct within the collective unconscious of us all, and cannot be excised. It is our desire to be spiritually complete that draws us to seek the Source. And we will seek through thousands of spiritual pathways until we find the one that brings us closest to reuniting with that Being. Humankind can no more give up worship of the Supreme Creator that we can give up breathing. It is our destiny, the primitive instinct, that draws us on toward the goal of perfection within the Light.

ENDNOTES

1. In *The Secret Teachings of All Ages*, Los Angeles, CA: Philosophical Research Society, 1977, Manly P. Hall writes about the very first dissentions between the Christians and the Pagan Mystery sects. He states that the Pagans opposed the Christians because even then there were falsehoods entering Christian worship. The Pagans had no quarrel, at first, as the vast majority of Christian ideals were lifted from the Mysteries. And the Mysteries used only symbolic forms to enlighten their initiates, knowing that humankind has no other way to relate to the unknowable Creator. For example, the priests and priestesses of the Eleusinian Mysteries, at the high point in the ceremony, held up a stalk of wheat before the worshippers. This symbolized the eternal creating power of the Mother Goddess, or female aspect of the Divine Creator. The Catholics today still hold up a wheat wafer at the high point of Mass. Although the Christians condemned the Pagan beliefs, they borrowed heavily from Pagan symbolism as they had no other method of explaining unexplainable things to their followers. Also see *The Myth of the Divine Child and the Mysteries of Eleusis* by C. G. Jung and C. Kerenyi; Princeton, NJ: Princeton University Press, 1973.

2. Campbell, Joseph. *Masks of God: Primitive Mythology*. NY: Penguin Books, 1978.

3. Jung, C. G. *The Archetypes and the Collective Unconscious*. Princeton, NJ: Princeton University Press, 1990.

4. H. P. Blavatsky, in *Isis Unveiled;* Pasadena, CA: Theosophical University Press, 1976, concludes that all religious faiths have been derived from one primitive source, that they are all expressions of the human soul to be reunited with the Supreme Being.

CHAPTER FOUR

RITUAL AND MAGICK

Magicians using rune staves

WEBSTER'S 7TH *New Collegiate Dictionary* lists religion as "the service and worship of God or the supernatural; a personal set or institutionalized system of religious attitudes, beliefs, and practices; a cause, principle, or system of beliefs held to with ardor and faith." It also gives ritual as "the established form for a ceremony; a ceremonial act or action; any formal and customarily repeated act or series of acts."[1]

However, no dictionary gives a really correct definition of magick. Magick is a deliberate process by which events occur that have no ready, visible explanation. The Christians call these happenings "miracles" and sanction their occurrence as long as the person or people involved use no means other than prayer to bring about the result.

Orthodox religions seem to be caught up in a power play based on their interpretation of certain words. Every Christian gathering, regardless of the subdivision of denomination, is a ritual, although this is something that will stir up trouble if you point out this fact. A set formula of action and prayer is followed, with little or no deviation; one New Age group I know insists that they must begin every service with the same song. But the quickest way to be

19

persecuted is to tell a Christian that he or she is using a form of ritual and magick, the same as Pagan worshippers do!

So how do Pagans define magick? Ritual magick is merely the taking of energy from another plane of existence and weaving that energy, by specific thoughts, words, and practices, into a desired physical form or result in this plane of existence.[3] The whole idea of magick is to contact various energy pools (Gods/Goddesses) that exist in a dimension other than our own. Magicians do this deliberately because these energies add a vast amount of power to the energy for manifestation that we hold within ourselves. And by doing this practice deliberately, Pagan magicians have a higher success rate than Christians do. The prime purpose of any ritual is to create a change, and we cannot do that without the combination of these energies, those of the Archetypes and our own. We need the assistance of those energy pools, which can be called gods, deities, or elementals.

Everything used during ritual is a symbol of an energy that exists on another plane. Whether or not the magician properly connects with that specific energy and believes one can work magick depends upon how well one understands its representative symbol that is used on this plane or world. Study of, and meditation on, ritual symbols is an important part of training.

In order to bring through the energy of the gods or energy pools, the magician must set up a circuit of communication along which that power can flow. This is done by ritual use of symbols, ritual itself, visualization, and meditation. To keep the incoming power from dissipating before being directed toward a particular goal, rituals are performed within a cast and consecrated imaginary circle. This provides a neutral energy area that will not siphon off or dissipate the incoming energy.

To further aid in this control and direction of power, the magician relies upon certain magickal tools to help his subconscious mind do the task at hand. Whether Ceremonial Magician, Pagan, or Witch, most of the ritual tools are the same: dagger, sword, wand, cup or chalice, incense and burner, lamp or candles. Shamanism uses different implements, but for the same results. These three types of ritual systems will be discussed in-depth in later chapters. Special dress (robes or costumes) is also worn explicitly for ritual as an influence on the mental participation of the magician.[4]

To correctly contact the appropriate energy pool, the magician uses as many symbols as possible that represent a specific deity, power, or archetypal energy. Only by contacting his subconscious mind and getting it to participate in the ritual can a magician expect to produce positive results. Since the subconscious mind speaks only in symbols, only symbols can attract its attention and solicit its aid. For example, the magician will choose a color, incense, plant, stones, statue or picture, or other tools to help in subconscious communication for a specific ritual.

At the end of each ritual, the godform or archetypal power is dismissed so it can manifest the desire called for during the ritual. This enables the magician to gain the manifestation for which the ritual was done and also enables him to function again in the physical world. To continue holding the power after the ritual is completed would make it impossible for you to live a normal life.

The magician sees the universe as an infinite organism with humankind made in its image. Thus, everything in the universe, including the universe itself, makes up

Ritual tools

"God." Because of this interaction and interpenetration of energies, the magician, by mystical means, can learn to extend his own being and influence the universe with his magical will. To do this, he must first reach his own center of being, the Light within each person where humankind becomes "God." This is the true meaning behind the phrase "the Great Work." Perfecting the Great Work may take a lifetime or many lifetimes to achieve.

Ritual magick opens the doors to your creative mind and the subconscious. To effectively do magick one must get the creative side of the mind, or right brain, to operate uninhibited by the analytical left brain. This is accomplished by a consistent routine of visualization and meditation.

The dominant left brain generally maintains control. It is closely connected with the conscious mind and deals totally with what it calls reality, or this world. It is the side of the brain that primarily deals with logic, mathematics, and other similar functions. Unfortunately, it is also the side of the brain that makes us feel guilty and criticizes us for things we do or do not do; it might well be called the seat of the conscience.

The creative right brain pertains entirely to what we call imagination, or other worlds. It is artistic, visualizing, creating new ideas and inventions from a spark of a thought. Without the balancing effect of the left brain, the right brain would allow us to do whatever struck our fancy at the moment, whether it was moral or not. However, it is also the powerful belief formed in the right brain that contacts the deity energy pools and creates manifestations.

One of the first tasks a magician must do is reprogram the subconscious mind to eliminate old messages of failure, dissatisfaction, and lack of belief in anything that cannot be seen, felt, or dissected and placed under a microscope. We all are constantly bombarded with these negative types of messages by family, so-called friends, and of course enemies; we have been conditioned in this manner from birth. That is why it is so important that friends and companions be chosen carefully, whatever age you are.

Ideas for limitations and failures must be kept to a minimum, whether this pertains to goal-planning or ritual. This programming can be changed into positive actions with certain techniques during meditation, such as visualizing yourself surrounded by white light and then dropping your problems and problem people down an imaginary well.

During ritual, the left brain is lulled into a false sense of control by the chants, tools, candles, and movements. All these tangible, logical things lead it to believe that everything is normal and explainable, that nothing illogical is happening. The left brain becomes so involved that it forgets to monitor the run-away creativity of the right brain. At the same time these tools and activities become symbols to the right brain for use in its creative work.

The left brain does not like emotion; emotion is not logical. But emotion is of vital importance in ritual and magick; unless you are emotionally involved, unless you really care about getting results, you may as well spend your time reading a book or watching a movie. Fluctuating emotions have no place in true magick, but controlled emotions are vitally necessary. The more emotionally involved you are, the more effective the manifestation. The trick is to release that emotion at the end of the ceremony.

To work effective magick, you must believe you can cause things to happen; that you have the power within yourself to change your life. Until you can reprogram your subconscious mind to believe this, manifestations will take longer to come into being.

To begin making the changes needed to do magick, you must start by working on your hidden or inner self. You must change bad habits: negative thoughts of yourself, lying, cheating, stealing, broken promises, addictive lifestyles (whether drugs, alcohol, temper, uncontrolled sex, or other negative problems). As you begin to create these changes, you will find that you will like yourself better and that magickal results flow more freely.

Some schools of magickal thought will tell you that doing magick for yourself is selfish and wrong. Throw out this negative thought immediately! This is an idea held over from Judeo-Christian beliefs and has nothing to do with ritual magick. The truth is, if you cannot manifest for yourself, you have little chance of manifesting anything for others.

There is, however, one great rule of morality in magick: Do what you will if you harm no other being. You can never really benefit by deliberately harming another creature through magick. The eventual backlash of karma is not worth the risk. However, one also must consider what happens if evil is left to flourish. Those in Witchcraft believe that allowing an evil to exist unchecked is harmful to everyone. If action must be taken, carefully consider all angles of positive magick before proceeding. It is essential to think through your reasons for doing magick. But be sure to protect yourself, your possessions, your family, and friends.

Witches brewing

Human willpower is a powerful and real force; it is quite capable of being disciplined and concentrated to produce what seems to be supernormal results.[5] The willpower is directed by imagination, that prerogative of the right brain. The universe does not consist of chance factors; it is an ordered system with correspondences in all things. Using correspondences and understanding their patterns will enable you to use archetypal energies for your own purposes, whether good or bad.

The Gods/Goddesses, archetypal energies, or spirits are morally indifferent or neutral.[6] The power is there, it exists; how it is used becomes the responsibility of the magician. Positive magick brings beneficial results; negative magick brings results, but the scales of karma must eventually be balanced and the price paid. Unfortunately, in the minds of many people the word *karma* has come to mean punishment. This is not an accurate definition. Karma, which is closely tied to reincarnation, merely means that every action causes an equalizing reaction: good begets reward; bad begets correction.

The Gods themselves are supernormal stimuli to be used by humankind as a catalyst for raising consciousness and improving the environment or immediate world surroundings. Ritual, in its fullest sense and by whatever manner it is performed, brings about changes in the interior and exterior environments of individuals and nations. Knowledge of this action and reaction is why magicians often work on global issues as well as their own immediate needs. This is also why the orthodox churches and religions fight so hard against Pagan religions; they do not want to change the existing condition. Change would strip away their power because there would no longer be a need for their stultified methods.

C. G. Jung says that ritual spiritual experiences in a group and those experienced alone are quite different, that personal experiences are of a higher level. This is entirely possible, particularly if group members are not all committed to a high level of morality and purpose. This is why most magickal ritual groups carefully screen applicants for membership. Disruptive people can either siphon off the energy for themselves or create such chaos that ritual achieves no positive results.

The whole idea behind participating in a ritual, or even entering a sanctuary (even a Christian, Hebrew, or Moslem one), is to reach a state known in India as "the other mind."[7] During this sacred drama, the participants are both audience and performers, thus activating areas of the mind that are not used during everyday activity. This "game," as it might be called, frees our minds and spirits from the bonds of theology, which pretends to know the laws of the Gods. It also frees us from the bonds of logic of the left brain so we can go beyond the known areas of human physical experience.

"The power of belief is more potent and active than the object or system believed in."[8] Every magician, sooner or later, discovers that the archetypal energy pools, or Gods, exist in a myriad of forms and patterns. Only political religions argue over the gender or will of deities. An effective magician goes beyond these petty, control-centered discussions, seeking only a specific aspect of archetypal energy to raise his consciousness and create environmental changes to better the world.

There is no basis, not even in Nature herself, for belief in only a male god. This tenet serves only to justify male control of social institutions.[9] The same applies to the "Chosen People Syndrome,"[10] where everyone who does not profess belief in a specific religion (or lack of it, as in Communism) is damned and evil. The reasoning of this Syndrome excuses its followers from recognizing the humanness of dissenters and treating them as they would treat their own members.

Ritual is essential to humankind. We cannot live productive lives without it. The drive to perform it, in whatever manner we choose, appears to be embedded deep within our collective unconscious; it is a logical path for humans to take in seeking either the inner self or the gods. And magick, the using of invisible, intangible powers, is a natural offshoot of ritual. The words a person uses to describe ritual and magick will often be different, according to their racial or religious background, but in the final analysis the words will mean the same thing. All peoples, all religions perform ritual and magick, however much some of them vehemently declare they do not. It is perfectly permissible—and desirable—for you to compose your own rituals or re-work old rituals. Our world is not the same as it was a thousand or even one hundred years ago. Change equates with growth. Some people do not feel comfortable working with ceremonies that use ancient-sounding language. They can only get into the rhythm of magick if the wording is in the modern vernacular. For others, modern verbiage throws them off stride. They need the more ancient formality to lift their thoughts and emotions above the everyday and commonplace.

By all means, feel free to worship in the style that works best for you. If you are not certain of your personal preference, try rituals in both styles. You may discover that you can use either type, depending upon the ceremony being performed. Whatever wording feels right for you is the style to use.

The same applies to the use of ready-made rituals. As long as you incorporate certain aspects of a ritual, there is no reason you cannot write your own. This often becomes necessary when you have definite personal goals in mind and are unable to find anything that fits your needs. After all, at the very beginning of all religions, someone had to write the first rituals.

However, there are a few guidelines that should be observed when composing rituals and ceremonies. First of all, do not mix pantheons. If you feel that you want to use the name of Isis, for instance, then write the ceremony with an Egyptian flavor, using the names of other Egyptian deities, if they are necessary. Do not use the names of Isis and Odhinn together, or Isis and Lugh. You want your subconscious mind to get a compact, orderly message that you are changing levels of vibration, that you are turning off your ordinary existence and moving into the realms of magick. This continuity must include symbols, robes (if any), and the whole general atmosphere of the ceremony.

As always, there are exceptions to the rule, but these must be carefully calculated and controlled. Dion Fortune gives excellent examples of the mixing of pantheons in her books *The Sea Priestess* and *Moon Magic*.[11] In salutations and praise to the Goddess, Dion Fortune lists the many diverse names by which the Goddess is known. The worshipper is acknowledging the honor given to the Goddess by all cultures, but dwelling upon the unchanging basic attributes of Her power.

Each ritual should have an opening, middle, and ending—or, in oversimplified terms, praise, petition, and thanksgiving. Depending upon the ritual system used (see later chapters on specific systems), the magician may cast a circle, set the Watchtowers, call upon power animals, ancestors, certain deities, or Nature spirits. Some magicians may not adhere completely to just one magickal system; rather, they are eclectic in nature, using different systems at different times for different projects.

According to personal inclinations, and whether a magician works solitary or in a group, one might include music and dance for an emotional response, intellectual exercises to stretch the mind, or spiritual contemplative devotions. Prayers, chants, invocations, any physical or mental activities that enable the magician to engage the subconscious mind can be worked into the writing of such rituals.

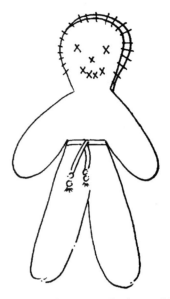

Poppet for sympathetic magick

Sympathetic magick includes probably some of the easiest rituals to do. Unfortunately, the widest-known example of sympathetic magick is the sticking of pins in a doll or poppet that represents a person, the idea being that the named person will feel pain in the area where the pin is stuck. However, sympathetic magick has much wider uses than this negative activity. Poppets can be used for healing by stuffing them with healing herbs. Green (for growth and money) candles are burned to bring prosperity and success. Salt (a sterilizing material) can be lightly sprinkled throughout a house to rid it of negative entities and vibrations. A very old example was the Pagan activity of jumping high or copulating in newly plowed fields to encourage the crops to grow abundantly.

It is a good idea to work out a number of various types of rituals, keeping them in a loose-leaf notebook at the beginning of your endeavors. When you have worked with several and find that they produce satisfactory results on your physical, mental, emotional, or spiritual levels, copy these into a permanent Book of Shadows,[12] or whatever you call your private ritual book. It is also a good idea to work up rites for special occasions: seasonal celebrations, New and Full Moons, healings, farewells for deceased persons, initiations, etc. There are many ready-made rituals in publications. If you copy these into your Book, please make a footnote about the publication and author. Then if you share these with other magicians, you can give credit where credit is due.

The Ancient and Shining Ones was written to be a reference guide for magickal practitioners to use in creating and performing rituals. The whole idea behind this book is to offer the magician a compact cross-reference whereby he can check to see which names in different pantheons symbolize the same aspect, or what each aspect represents in exact terms of petitioning for physical results. Wherever a particular name is used in a ritual, and you want to use a different pantheon or culture name, turn in this book to the pantheon (or cross-reference section) you want to use and choose a suitable substitute.

HOURS OF THE DAY							
	Mo	Tu	We	Th	Fr	Sa	Su
1	☾	♂	☿	♃	♀	♄	☉
2	♄	☉	☾	♂	☿	♃	♀
3	♃	♀	♄	☉	☾	♂	☿
4	♂	☿	♃	♀	♄	☉	☾
5	☉	☾	♂	☿	♃	♀	♄
6	♀	♄	☉	☾	♂	☿	♃
7	☿	♃	♀	♄	☉	☾	♂
8	☾	♂	☿	♃	♀	♄	☉
9	♄	☉	☾	♂	☿	♃	♀
10	♃	♀	♄	☉	☾	♂	☿
11	♂	☿	♃	♀	♄	☉	☾
12	☉	☾	♂	☿	♃	♀	♄

HOURS OF THE NIGHT							
	Mo	Tu	We	Th	Fr	Sa	Su
1	♀	♄	☉	☾	♂	☿	♃
2	☿	♃	♀	♄	☉	☾	♂
3	☾	♂	☿	♃	♀	♄	☉
4	♄	☉	☾	♂	☿	♃	♀
5	♃	♀	♄	☉	☾	♂	☿
6	♂	☿	♃	♀	♄	☉	☾
7	☉	☾	♂	☿	♃	♀	♄
8	♀	♄	☉	☾	♂	☿	♃
9	☿	♃	♀	♄	☉	☾	♂
10	☾	♂	☿	♃	♀	♄	☉
11	♄	☉	☾	♂	☿	♃	♀
12	♃	♀	♄	☉	☾	♂	☿

One of the earliest views of the Moon

It is also a good idea to use either one of the planetary tables or Qabalistic tables as a guideline to help in setting up rituals. (It is also advisable to check the phases of the Moon. Charts of the planetary hours are found on pages 26 and 27.) First, choose a table that matches the type of ritual you want to do. Use the colors, incense, plant, etc., listed there as part of the ritual makeup. As an example, if you planned to do a ritual for love, you might choose the planetary table for Venus. For the altar cloth you could use a light green or pink. Musk or rose incense along with roses or daffodils on the altar would help. Put a small statue or picture of a dove or cat where you can remind your subconscious mind in a visual sense. For jewelry you could wear copper set with jade or amber; if you cannot afford cut stones, simply set pieces of rough stones of the appropriate kinds or colors as focal points. As a further added focus for energy, you would set the ritual for a Friday in the hour of Venus and perhaps call upon the angel Haniel, if you practice Ceremonial Magick.

Before beginning any ritual, the magician should take time for physical cleansing (a bath[13]), and cleansing of the mental, emotional, and spiritual by meditation. This sets the stage for the subconscious mind to shift gears and prepare for magick.

The powers of the Moon phases are also ancient knowledge. It is traditional that ritual spellworking for banishing, decrease, or removal of problems takes place from after the Full Moon until the New Moon, with the day or night of the New Moon being strongest. Spellworking for increase, growth, and gain takes place from after the New Moon until the Full Moon, with the day or night of the Full Moon being the most powerful.

Most of the human body is made up of water or liquids. The type of energy from the phases of the Moon conceivably will be reflected in our bodies. Therefore, it is logical that the Moon should affect your body and emotions just as it affects the tides of the Earth. It is more efficient to work magick in concert with the Moon energy than against it.

Whatever magickal system you choose to follow, it would be wise to heed the "Four Powers of the Magus (Magician)," a very old teaching in magick. It is: *to know, to dare, to will, to be silent. To know* means to gain the knowledge to do ritual magick; *to dare* to practice it; *to will* the manifestation; and *to be silent* about what you are doing. The last part is especially important. Talking about magick diffuses the energy flow. Silence also keeps unsympathetic people from directing negative thoughts toward your efforts. People who talk about their magickal operations seldom achieve real magick.

There are essentially two types of ritual magick: evocation and invocation. Evocation is primarily used in Ceremonial Magick and is the commanding of certain forces and entities by Names of Power and sigils. These rituals are done in a mixture of Greek, Hebrew, and unknown languages. They are ordinarily based on a framework of Judaism or Christianity, with belief in the power of angels. The compelled entity is forced into a magickal triangle drawn outside the circle. Only the lower orders of spirits are evoked, and it can be extremely dangerous if you do not know exactly what you are doing.

Invocation is used by Witches and most Pagans and is the safest and easiest form of magick to perform. It invites higher spirits and the gods to enter the magickal circle. This type of ritual does not use strange tongues and is never a command. It is much more harmless to invoke than evoke. It is also spiritually uplifting because the practitioner is dealing with more spiritual, higher entities. This is not to say that Ceremonial Magicians are not spiritually minded; they use both invocation and evocation.

Being responsible in the use of magick is very important. Spellworking, especially that done in a moment of pain and anger, that harms others, harms you in the long run. Karmic debt cannot be avoided, although sometimes it appears to be delayed, as we have all noticed when someone who terrorizes and brutalizes others seems to get away with such behavior.

However, karmic scales demand balance; sooner or later the retribution comes. The important point for every magician to learn is to seek ways of positively using magick. Protect yourself, your loved ones, and your possessions. Refusing to protect yourself only opens you to more of the same treatment. For example, if you must deal with a harassing landlord, you can spell for another, better place to live. The landlord's karma will balance itself.

We ran into a sticky problem when we tore up a hearth in our new home. Underneath the hearth was a detailed curse, written by two men who had previously rented

the house. I took the paper to my altar and had a long talk with the Goddess about the problem; I did not specify any punishment, only the protection of my family, pets, and property. Then I carefully built a mental brick wall around the property and burned the paper in my cauldron. Several weeks later, we heard of the harsh fate that had befallen the two men in question. It just does not pay to threaten a magician; they have friends in high places.

Ritual can be any predetermined performance by a person, whether or not one calls oneself a magician, with a specific goal in mind. The goal can be physical, mental, emotional, or spiritual. Everyone performs rituals, from brushing

Libra, the balance

their teeth in the morning to worship of a deity. To use a ritual to gain the best results requires dedication and determination on the part of the individual. Each ritual, whatever its goal, needs to be personal and planned. The responsibility for the results lies with each practitioner.

ENDNOTES

1. *Webster's 7th New Collegiate Dictionary.* G. & C. Merriam & Co., Springfield, MA: 1967.

2. Adler, Margot. *Drawing Down the Moon.* MacGregor Mathers wrote that magic is "the science of the control of the secret forces of nature." Crowley and others also came up with similar, although differently worded, statements. They all mean the same thing.

3. Conway, D. J. *Celtic Magic.* St. Paul, MN: Llewellyn Publications, 1990.

4. The costume details given in each chapter are not meant to be all-inclusive. Each magician may choose what seems best, for him or her, adding or subtracting details.

5. King, Francis, and Skinner, Stephen. *Techniques of High Magic.*

6. Jung, C. G. *The Archetypes and the Collective Unconscious.*

7. Campbell, Joseph. *The Masks of God: Primitive Mythology.* The Sanskrit word *anya-manas* means absent-mindedness or possession by a spirit. This is the state of mind where a person separates from personal logic of self-possession and is overcome by a creative logic, where, Campbell says, A is B and C is also B.

8. Stewart, R. J. *Living Magical Arts.*

9. Daly, Mary. *Beyond God the Father.*

10. Starhawk. *The Spiral Dance.* When a religious group with these delusions is in control of an area or nation, they soon institute inquistions, Witch-hunts, pogroms, executions, censorship, and concentration camps.

11. Fortune, Dion. *The Sea Priestess; Moon Magic.* York Beach, ME: Samuel Weiser, 1985.

12. The Book of Shadows, as it is called in Witchcraft, is a book in which Witches write rituals, invocations, and spells. Its name comes from the fact that everything in it is only a shadow of reality of the Other World.

13. Ritual baths are important for several reasons. During this time, the magician begins attuning his subconscious mind to switch over to magickal work. The magician removes the mundane vibrations from the physical body, some of them possibly negative which have been picked up in the course of the day's contact with other people. Water is universally considered a purifier, as is the salt (sometimes scented with appropriate essential oils) that is added to the bath. Some magicians also like to burn incense and a white candle during this

bath; this practice is a further suggestion to the subconscious mind to prepare for extraordinary experiences.

BIBLIOGRAPHY

Bias, Clifford. *Ritual Book of Magic*. NY: Samuel Weiser, 1981.

Bonewits, P. E. I. *Real Magic*. Berkeley, CA: Creative Arts Books, 1979.

Bouisson, M. *Magic: Its History and Principal Rites*. Trans. G. Almayrac. NY: Dutton, 1961.

Brennan, J. H. *Experimental Magic*. UK: Aquarian Press, 1984.

Butler, W. E. *The Magician: His Training and Work*. UK: Aquarian Press, 1969.

Cavendish, Richard. *The Black Arts*. NY: G. P. Putnam's Sons, 1967. (Not a book of black magick.)

Conway, D. J. *Celtic Magic*. St. Paul, MN: Llewellyn Publications, 1990.

Conway, D. J. *Norse Magic*. St. Paul, MN: Llewellyn Publications, 1990.

Conway, David. *Magic: An Occult Primer*. NY: E. P. Dutton & Co., 1972.

Cunningham, Scott. *Earth Power*. St. Paul, MN: Llewellyn Publications, 1983.

Crowley, Aleister. *Magick in Theory and Practice*. NY: Dover Publications, 1976.

Daly, Mary. *Beyond God the Father*. Boston, MA: Beacon Press, 1973.

Denning, Melita, and Phillips, Osborne. *The Magical Philosophy*, Vol. I-V. St. Paul, MN: Llewellyn Publications, 1974–1981.

Denning, Melita, and Phillips, Osborne. *Magical States of Consciousness*. St. Paul, MN: Llewellyn Publications, 1985.

Gray, William G. *Inner Traditions of Magic*. York Beach, ME: Samuel Weiser, 1984.

Gray, William G. *Magical Ritual Methods*. NY: Samuel Weiser, 1980.

King, Frances, and Sutherland, Isabel. *The Rebirth of Magic*. UK: Corgi Books, 1982.

Knight, Gareth. *The Rose Cross and the Goddess*. NY: Destiny Books, 1985.

Kraig, Donald. *Modern Magick: Eleven Lessons in the High Magickal Arts*. St. Paul, MN: Llewellyn Publications, 1989.

Shaw, S. Indries. *The Secret Lore of Magic*. NY: The Citadel Press, 1958.

Starhawk. *The Spiral Dance*. NY: Harper & Row, 1979.

Stewart, R. J. *Living Magical Arts*. UK: Blandford Press, 1987.

Stewart, R. J. *The Underworld Initiation: A Journey Towards Psychic Transformation*. UK: Aquarian Press, 1985.

Tyson, Donald. *The New Magus: Ritual Magic as a Personal Process*. St. Paul, MN: Llewellyn Publications, 1988.

Valiente, Doreen. *Natural Magic*. Custer, WA: Phoenix Publishing, 1985.

CHAPTER FIVE

WITCHCRAFT AND PAGANISM

Ancient Pagans in worship

THERE IS a difference between Witchcraft[1] and Paganism, although many of the basic beliefs are the same. Witchcraft, or the Craft, as many call it, is primarily a Goddess-based Nature religion, with a dual-deity foundation. Paganism believes in pantheons or pluralities of deities, with a God or Goddess predominating according to the system and worshippers. Witchcraft almost always does its rituals and spellworkings within a cast circle; Paganism sometimes does, sometimes does not, depending upon the group.

Witchcraft, or Wicca, if you prefer a more acceptable name, is both a religion and a magickal system.[2] However, it is also a way of life, of looking at everything around you. The word *Wicca* or *Witch* comes from the Anglo-Saxon language and means "wise one." Originally, the word for a male Witch was *Wicca* and a female *Wicce*, with the plural being *Wiccan*. Today, however, the common word for both sexes is Wicca.

Some Witches resist using the word Wicca, saying it only bows to orthodox demands for acceptability. The best statement I have heard on this subject comes from the song "Witch" by Lady Isadora:

I call myself a Witch because
A witch is what I am,
And like a Jew in Nazi Germany
I don't define my name
To suit the Master Plan . . .
I don't believe in Satan
He's a poor excuse for Pan.
I'm a child of Holy Mother Earth
And I'm gonna stand up to
The Propaganda Man
In every way I can.[3]

The word Pagan comes from the Latin *paganus*, meaning "country dweller." After Christianity began its militant takeover, Pagan and Heathen became derogatory terms. The Christians really meant they could not influence the country dwellers and people from the heath except by physical force, therefore, those people must be backwards and more than a little stupid. In fact, just the opposite was true; the Pagans and Heathens were extremely wise to the Christian takeover and wanted no part of being controlled and ordered around.

The Pagan healers and wise people were a real threat to the Christian church. First, because they were better at their chosen tasks of healing and divination than the Christian priests, helping for free or small donations when these priests demanded conversion to their way of religion and as much money as they could get. Second, a great many of these Pagans were priestesses, something abhorrent to the Christians who believed that only their male priests had "power" and could communicate with "God." Third, these healers and wise people clearly saw the dangers of Christianity and, until severe persecutions got under way, did not hesitate to point this out to the less educated commoners.

Paganism also tends to be a Nature-oriented religion, again depending upon the group practicing the rituals. It is based upon an ancient pantheon, such as Norse, Celtic, Roman, etc. There is usually no claim that they are practicing "real" ancient rituals; historical details are for the most part too sketchy to make such claims. Most of the Pagan groups write their rituals and spellworkings with the flavor of the selected pantheon, incorporating some aspects of both Witchcraft and Ceremonial Magick. This does not make the rituals any less effective or powerful; in my opinion, it strengthens them.

To be technically correct, I suppose one should say that practitioners of the Craft and Paganism today should be called Neo-Witches and Neo-Pagans, as they do not worship exactly as was done in the past.[4] However, I have never met a Witch or Pagan who really cared about the technicality of being semantically correct. Witches and Pagans are individualists who "do their own thing" and leave others to do theirs.

Witches and Pagans are practical people who seek hidden powers and knowledge, and usually do not conform, at least inwardly, to society's so-called "acceptable" molds. They have close ties with Nature and all other beings, living their lives with respect for other humans, animals, plants, and the Earth herself.

There are certain observances and beliefs that all Wiccan individuals and groups hold to be true, regardless of the deity names they choose to use. Witches believe in a main Goddess (the Lady) and a main God (the Lord), with the Goddess having primary importance. For example, the male and female aspects of Nature were personified by the Celts as the White Moon Goddess and the Horned God. The White Moon Goddess and her consort the Horned God are the oldest known deities. This is the basic idea still held by Witches, although they sometimes petition various aspects of each of these main deities, just as the Celts did. Witches believe that all Gods are one God, all Goddesses are one Goddess, and both are united. The Goddess is worshipped as a Triple Deity—Maiden, Mother, and Crone (Dark Mother, Wise Woman, the Hag). The God also is often seen in three aspects: Son, Lover, and Sacrifice, or Lord of Death.

The Maiden is essential to the continuation of all life; her color is white, denoting innocence and newness. She is the springtime, the dawn, eternal youth and vigor, enchantment and seduction, the waxing Moon.

The Mother is the ripeness of womanhood. Her color is red, the color of blood and the life-force. The Mother is summer, the day, lustiness, teacher, the Full Moon.

The Crone, or Dark Mother, sometimes called the Hag, has black as her color, the color of darkness where all life rests before rebirth. This aspect of the Goddess is winter, night, wisdom, counsel, the gateway to death and reincarnation, the waning Moon.

Neither Witches nor Pagans have anything to do with Satan or the Christian Devil.[5] First of all, they do not believe in the Devil; they do, however, believe there are evil spirits. Second, you have to be a Christian or believe in their tenets to be a Satanist, as Satanist ceremonies are a negative parody of Christian ceremonies.

Witches and Pagans believe that this world is only part of reality, that divinity is both male and female. They say humans have more than five senses and that they can be trained to be aware of the Other Worlds. The concept of the Ultimate Creative Force, or God behind the Gods, is the inexplicable life-force of the universe. The Pagans' pantheons of Gods and Goddesses who rule over different parts of Nature and help in the evolution of the universe are merely different aspects of this life-force.

The Craft uses certain symbols with a magickal significance, such as the pentagram.[6] They observe Moon phases in connection with spellworking. They believe that powerful Witches of the past are still able to help those practicing the Craft today. And they believe in magick and its powers.

Most Pagans and Witches believe in reincarnation and the destiny of karma. They say it is logical to believe in reincarnation

Triple goddess image

THE ANCIENT & SHINING ONES

rather than obliteration at death, because, as modern science tells us, nothing in this universe can be destroyed; it only changes its form. Karma, which is deeply involved in reincarnation, means simply that every action causes an equalizing reaction; it is not necessarily punishment. Between incarnations the soul is said to rest in a Pagan paradise called by various names. The statements that this afterlife land co-exists with our own identifies it with the astral plane.

Both Witches and Pagans believe in this other world or plane of existence that is made up of spirits, both human and elemental. The Ceremonial Magician and shaman share this belief in the astral plane. This other-world plane is made up of a different type of energy that vibrates at a higher rate than this physical world. At the same time, the astral plane and this world surround and interpenetrate each other. The astral plane is very responsive to thoughts and emotions. The souls of Nature spirits, animals, and beings created by many strongly projected human thoughts dwell on certain areas of this plane. Part of this world is the world of ghosts, or earth-bound human spirits; it is also the place where one can meet other astral travelers.

The human astral body,[7] which survives after death, is how humans function in the astral world. While still in this world, it is said that a person can travel on the astral during sleep or by deliberate out-of-body methods. This is the reality behind the old stories of Witches flying.

Higher levels of the astral plane contain departed higher souls, while the lower levels are inhabited by spiritual darkness and lower souls. The words "higher" and "lower" have nothing to do with the social classes, outward appearance while on Earth, or the amount of time a person spent in worship. Rather, these terms indicate areas of existence inhabited by evolved or devolved souls. Witches know that what appear to be opposites of matter, form, energy, and force are not really opposing at all. They are simply different manifestations of each other.

Witches celebrate eight yearly festivals and each Full Moon. There are eight traditional Wiccan holy days. The four Greater Sabbats are Imbolc,[8] Beltane, Lunasa, and Samhain. The four Lesser Sabbats are Spring Equinox, Summer Solstice, Autumn Equinox, and Winter Solstice. At the Equinoxes the flow of power is strong, while the tides of the Solstices are quieter. The wheel is the symbol of the year with the Solstices and Equinoxes as the main spokes, and the remaining four holy days as additional spokes. Monthly Wiccan meetings are held at or near the Full Moon, as the Full Moon is the high point of psychic power.

Imbolc, February 2, is a time of cleansing and newborn lambs. The name Imbolc comes from the word *oimelc*, or sheep's milk. It is a festival of the Maiden in preparation for growth and renewal.

Spring Equinox, about March 21, is when light and darkness are in balance but the light is growing stronger.

Beltane is May 1. Some of the other names for it are May Day or Lady Day. It is primarily a fertility festival. The powers of elves and fairies are growing and will reach their height at Summer Solstice.

Summer Solstice, about June 21, is when the hours of daylight are longest. The Sun is at the highest before beginning its slide into darkness. Traditionally, herbs gathered on this day are very powerful. On this night elves and fairies abound in numbers.

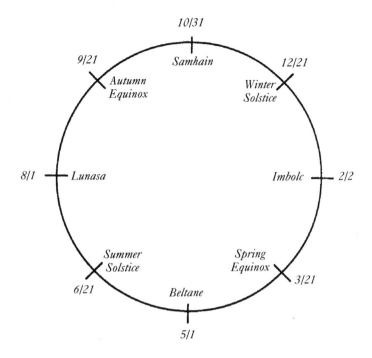

Pagan Wheel of the Year

Lunasa is August 1. It is a preharvest festival, the turning point in Mother Earth's year. The last herbs are gathered.

Autumn Equinox, about September 21, was a time of rest after labor, completion of the harvest. Again the hours of day and night are in balance, with the darkness increasing.

Samhain, pronounced SOW-en and called Halloween today, was also known as Ancestor Night or Feast of the Dead. Because the veil between the worlds is thinnest on this night, it was and is considered an excellent time for divination. Feasts are made in remembrance of dead ancestors and as an affirmation of continuing life. Many northern European cultures counted Samhain as the beginning of their year.

Winter Solstice occurs about December 21. This is the time of death and rebirth of the Sun God. The days are shortest, the Sun at its lowest point. The Full Moon after Yule is considered the most powerful of the whole year.

Other Pagans celebrate many of the same festivals with additional holy days, depending upon the pantheons and magickal systems they follow. The eight holy days of the Witches appear to be European in basis,[9] but nearly every magickal system and religion around the world noted and celebrated the Solstices and Equinoxes.

Most of the Pagan years were based on lunar months, thus having thirteen months to a year. Celebration of the Solstices and Equinoxes was and is done on a particular day when the Sun changes into particular zodiacal signs. This is listed on most calendars, especially the astrological ones such as published by Llewellyn, and varies slightly from year to year. The remaining six holy days are honored by many Wiccans on a specific day also.

Most of the ancient Pagan world counted days as starting at sunset or midnight. All their festivals were celebrated on the eve, or night before, the holy day. Therefore, Summer Solstice was celebrated on Midsummer's Eve, and so on.

Witches, Ceremonial Magicians, and many Pagans begin their ceremonies by casting a circle about the area or room where they are planning to do magickal work. To most cultures, the circle is a symbol of infinity and eternity. It has no beginning and no end. When properly drawn, with the candles of the Elements at the four directions and the altar in the center, the circle becomes a mandala,[10] or sacred symbol, upon which the magician stands.

The circle is drawn by the dagger or sword as protection against potentially dangerous forces or spirits. It also concentrates the cone of power that is raised within its boundaries. This cone of power, seen by outsiders, is most likely what brought about the idea of Witches or magicians wearing pointed hats. A properly drawn circle becomes an invisible boundary, having power in this and other realms. The energy of that boundary keeps out negative influences and contains the power raised until the practitioner is ready to release it. The circle is also a neutral working area, capable of regenerating and amplifying the kind of power the magician is creating.

In Witchcraft, it is traditional to "draw" or cast a circle with a nine-foot circumference. However, if the coven, or group of Witches, is large, this size circle is very crowded. It is not essential that the circle be a certain size. The concentration and visualization used during the casting determines the value of the circle.

The magick circle is an imaginary boundary (to the physical eye), but when properly drawn, has great power in both this world and other realms. Once drawn, practitioners usually do not cross the boundary until the ritual is finished. Cats, however, have the unusual ability of being able to cross the cast circle without disturbing the power flow. Casting a proper circle requires concentrated visualization of silver-blue light issuing from the dagger or sword and rising from the imaginary line. The line is begun in the east and drawn sunwise around the area, ending and overlapping in the east.[11]

Following the casting of the circle, the perimeter is sprinkled with consecrated salt and water, then cleansed with smoking incense. The four Element candles (see the chapter on Elements) are lit and the rulers of the Elements called upon for protection and assistance. At the appropriate point in the ceremony, a cup of wine is blessed and dedicated to the Gods, then shared by the participants. When the ceremony and any spellworking are completed, the Elements are dismissed and the circle ritually broken.

The pentagram, a five-pointed star, is an ancient symbol. Its five points represent the four Elements, plus Spirit. One can see it in mundane places, such as police badges and the top of Christmas trees, although the Christians now have declared a spiritual war on it. It was and is a favorite symbol of Witches and magicians, as it also represents the five Elements within humankind; the head corresponding to the top point, the arms to the two side points, and the legs to the two bottom points. The Satanists in the U.S.A., who seem to try to corrupt spiritual symbols, use the pentagram turned upside-down.

Sometimes the pentagram is called a pentacle, although that word now means any disk of metal or wood that is engraved with a pentagram and other magickal symbols. The disk is placed on a Witch's altar as a power-point for consecrating objects, such as water, wine, or ritual tools.

The use of certain gestures and words, when performed in a specific way with candles, herbs, or other magickal equipment, is known as spellwork or spelling. Spellwork was and is an important part of all Pagan religions. Pagans believe in actively participating in the unfolding of opportunity and development in their lives. They believe that it is their right to confidently petition their deities for what they want. Furthermore, they believe it is their responsibility to do whatever they personally can to aid in gaining their desires. To do this, all Pagans engage in a form of spellworking.

Spellwork is a type of magick, the drawing down of energy from another plane of existence. This energy is woven

The pentagram

into a specific physical form or result by the use of certain words, gestures, thoughts, and practices. Be aware that if you use magick or spellwork to interfere with another's free will, you involve yourself with that person's karma, whether positive or negative.

Witches and most Pagans use invoking magick for their rites. (See the chapter on Ritual and Magick.) Certain Archetypes are asked to enter the magickal circle and, sometimes, into the High Priest or High Priestess. It is a spiritually uplifting experience to feel the archetypal power build up during a ritual. And when the powers are released at the end of the ceremony, there is a void, exhausting yet fulfilling at the same time.

Witches and Pagans are not evil. They do not practice blood sacrifices, torture, or other despicable acts. They do not go about casting curses on people for infractions of courtesy; however, they also are not doormats and will protect themselves from persecution in whatever manner is necessary. Of course, someone is bound to point out an exception to this description of Witches and Pagans. The key word here is "exception." Everyone is probably aware that a few years ago a group of Christians were shown on television praying for the death of a Supreme Court judge who did not rule to their liking; the Christians would say this was an exception to what they actually practice.

The followers of Witchcraft and Paganism are individuals following a personalized spiritual path that is right for them. They tend to be tolerant of others who follow dissimilar paths, but with the same goal: to bring the human soul as close to the Ultimate Creating Force as possible. They believe strongly in free will, the freedom to worship in the manner that each chooses. And they continue to work for every person's right to these freedoms. The history of Paganism and Witchcraft is an ancient one, going back to the beginnings of humankind's searching for divine fulfillment. The methods of worship in Witchcraft and Paganism have been updated to suit the modern individual, but the intent and purpose remain the same.

Chinese Witches performing a ritual

ENDNOTES

1. Starhawk. *The Spiral Dance*. Starhawk and others write that Witchcraft is probably the oldest Western religion. It is not based on a sacred book, a human "saint" or leader, or a dogma. In 1484, the Papal Bull of Innocent VIII set into motion the reign of terror against Witchcraft propagated by the Inquisition.

2. Buckland, Raymond. *The Tree: The Complete Book of Saxon Witchcraft*. Mr. Buckland says that Witches do not seek converts, and this is very true. Those in Paganism, and particularly Witchcraft, believe that the people who would feel comfortable in those beliefs will find the right people in those areas to teach and guide them.

3. This song comes from the tape *The Queen of Earth and Sky* by Lady Isadora. She also has two other beautiful tapes available: *Priestess of the Pentacle* and *The Witching Hour*. All three can be obtained from Dance of Life Productions, P. O. Box 2483, Des Moines, IA 50311. Guenevere's Music (ASCAP); printed with permission.

4. Aidan Kelly, in *Crafting the Art of Magic*, reveals how Gerald Gardner went about evolving the rituals of Witchcraft. It is fairly obvious from Kelly's research that, however much modern Witches would like to believe in a direct link to Stone Age ritual, there is no evidence of a tie to any "ancient and authentic" way of worship. This statement does not make Witchcraft

false. In the beginning of all religions some person or persons were led to create the necessary rituals that would help their followers walk the revealed spritual path.

5. Glass, Justine. *Witchcraft: The Sixth Sense.* Ms. Glass and others state that the Horned God is more closely related to Pan and other Nature deities than to the Christian Devil. The Horned God was declared by the Christians to be the Devil when it became apparent that the common people were not giving up their fertility celebrations.

6. A pentagram is a star whose five points represent the four Elements and Spirit.

7. There is more than one explanation for the astral body, that form which vibrates on a higher level than the physical body. One description of this body is the soul itself. Another explains that it is a vehicle for the soul, a means for it to travel while the person still lives. This latter explanation seems more plausible to me.

8. Spellings of the festival names differ from group to group and system to system. To simplify things, only one spelling will be given in this text.

9. Murray, Margaret A. *The God of the Witches.*

10. A mandala is a Hindu or Buddhist graphic symbol of the universe.

11. Conway, D. J. *Celtic Magic* and *Norse Magic.* Both books give detailed rituals for casting the circle, setting up the four Elements, and performing spells and seasonal ceremonies.

BIBLIOGRAPHY

Adler, Margot. *Drawing Down the Moon.* Boston, MA: Beacon Press, 1981.

Bell, Jessie Wicker. *The Grimoire of Lady Sheba.* St. Paul, MN: Llewellyn Publications, 1972.

Briffault, Robert. *The Mothers*, 3 vol. NY: Macmillan, 1927.

Buckland, Raymond. *Anatomy of the Occult.* NY: Samuel Weiser, 1977.

Buckland, Raymond. *The Tree: The Complete Book of Saxon Witchcraft.* NY: Samuel Weiser, 1981.

Budapest, Z. *The Holy Book of Women's Mysteries.* Oakland, CA: Susan B. Anthony Coven No. 1, 1979.

Chappell, Helen. *The Waxing Moon: A Gentle Guide to Magick.* NY: Links Books, 1974.

Conway, D. J. *Celtic Magic.* St. Paul, MN: Llewellyn Publications, 1990.

Conway, D. J. *Norse Magic.* St. Paul, MN: Llewellyn Publications, 1990.

Crowther, Patricia. *Lid off the Cauldron.* York Beach, ME: Samuel Weiser, 1985.

Crowther, Patricia and Arnold. *The Witches Speak.* NY: Samuel Weiser, 1976.

De Givry, G. *A Pictorial Anthology of Witchcraft, Magic and Alchemy*. NY: University Books, 1958. (Reprint of 1931 edition).

Farrar, Janet and Stewart. *Eight Sabbats for Witches*. UK: Robert Hale, 1981.

Farrar, Janet and Stewart. *The Witches' Way*. UK: Robert Hale, 1984.

Farrar, Stewart. *What Witches Do*. Custer, WA: Phoenix Publishing, 1983.

Frost, Gavin and Yvonne. *The Magic Power of Witchcraft*. West Nyack, NY: Parker Publishing, 1976.

Gardner, Gerald B. *Witchcraft Today*. NY: The Citadel Press, 1955.

Glass, Justine. *Witchcraft, the Sixth Sense*. North Hollywood, CA: Wilshire Book Co., 1965.

Huson, Paul. *Mastering Witchcraft*. NY: G. P. Putnam's Sons, 1970.

Janus-Mithras, Nuit-Hilaria and Mer-Amun. *Wicca: The Ancient Way*. Ontario, Canada: Isis Urania, 1981.

Kelly, Aidan A. *Crafting the Art of Magic*. St. Paul, MN: Llewellyn Publications, 1991.

Leek, Sybil. *The Complete Art of Witchcraft*. NY: New American Library, 1971.

Leek, Sybil. *Diary of a Witch*. Englewood Cliffs, NJ: Prentice-Hall, 1968.

Leland. Charles Godfrey. *Aradia: Gospel of the Witches*. NY: Hero Press, 1971.

Lethbridge, T. C. *Witches: Investigating an Ancient Religion*. UK: Routledge & Kegan Paul, 1962.

Manning, Al G. *Helping Yourself with White Witchcraft*. West Nyack, NY: Parker Publishing, 1972.

Martello, Leo. *Witchcraft: The Old Religion*. Secaucus, NJ: University Books, 1973.

Murray, Margaret A. *The Divine King in England*. UK: Faber & Faber Ltd., 1954.

Murray, Margaret A. *The God of the Witches*. UK: Oxford University Press, 1981.

Murray, Margaret A. *The Witch-Cult in Western Europe*. UK: Oxford University Press, 1921.

Noteskin, Wallace. *A History of Witchcraft in England*. NY: Crowell, 1968.

Starhawk. *The Spiral Dance*. NY: Harper & Row, 1979.

Valiente, Doreen. *An ABC of Witchcraft Past and Present*. NY: St. Martin's, 1973.

Valiente, Doreen. *Witchcraft For Tomorrow*. UK: Robert Hale, 1983.

CHAPTER SIX

SHAMANISM

Native American family totem

THE SO-CALLED civilized world has always used the term *shaman* interchangeably with medicine man and witch doctor. People readily identify these practitioners with the cultures of Siberia, Alaska, Africa, and North America. Sometimes this combined thinking is appropriate, sometimes not. A shaman can be a medicine man, but a medicine man is not necessarily a shaman. A shaman can also belong to any culture in the world; there is evidence of shamanic knowledge in the Mediterranean and Western Europe. In the truest sense, the shaman is a healer, priest, mystic, and poet.

Shamanism in the strictest sense is part of the religion of Siberia and Central Asia. The word shaman, pronounced SHAH-maan, comes from the Tungus people of Siberia. In other Central and Northern Asian languages, similar words are: Tugusic *saman*, Yakut *ojuna*, Mongolian *buga* and *udagan*, Turko-Tatar *kam*, and the Pali *samana*.[1] In these societies the shaman is the predominant socio-religious figure. Anthropologists have widely adopted the word to apply to a great many cultures who view similar practitioners as wizards, magicians, seers, sorcerers, medicine men, etc.

A shaman can be either a man or a woman. In some cultures, a shaman dresses as a woman, so it is possible that originally shamanism was a female spiritual art.[2] A shaman enters an altered state of consciousness at will in order to contact and use other-world energies for gaining knowledge, healing people, or foreseeing the future.

43

Through journeys in consciousness to other realms, the shaman gains the help and support of at least one, if not more, spiritual "helpers." While in a trance, he believes that his soul leaves his body to ascend or descend into other-worlds where he finds the necessary information to perform his tasks on this plane of existence.

A true shaman is usually a healer first, a prophet second. He does not ordinarily deal in black magick, curses, control of others, or any of the other charges leveled at him by ignorant, narrow-minded people. Every time the shaman makes his journey into the Lowerworld or Upperworld, he is offering up his own self to help another.

Nevill Drury calls shamanism a visionary tradition,[3] while Michael Harner terms it a "great mental and emotional adventure."[4] Shamanism is an ancient mystical practice of using the altered states of consciousness as a means of contacting energies, gods, and spirits from this and other planes of existence. The shaman sees all aspects of the universe as interconnected, a network of energy patterns, vibrations, and entities. It is the shaman's responsibility to be an intermediary between the different worlds.

First and foremost, a shaman is a healer. The ancient shamans, and the new breed of shamans evolving today, both use the same old techniques to create self-healing within themselves or others. Shamanic methods the world over are intrinsically the same, even though the cultures in which they live may be vastly different. Although shamans can be separated by oceans or eons, the basic techniques and experiences are amazingly the same. Shamanism may have evolved because primitive peoples lacked medical technology. Faced with the necessity of heal or die, some gifted individuals probably discovered the capacities of the human mind to heal and provide prophetic, but accurate, information necessary to the health and well-being of the clan.

Even today the so-called scientific miracles of Western medicine are not often enough to solve health problems. Some health professionals and patients are seeking alternative or supplementary methods to surgery and chemicals. This applies to mental as well as physical healing. In fact, most of the field of psychotherapy is less accurate, efficient, and time-tested than the ancient art of shamanism.

A shaman expects the patient to participate one way or another in the healing process. The patient takes part in the actual shamanic ceremony, relying upon the shaman's interpretation of the other-world scenes and symbols which are shown to give him insight into the problem.

Although many of the sights and symbols often encountered by the shaman on his other-world journeys are quite similar to the things seen and experienced by schizophrenics, there is a vast difference in the personalities of the shaman and the mentally disturbed person. The shaman has complete control over beginning and ending his self-imposed journey. He fully knows the difference between the worlds, and can interact in this physical world in a normal manner. In short, the shaman has to become an expert in self-control, self-discipline, and reality in all its dimensions.

It has been proven that most Westerners have no difficulty learning the fundamentals of shamanic practice. The culture in which one has been raised appears to have no bearing on the matter. Also, most people will not have the opportunity to study under an authentic shaman. Again, this does not appear to be essential if one uses some of the excellent written material available.[5] Naturally, it would be beneficial to study under a professional, but it is not absolutely necessary.

A shaman can freely move between what Harner calls an Ordinary State of Consciousness (OSC) and a Shamanic State of Consciousness (SSC). In the SSC, dragons and other "mythical" animals are "real," as is flying, conversing with animals and plants, or experiencing symbols. In the OSC, these things are considered fantasy. Robert Lowie calls the SSC "extraordinary manifestations of reality."[6] Since no one can incontestably prove that there is only one state of consciousness, both states, the Shamanic State of Consciousness and the Ordinary State of Consciousness, are valid realities for firsthand observations. If more people would become shamans and experience the SSC for themselves, their diverse descriptions of the SSC would further the understanding of that non-ordinary reality for those who never enter it.

In a few cultures, hallucinogens have been used to help alter the consciousness of shamans. This is not a necessary or positive procedure in which to become involved. Advances in neurochemistry have recently shown that the human brain produces its own consciousness-altering drugs, one of which is dimethyltryptamine. This fact shows two things: first, that one does not need to add dangerous chemicals to the body to produce the SSC; and second, that Nature herself considers an altered state of consciousness viable on occasion. Many great athletes enter this altered state naturally during their finest achievements.

Mircea Eliade[7] writes that the shaman's universe basically has three levels. Humans live on the Earth in a kind of middle zone between a Lowerworld and an Upperworld. The three are joined by a central axis, symbolized by various means in different cultures. The central sacred mountain of the mythology of India is an example, as is the World Tree of Scandinavian legend. Even the spiral path or labyrinth of Celtic mythologies represents the central axis between worlds.

The term "ecstasy" is applied by Mircea Eliade to shamanism. The SSC is a state of exaltation or rapturous delight, which is also a description of the state experienced by Christian mystics. The shamanic trance-state is much safer than dreaming. In a dream, a person often cannot voluntarily awaken and thus remove himself from an unwanted experience, particularly in a nightmare. In the Shamanic State of Consciousness, the shaman wills himself into the altered state of mind and is able to remove himself at any time. There are no uncontrolled, inescapable "bad trips," such as occur under the influence of psychedelic drugs. Social or political repercussions are the only possible bad effects that can stem from practicing shamanism.

A Native American shaman dances into trance

Shamanic tools

Obviously, not everyone who enters an ecstatic or trance state is a shaman. A similar experience can happen during periods of contemplation or meditation. There are also varying degrees of shamanic trance. They range from very light, such as experienced by many Native American shamans, to very deep and comatose in appearance, as with the Lapps. For most modern shamans, entering this state does not mean unconsciousness, but an altered state of consciousness where the shaman still has complete control. The other criteria, such as believing that the soul journeys to the other-worlds and the reasons for journeying, must also be met.

The shaman must always be aware that he has a definite mission in the SSC; entering this state of consciousness is not for play, but for serious purposes. And when he re-enters the OSC, he must know what to do with the information he has retrieved.

Of course, shamanism, like any other practice, including Christianity, can be misused and perverted to negative ends. As with meditation, any person who is not being truthful with himself can see and hear whatever he wants to see and hear. A true shaman has seen the depths of his soul, all the positives and negatives buried within his subconscious mind, and taken a stand for truth and Light.

The shamanic journeys all take place within the mind. This makes them very difficult to explain to other people who rely totally upon the five physical senses for information. If these experiences are written about, and not carefully explained as shamanic journeys, they are completely misunderstood or criticized as fantasies. Some of the writings of Carlos Castaneda and Lynn Andrews fall into this category.[8]

The shaman's journey into other-world realms is one of the most important tasks of his profession. It is also one of the easiest to learn. The shaman begins by selecting a special entrance or hole by which he mentally enters the Lowerworld; this is most often a real place in Nature, such as a cave, a hollow tree, a spring, etc. Following his entrance into the hole, he finds himself moving down a tunnel. When the shaman travels to the Upperworld, he generally mentally climbs a tree or ascends a spiralling tunnel, but we shall deal only with Lowerworld journeys here.

After making his way through the tunnel, the shaman finally comes to an exit point that opens into a beautiful landscape. Usually, this land is very much like, if not identical to, this plane of existence. The only difference is that animals, plants and inanimate objects, such as stones, are capable of communication; so-called "mythical" beings may also be present. By communing with the creatures of this world, the shaman is able to obtain the information he needs to correct the problems of his patient in the ordinary world.

Mircea Eliade wrote that he found that modern-day male shamans rarely took a journey to the Lowerworld; the journey there was feared as the realm of the Dark Mother, the area of death and magickal darkness.[9] The accepted journeys to the Upperworld, the realm of the Sky Father, may have superseded Lowerworld journeys when the male Gods took over from Goddess worship.

Skilled shamans learn to see, feel, and hear—in fact, experience—all senses in the SSC. Their experiences in the Lowerworld have as much validity and reality as happenings in the OSC. Minutes or hours may pass before the shaman returns through the tunnel to his body. This world's definition of time has no reality at all in the shamanic journeys. The shaman is unaware of the passage of time while in a journeying trance.

The two most important tools for shamanic journeying are the drum and the rattle. The drum, usually employed by an assistant, has been called the shaman's "horse," or "steed" or "canoe" by many cultures. The drum beat, set at heartbeat rhythm, helps the shaman to switch levels, to ride the sound of the beat down into the tunnel or up the tree. The steady, monotonous sound is a signal to his mind that serious work must be done. It has been scientifically proven that the drum beat frequencies of certain shamanic ceremonies match the EEG theta wave cycle (4–7 cycles per second).

The rattle has a higher, sharper pitch of sound. Sometimes the rattle is shaken throughout the ceremony, sometimes just as a signal to begin and end the journey. Since the sharper pitch of the rattle can be grating to some people, both methods of use should be tried before deciding upon its incorporation into the ceremony. Among the Tungus shamans, the rattle is not used. Instead, the costume of the shaman is decorated with bells and small iron ornaments which clash and jingle while he dances his way into the trance.

If the shaman begins his ceremony by dancing to the drum beat, he lies down when he feels his journey beginning. If he is journeying to help a patient, the shaman will lie down next to that person, who is lying in the center of the ritual area. The assistant continues to beat the drum until the shaman is ready to re-enter the OSC. Because of this close working relationship with the shaman, the assistant must be someone who is sympathetic to the task at hand, alert to what is going on, and sensitive to the other-worlds.

When first embarking upon his career, a shaman has to acquire a guardian spirit or animal. Among the Plains Indians of North America, this was accomplished only by going on a vision quest in a solitary area. This required long fasts in isolation. However, both the Jivaro of South America and the Southern Okanagon of Washington State believe that a guardian can be acquired without a quest. It is quite likely that the European idea of a Witch's familiar came from the use of a SSC power animal or spirit guide.

The prerequisite to obtaining the help of a guardian spirit or power animal seems to be the desire to do so and the belief that it is possible. A deep-level meditation, perhaps performed repeatedly over several weeks, can produce satisfactory results. Tradition says that any animal seen three times during such an inner or outer vision quest is offering its help as a guardian.

Many cultures say that everyone has a guardian spirit or animal whether they know it or not. The difference between the shaman and an ordinary person is that the shaman actively works with his guardian or power animal. The guardian helps to increase physical energy and mental alertness, and to resist disease. In shamanic tradition, this helper also makes it more difficult for a shaman to die. The Jivaro believe that the guardian mainly resides in the chest area; Australian and western North American tribes also believe this. Other shamanic cultures believe that the guardian enters and leaves through the fontanelle area at the top of the head.

Shamanic cultures believe a person can become diseased, or open to disease, if that person's guardian spirit has left or been lost. It is the function of the shaman to travel to the Lowerworld and retrieve the spirit; at the close of his journey back, he blows the spirit back into the patient, sometimes into the chest, sometimes into the head. If the lost spirit cannot be found, the shaman will attempt to bring back another guardian spirit. When this happens, the patient must dance the new spirit to make it feel at home and stay with him. During this dance, the recipient makes the movements and noises of the spirit animal. This is a conscious participation, not uncontrollable possession, as in Voodoo.

Even though a guardian spirit works with a shaman or any person, it does not always stay in the immediate vicinity. It moves around freely, coming and going as it wishes, entering and leaving the body according to its own will. During the shamanic journey, the power animal or spirit will generally meet the shaman somewhere inside the tunnel or just as he exits it into the Lowerworld.

Power animals can be any kind of animal, even those termed "mythical." In the SSC reality, there is no such thing as a nonexistent creature; dragons, griffins and other such beings are as real there as any other creature. Generally speaking, the power animal will offer a balance in strength, cunning, or power that is needed by the shaman. The power animal may appear in human form during a shamanic journey.

It is essential that a shaman have a guardian spirit or power animal so that he will have help and guidance in mastering the non-ordinary powers with which he comes in contact during his Lowerworld journeys. However, not every person who has a power animal is a shaman.

Besides the main guardian spirit, the shaman usually has a number of other spirit helpers. These may number from just a few to several hundred, depending upon the shaman's dedication and the years he has practiced his craft. Spirit helpers each aid in specific activities, while the guardian spirit is a general all-purpose helper with a wide range of powers and knowledge. Spirit helpers can be animals, plants, and even inorganic objects.

A shaman on the true shamanic path does not challenge or try to invalidate anyone else's experiences. He will never tell another that only a fantasy was experienced.

He completely understands that everything occurring in the SSC is "reality," that every symbol in a shamanic journey, no matter how inexperienced the person, has a message. He will contemplate even the most unusual happenings and see how they fit in with what he already knows, for all things are part of the truth.

Among most primitive groups that incorporate shamanism, the master shaman takes part in everyday activities like everyone else. He does not seclude himself from the world. It is common for him to be an accomplished hunter, craftsperson, or artist; in short, he is a responsible member of the community, earning his own way and not living off others. The modern-day shaman should accept the same responsibility.

A shaman has other magickal tools besides the drum and rattle. Sometimes he wears a small leather bag, known as a medicine bag, around his neck. Very small objects and plants that symbolize his helpers go into this pouch. The medicine bundle is a much larger bag or folded piece of leather that contains power objects that generally come to him, either in Nature or in unexpected places, such as shops. These objects may be feathers, stones and crystals, pieces of fur, etc., that have vibrations that speak to him of shamanic powers. The items of the medicine bundle usually represent the animal, plant, mineral, and human worlds. These objects can be used during healing and prophetic ceremonies; it is unlikely that a shaman would use them all at any one time.

Some shamanic cultures use masks to represent a connection between the shaman and the worlds of Nature and Spirit. Sometimes these are worn by the shaman during his ritual, other times only displayed. The original mask was a simple painting of the face with colors and symbols significant to each shaman.

Many shamans use a staff or walking stick to direct and receive the higher spiritual energies. This staff is often decorated with symbols of shamanic power, such as colored ribbons, feathers, fur, small bells, etc.; these decorations represent the natural Elements with which the shaman works. Although the shaman may change the contents of his medicine bag and medicine bundle as his needs change, the staff is a permanent part of his life. Although the staff is commonly of wood, it can be of metal; if you choose metal, however, wrap the staff with leather strips to avoid getting shocked.

Northwest coast masks

Chilkat dancing shirt

Some shamans, such as those of North American tribes, use large shells for smudge pots. In these they burn such things as sweetgrass, sage, thyme, and cedar. This uses the same principle as an incense burner. The smoke of the burning herbs is fanned, with either the hand or a feather, over people or objects to purify them. A single feather or a whole wing may be used; traditionally, feathers are the channels for energy and symbolic of the Winged Clans.

Every shaman must learn to use the energies and powers offered to him by the animal, plant, and mineral worlds, particularly the energies of those beings who are his spirit helpers and guardians. Often these powers are not what would be considered usual; they can appear in different energies and powers to each shaman.

The costume worn by a shaman is a personal representation of what he is as a practicing shaman. He does not have to clank and bang at every step with bones and beads and decorations, but his costume and appearance should signal to everyone present that he has now changed from his everyday character to a person who is serious about shamanic work. It is not imperative that the shaman own a totally authentic costume, although a set of clothes, especially made and perhaps decorated for that purpose, helps his subconscious prepare for the work at hand.

The prime purpose of a shaman's work is to help others, whether this is prophetic or simply involving the patient in self-healing. By helping someone transcend ordinary reality, the shaman can help him transcend his picture of himself as sick or diseased. When he can do this, he knows from the results of his work that he has becomes a true shaman.

ENDNOTES

1. Eliade, Mircea. *Shamanism: Archaic Techniques of Ecstasy.*
2. Neumann, Erich. *The Great Mother.*
3. Drury, Nevill. *The Elements of Shamanism.*
4. Harner, Michael. *The Way of the Shaman.*
5. Harner, Michael, *The Way of the Shaman* and Wolfe, Amber, *In the Shadow of the Shaman* are the two best books on the subject. Both give practical information in distinct styles. Harner gives a traditional shamanic approach with some modernization, while Wolfe gives a practical blend of shamanism and Pagan ideas.
6. Lowie, Robert. *Primitive Religion.*
7. Until his death, Eliade was considered the foremost authority on shamanism. His books are still available and widely read. Although he took little or no part in the proceedings, Eliade was a meticulous observer and recorder.
8. Nevill Drury in *The Elements of Shamanism* gives detailed criticisms of both Castaneda and Andrews, but I personally find Drury's work incomplete and dry. By his own admission, he also has a propensity for messing about with

drugs. Drury does praise Harner as having excellent credentials, which he does, being both an academic and a practicing shaman.

9. Sjoo and Mor. *The Great Cosmic Mother.*

BIBLIOGRAPHY

Aswynn, Freya. *Leaves of Yggdrasil.* St. Paul, MN: Llewellyn Publications, 1990.

Drury, Nevill. *The Elements of Shamanism.* UK: Element Books, 1989.

Drury, Nevill. *Vision Quest.* UK: Prism Press, 1989.

Eliade, Mircea. *Rites and Symbols of Initiation.* Trans. William Trask. NY: Harper & Row, 1958.

Eliade, Mircea. *Shamanism: Archaic Techniques of Ecstasy.* Trans. W. R. Trask. Princeton, NJ: Princeton University Press, 1964.

Harner, Michael. *The Way of the Shaman.* NY: Bantam, 1982.

Kalweit, Holger. *Dreamtime and Inner Space: The World of the Shaman.* Trans. Werner Wunsche. Boston, MA: Shambhala, 1988.

Lowie, Robert. *Primitive Religions.* NY: Grosset & Dunlap, 1952. (Originally published in 1924.)

Schultes, Richard Evans. *Plants of the Gods.* NY: McGraw-Hill Books, 1979.

Wolfe, Amber. *In the Shadow of the Shaman.* St. Paul, MN: Llewellyn Publications, 1988.

CHAPTER SEVEN

CEREMONIAL MAGICK

A circle for Ceremonial Magick

CEREMONIAL MAGICK is one of the few systems in this book that can be practiced without a belief in any religious system, beyond the acknowledgement of a Supreme Creator and what are called angels and demons, which are really human names for types of powers. Although this system is a very old one, dating from ancient Mesopotamian and Egyptian times, it was widely used during the Medieval era and is still practiced today. Because the magicians practicing this type of magick could profess a basic belief in a Supreme Creator such as that of the ruling Christian church, they often felt comfortable participating in the accepted religion of the day. This participation kept most of them free from persecution; the majority of these magicians also were very secretive about their magical work, which helped them live fairly safe lives. Furthermore, many of the clergy delved into Ceremonial Magick, until even this was declared anathema by the powerful Christian church.

Although Ceremonial Magick believes in the existence of a Supreme Creator, the practicing magician does not grovel before the deity, cower before the so-called demons, or engage in long prayer sessions. He fully understands that what is called

53

God and angels and demons are really only living symbols of matrices of power.[1] His rituals are merely a pattern-making system for contacting and using these powers.

The archetypal images used in magick are shared by everyone; they are all embedded in what Jung called the collective unconscious. These images are found, in similar forms, worldwide in myths, legends, and folklore.

Ceremonial Magick is often said to be divided into High Magick and Low Magick. High Magick is very demanding, detailed, and uses many languages, including ancient Greek, Hebrew, Latin, and what John Dee called the angelic language. (See charts on pages 55–57.) Low Magick is in the common tongue of the country in which it is practiced. High Magick deals directly with God, angels, and demons. Low Magick deals with pantheons of deities and Nature spirits. High Magick was generally studied from teachers and written sources. Low Magick was passed orally from one person to another in small villages; the goodywives, wise men and women, and illiterate psychics used Low Magick for healing, spellwork, and generally helping their fellow neighbors. In very simplistic terms, High Magick was the magick of scholars, Low Magick of the peasantry. These terms no longer apply; High Magick is no longer considered the Cadillac of Ceremonial Magick.

Regardless of the differences between the two, both magicks use ceremony and technically are Ceremonial Magick. However, this chapter will deal primarily with High Magick, which is what is generally meant when one speaks of Ceremonial Magick.

Low Magick is not to be despised as an inferior type of magick. It definitely has its place in the scheme of magickal training. It is an excellent proving ground for the novice magician, allowing him to sharpen his skills before moving on to the extremely demanding and often dangerous task of dealing with the evocation used in High Magick. It can also be an end unto itself, if the magician feels more comfortable working directly with archetypes and energies. The invocation used in Low Magick is not to be sneered at; it takes great preparation and self-knowledge to call a godform down into the circle without repercussions.

High Magick tends to think of the Supreme Creator as a combined male/female God. This type of magick calls upon angels, the rulers of the Elements, demons, and other forces which can be unpredictable. In order to do this safely, the Ceremonial Magician works within a cast, consecrated circle, but also sets up a consecrated triangle outside of the circle. This triangle is for the occupation of the powers he is calling upon, the angelic or demonic forces, the rulers of the Elements, Nature spirits. He does not call upon the Supreme Creator to manifest itself, only the powers ranking below God.

Practitioners of either High or Low Magick do not sell their souls to the Devil, although the fundamentalist Christians would like everyone to believe they do. The bad press comes from the mentally unbalanced individuals who dabble in whatever type of magick; they would exhibit the same sick, bizarre traits and mental imagings, and do, if they participated in born-again Christian services. The media encourages an immoral image of magick because it sells books and papers, the Christians because it keeps people from being curious and asking probing questions.

Malachim or Language of the Magi

A	B	G	D
H	I, J	K	L
M	N	O	p
Q	R	S	T
V	Z	CH	TZ
SH	TH		

Passing the River Script

A	B	D	G
H	I	K	L
M	N	O	p
Q	R	S	T
V	Z	CH	SH
TH	TZ		

Celestial or Angelic Alphabet

A	B	D	G
H	I	K	L
M	N	O	p
Q	R	S	T
V	Z	CH	SH
TH	TZ		

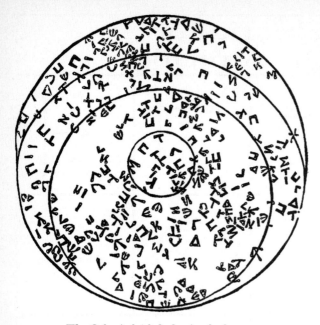

The Celestial Alphabet in the heavens

Isaac Bonewits writes that the only difference between magick and science is that the knowledge used by magick has not yet been confirmed and accepted by the scientific community.[2] Many of the things we now take for granted, such as astronomy, chemistry, medicine, physics, reading, mathematics, and writing, were originally occult secrets.[3] It may be centuries before other psychic and magickal arts are accepted by the general populace and the powerful scientific community. This is because the curious magician, who delves into other-worlds for his knowledge and enlightenment, works according to his own rules and comes up with answers without physical proof, beyond the desired results, that is. People accept the existence of atoms without ever seeing one, just because science says they are there. A magician knows he cannot prove the existence of angels or elementals and does not have the political clout to make anyone else believe him. But he really does not care if anyone else believes in his work; he gets the desired results and that is all that matters.

The Ceremonial Magician, like all magicians, is an artist, one who goes deep within his subconscious mind in order to reach the doorway to other dimensions of existence. His practice of self-discipline, self-knowledge, and self-control enable him to pass unharmed into other-worlds. His training helps him to find and see universal symbols and understand their meaning and application to his everyday life. Because he has few preconceived ideas about what he will find, the magician is open to discoveries that can revolutionize thinking, science, and humankind's relationship with the universe.

The most effective magicians probably could be said to practice grey magick. White and black magick definitely limit the exploration of truth and knowledge.[4] White magick could be said to be simple poetry and prayer to the Supreme Creator. Black magick, of course, is dealing wholly with demons[5] and immoral acts to gain results, usually personal power over others. Grey magick uses everything white magick does: healing, beneficial outcomes, expansion of consciousness, plus it adds the elimination of evils; stopping criminals, rapists, and murderers has as high a priority as removing disease in the physical body. The Ceremonial Magician must walk a tightrope, controlling negative entities but not falling under their influence, and avoiding any immorality that will cause him karmic repercussions.

It is my opinion that blood sacrifice falls into the category of immoral actions, bearing with it karmic consequences better done without. Aleister Crowley, who did indulge in many questionable activities, states that the incense of Abramelin[6] or Dittany of Crete are acceptable replacements for blood sacrifice; they are both also excellent for materializations.[7]

The Ceremonial Magician uses ritual tools similar to those used by most followers of Witchcraft: the sword, dagger, wand, chalice, incense burner, candles. He uses special incense blends for specific purposes, following ancient correspondence tables for choosing the ingredients. He wears ceremonial robes, used only for ritual. And he may work solitary or with a small number of like-minded individuals.

It is not necessary to belong to a group in order to perform Ceremonial Magick. Beware of groups or individuals who claim that they are the practitioners of an ancient method; they will often offer to teach "selected" students—for a fee, of course. If you become acquainted with anyone with a guru or master teacher complex, retreat as fast as you can.

The magician casts his protection circle with the sword at the beginning of each ritual, then sprinkles the imaginary outline with salt and water and fumigates it with smoking incense. At the four directional quarters, he calls upon the Archangels of the Elements to stand guard and help him. After this initial part of the ritual, the magician then continues on to whatever spellwork he has planned. To close, he dismisses the Archangels and "cuts" the circle.

The novice magician generally begins with the idea that he is practicing magick in order to contact the Supreme Creator and higher spirits.[8] No matter where his studies lead him, he will eventually return to this premise. The dedicated true magician seeks knowledge and wisdom in order to better himself and the world. He cannot do this by consorting only with lower spirits and powers. Whether he starts out to or not, his magickal work will precipitate a change in the consciousness of groups and nations.

The Ceremonial Magician works with the Qabala and the Tree of Life glyph. (This is explained in another chapter.) He also uses a technique known as "Assuming the Godform" in order to bring certain forces within himself into better balance. This technique is also used in Witchcraft, but not for quite the same purposes. In both magickal systems, it is called invocation.

Evocation is the calling into the magick triangle of powers or entities that one does not wish to directly associate with. These types of powers are too destructive and dangerous to the magician to make direct physical contact. The grimoires of the fourteenth to the nineteenth centuries speak of evocation as a major part of magick. However, the writings of Paracelsus, Cornelius Agrippa, John Dee, and Francis Barrett put evocation into a better perspective in relation to the rest of traditional magick. Evocation is not as beneficial to the magician as invocation.

The ancient grimoires, or books of magickal knowledge, carefully detail the extensive preparations for evocation, some of which border on the absurd. Grimoires which deal primarily with evocation are the *Goetia* or *Lesser Key of Solomon*, the *Grimoirium Verum*, the *Greater Key of Solomon*, and many others.[9]

To assume a godform, the magician studies the archetypal god or goddess in which he is interested. In preparation for the ritual, he assembles certain items known to magickally correspond to that particular energy, such as stones, colors, plants, incense, statues, etc. By meditation and mental discipline he calls upon the archetype in ritual; he feels the type of power that he wants to enter within him. He will intone the god-name, imagine himself in the god's form. At the end of his ritual he dismisses the power so that he can operate normally in his physical body.

Each archetypal energy form, or deity, has both a positive and negative side. Negative does not automatically mean evil or bad. An example would be Mars or Ares. The negative energy of Mars would exhibit itself in anger; this energy has its place at the proper time and in certain circumstances. But if there is a predominance of this energy within the magician's life, he will need to balance it in order to have greater harmony. He would not attempt to balance this by calling upon Jupiter, but rather by calling upon the positive powers of Mars: courage, strength, steadfastness. Thus empowered, he could also send energy to an imbalanced situation in the neighborhood, region, or nation, in order to correct it.

Each magician must pass through an initiation. It is not necessary to gain initiation by going through a ritual and being sprinkled or whatever by someone else. The outer trappings do not guarantee that a magician is initiated; that process can only take place within the heart and mind of the individual. It can occur spontaneously, as happens with many shamans, or it may occur during a profoundly enacted ritual.

High Magick speaks of having to pass the Dweller on the Threshold. This mystical guardian to the door to other-worlds lies deep within each individual. The Dweller is the guardian of a magician's sanity; without the correct mental and spiritual preparation, the magician can run into serious trouble if he manages to force his way into unknown realms, such as with the use of drugs. Joseph Campbell speaks of three stages that initiates undergo; he calls them Separation, Initiation, and Return.

SALOMONIS
(CITATIO)

XYWOLEH.VAY.BAREC
HET.VAY.YOMAR.HA.ELOHE
ELOHIM.ASCHER.TYWOHE
HYTHALE.CHUABOTAY.LEP
HA.NAWABRA.HAMVEYS.HA

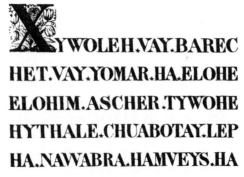

Magickal incantation according to the Key of Solomon

Separation is when the novice magician releases his preconceived ideas about reality; something snaps, and he is faced with admitting that he knows little, if anything, about true reality, particularly of the mind and other-worlds. This leads him to deeper levels of his subconscious mind where he encounters the Dweller. It can be a frightening experience, particularly if one has no preparation. The Dweller appears to be all the things that make up the personality, good and bad. Seeing oneself as one really is takes a tremendous amount of courage, but this must be accomplished and acknowledged if the magician is to pass safely through the door to other-worlds. The Return is simply that, a return to ordinary existence. However, the magician will not be the same; he cannot be because of the deep spiritual experience which he endured.

When the magician comes to terms with the existence and reality of the Dweller on the Threshold, he must convert this entity into a Doorkeeper. This turns the Dweller into a Protector, whose function then becomes one of keeping the magician in line, so to speak, and refusing him entry to the other-worlds if there is danger to him. The Dweller also keeps out of the magician's mind and body any entities or power that would harm him.

The ancient Egyptians understood the dangers of wandering about in other-worlds, uninitiated and without the proper preparation. Therefore, they used archetypal guides, such as Thoth, and Anubis, who was called the Opener of the Way. Western magicians may feel more comfortable calling upon Merlin or the Guardian Angel. By calling upon such powers before journeying into other-worlds, the magician has access to great wisdom and counsel.

Most practitioners of High Magick try to have a room set aside especially for their ritual work. The sphere of power built up within such a room becomes palpable to even a non-believer. By having a separate room such as this, the magician can leave out his altar and ritual paraphernalia. However, to many people this is not possible. They build their temple in their minds, as they wish it were, each time they set up their altar for a ritual. This is a great deal harder than having a consecrated room, but it is possible to practice magick in this manner. It is not necessary or desirable that the ritual room take on the appearance of a museum stuffed with useless but impressive-looking objects.

Rather than wait until you can have all the ritual tools you want for High Magick, begin with what you have. A kitchen knife can replace sword and dagger, a glass the chalice, a tree branch the wand, and so on. Of course, there will come a time when you can replace each of your substitute tools, but even then one does not have to spends hundreds of dollars for equipment. The tools a magician makes for himself, imbuing them with his personal power just by making them, are the best in any circumstance.

There comes a time in every Ceremonial Magician's life when he feels that he can advance no further, that everything he has done to that point has been wasted effort. High Magick often refers to this as the Lesser Abyss.[10] In order to pass by this obstacle, the magician must do some soul-searching; a change of consciousness is required if he is to advance further.

High Magick uses the magician's native language, but interposed with ancient Greek, Latin, Hebrew, Enochian, and unknown languages. The use of such unfamiliar languages helps the magician's mind to switch to ritual purposes. The Names of Power are usually in another language; this is a human attempt to expand consciousness, to delve into other dimensions of existence. In order to advance spiritually, the magician must be able to form relationships through ritual and magick with nonhuman entities. After all, the Ceremonial Magician knows that this physical world is not the only sphere of existence and power.

The Ceremonial Magician is not chained to performing ancient rituals word for word, or even anything like they were performed in centuries past. The magician must learn what works best for him and perhaps write his own, taking into account, of course, that certain elements must be included. The circle casting and consecration, the calling of the Elements, the dismissal of such upon completion of the ritual, all these must be incorporated into each performance. It is good to remember that many of the techniques used in magick act as filters, allowing a smooth and safe flow of energy between the magician and the power upon which he is calling. But as the magician is the only one who can consecrate his ritual tools, so is he the best one to know what works for forming his mental and spiritual link with the invoked deities or powers.[11]

Chanting, music, and dance all help direct the mind and locate the energies or entities needed for the ritual. However, there are no secret ancient words of power that will create magick all by themselves. The "calls" used in High Magick connect with the rest of the ritual to produce the desired affect.

Ceremonial Magick can and should be a method by which the practicing magician raises his own levels of spirituality. By precipitating his own growth, he thereby improves the condition of those around him and of the world in general.

ENDNOTES

1. Stewart, R. J. *Living Magical Arts.*
2. Bonewits, Isaac. *Real Magic.*
3. Kraig, Donald. *Modern Magick.*
4. Richardson, Alan. *Gate of Moon.*
5. The word "demons" is not used in the Christian sense or interpretation. Demons are best described as negative spirits or energies, not related in any manner to the Christian Devil, who can be controlled and coerced into helping the magician. The study of demons (demonology) has been around for a very long time. The Babylonians, Egyptians, and many other cultures wrote detailed accounts of these spirits.
6. Slater, Herman. *The Magickal Formulary.*
7. Crowley, Aleister. *Magick in Theory and Practice.*

8. Richardson, Alan. *Gate of Moon*. Richardson quotes Guirdham in *Beyond Jung*, saying that there eventually comes an experience that raises the magician about the functions of the archetypes.

9. Richard Cavendish, in *The Black Arts*, lists twelve grimoires of Ceremonial Magick:

    1. *The Key of Solomon*. A Greek version in the British Museum may date from as early as the twelfth century; it was prohibited by the Inquisition as dangerous in 1559.

    2. *Lemegeton*, or *Lesser Key of Solomon*. Divided into the Goetia, Theurgis Goetia, the Pauline Art, and the Almadel. Mentioned in writing about 1500; origin and meaning of "Lemegeton" unknown.

    3. *Testament of Solomon*. A version in Greek from about AD 100–400.

    4. *Grimoire of Honorius*. Probably dates from the sixteenth century.

    5. *Grimorium Verum*. Written in French; probably from the eighteenth century. Based on *The Key of Solomon*.

    6. *Grand Grimoire*. Written in French, probably during the eighteenth century.

    7. *Red Dragon*. A version of the *Grand Grimoire*.

    8. *True Black Magic*, or *The Secret of Secrets*. Published in 1750; a French copy of *The Key of Solomon*.

    9. *Arbatel of Magic*. A Latin grimoire published at Basle in 1575.

    10. *The Black Pullet*. Probably dating from the late eighteenth century.

    11. *Fourth Book*. Added to Agrippa's *Occult Philosophy* after his death.

    12. *The Magical Elements*, or *Heptameron*. Probably written in the sixteenth century as a supplement to the *Fourth Book*.

10. Gray, William G. *Inner Traditions of Magic*.

11. King, Francis, and Skinner, Stephen. *Techniques of High Magic*.

BIBLIOGRAPHY

Barrett, Francis. *The Magus*. Secaucus, NJ: Citadel Press, 1980.

Bias, Clifford. *Ritual Book of Magic*. NY: Samuel Weiser, 1981.

Bonewits, Isaac. *Real Magic*. NY: Berkeley Publishing, 1972.

Brennan, J. H. *Experimental Magic*. UK: Aquarian Press, 1984.

Buckland, Raymond. *Anatomy of the Occult*. NY: Samuel Weiser, 1977.

Burland, C. A. *The Magical Arts*. UK: Arthur Barker Ltd., 1966.

Butler, W. E. *The Magician: His Training and Work*. UK: Aquarian Press, 1969.

Cavendish, Richard. *The Black Arts*. NY: G.P. Putnam's Sons, 1967. (Not a book of black magick.)

Conway, David. *Magic: An Occult Primer*. NY: E. P. Dutton & Co., 1972.

Crowley, Aleister. *Magick in Theory and Practice.* NY: Dover Publications, 1976.

deLaurence, L. W. *The Greater Key of Solomon.* Chicago, IL: The deLaurence Co., 1914.

deLaurence, L. W. *The Lesser Key of Solomon: Goetia, the Book of Evil Spirits.* Chicago, IL: The deLaurence Co., 1916.

deLaurence, L. W. *The Sixth and Seventh Books of Moses.* Chicago, IL: The deLaurence Co., no date.

Denning, Melita, and Phillips, Osborne. *The Magical Philosophy,* Vol. I-V. St. Paul, MN: Llewellyn Publications, 1974-1981.

Eliade, Mircea. *Myths, Dreams and Mysteries.* NY: Harper & Row, 1967.

Fortune, Dion. *Applied Magic.* UK: Aquarian Press, 1962.

Fortune, Dion. *Esoteric Orders and Their Work.* UK: Aquarian Press, 1983.

Fortune, Dion. *The Training and Work of an Initiate.* UK: Aquarian Press, 1982.

Highfield, A. C. *The Symbolic Weapons of Ritual Magic.* UK: Aquarian Press, 1983.

King, Francis, and Skinner, Stephen. *Techniques of High Magic.* UK: Sphere Books Limited, 1981.

Kraig, Donald M. *Modern Magick: Eleven Lessons in the High Magickal Arts.* St. Paul, MN: Llewellyn Publications, 1989.

Mathers, S. L. MacGregor. *The Book of the Sacred Magic of Abramelin the Mage.* NY: Dover Publications, 1975.

Mathers, S. L. MacGregor. *The Grimoire of Armadel.* UK: Routledge & Kegan Paul, 1980.

Regardie, Israel. *The Golden Dawn.* St. Paul, MN: Llewellyn Publications, 1982.

Schueler, Gerald J. *Enochian Magic: A Practical Manual.* St. Paul, MN: Llewellyn Publications, 1985.

Slater, Herman, ed. *The Magickal Formulary.* NY: Magickal Childe, 1981.

Stewart, R. J. *Living Magical Arts.* UK: Blandford Press, 1987.

Torrens, R. G. *The Golden Dawn: The Inner Teachings.* NY: Samuel Weiser, 1973.

Tyson, Donald. *The New Magus: Ritual Magic as a Personal Process.* St. Paul, MN: Llewellyn Publications, 1988.

Wang, Robert. *The Secret Temple.* NY: Samuel Weiser, 1980.

Zalewski, Pat. *Golden Dawn Enochian Magic.* St. Paul, MN: Llewellyn Publications, 1990.

CHAPTER EIGHT

THE QABALA

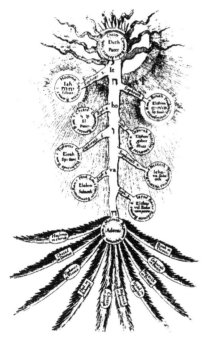

Diagram of the
Qabalistic Sephoritic Tree, 1621

THE QABALA is a form of mysticism based on Jewish tradition, literature, and language that works very well for all aspects of magickal rituals and spiritual seeking. Its various spellings are *Kabalah*, *Qabalah*, *Qabala*, *Kabala*, etc. The Qabala is a living system of spiritual development, the foundation of Western Esoteric Tradition as the *Bhagavad Gita* is to the Eastern Tradition. There seem to be elements from ancient cultures within the teachings of the Qabala, including Chaldean, Egyptian, and perhaps even pre-Aryan Indian.

I have included a brief discussion of the Qabala because it can be used in any Pagan ritual situation, without reference to its Jewish background. Its Tree of Life diagram is useful in determining the powers and ritual uses of any deity. By deciding where the deity goes on the Tree of Life (and a deity may belong in one place one time, another place another time, depending upon the aspect you plan to call upon), the magician can then find appropriate symbols that will enhance a ritual.

The Qabala's Tree of Life diagram, or glyph, of ten circles (singular, Sephirah; plural, Sephiroth) connected by twenty-two Paths is an outline of both the universe (macrocosm) and the human being (microcosm), and the mutual relationship of the underlying forces in both. It is valuable as a meditation source and tool, the classification and organization of ideas and symbols. Each Sephirah, or sphere, on the Tree of

Life represents a cosmic force or factor. When the mind concentrates on a particular Sephirah, you come in touch with the force of that Sephirah. This gives a tremendous access to energy that can be used for both magickal and spiritual workings.

The word "Qabala" comes from a Hebrew word meaning "to receive." The word Qabala itself means a tradition, a very definitive system of metaphysical thought. Originally the word meant the Law. It is also called the Secret Wisdom because in the beginning it was orally transmitted from Adept to Pupil on a one-to-one basis only. Its most valuable use is to help a seeker proceed from the known to the unknown by use of the symbols associated with the Sephiroth on the Tree of Life.

It was not until the twelfth century that the Qabala developed the connotations that describe it today.[1] About the second century AD the Western version of this Mystery Tradition began to be known; this is generally called the Hermetic Qabala and was probably based on knowledge passed down from a very ancient, oral tradition of magick.

Although there are two distinct and separate schools of Qabalistic teaching, that of Judaism and that of Hermetic Qabala, there are many practices within the two that are the same. In all forms of Qabala the God names used are those listed in the Old Testament, and Hebrew is the language used for these names. The main texts are those of the Jewish tradition.

The most important difference between the two Qabalistic schools deals with images. Mosaic law forbids showing the human form, such as a full face; however, a profile is not forbidden.[2] This intolerance is carried to such an extreme that the Tree of Life glyph is often not depicted in Jewish writings on the subject. The Jewish mystic will not mentally picture any image when meditating upon the Sephiroth or Paths, but will seek instead a pure consciousness experience, while the Hermetic Qabalist tries for a pictorial vision to help him with his inner exploration.

Many Qabalistic writings claim that the Qabala was given to Moses on Mount Sinai and is therefore the inception of Jewish Law. Others, including the Hermetic Order of the Golden Dawn, believe that it was given by angels to Adam. Both legends are fascinating but highly unlikely. The Qabala can be traced through a very long series of development beginning with the Merkabah Mysticism.[3]

The *Sepher Yetzirah*, or Book of Formation, is a collection of six very short chapters on the Qabala dating from some time between the third and sixth centuries AD; it is extremely important as in it for the first time the word Sephiroth[4] appears. It is most likely a summation of earlier teachings in Jewish mysticism. The *Sepher Yetzirah* details the creation of the universe in relationship to letters of the Hebrew alphabet; it also relates this action to numbers in much the same manner as used by neo-Pythagoreanism. It is a difficult book that only becomes understandable when used with the Tarot. Usually a later treatise, named the *Thirty-Two Paths of Wisdom*, is included with it.

During the late medieval era, Qabalistic scholars added a very important idea to the study of the Qabala, the idea of Gematria. Gematria, according to Donald Michael Kraig, is a method that assigns numbers to each of the Hebrew letters; words of equal value are then assumed to be related.[5] The scholars said that links could be found

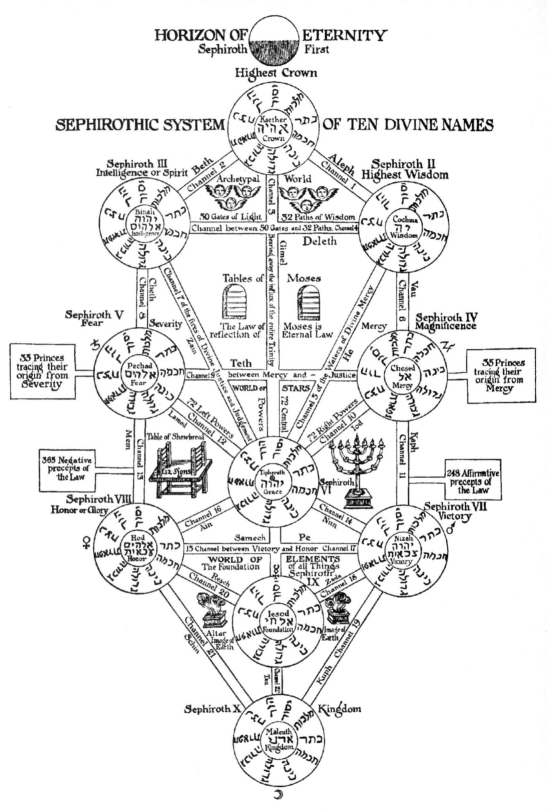

Kircher's Sephirotic Tree

between words by using this system. It also helped to assure that scribes could spell names precisely, and was an incentive for serious meditation on the God Names.

Another important Qabalistic work appeared in southern France between 1150 and 1200; this was the *Sepher-ha-Bahir*. Although it was supposed to be a very ancient writing, it is more likely that it was a compilation of several works from Germany or possibly the East.[6] However, the *Bahir* was the first work to refer to a "secret Tree" and also the first to call the Sephiroth vessels of Divine Light.

After Isaac the Blind from Narbonne wrote on the *Sepher Yetzirah* during the thirteenth century, scholars began to combine the study of the Ten Sephiroth and the Thirty-Two Paths.[7] At this same time in France and Spain arose the idea there were ten evil Sephiroth, counterparts of the good ones; the Hermetic Order of the Golden Dawn (late 1800s to early 1900s) expanded greatly upon this theory.

Between 1280 and 1286 Moses de Leon published the *Zohar*, a series of commentaries on the Bible and mystical cosmology. The five volume set in English, by Maurice Simon and Harry Sperlin, is only about 35% of the total *Zohar*. It has never been translated completely from the ancient Aramaic into a European language.

John Dee (1527-1608) was a great Elizabethan scholar who, with Edward Kelly, discovered and developed the system of Enochian Magic while working with the Qabala; this was later expanded upon by MacGregor Mathers of the Hermetic Order of the Golden Dawn. Dee also wrote *The Hieroglyphic Monad*, a paper on spiritual alchemy and mathematics; *A True and Faithful Relation of What Passed for Many Years Between Dr. John Dee and Some Spirits*, by Meric Casaubon (published in 1659), concerns Dee's work with Kelly when they were given the Enochian system by spirits.

The present-day version of the Tree of Life, the glyph used in study of the Qabala, was first published in 1652 in Kircher's *Oedipus Aegyptus*. The Tree obviously has undergone development over the centuries, its roots buried in an ancient mystical tradition.

The Qabala envisions four worlds in connection with the Tree, or actually four separate trees interacting with one another so closely there is almost no separation. These are the World of Atziluth, the World of Briah, the World of Yetzirah, and the World of Assiah. Each World has its own set of colors to represent each Sephirah.

The first World, or Atziluth, is the world of Emanation and is the highest of all. This is the plane of the Vital Spirit or Soul of the universe, the Ethereal and Reasoning Spirit, and the highest soul of humanity.

The second World, or Briah, is the world of Creation. Its ruler, the angel Metatron, governs the visible world, preserves harmony, unity, and the order of celestial bodies.

The third World, or Yetzirah, is the world of Formation. It is the plane of the Angels, the Intelligences of the planets and stars.

The fourth World, or Assiah, is the world of Material or Action. All substances of this world are subject to change, birth, death, and rebirth, yet nothing in it is ever totally destroyed.

The Tree is also divided into three triangles. The three top Sephiroth embody the Supernal Triangle, the middle three the Ethical Triangle, and the bottom three the Astral Triangle. The Sephirah Malkuth, which is at the very bottom, receives influences from all the others.

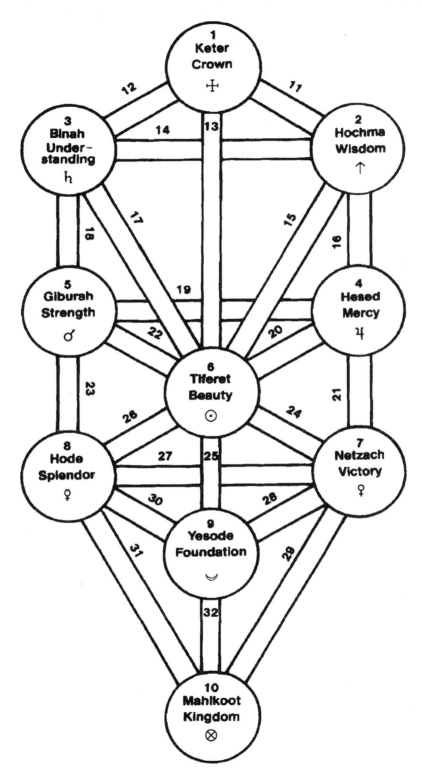

A modern Tree of Life

Furthermore, the Tree is divided into three pillars. The Sephiroth aligned on the right side are said to be the Pillar of Mercy, those on the left the Pillar of Severity, and those in the center the Middle Pillar.

Above the Tree, over the Sephirah of Kether, lie what are called Three Veils of Negative Existence. It is from these Veils that Kether, the prime source of creation, draws its powers. These Veils are named Ain, Ain Soph, and Ain Soph Aur, or Or; literal translations being Nothingness, Without Limit, and Limitless Light. Out of Ain, or Absolute and Limitless Void, rises Ain Soph, or Endless and Boundless Infinity, out of which rises Ain Soph Aur, or Limitless Light. Although they emanate from each other, they are undivided. These Three Veils might be called anti-matter.[8]

The Sephirah called Daath is not actually situated on the Tree of Life, although it is often shown by a faint circle between Binah and Chokmah, above Tiphareth and below Kether. In fact there is some question whether it should be called a Sephirah as it has no number. Daath means Knowledge, the expression of spiritual knowledge. It is the center of generation and regeneration, or the idea of becoming. It is sometimes even said to be knowledge without understanding; that is, without the understanding gained by traveling through the Sephirah of Binah and all it represents. In other words, all knowledge without spiritual understanding is false.

Daath is also the gateway to the reverse side of the Tree, the area governed by the Qlippoth, or demons.[9] Daath lies in the Abyss that is the gulf between spirit and everything that is not spirit, between reality and illusion, between the potential and the manifest. In the Abyss dwells a great demon named Choronzon.[10] This arch-demon is the master of false knowledge and illusion, which every mystic and magician must conquer before he can move to the higher Sephiroth where no duality exists.

Each Sephirah is balanced by its opposite. Between the Sephiroth are the Paths, the necessary roads to and entry points of a Sephirah. The departure point and return for each Pathworking journey is through the Sephirah of Malkuth at the bottom of the Tree. By meditating upon the symbols connected with a particular Path, a Qabalist visualizes the journey along that Path up the Tree to a specified destination or Sephirah. The Tarot card assigned to each Path is a symbol of experience along that Path, a guide for astral projection for spiritual growth.

Pathworking is a subjective experience.[11] That is, the journey is all done within the mind; this does not exclude astral projection that is also an activity of the mind. By learning to visualize fully, even to the extent of sensory perception, is a necessary part of a magician's training. It is also a necessary requirement for a spiritual mystic, as one realizes upon reading the visions of mystics of all countries and ages.

The whole idea behind meditation and use of the Tree of the Life glyph and the Qabala is to better integrate the personality of the magician or mystic and to create changes that will aid spiritual development. By traveling all the Paths, we force ourselves to face parts of our personality that we may not like, and do something positive about changing them.

In practical magickal terms, the Tree of Life helps the magician to place his ideas in proper position, see what Paths he needs to travel to reach that position and by which he will draw down specific power to create his desire. All work is done by visualization and astral travel, the prime ingredients of any good magician's rituals.

It should be clear at this point that study of the Qabala and the Tree of Life glyph can be used in several ways. First, one can use the Tree solely as a method of raising spiritual consciousness and balancing the personality. Second, a magician may use the Tree as a guide to finding a specific type of energy and drawing it down during ritual. Third, of course, is a combination of the above two methods. One does not have to be a Christian mystic or follower of Judaism to gain knowledge from the Qabala. Its system can easily be applied to any Pagan culture or magickal practices. The only limitations are in the mind of the user.

The Qabala is not a dogmatic form, but an aid for your journeying. It is not a goal, but a method of going. It is the most perfect instrument there is for practical research into magick, spiritual growth, or almost anything else that has ever been devised. When one explores unknown territory, one is well advised to take along a map. The Qabala is that map.

Qabalistic allegory

FIRST SEPHIRAH, KETHER[12]

Zeus

Titles: the Crown; First Mover; First Cause; Life Principle; the Divine Plane; Supreme Emanation; Ancient of Ancients; Ancient of Days.

Intelligence: Admirable or Hidden.

Pronunciation: as it reads.[13]

Place: First plane, middle pillar, Supernal Triangle

God-Name: Eheieh, Ehyeh.

Archangel: Metatron, World-Prince, Angel of the Presence.

Order of Angels[14]: Chaioth, or Chayoth, ha Qadesh; Holy Living Creatures.

Qlippoth[15] (Demons): Thaumiel; the Twins of God.

Arch-Demon[16]: Moloch and Satan.

Virtue: completion of the Great Work.

Vice: too high to have any vice.

Godforms: Creator God/desses—Ymir, Odhinn, Audhumla, Freyja, Gaea, Cronus, Ptah, Brahma, Shiva, Gaea, Jumala, Cagn, Zeus, Ra, Iacchus, Jupiter.

Color Atziluth: brilliance.

Color Briah: pure white swirling.

Color Yetzirah: pure white brilliance.

Color Assiah: white flecked with gold.

Incense: ambergris.

Animals: swan, hawk.

Stones: diamond.

Plants: almond in flower, chamomile.

Tree: almond.

Sphere of: Pluto, Primum Mobile.

Tarot Cards: the four Aces.[17]

Symbols: a brilliant glowing crown.

Correspondence to Human Body: the Self.

Being: spirit.

Consciousness: spiritual.

Power: incarnate will.

Disease: death.

Magickal Powers: union with self, union with God.

Magickal Symbols: crown, head-band, headdress.

Rituals Involving: divine consciousness; illumination; enlightenment; spiritual development and attainment; finding your karmic purpose in life.

SECOND SEPHIRAH, CHOKMAH

Beelzebub

Titles: Wisdom; Crown of Creation; the Second Glory; Theoretical Wisdom; the Supernal Father; the Great Stimulator; the Idea of Spiritual Force.

Intelligence: Illuminating.

Pronunciation: HOKE-muh.

Place: Second plane, right pillar, Supernal Triangle.

God-Name: Yah, Jehovah.

Archangel: Ratziel.

Order of Angels: Auphanim/Ophanim; the Wheels of Whirling Forces.

Qlippoth (Demons): Ogiel/Ghagiel/ Chaigidel/Chaigidiel; Hinderers.

Arch-Demon: Samael, Beelzebub.

Virtue: devotion.

Vice: too high to have a vice.

Godforms: All-Father Deities, Priapic Gods—Amen, Thoth, Isis, Odhinn, Uranus, Njord, Freyr, Zeus, Jupiter, Pan, Athene, Poseidon, Osiris, the Dagda, Cernunnos, Nuada, Asshur, Olorun, Deus Pater, Shiva, Janus.

Color Atziluth: soft pure blue.

Color Briah: grey.

Color Yetzirah: iridescent blue-grey.

Color Assiah: white flecked with red, blue, and yellow.

Incense: musk.

Animals: human.

Stones: star ruby, turquoise.

Plants: amaranth, Solomon's seal.

Tree: beech.

Sphere of: the Zodiac and Neptune.

Tarot Cards: the four Knights and the four Twos.

Symbols: phallus; standing stones; towers; straight line.

Correspondence to Human Body: spiritual will or purpose.

Being: spirit.

Consciousness: spiritual.

Power: purposeful will.

Disease: insanity.

Magickal Powers: vision of the self, vision of God face to face.

Magickal Symbols: inner robe.

Rituals Involving: achieving equilibrium; spiritual manifestations; creative force; divine inspiration.

THIRD SEPHIRAH, BINAH

Isis

Titles: Understanding; the Dark Sterile Mother; the Bright Fertile Mother; the Creator of Faith; the Great Sea; the Great Mother.

Intelligence: Sanctifying.

Pronunciation: BEE-nuh.

Place: 2nd plane, left pillar, Supernal Triangle.

God-Name: Yahveh, or Yahweh, Elohim.

Archangels: Tzaphkiel.

Order of Angels: Aralim; the Thrones, the Mighty Ones.

Qlippoth (Demons): Satariel; the Concealers.

Arch-Demon: Lucifuge.

Virtue: silence.

Vice: avarice, wrong idea of the self.

Godforms: Great Mother Goddesses, God/desses of the Underworld—Frigg, Freyja, Isis, Nephthys, Ta-urt, Danu, Demeter, Maya, Kuan Yin, Branwen, Bran, Tiamat, Asherat, Gefion, Parvati, Maat, Cybele, Demeter, Rhea, Hera, Juno, Saturn, Hecate.

Color Atziluth: crimson.

Color Briah: black.

Color Yetzirah: dark brown.

Color Assiah: grey flecked with pink.

Incense: myrrh, civet.

Animals: bee, woman, crow, raven.

Stones: star sapphire, pearl, onyx.

Plants: lotus, lily, comfrey, thyme.

Tree: alder.

Metal: lead.

Sphere of: Saturn.

Planetary Spirit: Arathron/Arathor.

Tarot Cards: the four Queens and the four Threes.

Symbols: chalice, cup, triangle, diamond, circle, oval, the sea.

Correspondence to Human Body: spiritual love and awareness.

Being: spirit.

Consciousness: spiritual.

Power: collective will.

Disease: amnesia.

Magickal Powers: vision of wonder and sorrow.

Magickal Symbols: outer robe.

Rituals Involving: stabilization of thought and life; help with groups; comfort in sorrow; contact with the Goddess; developing power of faith.

FOURTH SEPHIRAH, CHESED

Unicorn

Titles: Mercy; Greatness; Love; Pity; Majesty; Glory.

Intelligence: Cohesive or Measuring.

Pronunciation: HAY-sed.

Place: Third plane, right pillar, Ethical Triangle.

God-Name: El.

Archangel: Tzadquiel, God's Justice or Prince of Mercy.

Order of Angels: Chasmalim; the Brilliant Ones, Dominions or Dominations.

Qlippoth (Demons): Gha'ahsheblah/Gashekiah; the Breakers in Pieces, Disturbers of All Things, the Smiters.

Arch-Demon: Ashtaroth.

Virtue: obedience.

Vice: bigotry, hypocrisy, gluttony, tyranny.

Godforms: Benevolent Ruler Deities, Justice—Odhinn (as lawgiver), Forseti, Heimdall, Mimir, the Norns, Njord, Sin, Tyr, Zeus, Jupiter, Indra, Amen, Osiris, Poseidon, Brahma.

Color Atziluth: deep violet.

Color Briah: blue.

Color Yetzirah: deep purple.

Color Assiah: deep azure flecked with yellow.

Incense: cedar.

Animals: unicorn.

Stones: amethyst.

Plants: olive, poppy, balm, sage, mint.

Tree: birch.

Metal: tin.

Sphere of: Jupiter.

Planetary Spirit: Bethor.

Tarot Cards: the four Fours.

Symbols: pyramid, square, orb, wand, scepter.

Correspondence to Human Body: love, awareness.

Being: soul.

Consciousness: archetypal.

Power: good will.

Disease: dropsy.

Magickal Powers: vision of love.

Magickal Symbols: wand, scepter, crook.

Rituals Involving: magick; growth; expansion; help with order and neatness; emotional stability; mental creations; seeing truth behind the illusion; raising of consciousness.

FIFTH SEPHIRAH, GEBURAH

Magickal sword

Titles: Might; Strength; Justice; Severity; Fear.

Intelligence: Radical.

Pronunciation: ge-BOOR-uh.

Place: Third plane, left pillar, Ethical Triangle.

God-Name: Elohim Gebor.

Archangel: Khamael or Camael.

Order of Angels: Seraphim; the Flaming or Fiery Serpents, Powers.

Qlippoth (Demons): Golachab; the Burners.

Arch-Demon: Asmodeus.

Virtue: energy, courage.

Vice: cruelty, destruction.

Godforms: War Deities, the Smith Gods, Avenger Deities—Odhinn, Thorr, Hel, Loki, Ran, Vulcan, Hephaestus, Mars, Ares, Minerva, Athene, Bran, Kali, Morrigu, Lugh, Perun, Indra, Horus, Nephthys, Hades, Vishnu, Varuna.

Color Atziluth: orange.

Color Briah: scarlet red.

Color Yetzirah: bright scarlet.

Color Assiah: red flecked with black.

Incense: tobacco.

Animals: basilisk, wolf, horse, bear.

Stones: ruby, bloodstone, garnet, red topaz.

Plants: nettles, basil, tarragon.

Tree: holly, oak.

Metal: iron or steel.

Sphere of: Mars.

Planetary Spirit: Phaleg.

Tarot Cards: the four Fives.

Symbols: pentagram, sword, spear, scourge, chains.

Correspondence to Human Body: will-power.

Being: soul.

Consciousness: archetypal.

Power: strong will.

Disease: fever.

Magickal Powers: vision of power.

Magickal Symbols: sword, spear, scourge.

Rituals Involving: energy; courage; defense; will power; self-discipline; ridding oneself of garbage in order to attain higher aspirations; bringing rhythm and stability to life.

SIXTH SEPHIRAH, TIPHARETH

Belphegor

Titles: Beauty; Harmony; Majesty; Sovereignty; the Archetypal Man.

Intelligence: Mediating.

Pronunciation: TIFF-uh-reth.

Place: Fourth plane, middle pillar, Ethical Triangle.

God-Name: Jehovah Eloah va Daath or Tetragrammaton Aloah Va Daath.

Archangel: Raphael.

Order of Angels: Melechim; the Kings, Virtues.

Qlippoth (Demons): Thagirion; the Disputers.

Arch-Demon: Belphegor.

Virtue: devotion to the Great Work.

Vice: pride.

Godforms: Sun Deities, Holy Children, Healers, Sacrificed Deities, Illuminators—Osiris, Apollo, Helios, Adonis, Attis, Bran, Lugh, Dionysus, Ogma, Shamash, Surya, Amaterasu, Tezcatlipoca, Apu, Horus, Ra, Rama, Krishna, Buddha, Mithra, Vishnu.

Color Atziluth: clear rose-pink.

Color Briah: yellow.

Color Yetzirah: rich salmon-pink.

Color Assiah: golden amber.

Incense: frankincense, cinnamon, Egyptian Kyphi.

Animals: lion, phoenix, child.

Stones: topaz, yellow diamond, yellow jacinth, chrysoleth.

Plants: bay, vine, gorse, rosemary, laurel, acacia, coffee.

Tree: ash, bay.

Metal: gold.

Sphere of: Sun.

Planetary Spirit: Och.

Tarot Cards: the four Sixes and four Pages or Princes.

Symbols: Calvary-type cross, truncated pyramid, cube, hexagram.

Correspondence to Human Body: personal self.

Being: soul.

Consciousness: archetypal.

Power: skillful will.

Disease: heart diseases.

Magickal Powers: vision of harmony.

Magickal Symbols: lamen, rosy cross.

Rituals Involving: honor; power; life; growth; money; healing; understanding the deep Mysteries; building intuition; energy.

SEVENTH SEPHIRAH, NETZACH

Egyptian cat talisman

Titles: Victory; Conquest; Permanence; Firmness.

Intelligence: Occult.[18]

Pronunciation: NET-zack.

Place: Fifth plane, right pillar, Astral Triangle.

God-Name: Yahveh Tzabaoth.

Archangel: Haniel.

Order of Angels: Elohim; Gods and Goddesses, Principalities.

Qlippoth (Demons): A'arab Zaraq; the Dispersers.

Arch-Demon: Baal.

Virtue: unselfishness.

Vice: sexual immorality, lust.

Godforms: Love Deities—Freyja, Frigg, Venus, Aphrodite, Hathor, Rhiannon, Ishtar, Niamh, Cerridwen, Nike.

Color Atziluth: amber.

Color Briah: emerald.

Color Yetzirah: bright yellowish green.

Color Assiah: olive flecked with gold.

Incense: ambergris, rose, benzoin, red sandalwood.

Animals: lynx, leopard, cat, dove.

Stones: emerald, turquoise.

Plants: rose, damiana, birch, catnip, coltsfoot, daffodil, dittany of Crete, foxglove, mugwort, strawberry, thyme, violet, yarrow, feverfew, verbena.

Tree: apple.

Metal: copper.

Sphere of: Venus.

Planetary Spirit: Hagith.

Tarot Cards: the four Sevens.

Symbols: lamp, candle, rose, seven-point star.

Correspondence to Human Body: feelings.

Being: personality.

Consciousness: astral.

Power: emotional will.

Disease: skin troubles.

Magickal Powers: vision of triumphant beauty.

Magickal Symbols: lamp, girdle.

Rituals Involving: love; pleasure; the arts; music; writing; creativity; inspiration; building the intellect.

EIGHTH SEPHIRAH, HOD

Seal of Michael

Titles: Splendor; Glory; Fame; the Well of Truth.

Intelligence: Absolute or Perfect.

Pronunciation: rhymes with load and mode.

Place: Fifth plane, left pillar, Astral Triangle.

God-Name: Elohim Tzabaoth.

Archangel: Michael.

Order of Angels: Beni Elohim; Archangels, the Children or Sons of God.

Qlippoth (Demons): Samael; the Deceivers.

Arch-Demon: Adrammelech.

Virtue: truthfulness.

Vice: falsehood, dishonesty.

Godforms: Messenger and Teacher Deities—Bragi, Odhinn, Mimir, the Norns, Thoth, Mercury, Hermes, Ogma, Anubis, Loki.

Color Atziluth: violet purple.

Color Briah: orange.

Color Yetzirah: red-russet.

Color Assiah: yellow-brown flecked with white.

Incense: storax, mastic, white sandalwood.

Animals: jackal, twin serpents, swallow, ibis, ape.

Stones: opal, fire opal, agate.

Plants: moly, camphor, cloves, fern, honeysuckle, lavender, lily of the valley, marjoram, myrtle, orris, savory, valerian.

Metal: mercury or quicksilver.

Sphere of: Mercury.

Planetary Spirit: Ophiel.

Tarot Cards: the four Eights.

Symbols: eight-point star, caduceus, mantra, mandala.

Rituals Involving: contacting spiritual Masters; business; legal problems; travel; information; logic; writing; controlling runaway emotions; organization; learning; locating the proper teachers.

NINTH SEPHIRAH, YESOD

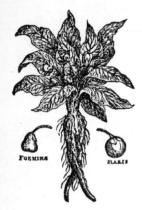

Mandrake

Titles: the Foundation; Base; the Sphere of Illusion; Treasurehouse of Visions.

Intelligence: Pure or Clear.

Pronunciation: YAY-sude.

Place: Sixth plane, middle pillar, Astral Triangle.

God-Name: Shaddai el Chai.

Archangel: Gabriel.

Order of Angels: Kerubim; Angels, the Cherubs.

Qlippoth (Demons): Gamaliel; the Obscene Ones.

Arch-Demon: Lilith.

Virtue: independence.

Vice: idleness.

Godforms: Moon Deities—Nana, Diana, Thoth, Ganesha, Hecate, Selene, Varuna, Soma, Ch'ang-o, Coyolxauhqui, Quilla, Hathor, Shu, Zeus, Vishnu.

Color Atziluth: indigo.

Color Briah: violet.

Color Yetzirah: very dark purple.

Color Assiah: citrine flecked with azure.

Incense: jasmine, ginseng, aloe, lotus.

Animals: elephant, hare, toad, dog.

Stones: quartz crystal, pearl, moonstone.

Plants: mandrake, orchid root, damiana, clary, cucumber, dogs tooth violet, orris, iris, lily, moonwort, mugwort, white rose, water lily, purslane, watercress.

Tree: willow.

Metal: silver.

Sphere of: Moon.

Planetary Spirit: Phul.

Tarot Cards: the four Nines.

Symbols: perfume, nine-point star, crescent Moon, magick mirror, crystal ball.

Correspondence to Human Body: subconscious, sexuality.

Being: personality.

Consciousness: astral.

Power: unconscious will.

Disease: impotency.

Magickal Power: vision of the working of the universe.

Magickal Symbols: perfumes, sandals.

Rituals Involving: change; divination; fertility; intuition; memory; use of the crystal ball, Tarot cards, or other divination helps.

TENTH SEPHIRAH, MALKUTH

Four Pages from an early Portugese deck

Titles: The Kingdom; Kingship; the Gate; the Inferior Mother; the Bride; the Virgin; the Queen; the Sphere of Form; Malkah or the Queen; Kallah or the Bride; the Gate of the Shadow of Death.

Intelligence: Resplendent.

Pronunciation: MAHL-kooth.

Place: Seventh plane, middle pillar.

God-Name: Adonai Malekh or Adonai ha Aretz.

Archangel: Sandalphon.

Order of Angels: Eshim; Souls of the Redeemed, the Flames.

Qlippoth (Demons): Lilith; Evil Woman.

Arch-Demon: Naamah.

Virtue: discrimination.

Vice: inertia.

Godforms: Earth and Grain Deities— Nerthus, Audhumla, Freyja, Frigg, Ymir, Gefion, Pan, Ceres, Demeter, Marduk, Mati, Nokomis, Niamh, Cernunnos, Persephone, Osiris, Isis, Nephthys, Adonis, Lakshmi.

Color Atziluth: yellow.

Color Briah: citrine, russet, black.

Color Yetzirah: citrine, olive, russet, and black flecked with gold.

Color Assiah: black rayed with yellow.

Incense: dittany of Crete.

Animals: cow, bull, snake, dog.

Stones: rock crystal.

Plants: corn, willow, lily, ivy, cereals.

Tree: oak.

Sphere of: Earth; the Sphere of the Elements.

Tarot Cards: the four Pages or Princesses and the four Tens.

Symbols: magick circle, altar, temple, equal-armed cross.

Correspondence to Human Body: body as a whole.

Being: personality.

Consciousness: etheric.

Power: manifesting will.

Magickal Powers: vision of the Holy Guardian Angel.

Magickal Symbols: consecrated circle, triangle.

Rituals Involving: contacting the guardian angel; organized material manifestations; healing mental and physical illnesses; seeing beauty and purpose in life; centering; healing plants and animals; trance; direct psychic contact with spirits.

DAATH

Osiris

Titles: The Abyss; Knowledge.

Pronunciation: DAY-ath.

Place: between Second and Third planes; below Kether, above Tiphareth; between Binah and Chokmah.

Angel: Zagzagel.[19]

Qlippoth (Demons): Belia'al; the Worthless.

Arch-Demon: Choronzon.

Virtue: getting beyond illusion to the truth.

Vice: self-delusion, ignorance.

Godforms: Freyja, Odhinn, Brahma, Danu, Osiris, Thoth; all ancient deities who grant spiritual wisdom and reveal the Truth.

Color Atziluth: lavender.[20]

Color Briah: grey white.

Color Yetzirah: pure violet.

Color Assiah: grey flecked with gold.

Incense: camphor.

Animals: extra-dimensional.

Stones: chrysocolla, sugilite.[21]

Plants: cuckoopint.

Planet: Uranus; the asteroids.

Symbols: the Veil.

Correspondence to Human Body: "the next step"; phase between the physical and the etheric.

Being: negative.

Consciousness: unfolding.

Power: no will.

Disease: complete soul loss.

Magickal Powers: dominion over darkness.

Magickal Symbols: chain.

Rituals Involving: controlling evil; getting past illusions to the truth of a matter; obtaining spiritual wisdom and discrimination.

PATH 11

Ox from The Book of Kells

Title: the Holy Ghost.

Intelligence: Scintillating Intelligence.

Place: joins Sephiroth 1-2.

Hebrew Name: Aleph; ox.

Number: 1.

Angel: Raphael.

Qlippoth (Demons): Oriens; air demon.

Demons of Hidden Paths: Amprodias.

Godforms: Odhinn, Maat, the Maruts, Dionysus, Jupiter, Bacchus.

Color Atziluth: bright pale yellow.

Color Briah: sky blue.

Color Yetzirah: blue-emerald green.

Color Assiah: emerald flecked with gold.

Incense: galbanum.

Animals: eagle, human, ox.

Legendary Beings: sylphs.

Stones: topaz, chalcedony.

Plants: aspen, grasses, peppermint, chamomile.

Tree: spruce.

Zodiac/Element: Air.

Tarot Card: the Fool; spirit of aethyr.

Correspondence to Human Body: respiratory organs.

Disease: fluxes.

Magickal Powers: divination.

Magickal Symbols: dagger.

Rituals Involving: reaching and using the superconscious.

PATH 12

Marjoram

Title: the messenger.

Intelligence: Transparent Intelligence.

Place: path joins 1-3.

Hebrew Name: Beth; house.

Number: 2.

Angel: Michael.

Qlippoth (Demons): Samael; the Deceivers.

Demons of Hidden Paths: Baratchial.

Godforms: Odhinn, Thoth, Vishnu, Hermes, Mercury.

Color Atziluth: yellow.

Color Briah: purple.

Color Yetzirah: grey.

Color Assiah: indigo rayed with violet.

Incense: sandalwood, mastic, storax.

Animals: swallow, ape, ibis.

Legendary Beings: disembodied voices, witches, wizards.

Stones: opal, agate.

Plants: vervain, palm, comfrey, marjoram, herb mercury.

Tree: ash.

Zodiac/Element: Mercury.

Tarot Card: the Magician; magus of power.

Correspondence to Human Body: cerebral and nervous system.

Disease: ataxia.

Magickal Powers: healing, language, knowledge of sciences.

Magickal Symbols: wand, caduceus.

Rituals Involving: auto-suggestion; controlling forces below the self-conscious level.

PATH 13

Moon

Title: the virgin.

Intelligence: Uniting Intelligence.

Place: path joins 1-6.

Hebrew Name: Gimel; camel.

Number: 3.

Angel: Gabriel.

Qlippoth (Demons): Gamaliel; the Obscene Ones.

Demons of Hidden Paths: Gargophias.

Godforms: Odhinn, Isis, Chandra, Artemis, Hecate, Diana.

Color Atziluth: blue.

Color Briah: silver.

Color Yetzirah: cold pale blue.

Color Assiah: silver rayed with sky blue.

Incense: camphor.

Animals: dog, camel.

Legendary Beings: lemures, ghosts.

Stones: pearl, moonstone.

Plants: hazel, buttercup, bay.

Tree: alder.

Zodiac/Element: the Moon.

Tarot Card: the High Priestess; priestess of the silver star.

Correspondence to Human Body: lymphatic system.

Disease: menstrual disorders.

Magickal Powers: clairvoyance, dream control, dream divination.

Magickal Symbols: bow and arrow, crystal ball, magick mirror.

Rituals Involving: seeing beyond the Veil; delving into the Deep Mysteries.

PATH 14

Title: the wife.

Intelligence: Illuminating Intelligence.

Place: path joins 2-3.

Hebrew Name: Daleth; door.

Number: 4.

Angel: Haniel.

Qlippoth (Demons): A'arab Zaraq; the Dispersers.

Demons of Hidden Paths: Dagdagiel.

Godforms: Freyja, Hathor, Aphrodite, Venus.

Color Atziluth: emerald green.

Color Briah: sky blue.

Color Yetzirah: early spring green.

Color Assiah: bright rose rayed with pale green.

Incense: sandalwood.

Animals: sparrow, dove, swan, lynx, leopard.

Legendary Beings: succubi.

Stones: emerald, turquoise.

Plants: rose, clover, cowslip, myrtle.

Lynx

Tree: pine.

Zodiac/Element: Venus.

Tarot Card: the Empress; daughter of the mighty one.

Correspondence to Human Body: genital system.

Disease: sex diseases (VD).

Magickal Powers: love philters and love magick.

Magickal Symbols: girdle.

Rituals Involving: enervating the creative imagination; seeking the Great Mother.

PATH 15

Minerva

Title: the mother.
Intelligence: Natural Intelligence.
Place: path joins 2-6.
Hebrew Name: Heh; window.
Number: 5.
Angel: Camael.
Qlippoth (Demons): Bahimoron; the Bestial Ones.
Demons of Hidden Paths: Tzuflifu.
Godforms: Mars, Ares, Minerva, Athene, Horus-Ra.
Color Atziluth: scarlet.

Color Briah: red.
Color Yetzirah: brilliant flame.
Color Assiah: glowing red.
Incense: dragons blood.
Animals: ram, owl.
Legendary Beings: mania, erinyes, furies.
Stones: ruby.
Plants: geranium, tiger lily.
Tree: yew, ash.
Zodiac/Element: Aries.
Tarot Card: the Emperor; the Sun of the Morning, Chief among the Mighty.
Correspondence to Human Body: head, face.
Disease: cystitis.
Magickal Powers: understanding esoteric astrology.
Magickal Symbols: censer, star charts.
Rituals Involving: seeking the Great Father; bringing reason and will into balance.

PATH 16

Theseus killing the minotaur

Title: the son; the priest.
Intelligence: Triumphal Intelligence.
Place: path joins 2-4.
Hebrew Name: Vau; nail.
Number: 6.
Angel: Asmodel.
Qlippoth (Demons): Adimiron; the Bloody Ones.
Demons of Hidden Paths: Uriens.
Godforms: The Vanir, Osiris, Shiva, Hera, Venus.

Color Atziluth: red-orange.
Color Briah: deep indigo.
Color Yetzirah: deep warm olive.
Color Assiah: rich brown.
Incense: storax.
Animals: bull.
Legendary Beings: gorgons, minotaurs.
Stones: topaz.
Plants: mallow, moss, archangel, figs.
Tree: birch.

Zodiac/Element: Taurus.
Tarot Card: the Hierophant; magus of the eternal.
Correspondence to Human Body: shoulders, arms.
Disease: indigestion.
Magickal Powers: secret of physical strength.
Magickal Symbols: energized sweat.
Rituals Involving: intuition; inner hearing; revelation.

PATH 17

Title: the twins emerging.
Intelligence: Disposing Intelligence.
Place: path joins 3-6.
Hebrew Name: Zain; sword.
Number: 7.
Angel: Ambriel.
Qlippoth (Demons): Tzalaimiron; the Clangers.
Demons of Hidden Paths: Zamradiel.
Godforms: Freyja, all twins, Castor and Pollux, Janus.
Color Atziluth: orange.
Color Briah: pale mauve.
Color Yetzirah: yellow-leather.
Color Assiah: reddish-grey to mauve.
Incense: wormwood.
Animals: magpie, all hybrids.
Legendary Beings: banshees, apparitions.
Stones: alexandrite, tourmaline, Iceland spar.
Plants: orchids, ragwort, all hybrids.

Gemini as the twins

Tree: oak, ash.
Zodiac/Element: Gemini.
Tarot Card: the Lovers; children of the voice.
Correspondence to Human Body: lungs.
Disease: pneumonia.
Magickal Powers: control of the double, prophecy.
Magickal Symbols: tripod.
Rituals Involving: messages from the superconscious; discrimination.

Path 18

Alchemists at the furnace

Title: the grail.

Intelligence: Influencing Intelligence.

Place: path joins 3-5.

Hebrew Name: Cheth; fence.

Number: 8.

Angel: Muriel.

Qlippoth (Demons): Shichirion; the Black Ones.

Demons of Hidden Paths: Characith.

Godforms: the Valkyries, Krishna, Apollo, Mercury.

Color Atziluth: amber.

Color Briah: maroon.

Color Yetzirah: rich bright russet.

Color Assiah: dark greenish-brown.

Incense: onycha.

Animals: crab, turtle, sphinx.

Legendary Beings: vampires.

Stones: amber.

Plants: lotus, angelica, watercress.

Tree: yew.

Zodiac/Element: Cancer.

Tarot Card: the Chariot; lord of triumph of light.

Correspondence to Human Body: stomach.

Disease: rheumatism.

Magickal Powers: enchantment.

Magickal Symbols: alchemical furnace.

Rituals Involving: seeking the Inner Self.

Path 19

Dragon

Title: the magickal union.

Intelligence: Spiritual Intelligence.

Place: path joins 4-5.

Hebrew Name: Teth; serpent.

Number: 9.

Angel: Verchiel.

Qlippoth (Demons): Shalehbiron; the Flaming Ones.

Demons of Hidden Paths: Temphioth.

Godforms: Freyr, Horus, Vishnu, Demeter, Venus.

Color Atziluth: greenish-yellow.

Color Briah: deep purple.

Color Yetzirah: grey.

Color Assiah: reddish-amber.

Incense: olibanum (frankincense).

Animals: lion.

Legendary Beings: dragons.

Stones: cat's eye.

Plants: sunflower, flax, saffron, marigold, tonics.

Tree: ash.

Zodiac/Element: Leo.

Tarot Card: Strength; daughter of the flaming sword.

Correspondence to Human Body: heart.

Disease: heart disorders.

Magickal Powers: power of dialogue with animals.

Magickal Symbols: heart.

Rituals Involving: work with the chakras; control over the biochemical workings of the body.

PATH 20

Title: the secret seed.

Intelligence: Willful Intelligence.

Place: path joins 4-6.

Hebrew Name: Yod; hand, sperm.

Number: 10.

Angel: Hamaliel.

Qlippoth (Demons): Tzaphirion; the Scratchers.

Demons of Hidden Paths: Yamatu.

Godforms: Frigg, Hel, the gopis, Attis, Vesta, Adonis, Isis, Nephthys, Balder.

Color Atziluth: yellowish-green.

Color Briah: slate grey.

Color Yetzirah: green-grey.

Color Assiah: plum.

Incense: narcissus.

Animals: cat, any solitary animal or person.

Legendary Beings: mer-people.

Stones: peridot.

Plants: snowdrop, lily, mint.

Tree: birch.

The Hermit

Zodiac/Element: Virgo.

Tarot Card: the Hermit; prophet of the eternal.

Correspondence to Human Body: back.

Disease: spinal disorders.

Magickal Powers: invisibility.

Magickal Symbols: lamp, wand, consecrated bread.

Rituals Involving: seeking silence of meditation; spiritual search.

PATH 21

Haida eagle totem

Title: the father of all.

Intelligence: Conciliating Intelligence.

Place: path joins 4-7.

Hebrew Name: Kaph; palm, egg.

Number: 20, 500.[22]

Angel: Tzadkiel.

Qlippoth (Demons): Gha'agsheblah; the Breakers.

Demons of Hidden Paths: Kurgasiax.

Godforms: Heimdall, Amen Ra, Brahma, Indra, Zeus, Fortuna.

Color Atziluth: violet.

Color Briah: blue.

Color Yetzirah: rich purple.

Color Assiah: bright blue rayed with yellow.

Incense: saffron.

Animals: eagle.

Legendary Beings: incubi, nightmares.

Stones: amethyst, lapis lazuli.

Plants: fig, arnica, thyme.

Tree: holly.

Zodiac/Element: Jupiter.

Tarot Card: Wheel of Fortune; lord of the forces of life.

Correspondence to Human Body: digestive system.

Disease: gout.

Magickal Powers: power of political and social control.

Magickal Symbols: scepter.

Rituals Involving: the study of karma and reincarnation.

PATH 22

Themis

Title: the sexually united.

Intelligence: Faithful Intelligence.

Place: path joins 5-6.

Hebrew Name: Lamed; ox-goad.

Number: 30.

Angel: Uriel.

Qlippoth (Demons): A'abirion; the Clayey Ones.

Demons of Hidden Paths: Lafcursiax.

Godforms: Tyr, Mani, Maat, Yama, Themis, Vulcan, Minerva.

Color Atziluth: emerald green.

Color Briah: blue.

Color Yetzirah: deep blue-green.

Color Assiah: pale green.

Incense: galbanum.

Animals: elephant, spider.

Legendary Beings: fairies, harpies.

Stones: emerald.

Plants: aloe, tobacco, sage.

Tree: oak.

Zodiac/Element: Libra.

Tarot Card: Justice; daughter of the lords of truth.

Correspondence to Human Body: liver.

Disease: kidney disorders.

Magickal Powers: power of equilibrium and balancing.

Magickal Symbols: equal-armed cross.

Rituals Involving: justice; equilibrium; study of metaphysical law.

PATH 23

Title: the water redeemer.

Intelligence: Stable Intelligence.

Place: path joins 5-8.

Hebrew Name: Mem; water.

Number: 40, 600.

Angel: Gabriel.

Qlippoth (Demons): Ariton; Water Demons.

Demons of Hidden Paths: Malkunofat.

Godforms: Njord, Balder, Soma, Poseidon, Neptune.

Color Atziluth: deep blue.

Color Briah: sea-green.

Color Yetzirah: deep olive-brown.

Color Assiah: white flecked with purple, like mother of pearl.

Incense: myrrh, onycha.

Animals: eagle, scorpion, snake.

Legendary Beings: nymphs, undines, nereids.

Stones: aquamarine, green beryl.

Plants: lotus, waterlily, leek.

Tree: willow.

Water demon

Zodiac/Element: Water.

Tarot Card: Hanged Man; spirit of the mighty waters.

Correspondence to Human Body: organs of nutrition.

Disease: chills.

Magickal Powers: skrying, creating talismans, crystal gazing.

Magickal Symbols: consecrated wine.

Rituals Involving: meditation and suspension of the mind's activities; controlled entry of the conscious mind into the pool of the subconscious.

PATH 24

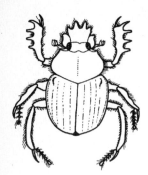

Scarab beetle

Title: the redeeming belly.

Intelligence: Imaginative Intelligence.

Place: path joins 6-7.

Hebrew Name: Nun; fish.

Number: 50, 700.

Angel: Barbiel.

Qlippoth (Demons): Necheshthiron; the Brazen Ones.

Demons of Hidden Paths: Niantiel.

Godforms: Odhinn, Set, Yama, Cronus, Mars.

Color Atziluth: green-blue.

Color Briah: dull brown.

Color Yetzirah: very dark brown.

Color Assiah: indigo-brown, like a beetle.

Incense: benzoin, oppoponax.

Animals: beetle, wolf, scorpion.

Legendary Beings: lamiae, hags.

Stones: snakestone.

Plants: cactus, mandrake.

Tree: yew.

Zodiac/Element: Scorpio.

Tarot Card: Death; child of the great transformer.

Correspondence to Human Body: intestines.

Disease: cancer.

Magickal Powers: necromancy, mediumistic ability.

Magickal Symbols: scythe.

Rituals Involving: willed transformation of the life; astral projection.

PATH 25

Temperance

Title: the pregnant womb.

Intelligence: Tentative Intelligence.

Place: path joins 6-9.

Hebrew Name: Samekh; prop.

Number: 60.

Angel: Adnachiel.

Qlippoth (Demons): Necheshiron; Snaky Ones.

Demons of Hidden Paths: Saksaksalim.

Godforms: Forseti, Nephthys, Vishnu, Apollo the Hunter, Artemis, Diana the Huntress, Iris.

Color Atziluth: blue.

Color Briah: yellow.

Color Yetzirah: green.

Color Assiah: dark vivid blue.

Incense: lignum aloes.

Animals: horse, dog.

Legendary Beings: centaurs.

Stones: jacinth.

Plants: rushes, reeds, wood betony, mallow.

Tree: oak.

Zodiac/Element: Sagittarius.

Tarot Card: Temperance; the bringer forth of life.

Correspondence to Human Body: hips, thighs.

Disease: apoplexy, thrombosis.

Magickal Powers: transmutation.

Magickal Symbols: arrow for the swiftness of willed force.

Rituals Involving: blending of the conscious and subconscious; rising in consciousness.

PATH 26

Title: the erect and glad.

Intelligence: Renovating Intelligence.

Place: path joins 6-8.

Hebrew Name: Ayin; eye.

Number: 70.

Angel: Haniel.

Qlippoth (Demons): Dagdagiron; Fishy Ones.

Demons of Hidden Paths: A'ano'nin.

Godforms: the Frost Giants, Set, Pan, Priapus, Bacchus, Saturn.

Color Atziluth: indigo.

Color Briah: black.

Color Yetzirah: blue-black.

Color Assiah: cold dark grey.

Incense: musk, civet.

Animals: goat, ass.

Legendary Beings: satyrs, fauns, panic-demons.

Stones: coal, black diamond.

Plants: thistle, wormwood, satyrion.

Tree: beech.

Zodiac/Element: Capricorn.

Wormwood

Tarot Card: Devil; lord of the gates of matter.

Correspondence to Human Body: genital system.

Disease: arthritis.

Magickal Powers: the evil eye, black magick, evocation, dialogue with Nature.

Magickal Symbols: elixir, lamp.

Rituals Involving: working with the Dweller on the Threshold of the Mysteries, working to transfer at will from intellect to intuition.

PATH 27

The furies

Title: the conquering child.

Intelligence: Exciting Intelligence.

Place: path joins 7-8.

Hebrew Name: Peh; mouth.

Number: 80, 800.

Angel: Camael.

Qlippoth (Demons): Golachab; the Burners.

Demons of Hidden Paths: Parfaxitas.

Godforms: Thorr, Odhinn, Horus, Menthu, Krishna, Ares, Mars.

Color Atziluth: scarlet.

Color Briah: red.

Color Yetzirah: Venetian red.

Color Assiah: bright red rayed with azure.

Incense: pepper, tobacco, dragons blood.

Animals: horse, bear, wolf.

Legendary Beings: furies, chimaeras, boars.

Stones: ruby, garnet.

Plants: wormwood, rue, absinthe.

Tree: oak.

Zodiac/Element: Mars.

Tarot Card: the Tower; lord of the mighty hosts.

Correspondence to Human Body: muscular system.

Disease: inflammation.

Magickal Powers: control of temporal imbalance, defense.

Magickal Symbols: sword.

Rituals Involving: working to access flashes of inspiration, creating needed changes of mind.

PATH 28

Nut

Title: the ruler.

Intelligence: Constituting Intelligence.

Place: path joins 7-9.

Hebrew Name: Tzaddi; fish-hook.

Number: 90, 900.

Angel: Malkiel.

Qlippoth (Demons): Ba'airiron; the Flock.

Demons of Hidden Paths: Hemeth-terith.

Godforms: Aphrodite, Nut, Athene, Juno, Venus.

Color Atziluth: violet.

Color Briah: sky blue.

Color Yetzirah: bluish-mauve.

Color Assiah: white tinged with purple.

Incense: galbanum.

Animals: man, eagle, peacock.

Legendary Beings: water nymphs, sirens, lorelei, mermaids.

Stones: glass, chalcedony.

Plants: olive, coconut.

Tree: elder.

Zodiac/Element: Aquarius.

Tarot Card: the Star; daughter of the firmament.

Correspondence to Human Body: kidneys, bladder.

Disease: apoplexy.

Magickal Powers: astrology.

Magickal Symbols: censer.

Rituals Involving: study of the emotional polarities of sex, meditation on astrology and charts.

PATH 29

Title: the elder witch.

Intelligence: Corporeal Intelligence.

Place: path joins 7-10.

Hebrew Name: Qoph; back of head.

Number: 100.

Angel: Barakiel.

Qlippoth (Demons): Nashimiron; the Malignant Ones.

Demons of Hidden Paths: Qulielfi.

Godforms: Odhinn, Freyja, Anubis, Vishnu, Poseidon, Neptune, Diana the archer, black Isis.

Color Atziluth: ultra-violet.

Color Briah: buff flecked with silver-white.

Color Yetzirah: light pinkish-brown.

Color Assiah: stone color.

Incense: ambergris.

Animals: fishes, dolphin.

Legendary Beings: phantoms, werewolves.

Stones: pearl.

Plants: poppy, raspberry leaf.

Fish

Tree: ash, elm.

Zodiac/Element: Pisces.

Tarot Card: the Moon; child of the sons of the mighty.

Correspondence to Human Body: legs, feet.

Disease: gout, VD.

Magickal Powers: bewitchments, casting illusions.

Magickal Symbols: magick mirror.

Rituals Involving: recognizing and understanding the primitive instincts.

PATH 30

Seal of Raphael

Title: the playing sun.

Intelligence: Collecting Intelligence.

Place: path joins 8-9.

Hebrew Name: Resh; head.

Number: 200.

Angel: Raphael.

Qlippoth (Demons): Thagirion; the Disputers.

Demons of Hidden Paths: Raflifu.

Godforms: Ra, Helios, Apollo.

Color Atziluth: orange.

Color Briah: gold-yellow.

Color Yetzirah: rich amber.

Color Assiah: amber rayed with red.

Incense: cinnamon, frankincense, Kyphi.

Animals: lion, birds of prey.

Legendary Beings: will-o'-wisps.

Stones: crysoleth, yellow jacinth.

Plants: sunflower, heartsease, laurel, heliotrope.

Tree: bay.

Zodiac/Element: the Sun.

Tarot Card: the Sun; lord of the fire of the world.

Correspondence to Human Body: circulatory system.

Disease: repletion.

Magickal Powers: power of acquiring wealth.

Magickal Symbols: lamen, talismans.

Rituals Involving: study of the personality.

PATH 31

Salamander

Title: the emerging goddess.

Intelligence: Perpetual Intelligence.

Place: path joins 8-10.

Hebrew Name: Shin; tooth.

Number: 300.

Angel: Michael.

Qlippoth (Demons): Paimon; Fire Demons.

Demons of Hidden Paths: Shalicu.

Godforms: Freyr, Freyja, Horus, Agni, Yama, Prometheus, Vulcan, Pluto, Hades, Vesta.

Color Atziluth: glowing orange-scarlet.

Color Briah: vermilion.

Color Yetzirah: scarlet flecked with gold.

Color Assiah: vermilion flecked with crimson and emerald.

Incense: olibanum.

Animals: lion.

Legendary Beings: salamanders, sphinx.

Stones: fire opal.

Plants: hibiscus, nettle, self-heal.

Tree: apple, oak.

Zodiac/Element: Fire.

Tarot Card: Judgment; spirit of the primal fire.

Correspondence to Human Body: organs of circulation.

Disease: fevers, death, insanity.

Magickal Powers: evocation, pyromancy, transformation.

Magickal Symbols: wand, lamp, pyramid, cloak.

Rituals Involving: reincarnation, cultural evolution, influence of temperament on previous incarnations.

PATH 32

Title: the pentacle of the whole.

Intelligence: Administrative Intelligence.

Place: path joins 9-10.

Hebrew Name: Tau; cross.

Number: 400.

Angel: Tzaphkiel.

Qlippoth (Demons): Satariel; the Concealers; Lilith; Earth Demons.

Demons of Hidden Paths: Thantifaxath.

Godforms: Odhinn, Sebek, Nephthys, Osiris, Brahma, Athene, Demeter, Persephone, Ceres, Gaea, Saturn, Ceres, the sorrowing Isis.

Color Atziluth: indigo.

Color Briah: black.

Color Yetzirah: blue-black.

Color Assiah: black rayed with blue.

Incense: storax, meadowsweet.

Animals: crocodile, bull.

Legendary Beings: gnomes, Mother Nature, Dweller on the Threshold.

Stones: onyx, salt, star sapphire.

Plants: ivy, rue, cypress.

Tree: beech, ash, hawthorn, oak.

Saturn

Zodiac/Element: Saturn.

Tarot Card: the Universe or World; great one of the night of time.

Correspondence to Human Body: excretory system, skeleton.

Disease: arteriosclerosis, sluggishness.

Magickal Powers: astral vision, manipulation, dialogue with plants.

Magickal Symbols: sickle, shadow, pentacle.

Rituals Involving: communication with the Dweller on the Threshold, initiation, descent to the Underworld, meditation on death of the physical body.

ENDNOTES

1. Scholem, Gershom. *Kabbalah*. NY: 1974.
2. Ganzfried, Rabbi Solomon. *Code of Jewish Law*. NY: 1963.
3. Scholem, Gershom. *Major Trends in Jewish Mysticism*. NY: 1977.
4. Gershom Scholem, *Kabbalah*, says that originally the word Sephiroth was used to mean numerical stages in creation. During the Middle Ages the word evolved to mean a system of divine emanation.
5. Kraig, Donald Michael. *Modern Magick*.
6. Scholem, Gershom. *Kabbalah*.
7. Actually there are only Twenty-two Paths, but often the Ten Sephiroth are called Paths and added to this number.
8. Science doesn't acknowledge the existence of the Veils, let alone magick. But theoretically speaking, there should be both matter and anti-matter (positive and negative, male and female energies) to create.
9. Dion Fortune, in *The Mystical Qabalah*, states that there is only one tree, not two. The area of the Qlippoth is the reverse side of the Tree of Life.
10. Parfitt, Will. *The Living Qabalah*. David Godwin says that this demon was "discovered" by Dee and Kelly and "popularized" by Aleister Crowley in his Enochian workings and, although it/he is a handy concept, is not an integral or necessary part of Qabalism.
11. Ashcroft-Nowicki, Dolores. *The Shining Paths*.
12. All correspondences of the Sephiroth and the Paths are taken from Godwin, David, *Godwin's Cabalistic Encyclopedia*; Wang, Robert, *The Qabalistic Tarot*; Regardie, Israel, *The Godlen Dawn*; Parfitt, Will, *The Living Qabalah*; Fortune, Dion, *The Mystical Qabalah*; Crowley, Aleister, *777*; Cavendish, Richard, *The Black Arts*. My own observations and knowledge gained from ritual have also been incorporated.
13. Regardie, Israel. *The Golden Dawn*. Regardie writes that the Dagesh, which represents the vowel sounds in modern Hebrew script, was invented a long time after the original Qabala. The Dagesh, or pointing, came into being to standardize pronunciation. Although there are many dialects of Hebrew, the two most important ones are the Ashkenazic, a dialect used mostly in Germany, Poland, and Russia; and the Sephardic, used mostly in Spain, Portugal, and the Mediterranean. The magickal society calling itself the Golden Dawn used the Sephardic dialect, while Regardie himself in *Garden of Pomegranates* used the Ashkenazic.
14. The Angelic or Formative World is the third of the four Qabalistic worlds. The choirs of angels associated with Yetzirah, or the third world, are also called Olam ha-Yetzirah.
15. The Qlippoth (spelled *Qliphoth* by Parfitt) are Shells of the Dead or Evil Demons of Matter. Godwin says that the Infernal Orders of Qlippoth corre-

spond in many ways to the Orders of the Angels. There are Qlippoth connected with the higher levels above the Tree of Life also; these are Qemetiel, or the Crowd of Gods, for Ain; Belial, Without God, for Ain Soph; and Athiel, Uncertainty, for Ain Soph Or. Mathers, in *The Book of the Sacred Magic of Abramelin the Mage*, goes into great detail about these demons and their characteristics. The idea of the ten evil Sephiroth had developed by the thirteenth century. Cermonial magicians considered salt and other preservatives, such as frankincense and myrrh, as poisons to demons. Tradition also says that if the demons see themselves in a mirror they will flee.

16. The Arch-demons given here are the ones listed by MacGregor Mathers. These Arch-demons are said to be under the supreme command of Sammael, the evil angel of poison.

17. There is often a difference in the placement of Tarot cards from book to book. However, the Golden Dawn system of correspondence of Tarot to the Qabala feels the most accurate. Although I enjoyed *Living Magical Arts* by R. J. Stewart, I would not recommend that anyone follow his outline of the placement of the Tarot cards on the Tree. Stewart's placement of the Tarot matches no other that I have ever seen, and frankly does not make sense.

18. The true meaning of the world "occult" is "hidden." This is the correct interpretation to be given to the Occult Intelligence.

19. Although most Qabalistic writers list demons for Daath, for some reason they do not give angels. Zagzagel is the angel of wisdom as listed in *A Dictionary of Angels* by Gustav Davidson.

20. Regardie, Israel. *The Golden Dawn*. Regardie is the only authority I know who even begins to cover the significance of the Sphere of Daath.

21. These stones were chosen for their magickal meanings as listed in *Cunningham's Encyclopedia of Crystal, Gem and Metal Magic* by Scott Cunningham.

22. Regardie, Israel. *The Golden Dawn*. Regardie not only gives the dual numbers for some of the Paths, but also the aphabetical equivalent to each.

BIBLIOGRAPHY

Aima. *The Ancient Wisdom and Rituals*. Hollywood, CA: Foibles Publications, no date.

Andrews, Ted. *Simplified Magic: A Beginner's Guide to the New Age Qabala*. St. Paul, MN: Llewellyn Publications, 1989.

Ashcroft-Nowicki, Dolores. *The Shining Paths*. UK: Aquarian Press, 1983.

Barrett, Francis. *The Magus*. Secaucus, NJ: Citadel Press, 1980.

Bias, Clifford. *Ritual Book of Magic*. NY: Samuel Weiser, 1981.

Brennan, J. H. *Experimental Magic*. UK: Aquarian Press, 1984.

Butler, Bill. *Dictionary of the Tarot*. NY: Schocken Books, 1977.

Butler, W. E. *Magic and the Qabala*. UK: Aquarian Press, 1964.

Butler, W. E. *The Magician: His Training and Work*. UK: Aquarian Press, 1969.

Cavendish, Richard. *The Black Arts*. NY: G.P. Putnam's Sons, 1967.

Conway, David. *Magic: An Occult Primer*. NY: E. P. Dutton & Co., 1972.

Crowley, Aleister. *The Book of Thoth*. York Beach, ME: Samuel Weiser, 1981.

Crowley, Aleister. *Magick in Theory and Practice*. NY: Dover Publications, 1976.

Crowley, Aleister. *777 and Other Qabalistic Writings of Crowley*. York Beach, ME: Samuel Weiser, 1986.

Cunningham, Scott. *Cunningham's Encyclopedia of Crystal, Gem and Metal Magic*. St. Paul, MN: Llewellyn Publications, 1990.

Davidson, Gustav. *A Dictionary of Angels*. NY: The Free Press, 1967.

deLaurence, L. W. *The Sixth and Seventh Books of Moses*. Chicago, IL: The deLaurence Co., no date.

Denning, Melita, and Phillips, Osborne. *The Magical Philosophy*, Vol. I-V. St. Paul, MN: Llewellyn Publications, 1974-1981.

Denning, Melita, and Phillips, Osborne. *Magical States of Consciousness*. St. Paul, MN: Llewellyn Publications, 1985.

Denning, Melita, and Phillips, Osborne. *The Magick of the Tarot*. St. Paul, MN: Llewellyn Publications, 1983.

Denning, Melita, and Phillips, Osborne. *Planetary Magick*. St. Paul, MN: Llewellyn Publications, 1989.

Fortune, Dion. *The Mystical Qabalah*. NY: Ibis Books, 1981.

Frater A.H.E.H.O. *Angelic Images*. The Sorcerers Apprentice Press, 1984.

Ginsburg, C. D. *The Kabbalah*. UK: Routledge & Kegan Paul, 1955. (Reprint of 1863 edition).

Godwin, David. *Godwin's Cabalistic Encyclopedia*. St. Paul, MN: Llewellyn Publications, 1979.

Gray, William G. *Inner Traditions of Magic*. York Beach, ME: Samuel Weiser, 1984.

Hawkridge, Emma. *The Wisdom Tree*. Boston, MA: Houghton Mifflin, 1945.

Highfield, A. C. *The Symbolic Weapons of Ritual Magic*. UK: Aquarian Press, 1983.

Knight, Gareth. *Knight's Practical Guide to Qabalistic Symbolism*. UK: Helios, 1970.

Knight, Gareth. *The Practice of Ritual Magic*. NY: Samuel Weiser, 1976.

Kraig, Donald M. *Modern Magick: Eleven Lessons in the High Magickal Arts*. St. Paul, MN: Llewellyn Publications, 1989.

Langton, E. *Essentials of Demonology*. UK: Epworth Press, 1949.

Levi, Eliphas. *The Book of Splendours*. UK: Aquarian Press, 1981.

Levi, Eliphas. *The Mysteries of the Qabalah*. UK: Aquarian Press, 1981.

Levi, Eliphas. *Transcendental Magic*. York Beach, ME: Samuel Weiser, 1981.

Mathers, S. L. MacGregor. *The Book of the Sacred Magic of Abramelin the Mage*. NY: Dover Publications, 1975.

Parfitt, Will. *The Living Qabalah*. UK: Element Books, 1988.

Paulsen, Kathryn. *The Complete Book of Magic and Witchcraft*. NY: New American Library, 1970.

Reed, Ellen Cannon. *The Witches' Qabala*. St. Paul, MN: Llewellyn Publications, 1985.

Regardie, Israel. *A Garden of Pomegranates*. St. Paul, MN: Llewellyn Publications, 1978.

Regardie, Israel. *The Golden Dawn*. St. Paul, MN: Llewellyn Publications, 1982.

Regardie, Israel. *Middle Pillar*. St. Paul, MN: Llewellyn Publications, 1970.

Richardson, Alan. *Gate of Moon*. UK: Aquarian Press, 1984.

Schaya, L. *Universal Meaning of the Kabbalah*. Secaucus, NJ: University Books, 1971.

Skelton, Robin. *Talismanic Magic*. York Beach, ME: Samuel Weiser, 1985.

Stewart, R. J. *Living Magical Arts*. UK: Blandford Press, 1987.

Torrens, R. G. *The Golden Dawn: The Inner Teachings*. NY: Samuel Weiser, 1973.

Tyson, Donald. *The New Magus: Ritual Magic as a Personal Process*. St. Paul, MN: Llewellyn Publications, 1988.

Valiente, Doreen. *An ABC of Witchcraft Past and Present*. NY: St. Martin's, 1973.

Wang, Robert. *The Qabalistic Tarot*. York Beach, ME: Samuel Weiser, 1983.

Westcott, W. W., Trans. *Sepher Yetzirah*. NY: Occult Research Press, no date.

Detail from Egyptian tomb painting, XVII Dynasty, New Kingdom

Chapter Nine

EGYPT

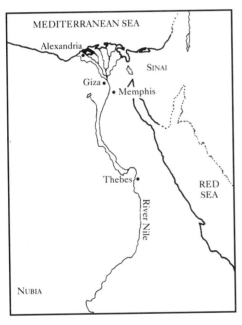

ANCIENT EGYPT, that narrow, fertile land bordering the Nile River, has always seemed to draw humankind's attention and imagination. We know much about Egypt, yet there still remain many unanswered questions, suppositions, and just plain guesses about their beliefs and culture. The culture of long ago Egypt is still covered with a mystique that fascinates people. What is really remarkable is that this civilization remained virtually unchanged for over 3000 years.

This great civilization began about 4500 BC. The four greatest periods in its history were the Old Kingdom (2686–2181 BC, Dynasties III–VIII), the Middle Kingdom (2134–1786 BC, Dynasties XI and XII), the Second Intermediate Kingdom (1786–1570 BC, Dynasties XIII–XVII), and the New Kingdom (1570–1085 BC, Dynasties XVIII–XX).[1] The Persians, Greeks, and Romans, who ruled Egypt from 525 BC to AD 324, did little, if anything, to restore the former glory and advancement of the culture.

During these periods, there were several individuals and one group that made their mark on Egyptian history. In the Old Kingdom, Khufu was responsible for building one of the magnificent pyramids, but little is known of his life.

During the Second Intermediate Kingdom, the Hyksos (Shepherd Kings) came out of the east to conquer Egypt in the middle of the eighteenth century BC, and continued to rule by force for about 150 years. The Egyptians called them Aamu (Asiatics).

Although some of their rulers had Semitic names, it is impossible to identify their country of origin. It is likely that the Hyksos introduced the horse and chariot into Egypt, an innovation that may have contributed to their downfall.

In the New Kingdom Dynasty XVIII, arose a very singular pharaoh, a woman named Hatshepsut. Hatshepsut was the first, and probably the only, woman to ascend the Egyptian throne. She began as the wife of her half-brother Thutmose II. Only daughters came from this union, but Thutmose had a son by a concubine. Thutmose II died while the son was still very small; Hatshepsut seized the throne and ruled for more than twenty years. She added to the Temple of Amen at Karnak and also built the magnificent temple at Deir el Bahri (called Djeser-djeseru in Egyptian). When Thutmose III came to the throne at her death in 1481 BC, he obliterated her name on everything, destroyed many of her statues, and persecuted anyone who had upheld her claim to rule.

Akhenaton (also known as Ikhnaton), born about 1370 BC, is remembered for the controversy he created when he tried to force the Egyptians into the worship of one god. He reigned in the same Dynasty as Hatshepsut. At his birth his father, Amenhotep III, gave him the name Akhenamen (meaning "Amen is satisfied"). His mother Ti was a commoner, raised to royal status by the marriage. In the sixth year of his reign, Akhenaton changed his name to reflect his new religious interest. He moved his capital from Thebes (home of the god Amen) to a new city, Akhetaton (the Horizon of Aton), 300 miles to the north. Soon he forbade worship of the old gods, especially Amen-Ra, whose name was obliterated from all temples, tombs, and monuments. He decreed that Aton was the one and only god to be worshipped. There was so much controversy over his dictatorial religious laws that there was little mourning at his death.

Tutankhamen was Akhenaton's son-in-law, ruling after Akhenaton, and related in some way to Amenhotep III. It is possible that he was the son of Akhenaton by a lesser wife or concubine. When he became pharaoh he was somewhere between nine and twelve years old and his wife, Ankhesenamon, about eleven or twelve. We do know that his original name was Tutankhaton, but he changed it to Tutankhamen when, after three years of rule, he moved his court back to Thebes. One of Tutankhamen's first projects was to restore the temples that Akhenaton had desecrated. It is known from his mummy that he died violently at age eighteen, but history is silent about the actual events.

Egyptian pharaohs usually were born into or married into the ruling family of a Great Queen or Great Royal Wife. Remnants of the Goddess-civilization were evident in the fact that no man became pharaoh except by marrying a daughter of the ruling house. Inheritance of the throne and power descended through the female lineage.[2]

Lily design from Tutankhamen's tomb

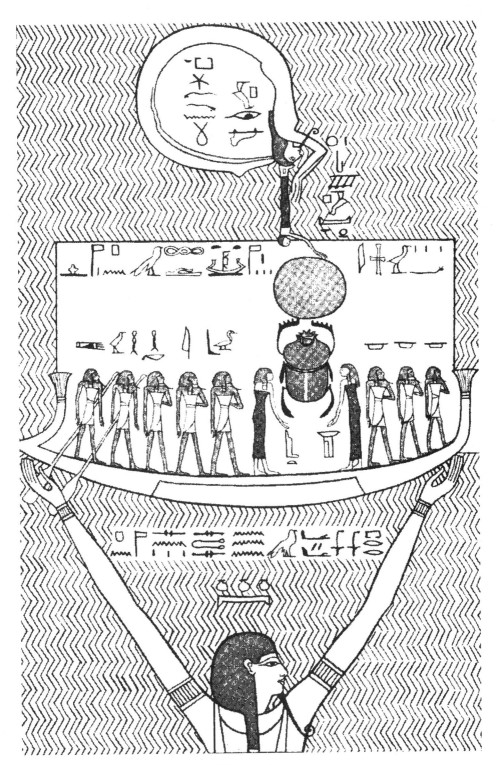

The creation

RELIGION

From early in their history the Egyptians held the concept of continuation of life after death. They perfected the art of embalming and built magnificent tombs and pyramids. Their environment was reflected in the nature, aspects, and appearances of their deities.

In the Old Kingdom, the three important religious centers were Memphis, Heliopolis, and Hermopolis. (I am using the more familiar Greek names for these cities.) By the time of the New Kingdom, the priests of Amen at Thebes had gained supremacy, making that city the ultimate religious power, and their god ruler of the Egyptian pantheon.

Egyptian deities did not require human sacrifice or annihilation of people with other religious beliefs. Temples were not considered a place of communal worship. They were looked upon as houses for the deities; there, statues were kept and attended by priests and priestesses.[3] The priesthood was not celibate. The pharaoh was considered an incarnated god upon Earth.

The life of the average Egyptian was a blend of religion and the use of magick. Magick was a vital part of everyday life. The people believed that worship was basically a private, personal concern and duty. After all, the ancient Egyptians said, when you stood in the Hall of Judgment after death, no one could tamper with the scales that weighed your heart for truth and goodness. Your soul was laid bare; everything was revealed.

Individual worship was performed at home altars and certain shrines, with the populace as a whole participating in the great seasonal festivals. The common people were not admitted to the great temples, but they made pilgrimages to certain shrines.

National or regional festivals of deities were primarily journeys of the appropriate statues through the local streets or on the Nile, as in the case of Amen's Feast of Opet, when his statue was taken from Karnak to his temple at Luxor and back.

Since worship was considered a private concern, the ordinary person visited the temple of his choice for healing or to present petitions when he needed something. Even then, he entered only the outer courts of the temples. The inner sanctuary of the deity was entered only by the highest priests, priestesses, or the pharaoh.

Originally, the priests and priestesses did not believe in polytheism or animal worship. They believed that the god-forms each represented a principle or aspect of the Supreme Creator. They believed that as long as the spiritual needs of humans were met, it did not matter how the Ultimate Spirit was pictured. These priests/priestesses used a sacred language known only to them for all rituals and worship, probably the remnant of a very ancient language.

Some temples were centers of healing, "sleep houses," where dream therapy and hypnosis were used to cure the sick. In these places, quiet music of special sounds and rhythms was employed for healing the whole person—body, emotions, mind, and spirit.

At sunrise each morning, the priest or priestess in charge of the day's rituals entered the deity's sanctuary and broke the seals on the doors of the shrine. The statue of the deity within, usually made of gold or other precious metals and gems, was washed, anointed, dressed in fresh clothing, and hung with jewelry. Fresh offerings of food and wine were laid out. The Singers chanted hymns, and the day's regular duties began. More rituals were held at high noon.

The altar faced east at dawn, south at noon, and west at sunset. Much incense was used, especially Kyphi,[4] a sacred blend burned only in the sanctuaries. This particular incense had such high vibrations that it was also used later by the Greeks. It was believed that the incense smoke rising towards Heaven, or the gods, bore with it words of power. This was deemed pleasing to Osiris who heard the prayers and did as the petitioner asked.

At sundown the priest/priestess in charge closed the shrine and sealed the doors. Carefully backing out of the sanctuary, he or she swept away all traces of footprints, literally and symbolically, so that the sacred place would be ritually clean. During this, the Singers chanted more hymns.

Egyptian worship was intertwined with music and dancing. The Singers could be either male or female, depending upon the deity they served. The Temple Dancers were most often female, spending their early years actively participating in the sacred dances, and their later years instructing the new Dancers.

Dancing and chanting made it necessary to have musicians. These were attached to the temples, as were the Dancers and Singers, and were usually female. Sometimes there were dramatic performances for very special religious rites.

Small drums, tambourines, flutes, the lute, the lyre, and the oboe (or a similar instrument) were used. There were many types of harps, from lap-size to the tall floor models.[5] Music was accompanied by hand clapping and finger snapping of the Dancers. And there was the ever-present *sistrum* (plural *sistra*), especially in the temples of Bast, Isis, Hathor, and Sekhmet.

The ancient Egyptians were well aware that humans had more than just a physical body. They said that humankind had seven souls. Much of the esoteric meaning of these forms has been lost. What we now know of these "souls" is limited, but vastly interesting and informative.

The physical body of humankind was called the *khat*. The *ka* (double) came into existence when the body was born. It continued to live in the body but was independent and distinct from it. It could assume any form and travel wherever it pleased in the realms of the gods. The ka did not die at the death of the body, but continued to

The deities of the planets

Ceremonial scene connected with the resurrection of Osiris

live in the tomb statues of the deceased. The Egyptians knew it as the body-soul; in their hieroglyphs it was pictured as a bird with a bearded human head.

The *ab* (heart) was believed to be the seat of the life-force and the home of emotions and passions. The Egyptians said that it was formed from the mother's heart blood. The *ba* (soul) was intimately connected with the heart; they called it the heart-soul. It was a kind of ghost or astral form that appeared at death.

The *khu* or *aakhu* (spirit) was known as the spirit-soul. It was eternal and could not be injured or killed. The Egyptians thought it resided in the blood as a primordial life force. It was the spiritual part of humankind. Sometimes its meaning is translated as intelligence.

The *khaibit* (shadow) was closely tied to the *sah* (spiritual body). Resurrection was not considered complete unless the sah had its shadow. If the shadow was lost or stolen while the person was alive, it was believed that the physical body would exist in a diseased or dying state. In many cultures besides ancient Egypt, to steal a person's shadow meant to steal their magickal power and their life; such a theft was considered a crime.

Other important forms of each person were the *sah* and the *sekhem*. The *sah* or *sahu* (spiritual body) was the eternal dwelling place of the soul. It had the power to travel anywhere on Earth and among the gods. The khu lived within it. The *sekhem* (power) animated the sah; we might term the sekhem willpower or purpose. At death, religious rites freed the sah from the physical body. The existence of the eternal sah is the idea behind the Egyptian belief in resurrection. The sah, in actuality, is the total of all incarnations, the spiritual form that must always return to the Hall of Judgment at the death of the physical body.

The *ren* (soul-name) was believed to be a vital part of every person. It was given to each person at birth by the goddess Renenet. The Egyptians believed that only by knowing the correct soul-name of a person, animal, or object could you have power over it. This, of course, had its positive and negative sides. The true name of every person had to be given to the gods when the heart was weighed on the scales of truth in the Hall of Judgment. Knowledge of a name also made a person vulnerable to black magick.

To the Egyptians the zodiac was: Aries, En-me-shar-ra; Taurus, Gud-an-na; Gemini, Tuamu; Cancer, Al-lul; Leo, Ur-gu-la; Virgo, Ab-sin; Libra, Zi-ba-ni-tum; Scorpio, Gir-tab; Sagittarius, Pa-bil-sag; Capricorn, Uz or Enzu; Aquarius, Gu-an-na; Pisces, Nu-shame.

The planets were: Jupiter, Heru-ao-sheta-taui (without a god); Saturn, Heru-ka-pet (Horus); Mars, Heru-khuti (Ra); Mercury, Sebku (Set); Venus, Bennu-Asar (Osiris).

The Egyptian calendar consisted of twelve months of thirty days with an adjustment period made up of the extra days. Originally, they may have used a lunar calendar of thirteen months, but changed to the solar calculation when the Sun gods became prominent.

The culture of the Nile was based primarily on agriculture. The people were attuned to the seasons, equinoxes, and solstices. Their year was divided into three seasons of four months each: inundation from July 19–November 15; winter from November 16–March 15; summer from March 16–July 18. There is also strong evidence in their writings that seasonal solar changes were celebrated.

Certain religious festivals (actual dates now unknown to us) were known to have been celebrated by the majority of the people. The Festival of Thoth, Lord of the Holy Words and inventor of the Four Laws of Magick, was on New Year's Day. The Recovery of Isis celebrated the return of health to the goddess after the birth of the Sun god Horus. The Resurrection of Osiris and his ascendance to the heavens probably occurred near the spring equinox. The Festival of Bast was a summer celebration, while the Night of the Teardrop was in remembrance of the sorrows of Isis. Opener of the Way, also called the Feast of Bread, honored the goddess Neith and was a harvest festival. The times of Hathor's Feast Day and the Mummification of Osiris are unknown. The Birth of Horus occurred about December 23, shortly after the winter solstice, the time of the final entombment of Osiris (called the Night of Lamps, because lamps were set out to burn all night).

Each month had two Moon festivals: one at the New Moon with dance and song, and one at the Full Moon, a time of petitions and magick, rituals, and religious celebrations.

Gods and goddesses of the months were:

1. Goddess Tekhi/Tekh-Heb
2. God Ptah-Aneb-Res-F or Menkhet
3. Goddess Het-Hert
4. Goddess Sekhet
5. God Min or Amsu
6. God Rekeh-Ur
7. God Rekeh-Netches
8. Goddess Renenet
9. God Khensu
10. God Khenthi
11. Goddess Apt
12. God Heru-Khuti

Birthdays of the deities on the five extra days of each year were: first day, Osiris; second day, Haroeris or Heru, the Blind Horus; third day, Set; fourth day, Isis; fifth day, Nephthys.

The four gods called the four sons of Horus were really a personification of the four Elements. In the Pyramid Texts, they were known as the Shesu-Heru, or Shemsu-Heru (Followers of Horus). They were also said to hold the four pillars of

Heaven. However, even Budge has conflicting evidence whether the northern deity was Mestha or Hap. Tomb pictures of Mestha are identified clearly, though. The four sons of Horus were:

East, Air: Tuamutef/Duamutef (with a jackal head)

South, Fire: Akeset/Amset/Imsety (with a human head)

West, Water: Qebhsennuf/Qebhsnuf (with a hawk head)

North, Earth: Mestha/Hap/Hapi (with an ape head)

The god Hapi listed with the Elements cannot be the same as the river god Hapi, since the elemental god is always shown with an animal head and Hapi, the river god, is shown in human form.

There were also Egyptian gods and goddesses who represented the four directions. These were:

East: Bast, Min, Osiris, Ra

South: Nekhebet, Sekhmet

West: Ament, Hathor, Neith, Anubis, Temu, Sebek, Nephthys

North: Buto, Shu, Mehueret, Isis

Egyptian magick was primarily of two kinds: first, magick to benefit the living or the dead; second, the type used to harm people.[6] At the beginning of each ritual, four lighted lamps were set at the four quarters or directions. They represented the four sons of Horus. Symbols were also set at these quarters. At the east was placed a *tat*, and in the south a model of a palm tree. At the west was set a figure of Anubis; in the north a figure of a mummy, sometimes lying in a coffin.

The power of any spell, incantation, or any word of power was considered greatly increased by the use of magickal pictures and amulets. The ankh was a favorite symbol, along with the *tat* of Osiris (also called a *tet* or *djed*), the solar disk, the scarab, the lotus, the buckle of Isis, and the Eye of Horus.

Wax images were used in certain rituals, primarily for gaining someone's love or harassing enemies. The name of the individual was cut or written on the image. After spells were recited over the figure, it was stabbed, destroyed, or (for love) carried next to the heart. The priests of Amen-Ra at Thebes regularly burned a wax image of the evil god Apep. These wax serpent-forms were subjected to all kinds of abuse before they were destroyed in a fire.

Dress and Ornamentation

The only Egyptian material for clothing was linen, usually white. It was woven in a wide range of textures from a coarse, canvas-like cloth to a very delicate, semi-transparent gauze. By the time of the New Kingdom, women's dress had changed from a form-fitting ankle-length shift with slender straps covering the breasts to a very sheer pleated robe, open in the front and tied at the waist by an embroidered sash. The older shift was retained as an underdress. An accordion-pleated cape went over the shoulders, with the ends tied on the breast.

Egyptian dress

The basic kilt for men remained the same through all periods, except that the length went up and down. This kilt was a rectangle of linen (sometimes pleated), knee-length mostly, wrapped around the body at the waist and fastened in the front by knots, sashes, or overlap. Sometimes a long, elaborate robe, sheer and pleated, was worn over this.

Nearly everyone went barefoot, wearing sandals only for special occasions. These sandals were of leather and often decorated with lotus blossoms, beads, or sequins. A linen square, anchored by a band, was worn as a head-covering.

Sheer, elegant robes, worn by both men and women, were long and loose. Often they were fringed and covered with rich designs: animals, flowers, religious symbols, cartouches. Priests and priestesses frequently wore robes ornamented with blue and gold.

Men wore their hair much as they might today, and were clean shaven. Feminine hair styles were long. Sometimes the hair was braided into many tiny braids, sometimes left loose, sometimes shaped into ringlets bound with gold rings. Fillets and wreaths were common, as were diadems and ribbons.

Jewelry was popular with both sexes: earrings, necklaces, pendants, bracelets, amulets, talismans, anklets, finger rings. The most popular, beautiful adornment was the wide, flexible collar that covered the wearer from the base of the neck to the middle of the breast.

The main metals used were gold, copper, and electrum (a mixture of gold and silver). Gold was in a wide range of colors, from grey to rose-pink. The Egyptian artisans were experts at inlay, embossing, filigree, gilding, plating, and a kind of enameling. However, they only knew and used semi-precious gems, except pearls. The gems widely used were carnelian, turquoise, garnet, feldspar, rock crystal, and lapis lazuli. Faience in turquoise color was extremely popular.

The only cosmetics worn were rouge for the cheeks and lips, and liner for the eyes. Both sexes dramatically outlined their eyes with black, grey, and deep green. Scented oils, such as myrrh and other sweet resins, were popular. These scents were sometimes embedded in small cones of fat and worn on the head for special occasions.

SOME OF THE MYTHS

One version of the Egyptian creation legend states that in the beginning Khepera (the scarab beetle god) was the only thing in existence besides the watery abyss of Nu. Nu supplied the primeval matter while Khepera created everything by magickal rites.

Khepera was an androgynous being, capable of reproducing without a mate. As soon as Khepera produced Shu and Tefnut from seeds (sperm?) dropped into his

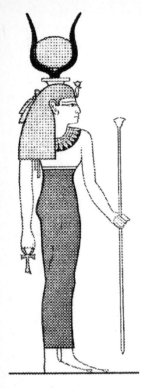

Hathor

mouth, the Sun emerged from the depths of Nu. Shu symbolizes daylight, the heavens, and the atmosphere; Tefnut symbolizes rain, dew, and moisture. Men and women were created from Khepera's tears dropping from his Eye (the Sun). Ra, the Sun god, was later called the Eye of Khepera.

Then the god made another Eye (the Moon) and went on to create plants, herbs, reptiles, and creeping things. Shu and Tefnut by this time were producing Seb, Nut, Osiris, Isis, Set, Nephthys, and Heru-Khent-An-Maati (the "Blind Horus"). Other versions list different names.

A second version of the creation story says that in the beginning was Nu, the watery abyss, and nothing else. Ra, the Sun god, produced himself from primeval matter, or nothingness, but did not appear at once. He enclosed himself in a lotus blossom for a time. When he decided to appear, he came with the goddess Maat and the god Thoth in his Sun-boat, rising from the waters of Nu. From his saliva (some texts say semen from masturbating), Ra made the god Shu. By a word of power he created the heavens, the Earth, the breath of life, everything. Then from his tears came vegetation, reptiles, animals, and finally humankind.[7]

Humankind became very wicked, distressing Ra greatly. Deciding to punish them, he called the goddess Hathor to carry out his vengeance. Turned loose on the Earth, the goddess slew until blood ran in rivers across the land. At last Ra pitied his creations and called for Hathor to stop. The goddess, blood-lust aroused, refused. In desperation, Ra set out 7,000 jars of beer spiked with mandrake and pomegranate, causing the liquid to resemble blood. Hathor drank them all, became very drunk, and forgot her battle fever.[8]

However, all this trouble caused Ra to lose his desire to rule among humans. He withdrew into the heavens, leaving his twin children, Shu and Tefnut, to rule. Shu in turn yielded the throne to his children, Seb and Nut.

Shu's son and daughter married against Ra's will and spent so much time copulating that Ra demanded that Shu forcefully separate them. Ra also declared that the pregnant sky goddess Nut could not give birth in any month of the year. Thoth felt sorry for her and, playing draughts with Selene the Moon, he won enough light to make five extra days for each year. Since these days did not belong to the regular Egyptian calendar of 360 days, Nut was able to give birth to five children: Osiris, Haroeris, Set, Isis, and Nephthys. (This list of names varies.) These children were born in five different parts of Egypt.

In the beginning of her life, the goddess Isis had no great magickal powers, although she knew many spells. She blackmailed those magickal powers from the old god Ra in exchange for his life.

At the end of his reign, the Sun god Ra was shaking and dribbling at the mouth. Isis used dirt and his saliva to make an invisible poisonous snake that bit the god. Ra could not cure himself since he did not know the cause of the wound. He had to rely on the goddess's healing, which she refused to do unless he revealed his secret name. At last, full of pain, Ra revealed his true name, passing the magickal knowledge directly from his heart to hers.

Nephthys, childless by her husband Set, lay with her brother Osiris. The child Anubis was born from this union and abandoned at birth because Nephthys feared Set would kill him. Isis found the baby and raised him. This god, with black skin and the head of a jackal, was devoted to her. When grown, Anubis accompanied Osiris on many of his journeys.

Isis married her brother Osiris. When their parents abdicated, the two ruled Egypt. While Osiris was spreading his civilizing ideas throughout the world, Isis ruled in his absence. Their brother Set, a jealous, violent god, wanted the throne for himself. When Osiris finally returned to Memphis, Set and 72 accomplices invited him to a banquet. Set brought out a beautiful chest, stating that whoever fit inside it would be the owner. Osiris fit perfectly. Set and his followers nailed shut the lid, covered the box with melted lead, and threw the box into the Nile. It floated out to sea. From there the chest floated to Byblos on the Phoenician coast where a tamarisk tree grew around it.

Because of Set's actions, Nephthys left him. Many of the other gods also abandoned him, hiding from the tyrant by taking refuge in animal bodies. Obviously Set did not care since he now was the ruler of Egypt.

When cut and placed as a pillar in the Phoenician king's palace, the tamarisk tree gave off such an exquisite odor that the story reached Isis in Egypt. She retrieved the chest and hid it from Set in the swamps belonging to Buto, the cobra goddess. Isis, with magick learned from the god Thoth, made light with her hair and stirred the air over her husband's body with her wings. This magick reanimated the body long enough for her to conceive a child. Isis remained hidden in the swamps until the child Horus was born.

Set, who had no intentions of giving up the throne, found the chest while hunting. Isis was gone, so he cut up the body of Osiris into fourteen pieces and scattered them throughout Egypt. Isis was brokenhearted. She searched until she found all the pieces of Osiris, except his phallus, which had been eaten by a Nile crab.

She and Nephthys joined the body pieces together. With the help of her nephew Anubis, the grand vizier Thoth, her young son Horus, and her sister Nephthys, Isis performed the first rites of embalming, thus giving Osiris eternal life. With Osiris ascended to the immortal world, Isis and her son hid from Set in the swamps of Buto until Horus grew old enough and strong enough to avenge his father.

As a child, Horus was exposed to many dangers. He was attacked and bitten by wild beasts, stung by scorpions, burned, and suffered intense intestinal pains. Thoth drove out the scorpion's poison; his mother's great powers saved him at other times. As he grew, Osiris came often to teach him the use of weapons so he could reclaim his inheritance and avenge himself on Set.

The day came when Horus challenged Set for the throne by presenting his petition to the Ennead, or supreme tribunal of the gods. The chief of the Ennead was Ra. The case was soon deadlocked over whether Horus or Set should have the throne of Egypt. To settle the dispute, the Ennead asked Thoth to contact the goddess Neith for advice. The goddess, without hesitation, said the throne belonged to Horus.

All the gods except Ra agreed with Neith. Ra called Horus a milk-drinking baby. In return one of the other gods insulted Ra, who then retreated to his house to sulk. To put Ra in a better mood, the goddess Hathor lewdly exposed herself and talked Ra into returning to the Ennead to hear the case.

Set did not have much going for him except a smooth tongue, so he based his case on his great strength that daily protected the Sun barge from enemies. Again the tribunal changed its mind, with all except Thoth voting for Set. Thoth spoke up for Horus and was roundly insulted by the gods. Furious, Isis began laying curses right and left, terrifying them. They tried to reassure her that everything would be fine.

This greatly infuriated Set, who promised to kill one god each day until they judged in his favor. He also refused any further discussion until Isis was removed from the tribunal. In an effort to please Set, Ra moved the Ennead to an island. He gave instructions to Anti, the ferryman, that no woman was to cross the water.

Isis had no intentions of giving up her battle. She disguised herself as an old woman and bribed Anti to take her to the island. There, she changed into a beautiful girl. It was no problem at all to entice Set away from the meeting. She proceeded to tell Set a sad tale of being a widow with a young son whose inheritance of cattle had been stolen by a foreigner. Set, besotted with love, magnanimously replied that the son was the rightful heir. Isis had him. Out of Set's mouth had come his own judgment. Set burst into tears and, returning to the Ennead, told them what had happened. The gods had no choice but to decide for Horus.

Set was a sore loser. He demanded trial by combat with young Horus. The two gods changed into hippos and plunged into the Nile to see who could stay down the longest. Isis began to worry, so she threw a magick spear into the water, but hit Horus. The young god came up onto the bank and demanded that she remove the weapon. Down Horus went again to do battle. And again Isis threw the spear, this time hitting her brother Set. He appealed to her to remove the spear, and she did.

Horus had had enough of this motherly interference. In a fit of anger, he cut off Isis's head for helping his enemy. Soon Ra became aware of a headless woman and told Thoth to do something about the situation. Thoth replaced the missing head with that of a cow. Another version says that Horus ripped off his mother's royal diadem, which Thoth replaced with a helmet in the shape of a cow's head.

During the great battle, Thoth was called upon to heal Set's emasculation with his saliva. As Horus lay sleeping, Set crept up and gouged out his eyes. The goddess Hathor stepped in and healed the young god.

During this terrible battle, it was Thoth's responsibility to see that a constant balance between Horus and Set was kept: a balance between good and evil, light and darkness, day and night.

Finally Osiris sent a threatening note to the Ennead: settle the dispute in favor of his son, or else. Horus was declared rightful ruler of the two Egypts. Thoth became grand vizier to Horus, later ruling in his place when the god resigned earthly power.

Everyone seemed satisfied with the verdict except Set, who periodically caused trouble. Isis again pleaded for her brother. The Ennead did not throw the troublesome god into the outer darkness, but instead gave him the desert and all foreign lands as his domain.

MAJOR GODS AND GODDESSES

The deities listed here are by no means all of those recorded in the Egyptian pantheon. It would be impossible to list them all. Anyone interested in an in-depth study of Egyptian deities should read *The Gods of the Egyptians* by E. A. Wallis Budge.

I have listed only a few important pronunciations for deity names; these pronunciations come from books by Budge and Barbara Mertz (who has a doctorate in Egyptology). There are vast differences of the spellings of Egyptian deity names. This has come about because Egyptian hieroglyphs had no vowels. Marilyn Seal Pierce in *Secrets of Egypt for the Millions* devotes a chapter to hieroglyphs and how the modern person can use them.

AMAUNET—Sometimes called the wife of AMEN; goddess of Heaven.

AMEN/AMOUN/AMUN/AMON/AMMON—"Hidden god"; "Great Father"; the great god of Thebes; similar to Jupiter and Zeus; a phallic deity. Sometimes pictured with the head of a ram; sometimes as a man with a crown with two tall straight plumes. Considered incarnate in the ruling pharaoh. Part of a trinity with MUT (pronounced Moot) and KHENSU. One of the universe creators and generous to all his devotees. The Phoenicians stole two of the priestesses from Amen's temple in Thebes and sold one to Libya, one to Greece. These two oracles founded schools of divination at Siwa in Libya and several famous centers in Greece. About the XII Dynasty, Amen became more than a god of local importance. At that time the princes of Thebes conquered their rivals to the throne, made their city the new capital, and their god the main deity in Upper Egypt at Karnak. Under the XIX and XX Dynasties, the priests of Amen gained supremacy over all other priests and temples. But the people were not satisfied. So the priests of Amen added the name of the great god RA to the name of Amen as a conciliatory gesture. Sacred animals were a ram with curled horns and a goose, both of which were kept at his temples at Karnak and Luxor. God of reproduction, fertility, generation, wind, air, prophecy, agriculture.

Amen

AMENT/AMENTI—"The Westerner"; "hidden goddess"; goddess of the land of the West or the Underworld; "goddess with beautiful hair." Consort of AMEN. Her emblems were the hawk and the feather. Ament was represented in human female form wearing either an ostrich feather on her head or an ostrich plume and a hawk. She welcomed all deceased people to the land of the dead with bread and water. If they ate and drank, they could not return to the land of the living.

Anubis weighing the heart

ANHUR/ANHER/ANHERT/ ONOURIS—"Skybearer"; official god of the nome Abt and its capital; very early aspect of OSIRIS. God of war, Sun, and the sky.

ANUBIS/ANPU/SEKHEM EM PET— Messenger from the gods to humans. His cult was very ancient, probably older than that of OSIRIS. He was pictured with the head of a jackal or dog, or as a dark-colored jackal. At the death of Osiris, Anubis invented embalming and funeral rites. To the Egyptians he was important as the god of embalming and tombs, protector of the dead, judge of the dead and god of the Underworld. He, with MAAT, weighed human souls for truth. He was the guide to the soul-judges after death. His duties included making sure that the funerary offerings reached the deceased. God of wisdom, intelligence, death, embalming, endings, truth, justice, surgery, hospital stays, finding lost things, anesthetics, medicine, journeys, protection, boats, diplomacy, astral travel (voluntary or involuntary), cemeteries; guardian against lower astral entities.

ANQET/ANUKET/ANUKIS—"The Clasper"; water goddess of the Nile Cataracts. Her symbol was the cowrie shell. KHNEMU's second wife, she had a special dwelling place on the island of Seheil. Also worshipped at Elephantine with Khnemu. Pictured as a woman wearing a tall plumed crown. Sometimes she was pictured as having four arms which represented the union of male and female principles. She was self-begotten and self-produced. Producer and giver of life, water.

APEP/APOPHIS—Demon enemy of the Sun; pictured as a huge snake, he was the eternal enemy of RA and lived deep in the Nile. Called the Great Serpent of Tuat (the Underworld); this realm of darkness with its chambers was actually the interior of Apep's body. The Egyptians said he was responsible for eclipses when he managed to swallow Ra's sacred Sun boat. Not the same deity as SET. Darkness, storm, night, the Underworld, death, eclipses.

AUF/EUF RA—Aspect of the Sun god RA. Pictured as a ram-headed man wearing the solar disk, he represented the Sun at night when the life-giving rays were concealed. The Egyptians believed that each night the Sun had to make its way through the caverns of the Underworld where he had to outwit APEP in order to ride again across the heavens. Peace, rest, sleep, courage.

BA-NEB-TETET/BANEBDEDET/BANADED—A ram-god; the Greeks knew him as MENDES. He was considered to be incarnate in the sacred ram kept in his temple. There was wide mourning when this ram died, and great festivals when the priests discovered a new one. God of discussion, arbitration, peace.

BAST/BASTET/PASHT (in her dark aspect)—Cat-headed goddess; mother of all cats; wife of PTAH. She was identified with ARTEMIS or DIANA who was also called the mother of cats. The living power and gentle heat of the sunlight. Lady of the East; associated with the god SEPT (Lord of the East). The cat was Egypt's most sacred animal but the black cat was especially sacred to her; Egyptian physicians used the black cat symbol in healing. Cats were sacred to her in general, kept in her temple, and embalmed when they died. To kill a cat meant a death sentence. Her sacred home was Bubastis in Lower Egypt. Bast carried a sistrum in her right hand and a basket in her left. She was generally draped in green. During her huge annual fair, thousands of worshippers journeyed on Nile barges, accompanied by flutes, castanets, and lots of wine. Splendid processions went through the streets to her temples. Goddess of fire, the Moon, childbirth, fertility, pleasure, benevolence, joy, jokes, sexual rites, music, dance, protection against disease and evil spirits, warmth, all animals (especially cats), intuition, healing, generosity, marriage.

BES—A guardian god; "Lord of the land of Punt." He was pictured as a leopard skin-clad dwarf with a huge head, prominent eyes and cheeks, a curly beard, and an open mouth with protruding tongue. Sometimes he was shown playing the harp or tambourine. Known as the protector of the dead; protected people from dangerous animals and night demons. His grotesque head was sculpted on pillars and over gateways as a guardian against all evils and dangers. God of luck, marriage, music, dance, childbirth, cosmetics, and female adornments.

BUTO/UAJYT/UATCHET/UTCHAT/PER UADJIT/UAZIT/UTO/URAEUS—Cobra goddess and ancient protectress of Lower Egypt and the Delta town of Uadjit. "Eye of Ra"; "Lady of Heaven." Lady of the North. At times she was portrayed as a cobra, sometimes winged, sometimes crowned. Other times she was shown as a woman wearing a vulture headdress and the red crown of the North; she held a papyrus scepter twined with a long snake. Goddess of protection, hiding from evil.

HAPI—Pictured as a very fat man with pendulous breasts, dressed like a boatman with a narrow belt around his great belly. Egyptians believed that Hapi lived near the First Cataract on the Isle of Bigeh in a cavern. In June they made offerings to him accompanied by poetic hymns. God of the Nile, crops, fertility, water, prosperity.

HATHOR/ATHOR/ATHYR/HET-HERT (House or Womb Above)/HAT-HOR (House of Womb of Horus)—"The golden"; "Queen of the West" (or the Dead); "the Lady of the Sycamore"; "House of the Face"; "House of Horus"; Mother Goddess; mother of all gods and goddesses; Queen of Heaven; sky and Moon goddess; similar to APHRODITE. Considered self-produced. The seven Hathors, or Holy Midwives, were associated with the seven planets. Cosmic goddess associated with

RA; she carried his Sacred Eye. Personification of the great power of Nature. The mirror and sistrum were sacred to her. Hathor's appearance could be as a cow-headed goddess or a human-headed woman with horns, cow's ears, and heavy tresses. She liked to embody herself in the sistrum to drive away evil spirits; another of her instruments was the tambourine. New Year's Day, one of her many festivals, was celebrated as her birthday. At that time her image was taken from the temple out into the rising Sun for a day of enjoyment, song, and intoxication. Her main sanctuary was at Dendera where she was worshipped with her infant son IHI (Ahi), "the Sistrum Player." She was also worshipped at Edfu with HORUS, her husband and Lord of the temple, as well as at Ombos. She cared for the dead, carrying them to the afterworld. Protectress of women; goddess of joy, love, pleasure, flowers, the sky, Moon, tombs, motherhood, beauty, marriage, cosmetics, singers and dancers, merry-makers, beautiful women, artists, artistic works, vine and wine, ale and beer, happiness, music, song, the dance, weaving garlands, good times in general, Nature, physical comforts, protection, astrology, prosperity, jewelry, strength, the arts, family.

HEH/NEHEB—A god shown as a man squatting on the ground and wearing on his head a reed, curved at the end. God of eternity, longevity, happiness.

HEQET/HEQTIT/HEKET—As a frog-headed goddess, she was one of the midwives for the birth of the Sun each morning and for the germinating grain. Goddess of creation, childbirth, fertility, corn, resurrection.

HORUS—Falcon-headed Sun and sky god; Divine Child or reborn Sun; identified with APOLLO. He was pictured as very fair with blue eyes, and associated with cats. As the divine falcon, his two eyes were the Sun and the Moon. From prehistoric times, the falcon was carried as a totem and considered an important powerful, divine being. The hieroglyph for "god" was a falcon on its perch. Some twenty

Horus the child

sanctuaries were dedicated to Horus in his different attributes. Some of the major aspects of Horus were: HAROERIS (Horus the Elder or Horus the Great), Sun and Moon god; HOR BEHDETITE, shown as a winged solar disk, a design placed over the porches of temples; HARAKHTY (Horus of the horizon), center of Sun worship; HERU-EM-AKHET (Horus who is on the horizon), symbol of resurrection; HOR-SA-ISET (Horus, son of Isis), falcon worship, avenger; HERU-PA-KHRET (Horus the child); HAR-END-YOTEF (Horus father-protector), skillful warrior; HAR-PA-NEB-TAUI (Horus of two lands) and HERU-SAM-TAUI (Horus, uniter of the two lands), ruler of humankind and Heaven. Lord of prophecy; a god of war, revenge, justice, success, problem solving, the Sun, music, the arts, beautiful things, weapons, beauty, family, home.

IMHOTEP/I-EM-HETEP—"He who comes in peace." He began as a deified human hero and later became a god. Another son of PTAH; similar to the Greek AESCULAPIUS. Study and knowledge, learning, medicine, healing, embalming, physicians, sleep to heal suffering and pain, magick, compassion, drugs, herbs.

ISIS/AS/ASET/ESET/TAIT—Supreme Egyptian goddess; Moon goddess; Great Mother; Great Goddess; Giver of Life. As Tait, Isis was the weaver and knotter of the threads of the Tat. She was pictured with dark hair, blue eyes, and fair skin. Identified with DEMETER, HERA, and SELENE. With OSIRIS, Isis (the mother) and HORUS (the divine child) made up the Holy Trinity. Legend says that Isis was born in the swamps of the Delta. North of Busiris at Perchbet, there was a renowned temple of Isis. Great festivals in the spring and autumn honored her with splendid processions, along with a June festival called the Night of the Teardrop.[9] Priestesses of Isis were said to control the weather by braiding or releasing their hair. ISIS-HATHOR was believed to bind or loose the lives of humans with the Tat (Knot of Fate); from her came the art of making and blowing on magick knots. Her priests were

Isis

called the *mesniu* (smiths) and worked with metals. As with many ancient cultures, these priest-smiths were said to receive their magick from secret connections with the Goddess and the female forces of Nature. The cow was sacred to her, as were the magick Buckle of Isis and the sistrum. Her sistrum was carved with a cat image that represented the Moon. Sometimes she was portrayed with protecting winged arms. Isis helped her brother-husband teach Egyptians to grind corn, spin flax, weave cloth, and cure disease. As High Priestess, she was a powerful magician. Goddess of marriage and domestic life, the Moon, motherhood, fertility, magick, purification, initiation, reincarnation, success, womanhood, healing, spinning, weaving, advice, divination, civilization, agriculture, the arts, protection, advice. The patroness of priestesses.

KHENSU/KHONS/KHONSU—"Traveller"; "The Navigator"; "He who crosses the sky in a boat"; God of the New Moon; son of AMEN-RA and MUT. He wore a skullcap topped by a disk in a crescent Moon. His head was shaved except for a scalp-lock tress of a royal child. His human body was swathed tightly, and he held a crook and flail. It was not until the New Kingdom that Khensu gained popularity as an exorcist and healer. The possessed and sick from Egypt and beyond flocked to his temples in Thebes, Ombos, and Karnak.

KHEPERA/KHEPRA/KHEPRI—"He who becomes"; god of transformations; the scarab beetle, symbol of creative energy and eternal life. A Creator God. The third form of the god RA. God of the rising Sun, emerging from its own substance and causing its own rebirth. Resurrection of the body, reincarnation, rebirth. God of the Moon, exorcism, healing, new beginnings, gentleness, literary abilities, miracles, compassion.

KHNEMU/KHNUM—"The Moulder"; "the Divine Potter"; the Ram God. Pictured as a man with a ram's head and long wavy horns holding a scepter and ankh. A Creator God; as an original river god of the annual Nile floods, his main sanctuary was near the Nile Cataracts on the Isle of Elephantine. In his temple he was worshipped with his two wives, SATI and ANQET; he watched over the sources of the Nile. Inventor of the potter's wheel, Khnemu was considered a builder, architect, controller of water, maker of human bodies before birth. God of arts and crafts, fertility and creation, gentleness.

MAAT/MAA/MAUT/MAYET (pronounced May-at)—"The Mother"; "Lady of the Judgment Hall"; the Virgin; cherished daughter of RA and wife of THOTH. Her law governed the three worlds; even the other gods had to obey ("live by Maat"). In the Hall of Double Justice where OSIRIS held his tribunal, Maat stood in one pan of the balance scale opposite the heart of the deceased when it was tested for truthfulness. There were 42 Assessors or Judges of Maat who passed judgment on souls. The heart had to be empty of evil to balance the feather weight on the scales. She was often pictured wearing an ostrich feather on her head while standing or sitting on her heels; she held a scepter and ankh. Associated with THOTH. Goddess of truth, right, justice, law, final judgment of human souls, order, divine order, reincarnation.

MEHUERET/MEHURT—A universal Mother Goddess; Lady of Heaven; Mistress of Earth. Associated with night.

MENTHI/MENTHU-RA/MENTU/MONT—Sun god, often with a bull head; wore a solar disk and two tall straight plumes on his head and carried a *khepesh* (a very curved scimitar). His wife was RAT-TAUI. "Lord of Thebes." In his war aspect he personified the destroying heat of the Sun and carried a bow and arrows, club and knife. The sacred bull of Mentu was considered the god reincarnated; it was kept at the temple at Hermonthis in Upper Egypt. Another place of the god's worship was at Medamud in the suburbs of Thebes. Protection, war, vengeance.

MESHKENT/MESKHENET—Goddess of childbirth and delivery, she brought relief to women in labor and often predicted the future of the new child. Sometimes an image of her head was carved on the two bricks on which Egyptian women crouched during delivery. Wife of SHAI. She was shown as a woman wearing two long palm shoots which were curved at the ends. Childbirth, rebirth.

MIN/MINU/MENU—"Lord of Foreign Lands"; god of the Eastern desert. A form of AMEN, the Greeks identified him with PAN. His sacred animal was a white bull, his ancient symbol the thunderbolt. The chief center of his cult was Coptos, the town of caravans, a departure point for commercial ventures. He was also worshipped in Akhmin, formerly Chemmis, later known as Panopolis to the Greeks. Min wore a crown with two tall straight plumes and held a flail in his right hand behind his head. As a fertility god, he was always portrayed with an erect phallus. God of sex, fertility, crops, harvests, roads, journeys; patron of the desert and travelers.

MUT (pronounced Moot[10])—"The Mother"; "Lady of Thebes"; "world-mother"; Great Mother; "The Great Sorceress"; "Mistress of Heaven"; "Eye of Ra"; a sky goddess who wore a vulture headdress. Associated with the cow, cat and lioness, her symbol was three cauldrons. Wife of AMEN-RA and identified with the Greek HERA. Sometimes shown winged, she was considered self-produced. Marriage, creation.

NEHEBKAU—A serpent god of the Underworld, dangerous to both the gods and humans. Death, cursing, vengeance.

NEITH/NEIT/NET/NIT (pronounced Night)—"The Huntress"; "Opener of the Ways"; Great Goddess; Mother of the gods; goddess of war and the hunt; goddess of the lower heavens; warrior-goddess and protectress; Lady of the West. Her name means "I have come from myself," or self-begotten. The Greeks identified her with PALLAS ATHENE, who also had a dual role of warrior and woman skilled in domestic arts. Eternal goddess, universal mother; the Spirit behind the Veil of Mysteries; World Body; Primal Abyss. Her cult was a very ancient one with two queens of the First Dynasty named after her. Often shown along side SELQET as mummy guardian and protectress of marriage. She wore the red crown of Lower Egypt. In her hands she held a bow and two arrows. At her temple in Sais, Plutarch read the inscription: "I am all that has been, that is, and that will be. No mortal has yet been able to lift the veil that covers me." Part of this sanctuary was a school of medicine, the House of Life, run by her priests. Her ceremonies were of a mystic nature. Herbs, magick, healing, mystical knowledge, rituals, meditation. Patroness of domestic arts, weaving, hunting, medicine, war, weapons. Protectress of women and marriage.

NEKHEBET—Guardian goddess, often in vulture form; identified with the Greek EILEITHYIA. Lady of the South. From earliest times she was the protective goddess of Upper Egypt. The center of her cult was at El Kab, the former Nekheb, capital of the oldest kingdom in the South. Often shown hovering over Pharaoh as a vulture, holding the flywhisk and the seal. As a woman, she was pictured wearing the white crown of Upper Egypt or a vulture headdress. She carried a scepter with a serpent twined around it. Goddess of motherhood, childbirth, protection.

NEPHTHYS/NEBT-HET/NEBTHET.NEBHET—"Mistress of the palace"; "Lady of the House"; "the Revealer"; Underworld

Neith

Goddess who represented life and death. The dark sister of ISIS; wife of SET; mother of ANUBIS. Pictured as fair with green eyes. Identified with the Greek APHRODITE and NIKE. Often shown as a woman with long winged arms stretched in protection; carried a basket on her head sometimes. Goddess of death and dark magick; guardian of hidden things; mystical things, protection, invisibility or anonymity, intuition, dreams, peace.

NUT (pronounced Noot)/NU—"Life-giver"; Mother of the gods; Great Mother; friend and protector of the dead. A sky goddess, often identified with the Greek RHEA. Personification of the heavens, sky, clouds, and stars. Reincarnation, weather.

OSIRIS—Lord of life after death; Sun god; Universal Lord; Nature god; Lord of Lords; King of Kings; God of Gods; Good Shepherd, Eternity and Everlasting. The Book of the Dead lists over two hundred titles by which Osiris was known. Primarily identified with the Greek DIONYSUS and HADES. Pictured with a tanned complexion and fair hair. He was shown sometimes standing, sometimes seated on his throne, tightly wrapped in mummy cloth, his freed hands on his breast holding the crook and flail. Sometimes his face was green; on his head he wore a high white miter flanked by two ostrich feathers. His birth was said to hail the rising of the Nile flood. His flesh was symbolically eaten in the form of a communion cake of wheat in his temples. Numbers sacred to him were 7, 14, and 28. Patron of priests; god of fertility, harvests, commerce, success, initiation, death and reincarnation, water, judgment, justice, agriculture, crafts, corn and vegetation, grains, religion, architecture, weaving, ceremonial music, civilization, composing rituals, codes of law (especially social laws), religion, power, order, discipline, growth, stability.

PTAH/PTAH-NEB-ANKH—"The Opener"; "the Divine Artificer"; "the Father of beginnings"; Creator god. He was the symbol of the creative power of the God behind the gods, the symbol of the Four Great Primary Forces (the Elements). Was identified with the Greek HEPHAESTUS. Ptah was usually portrayed with his skull wrapped in a headband and his body enclosed in mummy cloth. His hands were free and held a scepter, ankh, and tet. From early times, his main temple was at Memphis, south of the White Wall of Menes. His wife SEKHMET and his son NEFERTUM were worshipped there with him. In later times IMHOTEP took the place of Nefertum. The Apis bull, the living incarnation of Ptah, was kept near the sanctuary. Ptah's high priest was called the "Master Builder." The god was also invoked under the names PTAH TENEN, PTAH SEKER, and PTAH SEKER OSIRIS. Protector of artisans and artists; god of life, regeneration, crafts, builders, designers, metal workers, stone workers, engraving, carving, sculpting, all handcrafts, architects, masons, gentleness, miracles, science, manual skills, the arts.

RA/RE/PHRA—"The Creator"; "the Supreme Power"; "the only one"; Sun god; Creator God; Great Father; Father of the gods. Other aspects of Ra were: KHEPERA, the scarab, or Rising Sun; RA-HERU-KHUTI, the hawk, or Noon Sun; RA-TEMU, the Setting Sun. His main sanctuary was at Heliopolis. There he was worshipped in the form of a giant obelisk—a petrified Sun ray. In his temple at

Heliopolis were kept two sacred boats in a wooden tabernacle. One boat contained a hawk-headed figure of Ra, the other a man-headed figure of the god. He was also considered to take form in the bull MERWER and the bird BENNU. Often known as AMEN-RA or RA-ATUM, the god Ra was pictured in many forms: as a royal child sitting on a lotus; as a man, head topped with the solar disk surrounded by the sacred asp; as a man with a ram's head; as a man with a falcon's head. Source of all light and life; destroyer of darkness, night, wickedness, evil. Creator of Heaven, Earth, and the Underworld. Eternal god without end. God of agriculture, the Sun, magick, prosperity, spells, rituals, destiny, right, truth.

*The souls of Ra and
Osiris in Tattu*

RAT/TAT-TAIUT/RAIT/RAT (rate)—"Lady of the Heavens"; "Mistress of the gods"; "Mistress of Heliopolis"; Mother of the gods; "Goddess of the two lands." Mother of SELKHET and MAAT. Shown as a woman wearing a disk with horns and a uraeus. Wisdom, knowledge.

RENENET/RENENUTET/ERNUTET—"Lady of the double granary"; goddess of the eighth month of the Egyptian calendar. When a soul was weighed and judged, Renenet stood by with SHAI. She was shown as a woman with a serpent's head or a serpent wearing the solar disk. Other appearances of this goddess show her with a lion head or wearing the plumes of MAAT. She gave a baby its *ren* (soul-name), personality, and future fate at its birth. Children, luck, justice.

RENPET—"Mistress of eternity." She wore a long palm shoot above her head. Goddess of youth, springtime, the year, the general idea of time.

SATI/SATET—"To sow seed"; goddess of the Cataracts; one of KHNEMU's wives; similar to JUNO. Sister of the goddess ANQET. Her headdress was the crown of Upper Egypt with a pair of cow's horns. She was often shown as the Archer (representing the river's current), holding a bow and arrows. She was worshipped in the extreme south of Egypt on the island of Seheil. Fertility, the hunt, planting, water.

SEB/GEB/KEB—A fertility Earth god, similar to the Greek CRONUS; son of SHU and TEFNUT; brother and husband of NUT; father of OSIRIS, ISIS, SET, NEPHTHYS. "Father of the gods"; always shown with erect phallus. Shown in paintings lying under his sister-spouse Nut (pronounced Noot), who arches her body up on toes and fingers to form the sky. Fertility, new beginnings, creation, crops.

SEBEK/SOBK/SUCHOS—Lord of Death; "the hidden one"; "he who is shut in"; Creator god; crocodile god. He was said to live at the bottom of the Underworld in a secret pyramid filled with total blackness. His chief sanctuary was at Crocodilopolis, or Arsinoe. In a lake dug near the temple was kept an old, especially sacred, crocodile with gold rings in his ears and bracelets on his legs. God of death and the powers of darkness. Cursing, dark magick.

SEKER/SOKAR/SOCHARIS—The guardian god of the door to the Underworld. His sanctuary was called Ro Stau, "the doors of the corridors," a direct link to the Underworld. He was pictured as a greenish hawk-headed mummy.

SEKHET—Sister and wife of PTAH; mother of his son NEFER-TEM; sister of BAST. "Mighty lady"; "Lady of Flame"; personified the fierce, scorching, destroying rays of the Sun. Wore a red garment. Strength, might, violence, cultivated lands and fields.

SEKHMET/SAKHMET—"The terrible one"; "the Powerful"; "the beloved of PTAH"; dark sister of BAST; a lioness-headed goddess. She represented the destroying power of the sunlight and was crowned with a disk and coiled cobra. Goddess of war and battle, physicians and bone-setters.

SELQET/SELKET/SELQUET/SELCHIS/SERQET—Shown as a woman with a scorpion on her head, often with extended winged arms. Guardian after death of the canopic jars. Protectress of marriage; goddess of happy marriages and married sexual love.

SESHAT/SESHETA—"Mistress of the house of books"; "the secretary"; "mistress of the house of architects"; star goddess. The female equivalent and wife of THOTH, this goddess was in fact older than Thoth. At first Seshat was pictured as a woman wearing on her head a star, reversed crescent, and two long straight plumes. Later the crescent was replaced with two long down-turned horns. She was the record-keeper of the gods and keeper of the inventory of the pharaoh's enemy booty. Goddess of writing, letters, archives, measurement, calculation, record-keeping, hieroglyphics, time, stars, sky, history, books, learning, inventions.

SET/SETH/SETI/SUTEKH/SUTI—"He who is below"; God of the unclean, the terrible desert, the murderer and cruelty, evil, war, and the Underworld. Known to the Greeks as TYPHON. God of the northern sky, darkness, cold, mist, rain. Set was both a good and bad god, turning from one mood to another with lightning and unpredictable speed. But among the Egyptians, Set was worshipped just like any other deity. He had reddish-white skin and bright red hair—something hated by the Egyptians. This may have been emphasized by the fact that the conquering Hyksos rulers identified Set with their Sutekh, built a magnificent temple to him in Avaris, and elevated his worship over all others. The animal associated with this god had long pointed ears and looked rather like a dog, but the exact animal is not known. Animals belonging to Set were: asses, antelopes, the hippopotamus, the boar, crocodile, scorpion, black pig and other desert animals. God of hunger and thirst on the desert, thunder, storm, suffering, revenge, cursing, death, dark magick, darkness, evil, destruction, chaos, foreigners.

SHAI (male)/SHAIT (female)—Sometimes a goddess, sometimes a god. This deity had a role like a guardian angel, presiding over destiny and fate. One was born with each person and at death gave a true account of all sins and good works in the Hall of Judgment.

SHU—"Lord of the Sky"; god of Air, the North wind, and the atmosphere; similar to ATLAS. Seen in human form with an ostrich feather on his head. Connected with the heat and dryness of sunlight.

TA-URT/TAURET/APET/OPET/TAUERET/TAURT/THOUERIS/RERTRERTU/TAWERET—Hippopotamus goddess; sometimes an avenging deity. Her hieroglyphic sign was *sa*, meaning uterine blood of the Goddess that could give eternal life. She was pictured as a female hippo with pendulous breasts, standing upright and holding a plait of rolled papyrus (a sign of protection). In her darker aspect she was the goddess of darkness and revenge. Goddess of childbirth, maternity, nursing mothers, revenge, protection.

TEFNUT/TEFENET—Sometimes identified with the Greek ARTEMIS. Said to live at the bottom of the Underworld, Tefnut was fed by a group of Underworld gods, who hacked up dead bodies for the blood. Goddess of moisture, dew, rain, mist.

TEMU/TEM/ATEM/ATUM—Local god of Annu; the evening or night Sun (Dark Eye of Ra). Attributes of RA; often combined as RA-TEMU. Personification of God in human form and of the setting Sun. Father of the human race, he helped the dead. In one of his forms he was worshipped as a huge serpent. Two goddesses mentioned with him were IUSAASET and NEBT-HETEP. Originally a local god of Heliopolis. Temu was considered complete within himself, was the sum of everything that existed. Always represented as a man wearing the Egyptian double crown. Peace, help, rest.

THOTH (pronounced Toe-th)/TEHUTI/ THOUT/DJEHUTI/ ZEHUTI— "Lord of Books and Learning"; Judge of the gods; director of the planets and seasons; Great God; scribe of the gods; identified with the Greek HERMES. Considered self-begotten and self-produced. Thoth was called "Lord of Holy Words" for inventing hieroglyphs and numbers; "The Elder" as the first and greatest of magicians. He had greater powers than OSIRIS or RA. He was ibis-headed and the inventor of the Four Laws of Magick. He wore a lunar disk and crescent on his head and held the writing reed and palette of a scribe. At his center at Hermopolis Magna in Upper Egypt, his priests taught that Thoth created by the sound of his voice alone. In a crypt under his main temple were kept his books of magick which were open to disciples, and which the Greeks and later races translated into the works of Hermes Trismegistus and the *Kybalion* (not to be confused with the Jewish Qabala). In Lower Egypt his center was at Hermopolis Parva. He had two wives, SESHAT and NEHMAUIT. His chief festival was on the nineteenth day of the month of Thoth, a few days after the Full Moon at

Thoth

the beginning of the year. His disciples greeted each other at that time with "Sweet is the Truth" and made gifts of sweetmeats, honey, and figs. Patron of priests; Supreme Magus; god of all magick, writing, inventions, the arts, divination, commerce, healing, initiation, music, prophecy, tarot, success, wisdom, medicine, astronomy, geometry, surveying, drawing, sciences, measurement of time, all calculations and inventories, archives, judgment, oracles, predictions, rituals, the law, astrology, alphabet, mathematics, speech, grammar, arbitration, balance, mental powers, the Moon, botany, theology, hymns and prayers, reading, oratory, arbitration, peace, advice, learning, books, truth, Akashic records, the Moon, fate, arbitration, advice.

WEPWAWET/UPUAUT/OPHIS—"Opener of roads"; god of the Underworld. Pictured as wolf-headed; different from ANUBIS. At festivals of OSIRIS, his image on a shield led the way, representing his nocturnal guiding of the Sun's boat. His center was Siut, the Greek Lycopolis. He was often dressed as a soldier. War, protection, defense, martial arts, journeys.

Egyptian bowl design, fourth millenium BC

126

Dog-shaped cosmetic spoon from the XVIII Dynasty of the New Kingdom

SACRED ANIMALS, MORTAL AND SUPERNATURAL

This list has been included to show ancient Egyptian thought and correspondence to Egyptian deities. Pictures or statues of these creatures used during rituals will enable the subconscious mind to make a better link, thereby enhancing the ritual's power.

ASS—Evil; sacred to SET.

APE—Sacred to THOTH.

BULL—Apis bull was black with a crescent white spot on the right flank, a triangle on the forehead, and a flying vulture on the side. It was kept at the temple in Memphis where it was periodically sacrificed, embalmed, and buried in special tombs. It was known as Hap to the Egyptians or Apis to the Greeks, and was sacred to PTAH. The Bull of Mentu was sacred to the god MENTHU. A white bull was sacred to the god MIN.

CAT—Sacred to the goddess BAST and MUT; the cat decorated the sistrum and sometimes Hathor's mirror and represented the Moon. *Mau* was the Egyptian name for cat. The cat was domesticated very early and valued as a snake-destroyer. Anyone who killed a cat was put to death.

COW—Sacred to HATHOR, SATI, and MUT. The Egyptian word for cow was *kau*.

CROCODILE—Sacred to SEBEK of the Egyptians (called SOUCHOS by the Greeks), and to SET. A special crocodile was kept at the temple at Thebes.

DOG—Favorite animal of the Egyptians. Sacred to ANUBIS. Guardian and protector.

FROG—Sacred to HEQET and HATHOR.

GOOSE—Sacred to AMEN-RA, SEB, ISIS.

HAWK—Sacred to OSIRIS, HORUS, RA, SEKER, and others. Symbolic of the human soul. Sometimes the larger hawks were identified with the phoenix.

HERON—A sacred bird in general.

HIPPOPOTAMUS—Sacred to the goddess TA-URT and SET.

IBIS—Sacred to THOTH. Associated with the Moon.

JACKAL—Sacred to ANUBIS. Protector after death.

LION—Sacred to SEKHMET, MUT. Some lion deity names were AKER, ARI-HES-NEFER, URT-HEKAU, HEBI, and MA-HES.

LYNX—With tufted ears; a destroyer of serpents. Benevolent and protecting. Known to the Egyptians as Maftet.

PHOENIX—Sacred to OSIRIS. The Bennu, a bird of the heron species, was identified with the phoenix.

PIG—Sacred to SET. Considered very evil.

RAM—With flat branching horns, sacred to BA-NEB-TETET of the Egyptians or MENDES of the Greeks. With curly horns, sacred to AMEN. With long wavy horns, sacred to KHNEMU.

SCARAB—Sacred to KHEPERA.

SCORPION—Sacred to SELQET and SET.

SERPENT—Sacred to APEP, RENENET. Cobra sacred to BUTO. The uraeus was the hieroglyphic for "Goddess" and signified healing.

SHREW-MOUSE—Sacred to BUTO.

SPHINX—Also called Harmarkhis; human-headed lion statue; a symbol of the Sun god RA-TEMU. The famous statue existed in the time of KHEPHREN, the builder of the second pyramid, but was probably older. Guardian and protector.

SWALLOW—Sacred to ISIS.

TORTOISE or TURTLE—Greatly feared. Associated with the powers of darkness, night, evil. The enemy of RA.

URAEUS—Sometimes described as a cobra, other times as an asp. Sacred to BUTO. See SERPENT.

VULTURE—Sacred to NEKHEBET, MUT, NEITH and others. The hieroglyphic sign for "mother" was a vulture. Egyptian temples had a chapel on the east for BUTO to bring the Sun to birth and on the west where Nekhebet (the vulture goddess) daily ordained his death, thus preparing the Sun for rebirth.

WOLF—Sacred to WEPWAWET.

ENDNOTES

1. Chronologies differ from writer to writer. An in-depth chronology is given by Barbara Mertz in *Temples, Tombs and Hieroglyphs*.

2. Barbara Mertz in *Red Land, Black Land* has a different opinion on royal matriarchal lineage, although such authorities as Breasted and Frazer clearly state their reasons for coming to this conclusion.

3. Marilyn Seal Pierce in *Secrets of Egypt for the Millions* says that the Egyptian priests were not "dedicated" men, performing only the private rituals of the temples. Perhaps in later times this was the situation. However, in the beginning of organized rituals in Egyptian temples it is almost certain that both priests and priestesses were dedicated to a particular temple and deity.

4. Leo Vinci in *Incense: Its Ritual Significance, Use and Preparation* states that the Egyptian formula for Kyphi was given in the writings of Plutarch and that it contained 16 ingredients. He gives three different formulas for this incense in his book. My own personal formula contains more than 16 ingredients but smells much better than the ones given by Vinci.

KYPHI INCENSE

Red sandalwood	1 part	Bay laurel	1 part
Frankincense	1/2 part	Orris root	1/4 part
Myrrh	1/4 part	Henna powder	1/4 part
Galangal	1 part	Cinnamon	1/4 part
Juniper berries	1/4 part	Balm of Gilead	1/4 part
Dragon's blood	1/4 part	Styrax bark	1/4 part
Calamus root	1 part		

Add oils of amber, honey, acacia, orris, storax, lotus, and musk to personal preference.

5. Mertz, Barbara. *Red Land, Black Land.* Large harps are shown in tomb paintings.

6. Budge, in *Egyptian Magic*, devotes an entire book to this subject, giving many translated examples of ancient Egyptian magickal procedures.

7. There are several versions of the Egyptian creation myth, each designating a different deity as creator and each by a different methid of creating. Pritchard, James B., *The Ancient Near East* (Ptah with words of power); Neumann, Erich, *The Great Mother* (a goose laying an egg); Budge, E. A. Wallis, *The Gods of the Egyptians*, Volume I (Neith or Net bringing forth Ra who then created everything, or Isis as creator).

8. Pritchard in *The Ancient Near East* gives a very readable translation of this story in detail.

9. This festival has been preserved by the Arabs as their June festival Lelat al-Nuktah, which means Night of the Teardrop. See Walker, Barbara, *The Woman's Encyclopedia of Myths and Secrets*.

10. Mertz in *Red Land, Black Land* firmly states how Mut and Nut should be pronounced. Since Ms. Mertz has a Ph.D. and is a leading authority on ancient Egypt, I am listing her pronunciation. Besides, I have always detested hearing the goddess Mut's name pronounced as if she were a dog.

BIBLIOGRAPHY

Adams, W. Marsham. *Book of the Master of the Hidden Places.* UK: Aquarian Press, 1982.

Breasted, James H. *Development of Religion and Thought in Ancient Egypt.* NY: Charles Scribner's Sons, 1912.

Bromage, B. *The Occult Arts of Ancient Egypt.* UK: Aquarian Press, 1953.

Budapest, Z. *The Holy Book of Women's Mysteries*, Part I & II. Oakland, CA: Susan B. Anthony Coven No. 1, 1979.

Budge, E.A. Wallis. *The Egyptian Book of the Dead.* NY: Dover, 1967.

Budge, E. A. Wallis. *Egyptian Magic.* NY: Dover, 1971.

Budge, E. A. Wallis. *The Gods of the Egyptians*, Vol. I & II. NY: Dover, 1969.

Budge, E. A. Wallis. *Osiris and the Egyptian Resurrection*, Vol. I & II. NY: Dover, 1973.

Conway, David. *Magic: An Occult Primer.* NY: E. P. Dutton & Co., 1973.

Cottrell, Leonard. *Life Under the Pharaohs.* NY: Grosset & Dunlap, 1960.

De Lubicz, Isha Schwaller. *Her-Bak, Egyptian Initiate.* NY: Inner Traditions International, 1978.

De Lubicz, Isha Schwaller. *Her-Bak, the Living Face of Ancient Egypt.* NY: Inner Traditions International, 1978.

Durdin-Robertson, Lawrence. *Goddesses of Chaldea, Syria and Egypt.* Ireland: Caesara Publications, 1975.

Erman, Adolf. *The Ancient Egyptians: A Source Book of Their Writing.* NY: Harper Torchbooks, 1966.

Frazer, James. *Adonis, Attis, Osiris.* NY: University Books, 1961.

Gilbert, Katharine, ed. *Treasures of Tutankhamun.* NY: Ballantine Books, 1978.

Jung, C. G. *Psychology and Religion: West and East.* Princeton, NJ: Princeton University Press, 1969.

Knight, Gareth. *The Rose Cross and the Goddess.* NY: Destiny Books, 1985.

La Fontaine, J. S. *Initiation: Ritual Drama and Secret Knowledge Across the World.* UK: Penguin Books, 1985.

Macquitty, William. *Tutankhamun: The Last Journey.* NY: Crown Pub., 1978.

Mertz, Barbara. *Red Land, Black Land.* NY: Dodd, Mead & Co., 1978.

Mertz, Barbara. *Temples, Tombs and Hieroglyphs.* NY: Dodd, Mead & Co., 1978.

Patrick, Richard. *All Color Book of Egyptian Mythology.* NY: Octopus Books, 1972.

Pierce, Marilyn Seal. *Secrets of Egypt For the Millions.* Los Angeles, CA: Sherbourne Press, 1970.

Pritchard, James B. *The Ancient Near East.* Princeton, NJ: Princeton University Press, 1958.

Reader's Digest. *The World's Last Mysteries.* NY: Reader's Digest Association, 1978.

Skinner, Hubert M. *Readings in Folk-Lore.* NY: American Book Co., 1893.

Unknown Author. *Treasures of Tutankhamun.* NY: Ballantine Books, 1978.

CHAPTER TEN

MIDDLE EAST

THE ANCIENT Middle East generally covers the civilizations of Canaan, Babylonia, Assyria, Persia, Mesopotamia, Sumeria, Ur, Carthage, Phoenicia,[1] Akkad, Syria, Arabia, Elam, the territory of the Amazons, and other cultures that rose and fell in the great basin area of the Tigris and Euphrates rivers.

The origins of the Sumerians are uncertain but they likely were responsible for the Ubaid, Uruk, and Jamdet Nasr cultures, which existed about 3750 BC. Although the Akkadians arrived after the Sumerians, there were no clashes between the two. The Akkadian language later became the language of trade and diplomacy throughout the then-known world. During this period, city-states developed, that is, a city and surrounding fields and pastures irrigated by canals. Each city was politically independent until Sargon, an Akkadian from Kish, unified them by taking control.

Beginning in the twenty-fourth century BC, Sargon and his successors equipped their armies with superior metal weapons and built a vast empire extending from the Persian Gulf to the Mediterranean. During the reign of a successor, Naram-Sin, the kings began to use the names "god" and "divinity" to describe themselves. Kings and gods began to be pictured wearing horned helmets as a sign of their rank: one set of horns meant lower ranks, three sets highest rank.

About 2100 BC, Ur-Nammu of Ur forged Sumeria and Akkadian city-states into a new dynasty. This lasted about a century until it was displaced by the Elamites and the

Amorites, who also came from the East. By 1800 BC the Amorites founded the kingdom of Babylonia with Hammurabi as king. Hammurabi reorganized administration and codified the ancient Sumerian laws[2] that set down stiff penalties for offenders. The war chariot developed spoked wheels, and horses instead of asses were used to pull them. This dynasty ended about 1600 BC under attack of the Hittites and the Kassites. The land was further fragmented by the Mitanni, Babylonians, and Egyptians.

In about 1170 BC the Assyrians and Elamites again took control. The Assyrians proved the stronger, slowly expanding and gaining power, until by 900 BC they had a vast empire stretching from Iran to Jordan. They were destroyed by the Medes and the Babylonians. In turn these newcomers were overthrown by the Persians in 539 BC.

Alexander the Great conquered Persia in 332 BC. This Greek control lasted until 171 BC when the territory fell under Parthian rule.

The Parthian Empire lasted from the second century BC to the third century AD. The Sasanians took over in 224 and lasted until they fell in turn to the Muslims in 637. The greatest of the Sasanian kings was Shapur II, who was crowned before he was born, his sex having been assured by the Magi. He successfully defeated rebels of Kushan, nomads from the Russian steppes, and the Romans.

The Christian persecutions in his realm occurred because the Christians of the Mesopotamian areas were meddling in politics and supporting the pro-Christian Romans. Under a later king the Christians again brought royal wrath down on themselves for the same actions. The Sasanians steadily lost ground against the Muslims; in 636 the Iranian armies were defeated at the battle of Qadisiya.

In the seventh century AD there was a sudden eruption of the Arab population. In just three generations they went from nomadic tribes to a rich and powerful empire dominating the whole of the southern Mediterranean and Near East, from Afghanistan to Spain.

Islam, with its founder Mohammed, combined features from the old Arab Paganism, Judaism, and Christianity. However, Islam was not a pacifist religion; it aimed at world domination, if necessary by force. It claimed to purify and complete all other religions rather than reject them. When Mohammed died in 632, he had transformed the Arab world but reached little beyond it. That was left to his successor, his father-in-law Abu Bakr, who became ruler of the whole of Syria, Upper Mesopotamia, Armenia, Persia, and Cyrenaica. The fourth Caliph was Ali, Mohammed's cousin and husband of his daughter Fatima. Ali was opposed by Mu'awiya, cousin of the murdered third caliph, Uthman. This was the beginning of the Shiite faction in Islam that still exists today.

RELIGION

Religions in the Mesopotamian area are the oldest recorded religions of humankind, except perhaps for cave paintings. Most of the religions of this region were based on Sumerian beliefs. They provided the people with spiritual and ethical guidance and offered some sort of fairly acceptable explanations of the mysteries of life and death. Later cultures, such as the Babylonians and Assyrians, took over most of the Sumerian

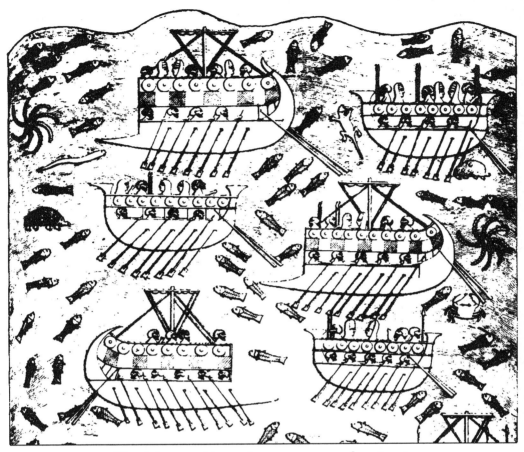

Phoenician warships and transports, seventh century BC

deities and religious practices, with some innovations, ideas, and changes of their own. All Mesopotamian pantheons were male-dominated.

In Sumeria the city was the actual property of its main deity, whose temple was the central feature.[3] Temples controlled the most land; the rest of the area around the city was owned by the palace or rich private individuals.

This was much the same in Mesopotamia where all religious and secular officials acted as servants of the deities. The temple was considered the god's earthly residence, housing not only the priests, but the deity's scribes, stewards, and those who administered his estates and engaged in commercial or manufacturing activities. These officials collected and distributed agricultural surpluses and the products of the specialized crafts and industries they sponsored.

Sumerian religious rites were performed by the priests in the sacred temples, with the common people taking part in the many festivals and several monthly feasts.[4] Daily temple sacrifices were made of meats, vegetables, water, beer, wine, fragrant spices, and perfumed incense.

Sumerian dream interpretation dates back to at least 2450 BC. Dreams were considered to be messages from the Gods and the dead, in both the prophetic and guidance senses.

Mesopotamian temples had much the same spiritual ranking, with a high priest or a high priestess. The next highest priests conducted the routine ceremonies; others pronounced incantations and interpreted omens; still others offered music or did sacrifices. There were also a great number of secular officials, workers, and servants who helped to carry on the business affairs of the temple.

There were a number of Babylonian festivals, the greatest being New Year, which took place during the first eleven days of the month of Nisan. This most important festival occurred around the Spring Equinox. This centered on the Sacred Marriage between the king, who took the role of Dumuzi (called Tammuz in the Bible), and a high priestess who played the part of Inanna. This was a re-enactment of the ceremony in the legend. At this festival, eggs colored red (the color of the life-force) were presented to friends.

The Mesopotamians used a lunar calendar of twelve lunar months. These months were 29 to 30 days long, and their names derived primarily from agricultural activities or from deity feasts. The names varied from city to city. Every three or four years an extra month was inserted to make the calendar equal the solar year. Each day technically began with sunset, with the time measured by water clock or shadow rod.

The Sumerians divided their year into two seasons: *emesh*, "summer," which began in February-March, and *enten*, "winter," which began in September-October.[5] Their New Year probably fell on the Spring Equinox. Regular monthly religious festivals were held on the day of the New Moon as well as the Full Moon, and on the seventh, fifteenth, and last days of each month.

Babylonians considered the physical presence of the god's statue necessary for worship and ceremony. They did not often carve new statues, but renovated the old ones with special ceremonies to imbue them with new life. Small replicas were made by the temples and sold to individuals for home use. Many shrines had pairs of horns at each corner of the top floor and horned crowns on the altar.

Both Babylonia and Assyria used a special gesture when greeting someone of higher rank and when addressing a god; the hand was placed in front of the mouth. The Persians crooked their forefingers as a sign of respect.

Commoners were not allowed inside the altar room of a temple and sometimes not within the temple. They had to watch the processions from a distance. However, each Babylonian had his own personal god or goddess to intercede with the other gods and protect him against the mass of devils and evil spirits. Prayers and sacrifices were made to these deities in individual homes.

The people of the many cultures occupying the Mesopotamian region believed strongly in all types of magick. They used the services of magicians and astrologers (Magi) on every possible occasion. These magicians were the Ashipu (priest-magicians) and the Ummati (priestess-magicians), who could heal, bless, or curse, according to the need. The Ashipu and Ummati were readily available to the common person for obtaining these protective charms. It was the duty of the Ashipu and Ummati to recite incantations and perform rituals to ward off evil.

When cursing during one type of ritual, the magician chanted spells while tying knots and blowing on them. In writing out magickal formulae, ink[6] perfumed with musk, rose, or saffron was used by the spell-worker. Usually this ink was red or black.

Arabian zodiac

While writing out these formulae, incense was kept burning as an offering to the deities being asked to help.

Although most magician-priests/priestesses were connected with temples, there were some free-lancers of varying abilities. They also made devil-traps,[7] many of which were uncovered in the ruins of private homes by archaeologists.

Divination was a basic feature of life. Its practitioners were men of influence and were consulted in all important matters, both by the individual and the state. Purification rituals *(namburbi)* could avert unwelcome predictions. Various methods of divination used were animal entrails,[8] oil in water, smoke from incense, behavior of birds and animals, and celestial phenomena. Astrology was used as a highly refined art. In the ancient Hittite empire, they developed a divinatory board game called Kin, possibly the forerunner of the Ouija board.

Mesopotamian deities were seen as great astral beings who loved, hated, fought, and connived much as humans do, although their powers were infinitely greater than those of humans.[9]

Being of an Oriental nature, the Mesopotamians bowed before their gods and pleaded their cases for help. They believed that the image of a deity held power, that the holy god-names written on objects imbued those objects with the force needed.

Statuettes of deities and animals were used for personal protection. Cylindrical seals made of precious and semi-precious stones doubled as talismans and official signatures for messages and contracts. Amulets and talismans[10] were made by the Ashipu or Ummati and carried by the people for specific purposes. Astrologers were consulted by all who could afford the service, from the king to the lowest merchant.

Some archaeologists say that the Mesopotamians did not believe in reincarnation because they consulted the dead in rituals. However, there are fragments of cuneiform tablets that suggest otherwise. It would be highly unusual if reincarnation had not been part of their belief system, but there is no complete information on which to make a definitive statement one way or the other.

The Sumerians invented and developed a system of writing, both cuneiform and a type of symbolic cursive, both of which became widely used in the region.[11] The letters of the alphabet were directly connected to the 28 days of the Moon, the planets, and zodiac signs.[12] Each letter had a numerical value, and some were believed to have more power than others.

Numbers and numerology were important to these ancient peoples. The number seven, for instance, was especially sacred, being considered a perfect and mystical number to the Persians, Sumerians, Babylonians, and Assyrians. In Babylonian literature there were seven gates to the Underworld, seven evil spirits of Heaven, seven evil spirits of Earth, seven stages or steps to a ziggurat, seven Tablets of Creation, seven layers of Heaven (the dwelling place of the Light Gods), and seven layers of the Underworld (the dwelling place of the Dark Gods).

The Persians adopted a totally new state religion, Zoroastrianism, remnants of which still exist today. This religion was named after Zoroaster, or Zarathustra, who was definitely anti-female. He taught that no woman could go to Heaven unless she was submissive to her husband's will, an idea adopted by the Jews and Christians.

This Persian religion centered around fire-altars and an eternal flame. The priests believed in free will, and posthumous reward and punishment. Their infernal deity, equal in power to their god, was later made into the devil by the Christians. Their ceremonies consisted of lighting and maintaining the sacred fire, drinking an intoxicating mixture made from a sacred plant called *haoma*, sacrificing a bull, and chanting for hours before the flame. They wore veils over their mouths to avoid contaminating the fire with their breaths.

The Chaldean astrologers (Magi), widely respected throughout the entire area, worked with seven planetary spheres and twelve zodiac signs. The planetary bodies known and used were the Sun, Moon, Mercury, Venus, Mars, Jupiter, and Saturn. A list of the zodiac signs as set up by the god Marduk follows:

MONTH	TRANSLATION	SIGN
1. Nisannu	The Laborer	Aries
2. Airu	The Star and the Bull of Heaven	Taurus
3. Simanu	The Faithful Shepherd of Heaven	Gemini
4. Duuzu	Tortoise	Cancer
5. Abu	Great Dog (Lion)	Leo
6. Ululu	Virgin with Ear of Corn	Virgo
7. Tashritum	Balance Scales	Libra
8. Arah Shamna	The Scorpion	Scorpio
9. Kislimu	The God Enurta	Sagittarius
10. Tebetum	The Goat-Fish	Capricorn
11. Shabatu	The Great Star	Aquarius
12. Addaru	The Star and the Band of Fishes	Pisces

Astrologers at work

The Magi, a hereditary priesthood, controlled Zoroastrianism and were renowned for their supernatural powers and skill in sorcery. They had a holy book of hymns called the Avesta and exposed their dead to the vultures. The floating winged disk symbolized Ahura Mazdah to them, as the rayed headdress represented Mithra, the warrior against evil.

The Chaldeans ("Moon worshippers"), who were also called the Magi, said that the sky was made of seven vessels (planetary spheres), one inside the other. They also believed that beneath the Earth were seven more nesting cauldrons. The word Chaldean was a common name for Mesopotamian astrologers who studied the movements of the Moon and stars. Their magical powers were respected throughout the ancient world.

Astrology played an important part in the lives of everyone, especially royalty. The ancient Chaldeans recorded that when all planets line up in the constellation of the Crab, Cancer, the world will return to its primordial elements and burn. The same doctrine appears in the cultures of India, Egypt, Persia, China, and pre-Columbian Central America. A future world-wide flood is supposed to take place when the planets line up in the sign of Capricorn.

The Canaanite religion had elaborate rituals, enacted in magnificent temples with every aid of art and music. The performance of rites was the responsibility of a large, highly organized priesthood under the leadership of a hereditary high priest. In addition, the temples had a large staff of priestesses so that the religious ideas of sex and fertility could be put into practice.

Assyrian court musicians

Musical instruments used in the Middle East were the sistrum; scrapers; bells; kettledrums; lyre; bronze, metal, or ivory clappers; cymbals; hourglass-shaped drum; arched harp; lute; castanets; finger cymbals.

Anatolia or Asia Minor, known as Turkey today, was one of the homes of many tribes of Amazons. The Amazons were ruled by sister-queens, and rode horses or drove them hitched to swift war-chariots. Their priestesses often wore vulture masks with wings. Not much is documented about these tribes of women, except that they were Goddess-worshippers. By the middle of the third millennium BC, they had produced a wealth of Goddess images which are still being uncovered.

DRESS AND ORNAMENTATION

The characteristic dress throughout the region was distinctly Oriental. All dignitaries wore voluminous robes or cloaks with added fringes. Everyone wore leather foot coverings tied around the ankles. The arts of weaving, dyeing, and embroidery were well known. Scarlet and purple dyes, fine linens, perfumes, and metallic work were widely used. Commonly used stones for jewelry were lapis lazuli, chalcedony, rock crystal, faience, agate, glass, hematite, green chert or serpentine, and mottled marble.

In Mesopotamia, the typical male garment was the flounced skirt, which varied in length according to the owner's wealth and rank. The upper body was left bare. Women's skirts and bodices were less elaborate but more varied in color. Both sexes wore large earrings, fillets, and necklaces. Robes had heavily embroidered edges. Sandals had upturned toes. Men wore their long hair held by a headband and their beards curled. Women's hair was done in long curls.[13]

The Babylonian men dressed much like the Mesopotamians, but the women wore flounced, pleated dresses and sometimes a turreted headdress.

In Assyria, the people wore Babylonian dress. However, the king's costume was more elaborate with fringes and folds. The men had mustaches, beards, and long hair. The women held back their long hair by a headband. Gold earrings were common.

The Akkadian men's garments were much the same as the Assyrian. They wore curled beards, their hair braided and clubbed in the back. Women's dress was similar to that of Babylonia. The high priestess of the Moon wore a pleated, many-tiered skirt, and had a magnificent necklace with enormous beads of banded agate set in gold.

In the Kassite empire, officials and wealthy men wore their hair long and clubbed in the back; they also had beards. They wore fringed garments and a fez-like hat. Their common symbols in embroidery were the cross, bee, rosette, and lozenge.

The Phrygians, who lived on the plateau of Anatolia, wore beautiful linens with gold and silver thread embroidery. The men wore a knee-length tunic with wrist-length sleeves under a second tunic that reached to the hips. Their fitted caps had flaps hanging to the shoulders. Women's tunics were the same, but longer. Both sexes wore silver and gold jewelry.

The Amazons ("Moon-woman" or "ample breasted") at one time ruled a great part of Asia, including Anatolia and the area of the Scythians. They were tribes of women only. At home, the Amazons wore short skirts of fine material, richly embroidered or painted. The skirt was worn over long, loose pantaloons, hanging in folds and caught in with the tops of their shoes. A little vest closed in the front was used as a bodice. Over this they sometimes added a wide sleeveless tunic clasped at the shoulders and girded at the waist. In war they donned skin trousers and often bared the right shoulder and breast for better use of weapons. They did not, as some historians hint, remove the right breast.[14]

The Persians, with their domed buildings, rich colors, and mosaic designs, were a luxury-loving people. Their fantastic silverwork on plates, jugs, bowls, and drinking cups portrayed many hybrid mythical animals, such as the *simurgh* (combination of peacock, lion, griffin, and dog).

The Medes and Persians dressed in linen vests and pantaloons. Over this they wore a long, sleeved robe, the length depending upon the wearer's rank. Both sexes dressed much the same. However, the Medes all painted their eyes and eyelids; they also favored more brilliant colors and much jewelry. Only the king could wear purple robes without sleeves; subjects were not allowed to bare their arms. The veiling of women's faces began with the Persians. They believed that women's mouths were obscene and dangerous, being symbols of the vagina, so they required all females to cover at least the lower part of their faces with veils.

The Parthians were noted for elaborate hair styles and magnificent jewelry. They dressed much like the Persians. The men wore long hair and elegantly curled beards; the women, mounds of ringlets.

The Canaanite men wore a version of the Oriental trousers and tunic, while the women's tunics were long with sleeves. Men's hair hung to the shoulders. Women wore stiff curls in the front and long ringlets in the back; they also painted their eyes with black antimony and used many ointments and perfumes. These women wore a great amount of jewelry: ankle bells; beads of semi-precious stones; bone pendants; bracelets; rings for the ears, fingers, and nose; combs.

Marduk destroying Tiamat

SOME OF THE MYTHS

The Babylonians and Assyrians took over most of the Sumerian gods and religious practices. What we know of their myths comes from the library of Ashurbanipal found in the ruins of Nineveh.

All in the Mesopotamian area believed that the Earth was a flat disk with mountains around the edge. The mountains supported the vault of Heaven. The Earth floated on the sweet waters of the Apsu. The atmosphere between the heavens and Earth was filled with a substance called *lil*. Around all this were the great seas, which anchored the universe.

In the Mesopotamian creation epic, everything began with watery chaos. Apsu, the sweet waters that produce springs and rivers, and Tiamat, the sea or salty waters, combined their forces to create the universe and the gods. But Apsu plotted against the gods because he did not like their new turbulent ways. The god Ea destroyed him. Tiamat, who had not supported the destruction of the gods, now fought against them.

Choosing a second husband, Kingu, the goddess Tiamat gave birth to a myriad of monsters to help her. All the gods were afraid to go against their mother in war until Marduk, son of Ea, took the field against her. The gods promised that if Marduk won, he would be king of the gods. After fierce fighting, Marduk was victorious.

He caught Kingu and all the monsters in his net and threw them in chains into the Underworld. He then used half of Tiamat's body to make the sky, the other half to make the Earth. He created humans out of the blood of Kingu. Marduk then made a dwelling place for the gods in the sky, fixed the stars in the heavens, and regulated the length of the year.

In the Canaanite version of creation, the god Ba'al slew the Chaos Monster, depicted as a sea dragon with seven heads. Ba'al then used the dragon's body to create the universe.

The Sumerians and Babylonians had the original deluge legend.[15] The great gods decided to destroy humans (the story tablet is broken and does not record why). However, the god Ea warned a man named Uta-Napishtim and instructed him to build a huge boat. The man did so, stocking the ark with provisions, then taking on board his family and some of the animals of the area.

For seven days and nights the rain fell until everything was gone, except Uta-Napishtim and those on his ark. After a long time, the man sent out a dove, then a swallow to find dry land. Finally, he sent out a raven that did not return. The ark landed on Mt. Nisr where Uta-Napishtim sacrificed to the gods. Uta-Napishtim and his family then settled at the "mouth of the rivers," possibly the Tigris-Euphrates valley.

In the Sumerian deluge legend the man's name was Ziusudra;[16] in Akkadia, Atrakhasis. In these two legends, the Great Goddess saved humans and set a rainbow in the skies as proof of her great powers.

The marriage of Dumuzi and Inanna ended in tragedy when Dumuzi became power-hungry. After marrying Dumuzi, the goddess Inanna wanted to become queen of the Underworld as well as of Heaven. Her attempt at the takeover failed. Ereshkigal, her sister and queen of the Underworld, put her to death. The god Enki allowed Inanna, accompanied by Underworld demons, to return to Earth to find someone to take her place so she could live again.

When Inanna returned to her city, she found Dumuzi sitting on her throne in her temple. He showed no signs of sadness at her absence. It seems he had secretly coveted the power and prestige of the goddess. Furious, Inanna ordered the Underworld demons with her to carry him away.

Dumuzi's sister, the goddess Geshtinanna, felt sorry for her brother and agreed to take his place in the Underworld for half of the year. The marriage ceremony from this legend was re-enacted each New Year by the king and a high priestess of Inanna, probably with admonitions from the priests not to covet heavenly thrones.

To the Babylonians, the land of the dead was called the House of Dust and the end of the Road of No Return. There the dead were clothed in feathers like birds. They sat in darkness, except when the Sun made his journey through their land at night and the Full Moon during his period of darkness on Earth. The Babylonians felt that the dead could be consulted at any time in rituals.

The Zoroastrians of Persia believed that Ahura Mazdah, the god of Light, and Ahriman, the god of Darkness, were born simultaneously from the womb of the primal Mother of Time. There was rivalry between the twins, much the same as between the Biblical Cain and Abel. Although Ahura Mazdah was considered the Heavenly Father of Light, Ahriman was not considered inferior. In fact, Ahriman's influence upon the Earth was greatest because he had created the material world. The essence of Zoroastrian belief is that God (Ahura Mazdah) is wholly good and that all evil and suffering come from Ahriman (the devil).

Zoroastrian priest

The great Ahura Mazdah was believed to express his will through the Holy Spirit, Spenta Mainyu. He also had six assistants called the Amshaspends, or Bounteous Immortals. There

141

was a continuous universal struggle between Spenta Mainyu and the Destructive Spirit called Angra Mainyu, or Ahriman (whom the Christians call the Devil).

The story of Ahriman's revolt against his brother became the basis of the Christian story of the fall of Lucifer and the battle between good and evil at the end of the world. To the Arabs, Ahriman became Iblis or Shaytan, leader of the djinn.

The Persians even had a garden of Eden story with Mashya and Mashyoi as the first couple. These unfortunates fell out of favor with Ahura Mazdah because they listened to the lies of Ahriman who appeared to them as a serpent.

Just before the end of the world, or doomsday, the Persian legends say that a messiah (Saoshyant) will appear. On that day of judgment at the end of all time, the Zoroastrians believe Ahura Mazdah will hand out to the good and the wicked what they deserve. However, the condemnation of the wicked will not last forever. The human body and spirit will be brought into balance with all wickedness destroyed, so each person can live with Ahura Mazdah in peace and harmony.

The Zoroastrian religion of Persia had vivid descriptions of a hell where the nastiest torments were reserved for women. Their legends of this place are a good example of the patriarchal preoccupation with pain, whereas the matriarchal religions are primarily concerned with pleasure. But none of these ancient Mesopotamian religions believed that hell lasted forever. That mental cruelty was left to the Christians.

In most Oriental religions it was recognized that the principle of Darkness was as necessary to life as that of Light. Only in the Underworld darkness could regeneration take place.

Babylonian kings and winged divinties before the sacred tree

142

MAJOR GODS AND GODDESSES

ACIEL—Chaldea. Black Sun of the Underworld; god of Darkness at the bottom of the seventh Pit. These Pits mirrored the upper seven levels where the Gods of Light lived.

ADDAD/ADAD/ADDU/HADDAD—Canaan, Babylonia, Assyria, Syria, Mesopotamia. God of the atmosphere; Lord of Foresight; The Crasher; Master of storms; consort of SHALA. With a voice like thunder, he rode the clouds. His symbol was forked lightning, his animal the bull. Often represented standing on a bull and holding thunderbolts. Clouds, storms, thunder, rain, lightning, foreseeing, floods, furious winds, earthquakes, destruction, the future, divination.

ADONIS/ADON—"Lord"; ancient Semitic god. His priests wore boarskins. Called the Anointed One (CHRISTOS in Greek). Corn, the harvest, death, resurrection.

AHRIMAN/ANGRA MAINYU—Persia; Zoroastrian. Destructive spirit; Spirit of Darkness and deception; Prince of demons; Great Serpent; Lord of Darkness. Twin spirit of AHURA MAZDAH, he introduced death into the world. Leader of the Daevas, whom Zoroastrians called devils, but which originally meant gods. God of evil, destructive pests, rumor, lies, doubt, idleness, death, trickery.

AHURA MAZDAH/MAZDA/ORMAZD/ORMIZD/HORMIZD—Persia; Zoroastrian. The Lord; Great God; Supreme God; Illumined Divine Being; Master of Heaven; Creator God; twin spirit and rival of AHRIMAN. He gave the Asha, or universal law. Light, goodness, faith, prophetic revelation, purification.

ALEYIN—Phoenicia. He who rode the clouds; god of springs and rain. The opponent of MOT and the son of BA'AL. He was accompanied by seven companions and a troop of eight wild boars. Vegetation, the harvest, springs, water.

THE AMSHASPENDS/AMENTA SPENTAS/AMESHAS SPENTAS—Persia, Zoroastrian. Benign Immortals. These were the assistants of AHURA MAZDAH: VOHU-MANO (Bahman), Spirit of Good; ASHA-VAHISHTA (Arbidihist), Supreme Righteousness or dharma; KHSHATHRA-VAIRYA (Shahriver), Ideal Dominion or dominion of the noble class; SPENTA-ARAMAITI (Sipendarmith), Benign Piety or selfless love; HAURVATAT (Khordadh), Perfection; AMERETAT (Mourdad), Immortality. They are similar to Archangels.

AMURRU—Phoenicia. God of the west; protector of sailors.

ANAHITA—Persia. Goddess of the waters and pro-creation.

ANA(I)T/QADESH (Holy One)/ANATU/ANAHITA—Phoenicia, Canaan, Ur. Warrior goddess; Mistress of the Lofty Heavens; Controller of Royalty; Virgin (meaning independent); Progenitor of People; Mother of All Nations;

Ahura Mazdah

143

THE ANCIENT & SHINING ONES

Anu

Sovereign of all Deities; Strength of Life; She Who Kills and Resurrects; consort of BA'AL. She carried an ankh and wore horns and a Moon disk. She was linked with the lion, wore coriander scent and purple makeup for battle. Her power was so great to curse and kill that even the greatest of gods were afraid of her; whatever she wanted was granted. Revenge, conflict, fearlessness, vegetation, dew, dogs, overcoming obstacles.

ANSHAR—Sumeria. Sky god; male principle of all life.

ANU/AN—Mesopotamia, Babylonia, Assyria, Sumeria. Sky; Father God; King of the Gods; Protector; Supreme God; God of Heaven. First god in the Sumerian pantheon; father of ENLIL; son of ANSHAR and KISHAR. Represented by a tiara on a throne, his symbols were a star, scepter, diadem, crown, and staff. Consort of the goddess ANTU, he presided over the fate of the universe. Power, justice, judgment, fate.

APSU—Mesopotamia, Babylonia, Assyria. First god; Primordial ocean; the watery abyss that encircled the Earth.

ARALLU—Assyria, Babylonia. Evil spirits from the Underworld. They brought all kinds of diseases to humankind.

ARURU—Sumeria. Goddess of creation.

AHERAH/ASHNAN—Mesopotamia, Phoenicia, Canaan. Holy Queen; Holy Mother; Exalted Mother; Holy Lady Who Walked the Sea; Mother of All Wisdom; Mother of the 70 Deities of Heaven; Great Goddess; Mistress of the Gods; Universal Law; Mistress of Wisdom. In special rites, the sacred *ashera* (woolen bands of mourning) were wrapped around her sacred tree or pole where her son/lover died. She gave to humankind the art of carpentry and the knowledge of building and making bricks. Oracles, prophecy, architecture, carpentry.

ASHERAT-OF-THE-SEA—Phoenicia. Mother of the gods; goddess of the sea. Motherhood, children, wisdom, art, religion.

ASSHUR/ASHUR—Assyria, Babylonia. National god of Assyria. King of gods; Warrior god; Sun god; Creator of humans; Supreme God; Self-Created; Maker of the sky and Underworld. Represented as a winged disk mounted on a bull, or winged disk flying through the air. Main consort of NINLIL. Fertility, time, skill with weapons, protection, victory, bravery, success.

ASHTART—Phoenicia. Also called BA'ALAT ASHTART. Of the sky of BA'AL; Goddess of the planet Venus; Queen of Heaven; Sovereign of Heaven; Guiding Star; Serpent Lady (in the Sinai). Byblos claimed she descended to Earth as a fiery star and landed in a lake near Aphaca. Her sacred stone (a meteorite) was kept in her

Byblos temple. This stone was said to heal and prophesy. Her symbol was an 8-point star. The word bibles came from Byblos where the earliest libraries were attached to her temple. See ISHTAR, ASTARTE, BA'ALAT.

ASTARTE—Babylonia, Assyria, Phoenicia. Lady of the Mountain; Queen of Heaven; Lady of Byblos; Mistress of horses and chariots; Maiden; Virgin; Mother Goddess. The fierce consort and sister of BA'AL of Canaan in her aspect as the goddess ANAT. Her temples had sacred prostitutes; sacred marriages were made by the priestesses with the kings. In her war aspect, she wore the horns of a bull. Her priestesses were famous astrologers. Revenge, victory, war, crescent Moon, astrology, sexual activities.

ATAR—Aryan, Persia. God of fire, celestial and Earthly.

ATARGATIS/TIRGATA/DERCETO—Syria, Canaan, Mesopotamia, Philistines. Possibly connected with the Syrian NINA or NAMMU. Sea Goddess, sometimes shown with a fish-tail. At her temple in Harran, her sacred fish were said to have oracular powers. Oracles, prophecy.

ATHIRAT—Canaan, Phoenicia. A goddess; consort of EL. Spinning, love, enchantments, beauty, persuasion.

BA'AL/BAAL/HADDAD—Canaan, Phoenicia, ancient Semitic god. Supreme God; Lord; Master; God of fertility and vegetation; Lord of the North; Lord of Lebanon. The son of ASHERAT-OF-THE-SEA; consort of ASHERAT. Often EL's enemy. Thunder, rain, fertility, death and resurrection, weather, lightning, sky, Sun, clouds, storms, the atmosphere, rebirth.

BA'ALAT—Phoenicia. Lady of Byblos; she wore either a cobra headdress or a disk between two horns. Similar to the Egyptian goddess HATHOR. Also known as BELIT, BELIT-ILI, BELTIS.

BA'AL-HAMMON—Carthage. God of the sky who wore rams' horns. Fertility, weather.

BA'ALITH—Canaan. Great Goddess. Love, the Moon, the Underworld, trees, wells.

BELIT-ILI/BELIT-ILLI—Mesopotamia. "Lady of the gods"; "Lady of childbirth." She set each human's fate at birth.

BELITIS/NINLIL—Mesopotamia, Babylonia, Assyria. Lady; Goddess of fertility.

DAGON/DAGAN—Philistines. Sea god shown as a merman, a fish-man or serpent-man. Mated to ATARGATIS. Patron of both fishing and farming.

DERCETO—Babylonia. Whale of Der; a fish-goddess and mother of Babylonia's foundress.

Astarte

145

Dagon

DUMUZI/TAMMUZ—Mesopotamia, Sumeria. Only-begotten Son; Son of the Blood; lover of ISHTAR. Called the Anointed One (CHRISTOS in Greek); a sacrificed god. The harvest, vegetation, the Underworld, fertility.

EA/ENKI—Mesopotamia, Babylonia, Sumeria. Water god; Creator God; House of the Water; Lord of the Earth; Lord of the sacred Eye (Ninigiku); Creator of Humans; Lord of the Underworld or primordial ocean. Consort of NINKI (Lady of the Earth). He taught humans the arts and crafts. Lived in the Apsu or fresh water that surrounded the Earth and universe. Represented as a man with a vase of flowing water, or as a goat with fish-tail. He was a friend of humankind and the source of all secret magickal knowledge. His priests wore fish-shaped garments when performing purification rituals. God of stonecutters, carpenters, goldsmiths. Sweet waters, wisdom, patron of all arts, oracles, incantations, magick, foretelling, skills and crafts, judgment, justice, knowledge, rain, weather.

EL—Canaan, Phoenicia, Akkadia, Babylonia. Master of time; Father of gods and humans; Benevolent and merciful Lord; Supreme God; Father of Years; Creator God; War god. Was shown seated wearing bull's horns. Strength, victory, fertility of the Earth, power, rain.

ENLIL/ELLIL/BEL—Sumeria, Babylonia, Assyria. Lord Wind; King of the gods; Lord; King of the Land; Lord of all regions; Lord of the world; Counsellor of the gods; God of Earth and Air; Dispenser of good and evil; son of ANU. Consort of NIN-HURSAG (Lady of the Great Mountain) and BELIT (Lady or Mother of the Gods). He held the Tablets of Destiny, or *me* (pronounced may), by which the fates of humans and gods were decreed. He invented the pickaxe. Wind (especially the destructive kind), hurricanes, floods, the forces of Nature, storms, rain, disaster, destiny, order, the laws, prosperity, influence, wisdom.

ERESHKIGAL—Mesopotamia, Babylonia, Assyria. Queen of the Underworld; the Crone aspect of the Goddess. Dark magick, revenge, retribution, the waning Moon, death, destruction, regeneration.

ESHMUN—Sedon. God of health and healing.

FRAVASHIS—Persia. Pre-existent souls or guardian angels.

GESHTIN—Assyria, Babylonia. Goddess of grape vines. Gardens, vegetation, fertility.

GIBIL/NUSKU—Assyria, Babylonia. God of the sacred fires used for offerings. He sat in judgment over the souls of unscrupulous judges. Justice, defense, destroyer of dark magick, intercession, purification, initiation.

GUHKIN-BANDA—Assyria, Babylonia. God of goldsmiths, jewelry makers.

GULA—Babylonia, Kassites. The Great Doctoress; daughter of ANU. Her symbol was a dog. She inflicted illness or restored health; also ruled fate.

HANNAHANNA—Hittite. Mother Goddess.

HAY-TAU—Phoenicia. God similar to ADONIS; his symbol was a bull. Forest vegetation, trees.

HUPASIYAS—Hittite. Weather god who slew the dragon Illuyankas in the Hittite story of Creation.

INANNA/NINANNA—Canaan, Phoenicia, Sumeria, Uruk, Babylonia. Mistress of Heaven; the Morning and Evening Star; War goddess; Sovereign Lady of the Land; Queen of the Assembly of Deities. The most important Sumerian goddess, she was represented riding on her sacred lion, sometimes with a pack of hunting dogs. Other times she was pictured as a winged goddess of war, armed with bow and quiver. One of her symbols was a gatepost hung with streamers; another, a serpent coiling round a staff; her planet was Venus. War, defense, victory, love, fertility, light, destiny, peace, prosperity, crops, sexual love, civilization, agriculture, justice, weaving and pottery, laws.

IN-SHUSHINAK—Assyria, Babylonia. Sovereign of the gods; Maker of the universe; Supreme God. The sky, storms, lightning, rain, fruit, fertility.

ISHTAR/INANNA/ASHTART/ASHTAROTH/ASHTORETH/ASTARTE/ANAITIS/ANAT/ATAR/ ATHTAR/MYLITTA/ESTHER—Mesopotamia, Babylonia, Assyria, Sumeria, Arabia, Phoenicia, Canaan. Lady of sorrows and battles; Queen or Lady of Heaven; Goddess of the Moon and evening; Great Mother; Shining One; Mother of Deities; Producer of Life; Creator of People; Guardian of Law and Order; Ruler of the Heavens; Source of the Oracles of Prophecy; Lady of Battles and Victory; Lady of Vision; Possessor of the Tablets of Life's Records. As a warrior goddess, she carried a bow and rode in a chariot drawn by seven lions. Other images show her seated on her lion throne, with horns, a bow and arrows, a tiara crown, a double serpent scepter, holding a sword, or with dragons by her sides. She was the sister of ERESHKIGAL. Her symbols were the eight-point star, the pentagram, dove,

Ishtar with lion

serpents, and the double-axe; her planet Venus. She wore a rainbow necklace much like that of the Norse goddess FREYJA; the Persians converted this necklace (the rainbow) into a razor-sharp bridge that led to the Mount of Paradise. In ancient Sumeria, she had 180 shrines where women gathered daily for prayer,[17] meditation, and socializing. The night of the Full Moon, known as Shapatu,[18] saw joyous celebrations in her temples. At these rites, called the sacred Qadishtu, women who lived as priestesses in her shrines took lovers to express the sacredness of sexuality as a gift from Ishtar. Men communed with the goddess in these rites through sex. Every woman once in her life had to sit in the temple grounds of Ishtar's temples and wait for a man to drop a coin in her lap. Then she had to lie with him. Until this was done, the woman could not marry. Goddess of the positive and negative sides of all she ruled. Radiant, sweet, and delightful, but also could be stern, cruel, and bad tempered. Patroness of priestesses. Love, fertility, revenge, war, resurrection, marriage, lions, lapis lazuli, irritability, violence, amorous desire, the dying and begetting power of the world, purification, initiation, overcoming obstacles.

JAHI THE WHORE—Persia. Great Mother who, as LILITH, mated with the serpent AHRIMAN. Moon, women, menstruation, sex.

KAMRUSEPAS—Hittite. Goddess of spells, magick and healing.

KHASIS—Canaan, Phoenicia. Craftsman god.

KISHAR—Mesopotamia. Earth goddess; female principle as her brother ANSHAR was the male principle of creation.

KOTHAR—Canaan, Assyria, Babylonia. Craftsman god. Skill in crafts, weapons.

KUSOR—Phoenicia. God of magick formulae, incantation and divination, fishing, navigation.

LAMA—Sumeria. Goddess who guided worshippers into the presence of the particular god they were praising. Intercession.

LATPON—Phoenicia. God of wisdom and magick.

LILITH/LILITHU—Hebrew, Babylonia, Sumeria. Moon Goddess; patroness of witches; female principle of the universe; demon goddess to the Jews and Christians. Her sacred bird was the owl. Protector of all pregnant women, mothers and children. Wisdom, regeneration, enticing sorcery, feminine allure, erotic dreams, forbidden delights, the dangerous seductive qualities of the Moon.

MAMMITU/MAMMETUN—Mesopotamia, Assyria, Babylonia. "Mother of destinies." Goddess who decreed the fate of humans and the destiny of newborn children. Goddess of each person's destiny.

Amulet of Lemashtu, Babylonian predecessor of Lilith, and her demons

MARDUK/MARDUC—Mesopotamia, Canaan, Sumeria, Babylonia, Assyria. National god of Babylonia. Bull calf of the Sun; Great God; Lord of Life; oldest son of EA. He had fifty names. As head of the Babylonian pantheon, he held the ring and rod symbols and carried a saw-toothed dagger in his belt. His robe was decorated with starlike rosettes. He killed TIAMAT and took from her the Tablets of Destiny, or Law. Governor of the four quarters of the Earth. His consort was SARPANITU. Patron of priests. Fate, courage, healing, magick, incantations, crops, agriculture, rain, resurrection, justice, law, water, hurricanes, winds, thunder, herbs, trees, the Sun, rebirth, victory, purification, initiation.

MARI/MARIHAM/MERI/MARRATU—Syria, Chaldea, Persia. Basic name of the Goddess; she wore a blue robe and a pearl necklace, both symbols of the sea. In the Amorite city of Mari, she had a six acre temple-palace. Fertility, childbirth, the Moon, the sea.

MITHRA/MITRA/MITHRAS—Persia; god of many Middle Eastern cultures. War god; God of the light that precedes the dawn; Guardian of sanctity; All-wise and knowing; Revengeful and merciless. His weapons were deadly arrows, a huge mace, incurable diseases, and the boar Verethraghna; his symbol, the rayed Sun disk. The son of AHURA MAZDAH, he was the protector of warriors in chariots. Only men were allowed to worship him. His birthday was celebrated on December 25. His followers considered caves so important to their worship that, if there were no natural ones available, they dug artificial ones. Wrath, death, contracts, sky, the Sun, moral

Mithra

Demon of disease and evil

purity, courage, light, oracles, clairvoyance, predictions, war, revenge, wisdom, diseases, sacred oaths, protection, prosperity, fertility, spiritual illumination, rituals.

MOT—Canaan, Phoenicia. God of death; Lord of the Underworld. His earthly domain was the dry plain where no rain fell. Spirit of harvest, regeneration.

NABU—Mesopotamia, Sumeria. Consort of TASHMETUM; son of MARDUK. God of writing and destiny; patron of scribes. It was believed he could increase or decrease the number of days allotted to a person. Represented death and sterility. His symbols were a serpent-headed dragon, an engraving tablet and chisel. Wisdom, accounting, intellect, literature, speech, writing, intercession.

NAMMU/AMU—Sumeria. Sea; the mother who gave birth to Heaven and Earth; Creatress Goddess; Mother of All Deities. Name of the Mother of the universe; identical with TIAMAT. Humans were made by her daughter NINMAH.

NANNA/NINA—Sumeria. Lady; Ancient Mother; Holy One of Many Names; Great Mother. The Judge of humankind on the last day of every year. An image of a winged lioness guarded her temple. A very ancient name, this goddess was represented with a fish-tail or serpent-tail. Herbs, Moon, healing, magick, intercession, interpretation of dreams, crops, civilization.

NANSHE—Assyria, Babylonia. Interpreter of dreams; sister of NISABA and daughter of EA. Her priests probably used a cup for divination. To acquire prophetic powers, the priests underwent an initiation of descent into a pit, a symbol of death and resurrection. Goddess of awareness and prophecy, springs and canals, dreams, regeneration, death.

NERGAL/MESHLAMTHEA—Babylonia. Lord of the great dwelling; Lord of attack; God of the Underworld; Judge of the dead. A form of the black Underworld Sun, his symbol was a sword or lion's head. Shown wearing a crown and attended by fourteen terrible demons. When he was exiled to the Underworld, he conquered ERESHKIGAL, who became his wife. Plague, destructive power of the Sun, battle, the desert, fierce winds, war, evil, death, wisdom, diseases, dark magick, fire, windstorms, revenge, destruction.

NINHURSAG/NINKHURSAG/NINTU/KI/NINMAH/INNINI—Sumeria, Assyria, Babylonia. Mother Goddess; Great Goddess; Earth Mother; Creative Principle; source of all life; Mountain Mother; She Who Gives Life to the Dead. Consort of EA, she wore a leafy crown and held a branch representing fertility. Regeneration.

NINTI—Sumeria. Lady of Life; Lady of the Rib. Birth goddess who enabled pregnant women to make the bones of babies out of their own ribs.

NINURTA/NINGIRSU—Sumeria, Akkadia, Assyria, Babylonia, Mesopotamia. The Throne Carrier; God of war; messenger from the gods to humans. Son of ENLIL; consort of BAU (one who breathed into humans the breath of life). The amethyst and lapis lazuli were sacred to him. War, wells, canals, south wind, hunter and destroyer of evil and enemies, agriculture, irrigation, fertility, hunting.

NISABA—Assyria, Babylonia. Daughter of EA and sister of NANSHE. Goddess of grain; similar to the Greek goddess DEMETER.

NUSKU—Mesopotamia. God of the sacred fire used to consume offerings. Justice, intercession.

RASHNU—Persia. Just Judge; impartial justice. Along with MITHRA and SAOSHYANT, he judged the souls of humans with his spiritual scales. The Persians believed that the soul stayed by the body for three days and nights while being judged.

RIMMON/RAMMON—Syria. God of weather, storms, thunder. The pomegranate, symbol of life and death, was sacred to him.

SAISHYANT/SRAOSHA—Persia. Savior; one who will come at the end of the world to remove all evil and renew all life. The wicked followers of AHRIMAN will be purged in a type of hell called Druj. Regeneration.

SHADRAFA—Phoenicia. "The Healer"; he stood on the back of a lion beneath a Sun symbol. Conqueror of evil, healing.

SHAMASH/UTU/CHEMOSH—Mesopotamia, Sumeria, Babylonia, Assyria. Sun God; Protector of the Poor; Judge of the Heavens and the Earth; Sublime Judge of the Anunnaki; Lord of Judgment. Son of the Moon god; consort of AYA; he rode in a chariot with Sun rays streaming from his shoulders. Shown with a scepter and ring in his right hand. Divination, retribution, vigor, courage, triumph, justice, eternity, the future, fertility, judgment, lawgiving.

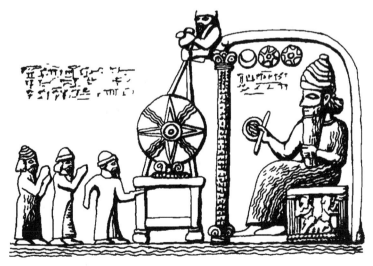

Shamash receives homage from the faithful

Sin

SHEDU/LAMASSU—Mesopotamia; many of the Mid Eastern cultures. Guardian spirits, similar to guardian angels. They defended against evil spirits and interceded with the gods for divine favors. They were shown as winged bulls with human heads. Protection, intercession.

SIN/NANNA/NANNAR—Mesopotamia, Ur, Assyria, Babylonia, Sumeria. Moon God; Lord of the calendar; Lord of the diadem; consort of NINGAL. He held the chief place in the astral triad along with SHAMASH and ISHTAR, both his children. He was shown as an old man with a long beard the color of lapis and wearing a turban. He rode in a boat (a brilliant crescent Moon) across the skies, with the Full Moon as his diadem. Enemy of evil doers; god of measurement of time. Destiny, predictions, air, wisdom, secrets, destruction of all evil, decisions.

TANIT/TANITH—Phoenicia, Carthage. Moon Goddess; Great Goddess; similar to ISHTAR.

TASHMETUM—Assyria, Babylonia. The wife of NABU. Writing.

TESHUB—Hittite. Weather god who carried a thunder hammer and a fistful of thunderbolts. Violent storms, destruction, damage.

TIAMAT—Mesopotamia, Babylonia, Sumeria. Goddess of the primal abyss. A she-dragon, she was sometimes evil, sometimes good. Shown as part animal, part serpent, part bird. MARDUK destroyed her, took the Tablets of Destiny, and built the universe out of her body. Destruction, revenge, karmic discipline, salt water, war, evil, despair, dark magick, death, regeneration, rituals.

ZABABA—Sumeria, Babylonia. Lord of hand-to-hand fighting. War, fighting, victory, destruction, weapons.

ZURVAN—Persia. God of infinite space and time. God of the four faces, which were Procreation, Birth, Aging, Return to the Infinite. In Zoroastrian symbolism, two-faced or two-sexed.

ENDNOTES

1. In *Amulets and Superstitions*, Budge writes that Phoenicia was the part of Syria that extended from the River Eleutherus in the north to Mount Carmel in the south. They were Semites and belonged to the Canaanite peoples, although their neighbors called them Sidonians. They were the most successful traders

of the ancient world, making the famous purple dye and fine linens; their ships went as far as the British Isles in search of metals.

2. James B. Pritchard, in his book *The Ancient Near East*, gives a translation of the Code of Hammurabi. The stela on which this code was carved was discovered by the French in 1901–1902.

3. There is an excellent description of the ziggurats of Ur and the temples of Babylon in *The World of the Past* by J. Hawkes. The original source for these descriptions is Herodotus.

4. In Babylonia, the common man was not allowed to enter the sanctuary of the god. See *Babylon* by Joan Oates.

5. Kramer, Samuel N. *The Sumerians: Their History, Culture and Character.*

6. The making of perfumed ink is quite easy. Simply purchase a bottle of ink, either black or colored, and add two to three drops of the appropriate essential oil to it. Let it sit on the altar overnight. This is best done on the Full Moon for positively charged inks, and on the New Moon for negatively charged inks. For a list of oils and their meanings, check books by D. J. Conway and Scott Cunningham. Chapter 10 of Cunningham's *Magical Herbalism* has a very good list of the meanings of oils.

7. The Babylonian devil-traps were pottery bowls with a spiraling spell written inside; this spell led down to the center of the bowl. They were found buried under the four corners of buildings.

8. There are records of the use of entrails for divination as far back as 300 BC in Mesopotamia. Until astrology became a more exact and powerful tool, about 650 BC, this form of divination was considered one of the most dependable.

9. Kramer, Samuel N. *Cradle of Civilization.* The Sumerian word for gods was *dingir.* They believed there were four supreme deities of four realms of the universe: An, god of heaven, the fire god; Enlil, the air god; Enki, the water god; Ninhursag, the Mother Earth Goddess.

10. Budge, E. A. Wallis. *Amulets and Superstitions.*

11. For examples of cuneiform and cursive writings, see both *Voices in Stone* by Ernst Dolbhoper and *The Story of Archaeological Decipherment From Egyptian Hieroglyphs to Linear B* by Maurice Pope.

12. In *Amulets and Superstitions*, Budge gives a list of Babylonian zodiac signs which are different from those given by Marduk.

13. Ceram, in *Gods, Graves and Scholars*, gives a rich description of the contents of a royal grave found at Ur. There is also a photograph of a beautiful headdress of a Sumerian queen.

14. Walker, Barbara; *The Woman's Encyclopedia of Myths and Secrets.* Stone, Merlin; *Ancient Mirrors of Womanhood.*

15. There is a very readable account of the flood legend in *Four Thousand Years Ago* by G. Bibby.

16. *The Masks of God: Oriental* by J. Campbell.

17. For translations of hymns to Ishtar, see *The Ancient Near East* by J. Pritchard and *The Woman's Enclopedia of Myths and Secrets* by B. Walker.

18. Stone, Merlin. *Ancient Mirrors of Womanhood.*

BIBLIOGRAPHY

Ceram, C. W. *Gods, Graves and Scholars*. NY: Bantam Books, 1972.

Childress, David Hatcher. *Lost Cities and Ancient Mysteries of Africa and Arabia.* IL: Adventures Unlimited Press, 1989.

Doblhoper, Ernst. *Voices in Stone.* NY: The Viking Press, 1961.

Driver, G. R. *Canaanite Myths and Legends.* Edinburgh: Clark, 1956.

Durdin-Robertson, Lawrence. *Goddesses of Chaldea, Syria and Egypt.* Ireland: Caesara Publications, 1975.

Frazer, James G. *Adonis, Attis, Osiris.* NY: University Books, 1961.

Godwin, Joscelyn. *Mystery Religions in the Ancient World.* NY: Harper & Row, 1981.

Herm, Gerhard. *The Phoenicians.* NY: Wm. Morrow & Co., 1975.

Hicks, Jim. *The Persians.* NY: Time-Life Books, 1975.

Hooke, S. H. *Babylonian and Assyrian Religion.* UK: Hutchinson, 1953.

Houston, Mary. *Ancient Egyptian, Mesopotamian and Persian Costume and Decoration.* NY: A. & C. Black, 1954.

Kramer, Samuel N. *Cradle of Civilization.* NY: Time-Life Books, 1967.

Kramer, Samuel N. *The Sumerians: Their History, Culture and Character.* Chicago, IL: University of Chicago Press, 1963.

Lenormant, F. *Chaldean Magic.* UK: Bagster, 1877.

Oates, Joan. *Babylon.* UK: Thames & Hudson, 1979.

Pope, Maurice. *The Story of Archaeological Decipherment from Egyptian Hieroglyphics to Linear B.* NY: Charles Scribner's Sons, 1975.

Pritchard, James B. The Ancient Near East: An Anthology of Texts and Pictures. Princeton, NJ: Princeton University Press, 1958.

Reader's Digest. *The World's Last Mysteries.* NY: Reader's Digest Association, 1978.

Ringgren, Helmer. *Religions of the Ancient Near East.* Trans. John Sturdy. Philadelphia, PA: Westminster Press, 1973.

Skinner, Hubert M. *Readings in Folk-Lore.* NY: American Book Co., 1893.

Chapter Eleven

GREECE

ANCIENT GREECE comprised the extremity of the Balkan Peninsula and included the islands of the Aegean Sea, the Dodecanese, the Ionian Islands, and at one time Crete. The first period of their culture was from about 3000 to 2000 BC. During this time, the Arcadians, Achaeans, Ionians, Boeotians, and Dorians expanded from the Balkan interior into the Peloponnesos. The second period, about 1000 to 499 BC, saw the expansion of the city-state aristocracies all along the Mediterranean basin. Landed nobility governed, replacing the earlier monarchs. There was extensive colonization and trade along the Mediterranean, including the African, French, and Italian coasts. During the internal wars of this period, Sparta and Athens emerged as leaders. About 600 BC, the Spartans reorganized into a military, authoritarian regime, dividing into citizens and noncitizens. Athens abolished its monarchy in 683 BC, gradually forming a republican form of government. By 500 BC middle class Athenians had gained control.

The third period saw the Persian Wars, 499–338 BC. The Persians, first under Darius in 499–490 BC, then under Xerxes in 480–479 BC, controlled Athens, only to be thrown out each time. Civil wars plagued Athens until 445 BC, with rival factions gaining and losing power in government, and Sparta always aiding one side or the other. Finally, a 30 years' peace was made between Athens and Sparta. However, even during this period, the Greek city-states had to fight off invaders.

During the fourth period, 359–146 BC, Philip of Macedonia occupied Thebes but not Athens. Sparta refused to join his Hellenic League. At Philip's death in 336 BC, his son Alexander the Great took over and forced his control over all Greece.

By 205 BC Greece had to accept Roman terms in the Peace of Phoenice, and by 149–148 BC were conquered territories of Rome. Even after Emperor Constantine made Christianity a state religion in AD 330, the Greek Pagan religion continued to exist until around AD 600.

Renowned deity centers were at Onchestus in Boeotia, at Calauria on the coast of Argolis, and later at Thermopylae and Delphi, among others. The oracles and shrines, of which Delphi was the most famous, were consulted by the cities and individuals throughout Greece; they grew to be national institutions.

The Greeks had what they called a civil year, which was divided into ten parts. The civil (government) year and the official year (general reckoning) were both based on solar calculations, but for a long time did not coincide on dates. The civil year was adjusted by Cleisthenes to correspond to the official year, thus bringing the two into balance. He adopted a cycle of five years, with once in every cycle an extra month of 30 days being inserted. The civil year began on the first New Moon after the Summer Solstice.

RELIGION

The main motive of Greek religion was to enlist the aid and placate the anger of the gods. Although there were no fixed daily ceremonies to observe, their belief gave occasion for some religious act each day. Before a cup of wine was drunk, a few drops were poured on the floor as a libation to the gods. If a coin was found, thanks was given to Hermes, god of treasure. If going on a voyage, there were prayers to Poseidon, god of the seas. Prayer to all gods, or a single one, began and ended each day, even in private dwellings. Prayer and libations began and ended each meal. Special prayers and sacrifices were done before special events or undertakings.

Greek religious philosophy was that of deep-thinkers. Although they believed in moderation, they were not a superficial culture. Attempting to understand the mystical was a consuming passion with many of them.

The Greeks wore many charms, amulets, and talismans, and believed in the significance of dreams. If something went wrong in their lives, they immediately asked which god they had offended. They considered life a magnificent adventure to be enjoyed to the fullest. Although they exhibited deep spirituality and avid performance of ritual duties, they also lived by the maxim, "Everything in moderation."

The Greeks had a strong sense of family and blood ties, shown by their festival, the Apaturia. At the Apaturia family and clans gathered; newborn children were presented, both to the family and to the gods (rather like a christening).

Each craft-guild had its patron deity and worshipped and sacrificed at fixed times. Women held ritual celebrations where no males were admitted. There were many national festivals asking for favor for crops or vintage. However, the temples were regarded as the dwelling place on Earth of the god, and people only went there to make special prayers.

There were four main national Greek festivals in honor of certain gods: the Olympian, Pythian, Nemean, and Isthmian. During these celebrations, wars between any Greek states were suspended so festival participants could move freely.

The Olympian, five to seven days in July, was held in honor of Zeus. It was open to all free-born Greeks, except those convicted of a crime; women were forbidden to attend. Every fifth year it was held on the plain of Olympia in Elis. The victory prize was an olive wreath, yet athletes trained hard and traveled long distances to compete. Kings sent their best horses for the races; winning was considered the highest point in

Greek athlete

any man's lifetime. The first Olympiad was said to have been held in 776 BC. The gold and ivory statue of Zeus in the temple there was considered one of the Seven Wonders of the ancient world.

The Pythian games were held near Delphi in honor of Apollo; this happened every five years, but not in the same year as the Olympiad. There were competitions in music and athletics, with prizes of laurel wreaths.

Prizes of ivy wreaths were handed out at the Nemean games in honor of Zeus. On the Isthmus of Corinth, in the autumn twice in each Olympiad, Poseidon was honored by the Isthmian games; these occurred every three years. Prizes of pine wreaths (originally of parsley), made from the trees in the sacred grove, were given to the winners.

The Greek gods were treated with respect and awe, but not love. The Greeks disliked the Oriental custom of groveling to a deity. In praying to most gods, they stood holding the arms upward. When praying to a sea god, the arms were held forward; to an Earth or infernal deity, the arms were held down toward the ground, at the same time stamping on the Earth to attract the god's attention. In all ritual positions, they faced east. When praying in the temples, they faced the altar and the god's statue.

To be successful in prayer, the Greeks believed that a person had to be bodily and morally clean. For this, and in case one was accidentally contaminated, a vessel of holy water and a sprinkler were kept near the temple entrance. Smoke of special ingredients was also used to purify. Birth, death, and murder (even an accidental one) made a person unclean. Some impurities required a special sacrifice where the person was sprinkled with blood.

Priesthood was limited to no specific age, sex, or marital status. There was no dogma to learn. The only requirements were legitimate birth, citizenship, bodily purity, good moral character, and occasionally strength or beauty. Sometimes priestesses were required to be virgins for the duration of their service, which was not

Victims for sacrifice

necessarily a lifelong occupation. Both priests and priestesses were elected by the people, chosen by lot, called by the gods, or inherited the position by birth.

Priests/priestesses performed prayers and sacrifices, offered prayers for others, kept the god's holy days, cared for the temple and divine images, guarded the temple treasures, and performed mysterious dedications and purifications. They usually lived in a house on the grounds and received a share of its income. They held places of honor in the theater and in public. They wore a long tunic of white or purple, had long hair, and carried a staff. Their assistants were either slaves owned by the temple, permanent servants, or occasional volunteers.

Any offering consumed by fire was considered a sacrifice, but the strongest were the blood sacrifices of animals. Poor people gave cakes in the shape of an animal. Horses were sacrificed to Poseidon and Helios; asses to Apollo; geese, doves, fowls, cocks to Aesculapius. White animals were offered to the gods of Light, black to the Dark gods.

Common incenses used were Kyphi[1] (brought originally from Egypt), frankincense, storax, laurel, olive, etc. Oak leaves were for Zeus, laurel for Apollo, ivy or vine for Dionysus, poplar for Herakles, wheat ears for Demeter, myrtle for Aphrodite, fir twigs for the fauns and silvans, reeds for the river gods. Tripods with basins containing coals burned these offerings. The *rhyton*, or drinking horn, was used with vases for religious rites. Lamps were squat, open vessels with a spout and wick.

The Greeks believed strongly in oracles, the best known being the oracle of Apollo at Delphi.[2] In fact, in Greece and Asia Minor there were several hundred places where prophecies were given. The best known of these were Delphi, Hysiae in Boeotia, Argos, Colophon, Miletus, Dodona in Epirus, the Peninsula Magnesia in Thessaly, Oropus, Lebadia in Boeotia, and the Libyan Desert.[3]

Musical instruments used were the phorminx, or large lyre (which had seven strings); cithara, or smaller lyre made of tortoise shell and goat horns; triangle; double flute; syrinx or panpipes (made of graduated reeds fastened together); tambourine (especially for festivals of Dionysus and Cybele); cymbals; castanets. Dances were varied: slow, quick, gay, somber, warlike, sexual. Women danced and played music at feasts to entertain guests.

Many wise men *(bakids)* and wise women *(sibyls)* were attached to no temple or sanctuary. They earned their living by going about the countryside prophesying, purifying, and healing.

The Greeks borrowed the concept of the zodiac and astrology from the Babylonians along with many other magickal practices, including numerology. They, like many other ancient cultures, recognized only seven planets: the Sun, the Moon, Hermes (Mercury), Aphrodite (Venus), Ares (Mars), Zeus (Jupiter), and Cronus (Saturn).

However, they apparently did have the twelve signs of the zodiac. Although the works of Gaius Manilius (48 BC–AD 20) give a different arrangement of deities, the following list appears in other writings: Ares, Aries; Aphrodite, Taurus; Hermes, Gemini; Demeter, Cancer; Apollo, Leo; Hestia, Virgo; Hera, Libra; Artemis, Scorpio; Athene, Sagittarius; Hephaestus, Capricorn; Poseidon, Aquarius; Zeus, Pisces.

The Greeks also borrowed their beliefs of certain mystic and sacred numbers from the Babylonians and Sumerians. Pythagoras (born about 580 BC) held that all things are basically numbers; therefore, the study of numbers was very important. The Greeks held that 3, 5, 7, 9, and 12 were very magickal. The most popular mystical number was three, a trinity, especially when pertaining to goddesses. Nine was considered a complete number, a triad of threes (three times three), as shown by the Nine Muses. Although unlucky in Babylon, twelve was a lucky magickal number to the Greeks, as seen in the twelve main gods of Olympus.

Interpretation of signs was used for divination, such as a flight of birds, signs in the sky, atmospheric phenomena, earthquakes, unusual behavior of animals, sneezing, the entrails of sacrifices, and especially dreams. The temple of Aesculapius was a dream temple where people went to pray and stay all night in order to be given a healing. The attending priests helped with the dream interpretations.

There were also certain national festivals. Panathenaea was celebrated at the end of July (Hekatombaeon) in honor of Athene Pallas. February (Agrae) 1–3 was the Lesser Eleusinia, or the Festival of the Returning Daughter, which celebrated Kore's return from the Underworld and the rebirth of vegetation. This festival was open to many people.

Initiation into the Eleusinian Mysteries was difficult and not for everyone. The Mysteries, open to both men and women, were bound by oaths of secrecy; to this day there are no records of exactly what went on during certain parts of these rituals. No Greek initiated into them ever broke the oath of silence; initiation into the deeper Mysteries granted the initiate immortality only if he obeyed the oath. We do know a few facts that picture these Mysteries as an intense spiritual experience. Many of Greece's highly educated thinkers were Eleusinian initiates.

The annual Sacred Festival of the Greater Eleusinia was celebrated September 23–October 1 in honor of Demeter of Eleusis,[4] Kore, Persephone, and the holy child Iacchus (Dionysus). During this secret autumn ritual, the Divine Child was displayed in a wicker winnowing basket as part of the ceremonies. It took place every five years and could be attended only by first or second grade initiates. And only the second degree initiates (the Epoptae) could participate in many of the rites. Eleusis means "advent," thus explaining the Divine Child in the basket of Demeter. Candidates for initiation had to fast all night in a vigil of silence. As the final act of their initiation,

Demeter, Persephone, and a youth

they went veiled into the deep caverns where a single ear of wheat and other secret symbols were revealed in flashes of light.

From March 19–23 were the Lesser Panathenaea in honor of Athene. Games of skill were open to all comers. Festivals honoring Cybele were held March 22–27. On August 13, Hecate as the Dark Mother was feasted, with pilgrimages to the cemeteries. The goddess Nemesis had a festival on August 23. The exact dates for the festivals of Artemis are unknown, but we know the Brauronia occurred every five years and a minor celebration was held annually.

The Thesmophoria came October (Pyamepsion) 9–13 every year in honor of Demeter and was confined to women only. This was a three day remembrance of Kore's (Persephone) return to the Underworld. At this festival the initiates shared a sacred barley drink and cakes. The abduction of Kore was enacted, followed by the *hieros gamos*, attended only by second degree initiates. This was the actual physical union or copulation of the hierophant (priest) and priestess, a representation of the union of Demeter and Zeus that had produced Kore.

There were four festivals of Dionysus in Athens every year: one in January, two in February, and the Greater Dionysia in March. The Anthesteria, or Lesser Dionysia, occurred about February 11–13; it was a fertility festival during which Dionysus was mated with the queen. These festivals were filled with sacrifices, games, and much wine. A much wilder, orgiastic type of Dionysia took place at Cithaeron and Parnassus, the Islands, and in Asia Minor every other year.

At Olympia in Elis, a festival only for girls and unmarried women was held in honor of Hera. This did not coincide with the festival for Zeus, although it also was held every five years. The contestants wore short dresses and raced for prizes, their hair unbound and streaming behind them. The judges were sixteen married women. Each year at this festival the statue of the goddess was draped in a new, richly embroidered *peplos* made by selected Greek women.

Every year on March 1, Hera's chief festival, the Matronalia, was celebrated only by women. The town of Argos was the oldest and chief center of her worship; in her main temple there was a beautiful statue carved by Polykleitos. She had other temples at Samos, Corinth, Eubaea, Boeotia, Crete, and Lakinion in Italy.

These holy days were only a few of the religious festivals celebrated by the ancient Greeks. There is evidence in their writings that they marked the solstices and equinoxes. Among followers of certain deities, rites were performed at the New and Full Moons. The life of the average ancient Greek was abundant with mystical opportunity.

DRESS AND ORNAMENTATION

The normal dress of both men and women was of two garments, each an oblong piece of woolen cloth. The tunic *(chiton)* for men, tunica for women, was worn around the body, pinned over each shoulder, and the hanging folds held in place by a girdle. This tunic for men came to about the knees; women wore it to the feet. Ordinarily both the tunic and *himation* (cloak) were white.

The Doric tunic was wool and shaped by pinning; the Ionic tunic was linen and sewed. Cotton, muslin, and silk were extremely rare, and worn only by the very wealthy. On festive occasions, women sometimes wore tunics of bright colors. When in mourning, a black tunic was worn, and the hair cut very short. On festive occasions, or if they were priests, harp players, flute players, charioteers, or other notable persons, men wore the longer chiton. Sometimes this was unpinned on one shoulder to leave the arm free.

In Sparta, women had special sports schools where they wore a short tunic with a girdle only a little below the hips, and left the right breast exposed.

Over the tunic, a himation for men, peplos for women, of thicker material was arranged. This was seldom pinned, but carefully draped and folded. Its draping became quite an art. The *chlamys* was a short oval cloak of light material, sometimes fastened by a brooch on the right shoulder. This was worn by soldiers and riders. It was the common cloak of young men as soon as they came of age and entered the cavalry. Both men and women pulled the cloak over the head during bad weather, mourning, or when performing sacred rites.

Women also wore a short mantle falling to just below the breasts. This had sleeves that were pinned by little brooches on the upper side of the arms. Very thin materials were worn by *hetaerae* (professional prostitutes); these women were classed in different grades according to their education.

Although the tunic and himation were usually white, they often had decorative borders. Checks and diamonds were popular designs, as were ivy leaves.

At home and in summer men usually went barefoot. In winter they wore sandals or boots. Heavy nailed sandals or boots were worn by soldiers and country people. Men wore flat broad-brimmed hats in bad weather, sailors a rimless conical cap. At the birth of a son, men donned a wreath of olive branches, and at weddings and festivals a garland of flowers around the neck.

Women used sunshades and wore a light tissue veil as both a sign of modesty and rank. This veil also covered the face of a bride during the marriage ceremony.

In the early periods, both men and women wore their hair in long curls. Later all the hair

Greek dress

was pulled back and held by ribbons. Heated irons were used to curl the hair and beard. In later periods, the men's long curls were clipped into ringlets hanging around the ears. The Grecian knot worn by women was made by combing the hair into a flattened knot low on the back of the head. They then wore a narrow band around the hair and forehead.

Many cosmetics were used: white lead for the forehead and chin; red of cinnabar, fucus, and bugloss for the cheeks; flesh tint for below the eyes; pine blacking or antimony for the eyebrows and dyeing the hair.

On their heads, women wore the *mitra* or bushel-shaped crown, the tiara or crescent diadem, rows of beads, wreaths of flowers, nets, fillets. For jewelry they wore earrings, necklaces, bracelets of hoops, snake bracelets for the upper and lower arms, clasps, and hairpins.

SOME OF THE MYTHS

In the beginning was Chaos, the vast, dark void, and Gaea, the broad-bosomed Earth. Chaos alone produced Erebus and Night; Gaea gave birth to Uranus (the sky). Then together Gaea and Uranus produced the Titans (six male and six female giants), the Cyclopes, and three monsters called the Centimanes. Of the Titans, the best known were Cronus, Oceanus, Rhea, Phoebe, and Themis; they were considered the ancestors of humankind, inventors of the arts and magick.

As soon as the Cyclopes (gods of storm, thunder and lightning) were born, Uranus shut them all in the Earth, angering Gaea. She made a sickle and talked her youngest son, Cronus, into castrating his father. Uranus' black blood on the Earth created the Furies; his genitals, thrown into the sea, brought forth Aphrodite. Then Cronus freed the other Titans and became their king. They all interbred, finishing creation and producing a host of other deities.

Finally Cronus married his sister Rhea. From them came Hestia, Demeter, Hera, Hades, Poseidon, and Zeus. Because of a prophecy that his children would supplant him, Cronus swallowed each at birth, except the unborn Zeus. To save her last child, Rhea hid in Crete and gave the newborn Zeus to Gaea at his birth. Then Rhea wrapped up a rock, which Cronus promptly swallowed.

The baby Zeus was smuggled to the island of Crete and hidden in a cave on Mount Ida. There the nymphs Adrastea and Ida cared for him. The goat Amalthea supplied the milk and the bees honey. Afraid that his cries might be heard by Cronus, the Kuretes, Rhea's servants, made a continual noise by dancing and clashing together their swords and shields.

Cronus devouring his children

162

When grown, Zeus talked Metis, daughter of Oceanus, into giving his father Cronus a potion that caused the old man to throw up all his children. Then Zeus chained Cronus in the depths of the universe. The stone which had been substituted for the baby Zeus was placed at Pytho at the foot of Parnassus.

Zeus and his siblings went to live in Olympus. The Titans, except Oceanus and a few of the others, declared war on them. The battle lasted ten years before the new gods finally chained the Titans in Tartarus, in the deep depths of the Earth. Sometime during all this turmoil, humans were created.

There were twelve major gods and goddesses on Olympus: Zeus, Poseidon, Hephaestus, Hermes, Ares, and Apollo; Hera, Athene, Artemis, Hestia, Aphrodite, and Demeter. Those of lower rank were Helios, Selene, Leto, Dione, Dionysus, Themis, and Eros. Of lower rank still were the Horae, Nemesis, the Charities, the Muses, Iris, Hebe, and Ganymede (the homosexual lover and cup-bearer of Zeus).[5] Hades, brother of Zeus, seldom visited Olympus, preferring to stay in his subterranean kingdom with Persephone and Hecate.

Athene

The name Olympus (or Olympos) was originally used to designate a specific mountain in Thessaly. Later the name was applied to as many as fourteen mountains throughout Greece. These other mountains were regarded as meeting places of the gods. Although Mount Olympus was the name given to a physical mountain, the Greeks understood the word to mean an area above the visible sky. It was said that Olympus was so high above the Earth that once an anvil fell nine days and nights before it reached the planet. At an equal distance below the surface of the Earth lay Tartaros; in this huge gloomy space, bounded by walls of brass, the Titans were imprisoned.

The Greeks believed that Zeus lived on the highest point of Olympus in his magnificent palace with his great throne. On lower plateaus were the palaces of the other gods.

Although Zeus was king of the gods and ruled Olympus with an iron hand, he certainly spent plenty of time marrying, seducing, and raping a long list of goddesses and mortal women. He first married Metis (wisdom). He promptly swallowed Metis[6] and her unborn child as soon as he learned that the baby would be more powerful than he. Next he married Themis (law), daughter of Uranus and Gaea. Their children were the Horae or Seasons, Eunomia, Dike, Eirene, and the Fates or Moerae. Next was the Titaness Mnemosyne, who conceived the Nine Muses. As Zeus' wife, the Oceanid Eurynome birthed the Graces.

Finally Zeus married Hera, his sister. However, this royal marriage did not stop the god's amorous adventures. He seduced or raped Demeter (who bore Kore), Leto (mother of Apollo and Artemis), Maia[7] (mother of Hermes), Semele (mother of Dionysus), Thymbris (mother of Pan), plus many other females who gave birth to heroes, founders of races, and beautiful daughters. Hera herself bore Hebe,[8] Ilithyia,[9] Ares, and Hephaestus.

In the midst of all the carousing and children, Zeus developed such a terrible headache that he begged Hephaestus for help. Knowing he could not kill a god, Hephaestus split his father's skull with a bronze axe. Athene, who had been swallowed unborn, sprang out, fully grown, fully armored, and shaking a javelin.

Athene was an absolute chaste goddess, a rarity among the Olympians, and only gave her aid to those she considered deserving. She helped Herakles through his twelve labors, and at his death, welcomed him to Olympus as a demigod. She was also the goddess of handcrafts, the arts, and weaving. But like the rest of the Olympians, Athene had great pride and temper when dealing with mortals. Arachne, a skilled mortal weaver, boasted that she was better at the loom than the goddess. Athene accepted the challenge. At the end of the contest, the goddess could find no flaw in Arachne's tapestry, a picture of the amorous adventures of the gods. Furious, Athene changed the girl into a spider, condemned to spin and weave forever.

Hera may have been queen of Olympia but she was extremely jealous and spiteful against her husband's lovers, whether forced or willing participants. She hounded them all, even killing some. Once she succeeded in binding Zeus with thongs but he escaped with the aid of Thetis[10] and a hundred-armed giant. In retaliation, Zeus hung Hera up by her hands from the sky with an anvil tied to her feet. Though she had to refrain from further attacks on unfaithful Zeus, Hera continued to vent her anger on his paramours and their children.

At the birth of Apollo and Artemis, Hera sent the serpent Python after their mother Leto, but Poseidon hid her. Apollo, fortified with nectar and ambrosia[11] and armed with the arrows forged for him by Hephaestus, sought out the monster in Parnassus. He slew Python, then purified himself in the Vale of Tempe before going to Olympus crowned with laurel leaves.

Like Athene, Apollo did not take kindly to being challenged on his talents. He was so gifted with the cithara, or large lyre, that wild animals gathered at his feet when he played. The satyr Marsyas challenged him to a musical contest; the judges were the Muses (Apollo's constant companions) and King Midas. Apollo won the contest and killed the satyr. Midas, who voted against Apollo, got a permanent pair of donkey's ears for daring to vote as he did.

Like his father, Apollo had a great number of mistresses, willing and unwilling. Some women escaped his ardor by being changed into trees or plants. Apollo's only son to join the ranks of Olympus was Asclepius, whom the god snatched from the mother's funeral pyre. Apollo also had affairs with several young men, none of which ended happily.

Leto defending her children

Artemis, twin of Apollo, was called the Virgin Huntress. Always with her were sixty young Oceanids, twenty nymphs, and her pack of hunting hounds, the Alani. For all her Amazonian attributes, Artemis loved singing and dancing. However, she was not one to overlook an insult, even if unintentional.

Admetus forgot to sacrifice to Artemis at his wedding and found his bride's chamber full of snakes. Oeneus forgot to offer for a good crop and found his kingdom besieged by a huge boar. The hunter Actaeon chanced upon the goddess bathing and made the fatal mistake of watching. Artemis changed him into a stag, which her hounds tore to pieces.

Hermes

The hunter Orion came the closest to becoming consort of the Huntress. But jealous Apollo challenged his sister to hit a black object in the ocean (Orion taking a swim). Her swift arrow killed him. Another version says that Orion dared to touch Artemis while they were hunting; the goddess directed a scorpion to sting his heel, and he died.

Hermes was a prankster from the day of his birth, and his half-brother Apollo was the first of the gods to be the victim. Not even 24 hours old, Hermes sneaked off to steal 50 heifers from the sacred herd entrusted to Apollo. The young god made the cows walk backward into a cavern where he hid them, then sacrificed two of them to the Olympians. The little boy hurried home and lay innocently in his cradle. Apollo, god of divination, knew immediately who was the culprit, but Hermes denied it. Furious, Apollo carried the child to Olympus, where Zeus made him return the heifers.

Reconciliation finally came between the two when Hermes invented the cithara and gave it to Apollo. In return the god gave Hermes the caduceus and entrusted him with the sacred herd. Thus, Apollo, originally a Nature god, became god of music, and Hermes became protector of flocks and herds. Theirs was a lasting friendship. Although Hermes was a malicious trickster, all the deities loved him. He became their messenger, wearing a winged hat and sandals.

At various times Hermes rescued Zeus, Ares, Dionysus, and several heroes. Like Zeus, Hermes had a way with the ladies, mortal and divine. He had affairs with Persephone, Hecate, and Aphrodite, and several nymphs and mortal women. A number of offspring are attributed to him. In one myth, Pan was said to be his son.

Ares was not popular with the Olympians because of his brutality, blind violence, and terrible temper. Ares enjoyed fighting and took part in all wars, but rarely emerged victorious. He and Athene hated each other and were often on opposite sides of mortal battles. Athene represented cool, intellectual courage, while Ares stood for blind rage and thoughtless reaction. Once he even had the audacity to attack the goddess. Athene knocked him out with a huge boundary stone. Later the god challenged

Herakles and returned to Olympus wounded and groaning. Zeus ended the dispute by dropping a thunderbolt between the two.

Ares fared no better in his love affairs. He and Aphrodite were trapped in a net while they were in bed. Hephaestus, Aphrodite's husband, then called all the deities to witness the couple's embarrassment; both had to endure divine ridicule. From this union between Ares and Aphrodite came Harmonia, who later married Cadmus, king of Thebes. Most of the god's other offspring fared worse; several died.

Hephaestus, divine smith of the gods, was lame in both legs and had twisted feet. At his birth, Hera was repulsed by the misshapen form and threw him into the sea where he was raised by Thetis and Eurynome.[12]

For nine years Hephaestus lived in the sea, out of sight, forging wonderful things for the nymphs and plotting revenge. One day a beautiful golden throne arrived for Hera. Delighted with its beauty, the goddess sat on it and could not get up again. None of the other deities could release her. Ares sped to the depths of the ocean and tried to drag Hephaestus to Olympus by force. Hephaestus threw burning brands at him and ran him off. Dionysus was more clever. He got Hephaestus drunk, perched him on a mule, and took him to Olympus. The smith god may have been drunk, but not so much that he did not get full revenge on his mother. He demanded, and got, the lovely Aphrodite as his wife.

Like the other gods, Hephaestus liked women. In return for freeing Athene, who was giving Zeus a splitting headache, the god demanded the new goddess as wife also. Athene refused to fulfill her father's promise; there was nothing Hephaestus or Zeus could do about it. The smith god had several children by nymphs and mortals, but none by Aphrodite. Hephaestus was aided at his forge by many subterranean deities, such as the Cyclopes.

The judgment of Paris

Aphrodite, the divine essence of feminine beauty, was born from the foam caused on the ocean when Cronus threw down his father's genitals. Her love powers were great; even Hera borrowed her magickal girdle to recapture Zeus's attentions.

The only immortals Aphrodite could not arouse to amorous adventures were Athene, Artemis, and Hestia. Aphrodite was never faithful to Hephaestus, having a long series of mortal and divine lovers. By the Trojan Anchises she had Aeneas, by Ares a daughter (Harmonia), and by Hermes a son (Hermaphroditus). Winged Eros, whose capricious arrows caused trouble for both men and gods, was her zealous servant, along with her companions the Charities.

Poseidon

One day Hera, Athene, and Aphrodite had an argument over a golden apple inscribed "to the fairest." Zeus, not wishing to get himself in difficulties, ordered them to get a judgment from a mortal man. They chose Paris, son of King Priam of Troy. Hera appeared to Paris, promising to make him lord of Asia. Athene promised to make him always victorious in battle. Aphrodite came, took off her robe, and promised him the most beautiful of mortal women. Poor Paris chose Aphrodite, thus winning Helen, wife of Menelaus, and also the death of his people and himself when they lost the Trojan War.

Poseidon, son of Cronus and Rhea, was ruler of the seas. His wife was Amphitrite, daughter of Oceanus. Because of the aid of Poseidon and Hades when Zeus fought the Titans and Giants, Zeus divided his kingdom. Zeus took the heavens and Olympus, Hades the Underworld, and Poseidon the seas. Poseidon had a thirst for possessions and was often in contention with Zeus over land. However, he never completely won, having to settle for only part of what he wanted. He drove a chariot pulled by Tritans blowing conch horns; tridents and horses were his symbols. He also had the power to summon monsters to avenge himself on humans, and did so on several occasions.

Poseidon also had many mistresses. By Gaea he had the monster Antaeus. Demeter, who tried to escape him by changing into a mare, found herself mounted by a stallion (Poseidon). She bore the wild winged horse Arion. Poseidon seduced Medusa, priestess of Athene (some say Aphrodite), in her temple; she became the mother of Pegasus.[13] In a fury, the goddess changed the hapless woman into a monster with snakes for hair. Poseidon even lay with the harpy Celaeno, producing two sons, one of whom distinguished himself at Troy. The list of Poseidon's offspring is longer than that of any other deity.

Hestia was a fire deity, goddess of the hearth and home. She was the first child of Cronus and Rhea and remained an eternal virgin. Her dignity and rights were unquestioned by the other Olympians. Both Poseidon and Apollo wanted her, but she put herself under the protection of Zeus by a solemn vow sworn on his head.

Helios was the Sun deity, while Apollo was god of solar light. Like the other gods, Helios had a number of loves and offspring; one of his daughters was Circe, mistress of evil spells and enchantments. His sister Selene was the Moon goddess; among her lovers was Zeus, by whom she had three daughters. Cybele, goddess of the mountaintops and caverns, was an Asiatic Mother Goddess, often pictured in a chariot drawn by lions.

The Greeks had many rites to honor their gods. One of the greatest was the October rite of Thesmophoria, which was celebrated in connection with Demeter and Kore (later known as Persephone). Part of the rite was the re-enactment of the disappearance and return of Kore.

Demeter's daughter Kore was out picking flowers when the Earth opened, and Hades dragged the girl into his subterranean kingdom to be his wife. For nine days Demeter looked everywhere. In despair she finally consulted Helios, who told her that her brother Zeus had given the girl to Hades. Furious, Demeter left Olympus, wandering on the Earth disguised as an old woman. She finally settled in her temple at Eleusis. She cursed the Earth and it yielded no crops; in answer to Zeus's frantic message, Demeter stated there would be no renewing vegetation until Kore[14] was returned to her.

Zeus sent Hermes into the kingdom of Hades for the girl. But Hades, not wanting to give up his wife permanently, enticed her to eat pomegranate seeds before she returned to her mother. Upon learning of this trick, Demeter again despaired, until Zeus declared that for one-third of the year Persephone-Kore would live with her husband and the rest of the year with her mother. In gratitude, Demeter lifted her curse on the Earth.

Major Gods and Goddesses

ADONIS/ADON/ADONAI—"Lord"; ancient Semitic god. Connected with APHRODITE and PERSEPHONE. Celebration of his death and subsequent resurrection was at the spring equinox. God of rebirth and seasons, love and beauty.

APHRODITE—"Foam-born"; Moon Goddess; "She Who Binds Hearts Together"; "She who came from the sea"; Goddess of the Western Corner. She was pictured as beautiful, voluptuous, with blue eyes and fair hair. At one time her name was Marianna or "La Mer," meaning "the Ocean." She was called virginal, meaning that she remained independent. Her priestesses were not physical virgins, but celebrated sexual rites; men were excluded from many of her rituals. Frankincense and myrrh were burned in her temples. The love of women, in whatever form, was sacred to her. She was strong, proud, loving. Her birds were the heron, lovebird, swan, and dove (yonic symbol). Her girdle, cockle shells, poppy, rose, golden apples, sweet fragrances and fruits, and pomegranate were some of her symbols. Patroness of prostitutes. Goddess of love, beauty, the joy of physical love, sensuality, passion, generosity, all forms of partnerships and relationships, affection, fertility, continued creation, renewal.

APOLLO—"Shining"; god of solar light; greatest of the gods after Zeus. Twin brother of ARTEMIS, his chariot was pulled by golden horses. He used the bow and lyre with skill. His arrows brought illness or death. Pictured as extremely handsome, perfectly built with fair hair. He was bi-sexual, a possible result of his worshippers overrunning and absorbing a matriarchy, such as at Delphi. He represented lawful punishment of crimes, not revenge; justified revenge. He demanded tolerance of his followers. The laurel was sacred to him. Patron of priests. God of prophecy, poetry, music, medicine, oracles, healing, reason, inspiration, magick, the arts, divination, harmony, spiritual goals gained through use of the arts, ravens, earthquakes, woodlands, springs.

Apollo and Hyacinthus

ARES—The Greeks did not care much for him as they thought this god was blood-thirsty and a liar. He wore a crested helmet, and was thought of as very tough, insensitive, and greatly concerned with his male image. God of war, terror, uncontrolled anger, revenge, courage without thought, raw energy, brute strength, untamed passions, any situation where sheer stamina is needed. Do not invoke Ares unless you are very self-disciplined.

ARTEMIS—Virgin Huntress; goddess of wild places and wild things; the Huntress; Maiden; Bear Goddess; Moon Goddess; Hunter of Souls; shape-shifter. In Ephesus she was called "many-breasted" and was the patroness of nurturing, fertility, and birth. In Greece she was sculpted as tall, slim, lovely, and dressed in a short tunic. Her chariot was pulled by silver stags. She roamed the forests, mountains, and glades with her band of nymphs and hunting dogs. She acted swiftly and decisively to protect and rescue those who appealed to her for help and was quick to punish offenders. She knew the deep secret places in Nature where one could rest and regain strength. The Amazons, who were loyal to her, worshipped one aspect of this Moon Goddess (the New Moon phase).[15] Acorns were the symbol of her association with forests and the woodlands. Goddess of the hunt accompanied by a stag and the Alani[16] (her pack of hounds), she carried a silver bow. Her priestesses did not consort with men, but the goddess helped women in childbirth. She could bring destruction but was usually benign. Her animals were guinea fowl, dog, horse, stag. Her symbols were the sickle, bridle, spinning distaff, hanks of wool. The sixth day from the New Moon was hers. Defender of women who were harassed or threatened by men. Very beneficial when dealing with animals or the elemental kingdoms. Patroness of singers; protector of young girls; mistress of magick, sorcery, enchantment, psychic power, women's fertility, purification, sports, exercise, good weather for travellers, countryside, the hunt, mental healing, dance, wild animals, forests, mountains, woodland medicines, juniper, healing.

ASCLEPIUS/ASKLEPIOS/AESCLEPIUS—Son of APOLLO; god of healing. He learned the arts of hunting and medicine from the centaur CHIRON. His sons MACHAON and PODALIRIUS served as doctors during the siege of Troy, while his daughters HYGEIA[17] (good health) and PANACEA[18] (helper) were temple physicians. These children founded the college of medicine, the Asklepiades, which taught medicine as a sacred secret. Pale brown harmless snakes were kept in his temples; they were considered sacred. Vast libraries were also in the temples. Symbols were mortar and pestle, garlic, squill. His cult was active at Cos, Epidaurus, and Pergamus, where there were sleep and dream temples for healing. God of snakes, revival of the dead, healing.

ATHENE/ATHENA—Holy Virgin; Maiden Goddess; Mother Goddess of Athens; Bright-Eyed. An all-powerful warrior goddess, but she disliked senseless violence. Sometimes called PALLAS (PAL-ass) ATHENE in memory of the goddess' close friend whom she accidentally killed in practice. The Parthenon, "Virgin Temple," was her shrine. Sacred to her were the owl, olive, oak, intertwined snakes. She wore a helmet and aegis (breastplate) and carried a shield and spear. She invented the plow, bridle, rake, ox yoke, chariot, and flute; also taught humankind to breed and break horses. She was celebrated at the Lesser Panathenaea in March and on the Day of the Geniae on December 25. She was a goddess of freedom and women's rights; patroness of craftsmen, especially smiths, goldsmiths, potters, dressmakers, shipbuilders, weavers and spinners. Also the patroness of career women. She was the protector of cities and patron of soldiers. She was the goddess of protection, writing, music, the sciences, sculptors, potters, architects, wisdom, arts and skills, renewal, true justice, protection (both psychic and physical), prudence, wise counsel, peace, embroidery, horses and oxen, snakes, pillars, trees, olive boughs, battle strategy.

BENDIS—Thracian goddess of the Moon and fertility. Her rites included orgies.

BOREAS—God of the North Wind; prosperity, growth, riches. He was pictured with a man's upper body and a serpent's tail; sometimes winged and with two faces, looking forward and backward. The most important of the four wind gods; others

Circe and friends of Odysseus, whom she turned into pigs

were: ZEPHYRUS, West, calm, peace of mind, love and the emotions; NOTOS, South, happiness, change, passion, bringer of rain; and EURUS/APHELIOTES, East, renewing, intelligence. AEOLUS was the keeper of the winds, but not always capable of controlling them.

BRITOMARTIS/DICTYNNA—(meaning "law-giver"): "Sweet Virgin"; Cretan virgin forest huntress; goddess of chastity. May have been a form of ARTEMIS.

CHARITIES/GRACES—Triad of Moon goddesses; Aphrodite's companions. Usually portrayed nude and dancing. They were AGLAIA (the shining one, glorious), THALIA (the flowering one, abundance), and EUPHROSYNE (the one who makes glad, joy).

Cybele

CIRCE—"She-Falcon"; Moon Goddess. Called the death-bird (*kirkos* or falcon). As the circle, or cirque, she was the fate-spinner, weaver of destinies. Ancient Greek writers spoke of her as Circe of the Braided Tresses because she could manipulate the forces of creation and destruction by knots and braids in her hair. Circe had her magnificent palace on a small isle *(aeaea)* in the Aegean Sea. The willow tree was sacred to her, as are honey and fruits. She was the goddess of physical love, sorcery, enchantments, evil spells, vengeance, dark magick, witchcraft, cauldrons.

CRONUS/CRONOS/KRONOS—Father Time; the Old King; Father of the Gods; the Great Lesson-Giver; Ruler of the Golden Age. Titan son of GAEA and URANUS. God of abundance and agriculture, Earth's riches, prosperity. Inventor of the arts and magick.

CYBELE/KYBELE—A Phrygian goddess of the Earth and caverns; Great Mother; associated with ATTIS, who was her son.[19] Her symbols were the crescent Moon, cymbal, libation bowl, sickle, honey, lions, pomegranate, caves, violets, meteorites, pine trees, and bees. She carried a scourge of knuckle bones and liked pearls and cypress. The greatest center of her worship was at Pessinus in Phrygia; there, under the shadow of Mount Dindymon, was a cave containing the tomb of Attis and an extremely ancient image of the goddess in the shape of a stone. She was the goddess of the natural world and its formations; wild beasts, especially lions; dominion over wild animals; dark magick, revenge.

Dactyls—"Fingers"; Divine Beings. They were spirits born from the fingerprints of Rhea: five males from her right hand, five females from her left. They were blacksmiths, magi, founders of meter, inventors of magickal formulae. A form of the Earth elementals.

Demeter—"Mother"; "Doorway of the Mysterious Feminine"; Eternal Mother; the Sorrowing Mother; Corn Goddess; "Grain Mother"; Mistress of Magick. She was shown as a matron with beautiful hair, wearing a blue robe and carrying a sheaf of wheat; crowned with ears of corn or ribbons and held a scepter. This goddess gave the first wheat seeds to humans, taught them how to cultivate the soil and make bread from the grain. She instituted the Eleusinian Mysteries,[20] the Lesser in February, the Greater in September. She was the protectress of women; goddess of crops, corn, the plow, initiation, renewal, rebirth, vegetation, fruitfulness, agriculture, civilization, law, motherhood, marriage, maternal love, fidelity, magickal philosophy, expansion, higher magick, soil, all growing things.

Dionysus—"Horned God"; "Savior"; "The bull-horned god"; also called Dithyrambos ("double-birth" or "twice-born");[21] the Roaring One; the Initiated. The vine, wine, and ivy were sacred to him. Symbols were the panpipes, thyrsus, rhyton, tambourine, wicker winnowing basket, chalice, and cymbals. His tutor was Silenus, a satyr. Most of his followers were women, called the Maenads,[22] who held drunken, orgiastic rituals; they were known to tear men apart with their bare hands. The Centaurs[23] and Satyrs[24] were also followers. At Eleusis, the god appeared as the Holy Child Iacchus laid in the winnowing basket. Dionysus was the great remover of inhibition and influences the human emotions. He was the god of pleasure, ecstasy, total abandon, woodlands, Nature, wine, initiation, rituals, rebirth, regeneration, civilization.

Eos/Aurora—Goddess of the dawn. Sometimes she rode on Pegasus, sometimes in a purple or gold chariot.

Erinyes/Eumenides—"The angry ones"; "Avengers"; "the kindly ones"; Children of Eternal Night; Daughters of Earth and Shadow. Punishers of sins, they had serpents twined in their hair and carried torches and whips.[25] They tracked down those who wrongly shed blood, especially a mother's blood. Three virgin goddesses: Allecto (beginnings, unending), Tisiphone (continuation, retaliation), and Megaera (death and rebirth, envious fury). They defended mothers and the laws of blood relationship; revenge; justice against those who broke customs or taboos, social and bloodline laws. Later identified with fairies.

Eros—God of Bringing Together; God of erotic love, both homosexual and heterosexual. Shown as a beautiful but wanton boy with a golden quiver of arrows of desire and physical attraction. He was a dangerous force that could drive men and women to useless self-sacrifice.

Gaea/Gaia—"Broad-bosomed"; Great Mother; Universal Mother; Supreme Goddess; Earth Goddess; Mother Earth; Primeval Prophetess; most ancient Earth; omnipotent. She was the greatest of oracles; the great center at Delphi was hers before Apollo came. Sacred oaths were made in her name. She had sanctuaries at Dodona, Tegea, Sparta, and Athens. Her priestesses were the sacred Sibyls, wise Pythias, and devout Mellisae. Into her sacred cauldron at Delphi, the priestesses threw barley and laurel. She was goddess of motherhood, agricultural fertility, marriage, dreams, trance, divination, oracles, healing.

THE GRAIAE/GRAEAE—Called the Mothers of Greece (Graecia). They lived in the Land of Rock-roses, a land of pathless forests and rock. Grey goddesses who shared one All-Seeing Eye. Their names were ENYO, PEMPHREDO, and DEINO (Fear, Dread, and Terror), and were associated with war, retribution, and divination.

HADES—"The invisible one"; brother of ZEUS; ruler of the Underworld and wealth. Absolute master in the Underworld. His helmet of invisibility allowed only the initiated to see him. Also called PLUTON, Lord of Riches. His principal temples were at Pylos, Athens, and Olympia in Elis. He was both the mysterious, terrifying god of death and the benign god of prosperity. The house of Hades was the place of shades, or the dead.[26] God of crops, minerals, spring water, gem stones, material gain, elimination of fear of death, astral projection.

HECATE—"Most lovely one"; "the Distant One"; Thracian goddess of the Moon, the dark hours, and the Underworld; the Crone; Queen of the world of spirits; goddess of witchcraft; snake goddess; Great Mother; Great Goddess of Nature; Lady of the Wild Hunt. Daughter of TARTAROS and NIGHT, two Titans; other versions says of PERSES and ASTERIA (Starry-Night), or of ZEUS and HERA. Another goddess of the Amazons, her chariot was pulled by dragons. She could change forms or ages and rejuvenate or kill. She was the third Moon aspect as the Hag (Dark Moon) or the Crone (revered as the Carrier of Wisdom). An ally of Zeus; accompanied by a pack of hounds. Her symbols were a key and the cauldron. The women who worshipped her stained their palms and soles with henna. Her festivals were held at night by torchlight. Every year on the island of Aegina in the Saronic Gulf, a mysterious festival was held in her honor. A huntress goddess who knew her way in the realm of spirits; all secret powers of Nature at her command; control over birth, life, and death. She was patroness of priestesses; goddess of witches, the waning Moon, dark magick, prophecy, charms and spells, vengeance, expiations, averting evil, enchantments, riches, victory, wisdom, transformation, reincarnation, incantations, dogs, purification, prosperity, destruction, limit, ends, choices, crossroads, annihilation, curses, sky, Earth fertility, victory, wealth, magickal charms, hauntings, destructive storms, revenge, change, renewal, and regeneration.

HELIOS—Sun God (of the actual Sun). Nine (some say seven) winged white fire-breathing horses pulled his golden chariot, and he wore a golden helmet and breastplate. God of riches, enlightenment, victory.

HEPHAESTUS—He was a magician of metal and gems for the Olympians; he made a scepter and the dreaded aegis for ZEUS (later worn by ATHENE), and armor for ACHILLES and MEMNON. His workshops were said to be under the Earth, one of them within Mount Etna in Sicily. The place most sacred to him, however, was Lemnos, at the foot of Mount Mosychlos; an ancient temple there was said to be

Hera

the place where PROMETHEUS stole fire to give to humans. He was also highly honored in Athens because of the large population of pottery-makers and metal-workers; every year in October he was honored in a festival called Chalkeia. Broad-shouldered and dark from the forges, he wore a leather apron and leaned on a great staff; considered the common person's deity. He could be found wherever molten metal was poured and forges were used. God of blacksmiths, metalworkers, thunder, lightning, fire, subterranean fires, volcanoes, industry, artisans, craftsmen, jewelry making, mechanics, micro electronics, manual dexterity, hard work, inventiveness, all creative crafts, engineering, building construction.

HERA—"Lady"; "Holy One"; "Great Lady"; Mother of the gods; Queen of Heaven; Earth Goddess; Great Mother. Her sacred bird was the peacock. Pictured wearing a veil and a matronly dress; very noble. She held a scepter and pomegranate; wild marjoram, the cow, the Milky Way, and lilies were sacred to her. The sickle she sometimes carried was made for her by HEPHAESTUS. To her belonged the tree of golden apples in Hesperides.[27] Some of her symbols were the double axe, sacred shield, helmet, spear, cows. Represented the stability of women in a male society. She was goddess of protection of the home, marriage, children, and all phases of feminine life. Invoke when facing infidelity and insecurity. She helped women's fertility, renewal, purification, the Moon, the sky, flowers, willow, myrtle wreath, death, pain, punishment.

HERAKLES—"Glory of HERA." A culture hero-demigod symbolizing strength and courage, joy, and wine.

HERMES—"The ram-bearer"; messenger of the gods. Sculpted as a slim athletic young man carrying a caduceus and wearing winged sandals and helmet. He invented the small lyre, boxing, and racing. He was patron of shepherds and flocks. As the "leader of souls," he lead the dead to the Underworld. God of roads, good luck and fortune, all kinds of profit (legal or not), commerce, transport, thievery, liars, treaties, boxing, gymnastics, alphabet, letters, orthodox medicine, occult wisdom, measuring and weighing, astronomy and astrology, music, divination by dice, cunning, success, magick, travel, profits, gambling, mischief, crossroads, athletics, eloquence, merchants, speed, ingenuity, intelligence, diplomacy, finding the way when lost, journalism. Helped in jobs connected with travel. He could control the four elements, four winds, four seasons, solstices, and equinoxes. He was the patron of alchemists, Hermetic magick, and philosophy.

HESTIA—Virgin Goddess; oldest of the Olympians; goddess of the domestic hearth and fire; a gentle, reserved goddess. She represented the quiet life, home and city. She had no temples in Greece; a house or temple was not considered sanctified until Hestia entered in the form of the hearth flame. Goddess of circles, discipline, dedication to duty, humility, modesty, prudence, acceptance, continuity, service to others.

HORAE—The Hours or Seasons. They were the guardian goddesses of Nature and rain: EUNOMIA (order), DIKE (justice), CARPO (fruit), and IRENE/EIRENE (peace). They ruled law, justice and peace, protected young people.

HYPNOS—He caused sleep by touching the eyelids with his fingers or fanning the person with his dark wings. His three sons were MORPHEUS,[28] PHOEBETOR, and PHANTASUS. It was their job to occupy the sleeper's mind with dreams while the soul traveled. Through dreams they entertained, warned, or punished.

IRIS—Rainbow goddess; HERA'S maid; messenger between the gods and humans; personal messenger of ZEUS. She had golden wings on her shoulders and carried the caduceus. Her sacred place was Delos where she was offered dried figs and cakes of wheat and honey as sacrifices. Now she carries the telepathic communications between the gods and humans.

MOERAE/MOIRAI/THE FATES—Three deities who decided the destiny of each individual. CLOTHOS spun the thread of life, LACHESIS measured it out, and ATROPOS cut it. Lachesis often added good luck which could change the destiny spun by Clothos. NEMESIS could intercede with Atropos to allow a longer life. Often accompanied by the KERES (Dogs of Hades), who were three beings with sharp teeth and robed in red. Invoked at weddings for a happy union.

THE MUSES—Companions of APOLLO; goddesses of springs, memory, and poetry. Their oldest sanctuary was at Pieria in Thrace. There were nine: CLIO (history), EUTERPE (flute playing), THALEIA (comedy), MELPOMENE (tragedy), TERPSICHORE (dancing and lyric poetry), ERATO (love poetry), POLYHYMNIA (mime), URANIA (astronomy), CALLIOPE (epic poetry). Their music was based on the seven-tone musical scale which came from the music of the seven spheres or planets. Willow wands were used to invoke the Muses.

NEMESIS—Also called ADRASTEIA (the inevitable). Shown with a wreath on her head, an apple in her left hand and a bowl in her right. Goddess of destiny, divine anger against mortals who broke moral laws or taboos. She was a harsh, unremitting force representing acceptance of what must be. At times she would intercede with the Fate ATROPOS to allow a longer lifespan.

NEREIDS—A Greek catch-all phrase for fairies, nymphs, mermaids, female Nature spirits. They were shapeshifters. Also the name of the sea nymphs of the Mediterranean; the

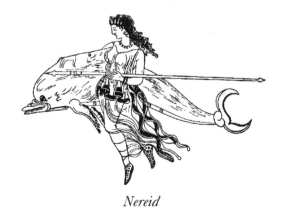

Nereid

50 granddaughters of PONTUS (sea god) and GAEA (Earth mother). They had beautiful fair hair, no fish-tails and accompanied the chariot of POSEIDON. THETIS and GALATEA were nereids.

NEREUS/PROTEUS/PHORCYS—"The old one of the sea"; god of the sea; a shape-shifter. He was a knower of the future, a just and kind god.

NIKE—Goddess of Victory; sister of BIA (violence), ZELOS (jealousy), and KRATOS (force). She was winged and carried a palm branch.

NYMPHS—Female spirits of water, plants, and Earth. The NAIADS were nymphs of brooks, the CRENAE or PEGAE of springs, the LIMNADS of stagnant waters, the OREADS of grottoes and mountains, the DRYADS of forests and trees, the HAMADRYADS of specific trees, and the NAPAEAE, the AULONIADS, the HYLAEO-RAE, and the ALSAEIDS of woods and valleys. They sometimes lived within the waters, sometimes in grottoes nearby. They gave the gift of prophecy and oracles, healed the sick, watched over flowers, fields, and flocks.

OCEANUS/OCEANOS—"He who belongs to the swift queen." An ancient sea god who took part in the creation of Cosmos out of Chaos, and whose power was later given to POSEIDON. The Greeks said that he surrounded the Earth and held his tail in his mouth. Inventor of the arts and magick.

PAN—"Little god"; Horned God; goat-foot god; the Horned One of Nature; very ancient. Horned and hoofed woodland god; one of the oldest in Greece. Shrines, altars, and caves were dedicated to him as late as the first century AD. He was the protector of flocks and the inventor of the syrinx or panpipes. Associated with DIONYSUS. He was called the Positive Life Force of the world. He was the ruler of all Nature spirits, god of male sexuality, animals, fertility, Nature, woodlands, vocal powers, gardening, healing, plants, music, dance, farming, medicine, sooth-saying, flocks, agriculture, bee-keeping, fishing, orchards, gardens. He also had a dark side, causing the wild and unreasoning terror which seizes humankind and animals in lonely woodlands or mountains.

PERSEPHONE—Corn Maiden; "Destroyer"; Queen of the Underworld. Daughter of DEMETER, her name was KORE before she became the wife of HADES. Crone aspect of the Goddess, she held the keys to Elysium and Tartarus. Sacred to her were the bat, willows, grain, corn, narcissus, and the pomegranate. She was pictured carrying a cornucopia. Seldom invoked without Demeter. Goddess of corn, the seasons and the Underworld; rest, winter, the survivor, overcoming obstacles.

POSEIDON—"Earthshaker"; god of the seas and earthquakes; Supreme Lord of the Inner and Outer Seas; Overlord of Lakes and Rivers. He was the god of every-thing that swam in or on water. His golden palace was said to be in the depths of the ocean. Pictured as a mature, bearded man; AMPHITRITE, nereid, was his immortal wife. His mortal wife was CLEITO; their ten sons were made rulers of Atlantis. Horses and bulls were associated with him. He was also master of storms, lakes, and rivers. He used his trident to stir the seas to furious storms and to spear the clouds to release floods. He was turbulent and independent. Invoke

Prometheus stealing the fire

this god when you want feeling but do not want to get caught in emotionalism. Storms, all marine life, intuition, human emotions, sailors, ships, hurricanes, rain, weather, revenge.

PRIAPUS—God of fertility and animals. Shown with an enormous phallus. The sick came to his healing temples for sleep treatment.

PROMETHEUS—"He who foresees"; "Forethought"; the Titan who stole fire from the forge of HEPHAESTUS and gave it to humans. The god of creation and fire.

RHEA—Cretan Universal Mother or Great Goddess; Supreme Queen of Heaven; Great Goddess; the Mother. Goddess of plant life and fertility; inventor of the arts and magick.

SELENE/MENE—The second aspect of the Moon; daughter of HYPERION and THEIA;[29] sister of HELIOS and EOS; Moon Goddess; the Moon as lover and bride. She was pictured as a beautiful woman with a gold crown. Great importance in magick, spells, enchantments.

THEMIS—Titaness daughter of URANUS and GAEA; mother of ATLAS and PROMETHEUS; mother by ZEUS of the HORAE and the MOERAE. Zeus's advisor and respected by all the Olympians. Her temple was in the citadel of Athens, and she carried a pair of scales. She was another form of the Earth Mother, personifying law and order. Her festival was near the end of September. She protected the innocent and punished the guilty. She was the goddess of the collective consciousness and social order, the Law, peace, settlement of disagreements, justice and righteousness, feasts, social gatherings, oath-swearing, wisdom and prophecy, order, childbirth, courts and judges. Inventor of the arts and magick.

TRITONS—Mermen of the Mediterranean, with fish-like tails, scales on the body, sharp fish teeth, and webbed fingers with long claws. They could change the tail to legs and walk on land. Their father was a peaceful, helpful deity who assisted sailors in trouble and caused the seas to calm by blowing on his conch shell. His sons, however, were carousers in seaports, causing all kinds of trouble. It was the duty of the Tritons to harness dolphins to POSEIDON'S chariot and blow conch horns as they swarmed before the Lord of the Ocean.

URANUS/OURANOS—Original Great God; husband of GAEA and father of the twelve divine Olympians. God of the sky and heavens.

ZEUS—Supreme God; Great God; Lord of the Heavens.[30] Pictured wearing a crown of oak leaves and a mantle with his chest and right arm bare; scepter in his left hand and a thunderbolt and eagle at his feet. His sanctuary at Dodona in Epirus contained his sacred oaks and tripods with cauldrons. Oracles were heard by listening to the rustling oak leaves; the cauldrons were struck and the sounds interpreted. His bird was the eagle. He was the protector of laws, justice, and the weak. He never refused genuine supplicants who asked for his aid, but he inflicted terrible punishments on those who offended him. He was god of all high things, clouds, rain, wind, thunder, lightning, mountain tops, wisdom, justice, popularity, the law, honor, riches, friendships, health, luck, the heart's desires.

ENDNOTES

1. For the ingredients that make up Kyphi, see endnote 4 in the chapter on Egypt.

2. *Temples and Sanctuaries of Ancient Greece,* edited by Evi Melas. In the beginning, Gaea ruled at Delphi; she was followed on the oracular throne by her daughter Themis, who in turn was succeeded by Phoebe. This goddess gave Delphi to Apollo as a birthday gift; Aeschylus in the *Eumenides* tells this story. In actual fact, this tale probably was fabricated to placate the people when a patriarchal religion supplanted the matriarchal one. During the time that Gaea was worshipped in Delphi, so was the god Poseidon, not as sea-king, but as the god of springs and earthquakes. Although the inner sanctum of Delphi has not been uncovered at this time, there are many ancient writers who detailed their experiences there and the sanctum's beauty and holiness.

3. In ancient Egyptian history, it was said that the Phoenicians stole two of Amen's oracular priestesses from Thebes, selling one of them to Greece.

4. Frazer in *The Golden Bough* says that the oldest literary manuscript telling of the Demeter-Persephone myth is a Homeric Hymn to Demeter. The main purpose of this hymn was to set down the traditional beginnings of the Eleusinian mysteries by the goddess Demeter.

5. (GAN-ee-meed); "rejoicing in virility"; a beautiful young man who replaced Hebe.

6. (MEET-iss); a Titaness of wisdom.

7. (MY-a); "grandmother of magic."

8. (HEE-bee); goddess of eternal youth. She served nectar and ambrosia to the gods in Olympus until Ganymede arrived. Also the virgin goddess who guarded the golden apples of eternal life in the garden of paradise, or Hesperides.

9. Also called Eileithyia (Eel-EE-thee-a); shown kneeling with a torch. She was the goddess of childbirth and brought both pain and relief.

10. (THEE-tis); lover of Zeus at one time. She married Peleus and became the mother of seven sons, one of whom was Achilles.

11. Food of the Olympian gods. Nectar filled the drinker with poetic inspiration. This food was needed to renew the strength of the ichor in the gods' veins and grant them immortality. This blue ichor was a substitute for blood.

12. Another myth says that Zeus threw Hephaestus out of Olympia and crippled him when the smith-god tried to protect his mother, Hera.

13. "Strong"; a winged, white, magnificent stallion with golden wings. He dug a well (the Hippocrene, or "horse well") for the Muses; its waters gave poetic inspiration.

14. (KORE-ee); "girl"; daughter of the Earth; she took the name of Persephone after her marriage to Hades. The pentacle, which can be seen in an apple core, was her symbol.

15. "Moon Women." From a Greek word *amazos* meaning "ample-breasted." They did not amputate the right breast as some writers speculate. (See further descriptions of the Amazons in the chapter on the Middle East. B. Walker in *The Woman's Encyclopedia of Myths and Secrets* also has an entry on Amazons.) Their society near the Black Sea was a matriarchy ruled by an elected queen. Children were conceived by annual visits to neighboring tribes; the girls were kept, the boys returned to the father. Strictly worshippers of the Great Mother. They used a Moon-sickle for rituals and battle, as they did the labrys, or double-bladed ax. The labrys was used by women in ceremonies, agricultural work, and battle. Its two blades represented the waxing and waning Moon crescents. See *The Great Cosmic Mother* by Sjoo and Mor.

16. The huntress aspect of this goddess was another form of the Crone or waning Moon. Her priestess wore dog-masks; the Greeks called her Scythian devotees Alani, or "hunting dogs."

17. (High-GEE-a); her features show a possible African origin. Symbol was the caduceus. She was shown with a boa constrictor and was the goddess of women physicians in her temples.

18. (Pan-a-SEE-a); her symbol was the caduceus.

19. He was served by a eunuch priesthood, the Galloi.

20. When Demeter rested at Eleusus during her search, she instructed Queen Metaneira to build a great temple. In return, the goddess taught the Queen the sacred rites that should be performed there. *The Triple Goddess* by A. McLean.

21. Semele, the mother of Dionysus, insisted that Zeus reveal himself to her in his true form. She was destroyed by the god's brilliance. The child she carried was rescued by Zeus and enclosed in his thigh until time to be born. Dionysus was raised in Thrace, suckled by goats and tended by satyrs. *Mystery Religions in the Ancient World* by J. Godwin. In *The Triple Goddess*, McLean says that the Horae were present at Dionysus' birth.

22. (MEEN-adds); originally they were priestesses of Dionysus. Their name comes from their original home, the holy mountain of Maenalus, where Pan also lived.

23. (SEN-tors); they had a human male head, arms, and chest, with the legs and bottom half of the body like a horse. Some were lecherous carousers, while others were skilled teachers. Their allegiance was only to Eros and Dionysus. Magic shape-shifters and teachers of the gods.

24. (SATE-irs or SAT-irs); sometimes described as young men with the ears and tail of a horse; other times as having the body, arms, and sex organs of men and the legs, hooves, and tails of goats. They loved music, dancing, women, and wine; extremely amorous mischief-makers. If you call upon their aid, you must use absolutely no drugs, alcohol, or stimulants. Use their aid to gain control of your lower self and a clearer idea of your cosmic role.

25. These three women were sometimes described as having snaky hair, clawlike fingernails, bloodshot eyes, and wearing long black robes. In later Greek mythology, they were portrayed as huntress-garbed, with snakes in their hair and scourges or sickles in their hands. *The Triple Goddess* by A. McLean.

26. Shades of the dead entered the Underworld by crossing the River Styx on the ferry; Charon (KA-ron), the ferryman who rowed the spirits across the River Styx for a fee of one obol, was pictured as a white-haired old man with fiery eyes and dressed in a hooded cloak. Styx means "shuddery" or "that which is taboo." The shades then had to cross four more rivers. When they came to the River Lethe, they drank and forgot their lives on Earth. Anyone wanting to remember previous incarnations had to endure great thirst, pass by, and drink from the spring of Memory. Next came the three-headed monster dog Cerberus (SIR-ber-us); he allowed people in but resisted anyone trying to leave. After all this, the dead stood before three terrible judges who decided their eternal fates. All who committed unnatural crimes were tormented forever by the Erinyes. Other sinners were thrown into the Rivers of Woe, Wailing, or Flame. The majority, who were neither good not bad, were sent to wander the bleak plains covered with the black lilies of asphodel. The blessed and virtuous ones went to the Elysian Fields. The River Acheron was created when the gods won the war against the Titans. Acheron has four tributaries: Styx, the River of Hate; Phlegethon, the River of Flames; Cocytus, the River of Wailing; Lethe, the River of Forgetfulness. The Acheron and its tributaries run in seven concentric circles within the underworld and divide it into Tartarus, the Plain of Asphodel, and the Elysian Fields. The shades of the dead have to cross all five rivers on their way to the underworld. The Greeks believed that

if a mortal bathed in the Styx and found his way back to Earth, he was invulnerable to manmade weapons. But if he swallowed any of the water, it would kill him. The gods, however, drank the waters of the Styx when binding solemn oaths.

27. Hera received the tree of golden apples as a wedding gift from Gaea. The tree was placed in the sacred orchard on Mount Atlas. *The Triple Goddess* by A. McLean.

28. (MORF-yoos); god of dreams; nephew of Thanatos, the god of death, who dressed in black robes and carried a sword.

29. (THEE-ya); a Titaness and mother of Selene, Helios, and Eos; also called Tethys. She symbolized the principle of light.

30. Four of his word-titles were descriptions of this god's other attributes. Keraunos (lightning) shows his connection with the weather, Katachthonios (the subterranean one) with the underworld, Meelichios (the gentle one) as a judge, and Eleutherios as the guardian of freedom.

Bibliography

Angus, S. *The Mystery-Religions.* NY: Dover Publications, 1975.

Bolen, Jean Shinoda. *Goddesses in Every Woman.* NY: Harper & Row, 1985.

Briggs, Katherine M. *Pale Hecate's Team.* UK: Routledge & Kegan Paul, 1962.

Budpest, Z. *The Holy Book of Women's Mysteries.* Oakland, CA: Susan B. Anthony Coven No. 1, 1979.

Bury, J. B. *History of Greece.* NY: Macmillan, 1956.

Ceram, C. W. *Gods, Graves and Scholars.* NY: Bantam Books, 1972.

Cumont, Franz. *Astrology and Religion Among the Greeks and Romans.* NY: Dover Publications, 1960.

Dickinson, Patrick, trans. *The Aeneid.* NY: New American Library, 1961.

Evans, Cheryl, and Millard, Anne. *Usborne Illustrated Guide to Greek Myths and Legends.* Tulsa, OK: EDC Publishing, 1986.

Fitzgerald, Robert, trans. *The Iliad.* NY: Doubleday & Co., 1974.

Fitzgerald, Robert, trans. *The Odyssey.* NY: Doubleday & Co., 1961.

Frazer, James G. *Adonis, Attis, Osiris.* NY: University Books, 1961.

Gayley, Charles Mills. *The Classic Myths in English Literature and in Art.* NY: Ginn & Co., 1939.

Godwin, Joscelyn. *Mystery Religions in the Ancient World.* NY: Harper & Row, 1981.

Gray, William G. *Evoking the Primal Goddess.* St. Paul, MN: Llewellyn Publications, 1989.

Herzberg, Max J. *Myths and Their Meaning.* Boston, MA: Allyn & Bacon, 1928.

Hope, Thomas. *Costumes of the Greeks and Romans.* NY: Dover Publications, 1962.

Jung, Carl J., and Kerenyi, C. *The Myth of the Divine Child.* Princeton, NJ: Princeton University Press, 1973.

Knight, Gareth. *The Rose Cross and the Goddess.* NY: Destiny Books, 1985.

La Fontaine, J. S. *Initiation: Ritual Drama and Secret Knowledge Across the World.* UK: Penguin Books, 1985.

MacKendrick, Paul. *The Greek Stones Speak.* NY: New American Library, 1966.

McLean, Adam. *The Triple Goddess: An Exploration of the Archetypal Feminine.* Grand Rapids, MI: Phanes Press, 1989.

Melas, Evi, ed. *Temples and Sanctuaries of Ancient Greece.* London: Thames & Hudson, 1973.

Mestel, Sherry, ed. *Earth Rites,* 2 vol. Brooklyn, NY: Earth Rites Press, 1981.

Mireaux, Emile. *Daily Life in the Time of Homer.* NY: Macmillan, 1959.

Mylonas, George. *Eleusis and the Elusinean Mysteries.* NJ: Princeton University Press, 1961.

Patrick, Richard. *All Color Book of Greek Mythology.* UK: Octopus Books, 1972.

Pomeroy, Sarah B. *Goddesses, Whores, Wives and Slaves.* NY: Schocken Books, 1975.

Quennell, Marjorie, and C.H.B. *Everyday Things in Ancient Greece.* NY: G.P. Putnam's Sons, 1957.

Robinson, C. E. *Everyday Life in Ancient Greece.* UK: Oxford Press, 1958.

Simpson, Colin. *Greece: The Unclosed Eye.* NY: Wm. Morrow & Co., 1968.

Spretnak, Charlene. *Lost Goddesses of Early Greece.* Berkeley, CA: Moon Books, 1978.

Vandenberg, Philipp. *The Mystery of the Oracles.* NY: Macmillan Publishing, 1982.

Warner, Rex. *The Stories of the Greeks.* NY: Farrar, Straus & Giroux, 1967.

Weed, Joseph. *Complete Guide to Oracle and Prophecy Methods.* West Nyack, NY: Parker Publishing, 1971.

Zimmerman, J. E. *Dictionary of Classical Mythology.* NY: Bantam Books, 1978.

CHAPTER TWELVE

ROME

THE ROMAN culture was of a much later origin than that of the Greeks. However, some writers think that the Romans may have been an early branch of Greek culture, which split off and went its own way; this theory could account for the similar pantheon of deities. We do know there were numerous Greek colonies in southern Italy. In fact, the region's connections with Greece go back to the thirteenth century BC. Even today there are more Doric temples in this region and in Sicily than are standing in Greece itself.[1]

Before these predecessors of the Romans arrived, there were immigrations of peoples from North Africa by way of Spain and from Asia Minor. The mysterious Etruscans were of these latter peoples.

About the eighth century BC, the tribes living on the original Seven Hills of Rome were united under the Etruscans, who dominated until late in the sixth century BC. At that time the Romans overthrew their conquerors and established their civilization, first under kings, then as a republic. Rome became one of the ancient world's largest and most prosperous empires before the decline in the late sixth century AD.

Traditionally, Roman history is divided into a Regal Period, when ruled by kings (753–509 BC); a Republican Period (509–27 BC); and an Imperial Period (27 BC–AD 476). The Imperial division is further divided into the Principate (27 BC–AD 285) and the Late Empire (AD 285–476).

The Romans learned early that conquer and rule worked better than mere self-defense of their existing territory. They annexed all Italy to their original Tiber settlements, then went on to conquer as far as Britain, Egypt, some of the Middle East, and the Balkans. They developed from farmer-warriors to conquerors, providing an excellent system of laws and organization. They made vast networks of roads, architectural advances and improvements, water and sewer systems, and were great patrons of the arts.

All religions were welcome within the Roman system, providing the ceremonies were not too gross, disruptive, or against the Roman pantheon of gods and goddesses. This policy continued, with worship of Isis forbidden for only a time and the Bacchanals broken up in 186 BC. When the Christians began their destructive rampages against temples, disrupting ceremonies and defacing property, the Romans took stern measures against them, outlawing the religion and killing many of the followers. It proved to be too little, too late; they could not entirely stop the unrest and rioting of the Christians, who seemed to have forgotten the precepts of their founder. Shortly after this, barbarians overran the Empire, plunging it into chaos and a time of darkness. Rome never recovered her former greatness.

RELIGION

The Romans readily accepted new gods/goddesses if they could be identified with an already existing Roman deity. A Roman's dealings with the gods were of a practical nature. He either wanted to avoid their ill will, or enlist their active support for definite material blessings. He offered sacrifices with the idea of getting some benefit in return. Roman religion was basically a family and home-oriented religion, as is seen in the worship of the goddess Vesta and the deep respect given to her priestesses.

Janus, Jupiter, Mars, Quirinus, and Vesta were considered by the Romans to be superior deities. Temples were raised to moral and civic qualities: Honor, Hope, Good Faith, Modesty, Concord, Youth, Public Safety, Peace, Victory, Liberty, and Fame.

The oldest Roman rites go back to a time before temples were built in Italy. These were probably processions and rituals held in the open, most likely in cultivated fields. These rituals consisted of purification ceremonies, blessing of the boundaries and animals, petitions for rich crops and the health of families, slaves, and livestock.

The use of *carmina*, or spell-casting, was forbidden early on if used negatively against another person. In Latin, carmina means a song or charm. In his Odes Horace describes his work as carmina; Virgil used the word in the same manner. The goddess Circe is said to have changed the companions of Ulysses into pigs by the use of a song or carmina. In the 5th century BC, Roman law specifically forbade the singing of carmina against anyone.[2] However, it was permissible to use carmina to increase abundance of a crop or business ventures.

The 15 Pontifices, their head being the Pontifex Maximus, controlled the State religion. They decided all religious matters, could discipline lesser priests, and made all rules for public worship, feasts, and sacrifices. The second strong order were the 16

Service in the temple of Vesta

Augurs, who interpreted omens, dreams, and oracles, and gave prophecies. The Augurs could carry the *lituus* (crooked staff) and wear the embroidered *toga praetexta*.

There were also 15 Flamines, actual priests, distributed among the various gods; the greatest of these was the Flamen of Jupiter. The priestesses of Carmenta cast fortunes of children at their birth. Twelve lesser priests of Mars were responsible for the twelve holy shields of his temple. The Haruspices, or Auspices, helped the Augurs interpret signs in the sacrifices. Six Vestal Virgins kept the Temple of Vesta. The famous sacred books of Oracles had 15 Keepers of the Sibylline Books.

There were about 45 Roman festivals each year. Temple sacrifices were accompanied by the music of pipes and harps. The animal to be sacrificed was decorated with flowers and ribbons, and sometimes with gilded horns. The entrails were examined by the Auspices for omens. The choicest parts were sprinkled with meal, wine, and incense, and burned on the altar. Frankincense was burned in braziers of charcoal. Lamps were small, flat, pitcher-like vessels with handles, spout, and wick; olive oil was burned in them.

The Dies Fasti were the lucky days each month when business could be done. The Dies Nefasti were the unlucky days when no business or sacrifices were done. There were three important days each month: Kalends on the first, Nones on the fifth, and the Ides on the thirteenth days. The exceptions were in March, May, July, and October when the Nones were on the seventh and the Ides on the fifteenth days.

The Lares and Penates were the guardian spirits of the private households, the Penates being guardians of the food supplies and the hearth, the Lar being in charge of the house and crossroads. Each house had a *lararium*, or shrine of the household gods. Here incense was burned, and oblations were poured into a special dish.

The Public Lares were the spirits of the gallant patriots. The Public Penates were the immortal "Twin Brethren," Castor and Pollux.

There was an annual festival called Mania for the ancestral Moon-mother. During this time the Lapis Manalis, or Stone of the Underworld or of the dead, was removed and spirits of the ancestors invited to join the feasts. This stone covered the pit of the manes located on Rome's Palatine Hill. Not much is known of this festival except that it was sometimes called Parentalia; this since the ghosts of the Underworld were considered to be the parent-ancestors of the Romans.

The month of Januarius had the festival of the important god Janus. Februarius was the month of ceremonial purification and was dedicated to Februus, later identified with Dis, the Latin Pluto. The City was purified by appeasing the dead with offerings and sacrifices called februalia. February 15 was the Lupercalia for protection of the flocks. On February 23, the boundary stones between neighbors were the scene of sacrifices to Terminus, the god of boundaries.

In Marius, the month of Mars, the Salii, or 12 leaping priests of Mars, performed an ancient dance with the holy shields *(ancilia)* to invoke both Mars and Saturn. This was to drive out evil spirits that might have entered the City during the winter and to stimulate crop growth.

Aprilis was the month of unfolding leaves and flowers. The Parilia, in honor of Pales, a very ancient country spirit, was held on April 21 (the founding day of Rome). Worshippers leaped over fires of straw and drove their herds through the fires. April 23 was the Vinalia for protection of the vines, and two days later the evil Robigus was propitiated.

Maius, sacred to Maia, the goddess of summer warmth, was the time of the Ambarvalia. This was a family crop festival for purification and protection of farm land. After a procession went three times around the fields, sacrifices and prayers were made to Mars and Ceres. On the fifteenth at the festival called the Fordicidia, a pregnant cow was sacrificed to Tellus, the Earth goddess. On the nineteenth, the Cerealis occurred.

On May 14 or 15, a solemn procession went through the city of Rome to collect straw dolls that had been placed in 27 of the city's chapels in March. These dolls were thrown into the Tiber by the pontiffs, the Vestals, and the praetors as offerings to the river god.

Junius was sacred to Juno and therefore was considered a lucky month for marriages. This was the time of the cleansing of the *penus* (a sacred vessel) in the Temple of Vesta by the Vestal Virgins.

Julius, originally called Quintilis, was renamed in honor of Julius Caesar. Julius Caesar claimed he was a descendant of Iulus, son of Aeneas, the founder of the Roman state, and Romulus and Remus, sons of Mars, and founders of the city of Rome. Romulus, after his disappearance, was worshipped by the name of Quirinus.

Augustus, originally called Sextilis, was renamed in honor of Augustus Caesar. In August special festivals were held for the gathered harvests. The most important of these was the Consualia on the twenty-first, with sacrifices to the underground god of the storehouse, Consus. The festival of Volcanalia was held on August 23 to ward off accidental fires; this was done outside the city boundaries.

Septem was the seventh month on the oldest Roman calendar, as Octem was the eighth month. On October 15, there was another purification of the City.

Decem, the tenth month on the old calendar, was the season of the Saturnalia (a time of gift giving) on the seventeenth, a second Consualia on the fifteenth, and the Opalia on the nineteenth, all agricultural festivals.

Dress and Ornamentation

The Romans thought it important to have good clothes and rings; these could be rented for special occasions if one didn't own them. The toga was a national garment worn only by Roman citizens. The toga was a very long rectangular cloth, draped and wrapped so no brooches were necessary. Freed slaves could wear it; banished Romans could not.

At a child's birth, the father hung a gold *bulla* (a type of locket) around the child's neck if he accepted the baby. A boy wore the bulla until he was old enough to become a citizen, around the age of fourteen or sixteen; then he offered it to the house *lares*. This ceremony was held on the Liberalia on March 17, if possible. A girl gave her bulla to the lares on the eve of her wedding.

Men wore shorts or a loincloth under the tunic. The tunica was ankle-length with short sleeves and belted, the excess length being bloused over the girdle-belt. An *eques* (horse soldier) had a narrow purple strip on the tunic, a senator a broad strip. Over the tunic, when outdoors or on business, the toga of white wool was worn. The toga had to be worn with shoes; sandals were worn only at home or while riding in a litter. For mourning, a dark colored toga was acceptable. Younger men often wore a light mantle *(lacerna)* over the toga, with a hood to conceal the face. Only one plain gold ring was considered the mark of a gentleman, although signet rings were worn by both sexes.

The Roman woman wore an undertunic and a stola, with a scarf or shawl *(palla)* when outdoors. Either over or under the tunic she had a sash to support the breasts. The stola had sleeves formed by the width of the garment over the shoulders; these were pinned together by small brooches. The extra length of the stola was bloused up over the belt at the waist. The lower edge had crimson or purple (for noble women) as a border and at the neck.

During hot weather, shawls, scarves, and veils were of thin material. Women's street shoes and sandals were of soft leather, either white, gilded, or bright colors, sometimes decorated with pearls. Parasols and fans were widely used, along with balls of amber or glass to keep the palms dry and cool. Long, straight hairpins were of ivory, silver, or gold. Stones used in jewelry were onyx, banded agate, amethyst, ruby, sapphire, and pearl.

Women's hair styles often changed, but the hair was never cut. Young girls wore their hair bound in coils or in clusters of curls. Older women wore high mounds of ringlets or plaits. Bleaches and dyes were sold, as well as wigs. Hair ornaments were pins; combs of metal, fine boxwood, ivory, or tortoise shell; snoods and wimples of scarlet, amethystine, or ivory; diadem chains set with pearls and jewels; hair nets of gold thread.

Perfumes were dissolved in olive oil and often turned rancid in a short time. Little shops that sold scented powders, oils, perfumes, and unguents in fancy jars were found everywhere. These shops were usually run by women.

SOME OF THE MYTHS

The twelve great Olympian deities of Greece were adopted by the Romans. Some authorities think this was because the Greeks and Romans may have been part of one band of people in the distant past. The Roman names of these deities were Jupiter (Zeus), Juno (Hera), Neptune (Poseidon), Vesta (Hestia), Mars (Ares), Minerva (Athene), Venus (Aphrodite), Mercury (Hermes), Diana (Artemis), Vulcan (Hephaestus), Ceres (Demeter). Two kept their Greek names: Apollo and Pluto, who was never called Hades by the Romans. Bacchus, also called Liber, was the wine god.

Some historians say that the Roman deities, before they merged with those of the Greeks, were vague, simply called the Numina—the Powers or the Wills—"those that are above." The original Numina had no myths attached to them. In fact, they were not even listed as male or female. A few of the Numina had no Greek counterparts: the Lares, the Penates, Terminus, Pales, Sylvanus, and Janus. However it came about, the Romans were deeply religious people. But they were also practical people who wanted useful gods.

Two myths were of Roman origin, or at least of Roman reconstruction: Romulus and Remus, and Castor and Pollux. The gods of the family were distinctly Roman: the Genius, the Penates, and the Lares.

The god Mars raped the Vestal, Rhea Silvia, while she slept, thus bringing into life twin sons, Romulus and Remus. For a Vestal to break her vows of chastity, even if forced, meant death. The Vestal Rhea Silvia was drowned in the Tiber. The babies were put into a winnowing basket and cast into the river. However, the river overflowed, leaving the basket in a safe place under a fig tree at the grotto Lupercal. A she-wolf found and nursed the babies who were later discovered and raised by a shepherd, Faustulus, and his wife Acca Larentia.

When Romulus and Remus were grown, they decided to found a city. First they carefully studied the flights of birds for omens. In Romulus's section of sky, he saw twelve vultures; Remus saw only six. Romulus harnessed a white cow and bull to a plough and made a furrow to mark his new city's boundaries on the banks of the Tiber River. The brothers then began to argue over a name for the new city, each wishing to name it after himself. Romulus killed Remus in combat.

Romulus now had his city but no inhabitants. He established the city as a place of refuge, where outlawed men from other communities could live. His neighbors did not like this situation and refused to allow their daughters to marry with these new upstarts. Romulus thought of a solution; he waited until the joyous festival of Consualia, then he and his men abducted the daughters of the Sabine tribe during the celebrations. The fathers gathered an army and advanced on Rome, but the daughters, now reconciled to their new husbands, begged them to make peace. The Sabines and the Romans did so by forming a single nation, over which Romulus ruled for 37 years.

In later years, Romulus mysteriously disappeared during a storm. Legend says that he was taken up to heaven in a fiery chariot by his father Mars. Both Mars and Romulus became identified with the name Quirinus and were sometimes worshipped under that name.

Roman concept of the founders of the race: Aeneas and Agamememnon

Some myths say that Castor and Pollux were Greek; but the Etruscans knew them as Kastur and Poltuke. Wherever their origin, the Romans made a definite claim to the Heavenly Twins. In 496 BC, the Roman dictator Aulus Posthumius was fighting against Latium at Lake Regillus. At that time Castor and Pollux were honored at Tusculum, an enemy of Rome's. The dictator promised the Heavenly Twins a great temple in Rome itself if they aided him. Within seconds, Castor and Pollux were seen at the head of the Roman cavalry, leading a victorious charge. That same evening the people of Rome saw two young men in purple chlamydes watering their horses at the fountain of Juturna in the Forum. This was the Heavenly Twins' way of announcing the Roman victory and that they had come to Rome to stay. Posthumius built a magnificent temple to them as he had promised. After that it was common to see them with the Roman cavalry during battles or calming storms at sea for Roman ships. Once, at Ostia, they quieted a terrible storm that was preventing shiploads of corn from entering the harbor.

One of the bravest men in the Trojan War was Aeneas,[3] son of Venus by a mortal, Anchises. The Romans traced their descent from him. In Virgil's *Aeneid* is told the story of how Aeneas escaped from Troy and was guided by a dream to seek a land in the west called Hesperia. He and his companions made their way to Italy where Aeneas founded the state of Latium.[4]

The Genius and the Penates were two classes of specific Roman deities. The Genius was the creative force affecting each individual's development; it came in at the birth and departed at death. If a child was male, the spirit was a Genius; if female, a Juno. These spirits had many helpers: Nundina for purification; Vaticanus for the first cry; Educa and Potina for learning to eat and drink; Cuba for keeping the child quiet; Ossipago and Carna for bodily development; Abeona and Adeona for walking; Sentinus for developing mentally, etc. The Genius of the head of a family was pictured as a man in a toga. His statue was placed between the Penates and the Lar with the Juno of the wife.

The Penates, whose name comes from *penus*, or storage room for food, were the overseers of food and drink. They shared the family's joys and sorrows, and were often called *dii* or *divi*, a name not used for the Genius or the Lar. There were always two Penates; they shared the hearth altar with Vesta. Their images stood before the Genius at the back of the atrium. At every meal they were offered the first of the food.

Lar was an Etruscan word meaning chief or prince. They were found among the beliefs of the Romans, Sabines, and Etruscans in ancient times. At first they were protectors of agriculture with Consus and Mars. Later, their functions and worship differed little from the Penates. They received similar homage at the hearth altar. At festive occasions, they were decorated with garlands and offered fruit and wine. There was only one Lar to a family, symbolizing the house, and pictured as a curly-haired youth, dancing in a short tunic; over his head he held a *rhyton* (drinking horn). He was invoked on all important family occasions: departures, marriages, funerals.

MAJOR GODS AND GODDESSES

APOLLO—"Shining"; god of the Sun. He used the bow and lyre with skill. His arrows brought illness or death. He was bisexual, pointing to the possibility that originally he may have been a goddess. He drove a four-horse chariot *(quadriga)* through the sky. He first came to Rome in the fifth century BC following an outbreak of plague. He represented lawful punishment of crime, not revenge; justified revenge. God of prophecy, music, healing, medicine, oracles, reason, inspiration, the arts, magick.

ASKLEPIOS—Similar to the Greek AESCULAPIUS; god of healing; son of APOLLO.

Apollo

BACCHUS/LIBER/LIBER PATER—Similar to DIONYSUS; consort of LIBERA. Called the Liberator, he carried a pine cone tipped *thyrsus* and sometimes rode a panther. He was shown accompanied by goat-foot satyrs, centaurs, and crazed female Bacchantes. He was honored on March 17 in the Liberalia, when boys put on the toga of manhood. At his other festivals people wore masks, sang crude songs, and indulged in unrestrained good times. The everyoung god of wine, good times, ecstasy, fertility, wild Nature.

BELLONA—Goddess of war; her temple in Rome was near the gate of Carmenta. In front of the temple was a "war column" which was struck ceremonially with a javelin when war was declared. Her festivals were March 24 and June 3.

BONA DEA—"Good Goddess"; fertility goddess worshipped only by women. During her rites, statues of men were covered. Her festivals were the night of May 3–4 and December 3.

THE CARMENAE—Similar to the MUSES. ANTEVORTA knew the past; POSTVORTA knew the future; EGERIA foretold the fate of new babies; CARMENTA knew prophecies in general and gave the alphabet.

CASTOR and POLLUX—Heavenly Twins; they rode winged horses and had influence over victories, commerce, weights and measures.

Faunus

CERES—Corn goddess; Eternal Mother; the Sorrowing Mother; "Grain Mother." Connected with GAEA and ISIS. She instituted the Eleusinian Mysteries. DEMETER, CERES, KORE and KORE-PROSERPINE or KORE-PERSEPHONE are aspects of one goddess. Her festival, the Cerealis, was celebrated April 19. Crops, initiation, civilization, lawgiver, protectress of women, motherhood, marriage.

CUPID—God of love; son of VENUS.

DIANA—Goddess of the wildwood, lady of beasts; Moon goddess. Goddess of mountains, woods, women, childbirth. Her title "Queen of Heaven" was the Roman name for the Triple Goddess; as the Roman Triple Goddess, her aspects were the Lunar Virgin, Mother of Creatures and the Huntress or Destroyer.[5] Her festivals were May 26–31 and August 13 and 15. Her animals were the dog and stag.

DIS PATER—See PLUTO.

FAUNA—Consort of FAUNUS. Also called BONA DEA and closely related to MAIA. She was a fertility goddess honored with a mysterious festival at the beginning of December. This festival was forbidden to men and ended in an orgy.

FAUNS—Roman satyrs; Latin rural deities with horns, pointed ears, beards, and tails. They accompanied BACCHUS and represented intense sexuality and fertility.

FAUNUS—Similar to PAN, he was a rustic god, also called LUPERCUS. "Little God"; Horned God; goat-foot god; the Horned One of Nature; very ancient. On February 15 the Lupercalia honored him with sacrifices of goats. The priests of his temple performed the rites naked. Protector of flocks and agriculture, bee-keeping, fishing, orchards, gardens, animals, fertility, Nature, woodlands, music, dance, farming, medicine, soothsaying; the positive Life Force of the world. He also had Pan's dark side, seizing men and animals with wild and unreasoning terror in high and lonely places.

FORTUNA/FORS/FORS FORTUNA—She was the goddess of Fate in all its unknown qualities. Her symbols were the wheel, the sphere, the ship's rudder and prow, the cornucopia. She ruled oracles, fate, chance; protectress of women married only once. Sometimes she was pictured with wings.

HECATE—The Crone; snake goddess; queen of the Underworld or world of spirits; Moon goddess; Lady of the Wild Hunt; goddess of witchcraft. A three-faced image represented her triple aspects; she was then called TRIFORMIS. Patroness of dark magick, priestesses, charms and spells, vengeance, expiations, riches, enchantments, victory, wisdom, purification, prosperity, ends, destruction, choices.

HERCULES—A deified hero, demigod, culture hero, symbolizing strength and courage, wine, women, superhuman strength; he protected travelers.

JANUS—Essentially a Roman god as he had no counterparts. Called JANUS PATER, god of gods, he came before even JUPITER. He was honored on the first day of every month; Januarius was named for him. He was pictured as a bearded older man with two faces or heads, each looking in opposite directions. His two faces represented past wisdom and future knowledge, all thing which had a sense of beginning and ending. God of good beginnings, doorways, journeys, public gates, departure and return, harbors, communications, navigation, daybreak, victory, endings, success, the seasons.

JUNO—Sister consort of JUPITER; most important primitive goddess.[6] Moon goddess; Queen of Heaven; "Lady"; Earth goddess; "She who warns"; Great Mother; protectress of women in general. Geese and peacock were sacred to her. Sometimes she held a scepter, thunderbolt, patera, veil, or spear and shield. Her festivals were the Matronalia at Kalends of March, June 1–2, and July 7–8. Protectress of marriage, the home, and childbirth. Light, women's fertility, the Moon, renewal, purification, the sky, death, pain, punishment.

JUPITER—"The smiter"; "Best and greatest"; "Stayer"; Supreme God; Great God; Lord of the heavens; sky god. He was invoked before any military actions, and portions of war booty were given to him. A warrior god but protector of youth. Protector of the laws, justice, and the weak. Lord of all high things, clouds, rain, wind, thunder, mountain tops, lightning. God of the Elements, agriculture, honor, riches, friendships, health, luck, the heart's desires, protection, light.

Janus

LAVERNA and SUMMANUS—Deities of thieves and impostors.

LUNA—The second aspect of the Moon; the Moon as lover and bride. Enchantments, love spells.

MAIA—Goddess of fertility; month of May named after her.

Mars

MARS—God of war and agriculture; god of spring. Originally Mars was an Etruscan fertility-savior MARIS; he was worshiped at a shrine in the Apennines.[7] He was pictured as bearded with a cuirass and helmet. He was considered important because he was the father of ROMULUS and REMUS. Sacrifices to him took place in his month of March, thus making it a dangerous time of the year.[8] Sacred to him were the woodpecker, horse, wolf, oak, laurel, dogwood, and the bean. War, terror, anger, revenge, courage.

MERCURY/MERCURIUS—As the messenger of the gods, he carried the caduceus and wore a broad hat and winged sandals; he also carried a purse in one hand. He invented the lyre, boxing, and racing. Commerce, transport, thievery, cunning, success, magick, travel, profits, gambling, mischief, crossroads, athletes, eloquence, merchants, messages.

MINERVA—Virgin warrior goddess. Maiden Goddess; goddess of women's rights and freedom. She was especially worshiped by guilds of artisans, artists, and professional men, flute players, schools, doctors. She was honored with MARS during five days at the spring equinox. She wore a helmet and breastplate and carried a spear. Sacred bird was the owl. Patroness of craftsmen, especially smiths, weavers, and spinners. Protection, writing, music, the sciences, sculptors, potters, architects, wisdom, arts and skills, renewal, prudence, wise counsel, peace, embroidery, horses and oxen, snakes, pillars, trees, medicine, war, schools.

NEPTUNE—Sea god; protector against drought. On July 23 he was honored in the Neptunalia. He carried a trident and whip. The sea, ships, earthquakes, horses, bulls, lakes, storms, rivers, fishermen.

OPS—A harvest helper, her festival was the Opalia on December 19. She was invoked by sitting down and touching the Earth with one hand. Goddess of the harvest, wealth, success.

PLUTO/DIS PATER—The Etruscans called him FEBRUUS; Februarius was named for him. God of death and the Underworld. Altars to him were rare although he was also a god of riches.

PROSERPINA/LIBITINA—Grain Maiden; goddess of corn, the seasons, and the Underworld; consort of PLUTO. Sacred to her were the bat and the pomegranate. Goddess of rest, the winter, the survivor, overcoming obstacles.

SATURN—Old god; similar to CRONUS.[9] Father Time; the Old King; Father of the Gods; the Great Lesson-Giver; Ruler of the Golden Age. His Saturnalia, beginning

Vulcan

December 17 and lasting seven days, was a period of unrestrained festivities. He was pictured with a half-bare chest and a sickle or ears of corn in his hand; his consort was the goddess OPS. God of abundance and agriculture, Earth's riches, prosperity, karmic lesson-learning, vines.

SATYR—Youthful male companion of BACCHUS with pointed ears but a human figure. Dressed in panther skins and carried a flute. Sometimes pictured with goat feet.

TELLUS MATER—An ancient Earth goddess; shown as a woman with children, fruit, flowers, and a swan. Fertility, marriage, children, fruitfulness of the soil.

VENUS—Moon goddess; patroness of vegetation and flowers. She was strong, proud, and loving. She was called virginal, meaning that she remained independent; her priestesses were not physical virgins.[10] Her sacred birds were the heron and dove. She had a place in the Floralia (April 28–May 3) and in the Vinalia Rustica on August 9. Another festival was June 24. Goddess of love, beauty, and the joy of physical love, fertility, continued creation, renewal, herbal magick.

VERTUMNUS—God of the returning seasons and Earth fertility. "Changer"; shape-shifter. He was venerated with the god of the Tiber, because he altered the course of the river. Fruit trees, fertility, changes.

VESTA—"The shining one"; "one of Light." Her priestesses were the Vestal Virgins who kept the sacred fire of Rome always burning. Six Vestals of good family background served her for thirty years, coming into her service when they were between seven and ten years old. Her priestesses offered no blood sacrifices. If a Vestal chanced to meet a condemned man, he was set free. Hearth and fire goddess; goddess of domestic and ceremonial fires. Her festival was Vestalia on June 7.

VULCAN/VOLCANUS—The Divine Smith; a tough practical craftsman.[11] He was worshipped outside the City on August 23 during the Vulcanalia, on August 17 at the festival of the Portunalia, and again on August 27 at the Volturnalia. Shown as bearded with a short tunic and hat, he was the consort of MAIA, mother of springs and an Earth goddess. Near him he kept a hammer, tongs, and anvil. God of the Sun, thunderbolt, fire, battles, blacksmiths, thunder, volcanoes, craftsmen, jewelry making, mechanics. A magician of metal and gems.

Endnotes

1. Perowne, Stewart. *Roman Mythology.* Perowne says that this area of Italy was actually known as Magna Graecia, or Great Greece.
2. This is listed in the Twelve Tables, the earliest known Roman code of law.
3. Goodrich, Norma Lorre, *Ancient Myths,* has an excellent readable version of the story of Aeneas. So does *Mythology* by Edith Hamilton.
4. Herzberg, Max J. *Myths and Their Meaning.* Aeneas married Livinia and named a city after her—Lavinium. His son Ascanius or Iulus was said to be the ancestor of Julius Caesar.
5. Walker, Barbara. *The Women's Encyclopedia of Myths and Secrets.* Walker says that Roman towns all over Europe called their local mother goddess Diana, which the Christians later changed to Madonna.
6. Walker, Barbara. Ibid. The name Juno comes from the Sabine-Etruscan Uni, or yoni. The Romans said that each woman held a piece of the Goddess' spirit within her; this was called her *juno,* or soul.
7. Walker, Barbara. Ibid. "Red" Mars is quite similar to the Indo-European Vedic god Rudra; it is possible that there was a cultural connection in the distant past.
8. This festival most likely took place on the Ides of March. March was also the beginning of the Roman year.
9. Gayley, Charles M. *The Classic Myths in English Literature and in Art.* Some mythologists say that Saturn and Cronus are the same god, but there is ample evidence that Saturn was strictly a Roman deity with a few similarities to the Greek god. For instance, the Greeks did not celebrate the festival of Saturnalia as did the Romans.
10. The Roman Venus was definitely a goddess of sexual activity, not necessarily having anything to do with marriage. Her temples housed sacred prostitutes and were such popular centers that they were among the first casualties of Christian fanaticism.
11. Vulcan's name probably came from that of the volcano god of Crete, Velchanos. His forges were said to be under either Mount Etna or Mount Vesuvius, or both. Later he evolved into Volund or Waylund the Smith in medieval times.

Bibliography

Angus, S. *The Mystery-Religions.* NY: Dover Publications, 1975.

Bailey, C. *Phases in the Religion of Ancient Rome.* UK: Oxford University Press, 1932.

Bloch, Raymond. *The Origins of Rome.* UK: Thames & Hudson, 1960.

Bolen, Jean Shinoda. *Goddesses in Every Woman*. NY: Harper & Row, 1985.

Budapest, Z. *The Holy Book of Women's Mysteries*. Oakland, CA: Susan B. Anthony Coven No. 1, 1979.

Carter, Jesse Benedict. *The Religious Life of Ancient Rome*. Boston, MA: Houghton Mifflin Co., 1911.

Casson, Lionel. *Daily Life in Ancient Rome*. American Heritage Publishers, 1975.

Croft, Peter. *All Color Book of Roman Mythology*. UK: Octopus Books, 1974.

Cumont, Franz. *After Life in Roman Paganism*. NY: Dover Publications, 1959.

Cumont, Franz. *Astrology and Religion Among the Greeks and Romans*. NY: Dover Publications, 1960.

Cumont, Franz. *The Mysteries of Mithra*. NY: Dover Publications, 1956.

Cumont, Franz. *Oriental Religions in Roman Paganism*. NY: Dover Publications, 1956.

Eliot, Alexander, ed. *Myths*. NY: McGraw-Hill, 1976.

Fowler, W. Warde. *The Religious Experience of the Roman People*. UK: Macmillan, 1940.

Fowler, W. Warde. *Roman Ideas of Deity*. UK: Macmillan, 1914.

Gayley, Charles M. *The Classic Myths in English Literature and in Art*. NY: Ginn & Co., 1939.

Godwin, Joscelyn. *Mystery Religions in the Ancient World*. San Francisco, CA: Harper & Row, 1981.

Grant, Frederick C. *Ancient Roman Religion*. NY: Liberal Arts Press, 1957.

Halliday, W. R. *Greek and Roman Folklore*. UK: Harrap, 1927.

Herzberg, Max J. *Myths and Their Meaning*. Boston, MA: Allyn & Bacon, 1928.

Hope, Thomas. *Costumes of the Greeks and Romans*. NY: Dover Publications, 1962.

Johnston, Harold W. *The Private Life of the Romans*. NY: Scott, Foresman & Co., 1903.

Jung, Carl G., and Kerenyi, C. *The Myth of the Divine Child*. Princeton, NJ: Princeton University Press, 1973.

Perowne, Stewart. *Roman Mythology*. UK: Paul Hamlyn, 1973.

Pomeroy, Sarah B. *Goddesses, Whores, Wives and Slaves*. NY: Schocken Books, 1975.

Rose, H. J. *Ancient Roman Religion*. UK: Hutchinson, 1949.

Talbott, David N. *The Saturn Myth*. NY: Doubleday, 1980.

Treble, H. A., and King, K. M. *Everyday Life in Rome*. UK: Oxford at the Clarendon Press, 1931.

Zimmerman, J. E. *Dictionary of Classical Mythology*. NY: Bantam Books, 1978.

CHAPTER THIRTEEN

AFRICA

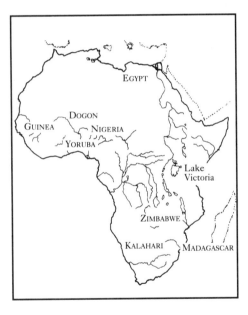

THE AFRICAN tribes have a rich background of social laws, religion, and art that is as old or older than those in Europe, the Middle East, or the Far East.[1] There are magnificent city or culture ruins, such as in Zimbabwe, that rival European castles for romance and mystery.

The continent of Africa is naturally divided into two sections. The northern part, from Egypt to Morocco and down the Nile to Ethiopia, primarily belongs to the sphere of Mediterranean influence. The southern portion, until the explorations of the Portuguese in the fifteenth century, remained virtually unknown to Europe. The area of Africa south of the Sahara Desert was called the Land of the Black People by Arab geographers.[2]

From east and west Sudan, through equatorial regions, completely down into South Africa, the black people are still the majority of the population. In Africa there is a wide range of sizes, colors, and body characteristics, and these are all characterized in the African languages. Most Africans are dark of skin with curly hair and distinct facial features from those of Europeans.

Some historians say that the Negro tribes came to Africa by sea from southeast Asia, but it is more likely that they are indigenous to the continent, as others now think. Anthropologists say there are two primary African races, the Forest Negro and Negrito, and two derived races, the Bushman-Hottentot and Nilotic. However the scholars strive to define and categorize them, the Black Africans have an extremely long oral history of life on the continent.

Three groups of Africans have different characteristics from the general African population: the Bushmen (including the Hottentots), Pygmies, and Hamites. The Bushmen are short in stature with yellowish-brown skin; they have been in Africa for centuries, as shown by their ancient rock paintings. The Pygmies (sometimes called Negritos) live in the Congo River forests and tend to shun modern civilization; they are very short with broad heads and noses. The Hamites, although sometimes mixed with African blood, are usually light-skinned and are related in some way to Europeans; they live in North Africa, Ethiopia, the Sahara, and some parts of the Sudan.

From early times myrrh and frankincense were taken from Somaliland; gold, ivory, and slaves came from farther down the coast. The Arabs controlled early trade with Africa, although the Phoenicians and Greeks did some trading on the east coast. Trading on the west coast was done mostly by Carthage. North Africa was controlled first by the Egyptians, then the Romans. From the seventh to the eleventh centuries, the Arabs and their religion came to invade and dominate northern Africa. The native Black Africans continued to control South Africa until the area was invaded by Europeans.

A scene from Haggard's King Solomon's Mines

Southeast of Fort Victoria in Rhodesia are magnificent ruins made famous by Rider Haggard in *King Solomon's Mines.* Archaeologists have discovered over 300 different areas of stone ruins in this and neighboring countries, but the stone buildings of Zimbabwe are the most famous. They have been dated from the ninth to the fifteenth centuries AD.

Section of Zimbabwe ruins

The name Zimbabwe comes from the Bantu language and can be translated as either "venerated houses" or "stone houses." The most impressive of these ruins are located at the head of a long valley of the Mtilikwe River. At one time this was a very large assembly of buildings, erected from granite blocks without any mortar. These ancient structures cover more than 60 acres.[3]

Written records of African history are incomplete, as the art of writing was unknown for centuries south of the tropical forests. However, there were other means of expression for thoughts and feelings: the beautiful and distinctive art work of the various African regions. Since religion was not separated from ordinary life, African art became a sacred literature, connecting the two. Although there are over 2000 languages and dialects on the African continent, study shows there are many similarities between groups totally isolated from one another.

RELIGION[4]

There are nearly as many religious beliefs in Africa as there are languages. Even within each religion there is a wide range of thought from the deeply philosophical to the rituals to help with everyday life. However, there are also many similar points of belief.

To the African the family unit is of prime importance, as is shown by the subjects of the many surviving wood carvings and other art work. However, their idea of family goes beyond the mother, father, child motif to include grandparents, siblings, and other relations. Older family members are cared for with honor.

The chief idea behind African religious thought is to produce power or vital energy. They considered a human to be more than body, in fact, each individual was thought to contain the breath of God. Therefore, the world was a place of power and those whose lives were the most fruitful and prosperous obviously had the most power and harmony with God.

As with most other cultures around the world, the Africans believed in a God behind the gods. One Supreme Creator made the world and its creatures, then turned

Ancestor statue, Zaire

it over for control and maintenance to lesser deities. The ancestors were also considered powerful in helping and affecting the lives of humans. Since animals and even inorganic forms of nature were believed to have power of one type or another, it became the duty of humans to keep themselves in balance with all powers of the world and harness these powers whenever possible. The knowledge of how to harness these powers became the prerogative of the sorcerer, witch doctor, or medicine man of each tribe. However, since humans are dependent upon God, it is humanity's responsibility not to abuse the use of any power.

An African medicine man is one who learns the secrets of plants and Nature in order to heal the sick. The witch doctor does not go about cursing people, as the Hollywood image would have us believe, but specializes in removing curses. Often these African professionals are priests, as well.

To the Africans, sorcery is very powerful. The world and everything in it is obedient to sorcerers, magicians with the power to command the Elements.[5] Sorcerers are said to call on the souls of the dead to aid them. Amulets are worn to protect against disease, wounds, thieves, murderers, or to increase wealth. The people also believe in transmigration of the soul to plants and animals. The Zulus won't kill certain species of snakes because they believe them to be the spirits of their relatives. The Dahomey wear snake bracelets with two heads as lucky charms; the round snake symbolizes life and eternity.

Many state and religious rituals call for the use of a symbolic sword, especially when oaths are sworn to a chief. The person swearing his loyalty must point the sword first to the heavens, then to the ground as a sign of his promise.

The Ijaw of the Niger Delta believe in mediumistic communication with the ancestors. To help in this, they carve wooden figures to represent their spiritual contacts. It is said that these figures will visibly tremble when a request for aid has been heard and acknowledged.

The Bushmen-Hottentots believe that the world is peopled with invisible beings seen only by sorcerers. To cause rain, this tribe lights large fires giving off black smoke.

The people of Angola believe fetishes or *muquixis* (statuettes of wood) protect them from evil spells and make them happy. A cock crowing or dogs barking at night are the signs of a death. The Mossi, Bobo, Gurusi, Senufo, and Mandinga all believe in evil spirits to which they sacrifice, on the assumption that the sacrifices will keep the evil ones away.

In West Africa there are several important beliefs and customs. Masks are worn to represent ancestors and spirits of wild places during ceremonies. The temples and shrines to the gods contain masks, figurines, and other ceremonial objects. Twins are considered special, uncanny, and are objects of cults. Among the Dogon of this region, blacksmiths have a high status. The Ashanti are matrilineal and believe that a person is formed from the blood of his mother's line or ancestry.

In a Dogo village, the ancestor shrines in individual houses are at the end of the passage to the work room. Liquid of crushed new corn is poured over the shrines. The village altar has diagrams of the 266 Signs painted under Amma's altar. Signs are also painted on the major totemic sanctuaries to perpetuate the totemic animals.

Among the Yoruba, yearly festivals commemorate Obatala's defeat by Odudua. During the ritual re-enactment of this legend, images of Obatala and his wife are taken out of the village. Then the Oni (king) sends gifts to them and receives the god's blessing for the coming year.

The Yoruba religion centers on the worship of a variety of divinities, called *orisha*, each having its own priesthood, temples, cult community, and special sections of town. But everyone shares a common belief in personal destiny determined by Olorun. Neither Olorun or Nhialic have temples, images, priesthoods, cult groups, or regular festivals. The Yoruba believe in a final judgment in the afterlife.

In most African societies, there are certain types of religious authorities, such as diviners, prophets, priests, and sacred kings, who perform specific ritual functions. Although these operate in different ways, they serve a common religious purpose— mediation between the human and the sacred.

Among the Ndembu of northwest Zambia, the diviner's task is a practical one of disclosing the causes of misfortune and death. He must uncover all acts of immorality that will cause problems.

The Yoruba diviner is concerned with forecasting the future. He must show his client his destiny and how to improve upon it. By contrast, the prophets go directly to the people and inspire religious and political movement.

The main task of any priest is to sustain and renew life in the community he serves. The Dinka call their priests "masters of the fishing-spear." They sacrifice animals and represent life to their people.

Each Dogon district has a priest chief called a Hogon. He is the head of a council of elders and head of the totemic priests. He is the mediator of Lebe's life-giving force, which visits him at night as a sacred serpent.

One of the most famous African secret societies is in Sierra Leone. These societies, found in one form or another throughout Africa, are used to initiate the young into the realm of adulthood; they also serve to continue ancestral customs. Their members often disguise themselves with frightening masks and lead the youngsters off into a special sacred place to undergo the rites of circumcision for boys and similar disfigurement for girls. The secret societies can be all male, all female, and a few allow both sexes to participate.

Sudanese dancer in ancestor mask

Musical instruments used in Africa include the sistrum, scrapers, pellet bells, pounding tubes, pit xylophone, ground zither, ground bow, rock gongs, sansa or thumb piano, slit drums, hourglass-shaped drum, barrel drum, frame drum, arched harp, lute, double flute, stopped flute, shawm, clappers, cymbals, percussion sticks, gourd rattles.

DRESS AND ORNAMENTATION

In North Africa, dress consists of sewn rectangular or T-shaped tunics, caftans, or big draped shawls, all acquired from the Arab conquerors but adapted by the local natives. Cotton, flax, and sheep wool or hair are used for fabrics. Layers of tunics and robes in bold geometric patterns and stripes keep out the heat. Rectangular head cloths and shawls keep out the sand. The burnoose (a big circular hooded cloak), a turban, a white muslin robe or long shirt, and wide-legged trousers are the typical male dress. For women, the *haik*, a huge rectangle that is draped, pinned, and tied to completely cover the body except for the eyes, is common. A caftan-like robe is worn underneath.

In South Africa, the dress varies according to the region and tribe, but there are some widely-used articles. Magick-making red and white paint are applied to the body by several tribes; they also wear ivory bangles and ostrich plumes for dramatic effect. White, yellow, red, and intense blue patterns on palmcloth and cotton sarongs are common. They oil their skin until it looks like polished ebony. Some tribes tattoo special patterns over some or all the body. They increase their height with lofty hair styles, plumes, and high, wrapped headdresses. Some tribes work their hair into tiny oiled braids; others crop it short in sculptured skullcaps. Some shape it back from the forehead into a tall dome. Heavy swirls of metal circle the arms, wrists, and ankles.

Costumes are of exotic pelts, cotton, hemp, and palm fiber. Jewelry is made of copper, gold, precious or colorful stones, shell, bone, ivory, and feathers. They use dyes of ocher, indigo, and saffron. Indigo dyed cloth from West Africa ranges from a delicate sky color to a rich blue-black. The rarest and best furs mark rank and status; among the furs are sable, leopard, white long-haired monkey, goatskin, cowhide, and civet.

Masai men wear a brown cowhide knotted on one shoulder; their hair is dusted with red ocher, and huge copper rings adorn their ears and necks.

The Bushmen and Pygmies are mostly naked, with the women wearing a soft leather wrap around the shoulders and a low girdle on the hips. The men wear a loin cloth. Both wear necklaces and earrings made of tiny beads.

At the west end of the Sudan, the children are naked until puberty when a skin apron or bead girdle is worn. A large cotton or palmcloth skirt is worn by women when married. Those of higher social status wears layers of cloth, masses of beads and bangles, feathers, and ceremonial robes.

Among the Yoruba, the men wear a skirtcloth knotted at the waist while the women knot theirs under the armpits. They wear ivory ornaments, beads, bracelets, and anklets. Heavy torque-like bands of gold, copper, brass, and bronze are at the neck, wrists, and ankles. Glass beads come in peacock, turquoise, deep green, red, and olive brown colors.

In Mali, the women sometimes wear silver or gold fillets hung with tiny bells and sarongs of fine cotton. The men wear long tunics and skullcaps. In Nigeria, the men wear a loose shirt and trousers. Their *gbariye* is coat-like with an immense skirt and huge flaring sleeves. The married women wear a *gele*, or headcloth, which is a long strip of cloth wrapped into a lofty pouf of color. Loose sleeved *buba* blouses are tucked into knotted and wrapped layers of skirt cloth.

SOME OF THE MYTHS

The Africans loved telling stories. Since the art of writing was unknown in most of the continent, the craft of story-telling by memorization was important to the social structure of the various tribes. Unfortunately, most of the African tales have not been written down until recently, and even now the collections are incomplete. With the resurgence of pride in ancestry, modern Africans and their descendants are beginning to record the myths and legends of their peoples so they will not be lost.

Nearly all, if not all, African tribes believe in a Supreme Creator in one form or another. From the myths it is apparent that this religious thought existed long before the invasions of Moslem and Christian missionaries. Most of the names of this Supreme Being vary, but there are some common names: Mulungu in East Africa; Leza in Central Africa; Nyambe or variants in the west tropics; Nyame in Ghana; etc.

God is considered a transcendent being who lives in heaven. Many myths say that he originally lived on Earth but retreated to his kingdom in the sky because of some human infraction. The Supreme Creator is the greatest of all beings, having brought forth in various manners the universe, Earth, and everything in them. Because he is such a remote deity figure, God created lesser beings or gods whose power is directly under his. These are the gods of storm, Earth, forest, water, etc., the prominent spirits of African worship. These deities are capable of answering human prayers by use of their own powers or can intercede on man's behalf with the Creator himself.

Although God is father and mother of people and animals, he is beyond sex, being both male and female. He has no form. He is thought of in an abstract manner, but is considered the last resort for justice, available to any man regardless of his position in life. A spark of his divine being dwells in and animates all things. The names given to him by the tribes describe his various attributes: Molder, Giver of Breath and Souls, God of Destiny, One Who Exists of Himself, God of Pity and Comfort, the Inexplicable, Ancient of Days, the One Who Bends Even Kings, the One You Meet Everywhere. There are many temples raised to him.

Among many tribes, including the Yoruba of Nigeria, in the beginning the Earth was a waste place of marsh and water with only the sky above. In the sky Olorun lived with other lesser deities. One day Olorun felt creative, so he gave directions to Orisha Nla (chief of the deities) to make solid ground upon the Earth. To do this, the Creator gave Orisha a snail shell with some dirt, a pigeon, and a hen with five toes. Orisha Nla climbed down a spider web and sprinkled the dirt upon a chosen spot; the pigeon and hen scattered it for him. The Creator sent down a chameleon to test for a wide, dry space, and when this was found, Olorun again sent Orisha Nla to plant trees that

203

would give food and wealth to men. The creation of the Earth took four days; the fifth was reserved for worshipping the Great God, Orisha Nla.

To people the Earth, Orisha Nla was set the task of forming bodies out of clay, but the life spark was secretly embodied in the forms made by the Creator. When Orisha tried to spy on him to learn the secret of life, the Creator put him into a deep sleep until the job was finished. Then the newly-made humans were placed upon the Earth to live.

Among the Macouas and the Banayis is a legend about the creation of the first man and woman by the supreme being Muluku. The god made two holes in the Earth and out of these holes came a man and a woman. Muluku gave them land to cultivate, a pick, an axe, a pot, a plate, and some millet. He told them how to cultivate, build a house, and cook the millet, but they did not follow his instructions. Instead they ate the grain raw, made a mess of everything else, and ran off to hide in the woods. Disgusted with the whole affair, Muluku gave the same implements and instructions to a male and female monkey. They did exactly as they were told, which pleased the god. So Muluku cut off their tails and attached them to the humans, thus giving the monkeys the right to be humans.

The Masai believe that the Earth has always existed. In the beginning there was only one man on Earth, and the daughter of Heaven fell in love with him. Through magick, Kintu, the first man, passed all the tests required of him and went to live on Earth with his heavenly wife. They were completely supplied with livestock and useful plants by her father. However, the girl's father told Kintu not to retrace his steps for any reason once he left Heaven. But Kintu forgot the corn for his chickens. Back he went to Heaven, deaf to his wife's pleas. One of the god's sons, Death, had not been invited to the wedding. Death was waiting and followed him back to Earth. There Death killed all the children of Kintu and the daughter of Heaven. Frantic, they appealed to the great god who sent another of his sons to expel Death. However, the god of Death escaped and established himself as lord of the Earth.

The Bushmen, who appear to be related to the Hottentots, believe that animals played an important role in the early world. Their legends tell of a tree called Omumbo-rombonga from which all men and cattle were born. Only the antelope know where their creator of all things, Cagn, and his wife Coti live. Lions could, at one time, talk by putting their tails in their mouths. Cagn could assume the form of any animal, and his power was in his teeth, like Samson and his hair. One day the thorns, that had once been men, attacked and killed Cagn; the ants then ate him. But Cagn's bones joined together again and he came alive.

According to the Zulu legend of the origin of the world, men came from a bed of reeds called *uthlanga*. The first man was Unkulunkulu, the Very Old, who taught men everything. Unkulunkulu sent a chameleon to tell men that they would not die, but the chameleon travelled slowly, stopped to eat, and fell asleep. In the meantime Unkulunkulu changed his mind and sent a lizard with a different message: men shall die. The lizard got there first and delivered his message. When the chameleon finally showed up, men would not believe him. No man has escaped death ever since.

The snake has an important place in African religious thought and in art. Because it moves about without feet and sheds its skin, yet continues to live, the

African snake of creation

snake is considered immortal. The symbol of a snake with its tail in its mouth, with no beginning or end, is common in African art in all forms. The favorite is the non-poisonous python which is often held to be sacred.

In Dahomey myth the Earth is supported by a coiled snake, with 3500 of its coils below the Earth and 3500 coils above. They say that at night, day, and twilight the snake puts on clothes of black, white, and red.

The Fon of Dahomey tell the story that in the beginning the Greatest of Snakes turned the stagnant water upon the Earth clean by making channels for streams and rivers. He carried the Supreme Creator about the Earth on his back. Wherever they stopped, mountains were formed. There soon became so many mountains, trees, and large animals that the Earth became unstable under its load; the Creator appointed the snake to lie coiled as a support for the Earth. Whenever the snake shifts, earthquakes occur.

In Africa the Sun is fierce and destructive, so men consider the Moon more kindly and beloved. It is during the evenings by light of the Moon that they gather to relax and tell old stories. The Dahomey believe that the Moon is called Mawu,[6] that the Moon is older than the Sun, that it is a woman and mother who is gentle with humans;

she is also called Wisdom of the World. Their Sun is named Lisa and is known as Strength of the World.

The God of the Ashanti is called Nyame and is sometimes personified as the Moon; in this aspect the Moon is represented on Earth by the queen mother of the tribe. The king is personified by the Sun, representative of the Great Nyame, Nyankopon.

MAJOR GODS AND GODDESSES

ADROA—Lugbara of Zaire and Uganda. "God in the sky"; "God on Earth"; Creator God; river god. Both good and bad, he is pictured as tall and white with only half of his body visible. Social order, law, death.

AKONGO—Ngombe of the Congo. Supreme God; Great God.

AKUJ—Turkana of Kenya. Supreme God. Divination.

ALA/ALE/ANE—Ibo of Nigeria. Extremely popular goddess and Earth Mother; creator goddess and queen of the dead. Community laws, morality, oaths, harvest.

AMMA—Dogon of Mali. Supreme God.

ANANSI—West Africa. Mr. Spider; the great Trickster; Creator God. The original source of the tar baby story.

ANAYAROLI—Temne. River demon. Wealth.

Behanzin

ASA—Akamba of Kenya. Father God; "the strong lord." Mercy, help, surviving the impossible or insurmountable.

ASASE YAA/ABEREWA/ASASE EFUA—Ashanti of west Africa. "Old Woman Earth." Goddess of creation of humans and receiver of them at death.[7] Cultivation, harvest.

ASIA—Agni. Goddess of the Earth.

ASIA-BUSSU—Agni. God of the bush.

BEHANZIN—West Africa. Fish god.

CAGN—Bushmen of south central Africa. Creator God; sorcerer and shape-shifter.

CHIUTA/MULENGI/MWENCO/WAMTATAKUYA TUMBUKA—Creator God; rain god; self-created and omniscient. Rain, help, plant growth, food.

CHUKU/CHINEKE—Ibo of East Nigeria. "The first great cause"; "creator." Father of ALE, the Earth goddess. Offerings and sacrifices done for him in groves or under trees. Help, goodness.

DANH—Dahomey. Snake God. The origin of the Haitian god DON PETRO. Described as the RAINBOW SNAKE and shown with his tail in his mouth (a universal symbol of wholeness and unity).

EN-KAI/PARSAI/EMAYIAN—Masai. Sky God. Grass used in his rituals. Rain, vegetation, blessings.

FA—Dahomey. God of destiny and the personal fate of each man.

FAMIAN—Guinea. God of fertility. Protector against sorcerers and demons. Grants good health.

Nigerian water spirit mask

GAUNA/GAWA/GAWAMA—Bushmen. Leader of the spirits of the dead. Disruption, harassment, death.

GE—Dahomey. Moon God; son of MAWU.

GU—The Fon of West Africa. God of war and smiths. Possibly linked with GE and OGUN.

GURUHI—Gambia. Evil god; meteors were considered his sign. Granted power and death over enemies.

HEITSI-EIBIB—The Hottentots. Benign sorcerer god. Shape-shifter, magician.

IMANA—Banyarwands. "Almighty God." Also called HATEGEKIMANA, HASHAKIMANA, HABYARIMANA, NDAGIJIMANA, BIGIRIMANA. Power, goodness, children, planning.

ISON/EKA OBASI/OBASI NSI—Ibibio and Ekoi of west Africa. Tortoise-shell goddess. Any fertility pertaining to the Earth.

JOK/JOK ODUDU—Alur of Uganda and Zaire. Creator God; "god of birth." Black goats were sacrificed to him when rain was needed.

JUOK—Shilluk of the White Nile. The god who created all men on Earth. Supreme God.

KAKA-GUIA—The tribes of the Volta area. A funerary god, he brought dead souls to the Supreme God. Also called NYAMI.

KATONDA—Ganda of East Africa. Also called LISSODDENE, KAGINGO, SSEWANNAKU, LUGABA, SSEBINTU, NNYINIGGULU, NAMUGINGA, SSEWAUNAKU, GGULUDDENE, NAMUGEREKA. Creator God; Savior; First King; Father God. Help, judgment, aid against all odds, control over spirits, divination, oracles.

Oba

KWOTH—Nuer of south Sudan. Great Spirit God. Natural phenomena, help, compassion, judgment.

LEGBA—Dahomey. Evil god; the original of the Haitian god of the same name.

LEZA/LISSA/LISA—Dahomey. Chameleon god/ goddess, depending upon the tribe. Formed a triad of deities with MAWU and GE. Protection, divination.

MBABA MWANA WARESA—Zulu of Natal. Goddess of the rainbow, rain, crops, cultivation, beer.

MAHOU/MAO—Dahomey. Good spirit; superior being.

MAWU—Dahomey. Supreme Goddess; creator of all things; Great Goddess. The Fon of Benin in West Africa worship Mawu as a Moon goddess and creator of all things.[8]

MINEPA—Macouas, Banayis. Evil spirit.

MUKURU—Herero of southwest Africa. "All alone"; Creator God. Rain, healing, protection.

MULUKU—Macouas of Zambesi, Banayis. Supreme God; creator of all things. Agriculture, architecture, the harvest.

MUNGO/MUNGU—Giryama of Kenya. Rain god.

NANA BULUKU—Fon of Dahomey. Goddess who created the world; mother of MAWU and her twin brother LISA.

'NENAUNIR—Masai of Kenya. Storm God; an evil god, linked to the rainbow. Called the RAINBOW SNAKE in Dahomey; dwelt in the clouds and was a dreaded spirit.

'NGAI—Masai. Creator God; giver of life and death.

NGAMI—Moon Goddess.

NJAMBI—Lele. Creator God; Great God. Protection, justice, help, forests, fertility.

NYAMBE—Koko of Nigeria. God; restorer of life.

NYAMBI/NYAMBE—The Barotse of Upper Zambesi. Great God; creator of all things.

NYAME—The Twi of West Africa. Great God. Prepared the soul for rebirth and gave out its destiny.

NYAMIA AMA—Senegal. God of storms, rain and lightning. Supreme God; sky god.

NZAMBI—The Bankongo of the Congo. Great Goddess; creator of all, she rewarded and punished according to man's deeds.

OBA—Santeria river goddess; wife of CHANGO.

OCHUMARE—Yoruba and Santeria. Goddess of the rainbow.

ODDUDUA—Yoruba. Primary Mother Goddess.

OGUN/OGOUN—The Nago and Yoruba of West Africa. God of iron and warfare, he removed difficulties, smoothed the way toward a desired end result. God of justice; god to smiths, hunters, barbers, goldsmiths, all who rely on iron and steel.

OLOKUN—Benin of West Africa. Sea spirit.

OLORUN/OLOFIN-ORUN/OLODUMARE—Yoruba. "Lord of heaven"; "almighty"; "supreme"; "owner"; sky god. Truth, control over the Elements, foreseeing, victory against odds, destiny.

PAN—Agni. Son of the Earth. Cultivation.

ROCK-SENS—The Serer of Gambia. Sky god; controlled the weather. Created rain, thunder and lightning.

RUGABA—Ankore of Uganda. Also called RUHANGA, KAZOOBA, MUKAMEIGURU. Creator God; Sun god; sky god. Life, healing, death, sickness, judgment.

RUHANGA—Banyoro. Great God. Fertility, plenty, children, animals, harvest, health, sickness, death, judgment, rebirth.

SAGBATA—Dahomey. Smallpox god; destroyer.

SAKARABRU—Agni of Guinea. God of medicine, justice, retribution. Swift to punish misdeeds. Strongest during critical phases of the Moon.

SHANGO/SCHANGO—Yoruba of Nigeria. Thunder, storm, and war god; a magician. Carried a double-headed axe like the hammer of THORR.

SOKO—Nupe of north Nigeria. Creator God. Control over the Elements, witchcraft, communication with the dead.

TILO—Mozambique. God of the sky, thunder, rain.

UNKULUNKULU/NKULNKULU—The Amazulu and Ndebele of Zimbabwe. Great God; Earth God; god of fertility, organization and order.

UTIXO—Hottentots. Sky god; spoke with the voice of thunder. Rain, storms, thunder, harvest, rebirth.

Shango

WAKA—The Galla of Ethiopia. Benign god who controlled all the rain.

WELE—Abaluyia, Bantu. "The high one"; "one to whom sacred rites are paid." Also called KHAKABA, ISAYWA. Sky God; Creator God. Rain, storms, lightning, creating, prosperity, harvest, celestial phenomena.

WERE—Luo of Kenya. Great God; Father God; Creator God. Birth, death, Nature, judgment.

WHITE LADY—Tassali of the Sahara. Goddess of agriculture, fertility.

XEVIOSO—West Africa. God of thunder, rain, fertility. He used a thunder axe.

YMOJA—Yoruba. River goddess. Women, children.

ENDNOTES

1. Stone, Merlin, *Ancient Mirrors of Womanhood*. Many writers, including Stone, say that Africa has evidence of the longest habitation of pre- and homo sapiens in the world.

2. Parrinder, Geoffrey, *African Mythology*. The Arab word for this region is *Bilad-as-Sudan*.

3. Reader's Digest, *The World's Last Mysteries*. David Randall-MacIver, a Scottish Egyptologist of the early 1900s, determined that the ruins of Zimbabwe were built by Africans as a type of control over the trade with the Arabs on the coast.

4. It is extremely difficult to get authentic material about ancient African cultures, myths, and ceremonies. Most of what is recorded, unfortunately, was done so by Europeans; most African-Americans are not happy with these texts. I cannot say that I blame them. I have tried to use only authenticated facts; this leaves a very narrow field of information. I chose to have this chapter short but as accurate as possible, rather than longer and full of controversial European-tinged ideas.

5. Parrinder, Geoffrey, *African Traditional Religion*. African sorcerers believe in contagious magick, as do many other peoples. This magick is based on the idea that something once joined can be used to harm the original part. This applies to hair, fingernails, spittle, blood, and even fidelity between married couples.

6. Sjoo and Mor, *The Great Cosmic Mother*. Mawu and Lisa are often spoken of as joint deities, creator gods, who remain separate yet work together. Sometimes their images are represented by a single serpent.

7. Monaghan, Patricia, *The Book of Goddesses and Heroines*. On Thursday, her sacred day, farmers did not till the fields. When the Christians arrived, the greatest controversy was over which was the most sacred day of the week.

Since Asase Yaa had no temples, her worship being performed in the open fields, the Ashanti were able to continue with their worship of her without the Christians realizing what was happening.

8. The god Lisa is often spoken of as her son. It is said that she sent him to Earth to teach humankind useful arts and to watch that they observed her rules. But Mawu is considered a gentle goddess, as seen in the proverb, "Lisa punishes, Mawu forgives."

BIBLIOGRAPHY

Arnott, K. *African Myths and Legends Retold*. UK: Oxford University Press, 1962.

Cardinall, A. W. *Tales Told in Togoland*. UK: Oxford University Press, 1931.

Childress, David Hatcher. *Lost Cities and Ancient Mysteries of Africa and Arabia*. IL: Adventures Unlimited Press, 1989.

Davidson, Basil. *The Lost Cities of Africa*. NY: Atlantic-Little, Brown, 1959.

Forde, D., ed. *African Worlds*. UK: Oxford University Press, 1954.

Herskovits, M. J. *Dahomey*. NY: Augustin Co., 1938.

Idowu, E. B. *Olodumare, God in Yoruba Belief*. UK: Longmans, 1962.

La Fontaine, J. S. *Initiation: Ritual Drama and Secret Knowledge Across the World*. UK: Penguin Books, 1985.

Lienhardt, G. *Divinity and Experience: The Religion of the Dinka*. UK: Oxford University Press, 1961.

Little, K. L. *The Mende of Sierra Leone*. UK: Routledge & Kegan Paul, 1951.

Murdock, George Peter. *Africa, Its Peoples and Their Culture and History*. NY: McGraw-Hill, 1969.

Parrinder, E. G. *West African Religions*. UK: Epworth Press, 1949.

Parrinder, Geoffrey. *African Mythology*. UK: Paul Hamlyn, 1975.

Parrinder, Geoffrey. *African Traditional Religion*. UK: Hutchinson House, 1954.

Rattray, R. S. *Religion and Art in Ashanti*. UK: Oxford University Press, 1927.

Ray, Benjamin. *African Religions*. NJ: Prentice-Hall, 1976.

Reader's Digest. *The World's Last Mysteries*. NY: Reader's Digest Association, 1978.

Smith, E. W., and Dale, A. M. *The Ila-Speaking Peoples of Northern Rhodesia*. UK: Macmillan & Co., 1920.

Spence, Lewis. *The History of Atlantis*. NY: Bell Publishing, 1963.

Werner, A. *Myths and Legends of the Bantu*. UK: Harrap, 1933.

Celtic knotwork design

CHAPTER FOURTEEN

CELTIC REALMS

THE CELTS[1] first appeared in history as they came out of the East[2] in the ninth century BC. They spread into Gaul, the Iberian Peninsula, north Italy, the Balkans, Asia Minor, Britain, and Ireland. They were not all of the same ethnic stock but spoke dialects of the same language.[3] By the fifth century BC, they were sacking towns in Italy, France, Germany, and Switzerland, areas where they finally settled for a time.

They were among the greatest technologists of the ancient world: craftsmen in metal, builders of roads and chariots, experts in agriculture and animal husbandry. They laid the foundation of western European civilization. They were great warriors, feared even by the Romans. At their height of power, their territory stretched from the British Isles to Turkey, but they finally fell to the Romans and Germanic tribes.

The Celts were brilliant, flamboyant, fearless, and dynamic, but also were poorly organized. They were first and foremost warriors, often hiring themselves out as mercenaries to any who could afford their high price. Among the Celts, women were held in high regard and were as good warriors as their men.

By the first century BC, the Romans began encroaching on Celtic territory, finally conquering most of their land, except for Wales, Scotland, and Ireland. Even after this, there were sporadic uprisings; the one led by Queen Boadicea in Britain around AD 61 nearly finished the Roman legions in that country.

213

The most important remaining Celtic writing containing their traditions are those from Ireland: the Books of Leinster, the Dun Cow, Ballymate, and the Yellow Book of Lecan. Surviving Welsh literature is preserved in the White Book of Rhydderch and the Red Book of Hergest.[4]

Children took the mother's name, and daughters inherited her possessions. A mother gave her child a secret name with the first breast milk; the secret name was carefully guarded so it could not be used in spells and curses. Virginity was not prized; twice the dowry was given for a woman with children. Abortion and choice or change of mate were a woman's right.

RELIGION

The Celts were religious to a high degree. They believed in reincarnation and transmigration of the soul. Their pantheon held a great number of female deities of primary importance—mother goddesses, war goddesses, tutelary goddesses. They also had the concept of the triune God/Goddess, three aspects of a single deity. The Celts did not believe in punishment after death. The ethical teaching of the Druids could be summed up as: worship the Gods, do no evil, be strong and courageous.

The Druids were the Celtic priesthood with an Arch Druid at their head. In the beginning, the Celts also had similar sacred organizations of women.[5] The Arch Druid's female counterpart was the High Priestess of the Grove.[6] These Druids and priestesses were the healers, judges, astronomers, teachers, oracles, and religious leaders of the clans.

Special schools were available for the fledgling priests and priestesses. It was no easy matter to become part of this elite religious community; up to twenty years of study were required. The Druids had three divisions within their order: the Bards (poets), who wore long blue robes; the Ovates (prophets, philosophers), who wore green; and the Druid priests, who wore white. They sang Veda-like hymns, sacrificed with special plants and occasionally animals or humans, and used sacred fires. Druid priests sometimes wore horns during certain ceremonies.

Human sacrifices by the knife, drowning, or burning were done because the Celts believed that a life must be given for a life, as in murder, accidental killing, extreme illness, or to be spared the perils of battle. These victims were generally prisoners of war or criminals. However, this practice does not appear to have been used much in Ireland and Britain.

The old priestesses were highly revered. Priestesses sang the dying to sleep, did enchantments, prophecies, charms, birthing, and healing. They knew the power of words, stones, and herbs. For their magick, they let their hair hang loose. A magick cauldron, bowl, or pool was one of the central features of their Groves. Curses were laid for any mistreatment of women. Red-haired women were sacred to the war Goddesses, as red was the color of blood and menstrual blood.[7] Odd numbers were sacred to the Goddess, even numbers to the God.

Certain hills, lakes, caves, springs, wells, monoliths, clearings within groves, and ancient stone circles were sacred worship places, but the Druids preferred oak groves

Celtic worship

and forests. They even used some large rectangular or horseshoe-shaped wooden buildings as temples. Roughly carved tree-trunk images or stones, ornamented with metal plates, were occasionally used as symbols of the deity for devotion. Offerings were sometimes thrown into lakes, wells, and springs. Most celebrations were held at night as the Celtic day began at midnight; their calendar, based on the Moon, had thirteen months.

Religious holidays centered on the solstices, equinoxes, and Moon phases. During the waxing Moon, they did positive magick; during the waning Moon, dark magick. There is also evidence that they observed Imbolc (February), Beltane (May), Lughnassadh (August), and Samhain (end of October). Special ceremonies were held at Samhain (Halloween) when they believed that the veil between the worlds was thinnest and the dead could be contacted for help and knowledge. Mai or Maj was the month of May, a month of sexual freedom. Green, worn during May to honor the Earth Mother, was later called unlucky by the Christians in hopes that the people, especially women, would discontinue wearing the color and engaging in sexual activities.

Feasting and games, particularly warrior skills, were part of the four seasonal holidays: Imbolc, Beltane, Lughnassadh, and Samhain. Pork was served at these festivals, along with mead, special breads, and other meats.

Celtic colors for the four Elements were red, east; white, south; grey, west; black, north.

The Triple Goddess, or triple aspects of the Goddess,[8] were well known to the Celts. To the Irish Celts these aspects were represented by Anu or Danu as the Maiden, Badb as the Mother, and Macha as the Crone. Sometimes the Morrigu, who

Holy ground

was in herself called triple, took the part of the Crone. To the Celts of Wales, the Maiden was Blodeuwedd, the Mother Arianrhod, and the Crone Cerridwen. Even in Arthurian times, we find the triplicity: Elaine as Maiden, Margawse as Mother, Morgan as Crone.

Blacksmiths ranked high in the social order because they were trained in magick. They trained for at least a year and a day on Scathach's Island (possibly Skye), learning metal magick and the martial arts. They were dedicated to the Goddess Scathach or Scath. They also could heal, prophecy, and make magick weapons.

Oak and mistletoe were sacred, as were wrens, which they considered prophetic. Holly was sacred to the Morrigu, underworld Goddess of death and regeneration; her symbol was a pentacle or five-point star.

DRESS AND ORNAMENTATION

Among the Celts, the men, and some of the women, wore blue tattoos or painted designs on their bodies. They played lyres and harps and loved song, music, and the recitation of legends and epic adventures. They used metal or ornamented natural horns for drinking.

Both sexes loved jewelry: brooches decorated with gold filigree, cuttlefish shell, garnets, lapis, and other stones; buckles of gold filigree and stones; pins and linked pins with animal decorations; necklaces of amber, granulation and chip carving. They wore torcs, pendants, bracelets, pins, and necklaces. The women sometimes sewed little bells on the fringed ends of their tunics. The elaborate intertwinings of their artwork was a guard against the evil eye or curses.[9]

Celtic women painted their fingernails, reddened their cheeks with roan, and darkened their eyebrows with berry juice. They wore their hair long and braided or piled up on the head. They wore a sleeved tunic tucked into a large, gathered, belted skirt or simply an ankle-length tunic with a belt.

216

Celtic men on the European mainland wore trousers with a tunic, but in Britain and Ireland the men wore a tunic and cloak, the ever-present dagger and sword, and leather or fur footgear tied around the legs. The clothing was usually wool and dyed in bright colors of red, green, blue, or yellow. Both men and women wore huge rectangular cloaks pinned at the right shoulder. These cloaks were usually woven in bright plaids, checks, or stripes.

SOME OF THE MYTHS

The tribe of the Fomorians was on the scene long before any other races came to Ireland. However, the Fomors lived mainly in the sea. The first outside race to invade Ireland was the race of Partholon; very little is known of them. After 300 years of struggle against the Fomors, the Partholons died of an epidemic.

Next came the race of Nemed who also suffered from an epidemic. This time, though, some of them survived, only to be oppressed by the Fomors. The Fomorian kings Morc, son of Dela, and Conann, son of Febar, built a glass tower on their stronghold of Tory Island. From there they taxed the Nemedians of two-thirds of the children born each year. During the battle that ensued over tax, all the Nemedians were killed.

Later came colonizers from Spain or Greece called the Fir Bolgs. They were actually three tribes: men of Domnu, men of Gaillion, and men of Bolg. They intermarried with the Fomors and held the country until the arrival of the Tuatha De Danann.

The Tuatha De Danann[10] invaded Ireland, defeating the Fir Bolg in battle. However, the De Danann king Nuada lost his hand. Because of this he had to step down, for no king was allowed to have any disfigurement. The Fomorian king Bres became ruler at the request of the De Danann, but he proved to be a harsh ruler. The De Danann people were living in hardship under him. The chief De Danann bard, Coirpre, satirized Bres in public, causing him to break out in a terrible red rash. The Tuatha De Danann insisted that Bres abdicate, but he refused. The Fomorian armies invaded Ireland to protect his kingship. In the meantime Diancecht the physician made Nuada a silver hand, making it possible for him to resume the kingship, which he did.

While Nuada was holding a great feast at Tara to celebrate his return, a strange warrior came to the gates and demanded entrance. The gatekeepers questioned him. The warrior revealed that his name was Lugh Samildanach, grandson of Diancecht. The gatekeepers answered that no man without a skill could enter Tara. Lugh then

Traditional Celtic design

217

listed his skills—wright, smith, champion, harper, hero, poet, historian, sorcerer, physician, brazier—but the men just sneered. The Tuatha De Danann had those already. So Lugh sent a message to Nuada, asking if he had a man among his people who could do all those skills.

The king still was not impressed and sent out his chess master with a board as a challenge. Lugh won all the games. Nuada then admitted the young man and set him in the seat reserved for the sage, for Lugh was a sage in all skills.

Nuada and his people decided that Lugh should command their armies against their enemies, the Fomorians, who were still causing problems. Just before the battle, the Dagda met the Morrigu, the war goddess, as she bathed in the river. In exchange for lying with her, she gave the Dagda a battle plan for victory.

The two armies finally gathered facing each other. For the Tuatha De Danann, Goibniu the smith made spearheads and swords, Creidne the brazier rivets that would not break, Coirpre the poet or bard satirized the enemy, Ogma supplied the warrior-power, the Dagda promised to slay with his massive club, and Diancecht prepared to bring the De Danann dead back to life by putting them into a magick well or cauldron.

Lugh was supposed to stay out of the battle because his mother's father, Balar of the Evil Eye, was leading the enemy. Whenever Balar's deadly eye was opened, it destroyed everyone in his sight. But in the heat of battle, Lugh sprang into action and met Balar face to face. As the eye began to open, Lugh threw a spear (some versions say a stone) and drove the eye back through Balar's head so that it looked upon the Fomorians. The Tuatha De Danann were victorious, driving the Fomorians back into the sea.

Lugh and his spear in battle

The Welsh legend of Branwen shows a connection with the Irish. Bran, one of the Welsh deities, was the brother of Branwen. King Matholwch of Ireland came to Wales to ask for Branwen in marriage. Efnisien, a giant Welshman, maimed Matholwch's horses because he was angry over being left out of the wedding feast. This action immediately caused trouble. Bran tried to smooth over the affair by replacing the animals with gold and silver. Branwen sailed to Ireland with Matholwch but was at once banished to the kitchens and servant duty. She had a son by Matholwch but her situation did not change. Finally, she managed to get a message to her brother by fastening a letter to a bird's leg.

The Welsh invaded Ireland to avenge the insult. Bran, a giant of a man, waded across the sea and forced the Irish to negotiate a peace. However, the troublemaker Efnisien killed the son of Matholwch and Branwen. The battle was renewed.

The Irish had the cauldron of rebirth, a wedding gift from Bran to Matholwch. They lit a fire under it and threw in their dead warriors to revive them. Efnisien could see that he was going to be killed by Bran if something was not done to rectify his hot-headed errors. So he hid among the Irish bodies and was thrown into the cauldron with the others. Once inside, he stretched himself out so that the cauldron burst. The Welsh won, but at a terrible cost. Only seven of the invading warriors and Branwen remained. Bran was mortally wounded. He ordered that his head be cut off at his death and buried on the White Mount in London with his face towards France. Branwen died of a broken heart.

Another Welsh legend tells the story of the well-known bard Taliesin. Originally, his name was Gwion Bach. As a young man he suddenly found himself at the bottom of Lake Bala in northern Wales where the giant Tegid and his wife, the Goddess Cerridwen, lived. The Goddess set Gwion to stirring a cauldron containing a special brew. At the end of a year and a day of stirring, the last three drops flew out and burned Gwion's finger; he thrust the finger into his mouth and at once realized the power of Cerridwen. He fled the lake in terror.

Furious, Cerridwen went after him. The two repeatedly changed shapes, Gwion to escape, and Cerridwen in an attempt to capture him. Finally, he changed into a grain of wheat and the Goddess as a hen ate him. Upon returning to her own shape, she discovered she was pregnant. When Gwion was reborn, the Goddess cast him into the sea in a little boat.

Elphin, son of a wealthy landowner, rescued the baby and named him Taliesin (radiant brow). Taliesin remembered all the knowledge he had gained from Cerridwen's magick potion. He became a great bard, magician, and counselor of kings.

Major Gods and Goddesses

Aine of Knockaine—Ireland. Moon Goddess; patroness of crops and cattle. Connected with the Summer Solstice.

Angus mac Og/Angus of the Brugh/Oengus of the Bruig/Angus mac Oc—Ireland. "Young son." One of the Tuatha De Danann. He had a gold harp that made

Harp of the Bard

irresistible sweet music. His kisses became birds carrying love messages. He had a *brugh* (fairy palace) on the banks of the Boyne. God of youth, love, and beauty.

ANU/ANANN/DANA/DANA-ANA—Ireland. Goddess of plenty, another aspect of the MORRIGU; Mother Earth; Great Goddess; greatest of all goddesses. The flowering fertility Goddess, sometimes she formed a trinity with BADB and MACHA. Her priestesses comforted and taught the dying. Fires were lit for her at Midsummer. Two hills in Kerry are called the Paps of Anu. Maiden aspect of the Triple Goddess in Ireland. Guardian of cattle and health. Goddess of fertility, prosperity, comfort.

ARAWN—Wales. King of Hell; God of Annwn, the underground kingdom of the dead. Revenge, terror, war.

ARIANRHOD—Wales. "Silver Wheel"; "High fruitful mother"; star Goddess; sky Goddess; virgin; Goddess of reincarnation; Full Moon Goddess. Her palace was called Caer Arianrhod (Aurora Borealis). Keeper of the circling Silver Wheel of Stars, a symbol of time or karma. This wheel was also known as the Oar Wheel, a ship which carried dead warriors to the Moon-land (Emania). Mother of LLEU LLAW GYFFES and DYLAN by her brother GWYDION. Her original consort was NWYVRE (Sky or Firmament). Mother aspect of the Triple Goddess in Wales. Honored at the Full Moon. Beauty, fertility, reincarnation.

BADB/BADHBH/BADB CATHA—Ireland. "Boiling"; "Battle Raven"; "Scald-crow"; the cauldron of ever-producing life; known in Gaul as Cauth Bodva. War Goddess and wife of NET, a war God. Sister of MACHA, the MORRIGU, and ANU. Mother aspect of the Triple Goddess in Ireland. Associated with the cauldron, crows, and ravens. Life, wisdom, inspiration, enlightenment.

BANBA—Ireland. Goddess; part of a triad with FOTIA and ERIU. They used magick to repel invaders.

BEL/BELENUS/BELINOS/BELI MAWR—Ireland. "Shining"; sun and fire God; Great God. Similar to APOLLO. Closely connected with the Druids. His name is seen in the festival of Beltane or Beltain. Cattle were driven through the bonfires then for purification and fertility. Science, healing, hot springs, fire, success, prosperity, purification, crops, vegetation, fertility, cattle.

BLODEUWEDD/WLODWIN/BLANCHEFLOR—Wales. "Flower Face"; "White Flower." Lily maid of Celtic initiation ceremonies. Also known as the Ninefold Goddess of the Western Isles of Paradise. Created by MATH and GWYDION as a wife for LLEU. She was changed into an owl for her adultery and plotting Lleu's death. The Maiden form of the Triple Goddess; her symbol was the owl; Goddess of the Earth in bloom. Flowers, wisdom, lunar mysteries, initiations.

BOANN/BOANNAN/BOYNE—Ireland. Goddess of the river Boyne; mother of ANGUS MAC OG by the DAGDA. Once there was a well shaded by nine magick hazel trees. These trees bore crimson nuts which gave knowledge of everything in the world. Divine salmon lived in the well and ate the nuts. No one, not even the high gods, were allowed to go near the well. But Boann went anyway. The well waters rose to drive her away, but they never returned to the well. Instead they became the River Boyne and the salmon became inhabitants of the river. Other Celtic river goddesses: SIANNAN (Shannon), SABRINA (Severn), SEQUANA (Seine), DEVA (Dee), CLOTA (Clyde), VERBEIA (Wharfe), BRIGANTIA (Braint, Brent). Healing.

BRAN THE BLESSED/BENEDIGEIDFRAN—Wales. A giant; "raven"; "the blessed." Brother of the mighty MANAWYDAN AP LLYR (Ireland, MANANNAN MAC LIR) and BRANWEN; son of LLYR. A giant. Associated with ravens. God of prophecy, the arts, leaders, war, the sun, music, writing.

BRANWEN—Manx, Wales. Sister of BRAN THE BLESSED and wife of the Irish king MATHOLWCH. Venus of the Northern Seas; daughter of LLYR (Lir); one of the three matriarchs of Britain; Lady of the Lake (cauldron). Goddess of love and beauty.

BRIGIT/BRID/BRIG/BRIGID/BRIGHID—Ireland, Wales, Spain, France. "Power"; "Renown"; "Fiery Arrow or Power" (Breo-saighead). Daughter of the DAGDA; called the poetess. Often called The Triple Brigids, Three Blessed Ladies of Britain, The Three Mothers. Another aspect of DANU; associated with Imbolc. She had an exclusive female priesthood at Kildare and an ever-burning sacred fire. The number of her priestesses was 19 representing the 19-year cycle of the Celtic "Great Year." Her *kelles* were sacred prostitutes and her soldiers brigands. Goddess of fire, fertility, the hearth and all feminine arts and crafts, and martial arts. Healing, physicians, agriculture, inspiration, learning, poetry, divination, prophecy, smithcraft, animal husbandry, love, witchcraft, occult knowledge.

CAILLECH—Great Goddess in her Destroyer aspect; called the "Veiled One." Disease, plague, cursing. See the CRONE.

CERNUNNOS/CERNOWAIN/CERNENUS/HERNE THE HUNTER—Known to all Celtic areas in one form or another. The Horned God; God of Nature; God of the Underworld and the Astral Plane; Great Father; "the Horned One." The Druids knew him as HU GADARN, the Horned God of fertility. He was portrayed sitting in a lotus position with horns or antlers on his head, long curling hair, a beard, naked except for a neck torque, and sometimes holding a spear and shield.

Cernunnos

His symbols were the stag, ram, bull, and horned serpent. Sometimes called BELATUCADROS and VITIRIS. Virility, fertility, animals, physical love, Nature, woodlands, reincarnation, crossroads, wealth, commerce, warriors.

CERRIDWEN/CARIDWEN/CERIDWEN—Wales. Moon Goddess; Great Mother; grain Goddess; Goddess of Nature. The white corpse-eating sow representing the Moon. Welsh Bards called themselves Cerddorion (sons of Cerridwen).[11] The Bard TALIESIN, founder of their craft, was said to be born of Cerridwen and to have tasted a potent from her magick cauldron[12] of inspiration. Wife of the giant TEGID and mother of a beautiful girl CREIRWY and an ugly boy AVAGDU. In her magickal cauldron, she made a potion called greal (from which the word Grail probably came). The potion was made from six plants for inspiration and knowledge. Her symbol was a white sow. Death, fertility, regeneration, inspiration, magick, astrology, herbs, science, poetry, spells, knowledge.

CREIDDYLAD/CREUDYLAD/CORDELIA—Wales. Daughter of the sea God LLYR. Connected with Beltane and often called the May Queen. Goddess of summer flowers. Love and flowers.

THE CRONE—One aspect of the Triple Goddess. She represents old age or death, winter, the end of all things, the waning Moon, post-menstrual phases of women's lives, all destruction that precedes regeneration through her cauldron of rebirth. Crows and other black creatures are sacred to her. Dogs often accompanied her and guarded the gates of her after-world, helping her to receive the dead. In Celtic myth, the gatekeeper-dog was named Dormarth (Death's Door). The Irish Celts maintained that true curses could be cast with a dog's help. Therefore, they used the word *cainte* (dog) for a satiric Bard with the magick power to speak curses that came true.

THE DAGDA—Ireland. "The Good God"; "All-father"; Great God; Lord of the Heavens; Father of the gods and men; Lord of Life and Death; the Arch-Druid; God of magick; Earth God. High King of the Tuatha De Danann. He had four great palaces in the depths of the earth and under the hollow hills. The Dagda had several children, the most important being BRIGIT, ANGUS, MIDIR, OGMA and BODB THE RED. God of death and rebirth; master of all trades; lord of perfect knowledge. He had a cauldron called The Undry which supplied unlimited food. He also had a living oak harp which caused the seasons to change in their order. He was pictured wearing a brown, low-necked tunic which just reached his hips and a hooded cape that barely covered his shoulders. On his feet were horse-hide boots. Behind him he pulled his massive 8-pronged warclub on a wheel. Protection, warriors, knowledge, magick, fire, prophecy, weather, reincarnation, the arts, initiation, patron of priests, the Sun, healing, regeneration, prosperity and plenty, music, the harp. First among magicians, warriors, artisans, all knowledge.

DANU/DANANN/DANA—Ireland. Probably the same as ANU. Major Mother Goddess; ancestress of the Tuatha De Danann; Mother of the gods; Great Mother; Moon

Goddess. She gave her name to the Tuatha De Danann (People of the Goddess Danu). Another aspect of the MORRIGU. Patroness of wizards, rivers, water, wells, prosperity and plenty, magick, wisdom.

DIANCECHT/DIAN CECHT—Ireland. Physician-magician of the Tuatha. Once he destroyed a terrible baby of the MORRIGU. When he cut open the child's heart, he found three serpents that could kill anything. He killed these, burned them, and threw the ashes into the nearest river. The ashes were so deadly that they made the river boil and killed everything in it. The river today is called Barrow (boiling). Diancecht had several children: sons MIACH, CIAN, CETHE, and CU, and a daughter AIRMID. God of healing, medicine, regeneration, magick, silver-working.

DON/DOMNU/DONN—Ireland, Wales. "Deep sea"; "Abyss." Queen of the Heavens; Goddess of sea and air. Sometimes called a Goddess, sometimes a God. The equivalent of the Irish DANU. In Ireland, Don ruled over the Land of the Dead. Entrances to this Otherworld were always in a *sidhe* (shee) or burial mound. Control of the elements, eloquence.

DRUANTIA—"Queen of the Druids"; Mother of the tree calendar; Fir Goddess. Fertility, passion, sexual activities, trees, protection, knowledge, creativity.

DYLAN—Wales. Son of the Wave; God of the sea. Son of GWYDION and ARIANRHOD. His symbol was a silver fish.

ELAINE—Wales, Britain. Maiden aspect of the Goddess.

EPONA—Britain, Gaul. "Divine Horse"; "The Great Mare"; Goddess of horses; Mother Goddess. Fertility, maternity, protectress of horses, horse-breeding, prosperity, dogs, healing springs, crops.

ERIU/ERIN—Ireland. One of the three queens of the Tuatha Da Danann and a daughter of the Dagda.

FLIDAIS—Ireland. Goddess of forests, woodlands, and wild things; ruler of wild beasts. She rode in a chariot drawn by deer. Shape-shifter.

GOIDNIU/GOFANNON/GOVANNON—Ireland, Wales. "Great Smith"; one of a triad of craftsmen with LUCHTAINE the wright and CREIDNE the brazier. Similar to VULCAN. He forged all the Tuatha's weapons; these weapons always hit their mark and every wound by them was fatal. His ale gave the Tuatha invulnerability. God of blacksmiths, weapon-makers, jewelry making, brewing, fire, metal-working.

Epona

223

The Horned God

GREAT FATHER—The Horned God; The Lord. Lord of the winter, harvest, land of the dead, the sky, animals, mountains, lust, powers of destruction and regeneration; the male principle of creation.

GREAT MOTHER—The Lady; female principle of creation. Goddess of fertility, the Moon, summer, flowers, love, healing, the seas, water. The "mother" finger was considered the index finger, the most magickal which guided, beckoned, blessed and cursed.

THE GREEN MAN—See CERNUNNOS. A horned deity of trees and green growing things of Earth; God of the woodlands. In Old Welsh his name is ARDDHU (The Dark One), ATHO, or the HORNED GOD.

GWYDION—Wales. Druid of the mainland gods; son of DON; brother of GOVANNON, ARIANRHOD, and AMAETHON (God of agriculture). Wizard and Bard of North

Wales. A many-skilled deity like LUGH. Prince of the Powers of Air; a shape-shifter. His symbol was a white horse. Greatest of the enchanters; warrior-magician. Illusion, changes, magick, the sky, healing.

GWYNN AP NUDD—Wales. King of the Fairies and the underworld. Later he became king of the Plant Annwn, or subterranean fairies.

GWETHYR—Wales. Opposite of GWYNN AP NUDD. King of the Upper World.

HERNE THE HUNTER—See CERNUNNOS and the HORNED GOD. Herne the Hunter has come to be associated with Windsor Forest and has taken on attributes of GWYNN AP NUDD with his Wild Hunt.

THE HORNED GOD—Opener of the Gates of Life and Death; HERNE THE HUNTER; CERNUNNOS; GREEN MAN; Lord of the Wild Hunt. The masculine, active side of Nature; Earth Father. His sacred animals were the stag, bull, goat, bear. Growing things, the forest, Nature, wild animals, alertness, annihilation, fertility, panic, desire, terror, flocks, agriculture, beer and ale.

LLYR/LEAR/LIR—Ireland, Wales. God of the sea and water, possibly of the underworld. The father of MANAWYDAN, BRAN THE BLESSED, and BRANWEN.

LUD/LLUD/LLUD LLAW EREINT/LLUD OF THE SILVER HAND/NUADA/NUDD /NODONS/NODENS—Ireland, Wales. "Silver Hand"; "He who bestows wealth"; "the Cloud-Maker"; chieftain-God. Similar to NEPTUNE. He had an invincible sword, one of the four great treasures of the Tuatha. God of healing, water, ocean, fishing, the Sun, sailing, childbirth, dogs, youth, beauty, spears and slings, smiths, carpenters, harpers, poets, historians, sorcerers, writing, magick, warfare, incantations.

LUGH/LUGH LAMHFADA (of the Long Arm)/LLEW/LUG/LUGUS/LUG SAMILDANANCH (many skilled)/LLEU LLAW GYFFES ("bright one of the skillful hand") /LLEU/LUGOS— Ireland, Wales. The Shining One; Sun God; God of war; "many-skilled"; "fair-haired one"; "white or shining"; a hero God. His feast is Lughnassadh, a harvest festival. Associated with ravens. His symbol was a white stag in Wales. Son of CIAN and ETHNIU. Lugh had a magick spear and rod-sling. One of his magick hounds was obtained from the sons of TUIRENN as part of the blood-fine for killing his father Cian. He was a carpenter, mason, smith, harper, poet, Druid, physician, and goldsmith. War, magick, commerce, reincarnation, lightning, water, arts and crafts, manual arts, journeys, martial arts, blacksmiths, poets, harpers, musicians, historians, sorcerers, healing, revenge, initiation, prophecy.

MACHA—Ireland. "Crow"; "Battle"; "Great Queen of Phantoms"; Mother of Life and Death; a war Goddess; Mother Death; originally a Mother Goddess; one of the aspects of the triple MORRIGU. Also called MANIA, MANA, MENE, MINNE. Associated with ravens and crows. She was honored at Lughnassadh. After a battle, the Irish cut off the heads of the losers and called them Macha's acorn crop. Protectress in war as in peace; Goddess of war and death. Cunning, sheer physical force, sexuality, fertility, dominance over males.

MANANNAN MAC LIR/MANAWYDAN AP LLYR/MANAWYDDEN—Ireland, Wales. He dressed in a green cloak and a gold headband. A shape-shifter. Chief Irish sea God, equivalent of the Welsh LLYR. Son of the sea God LIR. The Isle of Man and the Isle of Arran in Firth of Clyde were under his protection. At Arran he had a palace called Emhain of the Apple Trees. His swine, which constantly renewed themselves, were the chief food of the Tuatha De Danann and kept them from aging. He had many famous weapons: two spears called Yellow Shaft and Red Javelin; swords called The Retaliator, Great Fury, and Little Fury. His boat was called Wave Sweeper, and his horse Splendid Mane. He had magick armor that prevented wounds and could make the Tuatha invisible at will. God of the sea, navigators, storms, weather at sea, fertility, sailing, weather-forecasting, magick, arts, merchants and commerce, rebirth.

MARGAWSE—Wales, Britain. Mother aspect of the Goddess.

MATH MATHONWY—Wales. God of sorcery, magick, enchantment.

MERLIN/MERDDIN/MYRDDIN—Wales, Britain. Great sorcerer; Druid; magician. Associated with the fairy religion of the Goddess. Old Welsh traditions called him a wild man of the woods with prophetic skills. He is said to have learned all his magick from the Goddess under her many names of MORGAN, VIVIANE, NIMUE, FAIRY QUEEN, and LADY OF THE LAKE. Tradition says he sleeps in a hidden crystal cave. Illusion, shape-shifting, herbs, healing, woodlands, Nature, protection, counseling, prophecy, divination, psychic abilities, foreseeing, crystal reading, tarot, magick, rituals, spells, incantations, artisans and smiths.

THE MORRIGU/MORRIGAN/MORRIGHAN/MORGAN—Ireland, Wales, and Britain. "Great Queen"; "Supreme War Goddess"; "Queen of Phantoms or Demons"; "Specter Queen"; shape-shifter.[13] Reigned over the battlefield, helping with her magick, but did not join in battles. Associated with crows and ravens. The Crone aspect of the Goddess; Great Mother; Moon Goddess; Great White Goddess; Queen of the Fairies. In her Dark Aspect (the symbol is then the raven or crow) she is the Goddess of war, fate, and death; she went fully armed and carried two spears. The carrion crow is her favorite disguise. With her, FEA (Hateful), NEMON (Venomous), BADB (Fury), and MACHA (Battle) encouraged fighters to battle-madness. Goddess of rivers, lakes, and fresh water. Patroness of priestesses and witches. Revenge, night, magick, prophecy.

Merlin, detail from a fourteenth century enamel

NIAMH—Ireland. "Beauty"; "Brightness." A form of BADB who helps heroes at death.

OGMA/OGHMA/OGMIOS/GRIANAINECH (sun face)/CERMAIT (honey-mouthed)—Ireland. "Sun-face"; similar to HERCULES; carried a huge club and was the champion of the Tuatha. Invented the Ogam script alphabet. He married ETAN (daughter of DIANCECHT) and had several children. One son, COIRPRE, became the professional Bard of the Tuatha. Eloquence, poets, writers, physical strength, inspiration, language, literature, magick, spells, the arts, music, reincarnation.

Early representation of the Celtic goddess of death

PWYLL—Wales. Ruler of the Underworld at times. Also known as PWYLL PEN ANNWN (Pwyll head of Annwn). Cunning.

RHIANNON—Wales. "The Great Queen." Goddess of birds and horses. Enchantments, fertility, and the Underworld. She rides a swift white horse.

SCATHACH/SCOTA/SCATHA/SCATH—Ireland, Scotland. "Shadow, shade"; "The Shadowy One"; "She Who Strikes Fear." Underworld Goddess of the Land of Scath; Dark Goddess; Goddess in the Destroyer aspect. Also a warrior woman and prophetess who lived in Albion (Scotland), probably on the Isle of Skye, and taught the martial arts. Patroness of blacksmiths, healing, magick, prophecy, martial arts.

TALIESIN—Wales. Prince of Song; Chief of the Bards of the West; a poet. Patron of Druids, bards and minstrels; a shape-shifter. Writing, poetry, wisdom, wizards, bards, music, knowledge, magick.

WHITE LADY—Known to all Celtic countries. Dryad of Death; identified with MACHA; Queen of the Dead; the Crone form of the Goddess. Death, destruction, annihilation.

ENDNOTES

1. Matthews, Caitlin. *The Elements of the Celtic Tradition.* The Celts thought of themselves as Bretons, Irish, British, or Gaels; more likely as a member of a specific tribe. The term "Celt" came into being at a much later date.
2. Squire, Charles. *Celtic Myth and Legend.* Squire says that the Celtic language, along with Latin, Greek, Slavic, Teutonic, Persian, and a great number of Indian dialects, can all be traced back to the Aryan and Sanskrit. But if one

takes the hypothesis one step further, where did the Aryans come from? Tales in India says they also came conquering out of the east.

3. Matthews, Caitlin. *The Elements of the Celtic Tradition.* Scholars cannot agree on where the Celtic tribes originated. Some say they came from Greece; the Greeks mention battles with roving bands of fierce peoples whom they called *Keltoi* who fit the description of the Celts, but are clear to state that they did not originate in the areas of Greece, coming instead out of the east. The Greek writer Ephoros in the fourth century BC called the Celts one of the four great tribes of barbarians in the known world.

4. Squire, Charles, *Celtic Myth and Legend* and Gantz, Jeffrey, translator of *The Mabinogion.* One must read Celtic myths and legends fully aware that most, if not all, of the copies and translations we have today have been heavily influenced by Christian scribes. The Book of the Dun Cow was named for its being copied onto the skin of an animal belonging to Saint Ciaran who lived in the seventh century. In this manuscript is the only complete saga of the hero Cuchulainn's raid on the cattle of Cooley. The Book of Leinster was compiled by Finn mac Gorman, Bishop of Kildare, in the twelfth century. The Book of Ballymote and the Yellow Book of Lecan were written down at the end of the fourteenth century. Among the Welsh documents are the Black Book of Caermarthen (twelfth century), the Book of Aneurin (thirteenth century), the Book of Taliesin (fourteenth century), and the Red Book of Hergest (fourteenth century). *The Mabinogion* is a collection of legends from various sources and written by more than one person over a span of time.

5. Rutherford, Ward. *The Druids: Magicians of the West.* The ancient writer Strabo mentions a specific group of priestesses who lived on a channel island off the coast of Gaul. Women tribal leaders, such as Queen Boadicea and Queen Cartimandua, performed sacrifices and rituals for the benefit of their people.

6. Green, Miranda. *The Gods of the Celts.* The Celtic word for a sacred grove was *nemeton,* which is seen in place-names such as Aquae Arnemetiae in Briton. The comparative Irish word is *fidnemed.* Classical writers like Tacitus, Strabo, Dio Cassius, and Lucan all mention the use of sacred groves for training, ritual, and sacrifice.

7. Walker, Barbara. *The Woman's Encyclopedia of Myths and Secrets.* A Celtic name for this fluid was *dergflaith,* or "red mead" or "red ale." To be stained with red in Celtic Britain meant to be chosen by the Goddess as king.

8. Conway, D. J. *Celtic Magic.*

9. D'Alviella, Count Goblet. *The Migration of Symbols.* Count Goblet traces the migration of the gammadion or swastika out of the East through Europe and into the Celtic lands. This symbolic design can be seen in much elaborated form on Celtic brooches and other jewelry.

10. Some legends say the Tuatha De Danann came from the sky, others say from far away islands. The four cities from which they originated were Findias, Gorias, Murias, and Falias. They were skilled in poetry and magick. With

them they brought four great treasures: Nuada's sword from Findias, Lugh's terrible spear from Gorias, the Dagda's cauldron from Murias, and the Stone of Fal (Lia Fail or Stone of Destiny) from Falias. Bonwick in *The Irish Druids and Old Irish Religions* says the Lia Fail was the inauguration stone of Irish kings. Later the stone was taken to Scone and finally became the Coronation Stone in Westminster Abbey.

11. Walker, Barbara. *The Woman's Encyclopedia of Myths and Secrets.*

12. Walker, Barbara. Ibid. The Celts of Gaul and Britain considered the Cauldron of Regeneration the central theme of their mystery religion. It represented reincarnation within the womb of the Goddess.

13. Bonwick, James. *Irish Druids and Old Irish Religions.* Bonwick cites stories of the Morrigu being first in the form of a bird and then as a beautiful woman. She often spoke in a mysterious language.

BIBLIOGRAPHY

Adler, Margot. *Drawing Down the Moon.* Boston, MA: Beacon Press, 1981.

Atkinson, R. J. C. *Stonehenge.* NY: Macmillan, 1956.

Bonwick, James. *Irish Druids and Old Irish Religions.* NY: Dorset Press, 1986.

Briggs, Katherine M. *The Anatomy of Puck.* UK: Routledge & Kegan Paul, 1959.

Capt, E. Raymond. *Stonehenge and Druidism.* Thousand Oaks, CA: Artisan Sales, no date.

Chant, Joy. *The High Kings: Arthur's Celtic Ancestors.* NY: Bantam Books, 1983.

Conway, D. J. *Celtic Magic.* St. Paul, MN: Llewellyn Publications, 1990.

Davidson, H. R. Ellis. *Myths and Symbols in Pagan Europe.* Syracuse, NY: University Press, 1988.

Eliade, Mircea. *Shamanism: Archaic Techniques of Ecstasy.* Princeton, NJ: Princeton University Press, 1964.

Gantz, Jeffrey, trans. *The Mabinogion.* NY: Dorset Press, 1976.

Green, Miranda. *The Gods of the Celts.* Totowa, NJ: Barnes & Noble, 1986.

Hawkins, Gerald S. *Stonehenge Decoded.* NY: Dell Publishing, 1965.

Herzberg, Max J. *Myths and Their Meaning.* Boston, MA: Allyn & Bacon, 1928.

Higgins, Godfrey. *The Celtic Druids.* UK: Rowland Hunter, 1829.

Kendrick, T. D. *The Druids: A Study in Keltic Prehistory.* NY: Frank Cass & Co., 1966.

La Fontaine, J. S. *Initiation: Ritual Drama and Secret Knowledge Across the World.* UK: Penguin Books, 1985.

Laing, Lloyd. *Celtic Britain: Britain Before the Conquest*. UK: Paladin Books, 1984.

MacManus, Seumas. *The Story of the Irish Race*. Old Greenwich, CT: Devin-Adair Co., 1978.

Markale, Jean. *Women of the Celts*. Rochester, VT: Inner Traditions International, 1986.

Matthews, Caitlin. *The Elements of the Celtic Tradition*. UK: Element Books, 1989.

Murray, Liz and Colin. *The Celtic Tree Oracle*. NY: St. Martin's Press, 1988.

Neumann, Erich. *The Great Mother: An Analysis of the Archetype*. Princeton, NJ: Princeton University Press, 1963.

Newark, Tim. *Celtic Warriors: 400 BC–AD 1600*. UK: Blandford Press, 1986.

Norton-Taylor, Duncan. *The Celts*. NY: Time-Life Books, 1974.

Pennick, Nigel. *Practical Magic in the Northern Tradition*. UK: Aquarian Press, 1989.

Richardson, Alan. *Gate of Moon*. UK: Aquarian Press, 1984.

Ross, Anne. *Druids, Gods and Heroes from Celtic Mythology*. NY: Schocken Books, 1986.

Ross, Anne. *The Pagan Celts*. Totowa, NJ: Barnes & Noble, 1986.

Ross, Anne. *A Traveller's Guide to Celtic Britain*. Harrisburg, PA: Historical Times, 1985.

Rutherford, Ward. *The Druids: Magicians of the West*. NY: Sterling Publishing, 1990.

Squire, Charles. *Celtic Myth and Legend*. Newcastle Publishing, 1975.

Stewart, R. J. *The Underworld Initiation: A Journey Towards Psychic Transformation*. UK: Aquarian Press, 1985.

Stover, Leon E., and Kraig, Bruce. *Stonehenge: the Indo-European Heritage*. Chicago, IL: Nelson-Hall, 1979.

Webster, Graham. *Celtic Religion in Roman Britain*. Totowa, NJ: Barnes & Noble, 1986.

CHAPTER FIFTEEN

NORDIC-GERMANIC REALMS

THE NORDIC-GERMANIC tribes settled in the south of the Scandinavian peninsula, on the islands of the Baltic Sea, and in Germany between the Rhine and the Vistula about three or four centuries before the Christian era. Their ancestors were Indo-European, and though they fought each other, they had the same language, customs, and religious beliefs. They were a large group of tribes, politically independent, who later became the Viking raiders who terrorized and settled parts of Europe, Britain, Scotland, Ireland, Greenland, and Iceland.

These Teutons appear to have been divided into three groups. The Goths of the east first settled between the Oder and the Vistula, but emigrated towards the Black Sea in the second century AD. The Teutons of the north settled the Scandinavian countries. The west Germans were ancestors of the present Germans and Anglo-Saxons; they spread toward the Rhine, the Danube, and Britain.

In their own language, a Viking was a raider; the phrase *fara i viking* meant to go raiding over the seas. A typical Northman was tall and blond with blue or grey eyes. However, there were "black" Vikings—not black of skin, but with dark hair and eyes.

The Norsemen were Vikings for a number of reasons. Their countries had extremely short growing seasons, very poor rocky soil, and long winters. The land also became overpopulated. It was a hard life that shaped men to be daring, adventurous, and aggressive. Their ships and weapons were the finest in Europe. They were expert horsemen and sailors, ferocious but sometimes undisciplined fighters.

Luck ranked highest in desirable qualities. When fighting men prepared to go viking, they chose a leader known for his battle-luck. Christian priests were known for their lack of weather-luck among the Norse. No ship's captain willingly transported one. If he had to, and a storm arose, the priest was immediately thrown overboard.

The Norse left few written documents, as their *skalds*, like the Druidic bards, were the keepers of the legends and history. However, pictorial symbols of their legends can still be seen, cleverly carved in Christian churches among the standard orthodox symbols.

The skalds were skilled poets, whose responsibility it was to remember correctly the family genealogies, myths, and sagas. Unlike the Celtic bards, they could not scorn a king in song, but could use their skills to break bad news, give advice, buy life, or mock death. These poets held Odhinn in high regard and called poetry "sacred mead." Skaldic poetry was long and full of vivid descriptions and history.

For about a thousand years these people worshipped their gods without much interference from the rest of the world.[1] There was no universal faith or priesthood among the Norse and Germans. Each tribe probably had their own special rituals, festivals, and methods of worship. However, some of the festivals and procedures were similar, if not the same. The characteristics of their deities certainly were, although the names might be different from tribe to tribe. The Vikings particularly carried their cult of Thorr to every land they settled. In fact, the Irish called the Vikings of Dublin "the tribe of Thorr."

Conversion to Christianity nearly destroyed their mythological epics. Fortunately, Iceland, Norway, Denmark, and Sweden have carefully preserved the songs of the skalds and the sages, the histories, the sagas and epics.

Although from very early times the Norse were divided into three classes, Thrall (slave), Karl (farmer), and Jarl (chieftain or aristocrat), there was no purely warrior class. Every man had to be a fighter. Even women were trained to handle weapons for defense. Heimdall, in the disguise of Rigr, brought these three classes of men into being, thus becoming the genetic link between the gods and humans.

The Norse believed strongly in a code of freedom and honor. They were outspoken, fearless in battle, and steadfast in friendship, even to the taking of sworn blood-bonds. A man fostered to another family early in childhood could claim the same rights and help from his foster family as from kin.

On occasion, the Thing (court of law) would pass sentence, fine, or outlaw an uncontrollable man.[2] They had a detailed, strict code of repayment, or *weregild*, for the death or injury of any human or domestic animal. Since the Norse considered their good name of prime importance, gossip was regarded as one of the worst crimes possible. Offense taken at slurs to honor led to blood-feuds that lasted for generations.

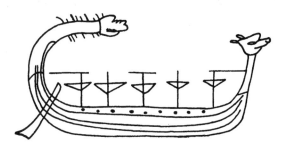

A Norse ship, early thirteenth century

Seldom was a woman married against her will. Weddings were formalized before witnesses by the bride and groom drinking the bridal ale. Divorces were simple—a declaration before witnesses at the Assembly (Thing) on the grounds for parting and a return of the dowry. No stigma was involved.

The Teutons were mainly monogamous; only kings and great chiefs had concubines. Their women were regarded as having the gift of prophecy, and none of their advice or answers were taken lightly. Illegitimate children were treated generously, often adopted by the father and given the same training as his other children.

These people built long houses, 40–100 feet in length, made of logs or planks and roofed with thatch or shingles. There was a door at each end, no windows, and long platforms along each inside wall. Two rows of wooden pillars helped to hold up the roof. A fire pit lay in the center of the pounded earth floor.

All types of wild game, beef, pork, chicken, and mutton were eaten with a variety of vegetables, fruits, and breads. Milk drinks, weak barley beer, and mead rounded out the meals. Mead made of fermented honey and water was drunk from tankards or drinking horns. Knives and spoons were known, but not forks.

RELIGION

Religious sacred places were on rocky hillsides, in groves, or in wild glens with mossy boulders. Rituals were also held before holy wells, special rocks, or trees. But there were wooden temples, too, probably built much like the Norse long houses, and marked off by fences built in a V-shape barrier. Inside these areas no blood could be shed or weapons carried. Sometimes wooden posts with human faces depicted the deities. The temples and even outdoor shrines were laid out on a north-south axis, and the people faced north to pray.

In some larger villages there were great wooden temples containing carved wooden statues of the three most important Gods: Thorr, Odhinn, and Freyr. Yarrow and mistletoe were among the herbs used for ceremonies.

The people knelt and chanted, arms upraised. The *lurs*, wailing sinuous horns about four feet long, were played during rituals. Animals, and sometimes humans, were sacrificed, using flint daggers. In later periods, wood, metal, or bread replicas replaced these blood offerings. Sacrifices of horses and humans were most commonly done to Odhinn or Wodan, God of death and battle. Other deities were given offerings dropped in lakes or bogs.

Miniature bronze chariots containing a gold Sun disk and pulled by a bronze horse represented the Sun god, as did ships. For this reason, burials or cremations in ships or plots outlined in stone to look like a ship were done for chiefs and warriors.

Sacred carving was done on great stones, using the runes (a magickal, sacred alphabet) and rough pictures of horses, ships, Sun wheels, trumpeters with lurs, charioteers, axes, etc.

The *landvaettir* were powerful land-spirits who lived in the Earth and were responsible for it. Offerings were placed for them at cairns, caves, and hillocks. The terrible dragon-heads on the Viking ships were removed before land was sighted so the landvaettir would not be frightened away.

There were full-time priests and priestesses in the temples. Among the people were men and women who practiced as seers, looking into the future and doing various magickal rites. A *vitki* was their name for a magician or wise one.

There is evidence to indicate that the terrifying berserkers were initiates of an Odhinn cult. These men were usually part of a chieftain's household. It was believed that they could change themselves into animals whenever they wished. They did leaping dances with spears and swords and wearing horned helmets. To induce their battle frenzies, they may have used a type of self-hypnosis, or trance-inducing plants. It was well known that neither fire nor steel could stop them in battle; only an instant death-wound could bring down a berserker.[3]

Nerthus, the Earth Mother, had a sacred grove on a sea island. In the spring of the year her chariot, drawn by cows, made a pilgrimage through the land. The chariot contained her image or a veiled priestess. No sword dared be lifted for any reason during this trek. At the end of her journey, the image was washed in the sea. Then the

Council of German chiefs, from the victory column of Marcus Aurelius

attending priest or slave, who had been chosen as her consort for the journey, was drowned as a sacrifice to her.

The God Thorr was called the common man's friend. Offerings of meat and bread were laid out in his temples. In these buildings were kept bronze hammers and a huge sacred arm-ring on which oaths were taken. His symbol, the double-bladed axe or hammer, was used to bless births, marriages, deaths, and cremations. The hammer was considered such a protection against all evil that men and women wore tiny hammer amulets. Fighting men worshipped Thorr as the strongest God, and Tyr for magickal influences in battle.

Freyr, as the god of fertility, was also called upon to bless marriages. Bells and hand clapping were performed in his rituals. Sacred horses were kept in some of his sanctuaries. In the Vatnsdaela Saga, there is mention of such a horse, a stallion called Freyfaxi (mane of Freyr).

Odhinn was not much trusted by the average Viking, although he was the chief God of Asgard and was worshipped by chieftains, skalds, and berserkers. Odhinn's main purpose was to fend off the terrible destiny he knew awaited the Gods and humans at Ragnarok. This put him and his actions above the human concept of good and evil.

A sacred symbol of both Freyr and Freyja was the boar. Boar images were used on ceremonial objects and war helmets. Some Teutonic tribes wore masks or helmets that covered the face and had a tusk protruding on each side. Neck-rings and arm-rings also carried the boar symbol.

Wise women, seeresses, rune-mistresses, and healers were closely connected with Freyja, Goddess of magick and love affairs (not marriages). The female *volva* went about the tribes giving predictions of the future through trance and were linked to cults of both Freyja and Odhinn. They also did healing and occasionally cursing. They did not tend to marry, but took lovers.[4] These women carried a staff with a bronze cap or mounting and wore capes, hoods, and gloves of fur.[5]

Seidr[6] was a form of magick, soul journey, trance, and divination that originated with Freyja and was a feminine mystical craft. It was fairly independent of runic magick, being more involved with shape-shifting, astral body travel through the nine worlds, sex magick, and other techniques.

Freyja was commonly known as the great *dis*. The *disir* (goddesses) were nine women dressed in black and carrying swords. Nine (a Moon number) was considered the most sacred and mysterious of numbers. At the beginning of winter, particularly in Sweden, these "spirits" and Freyja were worshipped in a ceremony called the *disablot*. The disir brought good luck, but they were also merciless in exacting justice.

Smithcraft was a mystical art as it included not only metalworking, but woodcarving, carpentry, bone carving, and other forms of magickal handicraft. A smith had to be knowledgeable about runes as it was his responsibility to engrave the correct ones on sword hilts.

The runes, which had few curved lines, were both magickal symbols and (at a later date) letters of the alphabet. Many leading Northmen learned them as part of their education. They believed that knowledge of the runes could save a man's life, blunt sword blades, calm the seas and winds, quench fire, and help to understand the language of birds.

Ancient runic alphabet

A *rynstr* or runester was very skilled in the knowledge of the runes. He had to know how the runes should be carved, how they should be read, how they should be colored, and how they should be used.[7] In ancient German, the words for "to make red" and "to endow with magickal power" were the same.

In Germany, the dragon was the guardian of the burial mound. German dragons had wings and a long tail, while Norse dragons were shaped like serpents. Jormungand, World-Serpent, who inhabited the Ocean surrounding Earth, was depicted as a long, slender, wingless dragon.

In Norse mythology, Asgard (Heaven) was the realm of the Gods where those who died violently, warriors, and righteous men went after death. There is nothing to suggest that women did not have the same privileges. Helheim, the kingdom of the Goddess Hel, had one section for criminals, and another for those who died of old age or illness. Oath-breakers and secret killers, two unforgivable crimes to the Norse, were also condemned to Hel's kingdom.

Predestination and predetermination were unknown to the Norse. They believed, however, that what each person did influenced the future. This idea is reflected in their descriptions of the Norns, or Fates. Urd was defined as "that which has become," Verthandi as "that which is becoming," and Skuld as "that which should become." The Vikings also believed in an afterlife and continuing contact between the living and the dead.

The Norse religious rituals encompassed the solstices and equinoxes, but primarily they were used for everyday happenings: plowing, harvest, birth, marriage, death, traveling, trade undertakings, etc. In other words, they approached the Gods whenever they felt a need. The most powerful times for rituals were thought to be dawn, noon, evening, and midnight.

An example of a personal ritual was the naming of a child. Not until it was certain that a new-born child would live was it sprinkled with water and given a name.

Germanic Runes

F	U,V	Th	A
R	C,K	G	W
H	N	I	J
E	P	Z	S
T	B	E	M
L	NG	D	O

DRESS AND ORNAMENTATION

Everyday clothing was simple among the Norse. The women wore ankle-length skirts embroidered in patterns of wool or woven in plaids. Their wide-necked bodices had elbow-length sleeves; they also wore jackets and openwork caps of horsehair or wool.

Men were clad in tunics, trousers, and close-fitting felt caps or metal helmets. If they were warriors, they wore chain link shirts over leather padding and usually a conical metal helmet with nose and cheek pieces. Helmets with wings and horns were rare among fighting men; these types of helmets were mainly used for religious ceremonies.

Everyone wore leather or fur moccasins tied around the legs. Furs used were fox, seal, marten, and bear; deerskin also was part of their apparel. On cool days they donned cloaks fastened at the shoulder with bronze pins and brooches.

Women either cut their hair page-boy fashion or wore it long and piled up in elaborate styles held by net caps. Usually men were clean shaven with short hair, but the warriors and Vikings tended to grow beards and mustaches and wore their long hair in braids. All women carried a dagger, distaff, and spindle at their belts. The common man carried a dagger, while the warriors carried the great carbon-hardened iron swords, daggers, and battle-axes.

Amber necklaces and amulets were used for luck in everything. Both sexes liked jewelry: bracelets, torcs, gold rings, bronze collars, earrings, necklaces, arm-bands, pins, coiled arm-rings, brooches, and pendants. Copper, bronze, and gold were the most common metals for these, and the smiths were honored and important members of each village.

SOME OF THE MYTHS

In the beginning the world consisted of only mist, ice, and frost. Audhumla, the great cow, and Ymir, the Frost Giant, were born from the warmth of the Sun touching the ice.[8] Ymir fed on Audhumla's milk, the only food available. The great cow licked the salty ice while the Frost Giant slept and licked into existence a man, Buri. Both Ymir and Buri were bisexual beings, capable of spawning offspring without a mate. Ymir perspired during his sleep; from his sweat were born his children, the Giants. Buri produced a male being called Borr. Borr married Bestla, one of Ymir's Giantess daughters; their children were Odhinn, Vili, and Ve.

Odhinn and his brothers eventually killed the Giant Ymir and built the worlds and the heavens out of the Giant's body. They also created the first human man (Askr, or ash) and woman (Embla, or elm) from two living trees by giving them a new form, intelligence, and a soul.

Maggot-like creatures crawling from Ymir's flesh were changed by Odhinn into Dwarves, small human-shaped creatures. However, he left them the color of the Earth in which they live. Their king was called Modsognir. There are said to be three tribes of Dwarves: one lives in mounds of earth, another in rocks, and the third in the high mountains. Four of the Dwarves were given the permanent task of holding up the sky.

They were named for the four directions: Nordhri (North), Austri (East), Sudhri (South), and Vestri (West).

Odhinn and his brothers then went on to create Midgard where mankind would live, and Asgard where the Gods would live. In all they created nine worlds, all held together by the World Tree, Yggdrasil.

Yggdrasil as a cosmic tree is sometimes called an ash and sometimes a yew. A clue to the correct name may be in another Norse word for yew, which is needle ash. Yggdrasil grows out of the past, lives in the present, and reaches toward the future. It nourishes all spiritual and physical life. Its roots reach into all the worlds; its boughs hang above Asgard.

Yggdrasil has three main roots that hold everything together. One root reaches into the Well of Urd in Asgard, another into the Fountain of Mimir in Midgard, and the third into the Spring of Hvergelmir in Hel. At Hvergelmir, the watchman Ivaldi and his sons defend Hel against the Storm Giants.

The World Tree is constantly under attack by evil creatures. In Niflheim, the dragon Nidhogg continually chews on its roots; in Midgard, four giant harts eat the buds and leaves. But the Norns sprinkle the tree each morning with water from Urd's fountain of life.

Of the nine worlds in Norse mythology, Asgard (home of the Aesir) is on the highest level, with Alfheim (home of the Elves) to the east and Vanaheim (home of the Vanir) to the west. The *Prose Edda* states that Midgard is in the center of Ginnungagap, an area of 11 rivers and frozen wasteland. It is Midgard that ties together all the other worlds. On the same level as Midgard is Svartalfheim to the south, Nidavellir to the east, and Jotunheim to the west. Below Midgard lie Hel and Niflheim.

Sometime after the creation of the nine worlds, the two races of gods, the Aesir and the Vanir, fell to fighting. This war lasted for some time before they decided to call a truce and exchange hostages. Mimir and Hoenir of the Aesir went to the Vanir, while Freyja and Freyr went to the Aesir. Hoenir was so indecisive that the Vanir took it as an insult and killed the wise Mimir in retaliation; they sent Mimir's head back to Odhinn. Odhinn preserved the head in herbs and oils and placed it by the Well of Mimir at the foot of the World Tree. There he could consult it as an oracle.

In the meantime the Aesir tried to torture to death the Vanir Goddess Gullveig, who had the ability to revive herself. When this did not work after three tries, the Aesir gave up. The Aesir and the Vanir decided that continued war was futile. Besides, they needed each other's strengths to fend off the Giants. They joined forces in Asgard and settled down to more or less peaceful living.

Odhinn had a very special horse, Sleipnir (offspring of Loki and the horse of a Giant), who had eight legs. Sleipnir could run the fastest, leap the highest, endure the longest of anything—human or animal. He even ran on water or in the air. However, Odhinn was jealous of Freyja's rune magick. She refused to share her knowledge with him. So he hanged himself from the World Tree Yggdrasil for nine days and nights. At the very last of his endurance, he saw the runes written clearly and understood their significance.

Dwarves, a group of supernatural beings, also played an important part in the legends. Skilled craftsmen, they made many of the Gods' weapons and possessions,

Fenrir

including Freyja's necklace Brisingamen. In order to obtain Brisingamen, Freyja had to sleep one night with each of four Dwarves; this meant that she had to master and understand completely the four Elements. Dwarves were greedy, cunning, and sometimes evil, but were usually enemies of the Giants. Dwarves hoarded gold and precious gems in their underground hiding places.

Elves were another group of supernatural beings and were divided into two categories: Light Elves and Dark Elves. The Light Elves were good and helpful; they lived in Alfheim. The Dark Elves were troublemakers who lived in caves and holes in Svartalfheim.[9]

There was a huge wolf monster in Asgard called Fenrir, a child of the God Loki. He was savage and unpredictable, even by the Gods' standards. So they decided that he must be chained. Every chain they bound on Fenrir, he broke to pieces. Then a magick chain was forged but Fenrir, fearing the seemingly innocent-looking chain, refused to cooperate. Tyr, God of justice and war, volunteered to put his hand into the wolf's mouth while the others chained the animal. When the bindings were tight, Fenrir struggled but found himself caught fast. Before Tyr could remove his hand, the wolf bit it off.

Thorr was the champion of the Gods, particularly against the Frost Giants. He had a magick hammer, Mjollnir, that was a short-handled, double-headed axe. Loki, the troublemaker, helped the Frost Giants to steal it, then repented his deed when he saw Thorr's anger. The Giants vowed they would return the hammer, but only in exchange for Freyja as a bride to their leader. Freyja was furious, so angry in fact that the Gods who had tried to talk her into accepting the bargain all fled before her wrath.

Thorr, dressed in a bridal dress and veil, took her place. He made the trickster Loki go with him. All through the wedding feast, Loki had to keep assuring the Giants that the bride who ate such huge amounts was only excited about the wedding. When Mjollnir was placed in the bride's lap to bless the marriage, Thorr grabbed it and slaughtered all the Giants there.

Loki, the troublemaker, made an occupation of lying. He liked nothing better than to stir up mischief among the Gods and Goddesses by going from one to another, spreading gossip, rumors, and jealousy. Unfortunately, the damage he did could not always be repaired. Odhinn's son Balder was a beautiful God, fully protected because his mother had petitioned every living thing to cause him no harm. But in her requests, she had missed the lowly mistletoe *(misteltein)*. Loki knew this and lied to the blind God Hodur. All the Gods were throwing objects at Balder, delighted to see everything swerve to avoid harming him. Loki took a stick of mistletoe and helped Hodur throw it. The shaft pierced Balder and killed him.

Hermod the swift, brother of Hodur, rode Sleipnir into the underworld where Balder's soul lay and bargained with Queen Hel. She finally promised that Balder could return to Asgard if everyone would weep for him. Full of hope, Hermod rode back with the message. The Gods went throughout the realms telling everyone to weep for Balder. However, they encountered a Giantess who absolutely refused. Balder could not leave the underworld.

It was not long before the Gods discovered the true identity of the Giantess—Loki in disguise. Loki was hauled before their assembly, and judgment was passed. He was bound with the guts of his son to a huge rock that went to the very depths of the Earth. Over his head the Gods hung a poison-dripping snake. Loki's wife Sigyn felt sorry for him and sits day after day with a dish to catch the burning poison. But the Teutons say that whenever she must leave to empty the dish, the poison causes Loki terrible agony. He writhes in pain, and the Earth quakes from his thrashing about.

However, Loki will have his revenge at Ragnarok (the end of the world) when he breaks free and leads the Giants against the Gods. Before Ragnarok, there will be a great winter (fimbulvetr) lasting three years with no summers in between. There will be constant war on Midgard; earthquakes and a great freeze will kill all humankind, except one man and one woman who will hide in Yggdrasil. The skies will darken; Jormungand will invade Midgard. The wolves Skoll and Hati will swallow the Sun and Moon. Hel, with her dead souls and the dog Garm, will burst out of Niflheim, crossing the Ocean in the boat Naglfari, which is made of dead men's nails. Hel will join with Loki, Fenrir, and the Giants in war against the Gods. Heimdall's horn Gjall will sound throughout the nine worlds as the combatants meet on the vast plain of Vigard.

Fenrir will kill Odhinn and then be killed by Odhinn's son Vidar. Garm and Tyr, Loki and Heimdall will destroy each other. Thorr will slay Jormungand but will die of its poison. The Earth will sink into the sea; however, Yggdrasil will survive. As new land rises, the two humans hidden in the World Tree will climb down to renew the race.

Some of the Gods will survive: Odhinn's sons Vidar and Vali; Thorr's sons Modi and Magni; Hodur and Hoenir. Balder and Nanna will return from the dead. And Thorr's hammer Mjollnir, wielded by his sons, will once again protect humans.

MAJOR GODS AND GODDESSES

AEGIR—"Alebrewer"; Vanir God of the sea; can be good or evil. He and RAN have nine daughters, or undines. Gold, prosperity, sailors, sunken treasure, brewing, control of wind and waves.

AESIR—Warrior-Gods; Keepers of the Dead; one of the races of Gods in Asgard.

ALAISIAGAE—War Goddesses. See VALKYRIES.

ASA-GODS—Aesir and Vanir deities.

THE ASYNJOR—Female attendants of FRIGG in Vingolf. One of them, a healer, was called EIR. Others were FJORGYN, FRIMIA, FIMILA, HNOSSA THE BEAUTIFUL.

AUDHUMLA—"Nourisher"; "Rich Hornless Cow"; Mother Earth; the great cow who produced BURI and nourished the Giant YMIR. Motherhood, child-rearing, home crafts.

Freyja

BALDER/BALDR/BALDUR—"The Bright One"; Aesir Sun God; Shining God; the Bleeding God; son of ODHINN and FRIGG. Sacred wells sprang up from the hoof marks of his horse. Light, advice, reconciliation, beauty, gentleness, reincarnation, wisdom, harmony, happiness.

BRAGI—Son of ODHINN and FRIGG; married to IDUNN. God of poetry and eloquence, he greets new arrivals to Valhalla with songs of their deeds. Wit, cunning, wisdom, music, writing, the arts; patron of skalds and minstrels.

FORSETI—Son of BALDER and NANNA. Justice, good laws, arbitration, peace, fairness, good judgment.

FREYJA/FREYA—*Syr* (seer); "Lady"; Great Goddess; "She who shines over the sea"; sister of FREYR and daughter of NJORD; Vanir Goddess. She was married to the God OD who mysteriously disappeared. She weeps tears of gold, but the tears which fall into the sea become amber. Her cats, Bygul and Trjegul, pull her chariot. She owns the necklace Brisingamen[10] and keeps half of the slain warriors in her hall. She is the mistress of cats, leader of the VALKYRIES, a shape-shifter, the sage or "sayer" who inspires all sacred poetry. Thirteen is her number and Friday her day. Love, beauty, animals, sex, cats, childbirth, fire, horses, enchantments, witchcraft, gold, wealth, trance, jewelry, wisdom, foresight, magick, luck, long life, fertility, the Moon, the sea, death, music, flowers, poetry, writing, protection.

FREYR/FREY/FRO—"Lord"; Vanir Sun God; "the Lover"; son of NJORD; God of Yule. He owns the boar Gullinbursti, the ship Skidbladnir, and a magick sword that moves by itself through the air. GERDA or GERD, a Giantess, is his wife. Sensual love, fertility, growth, abundance, wealth, bravery, horses, boars, protector of ships and sailors, peace, joy, happiness, rain, beauty, weather, guarantor of oaths, groves, sunshine, plant growth, sex.

FRIGG/FRIGGA/FRIJA—"Well-Beloved Spouse or Lady"; Aesir Mother Goddess; wife of ODHINN; queen of the Goddesses; a shape-shifter; knower of all things. Daughter of NOTT or NAT and sister of NJORD; mother of BALDER. Independence, childbirth, cunning, cleverness, physical love, wisdom, foresight, marriage, children, fertility, destiny, magick, enchantments.

GEFION/GEFJUN—"The Giver"; Fertility Goddess; a shape-shifter. May have been one of the Asynjor. Although not a virgin, she is the Goddess to whom virgins go at death. Magickal arts, prosperity, luck, plowing, crops, land, fortunate turn of events.

GULLIVEIG—Vanir Goddess and sorceress; "Golden Branch"; Mistress of Magick. Magick, seerers, prophecy, healing.

HEIMDALL—Vanir God of Light and the rainbow; "The White God"; guardian of Bifrost bridge. He has super sight and hearing. His horse's name is Golden Forelock. He is called "the Son of the Wave" because he was born from nine waves by ODHINN'S enchantment. Nine is a magick Moon number. Guardian, beginnings and endings, morning light, seriousness, defense against evil.

HEL/HELA—Queen of the Dead and Ruler of Niflheim; her home is called Sleet-Den or Sleetcold. Dark magick, revenge.

HERMOD—Aesir God and son of ODHINN; rode to Niflheim to try to get BALDER back. Honor, bravery.

HODUR/HOTH/HOTHR/BJORNO-HODER—"The blind God"; Aesir God of winter; son of ODHINN and FRIGG. Passiveness. Famous archer before he became blind.

HOENIR/HONIR—Aesir God; a great warrior but not clever. Aggressiveness, bravery.

HOLDA/HOLDE/HOLLE/HULDA (Benign)/BERTHA/BERCHTA (White Lady)—North Germanic name for HEL. "White Lady"; "Black Earth Mother"; Goddess of winter and Witchcraft; the Crone aspect of the Moon; rides on the Wild Hunt. She is sometimes seen riding on a goat with a pack of 24 spotted hounds (her daughters) running beside her. Fate, karma, the arts, dark magick, revenge.

IDUNN/IDUN/IDUNA—Aesir Goddess of immortality; wife of BRAGI; keeper of the golden apples. Youth, responsibility, beauty, long life.

LOKI—"Father of lies"; the Trickster; Sky-Traveller; Shape-Changer; Giant who is the blood-brother of ODHINN; son of the Giant FARBAUTI (Cruel Smiter); married SIGYN. He is attractive and free with the ladies. A dangerous god to invoke as one can never be certain how he will answer. Earthquakes, fire, forest fires, cunning, wit, stealth, deceit, mischief, daring, agility, trickery, thieves, revenge, destruction, lecherousness, death, lies, evil, dark magick.

MIMIR/MIMR/MIMI—Very wise Aesir God; his head kept at the Fountain of Mimir after his death. Wisdom, knowledge, springs, pools, inland lakes, peace, teaching, the arts.

NANNA/NANA/ANNA/INANNA—Aesir Goddess; "The Moon"; Great Mother; Earth Goddess; wife of BALDER. Love, gentleness.

NEHALLENNIA—Goddess of plenty, seafaring, fishing, fruitfulness. Her symbol is a cornucopia.

NERTHUS/ERCE—Earth Mother; Fertility Goddess. Peace, spring, fertility, witchcraft, wealth, groves, the sea, purification.

NJORD—Vanir God of the sea; father of FREYR and FREYJA. Lives in Noatun (Anchorage). His Giantess wife SKADI picked him for his beautiful feet. Rules fire, winds and seas. Fishing, sailors, prosperity, success, livestock, lands, journey-luck, guarantor of oaths, wisdom, stubbornness.

THE NORNS—The Fates; the Wyrd Sisters; three women usually found near the World Tree at the Well of Urd in Asgard. URD/URTH/WYRD/ERTHA/WURD/WEIRD (past, destiny), VERTHANDO/VERDNANDI (present), SKULD (the future).

ODHINN/ODIN/WODIN/WODEN/OTHINN—Aesir King of the Gods; "Allfather"; Sky God; Great Father; All-Seeing; "Frenzied, mad"; God of the hanged and the Wild Hunt; God of storm, rain, and harvest. A shape-shifter, he makes men mad or possessed with a blind raging fury. He produces the battle panic called "battle-fetter." Three different frenzies or madnesses are his gifts to man: the warrior in battle, the seer in trance, and the poet in creativity. Subtle, wily, mysterious, and dangerous, often ignoring pacts made in honor with men. Attended by his two ravens, two wolves, and the Valkyries. Feared by ordinary people and worshipped only by princes, poets, the berserkers, and sorcerers. Unpredictable when invoked. Runes, poetry, words of power, sacred poetry, magick, divination, storms, wind, death, rebirth, knowledge, weather, justice, reincarnation, wisdom, the arts, initiation, law, light, music, prophecy, patron of priests, war, inspiration, weapons, horses, deceit, medicine, fate, civilization; patron of poets, sages, and writers.

RAN—"The Ravager"; Vanir Goddess; wife of AEGIR. She is unpredictable, malicious. Drowning, the sea, sailors, storms, great terror.

Odhinn

SIF—Aesir Goddess; Earth Mother; wife of THORR. She is noted for her beautiful hair. Harvest, fruitfulness, plenty, generosity.

SIGYN/SIGUNA/SIGNY—Goddess wife of LOKI; two sons VALI and NARVI. Love, faithfulness, loyalty.

SJOFNA—Goddess of love. One of the Asynjor.

SKADI—"Harm"; daughter of the Giant THJASSE; wife of NJORD. Mountains, winter, hunting, revenge, dark magick.

THORR/THOR/THUNAR/THUNOR/ DONAR—Aesir God; "The Thunderer"; "High Thunderer"; champion of the Gods and enemy of the Giants and Trolls; protector of the common man; son of ODHINN and JORD. His symbol is his magick hammer Mjollnir (Destroyer). He has a magick belt (Megingjardar or Strength-Increaser) that increases his strength. He drives a chariot pulled by two giant male goats; his wife is SIF. Although he is sometimes overhasty in judgment, he is a totally reliable friend and battle-companion. He has wild red hair and beard; always in battle dress.

Thorr

Strength, law and order, defense, oaks, goats, thunder, lightning, storms, weather, crops, trading voyages, water, courage, trust, revenge, protection, war, battle.

TYR/TIU/TIWAZ/TIW/ZIU—Aesir God; "The One-Handed"; patron of the Thing or Assembly; called the bravest of the Gods. Giver of victory in battle against odds; he is never deceitful. He presides over law, legal contracts, assemblies of the people for judicial matters, awarded victory in combat. The sky, war, athletics, victory in battle, justice, meaningful self-sacrifice, order, bravery, honor, integrity, law and the binding of solemn oaths, courage.

ULL/ULLR—"The Magnificent"; "the Bow God"; sometimes known as the Death God; son of ORVANDEL-EGIL by the beautiful SITH. God of archery, skiing, winter sports; powerful enchanter. Thrown out of Asgard by ODHINN because the Allfather was jealous. Beauty, hunting, nobility, magick, single combats or contests.

VALKYRIES/WAELCYRIE/VALKYRJA/IDICI—"Choosers of the Slain"; female warrior-attendants of ODHINN,[11] they direct the course of battles, choosing the valiant warriors for Valhalla. Other names were VILAS, WILAS, WILIS, WAELCEASIG. Tradition says there are thirteen of them. BRYNHILD as SIGRDRIFA (Victory-Giver) was a valkyrie. She initiated SIGURD into runic wisdom. They are helmeted Goddesses with spears crowned with flames and mounted on flying horses whose manes drop dew or hail. They can also turn themselves into swan-maidens. They are death angels, mare-women. Associated with horses and wolves. Fearlessness, war, death.

VANIR—Fertility Gods of Asgard; second race of deities. Magick powers, witchcraft.

WELAND/WAYLAND/WIELAND/VOLUND/VOLUNDR—North Germanic God of smiths; Wonder Smith; prince of the fairies; supreme craftsman. A shape-shifter associated with horses. Mentioned in the tales of Siegfried and Dietrich of Bern. Strength, cunning, skill, healing, horses, magick, metal-working.

YMIR—First Frost Giant. Brutal, evil, violent.

Valhalla

ENDNOTES

1. Davidson, H. R. Ellis. *Gods and Myths of the Viking Age*.
2. Freya Aswynn, in *Leaves of Yggdrasil*, says that arbitration and law were the privileges of women in the old German tradition.
3. Davidson, H. R. Ellis. *Gods and Myths of the Viking Age*. Davidson quotes an example of this from the *Ynglinga Saga*.
4. Aswynn, Freya. *Leaves of Yggdrasil*. Another name for these priestesses was *seidkona*. In Old English she was called a *haegtessa*, in Iceland a *gythia*.
5. *Voluspa*, or the Sibyl's Prophecy, represent the type of prophecies and the manner in which they were given by the *volva* or *vala*. Elsa-Brita Titchenell, in *The Masks of Odin*, gives a very readable translation of this epic.
6. Davidson, in *Gods and Myths of the Viking Age*, uses the word *seidr*, while Thorsson, in *The Nine Doors of Midgard* and other of his books, uses the word *seith*.
7. Thorsson, Edred. *Futhark: A Handbook of Rune Magic*, and *Runelore*. Thorsson writes that the runes were divided into the Elder Runes, the Viking Runes, and the Medieval Runes. In both books he gives detailed information on their history, use, and the poetic verses that traditionally go with each rune.
8. Thorsson, Edred. *Runelore*. Thorsson has complete descriptions and diagrams of the nine worlds and their inhabitants in his books.
9. Thorsson says that Dark Elves and Dwarves are the same.

10. Crossley-Holland, Kevin. *The Norse Myths*. The poem *Husdrapa* has the earliest mention of the necklace of the Brisings. Davidson says that necklaces were associated with the Mother Goddess, particularly a fertility goddess.
11. Davidson, H. R. Ellis. *Gods and Myths of the Viking Age*. Davidson calls them a link between the living and the dead.

BIBLIOGRAPHY

Aswynn, Freya. *Leaves of Yggdrasil*. St. Paul, MN: Llewellyn Publications, 1990.

Barrett, Clive. *The Norse Tarot: Gods, Sagas and Runes from the Lives of the Vikings*. UK: Aquarian Press, 1989.

Branston, Brian. *Gods and Heroes From Viking Mythology*. NY: Schocken Books, 1982.

Branston, Brian. *The Lost Gods of England*. UK: Oxford University Press, 1974.

Chickering, Howell D., Jr. *Beowulf: A Dual-Language Edition*. NY: Anchor Press/Doubleday, 1977.

Chubb, Thomas Caldecot. *The Northmen*. Cleveland, OH: World Publishing Co., 1964.

Crossley-Holland, Kevin. *The Norse Myths*. NY: Pantheon Books, 1980.

Davidson, H. R. Ellis. *Gods and Myths of the Viking Age*. NY: Bell Publishing, 1981.

Davidson, H. R. Ellis. *The Journey to the Other World*. Totowa, NJ: D. S. Brewer Ltd. & Rowman & Littlefield for The Folklore Society.

Davidson, H. R. Ellis. *Myths and Symbols in Pagan Europe*. Syracuse, NY: University Press, 1988.

Eliade, Mircea. *Shamanism: Archaic Techniques of Ecstasy*. Princeton, NJ: Princeton University Press, 1964.

Ellis, Hilda Roderick. *The Road to Hel*. NY: Greenwood Press, 1968.

Evans, Cheryl, and Millard, Anne. *Usborne Illustrated Guide to Norse Myths and Legends*. Tulsa, OK: ECC Publishing, 1987.

Flowers, Stephen. *The Galdrabok: An Icelandic Grimoire*. York Beach, ME: Samuel Weiser, 1989.

Froncek, Thomas. *The Norsemen*. NY: Time-Life Books.

Gayley, Charles Mills. *The Classic Myths in English Literature and in Art*. NY: Ginn & Co., 1939.

Gibson, Michael. *The Vikings*. UK: Wayland Publishers, 1987.

Goodrich, Norma Lorre. *Medieval Myths*. NY: New American Library, 1977.

Herzberg, Max J. *Myths and Their Meanings*. Boston, MA: Allyn & Bacon, 1928.

Howard, Michael A. *The Runes and Other Magical Alphabets*. UK: Aquarian Press, 1981.

Kummer, Adolf. *Rune Magic*. Trans. by DuWayne Fish. Austin, TX: Rune-Gild, no date.

La Fay, Howard. *The Vikings*. Washington, DC: National Geographic Society, 1972.

Lindow, John. *Myths and Legends of the Vikings*. Santa Barbara, CA: Bellerophon Books, 1979.

MacCulloch, J. A. *The Celtic and Scandinavian Religions*. Westport, CT: Greenwood Press, 1973.

MacKenzie, D. A. *German Myths and Legends*. NY: Avenel, 1985.

Magnusson, Magnus. *Viking Hammer of the North*. UK: Orbis Publishing, 1979.

Neward, Tim. *Celtic Warriors: 400 BC-AD 1600*. UK: Blandford Press, 1986.

Palsson, Hermann, and Edwards, Paul. *Seven Viking Romances*. NY: Penguin, 1985.

Pennick, Nigel. *Practical Magic in the Northern Tradition*. UK: Aquarian Press, 1989.

Quennell, Marjorie. *Everyday Life in Anglo-Saxon, Viking and Norman Times*. NY: G.P. Putnam's Sons, 1955.

Rackham, Arthur. *Rackham's Color Illustrations for Wagner's "Ring."* NY: Dover Publications, 1979.

Serraillier, Ian. *Beowulf, the Warrior*. NY: Scholastic Book Services, 1970.

Simpson, Jacqueline. *Everyday Life in the Viking Age*. NY: Dorset Press, 1987.

Skinner, Hubert M. *Readings in Folk-Lore*. NY: American Book Co., 1893.

Sturluson, Snorri. *King Harald's Saga*. NY: Dorset Press, 1966.

Thorsson, Edred. *A Book of Troth*. St. Paul, MN: Llewellyn Publications, 1989.

Thorsson, Edred. *Futhark: A Handbook of Rune Magic*. York Beach, ME: Samuel Weiser, 1984.

Thorsson, Edred. *The Nine Doors of Midgard*. St. Paul, MN: Llewellyn Publications, 1991.

Thorsson, Edred. *Runelore*. York Beach, ME: Samuel Weiser, 1987.

Thorsson, Edred. *Rune Might*. St. Paul, MN: Llewellyn Publications, 1989.

Titchenell, Elsa-Brita. *The Masks of Odin*. Pasadena, CA: Theosophical University Press, 1988.

Wise, Terence. *Saxon, Viking and Norman: Men-at-Arms Series*. UK: Osprey Publishing, 1987.

CHAPTER SIXTEEN

FINNISH-UGRIAN REALMS

THE FINNISH-UGRIAN race comprises a great number of tribes who speak different dialects derived from the same language. They are divided into four principal groups: the Ugrians, Voguls, Ostyaks, and Magyars of West Siberia; Permians, Zyrians, Votyaks, Permyaks of the provinces of Vyatka and Perm in Russia; the Cheremis and Mordvins on the middle Volga; and the Finns, Karelians, Esthonians, Livonians, Lapps, Samoyeds, and Siryans in the West.

Sometime before the first century AD, they entered Russia and were slowly pushed north and west into the Baltic area. The last of these tribes to enter Europe were the Magyars, who entered Hungary in the ninth century. They tended to live in isolated groups and were basically nomads. They settled most of central and northern Sweden and Norway and all of Finland before either intermarrying with the Scandinavians or retreating to the far north. Because the Finnish tribes were separated from one another, they were influenced by a variety of other cultures: Iranian, Slav, Scandinavian. Today the religious beliefs of these people are almost entirely lost.

The Finns were a Mongolian, Ural-Altaic speaking people related to the Arctic Siberians. They differed in physical description from the Norse-Germanic peoples.

249

The Finns were smaller and darker in coloring. The North Germanic legends of the Dark Elves may have arisen from their encounters with the original Finnish people.[1] Today, the true Finns are found only in the far north in Finnmark or Lapland.

RELIGION

Sources for early Finnish beliefs are very few, far more scarce than even those of the Norse. The most important of these sources is a collection of chants called Magic Songs and the long epic heroic poem *Kalevala*.[2]

The *Kalevala* was compiled by the Finnish scholar Elias Lonnrot in the early 1800s. He traveled about the country, collecting a great number of songs or *runot* (runes) which had been handed down for generations among the peasantry. When first published in 1835, the *Kalevala* had about 12,000 verses. However, by the final edition in 1849 it had grown to 22,800 verses.[3] The theme of this mythic epic is the struggle between Kalevala or the "Fatherland of Heroes" and Pohja (Pohjola) or Northern Finland. Vainamoinen, son of the Virgin of the Air, is the main hero of the myth, along with Lemminkainen.

In the sacred chants of the Finnish clans in Estonia can be found bits and pieces of rituals and names. These groups call their Earth Goddess Maa Ema, while the Votyaks of Siberia call her Muzjem Mumi. Goddess names still known in Finland are Ilmatar, Mielikki, Maan Emoinen, and Rauni.[4]

The Goddess Rauni was associated with the rowan tree or mountain ash. Throughout much of Scandinavia the mountain ash tree became part of rituals performed on May 1, called Rowan Witch Day. Twigs and branches of this have long been used as a protection against evil in this section of the world.

Ilmatar was considered an ancient Creator Goddess, while Mielikki was called Mistress of the Forest. Very old sacred chants still used among the Finns call upon the spirits of Nature for help. Wild forest animals were considered the herds and property of the woodland God Tapio and his beautiful wife. Thus before any hunt, prayers and offerings had to be made. If a bear were killed, the hunter formally asked forgiveness of the dead animal and asked its spirit to join in the feast and celebration.

The Finno-Ugric races venerated ancestors, worshipped a variety of spirits, and believed firmly in magick and sorcery. They also believed in personal and Nature gods. Their belief in (and evidently their performance of) magick was so strong that in the Middle Ages Norwegian kings forbade their subjects to travel to Finland to consult magicians. During the sixteenth and seventeenth centuries Swedish authorities even went so far as to search out and confiscate the *quodbas* (magick drums) of the Laplanders.

The Finnish religious leaders were usually called shamans. But shamanism was not a religion in itself. The shamans did magick, conjuration, incantations, and spells to control men, animals, divine or demonic entities, and inanimate beings.

However, shamanism was the privilege of a gifted few. Only the highest grade of sorcerer was allowed to use a drum and raise spirits.

The drum was very important to the shaman. He used a single-head or frame drum that was called the "shaman's horse." Chanting was done to its beat. Often rattles, bells, and small images were tied to the drum frame. The drum was considered necessary in shamanic trances, as its beat allowed the shaman to fly through the air, carried him to the underworld, and helped him to summon and imprison spirits. Other instruments were scrapers, bells, and percussion sticks.

A Samoyed priest

The shaman performed the function of doctor and healer, magician, priest, mystic, and poet, protector of the tribe. He had little to do with birth or death, unless there was a difficult birth or the people feared the deceased would haunt the tribe.

A person became a shaman through hereditary transmission or by obeying the call of the gods and spirits. It was required that such a person have ecstatic experiences, such as special dreams or trances. Then he had to pass through certain initiatory ordeals and be instructed by the old master shamans. In a few tribes, shamanism was also transmitted in the female line. Anyone touched by lightning automatically became a shaman.

Sometimes there would be battles between shamans; this took place during trances when they went out from their bodies in animal forms. During these fights they would try to find and destroy the adversary's soul. Seeing and obtaining a spirit helper, either in dreams or awake, was required. A shaman could offer sacrifices to his particular helpers and guardians, but he did not participate in tribal sacrifices to the gods.

Shamanic costumes were cosmic symbols, magickal clothing that helped the shaman attune his mind to the spiritual level needed to do his work. He wore pendants and necklaces of special objects, a headdress or special cap, belt, and other magickal articles. The costume was considered full of "spirits" and necessary for trance journeys in particular. Bones, feathers, claws, and teeth were used. The shaman often carried a carved staff.

Among the Lapps and Samoyeds, natural stones of curious shapes resembling humans or animals were considered sacred; these were called *seide*. These objects were placed in a sacred spot and used to gain predictions or obtain desires. Wooden treetrunks or posts were used in the same manner.

The Finns, like most nomadic peoples, applied their spiritual, magickal beliefs to everyday survival and needs. In their original form, their rituals followed no discernable cyclic pattern, such as did the Norse or Celts. Where possible, most of their rituals were conducted within a grove or forest.[5]

Finnish wizards were believed to be capable of raising or stopping winds; the Esthonian peasants still fear the winds from Lappland, saying they are caused by Finnish wizards and can strike a man dead.

The Finlanders believed in the Little People in the forms of Dwarves and Kobolds. To them the Dwarves, who lived in a magnificent underground kingdom, were basically friendly toward humans if they were treated with respect and kindness. The Kobold was a home sprite also found in northern Europe. Although people made pacts with them, offering food and shelter in return for prosperity, the Kobolds were noted for causing mischief. The Kobold, called Para in Finland, could be enticed to become a willing servant of a human, but loved to do things like steal milk from cows.[6] Whether a Kobold was enticed into a house or came of his own will, they were considered notoriously difficult to remove. Some churches in the region kept exorcists whose primary job was to expel unwanted Kobolds.

DRESS AND ORNAMENTATION

The Laplanders, Samoyeds, and Siryans wore much the same clothing as the North American Eskimo: fur and hides. They often tattooed their faces with special patterns.

In Finland (Suomi is their word for the country), the people were orderly and particularly clean. The bathhouse was considered of great importance; this was really more of a sauna bath as large stones were heated and water thrown over them.

The women wore bright-colored aprons, long skirts, fringed jackets, and a head-dress or embroidered handkerchief. Sometimes they substituted a pinafore-type garment fastened at the shoulders for the skirt. Underneath they wore a long-sleeved blouse. The apron was heavily embroidered and fringed. The brooches that pinned the dress at the shoulders had a chain between them, supporting a small purse and other needed objects.

The men dressed in a jacket, pants to just below the knee, long stockings, and a tunic. The decorative belt at the waist was used for carrying weapons and other useful necessities. Everyone wore a type of flat shoe.

Red was the predominant color, and much embroidery was done on clothing. Geometrical designs were often worked in red cross-stitch and backstitch on white or

Finnish ornamental design

252

cream material. Blue in shades from light green-blue to dark violet-blue was favored, and often relieved by light, creamy yellow.

In the Russian areas, geometrical patterns were also used for decoration. Nearly every district had its own special costume, but the basic garments were much the same. A skirt called a *paneva*, made of thick checked material, was worn by women under a combined skirt and bodice called a *sarafan*. Over this they wore a short bodice with sleeves, usually of embroidered linen, but sometimes of silk brocade or velvet. The sleeves of this bodice alone required four to five yards of material. Embroidered slippers, hand-woven belts, and extravagant headdresses completed the outfit. Jewelry was chains of filigree work, crosses, earrings in gold or silver, and pearls threaded in the hair. Young girls could show their hair, but matrons had to wear a veil *(fata)* over the headdress.

The men donned shirts of white or colored linen that usually hung down over the trousers; the collars and cuffs were embroidered. Trousers of homespun cloth were tucked into leather top-boots. Both sexes wore fur capes during cold weather.

Some of the Myths

Most of the Finno-Ugric legends are contained in the *Kalevala*, the stories of their gods and heroes. In the beginning, the *Kalevala* says, Ilmatar, the Virgin daughter of Air, came down from the sky into the sea. The East wind made her pregnant with the hero Vainamoinen. The Goddess floated upon the water for seven centuries, unable to give birth because there was no land. She prayed to the God Ukko, the highest of gods, to help her. Ukko sent a teal to build a nest on her knee. When the teal's eggs fell and broke, the Earth, sky, Sun, Moon, and clouds were formed from them by the creative powers of the Goddess. However, she continued to carry the child within her for 30 summers.[7] After his birth into the cosmic ocean, it took Vainamoinen another 31 years to reach dry land and begin his life.

Another great hero was Lemminkainen. As a baby, his mother bathed him three times one summer night and nine times one autumn night so he could become a scholar, magician, singer, and a man of ability. But Lemminkainen tended to think of himself as invincible and finally overreached himself when he tried to kill the swan of Tuoni. He had not bothered to learn the magick words that gave protection from snake bites. It tore the hero to pieces and threw him into the river. Lemminkainen's mother patiently gathered up the pieces of her son, carefully fitted them back together with magick, and restored him to life. However, the hero could not speak. His mother called upon the bee Mehilainen to go to the ninth heaven and bring back the balm used by Jumala himself. When Mehilainen returned, the woman spread the balm on the terrible wounds. The hero's only comment when he awoke was: "I've slept a long time."

Another legend of the *Kalevala* tells of the origin of fire. Fire came from a spark made by Ukko when he hit his sword against his fingernail. He gave the spark to one of the Air virgins for safekeeping, but she carelessly let it escape. The spark rolled through the clouds and fell into a lake where a blue trout swallowed it. The trout was eaten by a red salmon, and he by a huge gray pike. Two heroes, Vainamoinen and

Ilmarinen, finally caught the gray pike and freed the spark. Before they could capture the spark in a copper jar, it caused many fires.

When the hot-head Joukahainen challenged the hero Vainamoinen, he called up all his magickal knowledge. Vainamoinen listened, and then sang his magick in turn. He overcame the young Joukahainen with spells. The hero changed the young man's sleigh into a withered shrub, his whip into a reed, his horse into a rock, and ended by throwing Joukahainen waist-deep into a swamp in a briar patch up to his ears. Joukahainen had to promise the hero the hand of his sister Aino in order to get out. Later he tried to avenge himself by shooting an arrow at Vainamoinen, but he only hit the hero's horse. Vainamoinen, thrown into the sea by the frightened horse, was rescued by an eagle.

In Finnish mythology, the kingdom of the dead, or underworld, was not a place of punishment. It was a land much like any other, except that it was darker. It had a sun to shine, and forests, rivers, and animals. The names for this underworld were Tuonela, land of Tuoni; or Manala, land of Mana. It was protected from the mortal world by a river with black billows. For a human to go into the underworld required an arduous journey: a week through thickets, a week through woods, and a week through deep forests. Only the hero Vainamoinen made a journey to the land of Tuonela and returned to Earth.

Major Gods and Goddesses

AHTO/AHTI—Chief god of waters and seas. His wife was the water Goddess VELLAMO.

AKKA/MAA-EMOINEN/MADER-AKKA/RAUNI—Earth Mother; Goddess of the harvest and female sexuality. Wife of the supreme sky God UKKO. Mountain ash was sacred to her. See RAUNI.

HIISI—Part of group of evil spirits along with LEMPO and PAHA. God of evil, skilled sorcerers, and necromancers; spells, sacred drums, trance, chanting.

ILMA—God of the air. Father of the Goddess LUONNOTAR/ILMATAR.

ILMATAR/LOUNNOTAR—Virgin daughter of Air; Sky Mother; Water Mother; Creatress Goddess; Daughter of Nature; Mother of the Waters. Immense powers.

ILMARINEN—In the *Kalevala*, the magickal smith who forged the mysterious, powerful talisman Sampo. He made the Sampo out of the point of a swan's feathers, milk of a sterile cow, small grain of barley, and wool of a sheep. God of smiths, magick, talismans, prosperity.

JUMALA/MADER-ATCHA—Supreme God; Creator God; originally probably a sky god. Oak was sacred to him. God of the sky and thunder, weather, twilight, dusk.

KALMA—"Corpse odor"; daughter of TUONI and TUONETAR. Goddess of death.

KIPU-TYTTO—Daughter of TUONI. Goddess of illness.

KUL/KUL-JUNGK—"Fish-spirit"; an evil Siryan water spirit; lived in deep water and had a human shape. When the ice broke in the late spring, wooden or birch fish images were taken to the fishing place and left as sacrifices.

Symbolic representation of the divine couple, Jumala and Akka

KUU—Moon goddess.

LEIB-OLMAI—"Alder man"; bear man; a Laplander bear god. At bear festivals, the hunters' faces were sprinkled with extract of alder bark, a ritual in honor of Leib-olmai. Luck in hunting, protection from injuries.

LOUHI—Fierce queen of the Arctic whose magickal battle with VAINAMOINEN is told in the *Kalevala*. Goddess of sorcery, evil, dark magick.

LOVIATOR—Daughter of TUONI and TUONETAR. Diseases came into being from her union with the Wind. Goddess of plagues; source of all evil.

MIELIKKI—Goddess of the Forest. Wife of TAPIO and mother of TUULIKKI and NYYRIKKI. Protector of woodland animals; Goddess of the Hunt. Bears, hunting, animals, archery, abundant grain.

MOTHER OF METSOLA— Forest goddess.

NUM—A Samoyed sky god; Supreme God. No images were made of him.

NUMITOREM—A Vogul sky god who created all animals.

OVDA—Unfriendly Finnish forest spirit. He was seen as a naked figure with his feet turned backwards, sometimes appearing as a man, sometimes as a woman.

PAIVA—Sun god.

PELLERVOINEN—God of fields; lord of the trees and plants.

RAUNI/MAAN-ENO/RAVDNA/ROONIKKA—Forest Mother; thunder Goddess; spirit of the mountain ash. One of the most powerful deities and wife of the oak-god of thunder. Childbirth, ease from pain.

TAPIO—"Dark beard"; God of water and woods. His wife was MIELIKKI, his son NYYRIKKI, and his daughter TUULIKKI. This triad had power over anyone who walked or hunted in the forest. Tapio wore a fir hat and a moss cloak. His realm of forest was called Tapiola. Abundance of game.

Tuoni—Lord of Tuonela or Manala (the underworld). His wife was Tuonetar. Their daughters were the Goddesses Kalma (death), Loviatar and Kipu-Tytto/Kivutar (diseases), and Vammatar (suffering). God of death.

Ukko—"Ancient father who reigns in the heavens"; god of the sky and air; Supreme God; highest of gods. Clouds, rain, thunder, help with the impossible.

Vainamoinen—Finnish sorcerer, archetypal magician of the North; son of Ilmatar, the Air goddess. He invented the zither and was a superb musician whose playing tamed animals.

Yambe-Akka—"Old woman of the dead"; the Lapps believed she had charge of the underworld.

Zaltys—Among the Balts, Lithuanians, Prussians, and Letts, a harmless green snake loved by Saule the Sun goddess. To kill it was sacrilege. It had an honored place in houses. Aitvaras was a flying zaltys which gave off light. Marriage, birth, fertility.

Endnotes

1. Stone, Merlin. *Ancient Mirrors of Womanhood.* Stone writes that although Finland is today considered a Scandinavian country, the Finn-Ugrian and Norse were two distinct, diverse cultures.
2. Kirby, W. F. *Kalevala.*
3. Guirand, Felix. *New Larousse Encyclopedia of Mythology.*
4. Holmberg, Uno. "Finno Ugric, Siberian Mythology" in *Mythology of All Races,* J. A. MacCulloch, editor. Boston, MA: 1928.
5. Frazer, James. *The Golden Bough.*
6. Keightley, Thomas. *The World Guide to Gnomes, Fairies, Elves and Other Little People.*
7. Campbell, Joseph. *The Hero With a Thousand Faces.*

Bibliography

Curtin, Jeremiah. *Myths and Folk-Tales of the Russians, Western Slavs and Magyars.* Boston, MA: Little, Brown & Co., 1890?

De Gerez, Toni. *Louhi: Witch of North Farm.* NY: Viking Penguin, 1988.

Holmberg, Uno. "Finno Ugric, Siberian Mythology" in *Mythology of All Races.* Ed. by J. A. MacCulloch. Boston, MA: 1928.

Kirby, W. F. *Kalevala.* Dent, 1907.

Lester, Katherine. *Historic Costume.* Peoria, IL: The Manual Arts Press, 1942.

CHAPTER SEVENTEEN

SLAVONIC-RUSSIAN REALMS

As far back as 2000–1000 BC, the Slavs began to emerge as a distinct racial group in the area of the Carpathian Mountains, but it was not until the sixth century AD that they emerged entirely as a separate ethnic unit distinguishable from the other cultures around them. They spread slowly to the Dnieper, Ukrain, Vistula, and Oder regions. They had early cultural contacts with various Iranian tribes, such as the Scythians and Sarmatians. During the sixth century, the Slavs crossed the Danube and went south through the Balkan peninsula, overrunning Thrace, northern Greece, and on to Constantinople.

Small family clans lived in forest areas that were cut up by marshes, lakes, and rivers. They survived by fishing, hunting, raising cattle, and some farming. Today they are known as the Russians, Byelorussians, Ukranians, Poles, Sorbs, Lusatians, Kashubians, Czechs, Slovaks, Slovenes, Croats, Serbs, Bulgarians, and Macedonians.

RELIGION

The only information available today about the religious beliefs and practices among the ancient Slavs was recorded from the eleventh to the fifteenth centuries, primarily by Christian monks. Unfortunately, this information is negatively colored by these writers, ones such as Thietmar of Merseburg, Adam of Bremen, Helmold and Saxo Grammaticus. This information mainly concerns the Russians and the Slavs living along the Elbe River. However, since tribal differences among the Slavs then were not as great as today, it is quite likely that these recorded customs were applicable to most clans.

The Slavic term for God is *bog*,[1] meaning "good" or "communicating." Early Slavs conceived that one of their gods was over all the others; this deity they called *boh bohov*, or the God of gods. This deity was Svantovit, creator of lightning, sole lord of all creation, ruler of the Sun and heaven, the one from whom all other deities came. Among the Russians, however, Perun was worshipped as the supreme God.

The Slavs believed that all life was unified, with even inanimate objects having an invisible agent controlling them. Trees and animals were considered older and wiser than man and were his ancestors. Animals possessed superior powers. For this reason, specific animals were never killed or eaten. Certain trees marked a sacred zone and were never cut. These trees were thought to be the dwelling place for souls. Cracks, caves, and holes in the Earth were gates to the underworld where most of the dead lived.

Ancestor worship was practiced, as it was said that the forefathers of the clans were still deeply concerned with their welfare and did all they could to help. Ancestor worship was widespread among the Slavs. They made small statues of them and gave them prominent places in their houses near the door or above the hearth. Czech was the leader of a tribe that still bears his name.[2]

The Slavs believed that the soul had a separate existence from the body, resided in the breast, and was revealed in the breath. They also believed the soul could leave the body during sleep and dreams, sometimes to protect property or trouble other sleeping people. When the body died, the soul was said to stay in the vicinity for 40 days, many times in the shape of animals or birds.

The *upir* or vampire[3] in Slavic belief was the soul of a dead person that came from the grave to harm others. These were the souls of sorcerers, murderers, or generally evil and bad people; the body did not decay. These souls came out only at night to suck blood from the living but had to return to the grave at cock-crow.

In contrast, the term werewolf *(vlkodlak)* was applied to a person who could change into a wolf-form during his lifetime. These people were also said to have the power to cause solar and lunar eclipses.

The ancient Slavs referred to death only indirectly by the term *sumirtu*. They cremated or interred their dead, but burial probably came in with Christianity. The burial, which had no particular place, was followed by a funeral banquet reminiscent of an Irish wake; this was called a *strava* or *kar*. A vacant place was set at the banquet for the deceased and he was invited to share the meal. Wine and honey were poured over the grave. Ceremonies were also held 3, 7, 20, and 40 days after the funeral. At six months and one year the family again held ceremonial rites.

The Slavs said there were several areas occupied by the dead: Nav (lassitude, death) was the general abode of the dead, a place of shadows with green fields and groves; Raj, a Pagan paradise of Sun over the eastern ocean; Peklo, a subterranean place of great warmth, a lake of fire and smoke, and the home of evil spirits. Sometimes the Slavs described the afterworld as a mountain of glass or iron that was very difficult to climb.

Vlad the Impaler (Dracula) eats while his victims suffer

The cult of the Great Goddess came from their contacts with the Scythians. She was pictured in human form with her arms upraised. After the Christians destroyed all her images, the Slavs still portrayed the Great Goddess in that form in their embroidery.

Festivals of the ancient Slavs and Russians were determined by the course of the Sun. The whole year was seen as a struggle between light and darkness, life and death. The year began in the turning of the Sun at winter solstice. The main festivals were Koleda, winter solstice; Rusalye, spring equinox; Kupalo, also known as Jarilo, summer solstice.

Koleda, for the god Kolyada at winter solstice, lasted about ten days. It was also a festival honoring Lada, the Goddess of love, spring, youth, and fertility, who was considered to be reborn each year with the Sun. The Russians called it *kutuja*, a term that was later applied to the Christian's Christmas Eve. An image of a wolf was carried about the village to signify the end of the rule of Chernobog, the Black God, which comes with the rebirth of the Sun. Each family burned a Yule log in personal celebration and invited their household gods to join in the festivities. Groups of children went from house to house singing and were rewarded with little gifts. Koleda was a seasonal festival of rejoicing, games, exchange of gifts, and the forgiving of enemies. Prophecy for the coming year was also practiced.

Spring was the time of Rusalye (also known as Rusadle), Turice, Letnice, and Trisna or Tryzna. The Rusalki (water nymphs) were honored at this time. In Russia, dolls called Morena (or death-doll) were thrown into rivers to gain the aid of the inhabiting rusalki. The Slavs buried, drowned, or burned dolls[4] to symbolize the end of winter and death.

Turice was associated with the war god Tur; the word Tur means steer or bison, and an image of such was carried about the village. Letnice is derived from the word *leto*, which means summer or year. During Trisna or Tryzna athletic contests were held.

The summer Sun festival was called Kupalo and Jarilo. Other names were Kostroma, Sobotka, Kresnice, and Vajano. Kupalo was the name of an ancient Slavic god or goddess of the Sun, treasure, and fertility. The main features of this festival

259

were lighting of fires, sprinkling of water, and foretelling the future. Because of the festival's connection with the Sun, it also may have been Svantovit's celebration. Another Sun festival was for Khors; his symbol was a tarred wheel, set on top of a pole, lit, and spun. During this season dead ancestors were remembered and marriages made.

Summer was sacred to Perun, god of thunder and lightning, similar to Zeus and Thorr. He was Christianized into St. Elias or Elijah the Prophet.

A special corner of each family hut was dedicated to the spirits of the ancestors. At harvest time, the little domestic shrine was specially decorated with freshly embroidered linen.

Some Slavic tribes built temples; others did not. Mostly, they worshipped in the open, in groves, at fountains or springs, on mountain tops, or by rivers. Actually, only the Polabian Slavs had a developed enough culture to include temples and statues in their religion. The inner walls of the temples were decorated with gold, red, and purple hangings. Carved or painted scenes were on the outer walls. These wooden temples had an inner sanctuary set apart by pillars and thick tapestries. In the center of this sanctuary was a statue of a chief deity, with minor divinities ranged on each side. Statues, pillars, and heads, all representing deities, were done in metal, stone, or wood.

Only among the Elbe Slavs did ritual include a priesthood. The western Slavs used the word *knez*, meaning prince, for priest; therefore, it is possible that royalty performed the duties of the priesthood in that clan. The Russians had only magicians called *vlukvu* or *volkhvy*, priest-sorcerers, who conducted all rites and did divinations and exorcisms. All priests were highly respected and considered of greater authority than kings.

It was the duty of a priest to offer sacrifice, pray, care for the God's shrine, and do divination, particularly to judge the outcome of proposed activities. Humans, particularly Christians, were sometimes thrown into rivers to appease the river gods.

The priest of Svantovit had charge of 300 horses that were set aside for the God; the soldiers who rode them were also considered sacred. A special white horse was designated as especially sacred to the deity and was only ridden by the priest. When an expedition was planned, this white horse was led between two spears stuck in the ground. If the horse crossed the line between the spears with his right foot first, it meant good luck. If he crossed with his left foot, the plans were dropped.

DRESS AND ORNAMENTATION

In Poland, they used unexpected color combinations for clothing and embroidery, such as orange-reds, violet-reds, vivid purples, and warm browns. Geometrics, birds, animals, and human figures were used in designs. Braid was used extensively with buttons and beads; lace ranged from very coarse to extremely fine. The women wore a long skirt with apron, a sleeved bodice, and short vest-jacket. The men dressed in baggy knee trousers, a fringed jacket, and top-boots.

The Balkans, Yugoslavia, Bulgaria, and Albania had many various national costumes, but basically they were similar. The women wore knee-length skirts with many petticoats, an embroidered apron, and a sheepskin jacket heavily decorated with buttons and beads. The men donned baggy knee-breeches resembling a divided skirt, a long tunic open in front, and a sleeveless jacket. Both sexes wore long stockings, knee garters, and flat shoes.

In Hungary and Czechoslovakia, the women had tight-fitting blouses with wide sleeves and skirts of dark material gathered up in the front to show the decorated petticoats. Black, yellow, and red colors were worn by unmarried women; black by married women. Their boots had upturned toes in the Persian fashion. In winter a fur-trimmed jacket ornamented with yellow lace was worn, with a handkerchief draped or tied over the top of the head.

Traditional Slavic design

The men donned long-sleeved blouses over their wide white trousers. Top-boots were common. During cold weather, they wore a sleeveless cape that hung to the knees.

SOME OF THE MYTHS

The Slavonic-Russians originally considered that creation came about through dualism: Byelobog (the White God) and Chernobog (the Black God). From the opposition of forces represented by these deities came the universe, planets, and Svarog, the Sky God. Svarog alone gave birth to two children; these were Dazhbog (the Sun) and Svarogich (Fire). Thus Svarog is considered the father of all gods.

The Russians said that the Sun had twelve kingdoms, or the twelve zodiac signs. He lived in the solar disk, and his numerous children on the stars.

The dawn was said to be a divinity called Zorya or Zarya. Aurora of the Morning (Zorya Utrennyaya) opened the gates of the celestial palace each day when the Sun began his journey across the heavens in his chariot drawn by twelve white horses

Russian elf

with gold manes. Aurora of the Evening (Zorya Vechernyaya) closed the gates when the Sun came home each evening. In some legends the Auroras are accompanied by the morning star Zvezda Dennitsa and the evening star Vechernyaya Zvezda, who share the work and tend the Sun's horses.

Several Slavic tribes also worshipped a god of the winds whose name was Stribog. The storm god Varpulis was considered as part of the retinue of the god Perun.

The Russians and Slavs had firm beliefs in various forms of the Little People. The Domoviye (singular, Domovoy) were a type of Slavic house elf; they were considered extremely loyal to the family they adopted, living behind the stove and doing favors for the family.[5] The Bannik lived inside the bath house and guarded it; however, it was considered polite and safer if one left a pail of clean water handy and the bath house empty after dark. The Vazila took care of the horses, while the Bagan protected all the farm animals, especially goats and horses. The Leshy was known as the Lord of the Forests; all woodland animals were his. He could be quite troublesome, even dangerous, but was active only from spring until autumn. The field elves, Poleviki, live in the grain and corn fields; they cause trouble and even death if they are not given respect and if the harvest is not done properly.

The Rusalki were believed to be the spirits of girls who drowned, especially in Russian rivers.[6] They were only active during the summer months, when they tried to entice humans into the water where they drowned them.

In Poland there is a story of the legendary hero Krak, who founded the city of Cracow. While Krak was journeying about, he discovered a simple peasant people living near Wawel (the later site of Cracow) who were ruled by a terrible dragon. No one seemed to know how to get rid of the animal, but Krak had an idea. He stuffed a sheep carcass with saltpeter and put it out for the dragon to find. This the beast swallowed whole, then suffered with an enormous thirst. Dragging itself to the river, the dragon drank half of the Vistula. This proved to be too much on top of the tainted dinner, and the dragon burst. Krak took control of the situation and built himself the city of Cracow on the Wawel heights.

Among the epic poems of the Russians is the story of the *bogatyr* (valiant champion) Ilya-Muromyets. He had a horse that flew through the air and a magick bow. Although later he was strong like Hercules, Ilya-Muromyets started life sickly. In fact, for 33 years he sat around, unable to participate in anything. Then two vagabond minstrels gave him a honey draught which cured and strengthened him. After this he went about defending people, once striving to rescue his friend, the bogatyr Svyatogor, who had shut himself into a gigantic treetrunk coffin. When Ilya-Muromyets died, his body turned into stone.

From the epics of the heroes of Novgorod comes the legend of why there are no longer any bogatyrs in Russia. After a victorious battle against invaders, one bogatyr bragged to his companions that if an army even came from "over yonder," they could beat them, too. Immediately two strange warriors appeared with a challenge. The bogatyrs sliced the warriors in two, but instead of dying, the two warriors became four. This slicing and multiplying went on for three days, three hours, and three minutes with the bogatyrs rapidly becoming outnumbered. Finally, in fear the valiant champions fled to the mountains and hid in deep caves where every one of them turned to stone.

MAJOR GODS AND GODDESSES

ANAHIT—Chief goddess of Georgia and Armenia; similar to APHRODITE. Fertility, wisdom.

ARAMAZD—Georgia, Armenia. The same as the Middle Eastern AHURA MAZDAH.

BABA-YAGA—Slavic. A tall gaunt hag with dishevelled hair. She ate humans and built her revolving house and stockade out of their bones. Her ally was the Snake, ZMEI GORYNICH. Evil, death, dark magick.

BANNICK—Slavic. A spirit who inhabited the bathhouse. He could predict the future.

BYELOBOG—Slavic. The white god; the positive half of the spiritual. Seen as an old man with a white beard, dressed in white. Light, good, creation, day.

CHERNOBOG—Slavic. The black god;[7] the negative half of the spiritual. Dark, evil, destruction, night.

DAZHBOG—Slavic. "Mighty lord"; god of the Sun; conqueror of shadows, cold, and misery. Happiness, fair judgment, peace, destiny, just rewards.

DIIWICA/DEVANA/DZIEWONA—Georgia, Armenia. Similar to DIANA; goddess of the hunt. Forests, hounds, horses, wild animals, victory, success.

Byelobog and Chernobog

DOGODA—Slavic. The west wind. Gentleness, love.

DOMOVOY—Slavic. "Grandfather"; spirit of the house. He lived by the stove or under the threshold of the front door. It was bad luck to see him, but he warned the family of coming troubles.

DZIDZILEYLA—Also called DIDILIA, DZIDZIS-LADO, ZIZILIA. Goddess of marriage, fertility, love.

KAJIS—Georgia, Armenia. Evil demons.

KHOPUN—Slavic. A river god who waited for bad men and drowned them.

KOSHCHEI THE DEATHLESS—Slavic. An evil entity who sometimes appeared as a reptile, sometimes as a bony human. He was a great horseman.

KRUKIS—Slavic. Patron of blacksmiths; he protected domestic animals.

KUPALA (goddess)/KUPALO (god)—Slavic. Goddess of springs, water. Plants sacred to her were the birch, fern, saxifrage, and purple loosestrife. Healing, exorcism, trees, herbs, flowers, luck, riches, prosperity, protection from evil spirits and demons, fire, purification.

KUPILA—Russia. God of abundance, harvest, fruits of the Earth.

LADO/LADA—Originally a goddess; god of rivers, merriment, and well-being. Especially honored between May 25 and June 25.

LESHY—Slavic. God of the forests. He was dangerous, especially in the spring after a long winter's sleep. He could be outwitted by putting clothes on backwards.

MATERGABIA—Slavic. Goddess of housekeeping. She was given the first piece of bread from a new batch.

MATI SYRA ZEMLYA—Slavic. "Moist Mother Earth"; Earth goddess; Great Mother. Agriculture, fertility, justice, solemn oaths, oracles, healing, crops, divination, truth, property disputes.

MHER/MEHERR—Georgia, Armenia. Same as the Middle Eastern MITHRA.

MOKOSH—Georgia, Armenia. A female deity similar to Middle Eastern ANAHITA. Water, rain, fertility, plenty, small animals.

MYESYATS—Slavic. Moon god; sometimes male, sometimes female. Spring, healing.

OVINNIK—Slavic. Deity of the barns. He looked like a black cat with burning eyes. He had to be placated to keep the barns from being burned.

PERUN/PYERUN/PIORUN/PERON/PERKAUNAS/ PERUNU—"Thunder"; "Lord of the universe"; Supreme God; Creator God; similar to JUPITER and THORR.[8] Pictured as a man holding a hammer or axe. There were wooden images made of him with a silver head and a gold mustache. If lightning struck a tree, rock, or man, it was believed that they became sacred as they then held some of Perun's heavenly fire. This god received sacrifices of a cock, goat, bear, or bull on his great feast days; the meat was then eaten by the people as it contained only *mana* (power) of the god. Eternal fires of oak wood were burned in his honor. Thunder, lightning, storms, warriors, purification, fertility, fire, oracles, defense against illness, war, victory, oaths, weapons, peace, rain, crops, forests, oaks.

POLEVIK/POLEVO/PULUDNITSA—Georgia, Armenia. God or goddess of the fields. Good crops.

RUSALKI—Slavic, Georgia, Armenia. Water and woodland goddesses; dangerous and evil. Weeping willow and birch were sacred to them. Abundance, good crops.

SICKSA—Georgia, Armenia. Forest sprite.

SIMARGL—Slavic. This entity guarded a tree which produced every kind of seed for every plant species. Pictured as a winged monster similar to the Iranian SIMURGH.

STRIBOG/STRIBOZH/VARPULIS—Slavic.[9] Wind god. Wind, storms, victory in battle.

Four sides of a statue of Svantovit

SVANTOVIT/SVANTEVIT/SVYATOVIT—Slavic, Georgia, Armenia. Four-headed god with faces turned towards all directions.[10] He was pictured with a sword, bridle, saddle, and white horse. Each of his major temples had 100 men as guards. Was called *boh bohov*, God of the gods. Divination, prosperity, war, victory, the Sun, fire, wine, plenty, warriors, weapons, horses.

SVAROG/SVAROGU/SVAROGICH—Slavic. "Bright, clear"; Sun, sky and fire god; father of all gods. He rode in a chariot drawn by twelve white horses with gold manes. Clouds, lightning, summer, abundance, heat, light, fire, metal.

SVAROZIC—Slavic. Fire god; son of SVAROG; similar to HEPHAESTUS.

VAHGN/VERETHRAGNA—Georgia, Armenia. God of battle. Similar to MARS.

VISHAPS—Georgia, Armenia. Evil attendants of the dragon and fish-like stone monsters. They could appear as men, serpents, or mermaids.

VOLOS/VYELYES/VELES/VLAS/VLAHO—Slavic, Georgia, Armenia. "God of cattle"; "god of beasts." Christianized into St. Blasius. God of horned animals, oaths, peace, war, protector of flocks and herds.

YARILO—Slavic, Georgia, Armenia. "Passionate"; "Uncontrolled." Similar to EROS. Carnal love, fertility, the harvest, white horses, wheat, spring, sowing, flowers.

ZOSIM—Georgia, Armenia. God of bees.

ZUTTIBUR—Georgia, Armenia. God of forests.

ZVEZDA/ZORYA/ZARYA DENNITSA—Slavic. Goddess of the Morning Star; dawn daughter. Patroness of warriors; a virgin warrioress. Associated with the planet Venus, she was the equal of all other gods, tending the horses of the Sun. Horses, protection, exorcism.

ZVEZDA/ZORYA/ZARYA VECHERNYAYA—Goddess of the Evening Star; evening daughter. Protection, exorcism.

ENDNOTES

1. Curtin, Jeremiah. *Myths and Folk-Tales of the Russians, Western Slavs and Magyars.* Curtin calls this a loan word which he says comes from the Iranian.

2. Curtin, Jeremiah. Ibid.

3. In 1985 the Associated Press ran an article on a rare disease, porphyria, which appears to be inherited. David Dolphin, a chemistry professor at the University of British Columbia, at a symposium of the American Association for the Advancement of Science, gave his view that this disease may possibly be behind the legends of vampires. The bodies of porphyria victims malfunction when it comes to creating *heme,* or red blood pigment. Sunlight causes skin and body deformities; the lips and gums pull back making the teeth more prominent; the person becomes more hairy. Today, victims of porphyria are treated with clinical injections of heme, but during the Middle Ages the only recourse would have been to drink a lot of blood. The aversion to garlic also has a medical background; garlic destroys a heme protein called cytochrome P450. As to becoming a vampire after being bitten by one, that too is a possibility if you are genetically predisposed to the disease. Most vampire legends originated in the Eastern European and Balkan countries during the Middle Ages. A Transylvanian warrior of of that era and area impaled his victims on spikes, among other heinous deeds (see illustration). The Dracula character became better known after the publication of the story by Bram Stoker in 1897.

4. The use of poppets, or small dolls, is known over much of the world. The uses are not always negative, as in cursing, as Hollywood and certain writers would have us believe. Poppets are used in rituals of healing, prosperity, love, etc. This is form of sympathetic magick, a visual tool to influence the subconscious mind to create the desired effect.

5. Arrowsmith, Nancy. *A Field Guide to the Little People.*

6. Page, Michael. *Encyclopedia of Things that Never Were.*

7. Znayenko, Myroslava T. *The Gods of the Ancient Slavs.* This writer quotes Tatis-cev (about 1746) but goes on to say that he erroneously reversed the descriptions of Chernobog and Byelobog. Later writers bear this out.

8. This god was worshipped by the Russians as late as AD 980. They had a wooden image of him with a silver head, gold beard, and iron feet.

9. The Russians considered this god the demon of the tempest and war. The winds were called his grandsons. A statue of him once stood in Kiev.

10. Curtin, Jeremiah. *Myths and Folk-Tales of the Russians, Western Slavs and Magyars.* Saxo Grammaticus described the god's image at Ruegen in the Baltic Sea as having four heads and four necks; two facing the breast and two facing behind.

BIBLIOGRAPHY

Curtin, Jeremiah. *Myths and Folk-Tales of the Russians, Western Slavs and Magyars.* Boston, MA: Little, Brown & Co., 1890.

Dolak, George. *The Religious Beliefs and Practices of the Ancient Slavs.* Springfield, IL: Concordia Theological Seminary, 1949.

Drahomaniv, Mykhailo Petrovych. *Notes on the Slavic Religio-Ethical Legends.* Bloomington: Indiana University Press, 1961.

Hubbs, Joanna. *Mother Russia: The Feminine Myth in Russian Culture.* Bloomington: Indiana University Press, 1988.

Kmietowicz, Frank A. *Slavic Mythical Beliefs.* Windsor, Ontario: Self published, 1982.

Kulikowski, Mark. *A Bibliography of Slavic Mythology.* Columbus, OH: Slavica Publishers, 1989.

Lester, Katherine. *Historic Costume.* Peoria, IL: The Manual Arts Press, 1942.

Oinas, Felix J. *Essays on Russian Folklore and Mythology.* Columbus, OH: Slavica Publishers, 1985.

Ralston, William. *The Songs of the Russian People, as Illustrative of Slavonic Mythology and Russian Social Life.* UK: Ellis & Green, 1872.

Warner, Elizabeth. *Heroes, Monsters and Other Worlds from Russian Mythology.* NY: Schocken Books, 1985.

Wilson, Richard. *The Russian Story Book.* UK: Macmillan & Co., 1916.

Znayenko, Myroslava T. *The Gods of the Ancient Slavs.* Columbus, OH: Slavica Publishers, 1980.

Om symbol

CHAPTER EIGHTEEN

INDIA

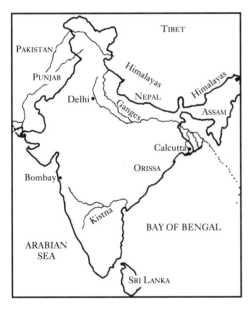

THE PROTO-DRAVIDIAN peoples of India entered the country about 4000 BC to 2500 BC and were called "dark-skinned."[1] Between 2000 BC and 1200 BC a group of tribes belonging to the Indo-European family invaded northwest India.[2] They called themselves Aryans and spoke a form of Sanskrit; they settled mainly in the Punjab area. The *Rig Veda*, the oldest Sanskrit text,[3] was a compilation of their religious beliefs. Usually each tribe was ruled by a hereditary king and had three social divisions: Brahmins, or priests;[4] Kshatriyas, or warriors; Vaisyas, or commoners. The *Rig Veda* mentions a fourth caste, the Sudras, or non-Aryan population. The *Brahmanas* and *Upanishads*, commentaries of the *Vedas*, give information on the last part of the Vedic Age (about 800–550 BC).

When Gautama, the Buddha or Enlightened One, came with his message of religious reform in the fifth or sixth century BC, it changed much of the East besides India. Another religious movement of this time period was Jainism, but it was less widespread.

From the fourth century BC, north India and especially the Punjab was influenced first by the Persian Empire, then by the Greeks and Alexander the Great. The Gupta kingdom, centered in the north in the plain of the Indus and Ganges, fell before the White Huns in the seventh century AD. The Huns did not rule in India, but established a stable government with the Rajputs (great fighting chiefs). After the fall of the Guptas, Buddhism virtually disappeared in India as a distinct religious body. Hinduism then became dominant.

269

The Moslems made a major invasion in the eleventh century. Although they established their rule in some of the north of India, they were blocked from further expansion by the Rajputs. In 1504 Baber, descendent of Tamerlane, invaded the Punjab and founded the Mogul dynasty. By the seventeenth century European traders were entering India and opening the way to later European rule.

Religion

Hinduism began in north India among the Aryans. Hinduism matured between the third millennium BC and the seventeenth century AD. Even the later, almost constant influx of conquerors and would-be conquerors did not damage the fabric of this religion. Hinduism co-existed with other religious viewpoints without harm to its original ideas or its social structure, but it did not absorb them. It assimilated them into its caste system, and life went on as usual.

Hinduism, probably more than Buddhism, contributed more to Western philosophy than any other Oriental religion. There are buried remnants of its influence as far north as the original Celtic practices. There are few people today who do not know something about chakras, meditation, karma, and reincarnation.

The Hindus believed in reincarnation, or the living of one life after another. However, they also believed that by living an unclean or non-spiritual life, a person could be sent back as an animal. This is the theory of transmigration of souls.

They practiced various types of yoga to raise spiritual awareness, Karma Yoga is the Path of Action; the surrender of one's life to Brahmin, or God, so a person ceases to be possessive of the body and ideas. Jnana Yoga is the Path of Knowledge, in which a person seeks to learn the difference between appearance and actual reality. Bhakti Yoga is the Path of Devotion; selfless adoration of God and surrender to him. Raja Yoga is the Path of Insight involving meditation and use of bodily postures known as Hatha Yoga; self-discovery and self-restraint (non-injury, truthfulness, non-theft, spiritual conduct, non-greed). Tantric Yoga is the Path of Transformation; to awaken and release the Kundalini energy, or the creative power; the fulfillment of natural desires.

Yoga means literally a binding or yoking together of psychic power and spiritual development. Yoga is practiced in order to bind the powers of the lower chakras with those of the higher chakras. The chakras are considered to be power-centers within specific areas of the body. There are three great books of yoga discipline: the *Upanishads*, Patanjali's *Yoga Sutras*, and the *Bhagavad Gita*. Not all yogis are celibate; those who follow Tantra Yoga specifically follow certain sexual practices.

On the concept of time, the Hindus believed that everything that happened had happened before and will happen again. Time was viewed as a revolving circle, without a beginning or an end. The repeating cycle of time bound everything together in the universe, including the Gods.

Their law of karma states that every act reaps a like reaction, the original basis for the golden rule of Christianity. Karma is neither manmade nor god-made, but is a natural, impersonal, impartial law. In each incarnation, man works out his karma, positive or negative. At the same time he must fulfill the law of *dharma* (rhymes with karma) so he can be reborn into better lives. Dharma can be translated as duty or the dutiful way of life. It is different for different people and directly influences karma and reincarnation.

Hinduism used mantras, which were actually one or more words or a series of sounds that promoted deep meditation. Om or Aum was considered the greatest sound possible. Mantras usually match the Elements that are inhabited by particular supernormal entities: Earth, Air, Fire, Water, Akasha (etheric fluid). The akasha is explained as being an invisible vital fluid that runs throughout all Nature and puts all beings in touch with one another. By learning to control this powerful Element, yogis can influence and manipulate all animate and inanimate beings, including spirits. The practitioner of yoga becomes more sensitive to akashic fluid and better able to mold it to his desire as he progresses in his spiritual pursuits.

Yantras, or geometric figures, represented thought-forms of the deities in visual symbols, as the mantras expressed them in sound. A yantra was a meditation graphic or symbol that visually helped to activate the mind on a spiritual level. Certain symbols have specific meanings: a circle for infinity; the triangle for everything subject to trinity; the serpent for wisdom and a warning to weak minds not to delve into things for which they are not prepared; the seven-knotted stick for the seven degrees of power (connected with the seven chakras) that can be achieved. Meditation, yoga exercises, and the burning of incense were other aids widely used.

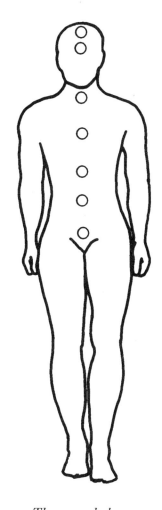

The seven chakras

Buddhism began as a branch of Hinduism in the sixth century BC. Its founder was the son of a king of a small north Indian state. Gautama, or the Buddha, taught the Four Noble Truths:

1. Suffering *(dukkha)*, miseries of existence common to all life.
2. Ignorant thirst for existence *(tanha)*, such as pleasure, is the cause of suffering.
3. Cessation of suffering, liberation from ego, is the extinction of craving that brings one to supreme happiness, or Nirvana.
4. The Eightfold Path shows the way to Nirvana.

This type of Buddhism, sometimes called Theravada, was primarily a religion for monks. Nirvana does not mean bliss, but means nothingness within God.

Representation of Kundalini

In Hinduism, the mantra Om was uttered before any prayer. Conch shells were blown from the temples to indicate offering of prayer or sacrifice. However, most of the people prayed at home and did not visit the temples, except for special devotions or needs. Each morning a man, upon rising, said the name of his particular god, bathed, and recited the Gayatri mantra text from the *Vedas*. Morning worship was done sitting, facing east. Water was sprinkled around the body, the breath controlled, and the deity invoked by touching the limbs in various places.

Most homes had a room or corner for worship *(puja)* where there was an image or symbol of the deity. Puja is the worship of a deity by means of an image or abstract symbol. Vishnu was represented by a stone with spiral markings, and Shiva by a short upright phallic pillar. Often bright colored pictures illustrated some episode in the myths. Incense sticks were lit, and lamps, flowers, and food were placed in front of the shrine. The images were sprinkled with water and offered fresh fruit. Worship was performed at dawn, noon, and in the evening. This was the accepted worship of upper caste Hindu males.

Women had their own deity images, such as the young Krishna. Symbols of the god Shiva were also revered by women. There were private writings (tantra) which taught spiritual disciplines in the service of the Divine Mother (Shakti or Kali); many women were devoted to these deities. Sex magick, or Tantra, in Hinduism is geared to the correct raising of the Kundalini through the chakras. The raising of the Kundalini is the pinnacle of spiritual experience, if properly done.

In the temples, worship was performed by priests who "woke" the deity with recitation of texts and music. The image or pillar was bathed and anointed with sandalwood paste; lamps and flowers were offered. No village was without a shrine; some quite small towns had many huge stone temples. Often associated with the temple was a large tank or artificial lake surrounded by steps for ritual washings. Visitors did not enter the shrine, but brought their gifts to the priests, circled the shrine clockwise, and bathed in the pool.

Pilgrimage was done to gain merit, and some pilgrims made the rounds of the sacred places. A great pilgrimage was held every twelve years, the Kumbha Mela, and attended by many ascetics and mystics.

All temples had annual festivals when images were carried in procession and bathed in rivers. Other popular festivals commemorated ancient rites or incidents in the myths. The New Year festival of Diwali, or Festival of Lights, was in honor of the goddess Lakshmi, wife of Vishnu; Goddess of wealth and prosperity. Hindu wives danced for their husbands; lamps were everywhere; good things to eat were produced. This is the Hindu New Year, a time of good luck and prosperity.

A spring festival, Holi, was an ancient fertility rite and concerned Krishna and Radha. To the Hindus, this rowdy, joyous festival celebrated the constant fertility of Nature as symbolized by the continuous lovemaking of Krishna and Radha. The Festival of Shiva required ritual purifications and meditations for spiritual growth; Shiva, the creating God of sexual ecstasy, showed the Tantric method of raising the Kundalini through ritual.

The Festival of Vishnu the Preserver was held when the monsoon rains began, and the land turned green and began growing once more. The Festival of Chauti was the time to honor Ganesha, the elephant-headed God. The Hindus said that anyone worshipping Ganesha at this time would have his wishes granted; however, it was considered unlucky to see the Moon. Flowers and dishes of rice were set before Ganesha's picture or statue. In Bengali, the businessmen and shopkeepers took their account books and little images of Ganesha to a riverside shrine for blessing. Ganesha is said to look after their interests, as well as those of writers.

Dasehra in the autumn commemorated the battle of Rama and Kali against the demon Ravana. At this time the Hindus also honored Samana the Leveller, or Lord of Death.

For four days in October the Durga Puja was held. Durga was considered a matriarchal figure and was very popular with the people. As the symbolic image of the Motherland, Durga was shown smiling, with many arms and in bright colors. Marigold garlands were draped on her statues. Her image was surrounded by those of other gods, including Shiva, her consort.

The Birth of Krishna symbolized a miracle to the Hindus. They believed that the death of Shiva under Kali's dancing feet brought forth Krishna, one of Shiva's incarnations.

One of the oldest Hindu *dharma* (holy laws of duty) stated that to kill any female, even a child, was the worst possible crime, for that act killed generations. Much later the Brahmans changed this law so that male dominance would rule. This belief in the creating power of the Goddess was so strong among the ancient Hindus that any yoni-shaped object was sacred and considered full of power: the cowrie shell, a cave, the triangle, the horseshoe, and the lotus.

Tantrism was, and is, a system of yoni-worship, or female-centered sex-worship. It was founded thousands of years ago by a female sect called the Vratyas, and was associated with written scriptures called the Tantras. Its basic idea was that women had

न हि ज्ञानेन सदृशं पवित्रमिह विद्यते ॥
तत्स्वयं योगसंसिद्धः कालेनात्मनि विन्दति ॥३८॥

This passage—chapter four, verse 38 of The Bhagavad Gita—*translates as:*
"Truly in this world there is nothing so purifying as knowledge;
he who is perfected in Yoga, in time finds this within."

Tantric yoga position

more spiritual energy than men, and that a man could only achieve realization of divinity through sexual and emotional union with a woman. The primary exercise to reach this realization of divinity is through controlled sexual intercourse with the male having no orgasm.

The Hindus said that no man came into this world or left it except through the Great Goddess. Therefore, man must love all aspects of the Goddess before he can get off the karmic wheel. This means humankind must understand the importance of and love Kali the Crone as well as the other, more beneficent Goddesses. The Left Hand Path, or Vama Marg, was known as the Female Way, the lunar, sensual path to the Goddess. Tantric yogis always enter a worship place with the left foot forward. The Right Hand Path was the solar, male, ascetic way to the God. Although the Goddess was considered of prime importance, Tantric yogis realized the necessity of union between the Goddess and her consort. This union came to be symbolized by the figure eight and the prayer position of the hands (palms pressed together). Their mantra "Om mane padme hum," or jewel (penis) in the lotus (vulva), was a prayer for oneness, not only of humankind and his soul, but of the Goddess and the God.

Musical instruments used were bells, drums, clappers, cymbals, hollow ring rattles, the sitar.

DRESS AND ORNAMENTATION

The main garment for men was the *dhoti,* or waist-cloth, a rectangular piece of cotton material. This was wrapped around the hips, fastened at the waist, and the ends passed between the legs to be tucked in the top of the cloth. The dhoti was usually about five yards long. A *kurta* (shirt) with long sleeves was worn with this, and hung loose to the hips or knees. Sometimes a jamal coat was worn over the top of the costume. The jamal coat was long, almost like a gown, and was commonly seen worn with a full pleated skirt; this outfit was brought to India by the Moguls. The double-breasted jamal coat was most often made of rich fabrics and was thickly embroidered. Sometimes sheer white muslin trousers, tied at the ankles, went with this coat. The leather slippers were also embroidered. Men had their heads wrapped in a very long, decorated turban.

Common dress for all women was the *sari,* a cotton or silk piece of fabric about six yards long and forty-five inches wide. Worn over an ankle-length petticoat, the sari was tied and pleated around the waist with the end drawn across the front of the body and draped over the left shoulder to fall down the back. The sari often had decorative borders done in silver or gold threads. Sometimes the folds of the sari covered the head, or a separate veil of thin material was used as a head-covering. The *choli* (short bodice) covered the breasts. Sandals covered the feet. Women outlined their eyes with kohl and, if their social position warranted it, placed a caste mark on their forehead. Rouge was also used on the cheeks and lips.

Men's hair styles varied from period to period and from place to place. Sometimes the hair was worn long and tied back; other times it was cut fairly short. The women wore their hair long and twisted up into a bun low on the head.

For jewelry, the men used talismans and arm-bands with an occasional necklace. The women wore a portion of the family wealth in their jewelry: silver or gold earrings, nose rings, necklaces, bracelets, armlets, finger and toe rings, anklets, and girdles.

Some of the Myths

There are many Hindu writings telling of the gods and their exploits, but the three best known are the *Rig Veda*, the *Bhagavad Gita*, and the *Ramayana*. The *Bhagavad Gita* (Song Celestial, or Song of the Divine One) is the dialogue between the god Krishna and a young human hero named Arjuna. The *Ramayana* is an epic of the hero Rama's trials and tribulations. In this story Rama's wife Sita is abducted by the demon king of Lanka (Ceylon) and is rescued by Rama's monkey friend Hanuman.

The Hindus have many legends in the *Rig Veda* about the beginning of the world. One story tells of the universe coming into being out of a state of chaos when a

Vishnu contemplating creation, with Brahma and Lakshmi

god (sometimes said to be Indra, other times Vishnu) separated the heavens from the Earth. The Sun rose from the navel of the Earth. A great pillar was erected at that place to hold apart the heaven and the Earth. This now made three worlds: heaven, Earth, and the air between. Some legends say that Vishnu measured out the three worlds by three steps.

A later account tells how a cosmic man, Purusha, was sacrificed and dismembered. Parts of his body went to create the cosmos and the four social orders, or castes.

One god gradually became known as the "Lord of Creatures," or Creator. This god was first called Prajapati and was considered to be multiple beings who acted as one. Later this form was said to be the god Brahma. Prajapati created four sons (fire, wind, Sun, and Moon) and a daughter (dawn). The god chased this daughter through her shape-shifting into every type of animal, mating with her until every species was created. Some of his seed fell on the ground, thus creating a golden egg. This egg split; half of the shell made the heavens, half the Earth. The yolk became the Sun.

The gods and the demons are said to share a single divine father but have different mothers. The gods are the children of Aditi, while the demons are sons of Diti. Thus, the constant struggle between the two is a matter of the older demons feeling they were cheated out of their rightful place. This battle immediately began upon creation and continues. The gods were more powerful and banished the demons to the underworld, while they rule in the heavens.

The universe to the Hindus consisted of fourteen worlds, or *lokas*. Bhuloka (Earth-world) is in the center; this is where humankind lives. Above this but below the Sun is the Bhuvarloka. Immediately below the Sun is the world of the eclipse-planet. Below this is the world of strange magickal beings; below this is the world of various demons. Below the demon world but above Earth is the world in which the winds move. The highest limit of the Bhuloka is the place where the superior birds fly.

Between the Sun and Dhruva is the Svarga world. This is the dwelling place of the devas (gods and goddesses) under Indra's command. In this region are Sukra (Venus), Buddha (Mercury), Bhauma (Mars), Brihaspati (Jupiter), and Manda (Saturn), and the Seven Rishis. Above them all is the star known as Dhruva; around him the whole starry universe moves.

Shri Yantra, Hindu diagram of the cosmos

Above the Svargaloka are four other worlds, three of which are defined. In the Mahar live seers like Sanaka and the other three sons of Brahma. In the Tapasloka (meditation world) live the Vairajas. The Satyaloka (world of being) is the home of Brahma. The Bhuloka, Bhuvarloka, and Svargaloka are destroyed and reformed during each age cycle.

Above the Satyaloka is a region called Vishnu-pada where the sacred Ganges begins. Beyond this are seven *avarnas* (envelopes). Below the Earth there are also seven lokas that give greater sense enjoyment than the home of the devas. In the first is the ruler Bala, son of Maya. In the second Rudra is surrounded by his attendants and makes love to his wife Bhavani; semen from their union turns into gold. In the third rules Bali, grandson of Prahlada. In the fourth lives Maya the Asura. In the fifth the great serpent-sons of Kadru reside. In the sixth reside demon enemies of the devas. In the seventh, Patala, the lowest world, live the lords of the Nagas. Light from their gems dispels the darkness of this world. Below them, and supporting the underworlds and the Earth, is the thousand-hooded serpent Sankarshana.

Krishna was born to Devaki, sister of King Kamsa. Kamsa killed

Krishna playing his flute

all of his sister's children as soon as they were born because he feared a prophecy that one of them would assassinate him. At Krishna's birth, his parents exchanged him for a cowherd's baby, thus saving him from his uncle. But soon Krishna began to exhibit his powers. He fought a huge water snake and, helped by his brother Balarama, destroyed a demon. He even played tricks on the god Indra.

Krishna talked some cowherds into paying honor to a mountain instead of the sender of rains (Indra), then appeared on top of the mountain to take the offerings for himself. Indra was furious. He poured down torrents of rain for seven days and nights on the herdsmen and their cattle. Krishna lifted the mountain and his friends into the air and protected them from Indra. Indra was so amazed at all this that he and his wife came down from heaven to ask Krishna to be friends with their son Arjuna.

Krishna was a mischievous young man, but he was adored and loved by the Gopis (cowherd girls). He stole their clothes while they bathed in the river. He danced with them by moonlight and made love to them all. Only one Gopi, the insatiable Radha, could satisfy and hold this lover-god. She became his mistress.

The god Shiva began as a dark outsider, separate from the gods and humankind. He came into the world from a great pillar of fire (another version of the world axis). This pillar was the cosmic form of his phallus, or linga. Without it the universe is said to be in darkness. This fact was discovered by seven sages who lived in a pine forest. Shiva disguised himself as a beggar and went to visit them. Because the sages were practicing asceticism, Shiva easily seduced their wives. The sages were furious and cursed him with castration. When Shiva's phallus fell to the ground, the universe was plunged into darkness. Horrified, the sages realized who the beggar was and what they had done. They begged him to undo what they had done, and the god agreed, but only if they would worship his linga.

The god Ganesha was made by the goddess Parvati from the sweat of her body mixed with dust. She then appointed Ganesha guardian of her gate. Ganesha worked at this job with much enthusiasm, so much in fact that one day he refused entry to the god Shiva. Shiva was in no mood to be kept out and had Ganesha's head cut off. Parvati was very upset; Shiva said that Ganesha could have the head of the first animal that came along. For better or worse, the first animal to pass by was an elephant.

In another legend, the god Shiva paid a visit to 10,000 heretic Rishis (hermits) to teach them the truth. The hermits received the god with curses, then called up a terrible tiger and set him on Shiva. Using his little fingernail, the god skinned the tiger and wrapped the skin around himself. The Rishis then sent a huge snake, but Shiva put it around his neck like a garland. The Rishis called up a black dwarf demon. Shiva calmly stepped on the demon's back and began to dance. The hermits silently watched the complex and splendid dance until the heavens opened and the other gods came to watch Shiva. At last convinced, the Rishis promised to worship Shiva.

Shiva is said to have three eyes, one of which is in the center of his forehead. These eyes represent the Sun, the Moon, and fire. One day Parvati, his wife, playfully covered his eyes with her hands. All light in the universe disappeared. A drop of sweat fell into Shiva's third eye and a blind child Andhaka was born. Because Andhaka was blind, he had demonic tendencies, one of which was his lust for his mother Parvati. Impaling him on his trident, Shiva held Andhaka in the burning gaze of his third eye until the lust and demonic tendencies were burned away. Andhaka then became one of Shiva's servants.

This story is symbolic of Shiva's mercy to all who display emotion toward him, even if it is hate. What seems like destructive behavior toward humankind is really Shiva's way of releasing man from the karmic wheel of rebirth.

Major Gods and Goddesses

ADITI—"The Unfettered"; "free"; "boundless"; Mother of the gods; sky goddess. She was mother of the ADITYAS, which were VARUNA, MITRA, ARYAMAN, INDRA, SAVITRI, BHAGA, ANSA, and PUCHAN. The sky, Earth, the past, and the future.

Agni

AGNI/PRAMATI—"Thrice-born"; demon-slayer; god of Fire; mediator between the gods and men; Earth, sky and storm god. Consort of AGNAYI, the fire goddess. He has seven tongues with which he consumes sacrifices. His fire represents the element of life in man and beast. His sacred symbols are the axe, fan, torch, sacrificial spoon. He purifies sacrificial offerings and solemn ceremonies such as marriage and death. Sometimes he appears as a man with three flaming heads, three legs, and seven arms, clothed in black, with smoke forming his standard and headdress. Sometimes he takes on the appearance of a hideous demon with two iron tusks. Other times he carries a flaming javelin and rides in a chariot drawn by red horses. Rain, weather, storms, protector of the home, wealth, power, new beginnings, Light, rebirth, immortality, justice, forgiveness, love, virility; mediator between the gods and men.

Brahma and Sarasvasti

ARYAMAN—God of the Heavens; source of all heavenly gifts. The Sun, Moon, winds, waters, seasons.

ASVINS/ASWINS/NASATYAS—Twin gods of the morning, DASRA and NASATYA; they rode in a gold car drawn by horses or birds. Physicians of the gods. Morning and evening stars; healing, old age; protectors of love and marriage.

BRAHMA—A form of PRAJAPATI (the creator); father of the gods and men; creator of the universe; guardian of the world. Part of the triad with VISHNU the Preserver and SHIVA the Destroyer. He is shown riding a swan and has red skin, four heads and wore white robes. In his four arms he carries his scepter (or a spoon or string of beads), the *Vedas*, a bow, and a water jug. He is the guardian of the *Vedas* because they sprang into being from his heads. Magick, wisdom, knowledge.

BRIHASPATI/BRAMANASPATI—Master of magickal power and the priesthood; master of created things.

THE BUDDHA—Divine teacher; the Enlightened One. An avatar, or incarnation, of VISHNU. Spiritual illumination, wisdom, self-realization.

CHANDRA/SOMA—Moon god whose name came from the intoxicating, hallucinogenic drink made for the gods. God of pleasant forgetfulness. Psychic visions and dreams, rising on the inner planes.

DEVI/MAHADEVI—"Shakti" or female energy; SHIVA'S consort. Great Goddess; the most powerful of the goddesses.

DURGA—"The inaccessible"; an aspect of JAGANMATRI, the Divine Mother; Great Mother. One of the triad with the goddesses UMA and PARVATI. This triad can be compared with the Celtic MORRIGU. In her aspect of DURGA PRATYANGIRA, she is a beautiful yellow woman with ten arms who carries a trident, sword, drum, and bowl of blood. She rides on a lion and uses the gods' weapons to defend them from demons. Her sacred festivals take place in Bengali in the autumn. Personification of the fighting spirit of a mother protecting her young. As the primary life force, Durga is a kind of female St. George, defending with serene dignity the gods and her children against enemies. The opening phrase of the national anthem of India praises her. She appeared to INDRA as the beautiful, awesome Great Mother, revealing to him that she was his true source of power. Death, destruction, futility, ruin, comfort, help, power, nurturing, protection, defense.

GANDHARVAS—Gods of the air, rain clouds, and rain; skilled horsemen and musicians. Connected with marriage and reincarnation. Truths, medicine, musical skills.

GANESHA/GANESA/GANAPATI/GAJANI—"Elephant-face"; Lord of obstacles; elephant-headed god of scribes and merchants. Pictured as a short, pot-bellied man with yellow skin, four arms, and an elephant's head with one tusk. In his hands he holds a discus, shell, club, and water lily. He rides on a rat. Removes obstacles from life. Thoughtful, wise, and knowledgeable of the scriptures, he is invoked before every undertaking to insure success. August is the time of a Hindu festival for Ganesha. Flowers and dishes of rice are placed before his statue. Ritual markings of red and yellow are placed on his forehead and trunk. It is said that if Ganesha is worshipped at this time, wishes will come true. However, it is unlucky to see the Moon during this festival. Wisdom, good luck, literature, books, writing, worldly success, prosperity, peace, beginnings, successful enterprises, journeys, building, overcoming obstacles, taming dangerous forces, combination of force and cunning.

GANGA—"Swift-goer"; goddess of the river Ganges. Purification.

GAURI—Golden One; the benign aspect of the Great Goddess. Wealth, good fortune.

INDRA/PARJANYA/SVARGAPATI (father of the shining palace)/MEGHAVAHANA (cloud-rider)/VAJRI (thunderer)/SASHRA—King of the gods; Lord of Storm; Great God; guardian of the Eastern quarter. He is pictured as fair with golden skin. He rides a horse, a massive white elephant named Airavata, or in a chariot drawn by two tawny horses. Carries the thunderbolt Vajra in his right hand. This thunderbolt is sometimes pictured as a club or hammer, sometimes as a discus with a hole in the center. Often his nature is violent; he has an insatiable thirst for *soma*, the drink of the gods. His consort is INDRANI, and his advisors the VASUS. War, weather, fertility, lightning, sky, warriors, violence, reincarnation, rain, strength, bravery, horses, elephants, love, sensual desire, rainbow, personal intervention, law, magick power, rivers, time, seasons, storms, opposition to evil, creativity, the Sun, hunting dogs, offerings.

Ganesha

JYESHTHA—Goddess of bad luck. Revenge, dark magick.

KALI/KALI MA—"The black mother"; Dark Goddess; the Terrible;[5] Goddess of Death; Great Goddess; the Crone; Mother of Karma. Dual personality exhibiting traits of both gentleness and love, revenge and terrible death; wife of SHIVA. Female Principle; patroness of witches. As the KALIKA, or

Crone, she governs every form of death but also rules every form of life. She is always a trinity manifested in three forms: three divisions of the year, three phases of the Moon, three sections of the cosmos, three stages of life, three types of priestesses at her shrines. As the female Holy Trinity she is called PRAKRITI (Nature); she commands the *gunas*, or threads of Creation, Preservation, and Destruction, and embodies the past, present, and future. She is said to command the weather by braiding or releasing her hair. Her karmic wheel devours time itself. She is pictured with black skin and a hideous face smeared with blood, four arms, and bare breasts.[6] She wears a necklace of skulls and is draped with snakes. Her brow has a third eye. Her four hands hold weapons and heads. Violence against any woman is forbidden by her. The Hindus revered the trefoil as an emblem of her three-fold divinity. Her worship includes garlands of marigolds, strings of tinkling bells, incense smoke, and gifts of sweetmeats and spices on fresh green leaves. Kali requires the blood sacrifice of a goat or sheep each day. Regeneration, revenge, fear, dark magick, sexual activities.

Kali

KAMI/DIPAKA (the inflamer)/GRITSA (the sharp)/MAYI (the deluder)/MARA (the destroyer)/RAGAVRINTA (the stalk of passion)/TITHA (fire)—God of desire; Great God. He bears a sugar-cane bow strung with humming bees and his flower-tipped shaft of desire. He is depicted as an ever-young man riding a parrot, and is accompanied by his wife RATI (passion), VASANTA (spring), and the APSARAS. Physical love, pleasures, sensual desire, spring, women, flowers.

KARTTIKEYA/SKANDA/SUBRAMANYA—Chief war god with six heads and twelve arms; defender of the gods; chief battle god. Women can not enter his temples. His mount is a peacock named Paravani; he carries a bow and arrow. He has six heads and six pairs of arms and legs. He is interested only in fighting and war. Revenge, dark magick.

KRISHNA—The Dark One; "Black"; "Stealer of hearts"; the Savior God. The most famous avatar, or incarnation, of VISHNU. Although he has 180 wives, his favorite mistress was the insatiable RADHA. His birth was announced by a star and angelic voices. Shepherds and wise men brought him gifts. He even survived a slaughter of the Innocents. He was sacrificed by hanging between heaven and Earth and fertilizing the soil with his blood. The Hindus call him Redeemer, Firstborn, Sin Bearer, Liberator, the Universal Word. It is said that Krishna returns at the end of each age to save the righteous, destroy sin, and establish goodness and holiness. God of erotic delights, sexual pleasures, love, music, savior from sins.

KUBERA/KUVERA/KHANAPATI/DHANAPATI (lord of riches)/JAMBHALLA—A dwarf god of Earth and treasures from the Earth; guardian of the North; enthroned in the Himalayas. Shown as a fat, white, bejeweled, hideous dwarf with three legs and only eight teeth. He carries a sack over his shoulder and a small chest in his right hand. He rides in a magick chariot called Pushpaka. Fertility, wealth, treasure, minerals, gold, silver, jewels, pearls, precious stones.

LAKSHMI/RUKMINI—Goddess of love and beauty. She gave INDRA the drink of *soma* (or wise blood) from her own body so he could produce the illusion of birth-giving and become king of the devas. She was born during the churning of the milk ocean. In September at a festival, wives dance for their husbands in honor of Lakshmi. This is the Festival of Lights. Lamps are placed everywhere and good things are set out to eat. Good fortune, prosperity, success, love, feminine beauty.

MANJUSRI—"The annihilator of YAMA, the lord of death." Patron of grammatical science. Enlightenment, wisdom, civilization, books and writing.

MARA—Master magician. Illusion, dark magick.

PARVATI/MENA/HAIMAVATI—Sister of GANGA; daughter of HIMAVAN, god of the Himalayas; wife of SHIVA; Mother Goddess. Virgin aspect of the goddess KALI. She seduced Shiva when she tired of his asceticism. She represents the union of god and goddess, man and woman. Desire, ecstasy.

PUCHAN/PUSHAN—"The nourisher"; conducted souls to the afterworld; protected travelers from bandits and wild animals or the exploits of other men. He was considered a good guide, leading his followers to wealth. Marriage, journeys, roads, cattle, meetings, prosperity, material gain.

RAMA/RAMACHANDRA— A princely incarnation of VISHNU; a hero-god.

RATI/MAYAVATI (the deceiver)—Goddess of sexual passions; the wife of RAMA. Lust, sexual activities.

THE RIBHUS—Artisan elves, sons of INDRA by SARANYU. Gods of crafts, horses, and the Sun. Herbs, crops, streams, creativity, blessings.

RUDRA/PASUPATI—"The howler"; Lord of Beasts; Dark God; the Red God. Also called TRYAMBAKA (He Who Belongs to Three Mother Goddesses). An ancient Vedic god of the dead and prince of demons; the original of SHIVA; father of the Maruts. A bull is sacrificed to him outside of villages to keep him away as he is considered dangerous. He is pictured as a ruddy or swarthy man with a wild temper; robber god of thieves; the divine archer who shoots arrows of death and illness. Supreme God; creator of all things; a skilled archer. Invoked for protection against the enmity of VARUNA; smiter of evil workers. Healing herbs, death, disease, the jungle, wild animals, the woodlands, cattle, intelligence, song, sacrifice, creation, prosperity, thieves, storms, wind, judgment.

SARASVATI—"Stimulator"; inventor of Sanskrit and discoverer of soma in the Himalayas. Consort of BRAHMA and mother of the *Vedas*. Represented as a graceful woman with white skin, wearing a crescent Moon on her brow, and seated on a lotus flower. The creative arts, science, music, poetry, learning, teaching.

SAVITRI— Morning and evening aspects of the Sun; golden-haired goddess who rides in a car drawn by two brilliant horses. Night, rest, healing, long life, immortality, dispels tribulation.

SHIVA/SIVA/MAHAKALA—Lord of the Cosmic Dance;[7] Lord of the World; Lord of Stillness and of Motion; Lord of Yoga; Great Lord; Beneficent One; He Who Gives and Takes Away; Great Ascetic; Cosmic Musician; Divine Hermaphrodite; King of Dancers; red god of storms and lightning; god of mountains, cattle and medicine; demon slayer; member of the Hindu triad with BRAHMA and VISHNU. God of contrasting characteristics representing the principle of unification. His power depends upon his union with KALI, without whom he can not act. His consorts are, at one time or another, Kali, PARVATI, and UMA. He wears his hair in an ascetic's knot, adorned with a crescent Moon and trident. He is pictured as a fair man with a blue throat, five faces, four arms and three eyes. His weapons are a trident called Pinaka, a sword, a bow called Ajagava, and a club with a skull on the end. He rides on a white bull, Nandi. Three serpents coil around him, darting out at enemies. Elephants are sacred to him. Sometimes he carries an hourglass drum and a rope for binding sinners. He is the god of all men who have no place in society. He is a merciful fertility god, yet also an ascetic, practicing yoga. He represented great power whatever aspect he takes. When in trance, he is approached only through his active force, *shakti*. His dance movements symbolize the eternal life-death rhythm of the universe. It is said that he brings the Ganges to Earth, breaking its fall from heaven by his curling hair as he sits in meditation. He has many names: LINGODBHAVA, phallic deity; RUDRA, lord of beasts; PASHUPA, protector of cattle; BHUTAPATI, father of demons; TRYAMBAKA, accompanied by three mother goddesses; DIGAMBARA, "clothed-in-space" or "sky clad"; NATARAJA, king of the Dance; NATESA, demon-slayer; SHIVA ARDHANARI, or Shiva in hermaphrodite form of half-male, half-female. Fertility, physical love, destruction, strength, medicine, storms, warriors,

Parvati and Shiva

long life, healing, magick, weapons, cattle, rivers, fire, death, dance, rhythm, meditation, war, righteousness, judgment.

SIVA JNANA-DAKSHINAMURTI—God of all wisdom; complete and rewarding meditation.

SIVA LINGODBHAVA—God of reproduction and fertility.

SURYA—Chief Sun God; Divine Vivifier; "the eye of VARUNA"; benefactor of man. Sometimes called the son of DYAUS, sometimes the son of ADITI and the sage KASYAPA. One story says he is the original source of soma which he gave to the Moon to be distributed to the gods. He is pictured as a dark red man with three eyes and four arms, as a man with golden hair, or as a copper colored dwarf with red eyes. He rides in a golden chariot pulled by seven mares, each one representing a day of the week. His symbol is the swastika, a sign of munificence. He is also the eternal enemy of demons. Measures, understanding, waters, winds, complete dominion, blessings, spiritual enlightenment.

TARA—"Star"; wife of BRIHASPATI. Great Goddess; Mother Goddess. She helped to control human sexuality in order to achieve spiritual enlightenment. Knowledge, compassion, punishment, threats, control, enlightenment.

TVASHTAR/TVASHTRI—Creator of all things; craftsman of the gods; son of DYAUS. He made the magickal weapons of the gods. Arts and crafts, skill with the hands, creativity, source of all blessings, granter of prosperity.

UMA—Corn goddess; Mother Goddess; part of the trinity of the Great Goddess. Called UMA HAIMAVATI, "daughter of the Himalaya Mountains." Golden goddess of light and beauty who mediates conflicts between BRAHMA and the other gods. Light, beauty, fertility, harvest, crops, the Earth, the dark seasons, yogic asceticism.

VAJRAPANI—God of lightning. Woodlands, physical love, ecstasy. Similar to PAN.

VARUNA—God of the Sun, Cosmic Law and Order; linked with MITRA. "The coverer"; creator of the Cosmos; judge of man's deeds; lord of creative power and life-force; sky god; guardian of the Western quarter. His palace is on a mountain called Pushpagiri which lies under water. Mover of the Universe; guardian of the cosmos; Great God. By using his *maya*, or creative will, he made the heavens, earth, and the air between them. Rain, wind, rivers, the Sun, truth, justice, punishment, heavenly gifts, law, magick power, snakes, demons, white horses, oceans, the creative will, seasons, death, rewards, prophecy.

VISHNU—Sun God; "the Preserver"; Lord of the principle of Light that permeates the entire Universe; conqueror of darkness. With three steps he measured the seven worlds. Intermediary between the gods and man. He is a handsome young man with blue skin, four hands, and dressed in royal robes. Often shown reclining on the coils of Ananti, the serpent. In his hands he holds a conch shell, a discus, a club or mace, and a lotus. He also has a bowl called Sarnga and a sword named Nandaka. LAKSHMI is usually beside him. Sometimes he rides the sunbird Garuda, half-man and half-bird. His heaven, Vaikuntha, is made entirely of gold and jewels, with the Ganges flowing through it. Five pools in this heaven grow red, white, and blue lotuses. A June festival at the time of the monsoon rains honors the pre-server god Vishnu. To help man, Vishnu appears on Earth as a human avatar (incarnation). Nine avatars are said to have already come, with a tenth yet to appear. At the time of the universal flood, Vishnu came as the horned-fish MATSYA. This fish saved MANU (equivalent of Noah) by hooking his ship on his horn. The second avatar, the tortoise KURMA, came after the flood to churn up the ocean for the soma of the gods. The boar VARAHA came after the second flood. He dug with his tusks under the water to bring up land again. The man-lion NARASIMHA killed the demon that BRAHMA had given invulnerability. The dwarf VAMANA became a giant to defeat a demon who sought control of the universe. Vamana measured out the heaven, air, and Earth in three steps. PARASURAMA was the sixth avatar; he killed all male warrior castes for twenty-one generations for robbing his father, a brahman. RAMA was India's greatest

Vishnu as Kurma

hero. He overcame the horrible demon Ravana. KRISHNA was the most important avatar of Vishnu; he was a hero-god much beloved by the people of India. BUD-DHA was the ninth avatar, exemplifying Hinduism's ability to absorb divergent religious ideas. He came primarily to teach the world compassion for animals. KALKIN, the last avatar, has not yet come. When he does ride up on a white horse, he will punish evil-doers and reward the righteous. Peace, power, strength, compassion, love, abundance, success, victory.

VISVAKARMA—The Divine Artificer; god of smiths and craftsmen; the creator and maintainer of everything in the universe, making things hold their individual shapes. Animals, horses, creativity, weapons making, architecture, building, smiths, craftsmen.

YAMA/DHARMARAJA—Judge of the dead; god of death, truth and righteousness; guardian of the Northern quarter. Also called SAMANA (the Leveller). He judges men's dharma. His messengers are the owl, pigeon, and brindled watchdogs with four eyes. As god of one of the "heavens" (where there were no sorrows), he is called PITRIPATI (father of fathers), SRADDAHEVA (god of funerals), SAMANA (the leveller), DANDADHARA (the beater or punisher). Judgment, destiny, death, punishment.

ENDNOTES

1. Campbell, Joseph. *The Masks of God: Oriental Mythology*. The Aryans were superior to the native existing cultures because they drove two-wheeled chariots pulled by well-trained horses. In other words, the Aryans were an advanced warrior people who had little trouble overcoming an agriculturally based society.

2. Stone, Merlin. *Ancient Mirrors of Womanhood*. Stone says that the *Vedas* show the extreme partiarchal orientation of the Aryans. Their religion centered around the male trinity of Indra, Mitra, and Varuna.

3. Written sometime between 1500 and 1200 BC in the Sanskrit language. The *Vedas* consist of hymns and epic adventures, but all are religious in orientation.

4. Official priests must be born into Brahman or higher caste families, but holy men come from all classes. The Brahams who want to gain supernormal powers with the help of spirits have to spend a great amount of time reading and studying the rules in the *Agrouchada Parikchai* (Book of Spirits). A priest believes that only by sacrificing all normal desires and activites, and by learning to manipulate the sound of Aum, can he control all spirits, Elements, and people. The highest initiate is called a *sannyasi*, or holy man; he lives in a temple and rarely appears in public. The Brahmas over seventy years of age guard the Law of the Lotus (or occult science) in order to protect it from the uninitiated. Any Brahman who divulges its secrets is put to death.

5. Neumann, Erich. *The Great Mother*. Kali Ma is considered the archetypal Crone, or the hungry Earth that devours and births her children or creatures.

6. Walker, Barbara. *The Crone: Woman of Age, Wisdom and Power*. The typical pose of Kali shows her squatting on top of her dead consort Shiva, pulling his intestines into her mouth while her vulva devours him sexually. Sometimes she has two hands, other times four.

7. Campbell, Joseph. *The Hero With a Thousand Faces*. The traditional statue of Dancing Shiva is executed in a very exact manner. Each position of the limbs has a meaning, as does each article of jewelry. For example, the living serpents around Shiva's arms, wrists, and ankles mean that he is made beautiful by the Serpent Power, or the creative energy of God.

BIBLIOGRAPHY

Bhushan, Jamila Brij. *The Costume and Textiles of India*. India: Taraporevalo, 1958.

Bouquet, A. C. *Hinduism*. NY: Hutchinson's University Library, 1948.

Budpest, Z. *The Holy Book of Women's Mysteries*. Oakland, CA: Susan B. Anthony Coven No. 1, 1979.

Charria-Aguilar, O. L., editor. *Traditional India*. Englewood Cliffs, NJ: Prentice Hall, 1964.

Chatterjee, Satis Chandra. *The Fundamentals of Hinduism*. Calcutta, India: Das Gupta & Co., 1950.

Chatterjee, Satis Chandra, and Dutta, D. M. *An Introduction to Indian Philosophy*. Calcutta, India: University of Calcutta, 1950.

Coomaraswamy, Ananda K. *The Dance of Siva*. NY: Farrar Straus & Co., 1957.

Danielou, Alain. *Hindu Polytheism*. NY: Pantheon, 1964.

de Bary, William T., editor. *Sources of Indian Tradition*. NY: Columbia University Press, 1958.

deLaurence, W. *The Great Book of Magical Art, Hindu Magic and Indian Occultism*. Chicago, IL: The deLaurence Co., 1915.

Dowson, John. *A Classical Dictionary of Hindu Mythology*. UK: Routledge & Kegan Paul, 1950.

Durdin-Robertson, Lawrence. *Goddesses of India, Tibet, China and Japan*. Ireland: Caesara Publications, 1976.

Embree, Ainslie T., editor. *The Hindu Tradition*. Encino, CA: Dickenson Publishing, 1971.

Epstein, Perle. *Oriental Mystics and Magicians*. NY: Doubleday, 1975.

Frost, Gavin and Yvonne. *Tantric Yoga*. York Beach, ME: Samuel Weiser, 1989.

Fuller, F. Max. *The Upanisads*. NY: Dover Publications, 1962.

Hall, Manly P. *The Light of the Vedas*. Los Angeles, CA: Philosophical Research Society, 1978.

Ions, Veronica. *Indian Mythology*. NY: Paul Hamlyn, 1973.

Kirk, James A. *Stories of the Hindus*. NY: Macmillan, 1972.

La Fontaine, J. S. *Initiation: Ritual Drama and Secret Knowledge Across the World*. UK: Penguin Books, 1985.

Levi, Eliphas. *The Book of Splendours*. UK: Aquarian Press, 1981.

Mascaro, Juan, trans. *The Bhaggavad Gita*. NY: Penguin Books, 1980.

Moorhouse, Geoffrey. *Calcutta*. NY: Harcourt, Brace, Jovanovich, 1971.

Morgan, Kenneth W., editor. *The Religion of the Hindus*. NY: The Ronald Press Co., 1953.

Norvell, Anthony. *Amazing Secrets of the Mystic East*. West Nyack, NY: Parker Publishing, 1980.

Piggott, Stuart. *Prehistoric India to 1000 BC*. UK: British Book Service Ltd., 1962.

Radhakrishnan, S. *The Bhagavadgita*. NY: Harper Torchbooks, 1973.

Reader's Digest. *The World's Last Mysteries*. NY: Reader's Digest Association, 1978.

Renou, Louis. *Hinduism*. NY: George Braziller Inc., 1961.

Rice, Edward. *Ten Religions of the East*. NY: Four Winds Press, 1978.

Ross, Nancy. *Three Ways of Asian Wisdom*. NY: Simon & Schuster, 1966.

Saraydarian, H. *The Bhagavad Gita*. Agoura, CA: The Aquarian Educational Group, no date.

Schulberg, Lucille. *Historic India*. NY: Time-Life Books, 1968.

Singer, Milton, editor. *Krishna: Myths, Rites and Attitudes*. Chicago, IL: University of Chicago Press, 1968.

Skinner, Hubert M. *Readings in Folk-Lore*. NY: American Book Co., 1893.

Thomas, P. *Epics, Myths and Legends of India*. Bombay, India: D. B. Taraporevala Sons & Co., no date.

Thomas, P. *Hindu Religion, Customs and Manners*. Bombay, India: D. B. Taraporevala Sons & Co., no date.

Walker, Barbara. *The Crone: Woman of Age, Wisdom and Power*. San Francisco, CA: Harper & Row, 1985.

Zimmer, Heinrich. *Myths and Symbols in Indian Art and Civilization*. NY: Pantheon Books, 1946.

CHAPTER NINETEEN

CHINA

THE HISTORIC Hsia dynasty ruled China from about 2205–1766 BC, with the early centers of civilization in the valley of the Hwang Ho, or Yellow River. The Shang dynasty, 1766–1122 BC, which replaced them developed the distinctive Chinese way of life. They developed a written language, cities and temples, used bronze, and fought from chariots. The Chous, who came from the western part of China, overthrew the Shangs and spread Chinese culture south to the Yangtze Valley and east to the sea.

During this period several religions and philosophies grew: Confucianism, Taoism, and Buddhism. The Great Wall of China was built as protection against the ravaging nomadic tribes.

The Ch'in dynasty followed but fell to the Han dynasty which ruled from 206 BC to AD 219. This era saw much territorial expansion, political growth, and cultural flowering. The religions of Confucius (which became the state religion) and Buddhism (which was persecuted under the Chous) again flourished.

The Sui dynasty, AD 589–617, built the canal linking the Hwang Ho and the Yangtze Kiang. Territorial expansion in the west was halted by the Arabs in 751, after the T'ang dynasty took over. This was the age of great Chinese poets and trading with outsiders.

The period of 907–960 was a time of political chaos. In 960 the Sung dynasty re-established control but lost the northern areas to nomadic tribes. In the thirteenth century the Mongols under Genghis Khan captured Peking and most of northern China. Kublai Khan, grandson of Genghis, made China part of the Mongol Empire. The Mongol dynasty ruled from 1279–1368 but were thrown out by the Ming dynasty (1368–1644).

In the early seventeenth century, the Manchus began to make their move. By 1644 the son of the Manchu chief was proclaimed emperor. The Ta Ch'ing or Ch'ing (Manchu) dynasty was one of the longest in Chinese history; it ran from 1644 until 1912. There were many uprisings during this period but all were ineffective.

The last great threat was from Europe and North America in the eighteenth century. Foreigners were confined to certain coastal areas and even then not allowed to interfere in any manner with the government and the people. Unfortunately, the British introduced opium, part of the reason for the Opium Wars.

RELIGION

In the traditional Chinese home was an ancestral hall and sanctuary. Here the main object was a large carved cabinet containing tablets listing the most recently deceased ancestors and a large tablet with five characters denoting Heaven, Earth, Highest Ruler, Government, and Teacher. Most homes also added little images to the tablets, figures from Buddhist and Taoist worship. These received much attention and prayer.

Morning and evening the father, or oldest person in the house, lit incense sticks and lamps on a shelf of the cabinet. A bell was rung to get the attention of the spirits. He bowed a certain number of times before the cabinet and presented food and drink. Incense was also placed outside in the open courtyard.

In the spring and autumn festivals, the entrance hall of the house served as a dining area for family pilgrims who came home to pay respects to their ancestors. At the winter and summer solstices, there were sacrifices of an ox, sheep, or pigs. Portions of the sacrifice, along with food, wine, and tea, were placed on the altar. Lamps and incense were burned; firecrackers were shot off. The eldest male of the family chanted, calling upon the ancestors to protect all the clan. These ceremonies lasted several days, and all families of the clan had to send representatives, no matter how far away they were.

Yin-Yang symbol

Those families belonging to Confucianism had tablets of the disciples of Confucius in their ancestral hall. Under a canopy in the center of the rear wall was a great red tablet, five feet high, with gold characters reading, "Master K'ung, the perfect, the teacher of 10,000 generations." The rites performed here were similar to the ancestor ceremonies.

In spring the blessing of the Earth God was asked for sowing of the crops, and gifts were made at his small altars at harvest. In the spring, the emperor, dressed as a peasant, sacrificed to the Ancestor of Agriculture by digging three shovels of dirt. The emperor also worshipped the Lord Above (Shang Ti), killing a young red bull with arrows; the sacrifice was burned while musicians chanted. Sacrifices were offered at the Temple of Heaven in the spring, and at the Altar of Earth and ancestral altars in the fall.

Tao (pronounced dow) means a path or way, a way of acting, or a principle or doctrine. It was believed that the Tao of man should be in harmony with the universe. Later in its development Taoism developed a magickal element.[1] The priesthood had the care of many town and village temples of various gods. Its priests, however, married, lived among the people, and were magicians. They also practiced yoga.

Tao magick was more closely related to European magick than that of India. Magicians used willow wands, wax dolls, water divining, geomancy,[2] yarrow sticks, and magick mirrors. These mirrors were decorated around the sides with unicorns, animals representing the four sides of the universe, and other mythical beings. Taoist magicians,

Early characters

through the use of symbols and spells, could raise thunder and storms, bring peace and prosperity. Symbols of the Sun, Moon, light, and fire were Taoist favorites to call upon for combatting evil influences. The picture-seal of Lao-tse was worn to bring good fortune.

Each Taoist sign or magickal symbol stood for a specific god. They used the words *shen* or *ling* as substitutes for the names of the gods themselves. Working with a like-minded group was believed to bring great amounts of power into being immediately. If the magician had to work alone, he would write the words *hiao* or *wao* on paper to aid in gaining power; these words were substitutes for group energy and meant "shouting with many mouths." Very experienced magicians were said to produce the same results by drawing the characters in the air with their fingers. This charm worked only when the Taoist concentrated deeply upon a particular god while inscribing the symbols.

The I Ching (Book of Changes) is still being used today as a divination aid.[3] It came into being about three thousand years ago as an oracle for the court of a Chinese dynasty. Both the Confucians and Taoists claim the I Ching as theirs.[4] The divination texts of the I Ching rhyme in modern Chinese. It is a philosophy of Yin, Yang,[5] and change; all things run in cycles with nothing being immutable.

Taoist priests could be male or female. However, most positions were inherited. The Wu (magician) could be an oracle, exorcist, or sacrificer. The Wu wore a *kang-i* (red garment), a robe for ceremonial and magical occasions. It was embroidered with trees, mountains, thunder spirals, and dragons to signify their control over Nature. The kang-i was formed from a square sheet of silk with a slit in front and a head-hole in the center. It was sleeveless with a wide blue silk border sewn at the bottom. Thick silk ribbons hung down the front. The hair was piled up on the head and covered with a round black cap embroidered with golden Sun rays.

The female Wu was thought to be particularly good at trance and mediumship. She worked in cooperation with a spirit called Lady Tzse. This class of women were shamanesses; they were feared and respected for their powers.

Certain items were part of the Taoist Wu rituals: swords, rice, water, and bells. Swords and daggers were primarily used for exorcisms. Symbolic swords were made from the joining of Chinese coins with holes in the center; these were hung in the home or ritual area for strong protection. Very small swords carved of willow were made to repel demons; these were decorated with red tassels and worn or hung near doors. Swords and *kiens* (double-edged daggers) were often made of peach wood for getting rid of demons. The hilts of ritual swords were wrapped in red cloth; when not in use the ceremonial swords were kept in silk cloth.

Chinese celestial sphere

The Chinese believed in astrology, but their system of casting charts was considerably different from the Western method. They used a cycle of twelve signs based on animals: Rat, Buffalo, Tiger, Cat, Dragon, Snake, Horse, Goat, Monkey, Rooster, Dog, and Pig. These signs were not based on the day and month of birth, but on the year.

A variety of drums, gongs, and bells marked the time for the recitation of the dialogues of Buddha. There was also religious chanting and meditation. The philosophy of the Buddha allowed for both priests and nuns.

The New Year festival was the most important festival of the year. It was calculated by the measurement of the lunar month and the solar year, falling no earlier than January 21 and no later than February 19. A few days before the New Year the paper image of the Kitchen God was burned, with a new picture being placed above the stove on the last day of the old year. Offerings were also made to him at the New and Full Moon. The Kitchen God was the deity who made a direct report to heaven on the behavior of the family each year, a type of secret police for the Immortals. The New Year was a time for settling debts, honoring ancestors, and celebrating family reunions. There was much feasting and visiting of friends. Paper images of dragons were carried through the streets; fireworks and firecrackers were widely used, the idea being that the noise would scare off any evil entities or misfortune.

Birthdays were observed, but with a difference to Western cultures. A child was considered one year old at birth, and at New Year each person was reckoned as being one year older. Thus, if a child was born just before the New Year, he was said to be two years old on the festival.

The Feast of Lanterns was held the night of the first Full Moon after the New Year. In the evenings, lanterns of every shape and description were carried through the streets or hung about the house.

Other festivals were the Feast of the Dragon that was held the fifth day of the fifth month of the Chinese year. The Feast of the Dead was observed twice a year, in spring and in autumn; at these times the family graves were cleaned and then decorated with gifts of food and candles. Gongs were sounded throughout the city.

Musical instruments used were bells, gongs, drums, flute, clappers, finger cymbals, percussion sticks.

DRESS AND ORNAMENTATION

Traditional Chinese costume for both sexes was the tunic or jacket *(san)* worn over trousers *(koo)*. The tunic was hip, knee, or ankle-length with a round neck and wide long sleeves that reached to the hands. It overlapped in the front at an angle and buttoned or tied on the right side. The trousers fastened at the waist with a soft girdle.

Long robes made of beautiful silk fabrics and richly embroidered in gold and silver thread were the clothing of both sexes of the upper classes. These robes had long flowing sleeves, very full skirts, and a slit at the sides. The feet were covered with slippers, or slippers mounted on high wooden blocks.

Until the twentieth century, it was common for the feet of upper class women to be bound; this produced what the Chinese called the lotus foot, and was considered highly erotic to the men. It was a terribly painful process that began in early childhood; as a result, the women could only walk for short distances in a swaying hobble.

The Chinese never kissed or showed emotion in public, never opened presents in front of the giver, and did not believe in saying "thank you," as that was considered an attempt to get rid of obligations.

Chinese men could discipline their wives for jealousy, adultery, stealing, being too talkative, being chronically sick, being barren, and other minor complaints. They expected to be waited on constantly with no complaints even though they visited courtesans ("flower girls") or brought home concubines. A barren wife, or one who had not produced a male child, would often give her consent or even choose a concubine to bear children; in this way, she kept her seniority in the household and was the only one to inherit upon the husband's death.

Among the poor, it was not uncommon for female babies to be drowned at birth. Boys were considered of value as they produced further family heirs, while the girls had to be supplied with a dowry upon marriage and then became part of the husband's family.[6]

Rattan hats were worn in summer; in winter, hats of silk, fur, or velvet. Most women did not wear hats, but used rice-paper parasols and delicately painted fans.

Before the Manchu dynasty, Chinese males wore their hair long and tied in a knot on top of the head. After the Manchus, the pigtail became compulsory. Women had elaborate hair styles piled on the head, held by wire frames, and ornamented with flowers and ribbons.

Certain beauty rituals among the women were in vogue for centuries. Face powder and rouge were heavily applied. Eyebrows were plucked and pencilled, nails were painted.

Jewelry was usually limited to earrings, talismans, rings, hairpins, and a great variety of necklaces made of jade, pearls, gold, silver, ivory, and precious stones.

The Chinese called jade the Stone of Heaven and valued it more highly than gold, not only because of its beauty, but because of its scarcity. The Chinese word for jade is *yu*, also a title of honor that means pure, precious, noble. Carving jade was extremely difficult; it was cut and polished by sawing, drilling, or rubbing it with garnet dust. Because of its beauty and rarity, jade became a symbol of wealth and authority. One of the jade objects that was used in religious ceremonies was a perforated disc called *pi* (pronounced bee); this disc was a symbol of heaven and the universe, a link between the Gods and humankind. One legend says that jade was the petrified tears of the Imperial Dragon who wept over the loss of North China to the Tartars in the fourth century.

SOME OF THE MYTHS

According to the Chinese, creation was an act of bringing order out of chaos. One such story tells the tale of Hu, emperor of the Northern Sea, and Shu, emperor of the Southern Sea. These two beings frequently met on the territory of the emperor of the Center, Hun-tun. Hun-tun was unusual as he did not have any body orifices for

Fu-hsi and Nu-kua, from a Han Dynasty stone rubbing

seeing, hearing, eating, or breathing. Hu and Shu decided to remedy the situation and, at the rate of one hole a day, they made openings for Hun-tun. However, Hun-tun (Chaos) died on the seventh day. At his death, the world came into being. The combined names of Shu and Hu mean lightning, thereby adding a very interesting interpretation to this story. When lightning or an illumination of Light falls upon Chaos, life is created.[7] The seven openings are also linked in Chinese thought with the mystical seven openings of the heart, the mark of a righteous man.

A legend of human creation tells the story of the Goddess Nu-kua, sometimes called the wife of Fu-hsi. Even after Heaven and Earth were separated, there were still no humans. Nu-kua modeled some out of yellow earth, but soon got tired of this process. Then she dipped a rope into the mud and dragged it about so drops fell off. Tradition says that those beings she modeled became the noble and rich, while the drops became the humble and poor.

The Chinese also have a legend that says the center of the star system contains the Pole Star and therefore the Middle Kingdom is off center. They say this happened when a monster named Kung Kung tried to seize power from Yao, the Fourth Emperor. The monster failed in his attempt and was so furious that he impaled Mount Pu Chou with his horn. This caused the mountain to break, tipped the sky to the northwest, and tore a hole in the sky. The Earth tipped in the opposite direction, and great floods rushed over the lands.

For a long time no one seemed able to do anything about the miserable situation. Then a man, K'un, tried to control the floods that were devastating everything. He built dams, but they collapsed. Then he stole the Swelling Earth, a material that grew endlessly, stopping all holes. This worked, but the god Huang Ti was angry and had the man executed. Three years later K'un's stomach was slashed open, and out came his son Yu. Without wasting any time (the floods were still raging), Yu went straight to Heaven and asked Huang Ti for a gift of the Swelling Earth. Because Yu had humbly asked, the god granted the gift.

Yu dammed up the springs that were adding to the problem, then built mountains at the corners of the Earth so there would be dry land. Next he dug ditches and tunnels to drain the water from the land back into the sea. While tunneling, Yu entered a cavern where he discovered the god Fu-hsi, who gave him a jade scale to measure Heaven and Earth.

In the beginning there were five islands of Pheng-lai, a paradise where the Immortals, or Gods, lived. These islands were free-floating, therefore drifting around the ocean and frequently bumping into the Chinese mainland. The islands were the only source of the herb of immortality; Chinese emperors were always sending out expeditions in search of the herb. Finally, the Immortals complained to the Celestial Emperor, who instructed the god of the ocean wind, Yu-chhiang,[8] to fasten three giant tortoises to each island. This arrangement worked quite well until a giant came from the realm of the Count of Dragons to fish. On his first cast he caught six tortoises, thus causing two of the islands to drift away and sink. The Emperor of Heaven was so angry that he shrank all the giants.

Chinese mythology looked upon the Earth as a square, with a huge mountain at each cardinal direction and another in the center. The Sun began its journey each day from the Thai Shan mountain.

The western mountain of Khun-lun was considered to be the home of the Lord of the Sky and several other deities. The Lord of Rain also lived on its slopes; he was dressed in yellow scale armor with a blue and yellow headdress. With a sword, another version says a watering can, he sprinkled rain upon the Earth.

The Royal Mother of the Western Paradise, Hsi Wang Mu, also had connections with Khun-lun. Originally, though, her home was on a jade mountain to the north of Khun-lun and to the west of the Moving Sands.[9] At first she was a terrible creature with a human face, tiger's teeth, and a leopard's tail, deity of plague and pestilence. By the time of Taoist literature, however, she had transformed into a beautiful, gracious Goddess who had a palace on Khun-lun and guarded the herb of immortality.

Kuan Ti, the God of War, was originally a kind of Robin Hood. He was one of three heroes whose stories are told in the Romance of the Three Kingdoms. There were more than 1,600 official temples, plus minor shrines, to this deity. His cult reached its peak during the Manchu era.

The Moon goddess, Ch'ang-o or Heng-o, was the wife of I, or Yi, the Excellent Archer. Her husband was renowned for having shot down the ten Suns of primitive times when they decided to all rise at once and cook the world. The gods had rewarded I with a drink of immortality that he saved. One day he returned home from one of his long ramblings to find that his wife had drunk the potion. He grabbed up his sword and had full intentions of doing the lady in. However, Ch'ang-o fled to the Moon and asked protection of Hare who lived there. Hare fought with and defeated her husband, then made him promise to give up his revenge. Ch'ang-o evidently knew I better than Hare did, for she decided to continue living in the Moon.

The Chinese even had a Hell, or rather eighteen of them all in one place. The Yama-Kings presided over this underworld, judging souls and handing out punishments that were put into effect by armies of helpers. Each Yama-King judged certain types of sinners, and there were certain portions of Hell designated for each. Each crime had its appropriate punishment, such as blasphemers having their tongues torn out, and misers and lying mandarins made to swallow melted gold and silver.

The *kuei* (spirits) were only one of a number of entities considered harmful to humans. Suicides, who could have no further incarnations, and drowning victims returned as dangerous ghosts to harass the living. Drowning victims could, however, reincarnate whenever another person drowned at the same place. There were other dangerous creatures besides the kuei; some were animals who, as they aged, developed the power to shape-shift into human form. The best known of these animals were the foxes. By taking on human form and seducing young men and women, the foxes could consume their life-energy and thus live to 800–1000 years old. Foxes were also thought to have the power to produce fire by banging their tails on the ground.

There is no complete list of the ancient Chinese gods; it is doubtful there ever was such a list, as there are thousands of them.

Major Gods and Goddesses

Ao—The four dragon kings, named Ao Ch'in, Ao Kuang, Ao Jun, and Ao Shun. Gods of rain and the sea. They were the subjects of the Jade Emperor (Yu-Huang-Shang-Ti). Each was responsible for a part of Earth and an area of sea; they each had a crystal palace staffed by fish and crabs. During droughts, the dragon kings were worshipped with noisy processions of music and dancing which followed a cloth effigy of a dragon. Rural areas honored local dragon kings; every stream and river had its own Ao.

Ch'ang-o/Heng-o—Goddess of the Moon and wife of I. She had her Palace of the Great Cold on the Moon.

Ch'eng-Huang—God of walls and ditches. Each town and village had its own Ch'eng-Huang. His festival came in the spring and included a procession with his statue and gongs. Protection, justice.

Chih-Nii/Chih Nu—Goddess of spinners, weavers and clouds; daughter of the Jade Emperor for whom she wove seamless robes and clouds. Handcrafts, rain.

Ch'in-Shu-Pao—Guardian god. A T'ang dynasty military hero elevated to the job of guarding doors. Protection, privacy.

Chuang-Mu—Goddess of the bedroom and sexual delights.

Chu-Jung—God of fire and executions. Justice, revenge, death.

Erh-Lang—"Second Lord"; the great restorer; the sustainer; god who chases away evil spirits. Shape-shifter who had up to 72 different bodily forms; widely worshipped. Protection from evil.

Chinese dragon motif

Kuan Yin

FENG-PO-PO—Goddess of winds; she replaced FENG-PO and rode through the clouds on a swift tiger. Storms, moisture.

FU-HSI/FU-HSING—God of happiness; his symbol was the bat. Destiny, love, success.

HOU-CHI—"Prince Millet"; ancient harvest god. He was shown as a kindly old man with millet stalks growing on his head. Harvest, crops.

HSI WANG MU/WANG-MU NIANG-NIANG/WEIWOBO—Queen of the West; highest Goddess of ancient China. Her palace is in the Khun-lun mountain; there she protects the herb of immortality. Cures disease.

HSUAN-T'IEN-SHANG-TI—"Supreme Lord of the Dark Heaven"; Regent of Water. God who removes evil spirits and demons. Exorcism.

HU-TU/HOU-T'U—Empress Earth; the Earth as a female deity; patroness of fertility. The Emperor offered sacrifices to her on a square marble altar in the Forbidden City each summer solstice.

I-TI—God of wine; he invented winemaking.

KUAN TI—God of war and fortunetelling; a famous martyred general of the Han dynasty. He was dressed in green and had a red face. Protection, valor, justice, divination, revenge, death, dark magick, prophecy.

KUAN YIN/KWAN YIN/KWANNON—Great Mother; goddess of compassion and mercy; "she who hears the weeping world"; patroness of priestesses. Sometimes shown holding a child. Her main temple was on Miao Feng Shan, where pilgrims used rattles and fireworks to emphasize prayers. It is believed that this Goddess sits on her paradise island of P'u T'o and answers every prayer to her. Success, mercy, purification, fertility, children, motherhood, childbirth, healing, enlightenment.

K'UEI-HSING/CHUNG-KUEI—Protector of travelers; god of tests and examinations, literature, and students.

LAN TS'AI-HO—One of the Eight Immortals of ancient China, this Goddess dressed as a woman but had a male voice; she carried a flute and a basket of fruit. Music.

LAO-TIEN-YEH—"Father Heaven"; the Jade Emperor; Great God.

LEI-KING/LEI-KUNG—God of thunder and retribution, he had few shrines. He was pictured as an ugly man with blue skin, wings, and claws, clad in a loincloth. He punished the guilty that human law did not touch.

LO SHEN—Goddess of rivers.

LU-HSING—God of salaries and employees, his symbol was a deer which he rode. Prosperity, success, law.

LU-PAN/LUPAN—God of carpenters and masons. Artistic abilities, fame.

MA-KU—Goddess of springtime.

MEN SHEN—Two deities who guarded the door against evil spirits and hostile influences. One had a red or black face, the other a white face; they were in military dress, holding a long-handled mace. Protection.

MENG-PO NIANG NIANG—Goddess who lived just inside the door to hell where those reincarnating would depart. Her secret brew, of which she administered a few drops to each departing person, made all humans forget previous lives.

NU KUA—Creator Goddess who made humankind.

PA—Goddess of droughts.

P'AN-CHIN-LIEN—Goddess of prostitutes.

PI-HSIA YUAN CHIN—"Princess of the Blue and Purple Clouds"; "Holy mother"; "Jade maiden." Goddess of childbirth and labor, she brings health and good fortune to the newborn and protection to the mother.

SAO-TS'ING NIANG—"Broom lady"; goddess of the clouds. End of drought.

SHAKA-NYORAI/SAKYAMUNI—The historical BUDDHA. Virtue, enlightenment, self-realization.

SHANG-TI—The Supreme God.

SHEN NUNG—God of medicine, pharmacy, and agriculture.

SHOU-HSING/SHOU/LAO—God of longevity and old people, keeper of the book of the life-span of men. He had a prominent bald head with white eyebrows and whiskers; with a stag beside him, he leaned on a staff and carried a peach, symbol of immortality. Life plan, date of death, reincarnation.

SHUI-KHAN—"Agent of Water"; he was offered cakes shaped like tortoises. The god who defends men against all evil and forgives sins. Averts evil.

T'AI-YUEH-TA-TI/TUNG-YUEH-TA-TI— "Great Emperor of the Eastern

Shou-Hsing riding in a peach

Peak"; god of the affairs of men; protector of men and animals. Children, fortune, honors, fate, animals, payment of good and bad karma, prosperity, success.

TIEN-HOU/TIEN FEI—"Empress of Heaven"; "Princess of Supernatural Favor." Protectress of sailors and others in time of danger.

T'IEN-KHUAN—Agent of Heaven. God who bestows happiness.

TIEN-MU—Goddess of lightning.

TI-KHUAN—Agent of Earth. God who grants remission of sins.

TI-TSANG-WANG-PU-SA—God of mercy, he visited those in Hell and tried to arrange for a good incarnation. He was shown as a smiling robed monk with a halo around his body; he carried a pearl that gave off light. Knowledge for reincarnation.

TOU-MOU—Goddess of the polestar and record-keeper; scribe of the Immortals; judge of all peoples.

TSAI SHEN/TS'AI-SHEN—God of wealth; the most popular of Chinese gods. Every year on the fifth day of the first month his birthday was celebrated in every household with the sacrifice of carp and cock. Shown dressed in exquisite silks. Abundance, success.

TSAO-WANG/TSAO-CHUN—The kitchen god; god of the hearth. Protector of the family and recorder of the actions and words of each family. He was represented by pictures painted on paper and had a daily offering of incense. His wife recorded the behavior of women in particular. His report each year to the Jade Emperor determined the family's coming fortunes.

TSI-KU/TSI KU NIANG—"Purple lady"; goddess of the outhouse. Tradition says that when a woman wanted to know the future, she went to the outhouse and asked Tsi-Ku.

TWEN-CH'ANG/WEN-CHANG-TA-TI—God of literature and poetry. He was represented by no pictures, only a tablet on which his name and title were done in fine calligraphy. His symbol was the crane. Writing, publishing, artistic fame.

YAO-SHIH—Master of Healing. Psychic abilities, healing powers.

YENG-WANG-YEH—"Lord Yama King"; foremost of the ten Yama Kings or Lords of Death; ruler of Hell. He screened all new arrivals and decided if they went to a special court for trial, were punished, or sent straight back to the Wheel of Life. Judgment, punishment, karmic justice.

ENDNOTES

1. Lao-Tse, a mystic who was born about 570 BC, transformed Chinese philosophy with his Book of the Tao. People of all classes believed in some form of spirit phenomena. The pattern of the occult world of the Chinese had the

Supreme Intelligence at the top, with descending planes of deities, angels, planetary spirits, and spirits of the dead.

2. This type of geomancy was called Feng Shui.

3. Huang, Kerson. *I Ching.* Carl Jung used this method as a psychoanalytic tool. The I Ching is actually a divination manual of two parts. The first part contains the rhymed verses, the second part an interpretation of the *pa kua* (the eight trigrams).

4. Huang, Kerson. Ibid. Kerson writes that the Taoists left the original untouched, but the Confucians came close to destroying it. The true interpretation of the I Ching had to wait until the passing of the Confucian state in order for scholars to study the process objectively.

5. The combination Yin-Yang symbol was considered the powerful masculine-feminine sign of Tao.

6. Latourette, Kenneth S. *The Chinese: Their History and Culture.* Marriages were arranged by the parents. A wife was sought who had equal or greater social standing and wealth than the son. Although a man could have only one wife, he could have as many concubines as he could afford; this practice was frequent among the well-to-do. Sometimes these women each had their own house; other times, they lived in one enclosure, each with separate apartments.

7. There is a similar idea contained in Norse mythology. They say that where Fire and Ice meet, the creative sparks of life came into being, thus creating the Giants and other beings.

8. Yu-Chhiang is not the wind god who is called the Count of the Wind. Yu-Chhiang is portrayed with a bird's body and a human face, green serpents at his head and feet. He is said to live in the north or northwest where he is god of the ocean wind.

9. This is according to the *Shan Hai Ching.*

BIBLIOGRAPHY

Appelbaum, Stanley, ed. *Traditional Chinese Designs.* NY: Dover Publications, 1987.

Birch, Cyril. *Chinese Myths and Fantasies.* UK: Oxford University Press, 1962.

Bloodworth, Dennis. *The Chinese Looking Glass.* NY: Farrar, Straus & Giroux, 1967.

Cammann, Schuyler. *China's Dragon Robes.* NY: The Ronald Press, 1952.

Chang, Kwang-chih. *The Archaeology of Ancient China.* New Haven, CT: Yale University Press, 1963.

Cheng Te-kun. *Archaeology in China: Prehistoric China.* Cambridge, MA: W. Heffer & Sons, 1959.

Cheng Te-kun. *Archaeology in China: Shang China.* Cambridge, MA: Heffer & Sons, 1961.

Christie, Anthony. *Chinese Mythology.* UK: Paul Hamlyn, 1973.

Delsol, Paula. *Chinese Astrology.* NY: Warner Books, 1976.

Durdin-Robertson, Lawrence. *Goddesses of India, Tibet, China and Japan.* Ireland: Caesara Publications, 1976.

Eberhard, W. *Folktales of China.* UK: Routledge & Kegan Paul, 1965.

Edwards, E. D., trans. *Festivals and Songs of Ancient China.* UK: George Routledge, 1932.

Epstein, Perle. *Oriental Mystics and Magicians.* NY: Doubleday, 1975.

Goodrich, L. Carrington. *A Short History of the Chinese People.* NY: Harper Brothers, 1959.

Huang, Kerson and Rosemary. *I Ching.* NY: Workman Publishing, 1987.

Huber, Richard. *Treasury of Fantastic and Mythological Creatures.* NY: Dover Publications, 1981.

Innes, K. E., and Brailsford, M. R., trans. *Chinese Civilisation.* UK: Kegan Paul, Trench, Trubner, 1930.

La Fontaine, J. S. *Initiation: Ritual Drama and Secret Knowledge Across the World.* UK: Penguin Books, 1985.

Latourette, Kenneth S. *The Chinese: Their History and Culture.* NY: Macmillan, 1946.

Leeming, Joseph. *The Costume Book.* Frederick A. Stokes, 1938.

Needham, Joseph. *Science and Civilisation in China.* Cambridge, MA: Cambridge University Press, 1956.

Norvell, Anthony. *Amazing Secrets of the Mystic East.* West Nyack, NY: Parker Publishing, 1980.

Rice, Edward. *Ten Religions of the East.* NY: Four Winds Press, 1978.

Riva, Anna. *Secrets of Magical Seals: A Modern Grimoire of Amulets, Charms, Symbols and Talismans.* Toluca Lake, CA: International Imports, 1983.

Rose, Donna. *Magic of Astrology.* Hialeah, FL: Mi-World, 1978.

Ross, Nancy. *Three Ways of Asian Wisdom.* NY: Simon & Schuster, 1966.

Scott, A. C. *Chinese Costume in Transition.* NY: Theatre Art Books, 1960.

Walters, Derek. *Chinese Astrology.* UK: Aquarian Press, 1987.

Werner, E. T. C. *Myths and Legends of China.* UK: George Harrap, 1922.

CHAPTER TWENTY

JAPAN

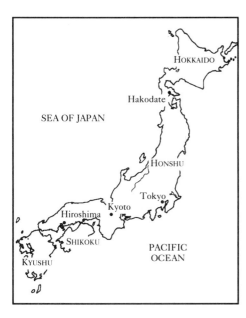

SOME TIME between 1000 and 500 BC, several waves of migrants arrived in the Japanese islands. The earliest were probably the Caucasoid ancestors of the Ainus, who today inhabit the northern island of Hokkaido. In about 300 BC to AD 300 a totally different racial group, the Japanese proper, entered Japan by way of Korea.[1]

Prominent among their leaders was a queen or princess named Amaterasu Omikami,[2] Heavenly Shining Great Female Person, later called the Sun goddess. One of her descendants, Prince Iware (Jimmu), became the first emperor of the Yamato dynasty. Neither Jimmu nor his early successors ruled over the whole of what is now Japan. Consolidation of the empire was gradual through a period of centuries.

By AD 11, the Shinto religion was established. Two of Japan's oldest books still in existence are the Kojiki (Record of Ancient Matters, compiled about AD 712) and the Nihonshoki or Nihongi (Chronicles of Japan, compiled about AD 720). The Emperor Tenmu instructed that these compilations be made so the genealogies, history, and mythologies of Japan would not be lost or become filled with mistakes.

Buddhism was introduced from China by way of Korea in AD 522. The Emperor Yomei (585–587) was the first of the royalty to accept this new foreign religion.

Japan controlled a large part of Korea in the fourth century AD but were defeated by the Chinese in 662. Kyoto, Japan, became the capital of the emperors in 795. Many luxurious palaces, temples, shrines, and gardens were built there. Art and literature reached a high level. Buddhism acquired great power. The era from 1118–1181 saw the rise of the samurai, or *bushi*, the warrior class, and of *bushido*, the Samurai code of loyalty.

The Kamakura era, beginning in 1185, saw the establishment of the *terakoya* (Buddhist temple schools). The austere life of the Kamakura Samurai and the influx of Chinese culture gave fresh impetus to art and literature. The Zen introspective doctrine of Buddhism rose to popularity between 1274 and 1281.

There was a conflict for the throne (1318–1392) between two rival branches of the Imperial family. They finally coalesced in Emperor Go-Komatsu. By then, the shoguns were either ruling or indirectly controlling the government. Many of the great Buddhist temples and monasteries became centers of armed strength, partly because of the need for protection from country-wide looting and conflicts. For thirty years, beginning in 1467, there was civil war. Corruption and intrigue among the shoguns became rampant. The stormy era of the Ashikaga shoguns ended in 1573. Three soldier-statesmen shaped Japanese history for the next three centuries, supporting the Emperor, establishing peace, and subduing the militant Buddhist strongholds.

The Ninja were formed as a counter-measure against the corrupt samurai. The Ninja were common people, both men and women, who learned to use the sword and other pieces of fighting equipment to defend themselves and their neighbors against the ambitious overlords who thought little of grinding down the peasantry in their search for power. Commoners were forbidden to carry swords, so the Ninja used whatever weapon came to hand. Their short swords are said originally to have been made from broken swords that the Samurai discarded; their other weapons were made to be inconspicuous.

The Samurai loyalty to their overlord was kept whether or not that leader was corrupt or insane, going to their death without question if so ordered. The Ninja believed that each person must judge a leader's moral values, then choose whether or not to follow that leader, questioning any irrational orders. If a ruler became corrupt and immoral, it was a Ninja's personal duty to abandon him.[3] In later years, the Ninja did come to fill the roles of assassins and spies. However, the current ideas of Ninjas, popularized by television, movies, and comics, is a misconception.

RELIGION

Shinto, or the Way of the Gods, was the original religion in Japan and had no written literature before the arrival of the Buddhists. However, all true Japanese mythology comes from this religion. Shinto believes that every natural thing, human, animate, or inanimate, has a *kami* or spirit in various degrees of vitality and strength. These noble spirits (kami) embodied fertility, productiveness, growth, natural objects such as trees and rivers, natural forces such as wind and lightning, and familial and Imperial ancestral spirits. The concept of interaction of the kami with human life is based on the embodiment of order, justice, balance, and divine favor or blessing. The Japanese call this In/Yo, which is much the same as the Chinese Yin/Yang.[4] Both Shinto and Buddhist shrines and temples are near or surrounded by Nature and natural beauty.

The concept of the dream oracle survived in Japan until the fifteenth century; this was found in Shinto and Buddhist temples. Village oracles, known as the Jor Takusen Maturi, could still be found as late as 1960.

At the Shinto center at Ise, the inner shrine (the Kotai-jingu) was sacred to the Sun goddess Amaterasu. The Kotai-jingu contained the mirror enshrining the soul of the goddess. The building was renewed every twenty years. The building was formed of cross-beams on top with exposed rafters. The shrine consisted of a number of wooden buildings in a dense forest within a series of enclosing fences.

Shinto shrine

Only the emperor and priests could enter the *shoden* (central shrine). The numerous small shrines and pavilions around it were for pilgrims.

Worship of the kami,[5] or higher spirits that can take residence in any object, especially unusual or natural ones, included various rituals, among them sacrifices of rice, rice cakes, and sake. Effigies of animals and humans were also used.

Worship could take place in the private home, or begin there and be completed in a shrine (the *miya*). The miya were wooden buildings consisting of a prayer hall and central hall. Originally, the worship was celebrated in the open near a rock, the ocean, or whatever held the presence of the god. At the miya, prayer was done by a priest standing inside for the people standing outside. The worship was obeisance, various offerings, prayers and petitions. A *goshei* stick tied with strips of cloth was placed on the altar, or suspended from the rafters.

Thirty days after birth, a child was brought to the local Shinto shrine and presented to the deities. This put the child under the care of the gods. Even when grown or moved away, that person would make visits to the shrine from time to time to let the gods know of changes in his life and to present requests.

There were three types of Shinto priests: the Imibe who maintained ritual purity of the people and of objects connected with ceremonies; the Nakatonu who communicated with the gods for the emperor and who performed the liturgies and rites; the Urabe who sought out the future and interpreted events. There was also a fourth class of priestly caste, who lived as laymen and discharged various religious duties.

Every holy place or object was guarded by a straw rope *(shimenawa)* to keep away evil; pieces of paper were hung from this. Inside the Shinto shrine, besides the mirror, were simple patterned curtains, some green twigs, white tablets, earthen vessels for offerings, and a grass mat for the priest to sit on.

In the homes the gods were honored with small shrines called god-shelves *(kami-dana)*, which were fastened high on the wall above the sliding screens. In front of these little shrines hung the twisted straw rope. Vases held small green branches, flowers, and leaves; bottles of water or sake were set out. Candles and incense were lit daily as the worshipper clapped his hands and chanted texts.

At the New Year the god-shelves were renewed or replaced by new ones. Doors were decorated with branches for good luck and new life. Demons were exorcised both from temples and many houses. In the spring and autumn the dead were remembered and the tombstones cleaned. There were also seasonal festivals for fishing, rice growing, and flowers.

Japanese Buddhists had images, incense, rituals, and sermons. They used gongs during rituals, and also practiced meditation. Although there were daily and weekly services at the black wood Buddhist temples with their Chinese-style roofs, worshippers only thronged there during special anniversaries. The people sat on the floor in dark kimonos, facing west toward the Western Paradise. Traditional music was played and, when the screen before the altar was opened to reveal the image and candles, everyone murmured, "Adoration to Amida Buddha."

Musical instruments used were bells, cymbals, drums, flutes, stringed instruments similar to the lute, percussion sticks, rattles, gongs, the *yotsu dake* (split bamboo clappers), the *hyoshige* (solid blocks of hardwood either struck together or with a board).

DRESS AND ORNAMENTATION

In early Japan, rank and office were judged by the dress[6] and the quality of materials used. Men wore a silk hat, lacquered and stiffened, called a *kammuri*. This was a skullcap with a tube at the back of the head; this tube held the hair at the crown of the head. Two flat pigtails of horsehair or lacquered silk hung down the back. Color of the kammuri denoted rank: the highest rank, dark and pale violet; then dark and pale green; dark and pale wine; and finally black.

Court dress for men consisted of one or more pairs of very full breeches *(hakama)*, undergarments with short sleeves *(kosode)*, and overgarments *(ho)*. Full ceremonial dress *(sokutai)* was a kind of uniform for all high court officials. The white train, up to three yards long, could be lined with colored silk. In winter every piece of clothing was lined with silk and quilted. Summer clothing was made of lighter materials. A sword *(tachi)* was held horizontally in the girdle. On the back went a quiver of arrows, carefully fanned out. To move freely, the end of the train was tucked into the girdle under the sword.

Japanese warriors

By the thirteenth century, the train had been done away with. Then the dress consisted of an outer robe with full breeches fastened at the ankles and almost concealing the shoes; the breeches could be of any color. Shoes were a kind of black lacquered wooden clog, padded inside and worn without socks. The color of the outer garment depended upon rank. Sometimes instead of an over-jacket, men wore a type of full, loose-fitting smock pulled in by a girdle.

Over a red *hakama*, women wore up to five silk kimonos (very long robes open down the front and trailing on the ground). The kimonos were arranged so each color showed and formed a train; the top one was the richest. Winter robes were very thick, lined with swansdown, and more undergarments were worn. In summer women wore lighter kimonos. At home they donned only a *kosode* and full length transparent kimono over the hakama of light silk. On the feet went straw sandals *(waraji)* or wooden pattens *(geta)*.

Both sexes of good rank (those belonging to families of nobles and warriors) wore makeup, the women wearing a greater amount than the men. They avoided the effects of the Sun, wind, and rain on the skin.

A very pale complexion was considered a sign of beauty among women. White coloring was enhanced by using a small cotton bag of rice powder that was dampened with perfumed water and smoothed over the face during the day. They made a red spot in the center of the lower lip with a paste of flower petals. This paste was kept in shells or small porcelain cups. Less of this paste was applied to the cheekbones with a large soft brush. The eyebrows were plucked to a very delicate arch or shaved off entirely, replacing them with two delicate black marks quite high on the forehead. Women and most of the men blackened their teeth; white teeth were considered uncouth.

Men wore small pointed beards and mustaches. Noble men fastened their hair up, the ends neatly cut, and gathered into a single knot. Women wore their hair long, both up in elegant styles or hanging down.

SOME OF THE MYTHS

One creation myth is the story of a giant carp that slept under the sea. When it awoke, it thrashed about, throwing up rocks and soil, thus creating the islands of Japan.

However, the most popular creation myth concerns a trio of beings who arose out of the primeval oily ocean mass. About all that is known of these first beings is that they produced generations of Gods and Goddesses, one pair of which was called Izanagi and Izanami. This brother and sister came down from heaven on the rainbow, but there was no land. Izanagi stirred the ocean with his spear; the drops from the tip formed the island of Ono-koro. There Izanagi and his sister Izanami married.

They learned the art of lovemaking by watching a pair of water birds. Their offspring included the rest of the islands of Japan, waterfalls, mountains, trees, herbs, and the wind. The last to be born was the god of fire, whose birthing killed Izanami.

Izanagi followed her spirit into the underworld, or Yomi, the Land of Gloom. She told him that she would return with him but he must not look inside a particular building in Yomi. When she entered the building, Izanagi could not resist peeking inside. There he saw the terribly decomposed body of Izanami. Enraged that he had broken his promise, Izanami with the help of horrible female spirits chased him back

Susanoo

to the world above. Izanagi blocked the entrance with huge rocks.

After purifying himself from his journey to Yomi, Izanagi by himself gave birth to the Sun goddess, the Moon god, and Susanoo the Storm god. One version says that these deities were made from Izanagi's eyes.

The god Susanoo was a mischief-maker whose idea of a joke was always a bad one; many times he was destructive on purpose. So when he showed up in Heaven to visit his elder sister Amaterasu, the Sun goddess, she was more than a little suspicious. She grabbed up her quiver and bow to meet him. Susanoo protested that he had only come to say good-bye before embarking on a long journey. The Sun goddess wanted proof of his good will. Susanoo suggested that they create children—his would be boys and prove his good intentions.

The Sun goddess took his sword, broke it into three pieces, and chewed them. Then blowing a light mist, she produced three goddesses. Susanoo took the five strings of jewels from around his sister's neck, cracked them with his teeth, blew a mist, and produced five gods. These eight deities were considered the ancestors of the Japanese.

However, Susanoo was so pleased with his success that he got carried away. He began destroying things; his final repulsive act was to drop manure in the sacred Temples. Amaterasu kept making excuses for her brother until one day he made a hole in the roof of her house and dropped in a dead horse while she and her women were weaving ceremonial clothing for the other gods. One of the women was so frightened that she stabbed herself with a shuttle and died. This was too much for Amaterasu. She was so upset that she fled into a cave and blocked the entrance with a boulder. The world was plunged into darkness by her absence.

This great darkness aided the evil gods and hindered the good ones. Finally the 800 good deities went for advice to the god Hoard-thoughts. Following his orders, they collected crowing roosters, hung mirrors and strings of jewels on a tree by the cave, and uttered ritual words. But the Sun goddess still hid.

The goddess Ama no Uzume took off her clothes, decorated herself with plants, and put a tub upside down before the cave. She began a lewd dance on top of the tub. The gods roared with laughter. This made Amaterasu curious, and she asked what was happening. The gods told her that they had found a better Sun goddess. Amaterasu peeked out of the cave but could only see the reflections from the mirrors. She crept out. The god of Force, who had been waiting, grabbed her hand and yanked her out. Quickly the other gods barred the entrance to the cave.

The gods decided that Susanoo must be punished and fined him heavily. Then they cut off his beard, mustache, and all of his fingernails. As a final punishment, they kicked him out of Heaven.

Susanoo wandered on the Earth until he came to Izumo Province. There he saw an old couple and a girl crying beside a river. When he asked what was wrong, they told him that the girl was to be a sacrifice to a terrible dragon that had already eaten her seven older sisters. The dragon had eight heads and his body covered eight valleys and mountains. Susanoo promised he would save the girl if she would marry him; naturally she agreed. He filled eight barrels with sake. The dragon appeared and each of the heads drank a barrel of the potent wine. When the dragon fell asleep, Susanoo took out his sword and cut the beast into little pieces. As he hacked up the tail, he discovered a divine sword, which he later gave to his sister, the Sun goddess. This sword is kept today in the Temple of Atsuta, near the town of Nagoya. Susanoo married the girl and built himself a palace at Suga.

Amaterasu, desiring to see if her Earthly kingdom was in order, sent her younger brother the Moon god to Earth to check on the food goddess, Uke-mochi.[7] Uke-mochi decided to entertain royally the Moon god, so she vomited boiled rice on the fields and

Amaterasu comes out of the cave

fish and edible seaweed into the ocean. On the wooded hills, she spewed out various kinds of game. The Moon god was so disgusted at this manner of providing food that he struck Uke-mochi and killed her. However, the creative powers of the food goddess did not stop with her death. From her head came cows and horses; from her eyebrows silkworms. Millet sprang from her forehead and a rice plant from her stomach.[8]

O-kuni-nushi (the Great Land Master) fell in love with the daughter of the Storm god Susanoo. In order to elope, the couple tied Susanoo's hair to the house beams and then fled with the god's bow and arrows and *koto* (harp). The harp strings rang as they took it and this woke Susanoo. When he caught up with the fleeing pair, he was so impressed that he agreed to the marriage and even let them keep the treasures. He also gave Oh-kuni-nushi the right to rule the province of Izumo.

Oh-kuni-nushi was aided in his rule by a dwarf god called Suku-na-biko (Small Renown Man). This dwarf was the offspring of the Divine Producing Goddess and arrived on the province coast on a small raft, wearing moth wings and tiny feathers. He was skilled in medicine; with Oh-kuni-nushi he cured diseases in the province and also cultivated many crops. This dwarf god is still associated with hot springs and healing.

MAJOR GODS AND GODDESSES

AMA NO UZUME—Fertility goddess; she performed the lewd dance to draw AMATERASU out of the cave. Good crops.

AMATERASU—Sun goddess; "great shining heaven"; guardian of the Japanese people; ruler of all deities. One of her tasks was to weave sacred robes for the gods, a habit kept alive today by modern Shinto priestesses. Her emblem of the rising Sun is still seen today on Japan's flag. Warmth, harvest, love, fertility, goodness, wisdom, peace, light, compassion.

Amida Buddha

AMA-TSU-KAMI—The name given to the gods of Heaven to distinguish them from the gods of the Earth (KUNI-TSU-KAMI).

AMIDA-NYORAI/AMIDA—"The Buddha of Infinite Light"; Ruler of the Pure Land; a form of the Buddha. Protection, forgiveness.

BENTEN/BENZAITEN—The only goddess of good luck; in one form a dragon woman with a company of white snakes, in another form a lovely human woman mounted on a dragon; queen of the sea. Protection from earthquakes; bringer of inspiration and talent, wealth and romance.

CHIMATI NO KAMI—God of crossroads and footpaths; the positive creative force of life; a phallic deity. Fertility.

EMMA-HOO/EMMA-O—Male Ruler of the Underworld. Death, revenge, destruction.

FUGEN BOSATSU—God of enlightening wisdom, intelligence, understanding, intuition, long life.

HACHIMAN—An historical figure, elevated to godhood after death. War, battle, bravery, honor, success in personal matters.

HAYA-JI/HAYA-TSU-MUJO NO KAMI—God of the winds and whirlwind.

IDA-TEN—Guardian of the Law. Justice, law, victory, purity.

INARI—Goddess, sometimes a god, of rice; very popular with many shrines. As a female, pictured as a woman with a fox-tail; could shape-shift into a fox. As a male, pictured as a bearded old man sitting on a sack of rice; foxes were his messengers. Shopkeepers, merchants, business, prosperity, smithing, sword blades.

ISHIKORE-DOME—Stone-Coagulating Old Woman; the smith-goddess who created the first mirror from copper stones out of the Isuzu River. It is said that this mirror is preserved as a sacred relic in the Imperial Shrine at Ise. No one is allowed to see the mirror, but tradition says that it has eight sides. Each of the Shinto shrines in Japan has a similar mirror as their most sacred object.

IZANAGI—Creator God; Earth God; Great Father; the Male Principle. Magick.

IZANAMI—Divine Mother; Great Goddess; Earth Goddess; the Female Principle. Magick.

JIZO BOSATSU—Protector of Mankind; rescuer of souls from hell; protector of women in childbirth. Children, the dead, comfort, rescue, counsel for the dead, protection from evil.

KANNON BOSATSU/KANNON/KWANNON—A male form of the Chinese KUAN YIN. Mercy and compassion.

KAYA NU HIMA—Goddess of herbs.

KISHI-MOJIN/KISHIMO-HIN—Protectress of children; Universal Mother. Compassion, childbirth, life, balance, fertility.

KONO-HANA-SAKUYA-HIME—"Lady who makes the trees bloom"; goddess of the cherry tree.

NAI NO KAMI—God of earthquakes.

NARU-KAMI/KAMI-NARU—Goddess of thunder; protector of trees; ruler of artisans.

O-KUNI-NUSHI/OKUNINUSHI—Earth God; "Great Land Master." Medicine, sorcery, cunning, self-realization.

O-RYU—Goddess of the willow tree.

O-WATA-TSUMI/SHIO-ZUCHI—"Old man of the tide"; most important of several sea deities. God of the tides and the sea creatures.

O-Yama-tsu-mi—First and most important of eight mountain gods. God of all mountains and volcanoes.

Rafu-sen—Goddess of the plum blossoms.

Sae no Kami—Collective name for the guardian gods of the roads; they protected people from misfortune.

Sakyamuni/Shaka-nyorai—Japanese name for the Buddha. Virtue, enlightenment, self-realization.

Shichi Fukujin/Shichi-Kukujin— "Seven Gods of Happiness."
1. Ebisu, patron of work;
2. Daikoku, god of prosperity;
3. Benzaiten, goddess of love;
4. Bishamonten, god of happiness and war;
5. Fukurokuju, god of happiness and long life;
6. Jurojin, god of happiness and long life;
7. Hotei Osho, god of good fortune.

Susanoo/Susanowo—An exuberant mischief-maker; god of storm and thunder. Agriculture, earthquakes, rain, storms, snakes, bravery, the seas, trees.

Toyota Mahime—"Lady Abundance of Jewels"; sea goddess.

Uso-Dori—Goddess of singing who appears in the shape of a bullfinch.

Japanese cosmogram

ENDNOTES

1. Campbell, Joseph. *The Masks of God: Oriental Mythology.*

2. Amaterasu Omikami is not a historical person verified by European historians, but this does not mean she did not exist. The Japanese people certainly look upon her as a real person, and that is good enough for me.

3. For more in-depth information on the Ninjas and their beliefs, see the books by Stephen K. Hayes.

4. Our female/male or negative/positive polarity is the same as both Yin/Yang and In/Yo. Because of this concept of duality, all Shinto deities were seen as having both positive and negative aspects.

5. The translation of the Japanese word *kami* is "god," but means much more than "god" or "deity." It means anything that is believed to possess supernatural power or beauty. This includes many inanimate objects as well as humans and animals.

6. The dress described here is that of court officials and Samurai, not of the common people.

7. This tale is found in the *Nihongi*.

8. The earliest record of this story says that Susanoo was the murderer.

BIBLIOGRAPHY

Adachi, Fumie. *Japanese Design Motifs*. NY: Dover Publications, 1972.

Anesaki, Masaharu. *The Mythology of All Races*, vol. 8, Japanese. UK: Harrap, 1932.

Aston, W. G., trans. *Nihongi*. UK: Allen & Unwin, 1956. (Originally published 1896.)

Benedict, Ruth. *The Chrysanthemum and the Sword: Patterns of Japanese Culture.* NY: Houghton Mifflin, 1946.

Davis, F. Hadland. *Myths and Legends of Japan*. UK: Harrap, 1913.

Dorson, R. M. *Folk Legends of Japan*. Tokyo: Charles Tuttle, 1962.

Durdin-Robertson, Lawrence. *Goddesses of India, Tibet, China and Japan*. Ireland: Caesara Publications, 1976.

Eliseev, S. *Asiatic Mythology: The Mythology of Japan*. UK: Harrap, 1932.

Frederic, Louis. *Daily Life in Japan at the Time of the Samurai*. NY: Praegar Publishers, 1972.

Hayes, Stephen K. *The Ancient Art of Ninja Warfare, Combat, Espionage, and Traditions*. Contemporary Books, Inc., 1988.

Hayes, Stephen K. *The Mystic Arts of the Ninja, Hypnotism, Invisibility, and Weaponry.* Contemporary Books, 1985.

Hayes, Stephen K. *Ninja Vol. III: Warrior Ways of Enlightenment.* Ohara Publications, Inc., 1981.

Hayes, Stephen K. *Ninja Vol. IV: Legacy of the Night Warrior.* Ohara Publications, no date.

Hayes, Stephen K. *Ninja Vol. V: Lore of the Shinobi Warrior.* Ohara Publications, 1989.

Joly, H. L. *Legend in Japanese Art.* UK: The Bodley Head, 1908.

Latourette, K. S. *The History of Japan.* NY: Macmillan, 1953.

McAlpine, Helen and William. *Japanese Tales and Legends.* UK: Oxford University Press, 1958.

Menten, Theodore. *Japanese Cut and Use Stencils.* NY: Dover Publications, 1980.

Minnick, Helen Benton. *Japanese Costume and the Makers of Its Elegant Tradition.* NY: Charles E. Tuttle Co., 1963.

Ozaki, Y. T. *The Japanese Fairy Book.* UK: Constable, 1903.

Piggott, Juliet. *Japanese Mythology.* UK: Paul Hamlyn, 1975.

Redesdale, Lord. *Tales of Old Japan.* UK: Macmillan, 1908.

Rice, Edward. *Ten Religions of the East.* NY: Four Winds Press, 1978.

Riva, Anna. *Secrets of Magical Seals: A Modern Grimoire of Amulets, Charms, Symbols and Talismans.* Toluca Lake, CA: International Imports, 1983.

Ross, Nancy. *Three Ways of Asian Wisdom.* NY: Simon & Schuster, 1966.

Seki, Keigo, ed. Trans. R. J. Adams. *Folktales of Japan.* UK: Routledge & Kegan Paul, 1963.

Smith, R. G. *Ancient Tales and Folklore of Japan.* UK: A. & C. Black, 1908.

Tilke, Max. *Oriental Costumes, Their Designs and Colors.* UK: K. Paul, Trench, Trubner & Co. Ltd., 1923.

Webster, R. G. *Japan: From the Old to the New.* UK: S. W. Patridge & Co., 1905.

CHAPTER TWENTY-ONE

TIBET

VERY LITTLE is known about Tibet before the introduction of Buddhism from India in the seventh century AD. An alphabet of Sanskrit origin was created to translate the Buddhist literature into the Tibetan language.

Early Tibetan kings sponsored the arrival of Buddhism. During the reign of King Srong-btsan sgam-po (who died in AD 650), a Buddhist temple was built in Lhasa. This temple, known as the Jo-khang, "temple of the Lord," contained an image of the Buddha. In the eighth century the first monastery was erected, and Tibetans were ordained as monks.

The period between the seventh and fourteenth centuries was one of rule by kings, with Buddhism and the priests emerging in a role of great influence and power. By the ninth century, the Buddhist priests exercised dominant political power. The region remained an independent state until late in the thirteenth century when it came under the nominal control of the Mongolian Empire. The rule of the Dalai Lamas, or "priest-kings," began in the thirteenth century, with the system of priestly incarnation beginning under the Second Dalai Lama late in the fifteenth century. The greatest of these rulers was the Fifth Dalai Lama in the seventeenth century who built the great Potala Palace in Lhasa. In 1720 the Chinese Manchu dynasty took control, but the Tibetans remained largely independent.

A few Europeans trickled into Tibet, but mostly they were discouraged from visiting and influencing the country. In 1904 the British, alarmed by Tibet's growing friendship with Russia, invaded. The Dalai Lama fled to Mongolia, where he stayed until 1911. The Chinese made Tibet part of the province of Sikang in 1908. But the Chinese revolution of 1912 enabled the Tibetans once again to declare independence; they fought against the Chinese until 1933. The Chinese Nationalist mission stationed at Lhasa was thrown out in 1949. Chinese Communist troops invaded Tibet in 1950 and took control. In 1959, a counter-revolution, led by monks and priests, was suppressed, and the Dalai Lama fled to India.

RELIGION

Bon is the primitive, pre-Buddhist religion of Tibet. The legendary founder of Bon was Mi-bo gshen-rab. Bon was a shamanistic belief, with priest-magicians called Bon-po. They believed in gods of the sky, Earth, mountains, and lower regions. Like most Orientals, the Tibetans had a great sense of sin, therefore believing in a purgatory and hell.

The shamans, or sorcerer-priests, of Bon possessed great occult strength and had to be able to control and appease the Nature spirits inhabiting rivers, mountains, trees, caves, etc. They had to know which rituals to use to keep spirits from taking over the body of someone ill, crazy, or dying. They learned to absorb the spirits into their own bodies so they could use those powers for their own purposes. One of the common homes of spirits was the juniper tree. For this reason, its berries, trunk, and branches were offered as sacrifices; the berries were used as a narcotic to induce ecstatic trances.

A great sacrifice was held every three years, with donkeys and humans offered to the gods of the three regions: Heaven, Earth, and Underworld. Sheep, dogs, and monkeys were sacrificed in less important rites. The victim was disemboweled and the blood scattered into the air.

The main celestial deity lived in Pagopunsum, a sacred peak in northeast Tibet. After the coming of Buddhism, Bon took on many of its aspects. Bon-po used the same language and literature as the Buddhists and even accepted the Buddhist pantheon, although they gave the gods other names.

The Bon-po, and later the Tibetan Buddhists, carried rosaries (some made of pieces of human skulls), a trumpet called a *longling* (also made of human bone), and a ritual knife. This magickal dagger had a triangular blade and a very ornate handle; it was used, not for sacrifices, but for ritual gesturing and the drawing of magickal symbols, etc.

Buddhist altars were very elaborate with a shelf above them full of statues. Over this hung a silk canopy with bells. Temple lamps were pedestalled bowls with a cotton wick in melted butter. A number of ritual items were used: flower vases, incense burners, five or seven offering dishes, disks picturing symbolic offerings, one or more sacred books, a *dorje* (thunderbolt knife of Indra), scepter, bells, large metal mirror, divining arrow bound with five colors of silk for demonic rites, holy relics, libation jugs. Fresh water and rice were placed on the altar each day.

To accompany the rites, certain musical instruments were used: a conch shell trumpet, a pair of copper flageolets, six-foot long copper horns, a pair of human thigh-bone trumpets to summon demons, a pair of tiger thigh-bones to summon demons, a rattle hand-drum, a large suspended religious drum, a human skull-drum.

Preparatory to all sacred rites, the fingers were dipped in water. Then the monk touched the forehead, chest, pit of the stomach, and both shoulders. The stages of each ritual followed the same pattern:

1. Invocation, calling to the sacrifice
2. Inviting the deity to be seated
3. Presenting the offerings, sacred cakes, rice, water, flowers, incense, lamps, music, sometimes a mandala
4. Hymns of praise
5. Special spells or mantras
6. Petition prayers
7. Benediction

Sacred images were made of clay, bread dough, compressed incense, papier-mache, copper, brass, wood, or stone. They were decorated with paint, gilt, and precious stones. The image was covered most of the time by a silk scarf decorated with sacred symbols.

For monks the New and Full Moons were for fasting, confession, and listening to or reading Buddha's Law. The Tibetan year began about the end of January. On February 15 was the festival of Buddha's Conception and the Feast of Flowers. His mother, Maya Deva, was worshipped with red flowers and asked for divine blessings. March 29 was the Expulsion of Demons of Bad Luck. A symbolic drama was held with the Grand Lama chasing out a priest representing the demon king. April 15 was the Sacred

Masks Festival. At this time temples exhibited the holy vessels, precious things, and pictures. On May 8, the Great Renunciation or attainment of Buddha-hood was celebrated. May 15 was the celebration of Buddha's Death and the Feast of the Dead. This was an old Nature festival for the beginning of summer and the rain deities. Deceased relatives were prayed for.

June 5 honored the Medical Buddhas. June 10 was the rite of the Birth of Padmasambhava. Masked sacred dances and mystery plays were held. July 4 was for Buddha's Birth and Preaching, also called the Picture Feast. August 10 was the Sikhim holiday of the birth of Padmasambhava. September 8 was the Water Festival, a thanksgiving feast and the special honoring of springs and water sprites. October

A Bon priest

Buddhist effigy

22 was the Descent from Heaven, the end of the rainy season, and the Buddhist Lent. November 25 was the Feast of Lanterns, winter festival of the shortest days of the Sun. December 1 was the old New Year. January 29 saw the Pantomime and expulsion of the Old Year. A dough image was made by each village. The demon of ill luck was invited to enter the image and was worshipped for seven days. Then it was taken beyond the village to a crossroad and abandoned.

In Tibet, Buddhism took on a number of shamanistic traits. The Tibetan Book of the Dead, the *Bardo Thodol*, was largely of Bon origin. Effigies of the dead were made. Animal masks were worn by Tibetan Buddhist priests for various rituals and mystery plays. They built temples and monasteries, while the Bon-po had lived among the people.

A reincarnating lama was regarded as the sPrul-sku (manifested body) of a particular Buddhist deity or renowned religious leader. The Dalai Lama was believed to be the reincarnation of the Bodhisattva Avalokitesvara, and the Panchen Lama the reincarnation of the Buddha Amitabha. Consultation of the state oracle in Nechung often played a key role in choosing a new Dalai Lama.

Prayer wheels with inscribed messages from scriptures were attached in long rows outside the temples and monasteries. There were also smaller individual ones. These were spun to send prayers to Heaven. Incenses were burned for all occasions, mostly sandalwood and other Indian imports.

Butter lamps were used in a form of divination known as Sman-gsal-mar-me-brtag-pa-ldep; this was done by the Mopa or diviner. Divination was also done on the rosary *(mala)*, which was also used for daily devotions.

At the beginning of each devotion, each lama or priest would touch his forehead while chanting Om, the top of the chest (Ah), the pit of the stomach (Hum), the left shoulder (Dam), and the right shoulder (Yam).[1]

The Kings of the four quarters of the heavens were known as Dhritarashtra, white guardian of the east; Virudhaka, green guardian of the south; Virupaksha, red guardian of the west; Vaisravana, yellow guardian of the north.[2] These kings were said to guard the heavens from the outer demons.

Ten Lokpals guarded the Earth from its ten directions: Indra, east; Agni, south-east; Yama, south; Sura, south-west; Varuna, west; Vayu, north-west; Kubera, north; Soma, north-east; Brahma, above; Bhupati, below.

Dress and Ornamentation

Both sexes in Tibet dressed primarily for warmth in the mountainous, cold region. The wealthier people wore full-length robes of silk on broadcloth, quilted or lined with fur; the sleeves were extremely long to protect the hands. The poorer people wore robes of rough-spun yak hair. Thick felt boots covered the feet. Women braided their hair in elaborate styles, the wealthy ones fastening the hair onto a cane frame covered with coral, turquoise, and other uncut stones.

Underneath the robes, men wore a knee-length tunic of thick material and trousers in the Magyar fashion. A turned-up cap of fur or felt protected their heads from the wind. Everyone wore a decorative amulet box around their neck to guard them against evil spirits.

Wealthy people trimmed their outfits with rich embroidery and wore elegant earrings, necklaces, and bracelets. Makeup was not much used, but the skin was protected against the elements by rubbing in rich perfumed oils.

The Tibetan monk wore a hat on his closely-shaven head, a robe and sash, an inner vest, cloak, trousers, and boots and carried his rosary and other implements. The robe was of saffron yellow or red, depending upon his religious affiliation. An ample deep garnet-red petticoat reaching from the waist to the ankles was worn by all sects. The sash color and the shape and color of the hat was determined by the sect. A long narrow shawl, several yards long, was thrown over the left shoulder, across the breast, and then around the body. From the sash hung a water bottle, pen-case, and a purse for food and things. In the upper flap of the coat were the prayer wheel, drinking cup, booklets, and charms. He carried his begging bowl and a trident-topped staff with jingling rings. The dress of nuns was very similar.

Rosary

Rosaries of sliding balls were carried by everyone, even lay men and women; they were used to keep count of prayers. The rosary was a string of 108 beads tied together with three larger beads at the end. The beads were made of everything from human bone, wood, pearls, gold, precious stones, conch shell, and glass, to seeds. Disks of human bone were used by the worshippers of Vajra-bhairava; those of snake spines by sorcerers in necromancy and divination. Worshippers of Tara used turquoise rosaries.

SOME OF THE MYTHS

The Bon legend of the creation of the world says that in the beginning was an uncreated being. From this being streamed out a white light from which emerged an egg. The egg had no moving parts but it flew about. After five months, the egg cracked open, and out came a man. He put a throne in the middle of the ocean, sat down, and systematically began to put the universe in order. Out of the void came forth wind, fire, water, foam, and a tortoise. The tortoise laid six eggs of six different colors; these eggs produced six kinds of serpents *(klu)* who were the origin of the six classes of living beings on the earth.

Another version of the creation story says that a female serpent came out of the void. The sky sprang from the top of her head; from her right eye came the Moon and from her left the Sun. From other parts of her body were produced the planets, thunder, lightning, clouds, rain, wind, the five oceans, rivers, soil, and mountains.

Western Tibet has a different legend. Here the world is symbolized as a tree with three tops and six branches. Each branch had a bird laying an egg; these eggs then produced various manifestations of the world.

In another legend (Buddhist but influenced by Bon), the Bodhisattva Avalokitesvara was told to convert Tibet to Buddhism. Instead of going there, Avalokitesvara sat on top of Mount Potala and produced from the palm of his hand a light ray. Out of this came a monkey, which he instructed in the Doctrine and sent to Tibet to meditate. There were no men living in Tibet then.

Buddha, detail from Tibetan woodblock

As the monkey was meditating, a rock-ogress came by and tried to seduce him by changing into all kinds of forms. The monkey was very upset about this and went back for advice. Avalokitesvara told him to mate with the rock-ogress because the descendants would become men. The monkey obeyed, and in nine months was the father of six dreadful looking beings. They had red faces, tails, were covered with hair, and had a liking for flesh and blood.

Finally the monkey took them to the Peacock Woods and left them with the monkeys who lived there. In a year the monkey returned to find that the six had become five hundred. The offspring were not monkeys or men, but suffered from heat and cold and had nothing to eat. The father monkey gave them food, but this caused them pain. Their hair fell off and their tails disappeared.

Avalokitesvara

Again he went to Avalokitesvara for advice. He was told that the offspring were now men. Avalokitesvara then went himself to convert the new beings. He gave them seven kinds of grain, and taught them how to cultivate land and produce food. And, of course, he instructed them in Buddhist Doctrine.

The Bon-pos said that the original king of Tibet came from the land of Mu by descending from Heaven on a sky-cord. At the end of each reign, the king would ascend the sky-cord and his successor would come to take his place. However, the seventh king lost the power because of his pride. He picked a fight with one of his ministers. The minister tricked the king into carrying a bag of ashes and slinging the carcasses of a fox and mouse over his shoulders. The protective gods, who stand by one's shoulders, disappeared because of the corpses. The minister could then break the bag of ashes with an arrow, which he did. The king lashed out with his sword and severed the sky-cord, cutting off all retreat on his part. The minister calmly finished him off with another arrow.

MAJOR GODS AND GODDESSES

AKSHOBHYA—"Imperturbable"; "Witness"; one of the Cosmic BUDDHAS. He was blue in color, and his symbol was a thunderbolt. Enlightenment.

AMITABHA—"Boundless Light"; the meditating BUDDHA; one of the Cosmic Buddhas. He sprang from a lotus and aided the weak and faltering. Uttering the holy formula of his name granted rebirth into the Pure Land (Heaven). His color was red, and his symbol a red lotus. Salvation, meditation, reincarnation.

AMITAYUS—"Infinite Light"; the BUDDHA of longevity; one of the Cosmic Buddhas. Long life, enlightenment.

AMOGHASIDDHI—"Perfect Accomplishment"; "Blessing of Fearlessness"; a Cosmic BUDDHA. He was green, and his symbol a thunderbolt. Spiritual attainment.

AVALOKITESVARA/AVOLOKITA—"Lord of Compassion"; "Keen seeing Lord"; "Lord of Mercy"; patron saint of Tibet. He was portrayed as a handsome young man with a lotus flower in his left hand. He was worshipped in many forms, the best known having one head and four arms, or eleven heads arranged on a cone and a thousand eyes. His *shakti* (female partner) was the Green TARA. He was believed incarnated in the Dalai Lama, the most senior monk. When the Dalai Lama died, the god's spirit passed to a newborn child, who was identified by the monks and brought up within the monastery. Shape-shifter, enlightenment, relief from problems, supreme knowledge.

BDUD—Evil-tempered demons of the higher spheres, shaped like birds, fish, herbs, or stones. All male, they were black and malignant. They required a pig sacrifice. Their leader was called "The Merciless Blood-head." Destruction, evil events.

BTSAN—A large group of gods inhabiting the sky, forests, mountains and glaciers. All male and red, these were vindictive ghosts of lamas and discontented priests who haunted temples. Some were protectors of the Buddhist Doctrine.

BUDDHA—"The Enlightened One"; Gautama Siddhartha (c. 563–479 BC); the Divine Teacher. There were 35 Buddhas of Confession; the eight Buddhas of Medicine were led by BHAISHAJYAGURU. Spiritual enlightenment, wisdom, self-realization, supreme knowledge, compassion, healing.

HAYAGRIVA/HEVAJRA—"Horse-Necked One"; protective and wrathful BUDDHA; Lord of Wrath. The terrible aspect of spiritual powers. Righteous anger.

LHA—Pre-Buddhist celestial entities; all male, colored white and generally benevolent. These included the shoulder gods (like guardian angels), gods of food, hearth, and roads. Protection, journeys, health.

LHA-MO/DMAGZOR RGYAL-MO—"The Great Queen"; "Queen of the warring weapons"; she-devil. Similar to the Indian DURGA, she loosed demons of disease.

MAITREIYA/METTEYYA—Name of the Buddha to come; "the Benevolent One"; BUDDHA of the Future.

MANJUSRI—"The sweet-voiced." He held a sword of divine knowledge and a book of wisdom. Metaphysical wisdom.

Manjusri

MARA—Lord of Death; the Evil One; demon of Desire. Master magician of illusion. Magickal powers.

RIN-PO-CHE/PADMASAMBHAVA—"Lotus-Born"; the Great Magician; Destroyer of Demons. He had extraordinary magickal powers.

SA-BDAG—Deities bound to the place they control, including individual mountains, villages, and fields. Although usually indifferent to people, they were easily provoked and caused harm. One of these was the door or house god, similar to the Chinese Kitchen God.

The White Tara

SAKYAMUNI—A Bodhisattva, "a being striving for enlightenment." He had indigo-colored hair, golden skin, and was seated on a grass cushion on a lotus-throne. See BUDDHA.

TARA—"Savioress"; Queen of Heaven; "Deliverer"; Universal Mother; Mother of All the Buddhas; Supreme Wisdom. She had 21 forms, the best known being the Green Tara and the White Tara. The Green Tara was called DOL-JANG, had green skin and was seated on a lotus holding a long-stemmed lotus flower. The White Tara, called DO-KAR and worshipped by the Mongols, had white skin, seven eyes, and was seated Buddha-like holding a lotus. She was the *shakti*, or female partner, of the BODHISATTVA AVALOKITESVARA. She was kind and loving, transcended social distinctions, and offered a personal relationship to her devotees.

VAJRASATTVA—"Wielder of the thunderbolt"; the primeval BUDDHA; meditation Buddha. He was invoked in the quest of enlightenment. His bronze statues portrayed the eternal embrace of the male and female principles of Tantric Yoga. His terrible aspect showed his violent fury in rain, hail, and snow. Attainment of oneness.

YAMA—"The Restrainer"; King of the Underworld and judge of people. Annihilation, funerals, death, destruction, punishment, judgment.

YAMANTAKA—"Destroyer of the Lord of Death"; "The Annihilator." He was the BUDDHA who brought civilization to the Himalayas and led sufferers to enlightenment. A protective god, he held a sword and a book. Enlightenment, rescue, protection.

ENDNOTES

1. It is very possible that the Catholic church took their signing of the cross from this Tibetan ritual.
2. Waddell, L. Austine. *Tibetan Buddhism.* Virupaksha was also known as king of the Nagas and Vaisravana, king of the Yakshas. Vaisravana was further known as god of riches.

BIBLIOGRAPHY

Andrews, Lynn V. *Windhorse Woman: A Marriage of Spirit.* NY: Warner Books, 1989.

David-Neel, Alexandra. *Magic and Mystery in Tibet.* NY: Dover Publications, 1971.

Durdin-Robertson, Lawrence. *Goddesses of India, Tibet, China and Japan.* Ireland: Caesara Publications, 1976.

Evans-Wentz, W. Y., ed. *The Tibetan Book of the Dead.* UK: Oxford University Press, 1975.

Frost, Gavin and Yvonne. *Tantric Yoga.* York Beach, ME: Samuel Weiser, 1989.

Knight, Gareth. *The Rose Cross and the Goddess.* NY: Destiny Books, 1985.

Norvell, Anthony. *Amazing Secrets of the Mystic East.* West Nyack, NY: Parker Publishing, 1980.

Rice, Edward. *Ten Religions of the East.* NY: Four Winds Press, 1978.

Ross, Nancy. *Three Ways of Asian Wisdom.* NY: Simon & Schuster, 1966.

Waddell, L. Austine. *Tibetan Buddhism.* NY: Dover Publications, 1972.

Walker, Benjamin. *Tantrism.* UK: Aquarian Press, 1982.

CHAPTER TWENTY-TWO

PACIFIC OCEAN

THE PACIFIC Ocean mythologies consist of at least four major cultures and divisions: Australia, Melanesia, Micronesia, and Polynesia. Polynesia is outlined in a great triangle extending from New Zealand to Hawaii and Easter Island; in its center are the island clusters of Tonga, Samoa, Tahiti, and Tuamotu. This area has seen several migrations of peoples, the main one about 2000 years ago when the first Polynesians came from southeast Asia. This triangle is more than 4,000 miles from Hawaii to New Zealand. The distance has produced many variations in cultures, languages, and deities. Cannibalism was practiced extensively until arrival of the Europeans. The eating of a human body was done to give the consumer more *mana*, or vital energy. Although the inhabitants of the Hawaiian Islands preferred man-slaying to man-eating, they had many details of the custom in their legends.

Melanesia is made up of Papua and a large ring of volcanic archipelagos, including the Admiralty Islands, Solomon Islands, Banks Islands, New Britain, New Hebrides, New Caledonia, and the Fiji Islands. Except for the fringes of this area, Melanesia remained isolated from about 3000 BC until AD 1567. British traders and missionaries arrived in the 1830s. In Melanesia there seemed to be no idea of a supreme deity. Headhunting was merely an assembly of the heads of defeated enemies and was a perverse idea of gaining mana. Some Melanesian cultures were matriarchal.

Micronesia is a group of scattered islands with four main archipelagos—the Gilbert, Marshall, Mariana, and Caroline groups. They were remote from early world trade routes and not influenced by the Europeans for some time. These people placed great emphasis on ancestor worship.

By 1788, when Britain annexed Australia, there were about 300,000 Aborigines there. They were divided into more than 400 tribes who did not know or use agriculture, metallurgy, pottery, writing, or domesticated animals, except the dingo. They were nomads who hunted animals and gathered wild fruits. Their arrival in Australia is so remote that no exact date can be given. They have been classified as a separate group, the Australoids, and are not considered a stone-age group. Although the Aborigines had a low-level material culture, they evolved a complex social structure and religion. They had limited contact with traders from New Guinea and Indonesia.

The Maoris of New Zealand have a legend about their settlement of the islands. A tenth century Tahitian navigator, Kupe, found the islands while exploring; 200 years later only a small colony had settled there. However, by the fourteenth century there was a major colonization by the Maoris, which changed them from a seafaring to a hunting people.

RELIGION

Throughout the region of Oceania, genealogy, mythology, and tribal histories were oral, taught by the elders to the young. Only one vegetable—the taro or babai—was cultivated with special care, although they used some breadfruit, coconuts, and bananas. The cultivation of babai was connected with magick because of its importance to the survival of the people. Its cultivation was the occupation of the men, as was fishing, because both were connected with high levels of mana. Mana was considered the soul, or spirit energy, in physical things. Men were thought to have more mana than women did.

In Melanesia, elaborate wooden masks *(matua)* were used for funeral rites of ancestors. Masks were also worn for both Nature and human fertility rites. The Melanesians were skilled sculptors in wood and highly advanced in astronomy and navigation. In navigation, they used the movements of birds, location of currents, known positions of floating seaweed, certain types of waves, certain types of fish that were close to the surface, etc. This all was taught in a building called the *maneapa*, the most important building on any island. Ceremonial axes of jadeite or serpentine had a circular polished blade lashed to a wooden handle and were used in rain making rites.

In New Guinea, the cult house, called the Haus Tambaran, contained drums and carved figures. Carved ceremonial shields were used as part of their rituals.

All of these seafaring cultures put special carvings for protection and good luck on their canoes. Tattooing was a religious rite, with different patterns and body locations in each culture. Tattooing was done by rubbing colored pigment into punctures or small cuts in the skin. In Australia, scar tattooing was used, while in the Fijis women sported wart-like burn tattoos. The Maoris tattooed elaborate swirls over most of the body and dyed their lips blue.

To make rain in New Guinea, the sorcerer took a branch from a certain kind of tree and dipped it into water. Chanting magick words, he then sprinkled water around. In contrast, on Bank Island, they made sunshine by winding red thongs around a round stone, sticking owl feathers on it, and hanging it in a high tree.

The culture of the Hawaiians is best known and represents the Polynesian cultures quite well. The Nature gods they worshipped played an important part of everyday life. Among the Hawaiians the word for god was *akua;* however, this word translated into a broad description that could even include a dead body, a living person, or a carved image. Every form of Nature

Oceanic festival

had a class god; these deities could become *aumakua*, or guardian god, of a family. In this manner so-called children of that deity were born in human form. These offspring, called *kupua*,[1] had to be worshipped by the family with prayers and offerings. The kupua's power was limited to the area where he lived.

A *lapu* was a ghost or mischievous spirit who frightens people at night. These differed entirely from the *akua li'i* (little gods) who lived in the many Nature forms; the akua li'i were regularly invoked in prayers for protection.

Every individual had his personal god, besides the national gods. The personal deity was represented by a carving in wood or stone and was carefully tended with sacrifices and prayers. Each family had its *mua* (house of worship) where a food gourd *(huililau)* called the *kuaahu* or *ipu* of Lono was kept. This gourd was covered with wickerwork and hung from a notched stick. Offerings of food and *awa*[2] were put inside it.

Throughout Polynesia, the great Gods Ku, Kane, Lono, and Kanaloa were invoked together in chants. Even thieves had their own patron deity.

The Hawaiians used complex vocal music and the hula. They expected help and guidance from the ancestors. There were many *tapus*,[3] and breaking them was a spiritual offense.

The people were divided into very strict social classes: chiefs, priests, commoners, and slaves.[4] These ranks were inherited and each had specific prerogatives. The chiefs who were descended from the god Kane were considered to rank among the *hoali'i* or high tapu chiefs; other chiefs were of lower rank. In fact, the high tapu chiefs were considered gods in name with power over life and death.

The only goddess to roam freely was the fire goddess Pele, who had special priests to keep track of her activities and keep her placated. Thousands of pigs, valuables, and humans were thrown into Mt. Kilauea to keep her from destroying crops and people with her lava.

Melanesian mask

Temples for other gods were erected on strategic promontories. Groups of priests made sacrifices amid statues, images, and altars. The temple, or *heiau*, was a very holy place, so taboo that no commoner was permitted to approach it. Only kings and high chiefs (the *alii*) regularly joined the *kahunas* (priests) in elaborate feasts there. Chanted prayers to the gods were probably the most important part of temple worship. The great gods each had his own style of worship, his priests and *heiaus*. The colors red[5] and yellow were sacred to chiefs; yellow was the Kane color.

There were also an infinite number of lesser gods who were said to have descended from the major deities; they were worshipped by families or individuals with special occupations. Spirits of deceased relatives were said to take the form of birds, thus helping their descendants. An example of this was the elepaio bird (flycatcher) worshipped by canoe makers. This goddess led the priest to a good tree for building a new canoe.

One particular holiday was island-wide and four months long. This was Makahiki, at the first harvest Moon in October, when priestly affairs, war, and work came to a halt. The patron god was Lono, and his image rode on the mast tip of a canoe during the opening processions. Makahiki was a time of games, sports, pageantry, the hula, surfing, feasting, and tax collection. It was also a mating season since it brought together couples from different villages. There was no taboo on sex, except that the elite class (the alii) had to be careful of the lineage. The hula was widely used in this celebration, being a mixture of Polynesian dance, music, poetry, pantomime, and drama.

Kane, a god of procreation, was the chief deity among the Hawaiians. He was worshipped as the ancestor of both chiefs and commoners. Worshippers of Kane were called *he papa la'a* (meaning a consecrated class), as opposed to image worshippers. A Pohaku-o-Kane (Stone of Kane), or family altar, was actually a single conical rock up to eight feet tall with ti planted around it. Here family members prayed to their aumakua and asked forgiveness for broken taboos. During the ceremony the stone was sprinkled with water or coconut oil and covered with a cloth. Kane did not require human sacrifice or rigorous labors.

In Tahiti, they celebrated the *parara'a matahiti* (a first-fruit festival) which began in December or early January. At this festival Ro'o-ma-tane (Roma-tane), the god of Paradise, was invoked. In Tonga, at a similar festival, the men indulged in wrestling, club-fighting, and boxing. Fiji imposed a Moon of silence as it was said that the Lord from Hades came in December to push the yam shoots through the soil; at the end of this time everyone gave a great shout and resumed their ordinary activities.

The bond between the Australians and Nature was a totemic one. They believed that this relationship began in the Eternal Dreamtime (mythic past) through such entities as the Sky Heroes or the Fertility Mothers. Some totemic forces were considered to be plants, animals, or natural occurrences, such as the wind. Many of the totemic beings were shape-shifters.

Each group often had a different totemic being as their prime spiritual source, with religious units within the group sometimes having their own special totem, which could be a different one from the general group. These religious units were the guardians of the myths, rites, sacred objects, and sites which were associated with that totem.

The group religious rites in Australia were controlled by the men. Women and children were banned from most rituals. In some areas the women had their own secret ceremonies, such as the love-magick rites *(djarada)* of Northern Australia. However, they could be summoned by the men to act as a chorus or to take a limited part, such as in the Kunapipi fertility cult in the north. There was a death penalty if a woman entered the sacred cult grounds or saw the sacred objects.

Boys were circumcised at puberty and had their front teeth knocked out. Then they were allowed to take part in the Kangaroo Dance, an imitation of a hunt. The bull-roarer was used as a warning for women to stay away during the ceremonies. Sub-incision was also used as part of a later ceremony. Carved and painted pubic shields were worn during cult ceremonies.

An important part of Australian religious culture was the re-enactment of the myths important to each group. Most of the time the entire group, including women and children, was allowed to either watch or participate in some manner. There was imitative totemic dancing to the rhythm of the clapping sticks and the *didjeridu* (drone pipe). The chants and songs were filled with beautiful imagery. Sometimes the men wore colorful headdresses, such as those of the emu men of the Aranda.

There were many sacred sites in Australia, such as waterholes and such natural phenomena as Ayers Rock. Stylistic totemic figures were painted in remote religious sites. The tribes said that Ayers Rock, which they called Uluru, rose out of a sandhill. This huge monolith is associated with ten different groups of totemic beings. The vertical marks on its sides were said to have been made during the battle between the Kunia (carpet snake-men) and the Liru, poisonous snake-men.

All men carried a dilly bag in which they kept their sacred objects. The bag was worn publicly but the contents were kept secret. The dilly bag sometimes symbolized the wombs of the Djanggawul Sisters and was said to have originated with them.

Pointing the bone, or cursing a person, was used over much of central Australia by anyone who had a need; in other places the ceremony had to be performed by a sorcerer. The thin bone, with a point at one end and a tip of grass resin at the other, had a human hair string attached to it. Usually the hair string was slowly burned in a fire to cause death.

Australian rock painting

When the Wawalug myth was re-enacted, the great snake Julunggul was represented by the drone pipe. This pipe, or symbolic snake, which was about eight feet long, would emerge from a clump of bushes that represented the sacred well. The drone pipe was blown over the prostrate men, who held their dilly bags in their mouths. Each man had a painting of an iguana on his chest to mark him as a member of that totem. This was primarily performed among the Gunwinggu tribe of the Liverpool River.

Musical instruments used throughout the Pacific Ocean were the nose flute, whistles, ukelele, gourds, drums, bamboo pounding poles, whirring tops, rattles. In Australia, men beat boomerangs together; in Borneo, they used hollow ring rattles.

DRESS AND ORNAMENTATION

Before the coming of the Europeans, the Oceanic cultures wore bark-cloth made by pounding a fibrous wood with a coral mallet. This made a surprisingly soft, fine apparel. Some areas added to this with a type of grass skirt. Clothing usually consisted of a loincloth for men and a short skirt or pubic apron for women.

They often put bones or pieces of carved wood through the nose septum, painted themselves in vivid colors, and draped themselves with garlands of native flowers. Nose rings, feathers, earrings, necklaces, and pendants of bone, coral, or shell were common. Hair was left long and flowing; in Fiji the hair was done up in a huge knot and often dyed black, white, or red.

Feathered capes of red and yellow were used by the Hawaiian kings as a sign of their rank. Everywhere in the Oceanic cultures red was considered a divinity color.

SOME OF THE MYTHS

The Polynesians believed in a pre-existent creator whom they called Tangaloa. This god lived alone in the Void and made all things. His messenger, the bird Tuli, flew over the vast oceans searching for a place to land, but found none. Tangaloa finally threw down a rock that turned into the island of Manu'a, the main island of the Samoan group. Then he went on casting rocks until he had formed all the islands. However, Tuli complained there was no shade on these islands. Tangaloa gave him the Peopling Vine to plant. This vine died, leaving behind a swarming mass of maggots, which Tangaloa formed into humans.

The Arawa tribe of New Zealand has a legend that says there was one pair of ancestors, Rangi and Papa. They clung so close together that their children Tane, Tangaroa, Tu, Rongo, Haumia, and Tawhiri were trapped between them in eternal darkness.[6] Finally Tane talked the others into separating their parents, but they failed. At last Tane put his head against his mother (the Earth) and his feet against his father (the Sky) and forced them apart. Tangaroa was furious at this, and the brothers have quarreled ever since.

In a Polynesian legend, the trickster-hero Maui went fishing often with his brothers, but he was not very good at it. Maui also had a bad habit of jerking the fish off his brothers' lines and claiming them as his. Finally, they refused to let him go along. His mother saw him as a failure and sent him to his father for a special hook, called Manai-ka-lani, that would catch all the fish they needed. His brothers still took a dim view of his going with them and threw him out of the canoe.

But the brothers continued to have such poor luck that they decided to let Maui go fishing with them again. They went far out to sea but caught nothing but sharks. Maui let down his hook, chanted special magick spells, and promised to catch a huge fish. The hook caught, the ocean moved, and all the brothers began to pull on the line. This went on for two days with the canoe being towed about on the sea.

Finally the tugging stopped; land began to rise from the water. Maui told his brothers that they must not look at this if they wanted to keep the fish. However, one brother, probably skeptical because of past pranks, looked. The line snapped, and the islands of New Zealand popped to the surface.

Maui

Maui continued his pastime of creating trouble until one day he took on more than he could handle, even with his magick. In a show of bravado, he tried to destroy the goddess of death. His attempt failed, and he was himself destroyed.

The Micronesians say that in the beginning the root crops of taro and yam were eaten, but only sun-baked as man had no fire. The people suffered stomach cramps and prayed for help. Immediately, lightning struck a tree; the thunder god Dessra found himself caught in the branches. The god's cries for help brought a woman named Guaretin who released him. In gratitude Dessra had her bring moist clay that he shaped into a cooking pot for her. Then he placed some sticks from the arr tree under his arm and made the beginnings of fire. The woman was delighted and showed the rest of the tribe how to cook food.

The Australian Aborigines have several myths stating why man dies. The Wotjo from Victoria say that once all animals were men and women. When some died, the Moon would say, "You up again," and they came to life. Finally the old man Moon tired of this and stated, "Let them stay dead." Since then, none except the Moon have ever come back to life.

The Lungga and Gidja of East Kimberley, Australia, say that Moon tried to seduce Snake, who was taboo to him. Snake and the other women were furious and cut off Moon's sexual organs, which turned to stone. Naturally, Moon was angry about this and cursed man with death.

In the legend of the Gunwinggu from west Arnhem Land, Australia, the red-eyed Pigeon man Yakul fell ill and was dying. Moon tried to help him, but Djabo, the Spotted Cat man, convinced Yakul that Moon did not know what he was talking about. Even when Djabo fell very ill, he refused to take Moon's advice and drink his urine. If Yakul and Djabo had listened to Moon, man would never have experienced death.

MAJOR GODS AND GODDESSES

AGUNUA—Solomons. Primary serpent god; creator god. God of fruits and vegetables.

ALULUEI—Micronesia. Two-faced god of knowledge, navigation. Sailors built miniature huts on outriggers and filled them with amulets and offerings to this god.

AMBAT—Melanesia. Hero-god who introduced commemorative figures for the dead. God of pottery and ritual.

ANULAP—Micronesia. Sky god; god of magick and knowledge.

APONIBOLINAYEN—Philippines. Sky woman who supported the heavens by a vine wrapped around her waist. Probably a Moon goddess as she bore children to the Sun.

ATANEA—Micronesia. Dawn goddess, daughter of ATEA. She created the seas from amniotic fluid when she miscarried.

ATEA/ATEA RANGI/RANGI—Polynesia. God who began all life. God of the sky, stars, regenerative life-force.

BAIAME—Australia. God of the sky, tools, weapons, rituals, initiation ceremonies.

BARA—Australia. Sun daughter of Arnhem Land.

BILA—Australia. Sun goddess cannibal.

BILIKU—Micronesia. Goddess who created the Earth; both kind and terrible, sometimes in spider form.

DARAGO—Philippines. Volcano goddess who demanded human sacrifices each year.

DARAMULUN—Australia. Sky god who carried a stone axe; his mouth was full of quartz and he had an exaggerated phallus. Bull-roarers were said to imitate his voice. Fertility, creation.

DJANGGAWUL SISTERS—Australia. Founder deities. They made ritual apparatus, water, trees, yams, babies, animals, sacred ceremonies.

EINGANA—Australia. Creator goddess in the form of a snake; said to still live in the ocean. Also the Death Mother. The life-tie of all creatures was said to be attached to her.

GAINGIN—Melanesia. Primordial beings, larger than life, who shaped the Earth. They were sky gods, but two of them took earthly forms and remained: BUGAL, the snake; and WARGER, the crocodile.

GIDJA—Australia. Moon god and totemic ancestor of the Dreamtime. God of dreams and sex.

GOGA—Melanesia. Old woman goddess from whom humans stole fire; said that she taught humans, who emerged from maggots, the rituals and skills of life.

GREAT RAINBOW SNAKE—Australia. Totemic deity of the Dreamtime; bisexual; Life-giver; Great God. God of rain, procreation, magick, life, blood.

HA'IAKA—Polynesia. Sister of the goddess PELE, she was born in the shape of an egg. Magick, flowers, healing.

HAUMEA—Hawaii. "Tree of changing leaves"; shape-shifter. Goddess of childbirth, productivity, wild plants. Capable of negative action.

HIKULEO—Hawaii. Goddess of the underworld (Pulotu).

HINA/HINE—Polynesia. Two faces; wife of TANE; Great Goddess. Goddess of darkness and death. Patroness of travelers.

HIT—Micronesia. Octopus goddess; grandmother of the hero Olifat.

IMBEROMBERA/WARAMURUGUNDJU—Australia. Consort of WURAKA; Great Goddess; Mother Goddess. Goddess of creation, the sea, children, animals, plants, languages.

JULUNGGUL—Australia. Rainbow snake goddess. See GREAT RAINBOW SNAKE.

JUNKGOWA SISTERS— Australia. Ancestor goddesses who formed the waterholes and the food producing areas of Earth. They were said to have invented the fire, dilly bags, amulets, yam sticks, and feather belts. They also invented all ceremonial rites, which were stolen from them by their sons.

KAMAPUA'A—Polynesia. Shape-shifter. God of rain, fog, mist, pigs.

KAPO—Hawaii. Goddess of childbirth and abortions.

KAPUA—Hawaii. Divine tricksters or mischief-makers. Shape-shifters of great strength and incredible mobility. Gods of cunning, thieves, multiple magick powers.

KOEVASI—Melanesia. Snake Goddess; Creator Goddess. Goddess of languages, dialects, the necessities of life.

KUKALIKIMOKU—Polynesia. War god who wore the crested feather helmet of Hawaii. Red and yellow were his colors.

KUNAPIPI/GUNABIBI—Australia. Great Goddess; Mother Goddess; creator of every living creature. Overseer of initiations and puberty rituals.

LA'I-LA'I—Hawaii. First goddess born after order was formed in the universe. By mating with the sky she produced humankind.

LAKA/RATA—Hawaii. Patron of hula dancers.

LONA AND LAKA—Polynesia. First fruits were offered to the god Lono. Laka, his sister, was goddess of the wildwood. Lono's festival in Hawaii was five days of merrymaking, sports and wrestling, processions with idols and feasts. God of agriculture and singing.

MAHUI-IKE—Polynesia. Goddess of fire, volcanoes, the underworld.

MARRUNI—Melanesia. Creator God; god of earthquakes.

MAUI—Polynesia. Great hero-god; "Maui of the thousand tricks"; helper of man; greatest of tricksters; shape-shifter. Magick, fishing, plants, stars, wind, rain, death, sorcery.

MIRU—Polynesia. Queen of the last three circles of the underworld.

NDENGEI—Fiji. Serpent god with stone flesh; created man. Yams, bananas, fire, boats, rain, floods, earthquakes.

NEVINBIMBAAU—Melanesia. Initiation goddess.

NYAPILNU—Australia. Ancestor goddess who invented household crafts, such as making shelters out of bark.

ORO—Maori. Son of TA'AROA; "Oro of the laid down spear." God of war and peace.

PAPA—Polynesia. Mother Earth.

PAREWHENUA-MEA—New Zealand. Rain goddess.

PELE—Hawaii. Personification of the female power of destruction, she came from Tahiti to settle in Mt. Kilauea. Her altars were erected beside lava streams, though only those who claimed direct family descent worshipped her. Goddess of volcanic fire, sorcery, the hula.

RATA—Polynesia. Grandson of TAWHAKI. Destroyer of demons, magick.

RUA—Tahiti. "The abyss"; god of wood carving, craftsmen, spells, magick, power.

TA'AROA—Maori. Creator God; personified primal darkness. Destructive power, moisture, oceans.

TANE—Maori. God of forests, craftsmen, knowledge, wood carving.

TANGAROA—Polynesia. Great God; Creator God. Fish, reptiles, carpenters, house builders.

TAWHAKI—Polynesia. God of thunder and lightning. Cunning, magick, spells.

TAWIRI/TAWHIRI—Polynesia. God of storms, winds, whirlwinds, hurricanes.

WALO—Australia. Sun goddess.

WAWALUG SISTERS—Australia. Pair of fertility goddesses. They were swallowed and regurgitated several times by the GREAT RAINBOW SNAKE, each time marking sacred spots for future ceremonies. Rituals.

YALUNGUR—Australia. "Eaglehawk"; also called WARANA. Created female sexuality.

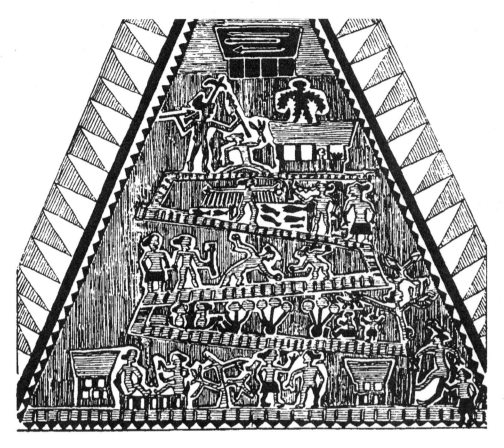

Spirits of slain warriors travel to the heavens, from a Palau Islands painting

ENDNOTES

1. Beckwith, Martha. *Hawaiian Mythology.* This name is derived from the word *kupu*, which means a type of plant that grows from a parent stock. The word *kupuna* means an ancestor.
2. *Awa* is the shrub of the pepper family, *Piper methysticum.* Only the rarer variety could be used by the chiefs as a drink. The most highly prized was the kind that grew on trees with their roots exposed.
3. Our word "taboo" comes from this word.
4. The slaves were considered outcasts and could associate with the freeborn only on a very limited basis. They had to live apart and were forbidden marriage with anyone who was not a slave.
5. Certain red flowers were sacred to the gods, such as the red iiwi blossom. A person would only dare pick and wear the iiwi if he was beloved by the gods; otherwise he ran the risk of being haunted by a headless woman.
6. This is very reminiscent of an Egyptian legend where the gods had to push the goddess Nut up into the sky.

BIBLIOGRAPHY

Beckwith, Martha. *Hawaiian Mythology*. Honolulu, HI: University Press of Hawaii, 1971.

Berndt, C. H. and R. M. *The World of the First Australians*. Australia: Angus & Robertson, 1965.

Berndt, R. M. *Djanggawul*. UK: Routledge & Kegan Paul, 1952.

Coates, Austin. *Islands of the South*. NY: Pica Press, 1974.

Codrington, R. *The Melanesians: Studies in Their History, Anthropology and Folklore*. UK: Clarendon Press, 1891.

Dixon, R. B. "Mythology of Oceania" in *The Mythology of All Races*. NY: Cooper Square Publishing, 1922.

Elbert, Samuel H., ed. *Selections from Fornander's Antiquities and Folk-lore*. Honolulu, HI: University of Hawaii Press, 1959.

Grey, Sir George. *Polynesian Mythology*. UK: Whitcombe & Tombs, 1965.

Howitt, A. H. *The Native Tribes of South-eastern Australia*. UK: Macmillan & Co., 1904.

Izett, James. *Maori Lore, the Traditions of the Maori People with the More Important of Their Legends*. Wellington, NZ: self-published, 1923.

La Fontaine, J. S. *Initiation: Ritual Drama and Secret Knowledge Across the World*. UK: Penguin Books, 1985.

Lee, W. Storrs. *The Islands*. NY: Holt, Rinehart & Winston, 1966.

Long, Max Freedom. *The Secret Science Behind Miracles*. Los Angeles, CA: Kosmon Press, 1948.

McConnel, Ursula. *Myths of the Munkan*. Cambridge University Press, 1957.

Poignant, Roslyn. *Oceanic Mythology: The Myths of Polynesia, Micronesia, Melanesia, Australia*. UK: Paul Hamlyn, 1975.

Reader's Digest. *The World's Last Mysteries*. NY: Reader's Digest Association, 1978.

Strehlow, T. G. H. *Aranda Traditions*. Australia: Melbourne University Press, 1947.

Suggs, R. C. *Island Civilisations of Polynesia*. UK: Mentor Books, 1960.

Westervelt, William D. *Hawaiian Historical Legends*. NY: self-published, 1923.

Wheeler, G. C. *Mono Alu Folklore*. UK: Routledge & Kegan Paul, 1926.

CHAPTER TWENTY-THREE

NATIVE NORTH AMERICANS

ANTHROPOLOGISTS ARE uncertain as to just when the Native American culture came to North America. They estimate there was a long series of migrations across the Bering Strait, which at that time was connected to the North American continent. This probably occurred about 2000 to 10,000 years BC. These groups of people gradually worked their way south as far as Tierra del Fuego. It is possible that many languages already existed before the emigration began. Eventually eight great linguistic languages developed in North America; from these came more than 200 ethnic dialects.[1]

In areas where food was abundant and crafts were practiced, there arose priesthoods, scholars, and artists. These were generally members of great centers of Native American civilization, ruled by an emperor, chief, or other single controller, and protected by large bodies of able warriors. Legends, religious beliefs, and practices differed from tribe to tribe.

The Eskimo,[2] or the Iniut or Inniut ("the people"), as they call themselves, range from Greenland to the Bering Strait in Arctic America. There is much speculation about their origins, but archaeological evidence seems to point to Asiatic ancestry. Changes from a rather elaborate culture based on hunting sea mammals to the somewhat simpler culture of today can be traced. The earliest known levels of Eskimo culture, which are far from primitive, appear to have their closest counterparts in Arctic Asia. Modifications of the early culture swept across the Arctic Zone, eventually reaching Greenland. The earliest settlers had long, high heads with very broad faces and large, straight noses. Their skin color was like southern Europeans, but the hair was coarse and black. Eskimos did not form tribes but lived in small, closely related groups without much formal organization.

The Native Americans of the USA and Canada generally appear to have Mongoloid ancestors. They usually have straight black or brown hair, broad faces, reddish to brown complexions, and little facial or body hair. They were essentially one people, although there were wide variations in living habits, physical types, and languages.

The principal stocks or tribes of North America are:

1. The Athabascans, including the Apaches and Navaho.
2. The Algonquins, including the Abnaki, Delaware, Cree, Chippewa, Cheyenne, Arapaho, and Blackfeet.
3. The Iroquois, including the Cherokee, Mohawk, and Seneca.
4. The Lakota, including the Dakota, Omaha, Osage, Winnebago, Crow, and Calawba.
5. The Muskhogeans, including the Alibamus, Apalachis, Choctaw, Creek, Chickasaw, and Seminole.
6. The Caddoans, including the Pawnee, Arickaree, Wichita, and Caddos.
7. The tribes of the north Pacific Coast, including the Tlingit of Alaska.
8. The Yuman of Colorado River and California, including the Mariocopa.
9. The Shoshone, including the Utes, Comanche, and Hopi.
10. The Pueblo Indians of New Mexico and Arizona, including the Zuni.

RELIGION

To understand the Native Americans, one must understand their belief in their place with Nature and their deities. The Native American was a deeply spiritual person. To him, the world of spirit, the unseen and supernatural, was all about him at every waking and sleeping moment. Everything he saw, touched, or used was wrapped with a divine sense known as *mana*. To the Lakota it was the *wakan* or *wakonda;* to the Algonquians the *manitou;* to the Iroquois the *orenda*. Mana could attach itself to chiefs, medicine men, master craftsmen, outstanding warriors.

All Native Americans had an entire range of deities, from important gods to monsters and demons. Nature spirits were seen in everything; not even the smallest animate or inanimate being was without its guiding in-dwelling spirit. Gods were invoked by magickal rites for specific purposes. The Native American believed that his deities needed him as much as he needed them, thereby making them more able to aid the individual.

Almost every wild creature was held sacred in one place or another. This was because Native American gods and goddesses sometimes took the shape of animals, birds, and reptiles when they gave messages. However, there were also deities whose appearance was human only, such as Turquoise Woman among the Navajo. Many types of natural features were also considered the home of a guardian spirit.

The Native Americans' relationship with Nature, the gods, dreams and visions, and with signs and symbols provided them with endless inspiration. Native American art was steeped in religion; it was neither realistic nor abstract, but symbolic, rather like the art of ancient Egypt.

It was quite common for individual Native Americans to go alone into the wilderness to commune with their personal guardian spirits. This was an intensely personal part of their religious ideas, as it was believed that everyone had his personal and clan deities in addition to the tribal deities. Clan and tribal deities were inherited, but personal ones had to be sought. Initially, this personal searching was a vision quest to find out what power animal, spirit helpers, and guardians belonged to each individual. However, it was not uncommon for this quest to be repeated whenever an individual felt the need for guidance and answers. In many tribes, a youngster who had not had some visionary experience could not become a warrior or even a man.

The tribal worship was communal and formal, almost always led by a shaman (pronounced SHAH-maan). The shaman, or medicine man, was the primary religious leader in most Native American cultures.[3] The shaman's ceremonial costume was very symbolic. It consisted of eagle or other feathers; a rattle; frame or shaman drum; and small bags with rock crystal, stones, and other magickal objects. The bag with the accessories never left the shaman; at night he put it under his pillow or bed. Bones, feathers, wings, claws, and fangs were all important religious items. Some shamanic cultures used masks; others did not.

This religious person was trained to petition, or even coerce, the supernatural powers by certain rituals. Singing, dancing, and drumming were essential parts of the rites. A medicine lodge or tepee was frequently a main feature of a Native American village. Here, in private, the shaman called upon the spirits for individuals. In some tribes, these men were a distinct class.

All tribes distinguished between good and bad magick. Practitioners of black magick usually kept their activities quiet; they cast more effective spells if they had a lock of hair, drop of blood, dried spittle, nail clippings, etc.[4] So Native Americans took extreme caution to bury, burn, hide, or protect these by

*Zuni fetish and shield
of the Priesthood of the Bow*

Innuit seal mask

taboos. Sometimes a gifted sorcerer would use a man's shadow, his sleeping soul, or his aura. The only defense was to identify and kill the sorcerer as soon as possible.

There was a regular cycle of ceremonies relating to the personal lives of the tribe members: birth, puberty, marriage, and death. There were also rituals to do with agriculture, since Nature spirits included the plants. The Native Americans believed that people were privileged to assist the gods in keeping the wheel of existence turning.

Native Americans believed that man was inferior in many ways to the wildlife, to Nature.[5] The impersonation of animals was important to him. If he was taking part in a dance in which he wore the fur or feathers of his clan's spirit patron, he would draw down its essence into himself and enhance his own inner power. When he killed for food, he felt guilty of a crime against Nature. So he performed rituals for success in tracking and hunting, but also rituals in apology afterward. Because of these beliefs, he tended to kill as sparingly as he could, in order to disturb the balance of Nature as little as possible. The slain animal was thanked for its sacrifice of life, and all parts were used, right down to the bones and sinew.

Dreams and visions were considered very important. Native Americans particularly gifted in interpretation of dreams were held in high regard. Many tribes had Dream Societies, in which dreams and visions were induced, shared, and analyzed. They believed that dreams were messages from otherworld powers and from within, sent by the gods and the spirit helpers. Native Americans used the sweat bath, certain charms, and dream songs to stimulate the ability to dream and have visions. Shamans spent long hours in the sweat bath to sharpen their ability to dream.

Tobacco was central to almost all Native American ceremonies, except for the Eskimo ones. From the earliest times tobacco had religious connotations. Tobacco was seldom smoked in a pure state, but mixed with various herbs and sweet grasses. In the East and on the Plains it was combined with laurel leaves, squaw bush, maple bush, or the aromatic inner bark of the dogwood, cherry, red willow, poplar, birch, or arrowwood.

Pipes were considered sacred, as were the pouches used to hold them and the tobacco. The pipes were made of clay or cut from such stones as soapstone, catlinite, or pipestone. As a sign of their religious aura, they were often beaded, ribboned, sculptured, or decorated with feathers and claws. The leather pouches for the pipe and the tobacco were also elaborately decorated.

Smoking a pipe was an extremely solemn occasion. It sealed all contracts and agreements. Its clouds of smoky incense were sent toward the four directions, the sky, and Earth; also to certain sacred objects.

The Native Americans were fearless of death and dying. They rehearsed all their life their own personal death-song. Most Native Americans believed in an afterlife, but until the Christians came did not believe in hell. They buried their dead with grave goods. There was a taboo on mentioning a dead person's name as that could draw the spirit back among the living and cause problems.

The Medicine Wheel, sometimes called the sacred hoop or circle, was used for many important religious ceremonies. A circle was held to be sacred. Native Americans danced in a circle, and played mostly round drums. They purified themselves in the circle of the sweat lodge. They met in a circle in counsel so all voices were equal.

The Medicine Wheel, with its four divisions, is much like the present day magickal circle used by magicians and Wiccans. The sacred hoop represented the cycle of life that encompassed the whole world. The four divisions corresponded to the four directions, four winds, four seasons, four times of the day, and four ages of humankind.[6] The keepers and guardians of these divisions had different names in different tribes.

The year began at the winter solstice when the Native Americans said that Father Sun began his return from his journey to the south. Therefore, the first division was in the north of the Medicine Wheel, beginning at the winter solstice. The second division, in the east, began at the spring equinox; the southern division at summer solstice; the western division at the autumn equinox.

DRESS AND ORNAMENTATION

The dress of Native Americans varied according to the region, climate, and tribe. The following descriptions are simplistic, as it is impossible to list the myriad of differences.

Basically, women wore a one-piece skin dress, a blouse and skirt, or a long blouse and leggings. Men wore breeches and went bare-chested, wrapping themselves in capes or mantles when it was cold and rainy. Only men of high caste wore shirts, mainly on ceremonial occasions. Furs were of the highest quality. Skins of buffalo, elk, moose, deer, antelope, and other animals were made into war-shields, bindings, parfleches (a type of box), clothes, bags, pouches, shirts, leggings, footwear, arrow-cases, etc. Leather items were seldom left plain; they were fringed, embroidered, painted, or embellished with beads, shells, quills, or feathers. Other articles of dress were made by weaving: finger-weaving, twining, plaiting and braiding, or on looms.

The Native Americans often had more than one pair of moccasins: high tops, low tops, hard soles, soft soles; some for lounging, others for farming, working, tracking, and hunting. Some were for everyday, others for ceremonies.

Men as well as women wore earrings, the size depending on the importance of the wearer. Necklaces, pendants, rings, bracelets, anklets, and armbands were also worn. Some tribes, such as the Pima and Eskimo, practiced tattooing. Feathers worn in certain ways by men were badges of honor indicating rank and prestige. Paint markings on the faces of men indicated membership in religious societies, brave deeds, or personal decorations for war or raiding.

Musical instruments made and used were the frame (shaman) drum, double-headed drum, nose flute, flageolet, scrapers, rattles, whistles, clappers.

Stone pipe

Some of the Myths

Sedna (Eskimo)

In Eskimo legends there is a story of a beautiful girl, Sedna, who lived beside the sea. She rejected all her suitors until one day a handsome young man came in his kayak. He did not come ashore, but called to her from his kayak, promising her ivory necklaces if she would go with him. Sedna entered the boat and was carried away. She soon realized that her lover was not human; he was a Bird-spirit with the power to assume human form. Although he loved Sedna, the girl was very unhappy and unable to leave his island.

Her widowed father searched for her and finally found the island. The Bird-spirit husband was gone. The father put his unhappy daughter into his boat and started home. Meanwhile the Bird-spirit returned to the island and, finding his wife gone, went after the fleeing boat. The girl hid under some furs, but her husband begged her father to return his wife. The father refused, continuing on his way.

Wild with despair, the Kokksaut (supernatural creature) changed back into a bird and aroused a terrible storm as he flew away. The terrified father, unable to row against the storm, threw his daughter into the sea as a sacrifice. When Sedna tried to climb back into the kayak, her father seized an ivory axe and chopped at her hands. Her severed fingers became seals and walruses; her body became whales.

At last the sea was calm again, and the father headed for home as fast as he could. Exhausted, he fell into a deep sleep in his tent. That night an exceptionally high tide rose and claimed both the father and Sedna's dog. Thus father, daughter, and dog reign over Adliden, a place in the depths of the ocean where souls go at death to pay for sins, rather like purgatory.

First Light (Navaho)

The Navaho say that in the beginning of the world there was only darkness and silence. Far to the north, a little white cloud awoke and slowly began to travel eastward, looking for the light. It was not long before the white cloud discovered a fierce black cloud, the keeper of the darkness.

The two clouds began to fight. As the great battle went on in the darkened sky, the two clouds began to perspire from their efforts. The drops of sweat fell and became rain upon the Earth. Finally the water made a hole in the Earth, and out came the imprisoned animals. The animals peacefully divided the land and the hunting grounds and began to build their homes. However, there was still no light.

The little white cloud was in tatters after the fight but it called upon its friends, a blue cloud from the south and a yellow cloud from the west. They knew they could not create much light but they managed to show forth enough that the animals could see one another. Then the animals realized that it was their responsibility to find a greater light.

FINDING THE SUN AND MOON (ZUNI)

Before the appearance of man, the animals could talk. They were the original inhabitants of the Earth, the ancestors of humankind, and could put on or take off their skins. They were intelligent and helped with many of the creations and happenings of Mother Earth.

*Animal motif
from Zuni pottery*

There was no Sun or Moon at first in the world. Only the owl had the light from its eyes to see its way. Although Coyote was hunting every day, all he could find to eat were a few grasshoppers. Feeling terribly hungry, Coyote was sitting near his den when Eagle flew up for a visit. Coyote apologized for not having anything to share with his friend. Eagle took pity on the poor creature and they decided to hunt together.

During the hunting, Eagle did all the killing with Coyote eating the leftovers. After a while, Eagle complained. However, Coyote defended himself, saying that they needed light; Eagle agreed. Eagle had heard of big lights, the Sun and the Moon, hidden far away in the west.

The two friends journeyed long into the west in search of the lights. After a time, it began to grow lighter around them. Peering over a low hill they saw many strange beings, *kachinas*, dancing and singing. These beings were so hideously painted that Coyote's hair stood up in fright. As the two friends watched, they noticed two chests that the dancers opened from time to time. Out of these opened chests came streams of beautiful light.

As soon as the kachinas grew tired and slept, Eagle swooped down and stole the chests. Away the friends went on their journey home. But Coyote was very curious about what was in the chests, so he talked Eagle into letting him carry them for awhile.

Finally, curiosity getting the better of him, Coyote opened one chest. Out popped the Sun and immediately rose to its place high in the heavens. Coyote was very upset, besides having burned his paws. He opened the second chest to send the Moon to bring back the Sun. However, the Moon escaped and hid in the Sun's shadow.

Eagle scolded Coyote, but his friend said that at least the kachinas could not get the celestial bodies back, either. Eagle agreed but cautioned Coyote to say nothing about his part in the release of the Sun and Moon. Thus, the first day and night came to Mother Earth.

THE FLOOD (ALGONQUIN)

The Algonquins have a flood story concerning Michabo, or the Great Hare. Michabo was out hunting with his wolves when the animals fell into a lake and disappeared. Michabo found out from a bird where they were and tried to rescue them. However, the lake overflowed, covering the whole Earth. The Great Hare sent a raven for clay so he could remake the Earth, but the raven found none. Then he sent a diving otter, but the otter brought back nothing. Finally a muskrat managed to return with some soil that Michabo used to rebuild the Earth. After taking revenge on the Underwater Panthers who had kept his wolves in the lake, the Great Hare married a musk-mouse. Their children repeopled the Earth.

MEDICINE (CHEROKEE)

At one time animals and people lived in peace and harmony with each other. Then some greedy Native Americans hunted only to sell the meat and furs. The animal population was dwindling.

The white bear called a council of animals so they could decide how to avenge themselves. Although many of the animals had ideas, they could not agree on what to do until the oldest and wisest of the flies offered his suggestion.

"We will call upon the spirits," he said. "We will ask them to send great sicknesses upon the Indians, and we will carry the diseases."

Soon great illness spread through all the Native American villages, attacking both good and bad. The animals had only wanted the wicked people punished and were sad to see what was happening. They called another council and discussed what was to be done to remedy the situation.

The lowly herbs promised to heal the sick. Spirit dreams were sent to the Native American shamans to guide them to the herbs. In this way was healing medicine brought to the Indians.

WHITE BUFFALO WOMAN (DAKOTA)

In the Dakota myth of White Buffalo Woman, two men were hunting when they saw a beautiful women coming towards them. She was dressed in white buckskin and carried a bundle on her back. One of the men decided to rape her, but when he approached, he was surrounded by a mist that left him a skeleton eaten by terrible snakes.

The woman told the other man to return to his camp and prepare a huge lodge for her. The hunter returned to his tribe to arrange everything. White Buffalo Woman entered the village, and told the people that she came from Heaven to teach them how to live and what their future would be. She gave the people maize, taught them the use of the pipe and the seven sacred ceremonies, and gave them colors for the four winds or directions. As she walked away, she turned into a bison calf.

MAJOR GODS AND GODDESSES

AGLOOLIK—Eskimo god. Helper of hunters and fishermen.

AIPALOOVIK—Eskimo god. Evil being associated with murder, vandalism, and destruction.

ASAGAYA GIGAEI—Thunder god of the Cherokees.

ATAENTSIC—Iroquois/Huron goddess; Great Mother. Marriage, childbirth, feminine crafts.

ATIUS TIRAWA—Pawnee creator god; god of the Sun, Moon, and stars.

AULANERK—Eskimo god; sea god; rules the tides and waves; brings joy.

COYOTE—Many tribes; similar to the Nordic god LOKI. A trickster; demon clown figure who represented the breaking free of negative power from the universal order of things; he was always sneaking around causing trouble.

ESTSANATLEHI—Navajo. "The woman who changes"; a shape-shifter. Transformation, immortality.

GLUSKAP—Abnaki/Algonquin. A cultural founder hero; similar to King Arthur. Strength, wisdom, rescue.

HAHBWEHDIYU—Iroquois. Good creator deity and twin brother of HAHGWEHDAETGAH, an evil spirit. Creating, strength, victory.

ICTINIKE—Lakota. War god. War, treachery, deceit.

IGALUK—Eskimo. Moon god; Supreme God. Natural phenomena, animals, sea animals.

IOSKEHA—Iroquois/Huron. Creator God. Defeats demons, heals diseases, gives magick and ritual. Gave the ritual herb tobacco.

IYATIKU—Pueblo. Corn goddess; ruler of her underground realm where the dead go. Compassion, agriculture, children.

KITCKI MANITOU/KICI MANITU/MANITOU—Many tribes. "Great Spirit"; "the father." Supreme God; Father of Life; Master of Light; God of the Winds; the spirit in everything; Great God; Supreme Creator; Sun God. The Lakota called him WAKONDA, the Oglala called him WAKAN or TANKA. The Iroquois word was ORENDA, the Eskimo word INNUA.

KWATEE/KIVATI—Puget Sound. "The man who changed things"; creator of people; destroyer of monsters.

MICHABO—Algonquin. "Great Hare"; creator of man; creator of Earth and animals. Shape-shifter god, magician. Invented fishing nets.

NOKOMIS—Algonquin. "Grandmother"; Earth Goddess. She fed all living things, plants, animals, people.

ONATHA—Iroquois. Goddess of wheat and harvest. Similar to the Greek goddess PERSEPHONE.

PINGA—Eskimo. "The one on high." Goddess of game, the hunt, helper of medicine men and the living.

RAVEN—Many tribes. A trickster god, similar to COYOTE.

SEDNA—Eskimo. Goddess of the sea and its creatures, hunting, sorcerers. She was greatly feared, but sought by shamans for the release of seals for hunting.

Michabo

345

Pueblo thunderbird

SHAKURU—Pawnee. Sun God; worshipped in the ritual of the famous Sun Dance.

SPIDER WOMAN—Navajo. Goddess of charms and magick.

TEKKEITSERTOK—Eskimo. Most powerful Earth God. God of the deer and hunting. His favor was sought at hunting season with great sacrifices.

THUNDER BIRD/THUNDER BIRDS—God of many tribes; thunder god; messenger between man and the gods. His eyes flashed lightning and his wings made thunder. Symbols were hawks and eagles. Thunder, lightning, rain, growing things.

TIRAWA—Pawnee. Creator and sky god. He taught the skills of speech, clothing, fire-making, hunting, agriculture, body-painting, tobacco-smoking, religious rituals and sacrifices.

TONENILI—Navajo. "Water sprinkler"; rain god and full of mischief. In tribal dances he was represented by a masked man who played the part of a clown.

UNDERWATER PANTHERS—Many tribes. Evil gods of water but a source of great wisdom and healing power, particularly with herbs.

WAKONDA—Lakota. "The power above." Source of all wisdom and power, enlightened medicine men.

WISHPOOSH—Nez Perce. The beaver monster who drowned fishermen. Out of his body, COYOTE made the Native Americans of the northwest coast.

YANAULUHA—Zuni. The great medicine man. Civilization, agriculture, animal husbandry, social life, healing, knowledge.

YOLKAI ESTASAN—Navajo. "White shell woman"; Earth Goddess. Seasons, the land.

ENDNOTES

1. Marriott, Alice. *American Indian Mythology.*
2. The word Eskimo is used only for the sake of simplicity. The Inniut do not use this name in referring to themselves. In fact, the word Eskimo means "eaters of fat," not a name a proud people would call themselves.
3. See chapter 6 on Shamanism.
4. This method of spellworking is also known in many other cultures around the world. It is not always black magick to use these personal items in spellworking, as it is a form of sympathetic magick and can be used for good.

5. There are differences of opinion on this point, but from my research, the reading of many authentic works, and talks with knowledgeable Native Americans, this appears to me to be the case. Native Americans speak of the animals as brothers to humankind. They speak of them as being more intelligent, more cunning, of having been created before humans. When looked at without preconceived ideas, one can readily see that animals meticulously follow the laws of Nature; they do not declare war, nor are they destructive in the way that humankind is destructive.

6. For more information on this, read *In the Shadow of the Shaman*, by Amber Wolfe (I consider this the best text); *Teachings Around the Sacred Wheel*, by Lynn Andrews; and *The Medicine Wheel*, by Sun Bear. Also for more information on the colors attached to the four cardinal points, see the chapter on Elements.

Bibliography

Andrews, Lynn V. *Flight of the Seventh Moon: The Teachings of the Shields*. San Francisco, CA: Harper & Row, 1984.

Andrews, Lynn V. *Medicine Woman*. San Francisco, CA: Harper & Row, 1981.

Andrews, Lynn V. *Star Woman*. NY: Warner Books, 1986.

Andrews, Lynn V. *Teachings Around the Sacred Wheel*. San Francisco, CA: Harper & Row, 1990.

Brown, Joseph Epes. *The Sacred Pipe: Seven Rites of the Oglala Sioux*. NY: Penguin, 1985.

Budapest, Z. *The Holy Book of Women's Mysteries*, Part I and II. Oakland, CA: Susan B. Anthony Coven No. 1, 1979.

Drury, Nevill. *The Elements of Shamanism*. UK: Element Books, 1989.

Eastman, Charles A. *Indian Scout Craft and Lore*. NY: Dover Publications, 1974.

Eaton, Evelyn. *I Send a Voice*. Wheaton, IL: Theosophical Publishing, 1982.

Eaton, Evelyn. *Snowy Earth Comes Gliding*. Independence, CA: Draco Foundation, 1984.

Fitch, Ed. *Magical Rites From the Crystal Well*. St. Paul, MN: Llewellyn Publications, 1984.

Franklin, Paula A. *Indians of North America*. NY: David McKay Co., 1979.

Gorsline, Marie and Douglas. *North American Indians*. NY: Random House, 1977.

Harner, Michael. *The Way of the Shaman*. NY: Bantam Books, 1982.

Hill, Ruth Beebe. *Hanta Yo*. NY: Warner Books, 1980.

Hulpach, Vladimir. *American Indian Tales and Legends*. UK: Paul Hamlyn, 1966.

Hunt, W. Ben. *The Complete How-To Book of Indiancraft*. NY: Macmillan, 1973.

Hunt, W. Ben. *The Golden Book of Indian Crafts and Lore*. NY: Golden Press, 1954.

Kalweit, Holger. *Dreamtime and Inner Space: The World of the Shaman*. Boston, MA: Shambhala, 1988.

La Fontaine, J. S. *Initiation: Ritual Drama and Secret Knowledge Across the World*. UK: Penguin Books, 1985.

Marriott, Alice, and Rachlin, Carol K. *American Indian Mythology*. NY: New American Library, 1972.

Mason, Bernard S. *How to Make Drums, Tomtoms and Rattles*. NY: Dover Publications, 1974.

Mestel, Sherry, ed. *Earth Rites*, 2 vol. NY: Earth Rites Press, 1981.

Neihardt, John G. *Black Elk Speaks*. NY: Pocket Books, 1972.

Parker, Arthur C. *The Indian How Book*. NY: Dover Publications, 1975.

Sams, Jamie. *Sacred Path Cards*. San Francisco, CA: Harper & Row, 1990.

Sams, Jamie, and Carson, David. *Medicine Cards: The Discovery of Power Through the Ways of Animals*. Santa Fe, NM: Bear & Co., 1988.

Skinner, Hubert M. *Readings in Folk-Lore*. NY: American Book Co., 1893.

Stanley-Millner, Pamela. *Authentic American Indian Beadwork and How to Do It*. NY: Dover Publications, 1984.

Steiger, Brad. *American Indian Magic, Sacred Pow Wows and Hopi Prophecies*. New Brunswick, NJ: Inner Light Publications, 1986.

Steiger, Brad. *Indian Medicine Power*. Gloucester, MA: Para Research, 1984.

Stirling, Matthew W. *National Geographic on Indians of the Americas*. Washington, D.C.: National Geographic, 1955.

Storm, Hyemeyohsts. *Seven Arrows*. NY: Ballantine Books, 1972.

Sun Bear, Crysalis Mulligan, Peter Nufer, and Wabun. *Walk in Balance*. NY: Prentice Hall Press, 1989.

Sun Bear and Wabun. *The Medicine Wheel: Earth Astrology*. Englewood Cliffs, NJ: Prentice-Hall, 1980.

Sun Bear, Wabun, and Barry Weinstock. *The Path of Power*. NY: Prentice Hall Press, 1987.

Waters, Frank. *Book of the Hopi*. NY: Penguin Books, 1985.

Williams, Chuck. *Bridge of the Gods, Mountains of Fire*. NY: Friends of the Earth, 1980.

Wilson, Eva. *North American Indian Designs*. NY: Dover Publications, 1984.

Wolfe, Amber. *In the Shadow of the Shaman*. St. Paul, MN: Llewellyn Publications, 1990.

CHAPTER TWENTY-FOUR

MAYAS

THERE WERE several periods of Mayan history and growth. The first lasted from about 1000 BC to around AD 150. Towards the end of this period the Maya were building temples in Yucatan and the Peten. They changed from an agricultural people to rulers who used sophisticated systems of chronology, numbers, astronomy, and weather prediction.

The second period, which lasted from AD 150–300, and the third period, from 300–925, were the flowering eras of Mayan culture. Architecture, sculpture, painting, ceramics, jade engraving, weaving, and featherworking became quite advanced. However, from 800–925 there were signs of decline and decay. By the tenth century, Mayan civilization sank back to its original cultural level.

From this time until about 1697, there began a resurgence of culture, with new cities being built. However, in 1697 their independence ended with the fall of Tayasal, the city-capital in the Peten. The two most important sites in the Peten were Tikal and Uaxactun, with the ruins of Tikal covering more than 25 square miles. One of its eight pyramids was 229 feet high; its grand plaza measured 400 feet by 250 feet.

These magnificent cities were actually religious centers. The people lived outside these areas, their adobe and thatch houses clustering around the perimeter of the sites. It is very likely that the Maya cleared the land and cultivated it, thus not having the problem of mosquito infestation that rules these areas today. Slaves were widely used, especially for carrying burdens and doing all the hard, menial jobs; the Maya had no beasts of burden. Slaves also made up the bulk of human sacrifices performed in the many temples.

During what is known as the Old Empire, the Mayas stretched their area of power from western Honduras to central Chiapas, Mexico, then across the forested lowlands of northern Honduras and north into the Yucatan Peninsula.

Chichen Itza, built at the end of the seventh century, was the largest and holiest of Mayan cities of the New Empire era. Toward the end of the twelfth century, the Mayan ruler Hunnac Ceel brought in the Toltecs to help him in a civil war. The blending of Maya and Toltec ideas revived the stagnating religion and culture.

The *Popol Vuh* is one of the remaining sacred Mayan books. It was written down by native Mayan authors of Quiche in Guatemala shortly after the Spanish conquest, but there is no reason to suppose that it was much adulterated by Christianity at that point. It contained mythologies and traditions of the Maya that had been handed down through generations. The *Chilam Balam-Noob*, which were also sacred scriptures, contained prophesies of difficult times in the future.

The Spanish entered the picture in 1525, and by 1687 finally conquered the great civilization. As with the Inca, the accompanying Catholic priests proceeded to destroy all native religious beliefs with fanatic fervor.

Religion

The Mayas were a very religious people. They built a great number of pyramid and square temples. These were mounted on terraces and had outside sacrificial stones so the people could watch. The temples were richly carved and brightly painted with pictures of gods, warriors, and high officials. Sacrifices of birds, maize, and humans were offered on a daily basis to most deities.

All Mayan festivals, indeed, almost every aspect of life, was connected with religion. Undoubtedly, the Mayan festivals were based on agriculture and seasons, but little is definitely known about them. The Mayan ball games, as well as dancing, were religious exercises. There were 18 months in the Mayan calendar, and each of these had many ceremonies and feasts. In preparation for these holidays, the people fasted. Then during the festival they indulged in huge feasts, excessive drinking,[1] and sometimes in orgies. Dance, drama, and music were the prerogatives of the priesthood; the commoners could only watch.

The national ball game, called *pok-a-tok* or *tlachtli*,[2] was very popular. It had religious connotations, and the players had to be experts. The game was so popular that the ball court was a feature of most Mayan cities. The court was a long rectangular field surrounded by tiers of spectator seats. In the middle of a side wall was a vertical stone ring, sometimes 20–30 feet up on the wall. The players, wearing protective gloves, belts, and hip-padding, tried to bounce a six-inch rubber ball through the hoop using only their fists, elbows, hips, and buttocks. The possibility of scoring in this manner was so rare that most of the attention was riveted on the action of keeping the ball in constant motion. The scoring team had the privilege of confiscating all the jewelry and clothing from the spectators and the losing team. The winning captain also beheaded the captain of the losers.

Virginity was highly prized, as it produced "pure" children who could be sacrificed in specific rituals. Also important to most sacrifices was "virgin" water that had to be collected from underground springs or caves. "Virgin" fire for the temples was made by twirling sticks.

At Chichen Itza, there were two great natural wells. The well on the edge of the city was a sacrificial well, about 200 feet in diameter with the water 70 feet below the surface. In times of national necessity, such as drought, the priests threw into this well trea-

Athlete, on a ball court marker

sures, jewelry, statues, and live humans. Men, women, and children were sacrificed in this manner while clouds of sacred copal incense filled the air.

Dancing was an important part of most rituals. The prime purpose was to induce a kind of hypnotic trance in all the participants, even the spectators. The Maya had flutes, trumpets, rattles, and percussion instruments, but no stringed musical instruments. Bells were tied to the wrists, ankles, and belts of the dancers. The dances tended to be dramatic in nature; that is, they told a story in some form. They were very ritualistic and precise in style. Often the dancers wore fantastic masks and costumes.

The priests in Mayan society were numerous and had a strict hierarchy; they were both men and women. At the head was the hereditary high priest, or *ahaucan mai;* this position had considerable power. The highest Mayan lords came to this priest for advice. The ahaucan mai participated at the principal feasts or in times of general need.

The *chilan,* another of the most important priests, taught the sciences, decided the holy days, healed the sick, and offered sacrifices; when a response from the gods' was required, it came through the chilan.

The *ahuai chac* priest was responsible for bringing rains. The *ah macik* did magick for winds. The *ahpul* could cause sickness or induce sleep. The *ahuai xibalba* had to know how to communicate with the dead. At the very bottom of the priesthood was the *nacon* who opened the breasts of the sacrificial victims. The *chac*[3] was assistant to the high priest. He was usually a person of importance who was appointed to serve for one year and was never re-elected.[4]

An order of acolytes known as *ah men* addressed prayers to the gods (for a fee, of course) and passed on to the people a deity's instructions relayed through the higher priests. A priest was needed to determine the best day for such events as marriage or the puberty festival.

Human sacrifice was practiced by the Maya, but not to the vast extent of the slaughter perpetuated by the Aztecs. The method, however, is pictured in their temples as the same. A captive was held over a sacrificial stone by four strong men; the priest slashed an opening in his ribs and pulled out the still-beating heart, which was presented to the deity for whom the sacrifice was performed.[5]

Mayan priests sat in the lotus position, but with their hands across their chests. During rituals they wore a special sacred apron. In sculptures the illumination of a priest is shown by lines or feathers surrounding the head.[6]

During the most sacred times of a ritual, the watching populace knelt in adoration of the deity.[7] An endless round of rituals and ceremonies was considered vitally necessary in order to maintain the help of the good gods and propitiate the evil ones. There could be thousands of ceremonies a year to just one god. Add to this the annual seasonal festivals, the rites of each guild or occupation, those of a personal nature, and the special ceremonies for drought, famine, pestilence, war, victory, and defeat, and you have a staggering amount of religious activity. The greatest percentage of these ceremonies all required human sacrifice, which meant tens of thousands of victims going under the obsidian knife in the temples.

The Mayas had a very elaborate, complex calendar system, primarily used by the priests. In actuality, they had three calendars: the Haab year, or Vague Year, which roughly corresponded to our own; the Tzolkin year; and the Long Count. The Long Count was really an extension of the Haab year in that it began with one Haab year of 360 days (a *tun*) and led back to what was known as the mystic year of 3113 BC. Each day of the Tzolkin coincided with the same day of the Haab only once every 18,980 days. Therefore, 73 Tzolkin equalled 52 Haab; at the end of this cycle everything began all over.

The primary unit of the Maya was the day, which they called *kin*. Each day, of which there were twenty, was named: Imix, Ik, Akbal, Kan, Chicchuan, Cimi, Manik, Lamat, Muluc, Oc, Chuen, Eb, Ben, Ix, Men, Cib, Caban, Eznab, Cauac, Ahau. When this cycle had run its course, it began again with Imix, thus repeating itself without interruption forever. To differentiate, the name of each day was prefixed by a number from one to thirteen. This action also repeated itself without interruption up to a cycle of 260 days when the sequence began all over. This total cycle of 260 days was called a Sacred Year, or Tzolkin.

The festival of carving of new masks

Glyphs for the months of the Mayan year

To add to the confusion, the Mayas also had a Solar Year that consisted of 365 days. This was known as a Haab. The Solar Year was made up of eighteen months *(uinal)* of twenty days each, with a five-day closing period at the end known as the *xma kaba kin,* or "days without name." These nineteen months were named: Pop, Uo, Zip, Zotz, Tzec, Xul, Yaxkin, Mol, Chen, Yax, Zac, Ceh, Mac, Kankin, Muan, Pax, Kayab, Cumhu, Uayeb.[8]

The Mayas also knew and used both a lunar and Venusian calendar. Their mathematicians were so accurate that they could calculate the lunar months to a remarkably exact figure: 29.53020 days.[9] With this strange conglomeration of calendars, the Mayan priests could predict eclipses of the Sun and Moon. In this manner they were able to ascertain the appropriate times for rituals and sacrifices.

There were about a dozen major Mayan deities and hundreds of lesser ones, each with its specific powers and required rituals and sacrifices. Most, if not all, of the deities had dual personalities. For example, the Sun god was benevolent for providing warmth and light, but evil for producing drought and thirst.

The head deity was Itzamna, father of the gods (except Hunab Ku) and creator of humankind. He personified the East, the rising Sun, light, life, and knowledge. He was considered the founder of the Mayan civilization, the inventor of writing and books, and a great healer.

However, Kukulcan (Feathered Serpent) was hardly less important. He was a personification of the West, out of which legend said he came; he was often pictured as white, bearded, blue-eyed and tall.[10] Legend says that Kukulcan came to Yucatan and settled at Chichen Itza where he ruled many years. At the end of his time, he returned to the West. He was considered a great organizer, founder of cities, law-giver, calendar founder; god of light, learning, culture.

The most feared and hated of Mayan gods was Ahpuch, the Lord of Death, also called Barebones. This god was portrayed with a fleshless skull and a body spotted black with corruption; he wore a stiff feather collar with small bells attached. He was associated with human sacrifice, suicides who hanged themselves, death in childbirth, and beheading. Closely associated with Ahpuch was the God of War who had black lines painted on his face.[11] Ek Ahua (Black Captain) was also a war god; he was totally black in color, armed with a spear or axe, and accompanied by seven black warriors.

The Earth deities were male and not thought of as having made the soil but owning it. Such a spirit was often called Lord of the Hills, or Lord of the Hills and Valleys. They were also seen as having power over animals and wild game.

Creation of the world was seen as action resulting from the alternating control and powers of the gods of wet and the gods of dry.

Yum Caax (Lord of the Harvest Fields) was the maize god, one of the important Mayan deities since maize was the staple crop of their civilization; they depended upon successful maize crops for survival. This deity wore a hat made from a sprouting ear of corn surrounded by leaves; he was considered kindly towards humans.

Nine deities were said to be lords of the night or the underworld.[12] This group was balanced by thirteen deities of day or the sky world. Religion was seen as a constant struggle between the powers of light and darkness.

The Mayas pictured the Earth as a cube that supported a heavenly vase. This vase rested on four legs, or the four cardinal points. Out of the vase grew a Tree of Life, whose flowers symbolized the souls of humans.[13]

DRESS AND ORNAMENTATION

Mayan dress was very similar to Aztec. The women wore sleeveless dresses that went to below the knee. Their hair was long and sometimes wound elaborately around the head, fixed with exotic decorations. Sandals for both sexes were decorated down the front and around the ankles. Women adorned themselves with huge earrings, necklaces, and bracelets.

The everyday dress of men was the loincloth. This garment among the warriors and high social ranks was fringed and decorated. Over this went a mid-thigh length skirt, woven in bright colors; down the front hung a series of masks, tassels, and other fanciful decorations. Large carved headdresses with myriads of feathers were the special property of warriors, nobles, and priests. Men adorned their bodies with collars, necklaces, bracelets, arm-bands, leg-bands, and earrings. High officials and priests carried carved and feathered staffs. Some priests wore exotic animal pelts, such as jaguars, as skirts. Priests were privileged to wear feathered cloaks and richly embroidered cottons.

Mayan design

SOME OF THE MYTHS

In the beginning, after the gods were formed (which is an undisclosed process), there was only sky and water. Two of the gods, usually named Quetzalcoatl and Tohil, took Hungry Woman and threw her down upon the ocean. Then they each took hold of an arm and leg, stretching her until the Earth was formed. Since these gods had treated Hungry Woman so roughly, they gave her the right to a type of human sacrifice, the right to eat the dead when they were buried within her.

After this the deities decided that they needed creatures who could talk to them by prayer and ritual. They created three races of beings before they finally managed to form humankind. The beings of the first race were the ancestors of the animals that live today; they were totally unsatisfactory as they could communicate only with noises. The second race was made of mud, and also proved unsatisfactory. The third time the deities formed creatures out of wood, but this too was troublesome. Although these wooden creatures could multiply, they had blank minds and no knowledge or care for their creators. Finally, humankind was created, to the delight of the gods. Here was a race of creatures that could learn and were able and willing to communicate with the deities.

These first people (listed in the *Popol Vuh* as the Quiche Maya) awoke into a world of darkness. They all met together at a place in the east known as Tulan Zuya, or Seven Caves. This place was considered the world-center. Here they were given fire, an essential for civilization, and symbol of the god Tohil.

When the first dawn came into being, the deities were hardened by the Sun's light into idols. However, the Maya had already been given the gift of civilization, which also contained the stipulation of blood sacrifice. At first they captured strangers and sacrificed them to Tohil. It was not very long before their neighbors realized what was happening and came to fight them. Thus, warfare was born.

One of the oldest stories in the *Popol Vuh* is the tale of twin brothers, Hunahpu and Xbalanque. The father and uncle of these boys had descended into the underworld and been defeated and slain there. In fact, the father's head had been placed as a trophy in a calabash tree near a ball court. The hero twins received an invitation from the lords of the underworld to come down for a ball game of *tlachtli*. The brothers accepted and descended into the lower realms. They were forced to go through a series of initiatory rites and ordeals, which they failed. But the hero twins had magickal abilities by which they were able to regenerate themselves.

They finally escaped but, instead of returning to the upper world, they disguised themselves as traveling magicians. In this manner they entered the courts of the underworld lords as entertainers. There they demonstrated that they could raise each other from death, which was very impressive. Finally, they talked the principal pair of lords into letting themselves be sacrificed, but the cagey brothers did not raise them from the dead. The remaining underworld lords were terrified. The twins revealed their identity and told them that from that point on the lords of the underworld would only receive sacrifices of rotten bodies in the grave, not the fresh blood of sacrifices. They retrieved their father's head and went home.

MAJOR GODS AND GODDESSES

ACAT—God of life; responsible for the development of children in the womb.

AHPUCH—"Lord of Death"; "Barebones." Associated with human sacrifice, suicide by hanging, childbirth death, and beheading.

BACABS—Gods of the four winds, the four directions; they held up the heavens in one legend.[14] The chief Bacab was HOBNIL, the patron god of beekeepers.

CHAC—"Long-nose." Rain and vegetation god. He was very popular and the most worshipped deity in the late Maya period. He rode on a serpent (symbol of rain) and carried a snake-shaped water bottle and torches. Sometimes pictured with a trunk-like nose and fangs sprouting from his lower jaw.

CIT CHAC COH—"Image of the red puma"; war god. At his festival, soldiers danced in his temple and sacrificed a dog to his image.

EK AHAU—"Black Captain"; war god.

EK CHUAH—Black scorpion-tailed god; patron of merchants and cocoa planters in one aspect, in another god of war. Participants were not allowed to get drunk at his festival as they did at others.

GUCUMATZ—"Feathered Snake." God of agriculture and civilization; a shape-shifter. He lived in both heaven and hell, and was associated with HURUKAN.

HUN PIC TOK—"Eight thousand stone knives"; war god. His pyramid temple was among the most important in Izamal in Yucatan.

HUNAB KU—Supreme, but remote and impersonal, god.

Mayan gods of death, maize, and the north

HURUKAN—"Triple Heart of the Universe"; very ancient god who created Earth, animals, fire, and people. The whirlwind, hurricanes, thunder, spiritual illumination.

ITZAMNA—Sky god; father of the gods and creator of humankind; lord of day and night; considered omnipotent and rather remote. Personified the East, the rising Sun, light, life, knowledge; founder of Mayan civilization, inventor of writing and books, first priest of the Mayan religion. God of healing, drawing, letters, crops, fertility, water, regeneration, medicine. His sign was a red hand to which the sick prayed for healing, or a lizard. Depicted as a cross-eyed, toothless old man with a lizard's body. Sometimes he was shown between a Sun and Moon or between two jaguars.

Itzamna

IXCHEBELYAX—Goddess-inventor of painting and fabric color designing.

IXCHEL—"The Rainbow"; consort of ITZAMNA. Goddess of childbirth, medicine, the Moon, pregnancy, floods, weaving, domestic arts.

IXCHUP—"Young Moon Goddess"; wife of a Sun god named AH KINCHIL.

IXTAB—Patroness of hunting and hanging.

IXTUBTUN—Protectress of all jade cutters.

TKINICH KAK MO—"Sunface fire macaw"; Sun god connected with lighting of the sacrificial fire.

KUKULCAN—"Feathered Serpent"; a form of QUETZALCOATL. The city of Quirigua was devoted to his worship. Personification of the West; god of light, learning, culture, organization and order, laws, calendar.

MAM—Earthquake god of Yucatan.

MASAYA—Niquiran of Nicaragua. Goddess of volcanoes and divination. She was pictured as a hideous old woman and required human victims thrown into volcanic craters.

NOHOCHACYUM—God of creation; defender from evil.

XAMAN EK—"Guide of the merchants"; the North Star. Business, peace, plenty.

YUM CAAX—God of maize or corn; "Forest Lord"; "Lord of the Harvest Fields." Granted riches, husbandry, fertility, growth, life, joy, good crops.

Endnotes

1. The national drink was *pulque,* an agave beer made from the fermenting of maguey cactus.

2. Whitlock, Ralph. *Everyday Life of the Maya.* This game was very probably the exact same game as played by the Aztecs.

3. Ralph Whitlock says that sometimes there were four *chacs;* they were responsible for holding the four corners of a rope enclosure where adolescents were held during puberty ceremonies. He writes that they also had to hold the four limbs of sacrificial victims. If this was the case, it is highly unlikely that the chacs were elderly men, as it would take considerable strength to hold down a victim while his heart was being cut out.

4. Morley, Sylvanus Griswold. *An Introduction to the Study of the Maya Hieroglyphs.*

5. References in the *Popol Vuh* to being "suckled by the god" meant that one was sacrificed to him. Tedlock, Dennis. *Popol Vuh: The Definitive Edition of the Mayan Book of the Dawn of Life and the Glories of the Gods and Kings.*

6. The Mayan word for illumination or enlightenment was *cizin.* This has also been explained as radiating energy, much the same as the aura.

7. The word *xoltal* means "kneel before the sacred" and was applied to this action.

8. For more exact information on this subject, see Sylvanus Morley, *An Introduction to the Study of the Maya Hieroglyphs;* Hunbatz Men, *Secrets of Mayan Science/Religion;* Ralph Whitlock, *Everyday Life of the Maya.*

9. Most of the information we now have comes from the Dresden Codex, one of the three surviving books.

10. Hunbatz Men, however, says that this description was added after the Spanish conquest. In my opinion it is not logical to reject this portion of the ancient writing if one accepts the rest of it.

11. Although the Mayas had several deities of war, this particular one was specifically associated with mass death by violence. He also presided over death by sacrifice.

12. Heaven and Hell, or sky and underworld, were not considered places of reward and punishment among the Mayas. Rather, they were the afterlife abodes of various classes of people. A person was destined to go to the area reserved for his class and occupation. Each zone had its own god, but most of their names have not been deciphered. It is known, however, that an underworld deity ruled over each day of the Mayan calendar. The gods of the sky ruled over the *katun,* or the period of twenty years.

13. For more information on the colors associated with the four cardinal directions, read the chapter on Elements.

14. Each Bacab was associated with a color and a tree of the color. To the north was white, the west black, the south yellow, and the east red. A fifth tree, colored green, grew in the center. And in each tree was a bird of the appropriate color.

BIBLIOGRAPHY

Alexander, Hartley Burr. "Latin-American Mythology" in *The Mythology of All Races*. Boston, MA: J. A. MacCulloch, 1920.

Bierhorst, John. *The Monkey's Haircut and Other Stories Told by the Maya*. NY: Wm. Morrow, 1986.

Bierhorst, John. *The Mythology of Mexico and Central America*. NY: William Morris & Co., 1990.

Boone, Elizabeth, ed. *Ritual Human Sacrifice in Mesoamerica*. Washington, DC: Dumbarton Oaks Research Library & Collections, 1984.

Brundage, Burr Cartwright. *The Phoenix of the Western World: Quetzalcoatl and the Sky Religion*. Norman, OK: University of Oklahoma Press, 1982.

Budapest, Z. *The Holy Book of Women's Mysteries*. Oakland, CA: Susan B. Anthony Coven No. 1, 1979.

Ceram, C. W. *Gods, Graves and Scholars*. NY: Bantam Books, 1972.

Coe, Michael D. *The Maya*. NY: Penguin, 1966.

deLanda, Friar Diego. *Yucatan Before and After the Conquest*. NY: Dover Publications, 1978.

Edmonson, Munro S., trans. *The Book of Counsel: The Popol Vuh of the Quiche Maya of Guatemala*. New Orleans, LA: Middle American Research Institute, Tulane University, 1971.

Gossen, Gary. *Chamulas in the World of the Sun: Time and Space in a Maya Oral Tradition*. Cambridge, MA: Harvard University Press, 1974.

Hay, Clarence, ed. *The Maya and Their Neighbors*. NY: Dover Publications, 1977.

Laughlin, Robert M. *The People of the Bat: Mayan Tales and Dreams From Zinacantan*. Washington, DC: Smithsonian Institution Press, 1988.

Le Plongeon, Augustus. *Maya/Atlantis, Queen Moo and the Egyptian Sphinx*. NY: Rudolf Steiner Publications, 1973.

Men, Hunbatz. *Secrets of Mayan Science/Religion*. Santa Fe, NM: Bear & Co. Publishing, 1990.

Morley, Sylvanus Griswold. *An Introduction to the Study of the Maya Hieroglyphs*. NY: Dover Publications, 1975.

Nicholson, Irene. *Mexican and Central American Mythology*. NY: Peter Bedrick Books, 1985.

Reader's Digest. *The World's Last Mysteries*. NY: Reader's Digest Association, 1978.

Schele, Linda, and Miller, Mary Ellen. *The Blood of Kings: Dynasty and Ritual in Maya Art*. NY: Braziller, 1986.

Spence, Lewis. *The History of Atlantis*. NY: Bell Publishing, 1963.

Stewart, George E. *Discovering Man's Past in the Americas*. Washington, D. C.: National Geographic Society, 1969.

Stirling, Matthew W. *National Geographic on Indians of the Americas*. Washington, D.C.: National Geographic, 1955.

Tedlock, Barbara. *Time and the Highland Maya*. Albuquerque, NM: University of New Mexico Press, 1985.

Tedlock, Dennis. *Popol Vuh: The Definitive Edition of the Mayan Book of the Dawn of Life and the Glories of the Gods and Kings*. NY: Simon & Schuster, 1985.

Thompson, J. Eric S. *Maya History and Religion*. Norman, OK: University of Oklahoma Press, 1970.

Thompson, J. Eric S. *The Rise and Fall of Maya Civilization*. Norman, OK: University of Oklahoma Press, 1954.

Tompkins, Ptolemy. *This Tree Grows Out of Hell*. San Francisco, CA: Harper & Row, 1990.

Turner, Wilson G. *Maya Designs*. NY: Dover Publications, 1980.

Von Hagen, Victor. *World of the Maya*. NY: Signet, 1960.

Von Hassler, Gerd. *Lost Survivors of the Deluge*. NY: New American Library, 1976.

Whitlock, Ralph. *Everyday Life of the Maya*. NY: Dorset Press, 1976.

CHAPTER TWENTY-FIVE

AZTECS

THE AZTECS were a Nahuatl-speaking group who referred to themselves as the Mexica or the Tenochca. They entered the valley of Mexico early in the fourteenth century after a long journey, guided by a prophecy of an eagle eating a snake while sitting atop a cactus. They found such a sign on a swampy island in a large lake, Lake Texcoco.[1] They overcame the Toltecs and all other peoples living in the region.

There they founded their culture on two islands, each of which was an independent state, with the capital of Tenochtitlan. The sixth ruler of Tenochtitlan united these cities in the fifteenth century. The name of the main city, Tenochtitlan, meant "place of the prickly pear cactus." The Aztecs conquered and ruled the surrounding country with extreme fierceness and a bloody religion. However, they were also superb builders.

In the mid 1400s they constructed a great dike to prevent flooding of the island cities. Punishment for crimes was harsh. The warriors became an elite class. They spread their rule over most of Mexico, as far south as Guatemala, El Salvador, and Nicaragua, but did not consolidate their control very well. The cities were great ceremonial and political centers but the smaller villages continued life as before, being careful not to cross their Aztec rulers.

Finally, the reign of Montezuma II (1503–1520), earthquakes, and Spanish invaders ended the Aztec rule. Montezuma II welcomed Cortes to his capital in

November of 1519, but was soon imprisoned by the Spaniards. Cortes established control, systematically stamping out the civilization in the name of Spain, gold, and religion.

RELIGION

The Aztecs built pyramid temples with round, drum-shaped, carved sacrificial stones on top of them. Thousands of men, women, and children were sacrificed every year to the gods. Many of the victims were taken as war captives.[2] Each day, night, week, month, and year had its own god or goddess demanding blood. The Aztecs believed that failure to honor the deities with blood sacrifices would cause the world to end at the end of their 52-year calendar (equal to our century).

The sacrifices to Tezcatlipoca, among a great many other gods, required the living heart to be cut from the body of a human. The beating heart was shown to the Sun, then thrown onto the sacrificial fire. After this, the body was skinned and cut up for cannibalistic ceremonies by the priests and warriors. This rite was held every year; more elaborate forms of the rite were held every 13 years.

Incense of copal or rubber was burned before the sacred images four times each day, three times each night. The priests also offered food, clothing, and flowers. However, blood was considered the most important. Pigeons and quail were common offerings. The priests considered it their duty to offer their own blood as well, piercing their tongues, cheeks, and ears for the blood sacrifice. Flutes, trumpets, and shell horns were played during the rites; there was also singing and chanting.

The Aztecs differed from their neighbors, who also performed human sacrifice, only in that they practiced it in massive numbers. Strangely enough, many of the victims apparently went to the altars willingly, believing that when they died they would go straight to the paradise of the Sun.

The priests and priestesses to the gods numbered in the thousands. The Spanish writer Torquemada wrote that 5,000 priests were kept at the Temple of Huitzilopochtli. At the top of the priesthood in power were those belonging to the principal gods, Huitzilopochtli and Tlaloc. They were chosen especially for their sanctity, not their lineage.

All priests and priestesses were required four times during the day and five times during the night to pray and burn incense in the temple. Fasts were frequent, as was self blood-letting.

Under the high priests and priestesses were hundreds of lesser members who were responsible for a myriad of details involved with the temples and deities. Some priests were specialists in astrology, divination, the calendar, music, and learning. Sacred music was taught by the Ometochtzin (Lord of the House of Flutes). Often the priests were also judges, commanders in battle, and even warriors.

Since the priesthood controlled the calmecac schools where Aztec leaders were educated, they had supreme control over and influenced secular life. They were the guardians of knowledge and traditions.

The priests and priestesses commanded instant respect by their very appearance. They painted their bodies black and wore a black or dark green cloak that reached to the feet. Often these capes were embroidered with human skulls and bones. They never washed, cut, or combed their hair; because of the temple sacrifices, their hair was most often matted with blood.

The original creator deities of the Aztecs were called Ometecuhtli and Omecihuatl, sometimes called by the single name Ometeotl (God of the Duality). Although this combined deity was considered to be both male and female, it was referred to as "he." The name under which he was worshipped was Tloque Nahuaque (Lord of Everywhere); he was considered so remote that he was never pictured in sculpture or paintings and had only one temple, which was in Texcoco. Another of his titles was Moyocoyani (He who gives existence to himself).

Sacrifice to the Sun

Probably the most important deity to the Aztecs was Tlaloc, the rain god, without whose aid not even maize would grow. Tlaloc was sculpted with rings around his eyes, a fringe of curved tusks about his mouth, and raindrops falling from his hands. His colors were blue or green, the colors of water. During the first and third months of the Aztec year, small children were sacrificed to this god. The more they cried, the better chances for rain during the growing season.

Quetzalcoatl's rival, Tezcatlipoca (Smoking Mirror), was an extremely powerful deity who gave, but also took life. He was pictured as eternally young with an obsidian mirror on his forehead. His face was painted black with horizontal stripes, and his hair cut in the warrior style. It was said that in his mirror Tezcatlipoca could see everything that happened in the world. Sometimes he went about in the disguise of a jaguar. He was considered the god of the night sky, the patron of sorcerers and warriors. He was also a war god and protector of the *telpochcalli* schools that trained the young warriors. He always carried a shield and weapons.

The most impressive statue of Aztec sculpture remaining today is of Coatlicue (Lady of the Serpent Skirt). She was an Earth goddess, mother of the Moon, the stars, and Huitzilopochtli. The sculpture shows her wearing a skirt of intertwining snakes, her breasts bare. As a death aspect of the Goddess, Coatlicue has claws on her hands and feet and a skull-pendant hanging on a chain of humans hearts and hands about her neck. In place of her severed head are two streams of blood shaped like serpents.

The Aztecs used a calendar that was shared by all the civilizations of Mexico. This was a 365-day calendar based on the solar year; it was divided into eighteen months of twenty days each, with five days called the "hollow days" at the end. The hollow days were considered very unlucky; any people born on these days were automatically assumed to be sorcerers and such. There is evidence to indicate that they knew enough about the correct length of the solar year to include a sixth "hollow" day every four years.

Aztec calendar stone

The year was named after the Sacred Almanac day on which it began. Thus, the eighteen months were the basis for both the agricultural and ritual years. Names of the months came from either monthly ceremonies and festivals or agricultural concerns.[3]

1. Stopping of the Water
2. Flaying of Men
3. Lesser Vigil
4. Greater Vigil
5. Drought
6. Eating of Bean Porridge
7. Lesser Feast of the Gods
8. Great Feast of the Lords
9. Offering of Flowers
10. Fall of the Fruits
11. Month of Sweeping
12. Return of the Gods
13. Feast of the Mountains
14. Quecholli (a bird)
15. Raising of the Feather Banners
16. Fall of the Waters
17. Severe Weather
18. Growth

The Sacred Almanac (also called the "Count of Days") was used by the priests in divination. This was a 260-day cycle arrived at by combining the numbers 1–13 with the twenty named days of the regular calendar. Each day had its own sign or symbol, important in the foretelling of events or the future.[4]

Priests, who were responsible for the calendar, also measured the correct length of the Venusian year, based on the rotation of the planet Venus. By this data they could predict eclipses.

DRESS AND ORNAMENTATION

The everyday dress of an Aztec man was a breechcloth, hipcloth, mantle or cape, and sandals. The mantle and ends of the breechcloth were long and embroidered only for those of high stations in society. All men wore ear plugs in the lobes, often heavy necklaces, bracelets, arm-bands, and nose ornaments. The hair never hung longer than the shoulders. High officials were allowed to wear a white mantle and carry a large fan.

Among the warrior class, the hair was cut to just below the ears. Warriors often wore elaborate feathered headdresses and body decorations. They had masks and helmets imitating in looks wild animal heads. Sometimes they even wore the animal skins.

Women cut their hair out around the ear with a piece hanging down in front of the ear; the back length was below the shoulders. They also wore ear plugs, headbands, and necklaces. Female everyday dress was a bordered short skirt and sleeveless blouse. Featherwork, gold, and wood crafts were unparalleled for the time period.

Aztec priests paraded their gory religion in their dress and looks. They usually dressed in black and stained their bodies the same color. However, the robe of the sacrificial priest was always blood red, and he carried a grotesquely carved staff. Shorter staffs were carried as an emblem of office by lower priests. Their hair was matted with sacrificial gore until it stood in a stiff Medusa-like mass on their heads. They wore fancy plugs in their lower lips as well as the ear lobes. Headbands were replaced by exotic headdresses during ceremonies.

SOME OF THE MYTHS

The most famous of the paired creator gods of the Aztecs were Quetzalcoatl and Tezcatlipoca. They appear as adversaries in several myths.

In the myth of why the Earth eats the dead (see the Mayan myth of the same name), Quetzalcoatl and Tezcatlipoca stretched Hungry Woman to make the Earth. In an effort to soothe her injured feelings over being treated so roughly, the gods filled the Earth with forests, flowers, valleys, and other pleasant places over her surface. However, this did not stop her craving for human hearts and human blood.

Later when all the gods had made the first Sun, Tezcatlipoca stole it. Tying it around his waist, he rose into the sky. Quetzalcoatl grabbed up a big stick and followed him. With one mighty blow, Quetzalcoatl knocked Tezcatlipoca back to the Earth where the dark god became the jaguar that ate the first people.

One day Quetzalcoatl noticed a trail of ants carrying some strange kernels into their hill. Curious, the god changed himself into an ant and followed them down their tunnels to their storage area. The ants' hill was filled with the strange food. The god tasted one of the kernels, which proved to be sweet maize. He thought that this would be a good food for humans. So he stole some kernels from the ants and gave them to humankind. Maize, the versatile grain, was considered by the Aztecs to be a gift from the gods.

Huitzilopochtli (hummingbird of the South) was the god of war to the Aztecs. In his temple of Tenochtitlan, many human sacrifices were made to him. He was the son of Coatlicue. One day before his birth his mother was sweeping and found a tuft of feathers. Tucking the feathers into her skirt, she went on with her work. She discovered a short time later that she was pregnant; she already had 400 sons and a warrior daughter. Her daughter, upon learning of the pregnancy, was extremely angry. She thought her mother had been dishonored and decided to kill the baby when it was born. When Coatlicue went into labor, the 400 sons, led by the warrior daughter, charged up the hill to kill the baby. Huitzilopochtli was born prepared to take care of his trouble-making sister. He leaped out of the womb with a blue javelin and killed the sister and the 400 brothers.

Tezcatlipoca (Smoking Mirror) was the dark aspect of the Aztec Sun god and was greatly feared. Any sensible Aztec stayed on the god's good side, or at least out of the reach of his priests who laid freshly cut-out hearts on the deity's altars.

Tezcatlipoca was the great enemy of Quetzalcoatl, who was chief god of the Toltecs until they fell under Aztec dominion. Then Quetzalcoatl became one of the chief Aztec deities. Tezcatlipoca plotted long over the destruction of the Toltec peoples. Once he appeared as a handsome young man and seduced three of Quetzalcoatl's nieces. Then he showed up during a festival, enticed a great number of people onto a bridge, and caused it to collapse. After several other killing escapades, Tezcatlipoca

Quetzalcoatl

convinced the Toltecs to stone him for his wickedness. They did, but the stench of his decaying body killed even more of them.

The Toltecs finally succeeded in dragging him out of town, but by that time Quetzalcoatl had enough. He burned his palaces, buried his treasure, and sailed off on the eastern sea for his old home land. He told his people that some day he would return. When the Spaniards showed up in their ships and shining armor, the Aztecs thought Quetzalcoatl had returned.

Once Quetzalcoatl spilled his semen on the ground, where it became a bat. The bat flew off to where Xochiquetzal, goddess of love, lay sleeping and bit off a piece of flesh inside her genitals. The bat returned with this piece of flesh to Quetzalcoatl, and the god transformed it into flowers.

The Aztecs even had a flood myth. After humankind was made by the gods, the creatures angered the deities by not sacrificing with human blood. The deities decided to punish their creations and caused all the rivers, streams, springs, and oceans to overflow and cover the Earth. A few people managed to survive and went back to worshipping the gods in the manner they preferred, which was human sacrifice. During this flood in ancient times, the sky fell down onto the Earth. Quetzalcoatl and Tezcatlipoca changed themselves into two trees that grew so tall that they pushed the sky back to its normal position. Then, leaving the trees in place, one at each corner of the Earth, the two deities climbed to the center of the Milky Way. Because of this action, the Aztecs called them "the lords of heaven and of the stars."

A few men actively sought the god Tezcatlipoca. One of these men was instructed by the deity through his priests to fetch musicians from the Sun. In other words, the man had to steal something that belonged to the opposing god, Quetzalcoatl. After several attempts and long trials, the man accomplished his mission. Thus, it was said, music, which was born in the sky, was brought to Earth for humankind to use in praising all deities.

Major Gods and Goddesses

ACAT—Toltec, Aztec. God of life who shaped bodies before birth.

CENTZON TOTOCHTIN—"Four hundred rabbits." Gods connected with the Moon. Depicted with black and white faces, crescent-shaped nose ornaments. Associated with pulque beer.[5]

CHALCHIHUITLICUE—"Precious green lady"; "Precious jewel lady"; "Precious jade skirt." Wife of the rain god TLALOC. Her special colors were blue and white, and she loved flowers. She had an unpredictable temper, though. Offerings of flowers, hallucinogenic mushrooms, and cotton headdresses were made to her. Goddess of storms, youthful beauty, whirlpools, spring growth, love, flowers, spirits, streams.

CHANTICO—Goddess of fire, home and fertility, she symbolized pleasure and pain together. Her symbols were a red serpent and cactus spikes. She ruled wealth and precious stones found in the Earth.

Coatlicue

CHICOMECOATL—Maize goddess; very popular as maize was considered the staple of life. Wore a huge four-sided headdress and carried a twin maize cob.

CIHUACOATL—"Woman snake"; goddess of childbirth.

CINTEOTL—God of corn, although he had female forms. Took over the original place of CHICOMECOATL; always protected by water gods. During his April festival reeds smeared with blood were put at the house doors as an offering. Corn Spirit; supplier of earthly food.

COATLICUE—"Snake Skirt"; "Serpent Lady"; Earth Goddess; Great Mother; "She of the serpent skirt." She was both positive and negative, could bless or punish.[6] Shown with claws and a skirt of snakes. Mother of all life, famines and earthquakes.

COYOLXAUHQUI—"Golden Bells"; Moon goddess. Shown with golden bells on her cheeks.

HUEHUECOYOTL/UEUECOYOTL—"Old, old Coyote"; a back-biting, mischievous deity who was associated with gaiety, physical sex, and irrational fun. He was uncontrolled and a trickster god.

HUEHUETEOTL—"Old God"; god of fire; also called XIUHTECUHTLI, "Turquoise Lord." Patron of warriors and kings. His festival was August 1, when slaves were roasted alive. God of domestic and spiritual fire, ritual, and the calendar. Pictured as a bent old man sitting with a shallow bowl for burning incense on his head.

HUITZILOPOCHTLI—"Hummingbird on the Left (South)"; "Left-Handed Humming Bird"; national god of the Aztecs;[7] possibly an aspect of TEZCATLIPOCA. His festival was one of 25 days of a blood orgy with hearts and blood of prisoners poured on his altar. Sun, death, war, young men, warriors, storms, guide for journeys.

ILAMATECUHTLI—Mother Goddess; terrible aspect of the Goddess. During her winter festival, a woman's heart was cut out and the severed head carried during a procession.

ITZCOLIUHQUI—"Twisted obsidian one"; "Curved obsidian knife"; an aspect of TEZCATLIPOCA. God of darkness, terrible cold, volcanic eruptions, disaster.

ITZPAPLOTL—"Obsidian knife butterfly"; a beautiful female demon with death symbols on her face. A mixture of sensuality and death. Goddess of fate, stars, agriculture.

MAYAUEL—Goddess who discovered and introduced the gods to pulque. She was pictured naked, holding up a bowl of pulque and seated on a throne of a tortoise and a snake. Night was her special time, and she carried a cord that she used to help women in childbirth.

MEZTLI/TECCIZIECATL—The material Moon at its height; "He from the sea snail." Represented as an old man with a white shell on his back and sometimes with butterfly wings. Was replaced by the goddess COYOLXAUHQUI.

MICTLANTECUHTLI—"Lord of the land of the dead"; god of the Underworld[8] and the North; "Dead Land Lord." Shown as a skeleton with red bones; his consort was MICTLANCIHUATL.

MIXCOATL—"Cloud serpent"; God of the Pole Star and national god of the Chichimecs. Sacrifice victims were painted white or red; it was believed that they turned into stars which were considered food for the Sun. God of hunting and weapons that strike from afar, such as javelins and spear-throwers.

QUETZALCOATL—"Most precious twin";[9] "Feathered serpent"; "Plumed serpent"; "Morning Star." Great Priest; Master of Life; god of the wind, sea breeze, and life-breath. Creator god, identified with the planet Venus. He was considered a good god as he required only one human sacrifice a year. Civilization, the arts, metallurgy, fate.

TEZCATLIPOCA—"Mirror that smokes"; "The shadow"; "He who is at the shoulder"; "Smoking mirror"; "It causes the Black Mirror (night) to shine." One of two most prominent gods of Mexico, he was a local deity of the Toltecs adopted by the Aztecs. The dark aspect of QUETZALCOATL; his symbol was the jaguar. Evil god of warriors, magicians and sorcerers. Divination, especially black mirrors. Drought, harvest, dancing, music, warriors, magick, cold and north, night.

TLALOC—"The one who makes things sprout"; "Lord of the sources of water"; Lord of the Waters. An ancient Nature and fertility god who required unending human sacrifice. Shown holding four pitchers from which he pours rain. Consort was CHALCHIHUITLICUE. God of thunder, mountains, rains, hail, fertility, water, clouds, thunder, and lightning.

TLAUIXCALPANTECUHTLI—"Lord of the house of dawn"; the morning star Venus. An aspect of QUETZALCOATL.

TLAZOLTEOTL—"Goddess of filth";[10] "Dirt Goddess"; Earth Goddess; Lady of Witches. Goddess of the crescent Moon. Terrible aspect of the Goddess. She rode naked on a broom holding a red snake and a blood-stained rope. Physical love, fertility, death.

TONATIUH/PILZINTECUTLI—"Royal Lord"; Sun God; ruler of fate; god of warriors who died in battle and women who died in childbirth. He received daily sacrifices of human hearts and blood.

TOZI/TETEOINNAN—"Our grandmother"; mother of the gods; personification of the powers of Nature. She had a popular festival in August which honored midwives and women healers. Goddess of healing and the sweat baths.[11]

XILONEN—Goddess of maize. Her festival involved feasts of maize, gruel, and tamales.

XIPE TOTEC—"The flayed one"; god of agriculture, the west, goldsmiths, and penitential self-torture. The Aztecs celebrated his festival on February 22 by skinning captives alive to help the growing corn.[12]

XOCHIPILLI—"Flower Prince." Originally a Mixtec Sun god whose helmet-mask was the jungle fowl who first voice dawn. God of music, dance, ball players, flowers, feasting, and pleasure.

XOCHIQUETZAL—"Flower plume"; "Flower Feather." Mother of the maize god. Goddess of the underworld and flowers (particularly marigolds which are laid on graves), sexual love, twins, children, and craftsmen.

Xolotl

XOLOTL—"The Animal"; Lord of the Evening Star; Lord of the Underworld. A monster animal with feet on backwards. The evil form of the planet Venus and opponent of the Sun; however, he did bring humankind and fire from the underworld. Giver of bad luck.

YACATECUHTLI—"Lord Nose"; "He who goes before." God of merchants and traders.

ENDNOTES

1. These original ruins are some 300 miles north of Mexico City, the site of Tenochtitlan, the Aztec capital.

2. In some cultures, it was common for volunteers to be sacrificed, but from all the evidence this was rarely the case in the Aztec culture. These unwilling sacrifices were captives from wars, subjugated tribes, and people dragged off the street.

3. It was said that the Aztec year began on February 2 by our calendar.

4. For a modernization of this technique, see Schofield and Cordova, *Aztec Wheel of Destiny.*

5. Pulque was a fermented juice of the maguey cactus and extremely potent.

6. As an Earth Goddess, she represented both life and death, the womb and the grave. In her most destructive aspect, she was called Cipactli, a monster who swallowed all living beings. Mother of Huitzilopochtli.

7. Although Huitzilopochtli was a national god, he had no great following outside Tenochtitlan and Tlatelolco. During their wanderings, the Aztecs carried with them a human mummy, which may have been the body of

Huitzilopochtli, a hero turned into a god. He is depicted in legend as a Sun god, opponent of the dark god Tezcatlipoca. Human heart sacrifice was offered to him to ensure his strength. He had a great temple on the Great Pyramid in Mexico City.

8. Mictlan, or Mictlampa, was the deepest underworld and the region of the dead.

9. The morning star, or Venus, was called Quetzal, or precious one; since Venus rises both morning and evening, the Aztecs called it a twin star. The Maya knew him as Kukulcan. Only priests or nobles could enter his great temple-pyramids.

10. The Aztecs considered sin, especially sexual sin, as filth. Her priests heard the confessions of adulterers. Her four phases were those of the Moon, and in her third phase her power of purification could wash away sin.

11. In Mexico the sweat bath was used as a cure for all sicknesses. People went there to cleanse both their bodies and souls. An image of Tozi was placed above the door to the sweat bath.

12. This god was represented by a mask of a human skinned face. Originally, Xipe Toltec was said to have skinned himself to help the corn shoots break out of the ground.

BIBLIOGRAPHY

Alexander, Hartley Burr. "Latin-American Mythology" in *The Mythology of All Races*. Boston, MA: J. A. MacCulloch, 1920.

Bernal, Ignacio. *Mexico Before Cortez: Art, History and Legend*. NY: Anchor Books, 1973.

Bierhorst, John, trans. *Cantares Mexicanos: Songs of the Aztecs*. Stanford, CA: Stanford University Press, 1985.

Bierhorst, John, ed. and trans. *The Hungry Woman: Myths and Legends of the Aztecs*. NY: Wm. Morrow, 1984.

Bierhorst, John. *The Mythology of Mexico and Central America*. NY: William Morrow & Co., 1990.

Blacker, Irwin, and Eckholm, Gordon. *Cortes and the Aztec Conquest*. American Heritage, 1965.

Boone, Elizabeth, ed. *Ritual Human Sacrifice in Mesoamerica*. Washington, DC: Dumbarton Oaks Research Library & Collections, 1984.

Bray, Warwick. *Everyday Life of the Aztecs*. NY: Dorset Press, 1968.

Brundage, Burr Cartwright. *The Fifth Sun: Aztec Gods, Aztec World*. Austin, TX: University of Texas Press, 1979.

Brundage, Burr Cartwright. *The Jade Steps: A Ritual Life of the Aztecs*. Salt Lake City, UT: University of Utah Press, 1985.

Brundage, Burr Cartwright. *The Phoenix of the Western World: Quetzalcoatl and the Sky Religion*. Norman, OK: University of Oklahoma Press, 1982.

Brundage, Burr Cartwright. *A Rain of Darts: The Mexica Aztec*. Austin, TX: University of Texas Press, 1972.

Burland, Cottie, and Forman, Werner. *The Aztecs: Gods and Fate in Ancient Mexico*. UK: Orbis, 1985.

Caso, Alfonso. *The Aztecs: People of the Sun*. Norman, OK: University of Oklahoma Press, 1958.

Ceram, C. W. *Gods, Graves and Scholars*. NY: Bantam Books, 1972.

Churchward, James. *The Children of Mu*. NY: Paperback Library, 1969.

Coe, Michael. *Mexico*. UK: Thames & Hudson, 1962.

Davies, Nigel. *The Aztecs*. Norman, OK: University of Oklahoma Press, 1980.

Du Solier, W. *Ancient Mexico Costume*. South America: Ediciones Mexicanas, 1950.

Leon-Portilla, M. *Aztec Thought and Culture: A Study of the Ancient Nahuatl Mind*. OK: University of Oklahoma Press, 1963.

Nicholson, Irene. *Mexican and Central American Mythology*. NY: Peter Bedrick Books, 1985.

Reader's Digest. *The World's Last Mysteries*. NY: Reader's Digest Association, 1978.

Scofield, Bruce, and Cordova, Angela. *The Aztec Circle of Destiny: Astrology and Divination From the Ancient Aztec World*. St. Paul, MN: Llewellyn Publications, 1988.

Sejourne, Laurette. *Burning Water: Thought and Religion in Ancient Mexico*. Berkeley, CA: Shambhala, 1976.

Soustelle, J. *The Daily Life of the Aztecs*. UK: Weidenfeld & Nicolson, 1961.

Spence, Lewis. *The History of Atlantis*. NY: Bell Publishing, 1963.

Steiger, Brad. *Indian Medicine Power*. Gloucester, MA: Para Research, 1984.

Stirling, Matthew W. *National Geographic on Indians of the Americas*. Washington, D.C.: National Geographic, 1955.

Tompkins, Ptolemy. *This Tree Grows Out of Hell*. San Francisco, CA: Harper & Row, 1990.

Weed, Joseph. *Complete Guide to Oracle and Prophecy Methods*. West Nyack, NY: Parker Publishing, 1971.

CHAPTER TWENTY-SIX

INCAS

THE INCAS were not a single tribe but rather a conglomeration of tribes who banded together and took their name from the title of their leader, Ynca, or "prince of the ruling family." About AD 1100 the Incas were only a small tribe of llama herders on the high plain some distance southwest of Cuzco, Peru. Their tribe migrated down into the fertile Cuzco valley. There their leader, dressed in spangles of gold, was accepted by the valley dwellers as a monarch sent from the Sun. They began organizing the small tribes around them and soon were conquering the surrounding areas.

For a time the Incas were halted by the fierce Chancas, but these were defeated by Hatun Tupac (1347–1400). Long lines of forts were built on the east frontiers; the culture flowered. Swift messengers carried news to the emperor over a thousand miles of roads and bridges. Tupac Yupanqui (1448–1482) expanded the empire to include Ecuador.

However, Tupac's son (1482–1529) divided the great empire on his deathbed, thus opening the Incan defenses to Spanish conquest. Although the Inca Empire finally included all the Andean area from southern Columbia to southern Chile, Francisco Pizarro and his Spanish soldiers took the emperor Atahualpa captive in 1532 and ended the Inca reign.

RELIGION

The Incas were tolerant of the religious beliefs of their conquered subjects as long as the worship did not interfere with the obligations laid upon them by Incan religious leaders. However, the Incan pantheon was superimposed over these pre-existing deities and was considered of greater importance.

The Incas and their subjugated peoples believed that it was the duty of each person to insure his well-being by carefully observing all details of rituals and religious thought. If a life, whether personal or national, did not go well, it was assumed that an infraction against the gods had occurred.

The prime deity of the Incas was Viracocha, the creator god. However, he was considered remote and invisible; no temples were erected to him. Inti, the Sun god, was thought to be his visible representation.

Within the state religion of the Incas the god Inti headed all activities. Because Inti was considered the ancestor of the ruling Inca, and the source of Inca prestige and power, he had the dominant position among the other Incan deities. The Sun, called the "Giver of Life," was of great agricultural importance to the Incas; the 12-month solar calendar was based on agricultural practices. The Incas called their country "lands of the Sun." Temples to Inti were built by the government throughout the empire.

The Temple of the Sun, also known as the Coricancha, was the most sacred shrine in the Incan culture. Located in Cuzco, it was a huge building, or rather a group of connected buildings around a central courtyard; it had a thatched gabled roof and only one outer door. Clustered around this central complex were many smaller shrines and rooms for priests. Inside, it was beautifully decorated with gold objects, images of the main gods, and the bodies of deceased Incan kings. Adjoining the Temple was a great square where important ceremonies were held for the people, during which sacred objects were brought from the Temple and displayed there. The most sacred object in this temple was the immense golden disk with a human face in the center, the representation of the god Inti.

The high priest of the Sun in Cuzco was head of the hierarchy of priests in the empire. He was called Uillac Uma (the Highest Priest). Under him were ten Hatun Uillac, rather like bishops. Under these there were the Yana Uillac, the ordinary priests. The High Priest held the post for life, was married, and had great power rivaling that of the Emperor. He had power over all shrines and temples, and appointed priests. The other priests had the duties of divining, interpreting oracles, hearing confessions and giving penances, praying, interceding for the dead, performing sacrifices, presiding over a variety of rituals, and diagnosing and treating diseases. They may have been allowed to marry. Male priests officiated in most shrines.

There were priestesses in Cuzco and in other Incan temples who served shrines of the Moon and carried her silver image on special ceremonial occasions.

A group of Chosen Women also were consecrated to serve in the Sun temples; they were called the Aclla Cuna, or Virgins of the Sun. They formed an order under a high priestess. They were selected from young girls about ten years of age from all over the empire. Many of the Acllas were daughters of leading nobles. These girls were trained in convents called Aclla Huasi, mainly in Cuzco but also in a few other cities. From these Aclla Cuna were chosen the Mama Cunas, or superior officials. The Mama Cunas were teachers of the chosen Virgins. These Chosen Women were vowed to chastity.[1] They were all under the rule of the Coya Pacsa, a high priestess, who was considered the earthly wife of the god Inti, and who was chosen because of her noble birth.

After presentation of the new Acllas to the Emperor, they were divided into groups. The Virgins of the Sun had various functions. Some of them served in the temples (especially the cult of the Sun), some became Mama Cunas and were responsible for the education of the next generation of Acllas in the convents, some

An Incan coya

became sacrifices, and others were wed to the king or other important state officials.

The gesture of reverence before a deity or the Emperor was a low bow from the waist with outstretched arms above the head. The open hands were brought to the lips and the fingertips kissed loudly.

Prayers to the gods could be made silently, aloud, or with gestures. Traditional prayers were recited at important public ceremonies. Confession had to be made to a priest for sins, and penances done. Preparations for most ceremonies required cleansing and fasting, abstinence from meat, salt, spices, and sexual relations. Some animal sacrifices were done for divination and communication with the spirits. The priests did much chanting and chewing of coca leaves. Natural celestial phenomena and dreams were regarded as omens and analyzed.

The Capac Cocha or Hucha was the most sacred religious ceremony of the Incas. A sister of the king was sent to a conquered city in exchange for a daughter of the conquered ruler. This daughter became a Virgin of the Sun in the capital. After a period of time, though, the girl was returned to be sacrificed in the ceremonies of the Capac Cocha.

Huaca meant a sacred shrine; it also implied the deities connected with these shrines. The word was used to describe adobe pyramids, piles of stones, hills, and great temples; high mountains were especially sacred. Each Huaca was the dwelling place of spirits who required propitiation. There were said to be more than 350 Huacas around Cuzco, all on lines that radiated from the Temple of the Sun.

One of the private family rites that was important was the puberty rite. This took place for both boys and girls. When a girl had her first menstruation, she fasted for three days while her mother wove her a new outfit. On the fourth day she dressed in this new white garment, braided her hair, and took part in a two-day family feast. Her most important male relative gave her a new, permanent name[2] and gifts.

Celebration

The puberty ceremony for boys was called Huarachico; this occurred when they were about fourteen. It was held every year in Cuzco for the sons of noblemen. The great feast of Capac Raymi was held during the same month (December). This rite for boys was generally a mass public ceremony, in opposition to that of girls, which was private. During this ritual, the boys took part in endurance tests of running, mock battle, elaborate ceremonies, dancing, and sacrifices.

Sorcerers who practiced black magick were greatly feared by the Incas, as they had vast knowledge of poisons. These sorcerers began their spells by working sympathetic or suggestive magick, using hair, nails, amulets, figurines, and animal parts to create a general feeling of unease in their victims. If this did not work the desired results, the sorcerer went a step further by administering poison in a subtle manner. If he were caught and found guilty of these practices, he was killed.

Incan astronomers carefully observed the movements of the Sun, Moon, and stars. They learned to reconcile their twelve lunar months[3] with twelve solar months. For governmental and dating purposes, they used a solar calendar since their prime deity was a Sun god. The start of the agricultural year was calculated from the Sun's proximity to certain stone towers built on high locations to the west and east of Cuzco.[4]

The most important festivals were Inti Raymi (Feast of the Sun), winter solstice in June; Chahua-huarquiz, Chacra Ricuichic or Chacra Cona (Plowing Month) in July; Yapaquix, Chacra Ayapui or Capac Siquis (Sowing Month) in August; Coya Raymi in October; Ayamarca (Festival of the Dead) in November; Capac Raymi (Magnificent Festival) at December solstice; Camay quilla at the New Moon in January; Hatun-pucuy (Great Ripening) in February; Pacha-puchuy (Earth Ripening) in March at the autumn equinox; Ayrihua or Camay Inca Raymi (Festival of the Inca) in April; Aymoray quilla or Hatun Cuzqui (Great Cultivation) in May.

DRESS AND ORNAMENTATION

Incan clothing was made of alpaca or vicuna wool and was of very simple styling. Straight sides of rectangles were sewn together or held at the front with a knot or straight metal pins. Clothing had a variety of textures, weaves, and brilliant colors; ornate borders were made with gold thread and ornaments.

All adult males wore a breechcloth, which passed between the legs and was held front and back over a belt. Over this was worn a sleeveless knee-length tunic.

For special occasions, a series of decorated tunics were worn together. The priests had a long shirt tunic reaching the ground with a second robe over this. A cloak went over the outfit and was tied at the breast or over one shoulder. Sandals were worn by both sexes.

Males often added knee and ankle fringes; they wore jewelry to indicate rank. All men of royal lineage or "Incas by privilege" wore large cylindrical ear-plugs of gold, wood, or bone. Wide bracelets of gold and silver could be worn only by the highest officials. Feathers were also added to headdresses, collars, and clothing.

Incan women wore a long sleeveless dress fastened at the shoulders with pins. A long mantle hung from the neck to the feet. A very broad decorated sash was tied around the waist. Pins and necklaces were of gold, silver, copper, bronze, shell, or bone.

Incan dress

Headgear and hairstyling were extremely important as they indicated rank. Incan men had a fringe of hair over the forehead and a long bob behind and covering the ears. Beards were unknown. Women wore their hair parted in the middle and falling straight down or in two braids.

SOME OF THE MYTHS

The Incas say in their legends that the god Viracocha created the Earth, sky, and people, but no Sun in the beginning. But people disobeyed Viracocha so he decided to destroy them. The god raised a flood that drowned all but two, a man and a woman who hid in a box. When the water finally went down, the wind drove their box to Tihuanaco, the chief palace of Viracocha.

The god forgave the survivors and made many more different tribes of people out of clay. He gave them life and breath, their languages and songs, and seeds to sow. Then he sent them by underground routes to the land areas that they would inhabit. Each nation made a sacred place of the area where it emerged, mountain, caves, springs, etc.

Because it was still dark, Viracocha went on to create the Sun, Moon, and stars. He sent them into the heavens from Lake Titicaca. As the Sun arose from the island of Titicaca to its place in the heavens, it took the form of a man and called out to the Incan Manco Capa that he would become a great leader of a great people. The Sun told him further that he would conquer many nations, but Manco must worship the Sun as father. The Sun gave Manco a headdress and battle axe as a sign of this coming greatness.

After the Sun had been set in place, a large white man came from the south, a man of much power and knowledge. He instructed the people on how they should live, then went north into the highlands and disappeared. This was Viracocha. Some time later a similar man was seen. Everywhere this man went, he healed the sick and restored sight to the blind by words alone. The village of Cacha decided to stone him, but as they neared, he knelt and looked to the skies. A great fire came down from the heavens and scorched the Earth until the people begged him to cease. Then the man went on down to the seashore and, spreading his cloak, he moved out across the waves and was never seen again.

The Incan legend of the founding of Cuzco tells of three brothers and three sisters who emerged from a cave at Pacaritampo (camp of origin). They were well dressed in long blankets and colorful shirts of the finest wool; with them they carried gold vessels. One of the brothers was named Ayar Cachi; he was so strong that he could level hills with his sling and shoot rocks up to the clouds. In a fit of jealousy, the other brothers talked Ayar into going back into the cave for a gold goblet. Then they walled up the entrance with stones and went on to found the city of Tampo Kiru.[5]

Just as the consciences of the two brothers were beginning to bother them, they saw Ayar Cachi flying through the air wearing great wings of colored feathers and golden earrings. He told the frightened brothers that he came only to establish the empire of the Incas. He further instructed them to leave their settlement and go farther down the valley to the present site of Cuzco. There they were to found the capital city of the coming empire. Then he flew off to the hill called Huanacauri.

The brothers followed Ayar Cachi to the peak and were instructed by him as to who should be considered the nobles of their new empire; he also gave a variety of advice on other cultural laws. Then Ayar Cachi and one of the brothers turned into stone figures. The remaining brother took his three sisters and went down to the site for Cuzco. There he named himself Manco Capac, which means king and rich lord, and took his sisters as royal wives. Because of Manco's kind words and love, he attracted many people from surrounding clans to join him. When he finally died, a statue of him was placed in the Temple and he was worshipped as a child of the Sun.

The coastal people of Peru, subjects of the Incas, had a competing legend about the creation and perfection of humankind. Pachacamac was their supreme deity; his main sanctuary was in the valley of the Lurin to the south of Lima. These people said that Pachacamac renewed the world by changing the humans created by the god Viracocha. Pachacamac also taught humans the different arts and occupations needed for civilization to succeed. He may have originally been a fire god, for the Incas made him a son of the Sun,[6] the master of giants. His worship included the giving of mysterious oracles and human sacrifice. It was forbidden to make any images of this deity.

MAJOR GODS AND GODDESSES

AMARU—Mythical dragon; sometimes identified with the Earth Mother PACHAMAMA.[7]

APU PUNCHAU—"Head of the Day"; Sun God. Another name for the god INTI.

CHASCA—"The long-haired star (Venus)." Goddess who cared for princesses, girls, and flowers.

ILLAPA—Storm and weather god; pictured as a man with war club and sling.[8] Thunder and lightning.

INTI—Sun God of the ruling dynasty. He was represented by a great golden disk with a face,[9] but the Incas thought of him as having human form. Consort of MAMA QUILLA, the Moon goddess. The great annual festival of Inti Raymi was to celebrate the harvest of maize. Chanting lasted from sunrise to sunset with continual animal sacrifices. Fertility, crops.

MAMA COCHA—"Mother Sea"; worshipped especially along the Peruvian coast. Fishing.

MAMA QUILLA—"Mother Moon"; Moon Goddess; her image was a silver disk with a human face. Wife of the Sun god INTI. Although she had little worship, she was connected with the calendar and festivals.[10] Protectress of married women, the calendar, religious festivals.

MANCO CAPAC—Sun God; youngest son of the Sun; founder of Cuzco. Magick.

PACHACAMAC—"Lord of the Earth"; Supreme God; son of the Sun; god of Fire; Earth God. Pictured as a tall white man who worked miracles; also said to create earthquakes. Sacrifices of animals and humans were carried out every year to him, especially in his great temple in the city of Pachacamac.[11] Giver of the arts and occupations, oracles.

PACHAMAMA—"Earth Mother"; also represented by AMARU. Invoked in daily rites; presided over agriculture.

SUPAI—God of the Underworld and death. A hundred children were sacrificed every year to him. He was considered a greedy god, always wanting to increase the number of his subjects.

URCAGUARY—God of underground treasures. He was represented as a snake with a deer's head and a tail adorned with gold chains.

VIRACOCHA/HUIRACOCHA—The Creator; "Foam of the lake"; Great God; being without beginning or end. The Incas said he lived in heaven and maintained the world; however, they also thought he left many functions of the universe and humankind to lesser gods. He was portrayed in human form.[12] Giver of the arts of civilization. Sun, storm, lightning, oracles, languages, moral codes, rain, water, fertility.

Pachacamac

Incan cosmogram

ENDNOTES

1. If an Aclla was found guilty of sexual relations, she was buried alive. However, if she could prove she was pregnant, she was allowed to live as the child was automatically considered to be that of the Sun.
2. Girls were generally named after objects or abstract ideas, such as "gold" or "pure."
3. The lunar calendar may have been the first calendar of the Incas before their Sun god took control, as a great many of their religious ceremonies were oriented to the lunar cycle.
4. These towers were called *pacaomancaq*, or time-markers. The Sun rose from behind one of these towers on the first day of each month. This movement could be seen from the main square in Cuzco.
5. Another version of this legend tells that the youngest brother walled up the other two in order to remove them from his plans of building an empire.

6. The Incas said that the Sun god had three sons: Choun (one of the names of Viracocha), Pachacamac, and Manco Capac.

7. This dragon lived under the Earth and caused earthquakes. It also was considered present in the fire from volcanoes and in the landslides that occurred during the rainy season.

8. Mythology says that Illapa broke his sister's rain jug with his weapons. This action produced thunder and lightning. The Incas said that rain came from the "heavenly river," their name for the Milky Way.

9. He was represented in this form in all Incan Sun Temples. The immense disk in the great Temple of the Sun in Cuzco was taken by the Spaniards. The king was said to be the "Son of the Sun" and ruled by divine right; at death the king's body was mummified so that he could live forever with the wives and servants buried with him.

10. When an eclipse of the Moon occurred, it was said that a snake or a puma was trying to eat Mama Quilla. During these times, the Incas made threats and great noises to drive away the animals said to be attacking the Moon.

11. This great pyramid temple rivalled that of the Sun god and was a center for pilgrimages. Its ruins still cover about 12.5 acres and rise about 70 feet high.

12. In Cuzco there was a golden image of Viracocha. He was primarily worshipped by nobles as he was part of the official religion.

BIBLIOGRAPHY

Alexander, Hartley Burr. "Latin-American Mythology" in *The Mythology of All Races*. Boston, MA: J. A. MacCulloch, 1920.

Bandelier, A. F. A. *The Islands of Titicaca and Koati*. NY: The Hispanic Society of America, 1910.

Bierhorst, John. *The Mythology of South America*. NY: Wm. Morrow, 1988.

Bingham, Hiram. *Machu Picchu, Citadel of the Incas*. New Haven, CT: Yale University Press, 1930.

Brundage, Burr Cartwright. *Lords of Cuzco*. OK: University of Oklahoma Press, 1967.

Churchward, James. *The Children of Mu*. NY: Paperback Library, 1969.

Guerra, F. *The Pre-Columbian Mind*. UK: Seminar Press, no date.

Hemming, J. *The Conquest of the Incas*. NJ: Prentice-Hall, 1967.

Innes, H. *The Conquistadores*. UK: Thames & Hudson, 1970.

Kendall, Ann. *Everyday Life of the Incas*. NY: Putnam, 1973.

Lanning, E. *Peru Before the Incas*. NJ: Prentice-Hall, 1967.

Moore, S. Falk. *Power and Property in Inca Peru.* NY: Columbia University Press, 1958.

Osbourne, Harold. *South American Mythology.* NY: Peter Bedrick Books, 1986.

Reader's Digest. *The World's Last Mysteries.* NY: Reader's Digest Association, 1978.

Spence, Lewis. *The History of Atlantis.* NY: Bell Publishing, 1963.

Stirling, Matthew W. *National Geographic on Indians of the Americas.* Washington, D.C.: National Geographic, 1955.

Von Hassler, Gerd. *Lost Survivors of the Deluge.* NY: New American Library, 1976.

Willey, G. S. *Introduction to American Archaeology, Vol. 2, South America.* NJ: Prentice-Hall, 1972.

Zarate, Augustin de. *Discovery and Conquest of Peru (1555).* Trans. J. M. Cohen. NY: Penguin, 1968.

Chapter Twenty-seven

ANGELS AND ARCHANGELS

Traditional angel

A GREAT many cultures around the world have believed in beings that we call angels. These great helpers of humankind are described in nearly all the sacred books of the world religions. Among the ancient religions and races that believed in angels were the Egyptians, Romans, Greeks, Persians, Muslims, Japanese Shintoists, Jewish Qabalists, Hindus, and the Maoris. The deep teachings of the Jewish Qabala called them the "shining ones"; the Old and New Testaments and the apocryphal books of the Hebrews and Christians are full of references to these beings. Even the Arabic Koran tells of angels, especially the four main archangels. The Koran says that it is the responsibility of these archangels to watch over humankind from their vantage point near God's throne and record all their deeds.

Because the study and invocation of angelic beings are such integral parts of certain ancient cultures, and of Ceremonial Magick, I felt it was appropriate to have a separate chapter on these otherworld beings.

Some of the world's greatest thinkers and writers believed in angelic existence; references to angels can be found in the works of Socrates, Plato, St. Augustine,

Paracelsus, Thomas Moore, William Blake, Milton, Shakespeare, Pythagoras, Homer, St. Thomas Aquinas, Jacob Boehme, and Swedenborg.

In the Old and New Testaments of the Bible, angels were commonly written of as God's messengers. In fact, the Christians believed firmly in them until the First Council of Nicaea in AD 325 eliminated much of the writing about angels; apparently the early Christian power-holders were afraid that belief in the help and support of angels would lessen humankind's devotion to Jesus. For some reason, the apocryphal books managed to retain much of angelic reference.[1] In 1215 at the Lateran Council the Christian church returned to much of the recognition of the existence of angels.

The archangels and all classes of angels are considered spiritual, celestial beings said to be made of the Element of Fire,[2] or pure radiant energy. They are said to have evolved from a different line than humans.[3] In Rosicrucian and Illuminati writings, these celestial beings were further described as being like small suns with an aura of radiant energy that gives off streamers of force.[4]

In most descriptions this force is described as a brilliant light that comes from the crown of their head and encircles their form, giving them an appearance of having wings[5] of light. It was said that they propelled themselves by manipulation of this force-field. Ancient mystics were also unanimous in their denial that angels and other similar celestial beings had a totally human form, although they were often said to faintly resemble humankind. However, they did agree that strong negative emotions and passions tended to keep them away from humans.

The word angel (Hebrew, *malakh*) comes from the Sanskrit word *angiras*, a divine spirit; from the Persian *angaros*, a courier; and from the Greek *angelos*, a messenger or one sent. The meaning is actually closer to the Greek word *daimon*, a supernatural being who mediates between God and humans. The Hebrews derived their basic ideas of angels from the Persians and Babylonians during captivity. The term angel is generally used to indicate ministering spirits that are sent by God.

Archangel is a term applied to the pure spiritual-energy beings who have progressed to the top of the angelic hosts. In both Hebrew and Christian literature, archangels are listed as supreme beings, messengers of the Almighty God, defenders, teachers, and on occasion, punishers. Accepted archangels are Michael, Gabriel, Raphael, Uriel,[6] Raguel, Sandalphon, Haniel, Metatron, Barakiel, Jehudiel, Barbiel, Oriphiel, and Tzadkiel. Even the Koran recognizes the four main archangels under similar names: Mikhail, Jibril, Azrael, and Israfil. Often the names and/or their spelling change from source to source.

The Book of Revelation states there are three main classifications of the angelic kingdom: The Cloud of Silent Witnesses before the Throne, these being Seraphim,[7] Cherubim and Thrones; The Advanced Orders, these being Dominions, Principalities, Powers, and Virtues; The Ranks of the Angels, these being Archangels, Angel Princes, and all angels of specialized service and worship.

There are angels for the months: Gabriel (January), Barakiel (February), Malkiel (March), Asmodel (April), Ambriel (May), Muriel (June), Verchiel (July), Hamaliel (August), Uriel or Auriel (September), Barbiel (October), Adnachiel (November), and Haniel (December).

Zodiac angels are Malkiel (Aries), Asmodel (Taurus), Ambriel (Gemini), Muriel (Cancer), Verchiel (Leo), Hamaliel (Virgo), Uriel (Libra), Barbiel (Scorpio), Adnachiel (Sagittarius), Haniel (Capricorn), Gabriel (Aquarius), and Barakiel (Pisces).

Angels for the days of the week are Gabriel (Monday), Camael (Tuesday), Michael (Wednesday), Tzaphiel (Thursday), Haniel (Friday), Cassiel (Saturday), and Raphael (Sunday).

The acknowledgement of angelic beings is primarily used in Ceremonial Magick or in Christian or Metaphysical-Christian beliefs. In Ceremonial Magick, angelic beings are called upon for aid in rituals, in much the same manner as the gods. However, this type of magick sometimes also evokes the fallen angels.[8]

Angel from Doré Bible illustration

For most Ceremonial Magick, only five archangels are called upon. These are Raphael (east), Michael (south), Gabriel (west), Auriel (north), and Metatron (center). However, there are archangels and angels who deal in very specific areas and can be called upon for those activities.

The use of mystical alphabets and other secret codes originated with the Arabs; during the Middle Ages, they were renowned as magicians. It was not until the Arabs controlled Spain and this country became a center for the study and practice of magick and the occult that Western Europe branched beyond the secret runic alphabet it had always used. Toledo, Spain, had the only university at that time that taught magick and sorcery. In AD 855 the Arabic scholar Abu Bakir Ahmad first included magickal Arab scripts in his writings. This alphabet was based on Hebrew letters with certain changes. The Arabs often referred to this merely as *rihani* (magick) because of the power it contained. Several other alphabets and codes emerged in the Middle East. Then, in the thirteenth century, a Jewish Rabbi in Spain[9] wrote down the Qabala and paved the road to greater Western understanding of magick and its spiritual, as well as physical, uses.

Also in the thirteenth century lived Roger Bacon, a medieval alchemist and expert on magickal writings. In his book *Secret Works of Art and Magick*, he gave a list of seven codes for concealed writings of magickal texts; they were mostly composed of letters from ancient, dead languages or invented characters.

Several medieval magickal alphabets are still known and used today: the Theban or Honorian (named after the city of Thebes and the renegade Pope Honorious); Celestial; Malachim; Passing the River; the Enochian. (See Chapter Seven for some of these alphabets.) When Francis Barrett wrote his book *The Magus* in 1801 he included all of these alphabets; this book is available today.

Pages from The Book of Spirits, *according to Barrett*

However, one of the more famous alphabets, the Enochian or Angelic, came through the work of Dr. John Dee and Edward Kelly in England. John Dee (1527–1608) was an astrologer and mathematician during the rule of Queen Elizabeth I. He worked with the questionable Edward Kelly[10] because he had no personal mediumistic talents, but Kelly did. The crystal and waxen tablets used by Kelly and Dee are now owned by the British Museum.

This alphabet with its calls is said to be the most powerful there is. It is believed that these Enochian calls, or keys, can unlock the astral gateways to other dimensions and communications with spiritual beings. Dee considered this language to be so powerful that he wrote the names backwards to avoid calling up unwanted entities. The language was named after the Biblical Enoch.[11] The alphabet received its secondary name, Angelic, because of Dee's description that he was working with angels.

The Angelic or Enochian alphabet is still widely used by Ceremonial Magicians because of its power. Along with the other mentioned alphabets, or codes, it is used by a wide range of magickal practitioners for recording rituals, the results of magickal workings, or just sending messages.

ANGELIC AND ARCHANGELIC NAMES

ADNACHIEL/ADVACHIEL/ADERNAHAEL—Angel of November with rulership over Sagittarius. Alternates with PHALEG as ruling angel of the Order of Angels.

AMBRIEL/AMRIEL—Angel of May and prince of the Order of Thrones; dominion over Gemini. Cited for conjuring purposes under the Seventh Seal of Mars.

ASMODEL—Angel of April with rulership over Taurus. In the Coptic gnostic Pistic Sophia, he is listed as a demon of punishment. The Qabala listed him among the ten evil sephiroth.

AZRAEL/IZRAIL—The Angel of Death in Islamic mythology; one of the four archangels. This angel is not named in the Koran. Described as having four faces and four thousand wings. Although he is the Angel of Death, he does not know the date of a death.[12]

BARAKIEL/BARACHIEL/BARCHIEL/BARKIEL/BARAQIEL—One of the seven archangels, one of the four ruling Seraphim, angel of February, and prince of the Order of confessors. He has dominion over lightning; the ruler of Jupiter and Scorpio. Along with URIEL and RUBIEL, Barakiel is invoked for success in games of chance.

BARBIEL/BARBUEL/BARUEL—Angel of October and once a prince of the Order of Virtues and of the Order of archangels. In the underworld, Barbiel serves as one of the Seven Electors.

CAMAEL/CAMIEL/CAMIUL/CHAMUEL/KEMUEL/KHAMAEL/CAMNIEL/CANCEL—The Avenging Angel; Prince of Strength and Courage, his planet is Mars. Chief of the Order of Powers and one of the sephiroth. He is of the underworld; in Druid mythology he appears as the god of war. When invoked, he appears as a crouching leopard. His name personifies divine justice. Angel of vision of power, discretion, energy, courage, exorcism, purification, protection.

CASSIEL/CASIEL/CASZIEL/KAFZIEL—The angel of solitude and tears; one of the rulers of Saturn, a ruling prince of the Seventh Heaven, and one of the princes of the Order of Powers. He sometimes appears as the angel of temperance. Pictured as a bearded djinn on a dragon.

GABRIEL—Prince of Change, Alteration; Archangel of the Annunciation. One of the two highest angels. The ruling prince of Paradise, he sits on the left hand of God. He is the angel of annunciation, resurrection, mercy, vengeance, death, revelation, truth, hope. His planet is the Moon, his color blue. He rules Water and the West. Angel of visions, magick, clairvoyance, scrying, astral travel, herbal medicine. See JIBRIL.

Angelic talisman

Unnamed angel

HAMALIEL—Angel of August and Virgo, one of the rulers of the Order of Virtues.

HANIEL/ANIEL/HAMIEL/ONOEL/HANAEL—Prince of Love and Harmony, his planet is Venus. Angel of December and Capricorn; head of the Order of Principalities, Virtues, and innocents. He is invoked against evil. Angel of love, beauty, creativity, nature.

HARUT and MARUT—Two angels mentioned in the Koran in connection with Solomon (Suleiman). Fallen angels who chose to be punished in this world by being hung by their feet in a pit in Babil. Teachers of magick.

ISRAFIL—Archangel of Islamic mythology, but not mentioned in the Koran or the Traditions. Reads divine decrees to the other archangels. Called Lord of the Trumpet because he will sound the trumpet at the Day of Resurrection, thus bringing the dead back to life.[13] See RAPHAEL.

JEHUDIEL—Ruler of movements of celestial bodies.

JIBRIL/JABRAIL—Arabic version of GABRIEL; most popular of the Islamic angels. Said to have revealed the Koran to Muhammad.[14] Called the Faithful Spirit and the Supreme Spirit.

MALIK—To the Islamic culture the chief guardian angel of Hell. Mentioned in the Koran.

MALKIEL/MALCHIEL/MACHIDIEL/MALCHEDAEL—One of the numerous guardian angels of the gates of the South Wind.

METATRON/METRATTON/MITTRON/METARAON/MERRATON—Prince of Countenances; the Messenger; the Great Teacher. His color is white brilliance, and he rules the center or straight up, the Element of Spirit. The greatest of all the hierarchs; the first of the ten archangels of the Briatic world in Qabala. King of angels, prince of the presence, angel of the covenant, chief of the ministering angels. He is the link between human and divine. He appears as a pillar of fire, his face brighter than the Sun. His specialty is last minute intercession. Angel of completion of the Great Work, spiritual enlightenment, mystical illumination.

Hopi celestial being

MICHAEL/MIKHAIL—Prince of Splendor and Wisdom; Disperser of the Forces of Darkness. Ranks as the greatest of all angels in Jewish,[15] Christian, and Islamic[16] writings; one of the four great archangels who surround the throne of God, he stands on the right; ruler of Mercury. The Chaldeans worshipped him as a god. Chief of the Order of Virtues and archangels; prince of the presence; angel of repentance, righteousness, mercy, vengeance, sanctification, destruction, and defense. He is called the "Prince of Light" and the "leader of God's hosts." He rules the Element of Fire and the South; his color is

Qabilistic sign of Michael

red. Angel of truthfulness, intelligence, knowledge, divination, tarot, philosophy.

MURIEL/MURRIEL—Angel of June and Cancer. One of the rulers of the Order of Dominions.

RAPHAEL—Prince of Brightness, Beauty and Life. He also is of Chaldean origin. In Hebrew his name means "healing of God."[17] His planet is the Sun, his color yellow. He rules the Element of Air and the East. Angel of healing, harmony, balance, prosperity, success, honor, contacting your guardian angel.

RATZIEL/RAZIEL/AKRASIEL/BALLIZUR/SARAQAEL/SURIEL—Bright Angel of the Soul of Man; Prince of the Princes of the Knowledge of Hidden and Concealed Things. One of the ten archangels of the Briatic world of the Qabala. Chief of the Order of the Erelim; herald of deity. Angel of illumination, guidance, destiny.

SAMMAEL/SATINIL/SAMIL/SEIR/SALMAEL/SAMAEL—Angel of Death; prince of demons and magicians; regarded both as good and evil. The dark angel of death, temptation, severity, punishment, retribution, balance between good and evil.

SANDALPHON/SANDOLPHON/SANDOLFON—Prince of Prayer; the Dark Angel. One of the great angelic princes; twin brother of METATRON; master of heavenly song. Angel of prayers, vision of the guardian angel, stability, grounding, spirit evocation, guidance, protection.

SHAITAN—A fallen angel; the Arabic word for Satan, the Koran uses the word in both the singular and plural. Tempts humans to evil. His name is often used in place of that of the Devil, or Iblis in Arabic.

A fallen angel

TZADQUIEL/TSADKIEL/TZADKIEL/AZZA—Prince of Mercy, Justice, Beneficence. Rules the planet Jupiter and is among the guardians of the gates of the East Wind. Angel of vision of spiritual love, inner plane teaching, good fortune.

TZAPHIEL/TSAPHIEL—An angel of the Moon.

TZAPHKIEL/TZAPHQUIEL—Dark Angel of the Soul of Man; Prince of the Spiritual Strife Against Evil. Keeper of the records of evolution; mediates with the forces of karma. He rules the planet Saturn and is one of the archangels of the ten sephiroth. Angel of spiritual development, overcoming grief, balancing or changing karma.

URIEL/AURIEL/ORIEL—Prince of Knowledge and Truth; Angel of the Presence; Flame of God; Regent of the Sun; Archangel of Salvation; Heavenly Interpreter; Divine Light. ISRAFIL is his Arabic name. He rules the Element of Earth and the North;[18] his color is green. Angel of teaching, insight, stability, endurance, bringer of knowledge from God.

VERCHIEL/ZERACHIEL—Angel of July and Leo; one of the rulers of the Order of Powers.

Angelic ornament

ENDNOTES

1. For exact Biblical references, see the list in *Rediscovering the Angels* by Flower Newhouse.

2. Not to be confused with physical fire. See the chapter on Elements.

3. Blavatsky, H. P., in both *Isis Unveiled* and *The Secret Doctrine*.

4. Hall, Manly P. *The Secret Teachings of All Ages.*

5. Manly P. Hall writes that the ancient manuscripts say that these celestial beings inhabit the middle world between the gods and humans.

6. The four most important and powerful archangels who stand around the throne of God are Michael, Gabriel, Raphael, and Uriel.

7. The word Seraphs comes from the Hebrew root word meaning "love."

8. For more on this type of angelic beings, sometimes called a demon, see the chapter on Qabala.

9. See the chapter on the Qabala for more information.

10. His real name was Tabot; before he met Dee, he lost both his ears for dabbling in necromancy, but he did have mediumistic talents and was quite capable with a crystal ball or shew-stone.

11. Gerald Schueler in *Enochian Magic* goes into this subject in depth, even listing pronunciations.

12. It is said that "Izrail keeps the roll of humankind for God and that when God decides upon the date of a person's death, the angel has forty days to take away the soul." He was appointed because of his hardness of heart.

13. His name may come from the Hebrew word Seraphim. Described as huge in size, with his feet under the seventh earth and his head by the throne of God; four wings.

14. Other Arabic legends say that Jibril showed the site of Mecca to Adam, helped all the prophets, and announced to Zachariah the coming birth of John.

15. In Hebrew his name means "who is like God?" His name occurs three times in the Biblical book of Daniel, and once each in Jude and Revelation. Appears in the Talmud as the guardian angel of Israel.

16. Mikhail, or Mikal, in Arabic; his name appears in the Koran and in Islamic tradition where it says he protects Arab armies.

17. Does not appear in the Bible, but in the apocryphal book of Tobit. In the Talmud he is described as one of the four archangels who surround God's throne; he stands behind it and corresponds to the tribe of Ephriam.

18. In Hebrew this means "light of God." One of the four archangels around the throne, Uriel stands on the left, corresponding to the tribe of Dan in the north, according to the Talmud.

BIBLIOGRAPHY

A.H.E.H.O., Frater. *Angelic Images.* The Sorcerers Apprentice Press, 1984.

Bertiaux, Michael. *The Voudon Gnostic Workbook.* NY: Magickal Childe, Inc., 1988.

Blavatsky, H. P. *Isis Unveiled.* Pasadena, CA: Theosophical University Press, 1976.

Blavatsky, H. P. *The Secret Doctrine.* Wheaton, IL: Theosophical Publishing, 1979.

Causabon, Meric. *A True and Faithful Account of What Passed Between Dr. John Dee and Some Spirits* (originally published in 1659). UK: Askins, 1975.

Chappell, Helen. *The Waxing Moon: A Gentle Guide to Magick.* NY: Links Books, 1974.

Davidson, Gustav. *A Dictionary of Angels, Including the Fallen Angels.* NY: The Free Press, 1967.

Gray, William G. *Inner Traditions of Magic.* York Beach, ME: Samuel Weiser, 1984.

Hall, Manly P. *The Secret Teachings of All Ages.* Los Angeles, CA: Philosophical Research Society, 1977.

Howard, Michael. *Candle Burning: Its Occult Significance.* NY: Samuel Weiser, 1980.

Howard, Michael. *The Runes and Other Magical Alphabets.* UK: Aquarian Press, 1981.

Long, Max Freedom. *The Secret Science Behind Miracles.* Los Angeles, CA: Kosmon Press, 1948.

Mathers, S. L. MacGregor. *The Book of the Sacred Magic of Abramelin the Mage.* NY: Dover Publications, 1975.

Mathers, S. L. MacGregor. *The Grimoire of Armadel.* UK: Routledge & Kegan Paul, 1980.

McLean, Adam. *A Treatise on Angel Magic.* Grand Rapids, MI: Phanes Press, 1990.

Newhouse, Flower A. *The Kingdom of the Shining Ones.* Escondido, CA: The Christward Ministry, 1955.

Newhouse, Flower A. *Rediscovering the Angels.* Escondido, CA: The Christward Ministry, 1976.

Paulsen, Kathryn. *The Complete Book of Magic and Witchcraft.* NY: New American Library, 1970.

Schueler, Gerald J. *Enochian Magic: A Practical Manual.* St. Paul, MN: Llewellyn Publications, 1985.

Valiente, Doreen. *An ABC of Witchcraft Past and Present.* NY: St. Martins Press, 1973.

Chapter Twenty-eight

ELEMENTS AND ELEMENTALS

Hermetic circle, eighteenth century

THERE ARE four directions on the terrestrial plane—East, South, West, and North.[1] In magickal rituals these correspond to the four quarters of the universe, the zodiac, and the magick circle. As the first step in most magickal ceremonies, the four quarters and their rulers are invoked for power and protection. Specific parts of magickal ritual call to each elemental kingdom and its ruler to protect its quarter of the circle. Because of this ritual use, it is very important to understand completely what each Element is and does. Pagans, Witches, and Ceremonial Magicians all use the Elements. The Elements are also of vital importance to alchemists.[2]

All magick is primarily based on four Elements for spellworking. These are Earth, Air, Fire, and Water, which correspond to specific directions. The four Elements are actually four types of forces, energies, and substances that make up the universe and everything in it.[3] Science, with its limited knowledge, does not acknowledge these four Elements as building blocks in the same way that the magician does. However, science does agree that they exist, although scientists call them by other names.

When speaking of elementals, we do not mean creatures having total existence in the world of matter, because some of the Elements are not of a physical nature. Rather the Elements should be considered states of being. The Elements possess force as well as form, more like a tendency than an actual product. Each Element has certain qualities, natures, moods, and magickal purposes. Each can be called a kingdom; each has a ruler or king; each has positive and negative traits. Some cultures changed the descriptions of one or more of the Elements. Physical settings, such as climate, influenced the cultural belief of an Element's power; in Africa, the Sun and Fire were considered enemies.

When something has qualities like one of the Elements, it is said to be ruled by that Element. In other words, it is made of that ethereal, spiritual material. Most things in the visible world have qualities of more than one Element. Human personalities come under this multiple heading and are said to reflect the pattern of the soul by this action.

The elementals, sometimes called Nature spirits, are Earth, Fire, Air, and Water deities. This etheric world, which exists interpenetrating but separate from ours, can be seen with the "inner eyes" or perceived by "feelings." When speaking of the elementals, one does not mean the physical, chemical elements. The elementals are living spirit beings who are part of and can control the physical elements. They see, hear, and feel, although they have no physical organisms to register these senses as we do. They can mold the creative forces of the ethers to produce desired physical effects.

The elementals did not evolve along the same lines as humans, nor will they ever become human.[4] They do not intrude into any Element other than their own. Because they have only astral forms, they usually escape detection by physical senses but can be perceived by clairvoyant vision.

They can assume any likeness they want and generally match the picture imprinted in the human mind of those that are around at the time. Every country of the world has its fairy tales of elemental spirits. In the Qabala, they were known as the Shedim, which were further divided into four classes; to the Persians as devs; to the Greeks as daimons; to the Egyptians as afrites; to the people of India as the Daityas. Some African tribes called them Yowahoos.[5]

Sylph

Our names for specific elementals come primarily from Greek and Latin. In Greek *gnoma* (gnomes) meant knowledge or the knowing ones. *Unda* (undine) in Latin meant wave, creatures of the waves. The Greek word *silphe* (sylph) was a butterfly or being with gauzy wings. *Salambe* (salamander) in Greek described a fireplace; however, the actual being was more like a very small dragon, sometimes called a fire drake.

Elementals tend to take on racial characteristics; it would be highly unusual for a Chinese to see an elemental looking like an African. They also can take on mental characteristics of a person, such as the wild forms seen by alcoholics or drug users.

They usually take little notice of humans but do respond to harmonious and loving thoughts. They take varying forms from very tiny to quite large, usually having some human likeness about them. If provoked, they become very mischievous. If one believes in the "little people," if one loves them and works with them in harmony, they will in turn love and help you.

Gnomes

There are other types of elementals that are thought-forms, created by thoughts; these can be both positive and negative, depending upon the original thoughts. Undesirable spirits are often creations of the people they are around.

However, the Nature elementals are the ones that concern us here. The Earth spirits are called gnomes, dwarfs, and trolls; the Air spirits sylphs, zephyrs, and fairies; the Fire spirits salamanders and fire drakes; the Water spirits undines and nymphs. They do not suffer from sickness but do react to violence. If they feel that they are not loved or appreciated, it hurts them, and they move away. They can cooperate with each other but cannot merge into Elements other than their own. Fire cannot perform tasks dealing with Water or Air powers, for instance.

Earth elementals are entrusted with the Earth's mineral treasures and can be wooed to help you financially. Gnomes often appear with long beards, caps, tight leg coverings, and a jerkin or tunic. They are steady, stubborn, but very practical.

Water elementals are seen as nymphs, undines, mermen, and mermaids, and winged fairies around plants. They produce the essence of plant life for abundant growth and are closely associated with the healing of plants, animals, and humans. They also will cooperate easily with Earth elementals for prosperity. These creatures are sensitive but persistent, doing whatever is necessary to reach a goal.

Air elementals are sylphs, zephyrs, and another type of winged fairy that is seen in high mountainous areas. They are powerful, mysterious, wispy creatures of constantly changing form. These beings are seen in breezes or storms and are an unlimited source of inspiration, knowledge, and new ideas.

Fire elementals are seen in and around hearth fires, candles, forest fires, etc. They are the least interested in humans, but can help in clearing out obstacles, both psychic or psychological. These beings are usually small but can become enormous around huge fires. They are also the most mischievous of the elementals, especially if the place where they are has vibrations of inharmony or upset.

In initiations, both ritual and physical, Water elementals are involved for tests of emotion, Air for strengthening of the mental, Earth for freeing from the lower physical nature, and Fire for tests of love.

Statues, amulets, talismans, and sometimes specific places often have elementals attached to them, hence the story of the genie of the lamp or ring. Elementals attached to jewelry, for instance, can bring good luck to the owner if he or she treats that jewelry with love and respect.

The Tattwas

Excellent symbols to use for visualization of the Elements or Nature elementals are the Tattwas from India. These geometric symbols of the magickal Elements are plain, unadorned, basic and primitive, with a deep meaning to the subconscious mind. They can be used separately or together, as in the illustration.

The Tattwas symbols are called Prithivi for the Earth element and the North, and is a yellow square; Apas for Water and the West, a silver crescent; Vayu for Air and the East, a blue circle; Tijas for Fire and the South, a red triangle; Akasha for Spirit and the Center, a black or indigo ovoid.

Various cultures around the world assigned specific colors and symbols to the Elements, not always the same ones. The Celtic myths speak of the "castles of the four winds" that are guarded by Arianrhod; their colors were east, red; south, white; west, grey; north, black. Norse tradition says that Odhinn set four Dwarves to hold up the sky: Nordhri (North, ruling ice), Austri (East, ruling air), Sudhri (South, ruling fire), and Vestri (West, ruling water).

Enochian and Qabalistic magicians consider that the four main Hebrew archangels guard the quarters: Raphael, air; Michael, fire; Gabriel, water; Uriel, earth. The quarters in Hebrew are Yamin, south or right; Kedem, east or front; Shemal, north or left; Achor, west or behind. Each Enochian "Castle" is associated with a color: east, red; south, white; west, green; north, black.

Among the ancient Mayas, four deities called Bacabs held up the sky aided by trees: east, red; south, yellow; west, black; north, white. In ancient Mexico's other cultures, north was red, fire; west, yellow, earth; south, blue, air; east, green, water; and the center many colors.

China said that the four cardinal points were the Black Warrior, White Tiger, Vermillion Bird, and Azure Dragon; but they also spoke of the Four Hidden Dragons of Wisdom.[6] Talbott, however, writes that the Chinese used north, black, water, winter; west, white, metal, autumn; south, red, fire, summer; east, green, wood, spring; center, yellow, earth.

Native American tradition has several versions of this directional description, depending upon the writer and the tribe. In *Teaching Around the Sacred Wheel,* Andrews lists east, yellow (eagle); south, red (mouse); west, black (bear); north, white (buffalo). Sun Bear and Wabun, in *The Medicine Wheel,* do not list colors but say that each direction has a Spirit Keeper who brings wind and is responsible for teaching Earth's children: east, Wabun; south, Shawnodese; west, Mudjekeewis; north, Waboose. The Navaho say that the colors are east, white; south, blue; west, yellow; north, black. The Cheyenne of the Plains use red, yellow, white, and black instead.[7] The Zuni says that air is yellow; water, blue; fire, red; earth, white; and the center all colors.

AIR

Rulers: sylphs, zephyrs, and fairies who inhabit the world of winds, breezes, mountains.

Archangel: Raphael.

King: Paralda.

Supreme Elemental Kings: Tahoeloj.[8]

Demon King: Orions.

Property: hot and moist.

Plane: mental.

Senses: smell.

Tattwas: Vayu, blue circle.

Tarot Suit: swords.

Qabalistic World: Yetzirah, Formative World.

Attracted By: oils and incenses.

Color and Direction: yellow, East.

Astrological Signs: Gemini, Libra, Aquarius.

Magickal Tools: wand, dagger, incense, creative visualization.

Alchemical allegory for Air

Symbols: sky, wind, breezes, clouds, the breath, vibrations.

Ritual Work: dawn, sunrise, spring, knowledge, inspiration, hearing, harmony, herbal knowledge, plant growth, intellect, thought, ideas, travel, freedom, revealing the truth, finding lost things, movement, psychic abilities.

FIRE

Rulers: salamanders and fire drakes, the consciousness of flames.

Archangel: Michael.

King: Djin.

Supreme Elemental King: Ohoohotan.

Demon King: Paimon.

Property: hot and dry.

Plane: spiritual.

Senses: sight.

Tattwas: Tijas, red triangle.

Tarot Suit: wands.

Elemental fire

Qabalistic World: Atziluth, Archetypal World.

Attracted By: candles, lamps, incense burner, fire.

Color and Direction: red, South.

Astrological Signs: Aries, Leo, Sagittarius.

Magickal Tools: lamp or candles, incense burner, images, burned herbs, or requests on paper.

Symbols: fire, lightning, volcanoes, rainbow, Sun, stars, blood.

Ritual Work: summer, noon, freedom, change, sight, perception, vision, illumination, learning, love, will, passion, sexuality, energy, authority, healing, destruction, purification.

WATER

Mermaid

Rulers: nymphs, undines, mermen, and mermaids who live in the sea, lakes, streams, and springs, and fairies of plants.

Archangel: Gabriel.

King: Niksa or Necksa.

Supreme Elemental King: Thahebyobeaatan.

Demon King: Ariton.

Property: cold and moist.

Plane: astral.

Senses: taste.

Tattwas: Apas, silver crescent.

Tarot Suit: cups.

Qabalistic World: Briah, Creative World.

Attracted By: water, washes, solutions.

Color and Direction: blue, West.

Astrological Signs: Cancer, Scorpio, Pisces.

Magickal Tools: chalice, water, the sea, mirrors, cauldron.

Symbols: ocean, lakes, rivers, wells, springs, pools, rain, mist, fog.

Ritual Work: fall, sunset, plants, healing, emotions, taste, smell, absorbing, communion with the spiritual, purification, the subconscious mind, love, emotions, pleasure, friendships, marriage, fertility, happiness, sleep, dreams, the psychic.

Earth

Rulers: gnomes, dwarves, and trolls who inhabit the interior of the Earth and are the consciousness of precious gems, minerals, and the Earth itself.

Archangel: Auriel or Uriel.

King: Ghom, Ghob or Gob.

Supreme Elemental King: Tha-haaotahe.

Demon King: Amaimon.

Property: cold and dry.

Plane: physical.

Senses: touch.

Tattwas: Prithivi, yellow square.

Tarot Suit: pentacles, or disks.

Qabalistic World: Assiah, Material World.

Attracted By: salts and powders.

Color and Direction: green, North.

Astrological Signs: Taurus, Virgo, Capricorn.

Magickal Tools: pentacle, salt, images, gems, trees, cord magick.

Earth as medium between light and darkness

Symbols: rocks and gemstones, mountains, plains, fields, soil, caves, and mines.

Ritual Work: winter, midnight, riches, surrendering self-will, touch, empathing, incorporation, business, prosperity, employment, stability, success, fertility, money.

Fifteenth century personifications of Fire, Air, Water, and Earth

A fifth Element is sometimes given as Spirit. This corresponds to the center of the magickal circle and the altar which is placed there. This Element is said to be pure aethyr and has no elementals attached to it, unless one considers the archangels and angels as elementals.

SPIRIT

Infinity symbol

Rulers: archangels and angels.

Archangel: Metatron.

Color and Direction: white brilliance, the Center or straight up.

Magickal Tools: incense, secret forces.

Symbols: infinity, the cosmos, god-head, the creator.

Ritual Work: enlightenment, finding your life path, spiritual knowledge, seeing and understanding karmic paths in life.

ENDNOTES

1. The Elements used in magick are not the same as the elements spoken of in scientific circles. Existence of the Elements cannot be proved in scientific terms and conditions, but that does not invalidate them. For centuries scientists could not see bacteria or viruses; that did not mean that they were not there. Anyone who has ever experienced the presence of beings from an elemental plane, such as Nature spirits or even ghosts, does not require a scientific paper so he/she can believe in them.

2. Buckland, Raymond. *Anatomy of the Occult.* Alchemists did not call themselves by that name, but instead referred to themselves as philosophers and sages, their science as philosophy. No one knows for certain where the word alchemy came from, but Wallis Budge suggests that the Arabic word *al* was added to the Egyptian word *khemeia* to mean "the preparation of the black ore." Lewis Spence suggests the Arabic word *al* (the) and *kimya* (chemistry). Cavendish, in *The Black Arts,* writes that alchemy was used to transmute base metals into gold, create the elixir of life, produce the philosopher's stone which could transmute metals, and the transmutation of ordinary life into greater spiritual awareness.

3. Ancient occult philosophers stated that all life was made of these Elements and could not exist otherwise.

4. Blavatsky, H. P. *Isis Inveiled*. Blavatsky says that elementals are composed of sublimated material with a rudimentary mind. The rudimentary mind is true of some of them, but many others seem to have evolved mentally along with humans.

5. Blavatsky. Ibid.

6. Blavatsky, H. P. *The Secret Doctrine*. However, other sources list different guardians and colors.

7. Steiger, Brad. *Indian Medicine Power*.

8. Crowley, Aleister. 777. The Supreme Elemental Kings, the Qabalistic Worlds, and the Demon Kings are all from Crowley's writings.

BIBLIOGRAPHY

Andrews, Lynn. *Flight of the Seventh Moon: The Teaching of the Shields*. San Francisco, CA: Harper & Row, 1984.

Andrews, Lynn. *Teachings Around the Sacred Wheel*. NY: Harper & Row, 1990.

Barrett, Francis. *The Magus*. Secaucus, NJ: Citadel Press, 1980.

Bias, Clifford. *Ritual Book of Magic*. NY: Samuel Weiser, 1981.

Briggs, Katharine. *An Encyclopedia of Fairies*. NY: Pantheon Books, 1976.

Buckland, Raymond. *Anatomy of the Occult*. NY: Samuel Weiser, 1977.

Butler, W. E. *The Magician: His Training and Work*. UK: Aquarian Press, 1969.

Cavendish, Richard. *The Black Arts*. NY: G.P. Putnam's Sons, 1967.

Conway, D. J. *Celtic Magic*. St. Paul, MN: Llewellyn Publications, 1990.

Conway, D. J. *Norse Magic*. St. Paul, MN: Llewellyn Publications, 1990.

Crowley, Aleister. *The Book of Thoth*. York Beach, ME: Samuel Weiser, 1981.

Crowley, Aleister. *777 and Other Qabalistic Writings*. York Beach, ME: Samuel Weiser, 1986.

Cunningham, Scott. *Cunningham's Encyclopedia of Crystal, Gem and Metal Magic*. St. Paul, MN: Llewellyn Publications, 1990.

Cunningham, Scott. *Earth Power*. St. Paul, MN: Llewellyn Publications, 1983.

Cunningham, Scott. *Magical Herbalism*. St. Paul, MN: Llewellyn Publications, 1982.

Gray, William G. *Inner Traditions of Magic*. York Beach, ME: Samuel Weiser, 1984.

Healki, Thomas. *Creative Ritual*. York Beach, ME: Samuel Weiser, 1986.

Howard, Michael. *Candle Burning: Its Occult Significance.* NY: Samuel Weiser, 1980.

Howard, Michael A. *The Runes and Other Magical Alphabets.* UK: Aquarian Press, 1981.

Knight, Gareth. *The Rose Cross and the Goddess.* NY: Destiny Books, 1985.

Kraig, Donald Michael. *Modern Magick: Eleven Lessons in the High Magickal Arts.* St. Paul, MN: Llewellyn Publications, 1989.

Manning, Al G. *Helping Yourself with White Witchcraft.* West Nyack, NY: Parker Publishing, 1972.

Mathers, S. L. MacGregor. *The Book of the Sacred Magic of Abramelin the Mage.* NY: Dover Publications, 1975.

Raphael. *Raphael's Ancient Manuscript of Talismanic Magic.* Chicago, IL: The deLaurence Co., 1916.

Richardson, Alan. *Gate of Moon.* UK: Aquarian Press, 1984.

Schueler, Gerald J. *Enochian Magic: A Practical Manual.* St. Paul, MN: Llewellyn Publications, 1985.

Seleneicthon. *Gods, Spirits and Daemons.* Hialeah, FL: Mi-World, no date.

Steiger, Brad. *Indian Medicine Power.* Gloucester, MA: Para Research, 1984.

Stewart, R. J. *Living Magical Arts.* UK: Blandford Press, 1987.

Sun Bear and Wabun. *The Medicine Wheel.* Englewood Cliffs, NJ: Prentice-Hall, 1980.

Talbott, David N. *The Saturn Myth.* NY: Doubleday, 1980.

Thorsson, Edred. *Futhark: A Handbook of Rune Magic.* York Beach, ME: Samuel Weiser, 1984.

Uyldert, Mellie. *Metal Magic: The Esoteric Properties and Uses of Metals.* UK: Turnstone Press, 1980.

Valiente, Doreen. *An ABC of Witchcraft.* NY: St. Martin's, 1973.

Valiente, Doreen. *Natural Magic.* Custer, WA: Phoenix Publishing, 1985.

Chapter Twenty-nine

PLANETS

Detail from title page of Egypto-Persian Book of Planets, *1890*

THE PLANETS are used primarily for performing ceremonies or rituals on certain days and in certain hours. If this is to be part of your ritual methods, I suggest you carefully read the charts for both day and night planetary hours. (See Chapter Four.) Remember to adjust for daylight savings time.

The idea behind using planetary days and hours is that you are connecting with a stronger energy for use in your ritual work. As the Elements are the substance of the universe, the planets are more concerned with action and process. Only seven astrological bodies are used: Sun, Moon, Mercury, Venus, Mars, Jupiter, and Saturn. These correspond to the days of the week and the hours of each day. To use this system, find the planet that corresponds to the type of ritual you plan to do. Then select the proper day and hour in which to do it.

The waxing and waning Moon should also be taken into account. The waxing or increasing Moon is the time for spells of increase, building, growth; the waning or decreasing Moon is a time for decrease, destruction, removal, binding.

It is not absolutely necessary to use the Elements, the lunar phases, Angels, or planets in preparing for ritual, but taking their powers into consideration certainly enhances the flow of power and your success ratio. They provide a convenient system of classification and association.

The seven planets, 1536

We know that as long ago as the Persian Mithraic Mysteries the planets were used in the same method of power and correspondence as they were later in the Qabalistic practices. The magickal descriptions of the planets used today have been taken from the Qabalists. References to the planets are also found in the ancient writings of Hermes Trismegistus. The planetary influences were, and are, considered as archetypes of power, reservoirs of energy that can be used by any magician when correctly called upon.

The prime reason for using the planetary influences in magick is to sharpen the magician's focus on manifestation of a desired result. By drawing upon all areas of power, the magician is guaranteed a higher rate of success in his workings.

The following planetary tables list many items that may not be used by a magician in every ritual. However, by having the information consolidated in one place, the practicing magician can more easily work his/her magick without wasted effort.

SUN

Day: Sunday.

Godforms: Horus, Ra, Apollo, Bast, Sekhmet, Lugh, Bel, Adonis.

Description: the Great God.

Archangel: Raphael.

Angels: Malachim, the Kings.

Spirits: Sorath and Och.[1]

Intelligence: Nakhiel.

Sephirah: Tiphareth.

God Name: Jehovah Eloah va-Daath.

Color: yellow or gold.

Tarot: the Sun, the four sixes.

Metal: gold.

Stones: zircon, jacinth, goldstone, topaz, yellow diamond, chrysoleth.

Wood: laurel.

Plants: acacia, almond, ash, bay, chamomile, centaury, heliotrope, marigold, meadow rue, mistletoe, rosemary, rue, St. Johnswort, storax, sunflower, tormentil, vine, walnut.

Rules: Leo.

Sun as God

Incense/Oil: Egyptian Kyphi, heliotrope, orange blossom, cloves, frankincense, ambergris, musk, mastic, cinnamon, vanilla.

Animal: lion, hawk, phoenix.

Rituals Involving: health, healing, confidence, hope, prosperity, vitality, personal fulfillment, immediate family, life-energy, money, favor, honor, promotion, success, support of those in power, friendships, creativity, active change.

MOON

The man in the Moon

Day: Monday.

Godforms: Isis, Khensu, Neith, Diana, Hecate, Selene, Luna, Morrigu.

Description: Astral Plane, the Silver Huntress, Maiden of the Mysteries, the Mother, Queen of Heaven.

Archangel: Gabriel.

Angels: the Kerubim, the Strong.

Spirits: Chasmodai and Phul.

Intelligence: Malkiel.

Sephirah: Yesod.

God Name: Shaddai El Chai.

Color: lavender, silver, blue, pearl-white.

Tarot: the High Priestess, the four nines.

Metal: silver.

Stones: moonstone, quartz crystal, beryl, pearl.

Wood: willow.

Plants: clary, cleavers, cucumber, dogstooth violet, orris, iris, lily, moonwort, mugwort, white poppy, white rose, wallflower, water lily, willow.

Rules: Cancer.

Incense/Oils: white poppy, white rose, myrtle, mugwort, camphor, galbanum, lily, jasmine, lotus.

Animal: hare, hart, boar, dog, horse, elephant.

Rituals Involving: travel, visions, divinations, dreams, magick, love, agriculture, domestic life, medicine, luck, feminine aspects, water, birth, time, theft, emotions, reflection, passive manifestation, formation of emotions.

MERCURY

Mercury

Day: Wednesday.

Godforms: Mercury, Thoth, Hermes, Anubis, Maat, Odhinn, Ogma.

Description: Messenger of the Gods.

Archangel: Michael.

Angels: the Beni Elohim, the Sons of the Gods.

Spirits: Taphthartharath and Ophiel.

Intelligence: Tiriel.

Sephirah: Hod.

God Name: Elohim Tzabaoth.

Color: orange, violet, multi-colored, pale yellow.

Tarot: the Magician, the four eights.

Metal: quicksilver, alloys.

Stones: carnelian, fire opal, agate.

Wood: hazel.

Plants: fennel, vervain, marjoram.

Rules: Gemini, Virgo.

Incense/Oils: storax, mastic, white sandalwood.

Animal: ibis, twin serpents, ape, swallow, jackal.

Rituals Involving: intellect, memory, science, creativity, business, magickal conjurations, divination, prediction, eloquence, gift of tongues, speed, speech, writing, poetry, inspiration, improvement of mind power, healing of nervous disorders, reflective thought.

VENUS

Day: Friday.

Godforms: Venus, Aphrodite, Astarte, Hathor, Freyja.

Description: the Great Mother.

Archangel: Haniel.

Angels: the Elohim, the Gods.

Spirits: Kedemel and Hagith.

Intelligence: Hagiel.

Sephirah: Netzach.

God Name: Jehovah Tzabaoth.

Color: green, light blue, pale green, pink.

Tarot: the Empress, the four sevens.

Metal: copper.

Stones: amber, malachite, jade, peridot, coral, emerald, turquoise.

Wood: myrtle.

Plants: roses, birch, blackberry, bugle, burdock, catnip, coltsfoot, columbine, cowslip, daffodil, daisy, devils bit, dittany of Crete, elder, feverfew, foxglove, geranium, marshmallow, mugwort, orchis, pennyroyal, plantain, primrose, strawberry, thyme, vervain, violet, yarrow.

Venus

Rules: Taurus, Libra.

Incense/Oils: apple blossom, musk, verbena, damiana, rose, benzoin, red sanders.

Animal: dove, sparrow, swan, lynx, leopard, cats.

Rituals Involving: love, marriage, friendship, pleasure, beauty, artistic creativity, imagination, fertility, partnerships, sex, spiritual harmony, compassion, children, emotions, instincts.

MARS

The Tower

Day: Tuesday.

Godforms: Horus, Ares, Mars, Tyr.

Description: the Warrior God.

Archangel: Khamael or Camael.

Angels: Seraphim, the Fiery Serpents.

Spirits: Bartzabel and Phalegh.

Intelligence: Graphiel.

Sephirah: Geburah.

Color: red.

Tarot: the Tower, the four fives.

Metal: iron, steel.

Stones: garnet, bloodstone, red agate, ruby, red topaz.

Wood: cedar.

Plants: nettles, thistle, broom, chives, coriander, dragons blood, galangal, garlic, ginger, holy thistle, honeysuckle, hops, onions, peppers, pine, squill, tarragon, tobacco, woodruff, wormwood.

Rules: Aries, Scorpio.

Incense/Oils: tobacco, pepper, dragon's blood.

Animal: wolf, ram, bear, horse, basilisk.

Rituals Involving: energy, courage, battle, conflict, death, masculinity, surgery, physical strength, opposition, defense, endurance, destruction, conflicting manifestation.

JUPITER

Marduk

Day: Thursday.

Godforms: Jupiter, Zeus, Amen, the Dagda, Thorr, Marduk.

Description: the Greater Benefic.

Archangel: Tzadkiel.

Angels: Chasmalim, the Brilliant Ones.

Spirits: Hismael and Bethor.

Intelligence: Iophiel.

Sephirah: Chesed.

God Name: El.

Color: blue, purple.

Tarot: Wheel of Fortune, the four fours.

Metal: tin.

Stones: lapis lazuli, amethyst, turquoise, sapphire.

Wood: pine.

Plants: cedar, oak, cinnamon, cloves, balm of Gilead, betony, cinquefoil, carnation, costmary, dandelion, fir, grains of paradise, ladys thistle, linden, meadowsweet, myrrh, pinks, roses, sage, verbena.

Rules: Sagittarius, Pisces.

Incense/Oils: lilac, storax, aloes, nutmeg, cedar, saffron.

Animal: eagle, unicorn.

Rituals Involving: honor, riches, health, friendships, the heart's desires, luck, accomplishment, religion, trade and employment, treasure, legal matters, harmony, beneficial change.

SATURN

Day: Saturday.

Godforms: Saturn, Cronus, Nephthys, Isis, Demeter, Ceres, Nut, Cerridwen, Danu, Hecate.

Description: the Great Taskmaster, Father of the Gods, the God of Time, the Silent Watcher, the Wise One, the Taskmaster of the Zodiac.

Archangel: Tzaphiel.

Angels: Aralim, the Thrones.

Spirits: Zazel and Arathor.

Intelligence: Agiel.

Sephirah: Binah.

God Name: Jehovah Elohim.

Color: black, indigo.

Tarot: the Universe or World, the four threes.

Metal: lead.

Stones: onyx, jet, pearl, star sapphire.

Wood: oak.

Plants: cypress, yew, beech, comfrey, elm, fumitory, hemp, holly, horsetail, ivy, juniper, mullein, oak gall, patchouli, poplar, rushes, sloe, solomons seal.

Saturn

Rules: Capricorn, Aquarius.

Incense/Oils: pepperwort, black poppy seeds, myrrh, civet, storax.

Animal: ass, goose, dragon, crocodile, goat.

Rituals Involving: knowledge, familiars, death, reincarnation, protecting buildings, binding, overcoming curses, protection in general, retribution, duties, responsibilities, influences, doctrines, intuition, thought formation.

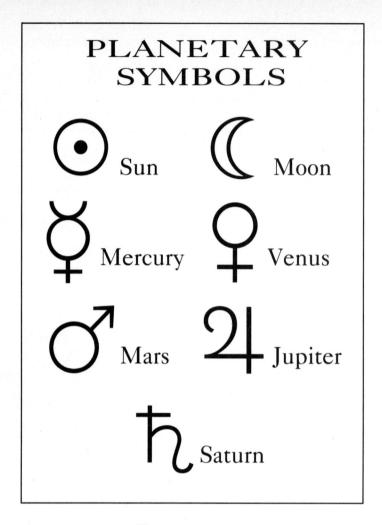

PLANETARY SYMBOLS

Sun

Moon

Mercury

Venus

Mars

Jupiter

Saturn

ENDNOTES

1. Crowley, Aleister. 777.

BIBLIOGRAPHY

Barrett, Francis. *The Magus*. Secaucus, NJ: Citadel Press, 1980.

Bias, Clifford. *Ritual Book of Magic*. NY: Samuel Weiser, 1981.

Beyerl, Paul. *The Master Book of Herbalism*. Custer, WA: Phoenix Publishing, 1984.

Cavendish, Richard. *The Black Arts*. NY: G.P. Putnam's Sons, 1967.

Conway, David. *Magic: An Occult Primer*. NY: E.P. Dutton & Co., 1972.

Corrigan, Ian. *The Book of the Dragon: A New Grimoire*. Publisher unknown, 1982.

Crowley, Aleister. *The Book of Thoth*. York Beach, ME: Samuel Weiser, 1981.

Crowley, Aleister. *777 and Other Qabalistic Writings of Aleister Crowley*. York Beach, ME: Samuel Weiser, 1986.

Crowther, Patricia. *Lid Off the Cauldron*. York Beach, ME: Samuel Weiser, 1985.

Cunningham, Scott. *Cunningham's Encyclopedia of Magical Herbs*. St. Paul, MN: Llewellyn Publications, 1985.

Cunningham, Scott. *Magical Herbalism*. St. Paul, MN: Llewellyn Publications, 1982.

Davidson, Gustav. *A Dictionary of Angels, Including the Fallen Angels*. NY: The Free Press, 1967.

Denning, Melita, and Phillips, Osborne. *Magical States of Consciousness*. St. Paul, MN: Llewellyn Publications, 1985.

Denning, Melita, and Phillips, Osborne. *Planetary Magick*. St. Paul, MN: Llewellyn Publications, 1989.

Dey, Charmaine. *The Magic Candle*. Bronx, NY: Original Publications, 1982.

Farrar, Stewart. *What Witches Do*. Custer, WA: Phoenix Publishing, 1983.

George, Llewellyn. *The Planetary Hour Book*. St. Paul, MN: Llewellyn Publications, 1975.

Healki, Thomas. *Creative Ritual*. York Beach, ME: Samuel Weiser, 1986.

Howard, Michael. *The Prediction Book of Practical Magic*. NY: Sterling Pub./Javelin Books, 1988.

Huson, Paul. *Mastering Witchcraft*. NY: G. P. Putnam's Sons, 1970.

Manning, Al G. *The Magic of New Ishtar Power*. West Nyack, NY: Parker Publishing, 1977.

New Age Fellowship. *Candle Burning Rituals*. UK: Finbarr International, 1983.

Parfitt, Will. *The Living Qabalah*. UK: Element Books, 1988.

Paulsen, Kathryn. *The Complete Book of Magic and Witchcraft*. NY: New American Library, 1970.

Riva, Anna. *Magic With Incense and Powders*. N. Hollywood, CA: International Imports, 1985.

Riva, Anna. *Modern Herbal Spellbook*. Toluca Lake, CA: International Imports, 1974.

Riva, Anna. *Secrets of Magical Seals: A Modern Grimoire of Amulets, Charms, Symbols and Talismans*. Toluca Lake, CA: International Imports, 1983.

Rose, Donna. *Magic of Astrology*. Hialeah, FL: Mi-World, 1978.

Rose, Donna. *Magic of Candle Burning*. Hialeah, FL: Mi-World, 1981.

Rose, Donna. *The Magic of Spells and Curses.* Hialeah, FL: Mi-World, 1984.

Rose, Donna. *Money Spells.* Hialeah, FL: Mi-World, 1978.

Seleneicthon. *Daybook of Ancient Spells.* Hialeah, FL: Mi-World, 1983.

Tarostar. *A Witch's Formulary and Spellbook.* Bronx, NY: Original Publications, no date.

Vinci, Leo. *Incense: Its Ritual Significance, Use and Preparation.* NY: Samuel Weiser, 1980.

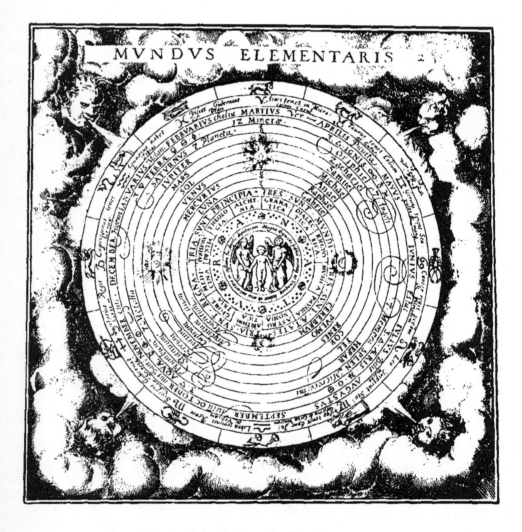

Alchemical cosmic diagram

SUMMARY

HOPEFULLY, THROUGH reading this book, you have explored new horizons and entered new doors of thought, of experience, of growth. As long as one continues to do these things, one continues to progress spiritually. And the upward spiral of spiritual growth is what each of us aspires to, even if that aspiration is only on the subconscious level.

The Ancient and Shining Ones was never meant to be the only book for someone to read. Rather, it was written as a sort of "appetizer," a spring-board to other, more detailed books. It is my hope that this book will remain on shelves as a well-used ready-reference volume for years to come. If I have succeeded in this, I have fulfilled my goal.

May the blessings of the Ancient Ones fill your life with joy.

CROSS-REFERENCE

ALTHOUGH THIS cross-reference section gives the attributes of the gods and goddesses, it is wise to double-check each deity within its particular section of this book before actually using it for ritual. For instance, both Freyja and Aphrodite are love deities, but they represent totally different aspects of love.

ABUNDANCE—Isis, Hecate, Ops, Thalia, Gauri, Lakshmi, Nerthus, Rusalki, Mokosh, Cronus, Saturn, Hades, Freyr, Njord, Hermes, Mercury, Agni, Kubera, Vishnu, Tsai Shen, Lu-hsing, Daikoku, Svantovit, Ilmarinen, Zeus, Jupiter, Pluto, Dis Pater, Bes, Osiris, Ruhanga, Svarog, Puchan, Onatha.

AGRICULTURE—Ceres, Demeter, Ops, Aglaia, Euphrosyne, Brigit, Persephone, Proserpina, Amaterasu, Heqet, Hecate, Mati Syra Zemlya, Gaea, Rhea, Flora, Tellus Mater, White Lady, Rusalki, Ama-no-Uzume, Nokomis, Cinteotl, Xilonen, Min, Osiris, Cronus, Saturn, Pan, Faunus, Odhinn, Mars, Amen, Hapi, Adonis, Marduk, Shen Nung, Loco, the Horned God, Agunua, Muluku, Gucumatz, Yum Caax, Yarilo, Susanoo, Ra, Hades, Jupiter, Ninurta, Bel, Thorr, Polevik, Perun, Lono, the Ribhus, Inari, Tirawa, Yanauluha, Paralda, Itzamna, Xipe, Carpo, Uke-mochi.

AIR—See SKY.

ANIMALS—Bast, Sekhmet, Artemis, Athene, Cybele, Freyja, Epona, Rhiannon, Frigg, Hecate, Pales, Mut, Cerridwen, Imberombera, Diana, Nymphs, Inanna, Ishtar, Flidais, Diiwica, Mokosh, Nokomis, Pan, Poseidon, the Horned God, Mars, Odhinn, Volos, Freyr, Faunus, Cernunnos, Nuada, Rudra, Tekkeitsertok, Hurukan, T'ai-yueh-Ta-Ti, Kamapua'a, Neptune, Vajrapani, Anubis, Hermes, Mercury, Ruhanga, Bel, Herne the Hunter, Thorr, Numitorem, Krukis, Volos, Indra, Puchan, Visvakarma, Igaluk, Niksa.

ARBITRATION—Ba-Neb-Tetet.

ARCHITECTURE—Athene, Minerva, Muluku, Osiris, Ptah, Khnemu, Thoth, Lugh, Tangaroa, Ganesha, Visvakarma.

ARTS AND CRAFTS—Athene, Holda, Brigit, Minerva, Ishtar, Astarte, Cerridwen, Pales, Juno, Hera, Isis, Neith, Hestia, Ataentsic, the Muses, Asherat-of-the-Sea, Seshat, Xochiquetzal, Khnemu, Ptah, Thoth, Apollo, Bragi, Mimir, Odhinn, the Dagda, Lugh, Manannan mac Lir, Ogma, Tvashtar, Lupan, Ebisu, Anubis, Taliesin, Nabu, Merlin, Hermes, Mercury, Osiris, Weland, Hephaestus, Ea,

415

Ambat, Rua, Tane, Itzamna, Pachacamac, Wen-ch'ang, Ganesha, Visvakarma, Vulcan, Kothar, Ogun, Bran the Blessed, Manannan mac Lir, the Ribhus, Itzamna, Quetzalcoatl, Hathor.

ASTRAL TRAVEL—Anubis.

ASTROLOGY—Hathor.

BEAUTY—Hathor, Aphrodite, Freyja, Arianrhod, Branwen, Isis, Creiddylad, Lakshmi, Venus, Chalchihuitlicue, Bast, Athirat, Lilith, Uma, Apollo, Balder, Bes, Adonis, Nuada, Hoenir, Freyr, Ull.

BEGINNINGS—Allecto, Janus, Heimdall, Ptah, Terminus, Svantovit, Agni, Ganesha, Clothos.

BLACKSMITHS—See METALWORKING.

BLESSINGS—Isis, Hera, Hathor, Danu, Demeter, Gaea, Osiris, Savitri, Surya, En-kai, the Ribhus, Tvashtar.

BOATS—Tien-hou, Manannan mac Lir, Njord, Janus, Neptune, Kusor, Aegir, Freyr, Aluluei, Ndengei, Anubis.

BREWING—Goibniu, Aegir.

CALM—Isis, Kuan Yin, Bast, Rhea, Gaea, Hera, Juno, Tara, Hathor, Rhiannon, Branwen, Creiddylad, Arianrhod, Lakshmi, Zephyrus, Fukurokuju, Jurojin.

CARPENTERS—Lu-pan, Ptah, Tangaroa, Khnemu, Ea, Lugh, Nuada.

CEMETERIES—Anubis.

CHANGE—Allecto, Hecate, Notos, Gwydion, Djin, Khepera, Janus. See MAGICK.

CHARMS—See MAGICK, ENCHANTMENTS.

CHILDBIRTH—Meshkent, Ta-urt, Hera, Juno, Frigg, Asherat-of-the-Sea, Kishi-Mojin, Renenet, Ataentsic, Artemis, Diana, Egeria, Freyja, Hathor, Heqet, Isis, Neith, Belit-Ili, Nekhebet, Demeter, Haumea, Kuan Yin, Cihuacoatl, Mayauel, Bes, Were, Nuada, Zaltys, Jizo Bosatsu, Bast.

CHILDREN—Kuan Yin, Hecate, Hera, Juno, Hathor, Isis, Nekhebet, Renenet, Artemis, Diana, Imberombera, Demeter, Gaea, Tellus Mater, Lilith, Asherat-of-the-Sea, Mammitu, Audhumla, Frigg, Iyatiku, Bes, Jizo Bosatsu, Imana, Ruhanga, Djanggawul, Acat.

CIVILIZATION—Demeter, Ceres, Gucumatz, Dionysus, Zeus, Jupiter, Horus, Osiris, Thoth, Quetzalcoatl, Enlil, Mithra, Odhinn, Manjusri, Yanauluha.

COMMERCE—Isis, Athene, Demeter, Ceres, Fortuna, Minerva, Ops, Nehallennia, Kuan Yin, Nzambi, Osiris, Hermes, Mercury, Lugh, Manannan mac Lir, Ganesha, Thoth, Castor and Pollux, Cernunnos, Herne the Hunter, Thorr.

COMPASSION—See MERCY.

CONTRACTS—Gaea, Mati Syra Zemlya, Mithra, Zeus, Jupiter, Tyr, Osiris, Njord, Freyr.

COURAGE—Athene, Artemis, Sekhmet, the Morrigu, Anat, Ares, Mars, Hercules, Thorr, Shamash, Marduk, Hoenir, Kuan Ti, Susanoo, Camael, Uriel, Auf.

CREATIVITY—Pales, Seshat, Isis, Ishtar, Anahita, Imberombera, Sarasvati, Odhinn, Khnemu, Ptah, Thoth, Khepera, Osiris, Ra, Wele, Byelobog, Daramulun, Indra, the Ribhus, Rudra, Tvashtar, Varuna, Visvakarma.

CREATOR GOD—Ptah, Osiris, Sebek, Khnemu, Rama, Rudra, Savitri, Buddha, Brihaspati, Tvashtar, Varuna, Visvakarma, Ea, Marduk, Kamapua'a, Ta'aroa, Tangaroa, Brahma, Cagn, Mawu, 'Ngai, Nyambi, Ioskeha, Michabo, Hurukan, Nohochacyum, Izanagi, Seb, Ra, Cronus, Odhinn.

CREATOR GODDESS—Nzambi, Sati, Tara, Demeter, Ceres, Hera, Juno, Rhea, Arianrhod, Danu, Freyja, Nerthus, Mati Syra Zemlya, Heqet, Isis, Anat, Anahita, Ninhursag, Imberombera, Koevasi, Gaea, Neith, Mut.

CROSSROADS—Hecate, Legba, Chimata-no-kami, Hermes, Mercury, Cernunnos, Herne the Hunter.

CRYSTAL READING—Isis, Gaea, Osiris, Merlin. See Psychic Abilities.

CUNNING—Circe, Hecate, Macha, Frigg, Hermes, Mercury, Bragi, Loki, Odhinn, Susanoo, Kapua, Maui, Tawhaki, Pwyll, O-kuni-nushi.

CURSING—See REVENGE.

DANCE—Bast, Hathor, Artemis, Thalia, Euphrosyne, Aglaia, Diana, Pele, Shiva, Bes, Pan, Faunus, Tezcatlipoca, Terpsichore.

DARKNESS—Hecate, Hel, Tiamat, Hina, Kali, Savitri, Hades, Loki, Chernobog, Apep, Set, Ahriman, Rua, Ta'aroa, Sebek.

DEATH—Isis, Nephthys, Ament, Persephone, Hecate, the Morrigu, Creiddylad, Freyja, Cybele, Hel, Durga, Jyeshtha, Kali, Astarte, Ereshkigal, Ishtar, Sekhmet, Ran, Kalma, Tiamat, Hina, Megaera, Proserpina, Hathor, Hera, Juno, Anu, Cerridwen, Macha, White Lady, Baba-Yaga, Itzpapalotl, Tlazolteotl, Guruhi, Huitzilopochtli, Mictlantecuhtli, Supai, Rudra, Ares, Apollo, Hades, Thanatos, Odhinn, Tyr, Mars, Chernobog, Tuoni, Anubis, Apep, Set, Adonis, Ahriman, Nergal, Sebek, Karttikeya, Shiva, Amen, Chu-jung, Kuan Ti, Shou-hsing, Yen-lo, Emma-Hoo, Jizo Bosatsu, Pluto, Arawn, Gwynn ap Nudd, the Dagda, Ogma, Osiris, Yama, Pwyll, Bes, Dis Pater, Ba'al, Mithra, Adroa, Gauna, Kaka-Guia, 'Ngai, Rugaba, Sagbata, Ruhanga, Were, Loki, Great Rainbow Snake, Maui, Agni, Mara, Aipaloovik, Itzcoliuhqui, Mictlantecuhtli, Huitzilopochtli, Xipe, Tonatiuh, Gabriel, Sammael, Apep, Atropos, Ahpuch.

DEMONS—See DEATH.

DESTRUCTION—Kali, Artemis, Hecate, Hel, Tiamat, Hina, Coatlicue, Sekhmet, White Lady, Bellona, Pele, Durga, Sagbata, Aipaloovik, Ares, Mars, Loki, Thorr, Horus, Set, Ahriman, Ta'aroa, Sebek, Enlil, Nergal, Chernobog, Kama, Shiva, Emma-Hoo, bDud, Yama.

DIPLOMACY—Anubis.

DISASTER—Tiamat, Hecate, Circe, Bellona, Ran, Pele, Durga, Coatlicue, Itzcoliuhqui, Enlil, Mars, Ares, Loki, Tezcatlipoca.

DISEASE—Hel, Febris, Gula, Caillech, Kipu-Tytto, Loviator, Lha-mo, Rudra, Nergal, Apollo, Mithra, Rugaba, Sagbata, Ruhanga, Vammatar.

DIVINATION—Masaya, Demeter, Gaea, the Graiae, Hecate, Diana, Fortuna, Freyja, Frigg, Mati Syra Zemlya, Artemis, Selene, Isis, Brigit, Akuj, Tezcatlipoca, Viracocha, Kuan Ti, Shiva, Apollo, Zeus, Faunus, Janus, Mithra, Odhinn, Svantovit, Hiisi, Thoth, Ea, Shamash, Merlin, Osiris, Thoth, Pan, Kusor, Katonda, Leza, Gabriel, Michael.

DOMESTIC ARTS—Neith, Vesta, Brigit, Athene, Hera, Juno, Isis, Hestia, Minerva, Pales, Cerridwen, Ataentsic, Athirat, Audhumla, Matergabia, Chih-nii, Ptah, Osiris.

DREAMS—Lilith, Gaea, Isis, Nanshe, Morpheus, Gidja, Osiris, Asclepius, Chandra.

EARTH GOD—Unkulunkulu, Tekkeitsertok, Pachacamac, O-kuni-nushi, the Dagda, Seb, Adonis, Enlil, Dumuzi, the Horned God, Pan, Cernunnos, Nuada, Osiris, Faunus, Ea, Adroa, Izanagi, Kuni-tsu-kami.

EARTH GODDESS—Cybele, Demeter, Gaea, Tellus Mater, Cerridwen, Nanna, Nerthus, Heqet, Audhumla, Anu, Blodeuwedd, Creiddylad, Ninhursag, Coatlicue, Inanna, Mati Syra Zemlya, Isis, Hera, Persephone, Juno, Asia, Uma, Izanami, Ninki, Ale.

EARTHQUAKES—Coatlicue, Poseidon, Neptune, Loki, Nai-no-kami, Enlil, Ndengei, Susanoo.

ECLIPSE—Apep.

ECSTASY—See PASSION.

ELEMENTS—Tuamutef, Akeset, Qebhsennuf, Mestha, nymphs, undines, salamanders, gnomes, Dhritarashtra, Virudhaka, Virupaksha, Vaisravana.

ELOQUENCE—Hermes, Mercury, Ogma, Ba-Neb-Tetet, Bragi, Nabu, Osiris.

ENCHANTMENTS—Circe, Hecate, Brigit, Cerridwen, the Morrigu, Rhiannon, Isis, Nephthys, Selene, Aphrodite, Artemis, Luna, Lilith, Freyja, Frigg, Kusor, Marduk, Gwydion, Math Mathonwy, Odhinn. See MAGICK.

ENDINGS—Hecate, Janus, Heimdall, Terminus, Svantovit, Anubis.

ENLIGHTENMENT—See BLESSINGS.

EVIL—Rusalki, Circe, Hecate, Tiamat, Kul, Loviator, Louhi, Baba-Yaga, Guruhi, Legba, 'Nenaunir, Aipaloovik, Loki, Chernobog, Leshy, Hiisi, Louhi, Nehebkau, Set, Ahriman, Nergal, Sebek, Ahriman, Minepa, Kajis, Khopun, Koshchei.

EXORCISM—Bast, Kupala, Zvezda Vechernyaya, Zvezda Dennitsa, Hsuan-t'ien-shang-ti, Bes, Camael.

FAMILY—See MARRIAGE, MOTHERHOOD.

FATE—Renenet, Shait, Holda, Isis, Aditi, Nemesis, Fortuna, Maat, Tiamat, Demeter, Frigg, Fa, Nyame, Legba, Shou-hsing, T'ai-yueh-ta-ti, Ti-tsang-wang-pu-sa, Tsao-wang, Varuna, Atropos, Nereus, Thanatos, Janus, the Dagda, Manannan mac Lir, Odhinn, Dazhbog, Ba-Neb-Tetet, Osiris, Nabu, Ra, Saturn, Enlil, Marduk, Sin, Yama, Fu-hsi, Yeng-wang-yeh, Quetzalcoatl, Tonatiuh, Ratziel, Tzaphkiel, Urd, Verthandi, Skuld.

FATHER OF THE GODS—Cronus, Saturn, Osiris, Uranus, Janus, An, the Dagda, Itzamna.

FERTILITY—Hera, Juno, Isis, Freyja, Arianrhod, Brigit, Cerridwen, Ishtar, Kuan Yin, Chantico, Ama-no-Uzume, Artemis, Bona Dea, Diana, Fauna, Flora, Maia, Pales, Venus, Aphrodite, Macha, Frigg, Nerthus, Mati Syra Zemlya, Bast, Heqet, Selqet, Lilith, Athene, Demeter, Gaea, Rhea, Tellus Mater, Inanna, Freyja, Gefion, Nehallennia, Anahit, Mokosh, Uma, Amaterasu, Kishi-mojin, Tlazolteotl, Pan, Faunus, Cernunnos, the Horned God, Min, Osiris, Freyr, Asshur, Indra, Shiva, Amen, Vajrapani, Dionysus, Bacchus, Itzamna, Unkulunkulu, Famien, Tlaloc, Legba, Chimata-no-kami, Kubera, Poseidon, Yarilo, Akka, Khnemu, Ba'al, Dumuzi, Gidja, Great Rainbow Snake, Viracocha, Vertumnus, Mithra, Njambi, Ruhanga, Xevioso, Bel, Herne the Hunter, Freyr, Bes, Hapi, Ninurta, Zaltys, Perun, Daramulun, Bast.

FINDING LOST THINGS—Anubis.

FIRE—Brigit, Sekhmet, Chantico, Hestia, Freyja, Kupala, Mahui-Ike, Pele, Vesta, Hephaestus, Vulcan, Loki, Bel, Agni, Chu-jung, Goibniu, Merlin, Svantovit, Gibil, Xiuhtecuhtli, Nergal, the Dagda, Perun, Svarozic, Svarog, Ndengei, Shiva, Tirawa, Ogun, Bast.

FISHING—Nehallennia, Agloolik, Michabo, Ebisu, Njord, Tangaroa, Pan, Faunus, Neptune, Kusor, Behanzin, Nuada, Maui.

FLOWERS—Flora, Venus, Aphrodite, Hathor, Chalchihuitlicue, Nymphs, Blodeuwedd, Creiddylad, Freyja, Ha'iaka, Xochiquetzal, Pan, Yarilo, Kama, Xochipilli.

FORESTS—See WOODLANDS.

FORETELLING—Gaea, Hecate, Isis, Cerridwen, Freyja, Frigg, Mati Syra Zemlya, Diana, Artemis, Nanshe, Aditi, Leza, Apollo, Thoth, Zeus, Jupiter, Janus, Mithra, Ea, Nereus, Pan, Faunus, Addad, Olorun, Merlin, Odhinn, Bannick, Kuan Ti.

FORGIVENESS—Ti-kuan.

FREEDOM—Diana, Artemis, Isis, Athene, Minerva, Vesta, Djin.

GAMBLING—Hermes, Mercury, Barakiel, Uriel.

GATES, DOORS, PORTALS, HARBORS—Janus, Men Shen, Legba, Bes.

GREAT GOD—Pachacamac, Amen, Osiris, Ra, Cronus, Uranus, Zeus, Jupiter, Ahura Mazdah, Anu, Ba'al, Ea, Enlil, Marduk, Adroa, Akongo, Akuj, Amma, Cagn, Chiuta, Chuku, Jok, Juok, Katonda, Kwoth, Mahou, Mawu, the Dagda, Odhinn, Jumala, Perun, Tangaroa, Indra, Kama, Rudra, Lao-tien-yeh, Shang-ti, Kitcki Manitou.

GREAT GODDESS—Demeter, Hera, Juno, Rhea, Cerridwen, Danu, Macha, the Morrigu, Nanna, Mati Syra Zemlya, Isis, Mut, Ninhursag, Hina, Imberombera, Brigit, Tiamat, Hecate, Freyja, Rhiannon, Gauri, Frigg, Nut, Kuan Yin, Venus, Aphrodite, Ishtar, Astarte, Audhumla, Uma, Tara, Sati, Parvati, Durga, Nzambi, Izanami, Gaea, Ceres, Inanna, Nzambi, Imberombera, Coatlicue.

GREAT MOTHER—The Lady; female principle of creation. Goddess of fertility, the Moon, summer, flowers, love, healing, the seas, water. The "mother" finger was considered the index finger, the most magical which guided, beckoned, blessed and cursed. See MOTHER GODDESS.

GROWTH—Demeter, Ceres, Gaea, Boreas, Eurus, Freyr.

GUARDIAN—Bast, Isis, Neith, Selqet, Shait, Heimdall, Anubis, Bes, Shai, Janus.

HAPPINESS—Aphrodite, Venus, Juno, Hera, Freyja, Bast, Hathor, Isis, Freyr, Dionysus, Aulanerk, Yum Caax, Fu-hsing, T'ien-kuan, Dazhbog, Nehebkau, Fukurokuju, Jurojin, Notos, Balder, Euphrosyne, Bishamonten.

HARVEST—Demeter, Ceres, Onatha, Persephone, Ops, Cerridwen, Heqet, Renenet, Gaea, Amaterasu, Balder, Saturn, Cronus, Ra, Amen, Dumuzi, Adonis, Osiris, Thorr, Yarilo, Akka, Hapi, Vertumnus, Agunua, Hou, chi, Cinteotl, Min, Muluku, Ruhanga, Utixo, Wele, Odhinn, Tezcatlipoca.

HATE—Fea, Nemon.

HEALING—Sekhmet, Brigit, Kuan Yin, Gaea, Minerva, Isis, Bast, Nymphs, Gula, Skadi, Kupala, Ha'iaka, Imhotep, Khensu, Apollo, Asclepius, Pan, Faunus, Cernunnos, Bel, Lugh, Yao-Shih, Loco, Thoth, Merlin, Asvins, Itzamna, Ioskeha, Bel, the Dagda, Diancecht, Gwydion, Nuada, Underwater Panthers, Yanauluha, Pachacamac, Faunus, Marduk, Shadrafa, Mukuru, Rugaba, Myesyats, Rudra, Shiva, Niksa, Raphael, Hygeia, Eir, Suku-na-biko.

HEALTH—Gaea, Brigit, Bast, Gula, Imhotep, Apollo, Asclepius, Famien, Fukurokuju, Zeus, Jupiter, Ruhanga, Asvins, Lha.

HEARTH—See HOME, MOTHERHOOD.

HEAVEN—See SKY.

HERBS—Isis, Hecate, Venus, Aphrodite, Kupala, Bast, Gaea, Brigit, Rudra, Marduk, Ioskeha, Pan, Merlin, the Ribhus, Tirawa, Paralda, Gabriel.

HOME—Chantico, Gaea, Hera, Juno, Hestia, Hathor, Isis, Selqet, Neith, Demeter, Vesta, Brigit, Tsao-wang, Bes, Legba.

THE HORNED GOD—Pan, Faunus, Cernunnos, Herne the Hunter.

HORSES—Athene, Minerva, Epona, Astarte, Rhiannon, Freyja, Valkyries, Diiwica, Zvezda Dennitsa, Odhinn, Poseidon, Neptune, Freyr, Weland, Gandharvas, Svantovit, Yarilo, Indra, the Ribhus, Varuna, Visvakarma.

HOSPITALS— Anubis.

THE HUNTER—Odhinn, Herne the Hunter, Cernunnos, Apollo.

HUNTING—Sedna, Diana, Artemis, Athene, Pinga, Agloolik, Tekkeitsertok, Mixcoatl, Asclepius, Apollo, Ogun, Ull, Leib-Olmai, Tapio, Indra, Tirawa.

THE HUNTRESS—Neith, Artemis, Diana, Holda, Hecate, the Morrigu, Diiwica.

HURRICANES, TYPHOONS—Hurukan, Haya-ji, Enlil, Marduk, Tawiri.

ILLNESS—See DISEASE.

ILLUSION—Merlin, Gwydion, Pan, Faunus, Loki, Odhinn, Kama, Mara. See SHAPE-SHIFTER.

INITIATION—Isis, Demeter, Cerridwen, Hecate, Neith, Ceres, Juno, Blodeuwedd, Osiris, Apollo, Odhinn, the Dagda, Lugh, Thoth, Merlin, Dionysus, Baiame.

INSPIRATION—Cerridwen, Isis, Badb, Brigit, Freyja, Apollo, Merlin, Osiris, Ogma, Odhinn, Paralda.

INTELLIGENCE—See WISDOM.

INVENTIONS—Fortuna, Diana, Artemis, Khnemu, Ptah, Thoth, Merlin, Pan, Mercury, Hermes, Enlil.

JEALOUSY—Zelos.

JEWELRY—Minerva, Ishtar, Freyja, Hephaestus, Vulcan, Lugh, Diancecht, Goibniu, Bes, Ptah, Kubera, Hathor.

JOURNEYS—Hecate, Sae-no-kami, Puchan, Janus, Njord, Thorr, Min, Hercules, Hermes, Mercury, Lugh, Ganesha, Lha, Legba, Huitzilopochtli, Anubis.

JUDGMENT—Nzambi, Artemis, Maat, Shait, Tiamat, Athene, Renenet, Hera, Juno, Tara, Ogun, Sakarabru, Varuna, Apollo, Zeus, Jupiter, Odhinn, Tyr, Dazhbog, Anubis, Horus, Osiris, Ea, Gibil, Ares, Mars, Ninurta, Shamash, Sin, Chu-jung, Kuan Ti, Lei Kung, Ida-ten, Shai, Thoth, Katonda, Kwoth, Ruhanga, Were, Rudra, Shiva, Yama, Yeng-wang-yeh, Sammael.

JUSTICE—Hecate, Hera, Juno, Mati Syra Zemlya, Maat, Shait, Tiamat, Diana, Artemis, Osiris, Apollo, Nereus, Zeus, Jupiter, Mars, Anu, Gibil, Shamash, Njambi, Ogun, Rugaba, Sakarabru, Tyr, Odhinn, Dazhbog, Agni, Ch'eng-huang, Chu-jung, Kuan Ti, Lei-king, Camael, Sammael, Anubis, Dike, the disir.

KARMA—See FATE, RETRIBUTION.

KNOWLEDGE—Athene, Persephone, Koevasi, Neith, Seshat, Brigit, Sarasvati, Tara, Aluluei, Ambat, Anulap, Tane, Imhotep, Eurus, Nabu, Sin, the Dagda, Taliesin, Mimir, Michael, Ratziel, Uriel, Osiris, Apollo, Janus, Odhinn, Brahma, Rudra, Surya, Fugen Bosatsu, Yanauluha, Paralda.

LAW—Athene, Maat, Kuan Yin, Demeter, Ceres, Odhinn, Lu-hsing, Ida-ten, Zeus, Jupiter, Horus, Varuna, Tyr, Osiris, Marduk, Forseti, Thoth, Apollo, Enlil, Adroa, Indra, Themis.

LEARNING—See KNOWLEDGE, ARTS.

LIFE—Isis, Hestia, Vesta, Ninhursag, Badb, Quetzalcoatl, Yum Caax, Legba, Shou-hsing, Varuna, Chimata-no-Kami, Osiris, Great Rainbow Snake, Ptah, Ninurta, 'Ngai, Rugaba, Kitcki Manitou, Acat, Anqet, Ninmah, Bau.

LIGHT—Hera, Juno, Isis, Neith, Vesta, Inanna, Uma, Amaterasu, Kitcki Manitou, Vishnu, Svarog, Osiris, Ahura Mazdah, Apollo, Balder, Odhinn, Mithra, Thoth, Zeus, Jupiter, Heimdall, Byelobog, Agni, Paralda.

LIGHTNING—Tien-mu, Juno, Agni, Indra, Hephaestus, Vulcan, Zeus, Jupiter, Thorr, Perun, Min, Ba'al, Tawhaki, Addad, Nyamia Ama, Rock-Sens, Wele, Svarog, Shiva, Vajrapani, Thunder Bird, Viracocha.

LONG LIFE—Renpet, Idunn, Hsi-wang-mu, Isis, Freyja, Hsi-wang-mu, Estsanatlehi, Nehebkau, Fukurokuju, Jurojin, Shou-hsing, Asvins, Shamash, Shiva, Fugen Bosatsu.

LOVE—Hathor, Aphrodite, Venus, Freyja, Branwen, Brigit, Creiddylad, Ishtar, Benzaiten, Frigg, Lakshmi, Astarte, Circe, Isis, Kali, Chalchihuitlicue, Bast, Selene, Luna, Inanna, Freyja, Amaterasu, Asvins, Krishna, Vishnu, Eros, Cupid, Yarilo, Bes, Adonis, Zephyrus, Fu-hsi, Dumuzi, Kama, Dogoda, Agni, Vajrapani, Djin.

LUCK—Hecate, Ops, Danu, Lakshmi, Isis, Fortuna, Freyja, Gefion, Kupala, Hotei Osho, Puchan, Hermes, Mercury, Saturn, Ilmarinen, Bes, Zeus, Jupiter, Odhinn, Ganesha, Tsao-wang, Tzadquiel, Lachesis, the disir. See SUCCESS.

MAGICK, DARK—Nephthys, Circe, Hecate, the Morrigu, Durga, Kali, Jyeshtha, Tara, Artemis, Ereshkigal, Tiamat, Skadi, Holda, Louhi, Baba-Yaga, Set, Pluto, Hades, Karttikeya, Kuan Ti, Nergal, Mara, Tezcatlipoca.

MAGICK, LIGHT—Isis, Circe, the Morrigu, Nephthys, Rhiannon, Cerridwen, Brigit, Selene, Spider Woman, Gaea, Banba, Freyja, Frigg, Kupala, Mati Syra Zemlya, Aphrodite, Artemis, Lilith, Banba, Danu, Skadi, Gefion, Thoth, Apollo, Hermes, Mercury, Odhinn, Ull, the Dagda, Gwydion, Lugh, Ogma, Marduk, Mithra, Varuna, Merlin, Heitsi-Eibib, Shango, Michabo, Tezcatlipoca, Brihaspati, Hephaestus, Zeus, Jupiter, Diancecht, Manannan mac Lir, Math Mathonwy, Loki, Ilmarinen, Louhi, Ea, Anulap, Great Rainbow Snake, Kapua, Maui, Rua, Tawhaki, Ioskeha, Manco Capac, Legba, Osiris, Ra, Vulcan, Kusor, Nuada, Taliesin, Odhinn, Brahma, Indra, Krishna, Shiva, Izanagi, Gabriel.

MARRIAGE—Aphrodite, Venus, Demeter, Ceres, Gaea, Hera, Juno, Frigg, Selqet, Isis, Hathor, Hestia, Ataentsic, Mama Quilla, Neith, Tellus Mater, Freyja, Asvins, Gandharvas, Puchan, Bes, Zaltys, Agni, Bast, Bes.

MECHANICS—Hephaestus, Ptah, Vulcan.

MEDICINE—Asclepius, Pan, Faunus, Lugh, Shen Nung, Loco, Sakarabru, O-kuni-nushi, Asvins, Apollo, Bel, the Dagda, Imhotep, Thoth, Gandharvas, Shiva, Wakonda, Gabriel, Sekhmet, Brigit, Gaea, Minerva, Bast, Gula, Pinga, Anubis, Suku-na-biko.

MEETINGS—Puchan, Ba-Neb-Tetet.

MEMORY—Janus, Odhinn.

MEN—Pan, Bacchus, Faunus, Cernunnos, Herne the Hunter, Odhinn.

MERCHANTS—Yacatecuhtli, Hermes, Mercury, Osiris, Ganesha, Inari. See COMMERCE.

MERCY—Kuan Yin, Maat, Amaterasu, Kishi-mojin, Tara, Iyatiku, Jizo Bosatsu, Kannon Bosatsu, Ti-tsang-wang-pu-sa, Kwoth, Avalokitesvara, Shiva, Ti-kuan, Amida-nyorai, Gabriel, Michael.

MESSENGER—Agni, Hermes, Mercury, Ninurta, Anubis, Khensu, Gabriel.

METALWORKING—Minerva, Athene, Brigit, Skadi, Ogun, Hephaestus, Vulcan, Lugh, Diancecht, Goibniu, Weland, Ptah, Gu, Visvakarma, Ilmarinen, Mimir, Lugh, Hades, Ea, Guhkin-Banda, Nuada, Inari, Quetzalcoatl, Creidne.

MISCHIEF—Mercury, Hermes, Anansi, Loki, Sicksa, Kapua, Maui, Susanoo, Coyote, Raven, Tonenili.

MOON—Hathor, Isis, Aphrodite, Venus, Artemis, Circe, Selene, Danu, the Morrigu, Ch'ang-o, Hera, Juno, Vesta, Frigg, Luna, Hecate, Ishtar, Brigit, Demeter, Ceres, Meshkent, Ta-urt, Kuan Yin, Lilith, Hina, Inanna, Kuu, Mama Quilla, Coyolxauhqui, Cybele, Diana, Ngami, Blodeuwedd, Cerridwen, Danu, Freyja, Nanna, Sarasvati, Khensu, Sin, Varuna, Horus, Cernunnos, Thoth, Nanna, Gidja, Jupiter, Myesyats, Chandra, Shiva, Ge, Ptah, Igaluk, Tzaphiel.

MOTHER GODDESS—Ataentsic, Coatlicue, Ilamatecuhtli, Demeter, Hera, Juno, Hathor, Isis, Gaea, Ceres, Ninhursag, Anu, Frigg, Imberombera, Aditi, Sati, Tara.

MOTHERHOOD—Isis, Demeter, Ceres, Hera, Juno, Vesta, Freyja, Kuan Yin, Kishi-mojin, Frigg, Brigit, Rhea, Gaea, Ishtar, Astarte, Artemis, Diana, Hecate, Selene, Meshkent, Ta-urt, Hathor, Nekhebet, Renenet, Gaea, Lilith, Epona, Audhumla.

MOUNTAINS—Artemis, Diana, Astarte, Zeus, Jupiter, Pan, Faunus, O-yama-tsu-mi, Tlaloc.

MUSIC—Bast, Hathor, Artemis, Diana, Rhiannon, Minerva, Athene, Freyja, Sarasvati, Bes, Apollo, Pan, Faunus, Bragi, Odhinn, Lugh, Ogma, Taliesin, Thoth, the Dagda, Nabu, Wen-ch'ang, Hermes, Gandharvas, Krishna, Mercury, Hiisi, Osiris, Bran the Blessed, Nuada, Vainamoinen, Lono, Rudra, Tezcatlipoca, Euterpe, Coirpre.

NATURE—See WOODLANDS.

NIGHT—The Morrigu, Ishtar, Nut, Hecate, Set, Apep, Auf, Wepwawet.

OATHS—Perun, Volos. See CONTRACTS.

OPPORTUNITIES—Ogun, Puchan, the Dagda, Jupiter, Zeus, Osiris, Odhinn, Renpet, Athene.

ORACLES—Gaea, Brigit, the Morrigu, Isis, Circe, Nymphs, Mati Syra Zemlya, Apollo, Pan, Faunus, Merlin, Osiris, Ea, Mithra, Katonda, Odhinn, Perun, Viracocha, Pachacamac.

ORDER—Unkulunkulu, Varuna, Osiris, Athene, Eunomia.

PASSION—Circe, Frigg, Parvati, Aphrodite, Ishtar, Lilith, Dionysus, Herakles, Notos, Pan, Faunus, Cernunnos, Kama, Krishna, Shiva, Vajrapani, Bacchus, Eros, Cupid, Fauns, Herne the Hunter, Yarilo.

PATRON OF PRIESTS—Osiris, Thoth, Odhinn, the Dagda, Merlin, Lugh, Freyr, Brihaspati.

PATRONESS OF PRIESTESSES—Isis, Hecate, Kuan Yin, Great White Goddess, the Morrigu, Freyja.

PEACE—Athene, Nerthus, Neith, Diana, Artemis, Minerva, Amaterasu, Ganesha, Forseti, Freyr, Dazhbog, Ba-Neb-Tetet, Oro, Imhotep, Osiris, Mimir, Perun, Volos, Vishnu, Paralda, Auf, Irene.

PLEASURE—See PASSION, SEXUAL ACTIVITIES.

POETRY—See WRITING.

POLITICS—Ogun, Forseti, Odhinn.

POWER—Herakles, Agni, Mithra, Marduk, Wakonda, Ogun, Camael, Olorun, Odhinn, Surya, Varuna, Vishnu, Osiris, Zeus, Jupiter, Mithra, Enlil, Guruhi, Imana, Katonda, Isis, Macha, Freyja, Tara.

PROBLEM-SOLVING—Artemis, Diana, Isis, Horus, Ganesha, Merlin, Osiris, the Dagda, Odhinn.

PROPHECY—Thoth, Apollo, Pan, Faunus, Odhinn, Bran the Blessed, the Dagda, Lugh, Addad, Varuna, Kuan Ti, Merlin, Gwydion, Osiris, Janus, Mithra, Sin, Gaea, Frigg, Brigit, the Morrigu, Isis, Nymphs, Ops, Nanshe, Skadi, Holda, Amen, Antevorta, Postvorta, Egeria, Carmenta.

PROSPERITY—Yum Caax, Tsai-Shen, Daikoku, Ganesha, Kubera, Puchan, Hades, Saturn, the Dagda, Njord, Ilmarinen, Bes, Hapi, Ra, Boreas, Cronus, Hermes, Mercury, Zeus, Jupiter, Pluto, Dis Pater, Enlil, Anayaroli, Wele, Bel, Cernunnos, Herne the Hunter, Aegir, Freyr, Agni, Rudra, Tvashtar, Vishnu, Lu-hsing, T'ai-yueh-ta-ti, Inari, Ghom, Raphael, Hecate, Ops, Danu, Nehallennia, Nerthus, Lakshmi, Isis, Anu, Gefion, Kupala, Chantico. See ABUNDANCE.

PROTECTION—Bast, Buto, Selqet, Athene, Minerva, Isis, Kuan Yin, Mama Quilla, Tien-hou, Hecate, Hera, Juno, Banba, Hathor, Neith, Diana, Artemis, Nekhebet, Ta-urt, Demeter, Ceres, Inanna, Lilith, Macha, Kupala, Zvezda Vechernyaya, Zvezda Dennitsa, Thorr, Min, Agni, K'uei-hsing, Jizo Bosatsu, Merlin, Famien, Leza, Ioskeha, Nohochacyum, Legba, Erh-lang, T'ai-yueh-ta-ti, Tsao-wang, Sae-no-Kami, Mithra, Puchan, Zeus, Jupiter, Odhinn, Volos, Anubis, bes, Horus, Sin,

Wepwawet, Asshur, Gibil, Ninurta, Shadrafa, Shedu, Asa, Mukuru, Njambi, the Dagda, Freyr, Heimdall, Leib-Olmai, Perun, Asvins, Indra, Karttikeya, Ch'eng-huang, Ch'in-shu-pao, Kuan Ti, Ma-mien, Men Shen, Amida-nyorai, Hayagriva, Lha, Yamantaka, Camael, Michael, Bes.

PROSTITUTES—P'an-chin-lien.

PSYCHIC ABILITIES—Brigit, the Morrigu, Isis, Artemis, Gaea, Freyja, Yao-Shih, Fugen Bosatsu, Merlin, Osiris, Pan, Faunus, Odhinn, Chandra, Djin, Niksa, Bast. See BLESSINGS, FORETELLING, MAGICK, ORACLES, SPIRITUAL ILLUMINATION.

PURIFICATION—Isis, Hecate, Kuan Yin, Pales, Kupala, Hera, Diana, Artemis, Juno, Nerthus, Faunus, Bel, Camael, Michael.

RAIN—Mungo, Nyamia Ama, Rock-Sens, Waka, Thunder Bird, Tlaloc, Susanoo, Agni, Gandharvas, Zeus, Jupiter, Addad, Great Rainbow Snake, Ba'al, Enlil, Chiuta, En-kai, Jok, Mukuru, Tilo, Utixo, Xevioso, Wele, Freyr, Odhinn, Ukko, Perun, Kamapua'a, Maui, Ndengei, Agni, Indra, Ao, Tone-nili, Viracocha, Tefnut, Mokosh, Chih-nii.

RAINBOW—En-kai, 'Nenaunir, Heimdall, Great Rainbow Snake, Indra.

REBIRTH—See Regeneration, Reincarnation.

REGENERATION—Hecate, Maat, Renenet, Aphrodite, Hera, Juno, Athene, Demeter, Persephone, Isis, Minerva, Venus, Lilith, Kali, Nyambe, Nyame, Izanagi, Ti=tsang-wang-pu-sa, Adonis, Mithra, the Dagda, Diancecht, Manannan mac Lir, Yarilo, Amen, Horus, Khepera, Osiris, Atea, Ptah, Asclepius, Dionysus, Ba'al, Dumuzi, Odhinn, Yarilo, Itzamna, Gabriel.

REINCARNATION—Gandharvas, Indra, the Dagda, Manannan mac Lir, Horus, Osiris, Adonis, Khnemu, Balder, Odhinn, Cernunnos, Ogma, Shou-hsing, Ptah, Dumuzi, Bragi, Khepera, Dionysus, Ba'al, Marduk, Nyambe, Ruhanga, Utixo, Herne the Hunter, Lugh, Agni, Ti-tsang-wang-pu-sa, Amitabha, Gabriel, Idunn, Maat, Renenet, Hecate, Isis, Demeter.

REMOVE DIFFICULTIES—Hecate, Persephone, Isis, Demeter, Ogun, Varuna, Vishnu, Horus, Osiris, Odhinn, Ukko, Ganesha, Indra, Yamantaka, Avalokitesvara, Gluskap, Gabriel, Michael, Metatron.

RENEWING—See GROWTH.

REST—Persephone, Auf.

RETRIBUTION—Kali, Hecate, Hera, Juno, Mati Syra Zemlya, Tiamat, Circe, Ereshkigal, Ishtar, the Morrigu, Holda, Jyeshtha, Sakarabru, Lei-king, Loki, Odhinn, Tyr, Horus, Set, Gibil, Nergal, Shamash, Njambi, Arawn, Lugh, Thorr, Karttikeya, Varuna, Yama, Chu-jung, Ma-mien, Yeng-wang-yeh, Emma-Hoo, Asmodel, Camael, Gabriel, Michael, Sammael.

REVENGE—Apollo, Horus, Set, Ares, Mars, Thorr, Lugh, Ninurta, Sin, Karttikeya, Chu-jung, Kuan Ti, Emma-Hoo, Mara, Odhinn, Circe, Hecate, the Morrigu, Anat, Durga, Kali, Jyeshtha, Tara, Sekhmet, Athene, Tiamat, Ta-urt, Astarte, Tisiphone.

RICHES—See ABUNDANCE.

RITUALS—Hecate, Freyja, Lama, Isis, Circe, Ioskeha, Mithra, Odhinn, Osiris, Thoth, Ea, Ra, Dionysus, Merlin, Ambat, Baiame, Djanggawul, Great Rainbow Snake, Tirawa, Legba, Xiuhtecuhtli.

ROADS—Cernunnos, Lugh, Chimata-no-Kami, Janus.

SCIENCE—Bel, Thoth, Mithra, Athene, Minerva, Sarasvati, Urania.

SEA—Khnemu, Poseidon, Neptune, Njord, Thorr, Dylan, Llyr, Enlil, Manannan mac Lir, Bel, Zeus, Jupiter, Janus, Nereus, Aegir, Ahto, Aluluei, Tangaroa, Aulanerk, Quetzalcoatl, O-wata-tsumi, Ea, Yam, Olokun, Ta'aroa, Varuna, Ao, Susanoo, Sedna, Tien-hou, Hecate, Fortuna, Nehallennia, Ran, Imberombera, Tiamat, Freyja, Nerthus, Pontus.

SEASONS—Demeter, Persephone, Ceres, Vertumnus, Adonis, Janus, Aryaman, Indra.

SEXUAL ACTIVITES—Dionysus, Eros, Pan, Bacchus, Cupid, Fauns, Faunus, Freyr, Yarilo, Gidja, Indra, Kama, Krishna, Shiva, Vajrapani, Xochipilli, Bast, Selqet, Aphrodite, Venus, Circe, Bona Dea, Ishtar, Lilith, Macha, Freyja, Frigg, Kali, Parvati, Itzpapalotl, Tlazolteotl, Bast.

SHAPE-SHIFTER—Diana, Artemis, Hecate, Flidais, the Morrigu, Estsanatlehi, Cagn, Heitsi-Eibib, Mich-abo, Gucumatz, Erh-lang, Nereus, Vertumnus, Manannan mac Lir, Loki, Kamapua'a, Kapua, Maui, Nereus, Gwydion, Merlin, Taliesin.

SKY—Nut, Freyja, Arianrhod, Aditi, Chih-nii, Hera, Juno, Hathor, Mut, Neith, Seshat, Ereshkigal, Tefnut, Shu, Uranus, Odhinn, the Dagda, Gwydion, Gwythyr, Varuna, Zeus, Jupiter, Enlil, Nyamia Ama, Rock-Sens, Asvins, Gandharvas, Indra, Thorr, Tyr, Svarog, Ilma, Jumala, Anhur, Horus, Addad, Ba'al, Anulap, Atea, Mithra, Sin, Adroa, En-kai, Olorun, Tilo, Num, Baiame, Daramulun, Atius Tirawa, Amaunet, Nwyvre.

SLEEP—Hypnos, Auf, Morpheus, Phoebetor, Phantasus.

SNAKE—Danh, Kulkulcan, Susanoo, Apep, Nehebkau, Agunua, Asclepius, Zaltys, Varuna, Quetzalcoatl, Chantico, Koevasi, Hecate, Athene, Minerva, Coatlicue.

SORCERER—Cagn, Heitsi-Eibib, O-kuni-nushi, Nereus, Vertumnus, Gwydion, Manannan mac Lir, Math Mathonwy, Loki, Hiisi, Louhi, Kapua, Maui, Rua, Tawhaki, Soko, Lugh, Merlin, Nuada, Taliesin, Odhinn, Tezcatlipoca.

SORCERESS—Sedna, Diana, Artemis, Hecate, Circe, Danu, Louhi, Pele.

SPELLS—Aphrodite, Circe, Hecate, Luna, Lilith, Brigit, Spider Woman, Ra, Ea, Kusor, Marduk, Merlin, Nuada, Ogma, Odhinn, Hiisi, Rua, Tawhaki. See Magick, Psychic Abilities, Divination.

SPIRITUAL ILLUMINATION—Kuan Yin, Tara, Isis, Artemis, Diana, Badb, Hurukan, Buddha, Shiva, Odhinn, Osiris, Thoth, Tane, Mithra, Avalokitesvara, Manjusri, Chandra, Surya, Shaka-nyorai, O-kuni-nushi, Akshobhya, Amitabha, Amitayus, Amoghasiddhi, Vajrasattva, Yamantaka, Djin, Niksa, Gabriel, Metatron, Ratziel, Tzadquiel, Uriel, Tzaphkiel.

SPORTS AND ATHLETICS—Hermes, Mercury, Ull.

SPRINGTIME—Blodeuwedd, Nerthus, Mars, Yarilo, Kama, Paralda.

STORMS—'Nenaunir, Nyamia Ama, Rock-Sens, Shango, Tlaloc, Thunder Bird, Viracocha, Susanoo, Zeus, Jupiter, Thorr, Perun, Jumala, Apep, Set, Addad, Enlil, Tawiri, Poseidon, Neptune, Ba'al, Nergal, Utixo, Wele, Manannan mac Lir, Odhinn, Stribog, Agni, Indra, Shiva, Haya-ji, Hurukan, Huitzilopochtli, Chalchihuitlicue, Hecate, Ran.

STRENGTH—Macha, Herakles, Shamash, Cernunnos, Herne the Hunter, Ogma, Hoenir, Odhinn, Thorr, Indra, Shiva, Varuna, Gluskap, Camael. See Power.

STIUDENTS—K'uei-hsing, Minerva.

SUCCESS—Horus, Osiris, Thoth, Hermes, Mercury, Tyr, Bel, Vishnu, Fu-hsi, Lu-hsing, Lu-pan, Tsai Shen, T'ai-yueh-ta-ti, Ganesha, Puchan, Saturn, the Dagda, Balder, Njord, Odhinn, Dazhbog, Cas-tor and Pollux, Janus, Raphael, Isis, Artemis, Diana, Hecate, Ops, Gauri, Rhea, Kuan Yin, Ishtar, Astarte, Lakshmi, Danu, Nehallennia, Nerthus, Diiwica.

SUMMER—Creiddylad, Gwythyr, Svarog, Djin.

SUN—Horus, Khepera, Menthu, Osiris, Ra, Apollo, Balder, Freyr, Bel, the Dagda, Lugh, Shamash, Mithra, Surya, Vishnu, Marduk, Dumuzi, Odhinn, Shakuru, Huitzilopochtli, Apu Punchau, Inti, Manco Capac, Viracocha, Agni, Vulcan, Dazhbog, Svantovit, Svarog, Anhur, Auf, Ba'al, Asshur, Bran the Blessed, Nuada, Aryaman, Indra, Varuna, Bast, Sekhmet, Amaterasu, Gauri, Kupalo.

SUPREME MAGUS—Thoth, Gwydion, Lugh, Varuna, Merlin, Cagn, Heitsi-Eibib, the Dagda, Odhinn, Vainamoinen, Mara, Rin-po-che, Michabo, Quetzalcoatl.

SURGERY—Anubis.

TAROT—Seshat, Brigit, the Morrigu, Isis, Fortuna, Mithra, Thoth, Merlin, Odhinn, Michael. See PSYCHIC ABILITIES.

TERROR—Pan, Leshy, the Horned God, Mars, Arawn, Cernunnos, Herne the Hunter, Hecate, Ishtar, Ran, Enyo, Pemphredo, Deino.

THIEVES—Hermes, Mercury, Summanus, Loki, Kapua, Rudra, Coyote.

THUNDER—Thunder Bird, Hurukan, Ogun, Lei-king, Susanoo, Zeus, Hephaestus, Jupiter, Vulcan, Thorr, Perun, Jumala, Set, Addad, Marduk, Tawhaki, Ba'al, Rock-Sens, Shango, Tilo, Utixo, Xevioso, Tlaloc.

TRADE—See COMMERCE.

TRAVEL—Artemis, Hina, Hermes, Mercury, Janus, Lugh, Thorr, K'uei-hsing, Njord, Hercules, Puchan. See Journeys.

TREASURE—Urcaguary, Kubera, Puchan, Saturn, Ghom, Chantico.

TRUTH—Apollo, Maat, Anubis.

THE UNDERWORLD—Persephone, Hel, Kali, Nephthys, Ereshkigal, Hikuleo, Mahui-Ike, Hecate, Yambe-Akka, Ament, Mictlantecuhtli, Xolotl, Yeng-wang-yeh, Rudra, Yama, Hades, Dis Pater, Arawn, Pwyll, Tuoni, Anubis, Apep, Nehebkau, Seker, Wepwawet, Dumuzi, Nergal, Set, Pluto, Gwynn ap Nudd, Yen-lo, Emma-Hoo, Ea, Supai.

VEGETATION—Thunder Bird, Adonis, Dumuzi, Dionysus, Faunus, Mars, Mithra, Vertumnus, Thorr, Akka, Hapi, Osiris, Agunua, Hades, Hay-Tau, Asia-Bussu, Chiuta, En-kai, Bel, Freyr, Ba'al, Demeter, Ceres, Persephone, Cerridwen, Imberombera, Gaea, Flora, Venus.

VICTORY—Hecate, Neith, Astarte, Inanna, Diiwica, Osiris, Castor and Pollux, Janus, Marduk, Shamash, Olorun, Tyr, Odhinn, Perun, Svantovit, Vishnu. See SUCCESS.

VIOLENCE—Bia, Kratos.

VOLCANOES—Itzcoliuhqui, Hephaestus, Vulcan, Enlil, Svarozic, O-yama-tsu-mi, Masaya, Mahui-Ike, Pele. See FIRE.

WALLS—Ch'eng-huang.

WAR—Horus, Menthu, Ares, Mars, Tyr, Thorr, Gwydion, Lugh, Asshur, Nergal, Ninurta, Indra, Karttikeya, Kuan Ti, Bishamonten, Gu, Ogun, Shango, Huitzilopochtli, Tezcatlipoca, Ogun, Zeus, Jupiter, Odhinn, Svantovit, Anhur, Oro, Kukalikimoku, Arawn, Bran the Blessed, the Dagda, Nuada, Volos, Vahgn, Shiva, Ictinike, Neith, Sekhmet, Athene, Minerva, the Morrigu, Anat, Ishtar, Durga, Kali, Bellona, Macha, Alaisiagae, Valkyries, Inanna, Tiamat, Freyja, Anhur, Ek Ahua.

WATER—The Morrigu, Kupala, Rusalki, Nanshe, Sati, Danu, Mokosh, Tlaloc, Itzamna, Viracocha, Hsuant'ien-shang-ti, Nuada, Ahto, Hapi, Ea, Marduk, Ninurta, Kamapua'a, Osiris, Hades, Mimir, Thorr, Ahto, Myesyats, Djanggawul, Aryaman, Shiva, Surya, Varuna, Itzamna, Viracocha, Anqet, Vellamo.

WEAPONS—Artemis, Athene, Neith, Inanna, Ishtar, Valkyries, Skadi, Mixcoatl, Ares, Mars, Goibniu, Odhinn, Thorr, Apollo, Asshur, Shango, Gwydion, Lugh, Nuada, Freyr, Perun, Svantovit, Baiame, Indra, Shiva, Tvashtar, Visvakarma, Inari.

WEATHER—Odhinn, Thorr, the Dagda, Manannan mac Lir, Ba'al, Addad, Agni, Indra, Vajrapani, Enlil, Marduk, Amen, Zeus, Jupiter, Hephaestus, Freyr, Jumala, Rock-Sens, Susanoo, Soko, Mi-lo, Tefnut, Hecate, Artemis.

WHIRLPOOLS—Chalchihuitlicue.

WIND—Boreas, Eurus, Notos, Zephyrus, Quetzalcoatl, Bacabs, Zeus, Jupiter, Haya-ji, Njord, Enlil, Ninurta, Tawiri, Marduk, Kitcki Manitou, Hurukan, Addad, Nergal, Odhinn, Stribog, Maui, Aryaman, Surya, Bade.

WINE—Dionysus, Bacchus, Saturn, Herakles, Svantovit, Flora.

WINTER—Holda, Persephone, Gwynn ap Nudd, Pluto, Hades, Nergal, Yama, Osiris, Anubis, Ghom.

WISDOM—Ganesha, Balder, Mimir, Odhinn, Thoth, Heimdall, Ea, Shamash, Sin, Anubis, Apollo, Eurus, Enlil, Manjusri, Merlin, Fugen Bosatsu, Fukurokuju, Janus, Mithra, Nabu, Nergal, Taliesin, Brahma, Buddha, Gluskap, Underwater Panthers, Wakonda, Michael, Athene, Minerva, Hecate, Frigg, Danu, Tara, Sarasvati, Maat, Artemis, Isis, Lilith, Badb, Blodeuwedd, Freyja, Anahit, Amaterasu, Metis.

WITCHCRAFT—Circe, Hecate, Holda, Brigit, Kali, Freyja, the Morrigu, Nerthus, Lilith, Kali, Tlazolteotl, Tlazolteotl, Soko.

WOMEN—Bes, Hercules, Kama, Mama Quilla, Gaea, Hera, Juno, Hathor, Isis, Nekhebet, Renenet, Lilith, Diana, Artemis, Neith, Aphrodite, Athene, Demeter, Hecate, Ceres, Minerva, Macha, Akka, Izanami.

WOODLANDS—Pan, Cernunnos, the Horned God, Leshy, Marduk, Tane, Rudra, Dumuzi, Faunus, Vajrapani, Merlin, Bacchus, Hay-Tau, Herne the Hunter, Thorr, Jumala, Pellervoinen, Tapio, Perun, Djanggawul, Susanoo, Thunder Bird, Artemis, Diana, Persephone, Blodeuwedd, Cerridwen, Creiddylad, Athene, Rusalki, Hecate, Cybele, Nerthus, Mother of Metsola, Diiwica, Kupala, Tane.

WRITING—Brigit, Seshat, Pales, Cerridwen, Athene, Minerva, Freyja, Sarasvati, Itzamna, Ganesha, Ogma, Bragi, Odhinn, Imhotep, Thoth, Ea, Nabu, Lugh, Taliesin, Manjusri, K'uei-hsing, Wench'ang, Njambi, Bran the Blessed, Nuada, Clio, Thaleia, Melpomene, Terpsichore, Erato, Calliope, Coirpre.

YOUTH—Artemis, Renpet, Dionysus, Zeus, Jupiter, Angus mac Og, Nuada.

INDEX

427

ILLUSTRATION CREDITS

Page 1. A scholar at work. Gaspard Lavater, *L'art de connaitre les hommes par la physonomie*, Paris: 1820.

Page 3. The Gateway to Eternal Wisdom. Heinrich Khunrath, *Amphitheatrum Aeternae Sapientiae*, Hanau: 1609.

Page 8. Hopi messenger of the gods. Paul E. Kennedy, *North American Indian Design Coloring Book*. New York: Dover Publications, 1971.

Page 9. Incarnation of Vishnu Inparting Wisdom. Thomas Bulfinch, *The Age of Fable*. Philadelphia: Henry Altemus Co., 1903.

Page 11. Greek pantheon in *Psyche Received into Olympus* from the painting by Carravaggio. John Clark Ridpath, *Ridpath's History of the World*. New York: Merrill Baker Publishers, 1897.

Page 12. Hopi mother goddess Hahhaiwugti. Ancient sand painting.

Page 15. The mystery of the Macrocosm. *Cesariano's Edition of Vitruvius*. Como: 1521.

Page 16. Ancient horned figure. Traditional image. Artist's rendition.

Page 17. Execution of Witches in England. Pen and ink drawing, 17th century.

Page 19. Magicians using rune staves. Woodcut print, 16th century.

Page 21. Ritual tools. Drawn by Alexandra Lumen after a sketch by D. J. Conway.

Page 22. Witches brewing. Ulrich Molitor, *De Lamiis*. 1489.

Page 25. Poppet for sympathetic magick. Drawn by Christopher Wells.

Page 28. One of the earliest views of the Moon. Johann Hevelius, *Selenographia*. Danzig: 1647.

Page 29. Libra: the balance. Medieval woodcut.

Page 33. Ancient pagans in worship. John Clark Ridpath, *Ridpath's History of the World*. New York: Merrill Baker Publishers, 1897.

Page 35. Triple goddess image. Drawn by Alexandra Lumen.

Page 39. The pentagram. Eliphas Levi, *Transcendental Magic*. Chicago: 1910.

Page 40. Chinese witches perforing a ritual. Lithograph, 18th century.

Page 43. Native American family totem. Ernst Lehner, *Symbols, Signs and Signets*. New York: Dover Publications, 1969.

Page 45. A Native American shaman dances into trance. Matilda Coxe Stevenson, *The Zuni Indians*. 1902.

Page 46. Shamanic tools. Drawn by Alexandra Lumen.

Page 49. Northwest coast masks. Le Roy H. Appleton, *American Indian Design and Decoration*. New York: Dover Publications, 1971.

Page 50. Chilcat dancing shirt. Le Roy H. Appleton, *American Indian Design and Decoration*. New York: Dover Publications, 1971.

Page 53. A circle for Ceremonial Magick. *The Complete Book of Magic Science*. Unpublished.

Page 58. The celestial alphabet in the heavens. Jacques Gaffarel, 1637.

Page 60. Magickal incantation according to the Key of Solomon. J. Scheible, *Das Kloster*. Stuttgart, 1847.

Page 65. Diagram of the Qabalistic Sephirotic Tree, 1621.

Page 67. Kircher's Sephirotic Tree. Athanasius Kircher, *Oedipus Aegyptiacus*. Rome: 1652.

Page 69. A modern Tree of Life. Drawn by Christopher Wells.

Page 71. Qabalistic allegory. Knorr von Rosenroth, *Kabbala Denudata*. Sulzbach: 1677.

Page 72. Zeus. Thomas Bulfinch, *The Age of Fable*. Philadelphia: Henry Altemus Co., 1903.

Page 73. Beelzebub. After Collin de Plancy, 1863.

Page 74. Isis. Ernst Lehner, *Symbols, Signs and Signets*. New York: Dover Publications, 1969.

Page 75. Unicorn. Konrad Gesner, *Curious Woodcuts of Fanciful and Real Beasts*. New York: Dover Publications, 1971.

Page 76. Magickal sword. Eliphas Levi, *The Magical Ritual of the Sanctum Regnum*. London: 1896.

Page 77. Belphegor. Collin de Plancy, *Dictionnaire Infernal*. 1863.

Page 78. Egyptian cat talisman. Fred Gettings, *The Secret Lore of the Cat*. London: Grafton Books, 1989.

Page 79. Seal of Michael. Francis Barrett, *The Magus*. London: Lackington, Allen, and Co., 1801.

Page 80. Mandrake. Richard G. Hatton, *The Craftsman's Plant Book*. 1909.

Page 81. Four Pages from an early Portugese Deck. William Andrew Chatto, *Origin and History of Playing Cards*. London: 1848.

Page 82. Osiris. Ernst Lehner, *Symbols, Signs and Signets*. New York: Dover Publications, 1969.

Page 83. Ox from *The Book of Kells*.

Page 84. Marjoram. Richard G. Hatton, *The Craftsman's Plant Book*. 1909. Moon. 20th century silver earring. Richard Huber, *Treasury of Fantastic and Mythological Creatures*. New York: Dover Publications, 1981.

Page 85. Lynx. Konrad Gesner, *Curious Woodcuts of Fanciful and Real Beasts*. New York: Dover Publications, 1971.

Page 86. Minerva. Thomas Bulfinch, *The Age of Fable*. Philadelphia: Henry Altemus Co., 1903. Theseus killing the Minotaur. From a 5th century Greek vase.

Page 87. Gemini as the twins. Hyginus, *Poetica Astronomicon*. 1504.

Page 88. Alchemists at the furnace. J. Scheible, *Das Kloster*. Stuttgart: 1845. Dragon. Joseph D'Addetta, *Treasury of Chinese Design Motifs*. New York: Dover Publications, 1981.

Page 89. The Hermit. French Tarot card, 19th century.

Page 90. Haida eagle totem. Le Roy H. Appleton, *American Indian Design and Decoration*. New York: Dover Publications, 1971. Themis. Thomas Bulfinch, *The Age of Fable*. Philadelphia: Henry Altemus Co., 1903.

Page 91. Water demon. 18th century engraving. Richard Huber, *Treasury of Fantastic and Mythological Creatures*. New York: Dover Publications, 1981.

Page 92. Scarab beetle. Eva Wilson, *Ancient Egyptian Designs*. New York: Dover Publications, 1986. Temperance. Court de Gebelin, *Le Monde Primitif*. Paris: 1787.

Page 93. Wormwood. Richard G. Hatton, *The Craftsman's Plant Book*. 1909.

Page 94. The Furies. Thomas Bulfinch, *The Age of Fable*. Philadelphia: Henry Altemus Co., 1903. Nut. E. A. Wallis Budge, *The Gods of the Egyptians*. Chicago: Open Court Publishing Co., 1904.

Page 95. Fish. Jorge Inciso, *Design Motifs of Ancient Mexico*. New York: Dover Publications, 1953.

Page 96. Seal of Raphael. Francis Barrett, *The Magus*. London: Lackington, Allen, and Co., 1801. Salamander. Paracelsus, *Complete Writings of Paracelsus*. Strasbourg: 1616.

Page 97. Saturn. Thomas Bulfinch, *The Age of Fable*. Philadelphia: Henry Altemus Co., 1903.

Page 102. Detail from Egyptian tomb painting, XVIII Dynasty, New Kingdom. Eva Wilson, *Ancient Egyptian Designs*. New York: Dover Publications, 1986.

Page 104. Lily design from Tutankhamen's tomb. Eva Wilson, *Ancient Egyptian Designs*. New York: Dover Publications, 1986.

Page 105. The Creation. E. A. Wallis Budge, *The Gods of the Egyptians*. Chicago: Open Court Publishing Co., 1904.

Page 107. The deities of the planets. E. A. Wallis Budge, *The Gods of the Egyptians*. Chicago: Open Court Publishing Co., 1904.

Page 108. Ceremonial scene connected with the resurrection of Osiris. E. A. Wallis Budge, *The Gods of the Egyptians*. Chicago: Open Court Publishing Co., 1904.

Page 111. Egyptian dress. Braun and Schneider, *Historic Costume in Pictures*. New York: Dover Publications, 1975.

Page 112. Hathor. E. A. Wallis Budge, *The Gods of the Egyptians*. Chicago: Open Court Publishing Co., 1904.

Page 115. Amen. E. A. Wallis Budge, *The Gods of the Egyptians*. Chicago: Open Court Publishing Co., 1904.

Page 116. Anubis weighing the heart. E. A. Wallis Budge, *The Gods of the Egyptians*. Chicago: Open Court Publishing Co., 1904.

Page 118. Horus. E. A. Wallis Budge, *The Gods of the Egyptians*. Chicago: Open Court Publishing Co., 1904.

Page 119. Isis. E. A. Wallis Budge, *The Gods of the Egyptians*. Chicago: Open Court Publishing Co., 1904.

Page 121. Neith. E. A. Wallis Budge, *The Gods of the Egyptians*. Chicago: Open Court Publishing Co., 1904.

Page 123. The souls of Ra and Osiris in Tattu. E. A. Wallis Budge, *The Gods of the Egyptians*. Chicago: Open Court Publishing Co., 1904.

Page 125. Thoth. E. A. Wallis Budge, *The Gods of the Egyptians*. Chicago: Open Court Publishing Co., 1904.

Page 126. Egyptian bowl design, fourth millenium BC. Eva Wilson, *Ancient Egyptian Designs*. New York: Dover Publications, 1986.

Page 127. Dog-shaped cosmetic spoon from the XVIII Dynasty of the New Kingdom. Eva Wilson, *Ancient Egyptian Designs*. New York: Dover Publications, 1986.

Page 133. Phoenician warships and transports, seventh century BC. David Hatcher Childress, *Lost Cities and Ancient Mysteries of Africa and Arabia*. IL: Adventures Unlimited Press, 1989.

Page 135. Arabian zodiac. Heinrich Daath, "Zodiacal Types and Affinities." *The Occult Review*, March 1908.

Page 137. Astrologers at work. Macrobius, *In Somnium Scipionis*. Venice: 1513.

Page 138. Assyrian court musicians. Traditional image. Drawn by Alexandra Lumen.

Page 140. Marduk destroying Tiamat. After Jastrow, *Bildermappe zur Religion Babyloniens und Assyriens*.

Page 141. Zoroastrian priest. C. W. King, *The Gnostics and their Remains*. London: 1887.

Page 142. Babylonian kings and winged divinities before the sacred tree. Bonomi, *Nineveh and its Palaces*. London: 1865.

Page 143. Ahura Mazdah. Traditional image. From a wall carving.
Page 144. Anu. Traditional image. Drawn by Alexandra Lumen.
Page 145. Astarte. Bronze sculpture. Drawn by Alexandra Lumen.
Page 146. Dagon. Athanasius Kircher, *Oedipus Aegyptiacus*. Rome: 1652.
Page 148. Ishtar with Lion .Traditional image. Drawn by Alexandra Lumen.
Page 149. Amulet of Lemashtu, Babylonian predecessor of Lilith, and her demons. Pen and ink drawing from stone carving. Mithra. Ernst Lehner, *Symbols, Signs and Signets*. New York: Dover Publications, 1969.
Page 150. Demon of Disease and Evil. After a wall carving at Nineveh. Ernst and Johanna Lehner, *Devils, Demons, Death and Damnation*. New York: Dover Publications, 1971.
Page 151. Shamash receives homage from the faithful. Traditional image. Drawn by Alexandra Lumen.
Page 152. Sin. Felix Lajard, *Sur le Culte de Mithra*. 1847.
Page 157. Greek Athlete. John Clark Ridpath, *Ridpath's History of the World*. New York: Merrill Baker Publishers, 1897.
Page 158. Victims for sacrifice. John Clark Ridpath, *Ridpath's History of the World*. New York: Merrill Baker Publishers, 1897.
Page 160. Demeter, Persephone, and a youth. John Clark Ridpath, *Ridpath's History of the World*. New York: Merrill Baker Publishers, 1897.
Page 161. Greek dress. John Clark Ridpath, *Ridpath's History of the World*. New York: Merrill Baker Publishers, 1897.
Page 162. Cronus devouring his children. Thomas Bulfinch, *The Age of Fable*. Philadelphia: Henry Altemus Co., 1903.
Page 163. Athene. Thomas Bulfinch, *The Age of Fable*. Philadelphia: Henry Altemus Co., 1903.
Page 164. Leto defending her children. Thomas Bulfinch, *The Age of Fable*. Philadelphia: Henry Altemus Co., 1903.
Page 165. Hermes. Thomas Bulfinch, *The Age of Fable*. Philadelphia: Henry Altemus Co., 1903.
Page 166. The judgment of Paris. John Clark Ridpath, *Ridpath's History of the World*. New York: Merrill Baker Publishers, 1897.
Page 167. Poseidon. Thomas Bulfinch, *The Age of Fable*. Philadelphia: Henry Altemus Co., 1903.
Page 169. Apollo and Hyacinthus. Thomas Bulfinch, *The Age of Fable*. Philadelphia: Henry Altemus Co., 1903.
Page 170. Circe and friends of Odysseus, whom she turned into pigs. Thomas Bulfinch, *The Age of Fable*. Philadelphia: Henry Altemus Co., 1903.
Page 171. Cybele. John Clark Ridpath, *Ridpath's History of the World*. New York: Merrill Baker Publishers, 1897.
Page 174. Hera. Thomas Bulfinch, *The Age of Fable*. Philadelphia: Henry Altemus Co., 1903.
Page 175. Nereid. Thomas Bulfinch, *The Age of Fable*. Philadelphia: Henry Altemus Co., 1903.
Page 177. Prometheus stealing the fire. Thomas Bulfinch, *The Age of Fable*. Philadelphia: Henry Altemus Co., 1903.
Page 185. Service in the temple of Vesta. John Clark Ridpath, *Ridpath's History of the World*. New York: Merrill Baker Publishers, 1897.
Page 189. Roman concept of the founders of the race: Aeneas and Agamemnon. John Clark Ridpath, *Ridpath's History of the World*. New York: Merrill Baker Publishers, 1897.
Page 190. Apollo. Thomas Bulfinch, *The Age of Fable*. Philadelphia: Henry Altemus Co., 1903.
Page 191. Faunus. Thomas Bulfinch, *The Age of Fable*. Philadelphia: Henry Altemus Co., 1903.
Page 192. Janus. Thomas Bulfinch, *The Age of Fable*. Philadelphia: Henry Altemus Co., 1903.
Page 193. Mars. Thomas Bulfinch, *The Age of Fable*. Philadelphia: Henry Altemus Co., 1903.
Page 194. Vulcan. Thomas Bulfinch, *The Age of Fable*. Philadelphia: Henry Altemus Co., 1903.
Page 198. A scene from Haggard's *King Solomon's Mines*. David Hatcher Childress, *Lost Cities and Ancient Mysteries of Africa and Arabia*. IL: Adventures Unlimited Press, 1989.
Page 199. Section of Zimbabwe ruins. David Hatcher Childress, *Lost Cities and Ancient Mysteries of Africa and Arabia*. IL: Adventures Unlimited Press, 1989.
Page 200. Ancestor statue, Zaire. Melita Denning and Osborne Phillips, *Voudoun Fire*. St. Paul, MN: Llewellyn Publications, 1979.
Page 201. Sudanese dancer in ancestor mask. Melita Denning and Osborne Phillips, *Voudoun Fire*. St. Paul, MN: Llewellyn Publications, 1979.
Page 205. African snake of creation. Traditional image. Drawn by Alexandra Lumen.
Page 206. Behanzin. Richard Huber, *Treasury of Fantastic and Mythological Creatures*. New York: Dover Publications, 1981.
Page 207. Nigerian water spirit mask. Richard Huber, *Treasury of Fantastic and Mythological Creatures*. New York: Dover Publications, 1981
Page 208. Oba. From the *Tarot of the Orishas* by Zolrak and Durkon. St. Paul, MN: Llewellyn Publications, 1994.
Page 209. Schango. From the *Tarot of the Orishas* by Zolrak and Durkon. St. Paul, MN: Llewellyn Publications, 1994.
Page 212. Celtic knotwork design. Courtney Davis, *Celtic Designs and Motifs*. New York: Dover Publications, 1991.
Page 215. Celtic worship. E. Wallcousins in Charles Squire, *The Mythology of the British Islands*. London: 1905.
Page 216. Holy ground. John Clark Ridpath, *Ridpath's History of the World*. New York: Merrill Baker Publishers, 1897.
Page 217. Traditional Celtic design. Courtney Davis, *Celtic Designs and Motifs*. New York: Dover Publications, 1991.
Page 218. Lugh and his spear in battle. H. R. Millar in Charles Squire, *The Mythology of the British Islands*. London: 1905.
Page 221: Cernunnos. From Gunderstrup, Denmark. Richard Huber, *Treasury of Fantastic and Mythological Creatures*. New York: Dover Publications, 1981.
Page 223. Epona. From a bronze statuette found in Wiltshire. Gray, *Mythology of All Races*. Boston: Marshall Jones, 1918.

Page 224. The Horned God. Medieval woodcut.

Page 226. Merlin, detail from a fourteenth century enamel. Ernst and Johanna Lehner, *Devils, Demons, Death and Damnation*. New York: Dover Publications, 1971.

Page 227: Early representation of the Celtic goddess of death. Traditional image. Artist's rendition.

Page 233. A Norse ship, early thirteenth century. From Bergen, Norway.

Page 234. Council of German chiefs, from the victory column of Marcus Aurelius. John Clark Ridpath, *Ridpath's History of the World*. New York: Merrill Baker Publishers, 1897.

Page 236. Ancient runic alphabet. John Clark Ridpath, *Ridpath's History of the World*. New York: Merrill Baker Publishers, 1897.

Page 240. Fenrir. Thomas Bulfinch, *The Age of Fable*. Philadelphia: Henry Altemus Co., 1903.

Page 242. Freyja. John Clark Ridpath, *Ridpath's History of the World*. New York: Merrill Baker Publishers, 1897.

Page 244. Odhinn. Thomas Bulfinch, *The Age of Fable*. Philadelphia: Henry Altemus Co., 1903.

Page 245. Thorr. Thomas Bulfinch, *The Age of Fable*. Philadelphia: Henry Altemus Co., 1903.

Page 246. Valhalla. John Clark Ridpath, *Ridpath's History of the World*. New York: Merrill Baker Publishers, 1897.

Page 251. A Samoyed priest. J. W. Buel, *The Story of Man*. Richmond, VA: B. F. Johnson & Co., 1889.

Page 252. Finnish ornamental design. Drawn by Alexandra Lumen from a sketch by D. J. Conway.

Page 255. Symbolic representation of the divine couple, Jumala and Akka. Traditional image. Artist's rendition.

Page 259. Vlad the Impaler (Dracula) eats while his victims suffer. Medieval woodcut.

Page 261. Traditional Slavic design. Drawn by Alexandra Lumen from a sketch by D. J. Conway.

Page 262. Russian elf. Gray, *Mythology of All Races*. Boston: Marshall Jones, 1918.

Page 263. Byelobog and Chernobog. Gray, *Mythology of All Races*. Boston: Marshall Jones, 1918.

Page 265. Four sides of a statue of Svantovit. Found in 1848 near the river Zbrucz. Gray, *Mythology of All Races*. Boston: Marshall Jones, 1918.

Page 268. Om symbol. Traditional image.

Page 272. Representation of Kundalini. From an 18th century painting. Drawn by Alexandra Lumen.

Page 273. Chapter 4, verse 38 of *The Bhagavad Gita*.

Page 274. Tantric yoga position. Traditional image. Drawn by Alexandra Lumen.

Page 275. Vishnu contemplating creation, with Brahma and Lakshmi. Edward Moor, *The Hindu Pantheon*. London: 1810.

Page 276. Shri Yantra, Hindu diagram of the cosmos. Traditional image.

Page 277. Krishna playing his flute. W. J. Wilkins, *Hindu Mythology*. London: 1882.

Page 278. Agni. Thomas Bulfinch, *The Age of Fable*. Philadelphia: Henry Altemus Co., 1903.

Page 279. Brahma and Saraswati. Thomas Bulfinch, *The Age of Fable*. Philadelphia: Henry Altemus Co., 1903.

Page 280. Ganesha. Ernst Lehner, *Symbols, Signs and Signets*. New York: Dover Publications, 1969.

Page 281. Kali. Moncure Daniel Conway, *Demonology and Devil-Lore*. London: Chatto and Windus, 1879.

Page 283. Parvati and Shiva. J. Hackin, *Asiatic Mythology*. New York: Thomas Y. Cromwell Co., no date.

Page 285. Vishnu as Kurma. J. Hackin, *Asiatic Mythology*. New York: Thomas Y. Cromwell Co., no date.

Page 290. Yin-Yang symbol. Traditional image.

Page 291. Early Chinese characters. Traditional image.

Page 292. Chinese celestial sphere. Medieval woodcut. Traditional image.

Page 295. Fu-hsi and Nu-kua, from a Han Dynasty stone rubbing. Drawn by Alexandra Lumen.

Page 297. Chinese dragon motif. From an enameled prcelain of the Kang xi period of the Qing Dynasty (AD 1662—1722). Joseph D'Addetta, *Chinese Design Motifs*. New York: Dover Publications, 1981.

Page 298. Kuan Yin. Hernry Doré, *Researches into Chinese Superstitions*. M. Kennelly, trans. Shanghai: 1914.

Page 299. Shou-Hsing. Hernry Doré, *Researches into Chinese Superstitions*. M. Kennelly, trans. Shanghai: 1914.

Page 305. Shinto shrine. Traditional image. Drawn by Alexandra Lumen.

Page 306. Japanese warriors. Braun and Schneider, *Historic Costume in Pictures*. New York: Dover Publications, 1975.

Page 308. Susanoo. J Hackin, *Asiatic Mythology*. New York: Thomas Y. Cromwell Co., no date.

Page 309. Amaterasu comes out of the cave. Traditional image. Drawn by Alexandra Lumen.

Page 310 Amida Buddha. Ernst Lehner, *Symbols, Signs and Signets*. New York: Dover Publications, 1969.

Page 312. Japanese cosmogram. Medieval woodcut. Traditional image.

Page 317. A Bon priest. L. Austine Waddell, *The Buddhism of Tibet*. London: 1895.

Page 318. Buddhist effigy. L. Austine Waddell, *The Buddhism of Tibet*. London: 1895.

Page 319. Rosary. L. Austine Waddell, *The Buddhism of Tibet*. London: 1895.

Page 320. Buddha, detail from Tibetan woodblock. Traditional image.

Page 321. Avalokitesvara. L. Austine Waddell, *The Buddhism of Tibet*. London: 1895.

Page 322. Manjusri. L. Austine Waddell. *The Buddhism of Tibet*. London: 1895.

Page 323. The white Tara. L. Austine Waddell, *The Buddhism of Tibet*. London: 1895.

Page 327. Oceanic festival. Traditional image.

Page 328. Melanesian mask. Richard Huber, *Treasury of Fantastic and Mythological Creatures*. New York: Dover Publications, 1981.

Page 329. Australian rock painting. Traditional image. Drawn by Alexandra Lumen.

Page 331. Maui. Traditional image. Drawn by Alexandra Lumen.

Page 335. Spirits of slain warriors travel to the heavens, from a Palau Islands painting.

Page 339. Zuni fetish and shield of the Priesthood of the Bow. *Authentic Indian Designs*. Maria Naylor, editor. New York: Dover Publications, 1975.

Page 340. Innuit seal mask. *Authentic Indian Designs*. Maria Naylor, editor. New York: Dover Publications, 1975.

Page 341. Stone pipe. Le Roy H. Appleton, *American Indian Design and Decoration*. New York: Dover Publications, 1971.

Page 343. Animal motif from Zuni pottery. Le Roy H. Appleton, *American Indian Design and Decoration*. New York: Dover Publications, 1971.

Page 345. Michabo. Traditional image. Drawn by Alexandra Lumen.

Page 346. Pueblo thunderbird. Le Roy H. Appleton, *American Indian Design and Decoration*. New York: Dover Publications, 1971.

Page 351. Athlete on a ball court marker. From Chinkultic, Chiapas, Mexico. Wilson G. Turner, *Maya Designs*. New York: Dover Publications, 1980.

Page 352. The festival of carving new masks. From the Madrid Codex. Wilson G. Turner, *Maya Designs*. New York: Dover Publications, 1980.

Page 353. Glyphs for the months of the Mayan year. Le Roy H. Appleton, *American Indian Design and Decoration*. New York: Dover Publications, 1971.

Page 354. Mayan design. Wilson G. Turner, *Maya Designs*. New York: Dover Publications, 1980.

Page 356. Mayan gods of death, maize, and the north. From the Dresden Codex. Wilson G. Turner, *Maya Designs*. New York: Dover Publications, 1980.

Page 357. Itzamna. *American Indian Design and Decoration*. New York: Dover Publications, 1971.

Page 363. Sacrifice to the Sun. After Codex Florentino. Drawn by Alexandra Lumen.

Page 364. Aztec·calendar stone. *Authentic Indian Designs*. Maria Naylor, editor. New York: Dover Publications, 1975.

Page 366. Quetzacoatl. Traditional image.

Page 368. Coatlicue. Melita Denning and Osborne Phillips, Voudoun Fire. St. Paul, MN: Llewellyn Publications, 1979.

Page 370. Xolotl. Richard Huber, *Treasury of Fantastic and Mythological Creatures*. New York: Dover Publications, 1981.

Page 375. An Incan coya. After Felipe Huaman Poma de Ayala, 1565. Drawn by Alexandra Lumen.

Page 376. Celebration. After Felipe Huaman Poma de Ayala, 1565. Drawn by Alexandra Lumen.

Page 377. Incan dress. After Felipe Huaman Poma de Ayala, 1565. Drawn by Alexandra Lumen.

Page 379. Pachacamac. Tapestry fragment. Drawn by Alexandra Lumen.

Page 380. Inca cosmogram. 16th century.

Page 383. Traditional angel. *Treasury of Book Ornament and Decoration*. Carol Belanger Grafton, editor. New York: Dover Publications, 1986.

Page 385. Angel from Doré Bible illustration.

Page 386. Pages from the *Book of Spirits*, according to Barrett. Francis Barrett, *The Magus*. London: Lackington, Allen, and Co., 1801.

Page 387. Angelic talisman. 19th century.

Page 388. Unnamed angel. *Treasury of Book Ornament and Decoration*. Carol Belanger Grafton, editor. New York: Dover Publications, 1986. Hopi celestial being. Le Roy H. Appleton, *American Indian Design and Decoration*. New York: Dover Publications, 1971.

Page 399. Qabalistic sign of Michael. 17th century. A fallen angel. Medieval woodcut.

Page 390. Angelic ornament. 19th century.

Page 393. Hermetic circle, eighteenth century. After Basil Valentine, *Musaeum Hermeticum*. Frankfurt: 1749.

Page 394. Sylph. 19th century.

Page 395. Gnomes. 19th century.

Page 397. Alchemical allegory for Air. "The Wind hath carried It in his Belly." Michael Majer, *Scrutinum Chymicium*. Frankfurt: 1687. Elemental fire. Robert Fludd, *Utriusque Cosmi Historia*. Oppenheim: 1617.

Page 398. Mermaid. Medieval woodcut.

Page 399. Earth as medium between light and darkness. 16th century. Fifteenth century personifications of Fire, Air, Water, and Earth. Woodcut.

Page 403. Detail from title page of *Egypto-Persian Book of Planets*, 1890. Woodcut.

Page 404. The seven planets, 1536. Woodcut.

Page 405. The sun as god. Medieval woodcut.

Page 406. The man in the Moon. Medieval woodcut. Mercury. Medieval woodcut.

Page 407. Venus. Medieval woodcut.

Page 408. The Tower. Tarot card, 19th century. Marduk. From a wall carving. Traditional image.

Page 409. Saturn. Medieval woodcut.

Page 412. Alchemical cosmic diagram. 19th century.

Page 414. *Treasury of Book Ornament and Decoration*. Carol Belanger Grafton, editor. New York: Dover Publications, 1986.

STAY IN TOUCH. . .